media environments

Edited by

Barry Vacker

Temple University

First published in the United States of America in 2011 by Cognella, a division of University Readers, Inc.

Trademark Notice: Product or corporate names may be trademarks or registered trademarks, and are used only for identification and explanation without intent to infringe.

Research Assistant: Carly Haines, MA

14 13 12 11 10   1 2 3 4 5

Printed in the United States of America

ISBN: 978-1-935551-34-8

www.cognella.com 800.200.3908

Contents

PART 2
ENLIGHTENMENT AND ENTERTAINMENT

PART 3
SEEING AND BEING SEEN

PART 4
REALITY OR SIMULATION

PART 5
BUYING IN AND SELLING OUT

PART 6
DESTINY AND THE FUTURE

Recommended Films

to Accompany Media Environments

CHAPTER 1. THE MEME

RECOMMENDED FILMS

Pulp Fiction (Quentin Tarantino 1994)
Whatever Works (Woody Allen 2009)

SECOND CHOICES

Waking Life (Richard Linklater 2001)
Network (Sidney Lumet 1976)
Meet John Doe (Frank Capra 1941)

CHAPTER 2. THE NETWORK

RECOMMENDED FILM

Star Trek (J.J. Abrams 2009)

CHAPTER 3. THE SPECTACLE

RECOMMENDED FILM

Network (Sidney Lumet 1976)

SECOND CHOICES

Strange Days (Kathryn Bigelow 1995)
Ace in the Hole (Billy Wilder 1951)

CHAPTER 4. THE HYPERREAL

RECOMMENDED FILM

The Matrix (The Wachowski Brothers 1999)

SECOND CHOICE

The Truman Show (Peter Weir 1998)

CHAPTER 5. NEWS

RECOMMENDED FILM

Good Night, and Good Luck (George Clooney 2005)

SECOND CHOICES

The Manchurian Candidate (Jonathan Demme 2004)
The Insider (Michael Mann 1999)
Wag the Dog (Barry Levinson 1997)
Broadcast News (James L. Brooks 1987)
The Year of Living Dangerously (Peter Weir 1983)
The China Syndrome (James Bridges 1979)

CHAPTER 13. THEME PARKS

RECOMMENDED FILM

The Truman Show (Peter Weir 1998)

SECOND CHOICE

Westworld (Michael Crichton 1973)

CHAPTER 14. CONSUMER CULTURE

RECOMMENDED FILMS

American Beauty (Sam Mendes 1999)
WALL·E (Andrew Stanton 2008)

CHAPTER 15. GLOBALIZATION

RECOMMENDED FILM

Slumdog Millionaire (Danny Boyle 2008)

CHAPTER 16. COUNTERCULTURE

RECOMMENDED FILM

Fight Club (David Fincher 1999)

CHAPTER 17. CATASTROPHE

RECOMMENDED FILMS

2012 (Roland Emmerich 2009)
The Day After Tomorrow (Roland Emmerich 2004)
Independence Day (Roland Emmerich 1996)
The Matrix (The Wachowski Brothers 1999)

CHAPTER 18. ELECTRONIC CONSCIOUSNESS

RECOMMENDED FILM

Vanilla Sky (Cameron Crowe 2001)

SECOND CHOICES

Artificial Intelligence: AI (Steven Spielberg 2001)
2001: A Space Odyssey (Stanley Kubrick 1968)

CHAPTER 19. SPACESHIP EARTH

RECOMMENDED FILM

WALL·E (Andrew Stanton 2008)

CHAPTER 20. TRAJECTORIES

RECOMMENDED FILM

Waking Life (Richard Linklater 2001)

SECOND CHOICES

Whatever Works (Woody Allen 2009)
Gattaca (Andrew Niccol 1997)
Ghost in the Shell (Mamoru Oshii 1995)
Blade Runner (Ridley Scott 1982)

Preface

Read a Movie, View a Text, See the Media

Media Environments is based on a simple concept: combine movies with texts to critique media and society in the 21st century.

If you are a student, you must be thinking: "Cool. This will be a fun class!" But don't forget, you are reading this in a book, a thick book.

If you are a professor, you might be thinking: "Oh no, more edutainment." But, like the students, you are reading this in an anthology full of critical theory.

Here's the general idea behind this book: Entertainment and enlightenment do not have to be in opposition, though they surely are in most of popular culture. "Fun" and "critical thinking" can coexist in a classroom. Art and theory can work together to educate and enlighten, sometimes in an entertaining way. And it is one way to address a daunting educational challenge. Let me explain in greater detail.

THE GOALS

The goal of *Media Environments* is to inspire students to think creatively and critically based on a broad cultural literacy that includes media and society, theory and technology, and the arts and sciences. Critical thinking and cultural literacy require learning at a deeper level, beyond the latest media trends and techno-gizmo, and being open to exploring the wider range of patterns in technological and cultural evolution. It also requires exploring our own beliefs and our place in the universe as revealed by media technologies.

We live in a 24/7, online, omnipresent, globally networked media universe. This anthology acknowledges that virtually all media technologies, industries, content, and usages have converged and work together to shape consciousness and culture as technological environments. Media-as-environments is the existential reality for college students in the 21st century. Rather than examine the media as separate industries (newspapers, radio, television, etc.), *Media Environments* explores these media in their totality and provides models for understanding and interrogating many universal themes that span media and global culture.

Media Environments combines popular art with text-based theory to creatively and critically map the "environments" of the media — the mental, material, and cultural environments.

THE CHALLENGE

Designed for media and society courses, this anthology directly confronts a fundamental challenge in the college classroom: how to inspire critical thinking and maintain relevance for students who have grown up with the internet, YouTube, Google, Wikipedia, Facebook, Twitter, and so on.

There exists an endless debate about how to best address this challenge, with little consensus other than colleges and universities inserting the internet into the classroom, making wireless access available to all students with a laptop or mobile phone. Of course, to maintain the students' attention, professors face two choices: 1) they can make the students turn off all electronic devices, or 2) they must compete with the entirety of the entertainment and information on the internet, plus all those urgent e-mails and text messages from students' friends. The first choice seems rather reactionary and draconian, while the other is a formidable challenge for any educator, choosing to stand before any audience with shrinking attention spans and unlimited electronic choices. Of course, the professor can have the students use their laptops for assignments during class, thus minimizing the random web surfing that may be happening.

Though the classroom use of such technologies may have some educational benefits and be relevant for today's student, it is arrogant or delusional to think the seamless introduction of the internet into the classroom will inherently instill or inspire critical thinking skills. Technological proficiency is not equivalent to reflective thinking. Hollywood, YouTube, TV news, and a zillion blogs illustrate this every day.

The "film-and-text" strategy emerged from my desire for an effective teaching method that combined contemporary relevance with critical analysis. The films provide relevance for today's students, while the diversity of readings provides analysis that complements the ideas in the films and promotes critical-thinking skills and deeper learning. One key advantage of the film-and-text approach is that the films serve as gateways into the world of critical thinking.

Does the combination of films and texts ensure that all students will be more reflective or better critical thinkers? No. Ultimately, it is up to each student to take responsibility for their own minds, beliefs, and behaviors, while learning what it means to think with greater depth and insight.

Here's the bottom line: critical thinking requires focusing one's attention on a topic and analyzing the subject matter with greater depth and from multiple perspectives. This means students should be able to focus their attention and concentration for the length of a film or long enough to read one or more articles. If college students cannot focus their minds for two to three hours in the world of ideas, then, in the famous words of *Apollo 13*: "Houston, we have a problem."

> If college students cannot focus their minds for two to three hours in the world of ideas, then, in the famous words of *Apollo 13*: "Houston, we have a problem."

THE FILM-AND-TEXT METHOD

In the spirit of pioneering media theorist Marshall McLuhan, I believe films can function as "probes" capable of providing deep insight into media and culture. Living in a world filled with media environments, it is often hard for us to get outside and view the larger patterns from different and deeper perspectives. That is why film and theory both play a crucial role in this anthology.

In the 1960s, McLuhan often referenced art to illustrate his innovative and often profound insights into the role of media in society. McLuhan believed that artists — writers, poets, painters, etc. — are capable of intuiting or anticipating patterns of cultural and technological change and that their artworks can serve as "counter-environments" that provide us with "the means of perceiving the environment itself."[1] As illustrated by the films referenced in this anthology, such artistic counter-environments can illustrate or critique media concepts that might be difficult to perceive or analyze in their totality, precisely because they are environmental in our global culture.

As the millennia of art history have shown, artworks can represent complex ideas in highly stylized and condensed forms, often to very powerful effect. Movies have been doing this for over a century. The art of film can entertain *and* enlighten students, and thus serves as the starting point for a deeper interrogation of the global media environments. If, as Aristotle believed, art is the fiction that can reveal truth, then surely the fiction of film can help reveal the truths of real-world conditions involving media, culture, and humanity.

As illustrated by the readings, this strategy and anthology provide much more than mere "edutainment." Rather then merely entertain, the films and readings encourage professors and students to see, read, contemplate, critique, and discuss. In effect, we learn to read a movie and view a text.

UNIVERSAL THEMES

Media Environments explores themes that are universal to media and society in the 21st century. The goal of these themes is to provide critical *grand narratives* for students living in media environments, with the purpose of uniting

---

1 Marshall McLuhan, *Understanding Media: The Extensions of Man* (New York: McGraw Hill, 1964): viii.

the students in discourse on intellectual topics that span cultures. These topics are highly interdisciplinary, situating media theory and media effects not merely within popular culture but also within the realms of science, philosophy, aesthetics, and cultural studies. Students are exposed to a diversity of cultural ideas and many specific media theories, all united and grounded upon a philosophical foundation toward media education.

This anthology purposely omits topics of class, gender, and ethnicity, as well as the typical textbook collection of factoids, time lines, new technologies, and industry hype. Politics and economics are minimized here, used only as parts of larger themes explored in this anthology. Topics such as class, gender, ethnicity, politics, and economics are amply covered in numerous other courses in the college experience. While teaching at one of the most culturally diverse campuses in America, I have found this approach to be effective in my courses.

With 20 chapters, *Media Environments* provides many options and topics for each week of the semester, while embracing this simple concept: combine movies with texts to critique media and society in the 21st century.

ADVANTAGES FOR TEACHING

For the college classroom, *Media Environments* provides pedagogical advantages in five areas:

> ➢ The anthology provides a wide range of media theory.
> ➢ The anthology presents four basic media models — The Meme, The Network, The Spectacle, The Hyperreal — and invites their application across the remainder of the themes covered in the chapters.
> ➢ The film-and-text approach embraces the diversity of learning styles among students.
> ➢ The anthology inspires creative and critical thinking necessary for deep learning and cultural literacy.
> ➢ The anthology unites the visual arts with text to present students with new models for understanding the global media environments.

The wide range of readings and films permits professors to tailor the theories to fit with their personal interests and expertise in teaching Media and Society or other media-related courses. Professors can select from among 20 chapters and numerous films.

The film-and-text approach uses four forms of communication for the exchange of ideas and enhanced learning in the classroom: oral, print, popular arts, and electronic screens, the last of which are perhaps the media most used by college students of this era. This combination also accommodates the differing and variable learning styles of students. Some students learn best via oral discussion, some via reading, some by seeing the ideas in visual form via film, which is one of the most popular of the arts.

POTENTIAL FOR "DEEP LEARNING"

Among college students, there is a spectrum of understanding that ranges between "surface" learning and "deep" learning in any given course. Between surface and depth, there is also the "strategic" learner.[2] Deep learning is what professors and students should desire, precisely because such learning will stay with the student long after the semester ends. To understand how *Media Environments* strives to motivate such deep learning, it is important to first understand the differences between surface, strategic, and deep learning, and the role of "models" and classroom "environments" in effecting deeper learning.

Surface learning involves the student replicating the ideas and information provided by the professor, without really understanding the ideas or grasping their fuller meanings or applications. Such learning among students may be motivated by the fear of being intellectually challenged or the lack of desire for deeper understanding. Students who remain on the surface are likely to forget what they "learned" soon after the completion of the semester. In effect this is the Xerox version of learning and, like most paper copies, it ends up sitting in a file folder or more likely, tossed in the trash can or recycling bin.

Deep learning happens when the student grasps the implications and meanings of the ideas and information. Such learning grasps the core of the idea, its foundations, and/or arguments. Deep learning is motivated in students

---

2   Much of the following discussion about student learning draws from insights shared by Ken Bain during a presentation to faculty at Temple University, January 12, 2010. The presentation explained some key ideas in his book, What the Best College Teachers Do (Cambridge, MA: Harvard University Press, 2004); student-learning patterns are discussed in Chapter 2, pp. 22–47.

by the desire to know and understand. Strategic learning is most often motivated by the desire for a good grade. As such, it involves surface learning and (sometimes) deep learning as needed to get the desired grade.

One method for inspiring deep learning is to make the course materials relevant to the students in their intellectual and cultural milieu. As with most college students of the past five decades, movies are intrinsic to the milieu of contemporary youth culture. In this anthology, the movies become the gateway to the texts, which can provide the potential for deep learning.

Another method for inspiring deeper understanding is to provide a natural critical "environment" that facilitates learning in the classroom. Since students are immersed in media environments, it makes sense to show movies on screens in classrooms, thus providing the counter-environment for understanding the very media environment that has permeated the classroom.

One of the obstacles to deep learning is overcoming the preexisting mental models about media that students have when they enter the classroom. One of the essential things humans do is integrate perceptual experiences and concepts into mental models (or schemata) that explain "the way the world works." These models can be simple or complex and have been constructed and modified in people's minds over the course of their lives. As illustrated most clearly in religion and politics, getting someone to discard one of their mental models is very difficult, often in the face of overwhelming evidence that contradicts or refutes their model. Students are no different and they may simply wrap the new information or model from the course into their preexisting mental models or discard the new ideas or model if it conflicts with what they believe they know.

Regarding deep learning, replacing outmoded or incorrect models in the minds of students is a formidable challenge. *Media Environments* addresses this challenge in two ways. First, the anthology combines text with powerful visuals to illustrate the models and themes covered in the anthology. Second, the four media models — The Meme, The Network, The Spectacle, The Hyperreal — can be applied to the remaining themes covered in the chapters. In the end, the "film-and-text" method is not a "perfect" method, but it does provide a model that has much potential for effectively teaching Media and Society (and other media-related courses) to the 21st century student.

A NOTE ABOUT THE READINGS AND FILMS

The readings selected for *Media Environments* were almost exclusively taken from books available in chain and independent bookstores, in the media, sociology, or cultural studies sections. It is assumed that if the readings are from publications in typical public bookstores, college students should be able to comprehend — with effort — the ideas in these readings, as organized in this anthology. That these readings appear in this anthology does not mean that the editor agrees with all the authors. This anthology is not a collection of the editor's favorite media theories. The readings were selected with one overall goal: to provide a variety of provocative ideas and arguments that mesh with the films to stimulate critical thinking among undergraduate students.

The films recommended in this anthology are not meant to be viewed as the "greatest" films of all time, nor are they the editor's favorite movies. Rather, these are some of the best popular films that dramatize complex media theory and its relations to culture and society. Professors are encouraged to be open minded about the learning potential of any given film, even though it is not one of their personal favorites. Since these topics and films obviously overlap, with some movies suitable for more than one topic, professors can use the films as they desire for each chapter.

The themes, films, and readings selected for this anthology are meant to provide new ways of looking at media and society. The readings within chapters are *not* arranged in a facile manner that suggests either/or, pro and con, or "both sides" of the issue. The world of memes and cultures is far more complex. The readings were selected to encourage creative and critical thinking. Though there is an overall structure, I want the films and readings to provide surprising juxtapositions, to flow imperfectly and embrace some turbulence, and to present models and memes in ways that are patterned and chaotic. That is the way the world actually works.

Acknowledgments

As with any textbook, this anthology would not have been possible without the efforts of many people. My thanks:

To Johanna Marcelino, the acquisitions editor at Cognella who initially approached me about doing an "innovative" anthology. To be honest, I was very skeptical about her interest because virtually all textbook publishers are ultraconservative in their approach and methodologies. That is why the media and society textbooks have hardly changed in style and structure over the past 30 years, despite the proliferation of media in our culture. Much to my surprise, Johanna immediately grasped the essence of my vision for this volume and paved the way for this book to happen. Thanks for getting it, Johanna!

To Al Grisanti, senior acquisitions editor at Cognella, for sharing his many insights into the mass media textbook marketplace. Our conversations helped shape the final selections and chapters included in this text. Thanks for sharing your expertise, Al.

To Monica Hui for making the cover look so great, for letting the image tell the story with minimal interference from text and graphics. Thank you for making it all work together, Monica.

To Jessica Knott for her "cool" design sensibilities. Most media and society textbooks offer a barrage of visual clutter, with pages packed with charts, photos, tables, timelines, and sidebars, all of which distract from concentrated reading and critical thinking. Jessica and I immediately connected in our visualization of the overall look and feel of the interior of the book: cool, clean, modern, minimalist, with just enough design elements to break up the text for easy readability. Your aesthetic talents are much appreciated, Jessica.

To all my colleagues in the School of Communications and Theater and the Department of Broadcasting, Telecommunications, and Mass Media at Temple University: Thanks to all of you who shared your ideas and offered useful suggestions for improving this anthology, especially Jan Fernback, Renee Hobbs, and Sherri Hope Culver. Thanks to Elizabeth Leebron Tutelman for providing me with the opportunity to teach so many of the large lecture courses in media theory at Temple and for supporting my experiments with different teaching styles and methods in these classes. Thanks to Paul Swann, Matthew Lombard, Nancy Morris, and Zizi Papacharissi, all of whom provided helpful feedback for teaching large and small theory-based courses. Thanks to Pamela Barnett and Carol Philips of Temple's Teaching and Learning Center; I have benefited from their workshops which provide numerous useful strategies for effective teaching. Thanks to everyone!

To Jarice Hanson at the University of Massachusetts Amherst for sharing many ideas and insights during our numerous conversations.

To Carly Haines for her diligent work as research assistant. Your cheerful assistance made working on this book easier.

To Gail Bower for her enthusiastic support of this anthology. Your patience and thoughtful advice was invaluable in helping me navigate the complexities of this project.

Finally, my thanks go to the many filmmakers and writers included in this anthology. Their individual and collective knowledge have furthered our understanding of the evolution and effects of the global media environments. How can anyone look at media, technology, humanity, and culture the same after reading Plato, Neil Postman, Jean Baudrillard, Susan Jacoby, Naomi Wolf, Stephen Hawking, Carl Sagan, and the many others? We all see further because of their visions.

We become what we behold.

— *Marshall McLuhan*

Media, Memes, and Moments

13 QUESTIONS

— Barry Vacker

You live in a 24/7, online, omnipresent, global network of media environments.

Screens and more screens, thousands of satellites surround the planet, millions of miles of fiber optics in the metropolises, computers, TVs, Kindles, iPhones, iPods, iPads, each storing and streaming music, videos, films, web sites, blogs, news, sports, opinion, art, and science — all connected via that vast network we call the internet. And there are newspapers and books, too, like the one you are reading now. Media are vast environments, environments of consciousness and culture, an electronic universe of space and time. It's like living in Times Square.

All this seems rather obvious.

But how can you begin to grasp the profound roles of these environments in shaping culture and human consciousness, including your own? Here's how:

Unplug. Disconnect. Turn off instant messaging. Tune down your iPod. Silence your cell phone. Yes, it is a challenge, but you can do it and survive, at least for a while. Your media environments are not going away and will be there when you plug in again shortly. The end of the world and *2012* will only happen in the movie theaters. For right now, just reflect on these next few sentences for a moment — a very long moment.

Let's begin.

Humans always exist astride an existential moment, the moment that is now, the moment between:

➢ Past and future
➢ Yesterday and tomorrow
➢ The world as it is and as it could be
➢ The world as it is and as we perceive it to be

➢ The world as it is and as it is represented to be by art, science, philosophy, and media.

This anthology is about these moments in the realm of media and culture. Since we exist astride these existential moments, we always face another moment, the moment between:

➢ Chance and choice
➢ Ignorance and knowledge
➢ Entertainment and enlightenment
➢ Dream and destiny.

This anthology is also about the moment of choice, the moment each of us faces in trying to shape our lives, to give us a sense of destiny that we control, to give meaning to our existence, to gain understanding of the culture and cosmos we inhabit. And perhaps nowhere are these questions clearer and more open to exploration than in a college classroom. These are the questions implicit in the worlds and worldviews represented in our global network of media environments, the worlds and worldviews explored in the films and readings in this anthology.

Implicit throughout this anthology is the question: "What is the role of media in human existence?" Here's the sound-bite answer: Media are how you come to know our universe and our planet and your place in that universe and your destiny here on Earth — in your life, in your career, in your network, in your reality. Those are a lot of big ideas implying many questions which are explored in this anthology. The 13 major questions in this introduction will be philosophical and/or rhetorical, designed to open your mind to thinking differently about your beliefs and the surrounding media environments! These questions also provide you with some context and additional explanations for the chapters, readings, and films.

> ➤ QUESTIONS 1–3: The Meme, The Network, The Spectacle, and The Hyperreal.
> ➤ QUESTIONS 4 AND 5: These questions help you think differently while exploring the ideas in the book and how you use media in your life.
> ➤ QUESTION 6: The Spectacle, News, Dumbed Down, and Science.
> ➤ QUESTION 7: Surveillance, Celebrity, and Social and Mobile.
> ➤ QUESTION 8: Hyperreality, Sports, Games and Virtual Reality, and Theme Parks.
> ➤ QUESTIONS 9–13: Consumerism, Globalization, Counterculture, Catastrophe, Electronic Consciousness, Spaceship Earth, Trajectories, and additional context for the films.

You can return to these questions and discussions as you work your way through the text over the course of the semester. The four media models — Meme, Network, Spectacle, and Hyperreal — can be applied to the topics and themes in the remaining chapters.

QUESTION 1
ARE YOU MASTER OF YOUR DESTINY?

You enrolled in college. Most likely you have met some new friends and heard some new ideas. You look forward to some of your classes, may dread others, and have dreams of life after graduation: career, fame, family, wealth, and so on. You may have declared a major, perhaps after a few changes and experiments in different classes. It's good to experiment. Changing your major is easy; changing your mind is a challenge.

What do you believe about the world, the universe, the role of media in human existence? Where did you get those beliefs? Do you know those beliefs to be true or are you just going along with your parents, friends, and society? Think it over.

Did you consciously choose those beliefs? Or did the beliefs choose you? That may sound like a strange question, but it is not. It is based on a very powerful idea. Maybe the

ideas and messages in the media replicate like genes and spread like a virus. Can activities, beliefs, and worldviews be thought contagions passed among minds? Douglas Rushkoff and Richard Brodie explain this possibility in the first chapter.

Facebook has friends and fans, Twitter has followers, and YouTube has viral videos. Let's think about these popular online communities by asking some questions:

> ➤ Did you find Facebook or did Facebook find you? Was it through the recommendation of a "friend?" Did you actively choose to become a "fan" of something — let's say the film *Fight Club* — on Facebook, or did it seem as if the *Fight Club* fan club chose you?
> ➤ Did you find Twitter or did Twitter find you? Did you actively choose to become a follower, or did the Twitter followers find you?
> ➤ Did you choose to find that viral video in YouTube, or did it seem as if the viral video found you?

Of course, these questions are rhetorical, yet they are meant to be seriously thought provoking at the same time. It is likely that you "found" Facebook, Twitter, and YouTube through a friend, long before your parents and grandparents ever heard of them. Once you found them, they were easy to use because it was easy to *imitate* what others were doing in these communities. That is why these communities grew so fast. Within but a few years, Facebook has reached over 300 million users, equaling the population of the United States. Some videos in YouTube have been watched tens of millions of times, often within a relatively short time frame. How these sites attain popularity and how you found and use these sites raise questions about the spread of ideas and beliefs via the networks of our media and culture.

Let's extend our analysis to sports teams and fans.

If you are a fan of a certain American football team, why are you a fan of *that* football team? Is it because they are intrinsically superior to all other football teams? If so, your team would never lose a game or fire their coach. More likely you are a fan because of sheer chance rather than pure choice. Maybe your fan preferences were determined by where you were born and/or raised by your parents; perhaps you grew up a city that has a professional football team such as Dallas, Philadelphia, or San Francisco. If you grew up in China, it is likely you are not a fan of an American football team and couldn't care less. Choice comes into the matter a little more if you chose to attend a college with a prominent football team like the University of Texas, Penn State, or the University of Southern California. But you might be a fan of college teams due to chance, just because you were born or raised nearby. Mostly, but not always, fan preferences are products of chance more than choice.

Of course, some teams find fans outside their regional areas, like the Dallas Cowboys and New York Yankees. They develop mystiques or followings because of their success, meaning they win much more often than they lose. Thus, they are on television more often. The meaning is simple: when teams win, they get more fans. Breathless sportscasters remind us that momentum changes, but winning is *contagious*! Being a fan looks like fun, except when your team loses.

Teams and fans have identifying slogans and regional nicknames, like "How 'bout them Cowboys" for the Dallas Cowboys and "Hook 'em Horns" for the Texas Longhorns. Fans often wear their team's logos or jerseys. Imitation is flattery and it is easy to do. I live in downtown Philadelphia and when the Phillies won the 2008 World Series, the celebration parade drew more than one-half million fans, all wearing red hats, T-shirts, and jerseys. From the balcony of my loft on the parade route, I watched the joyous fans stream in from every street; it looked like a species migration one might see on the National Geographic Channel. Perhaps sports taps into our tribal roots in hunter-gatherer societies. In Chapter 11, Carl Sagan's essay "Monday Night Hunters" explores this idea and gives new meaning to Tom Brady in the Super Bowl, Vince Young in the Rose Bowl, and Russell Crowe in *Gladiator*.

After all, cities and colleges build magnificent stadiums, which are temples and coliseums for their teams and fans. If you cannot attend the game, you can always migrate to the neighborhood sports bar or view the game on your flat screen in your dwelling. This explains how a lot of money is made off fans — many billions of dollars, in fact. To survive as economic and cultural entities, teams need fans and television needs viewers. They function together, always trying to acquire more fans by copying their beliefs into your mind.

And what better way to gain fans than to be celebrated on television in the annual rituals and spectacles of the Super Bowl and the Bowl Championship Series. "Super" games and "championships" are attractive and seductive, as are game-winning plays, heroic quarterbacks, and glamorous cheerleaders. So, did you *consciously* choose to be a fan because of the unique virtues of your team? Be honest. Or is your preference the product of chance (your parents and where you were born), the team, and the media, all of which combine in trying to choose you to be a fan?

Much like your fan preferences, many of your ideas and beliefs may have been passed down to you from your parents. Political, philosophical, and especially, religious beliefs strongly correlate to your parents' beliefs and/or which area, nation, or region of the world in which you were born. This means your beliefs and worldview are more likely the product of chance than your conscious choice. Just like teams need fans and TV needs viewers, political parties need voters and philosophies and religions need followers. When you agree with your parents in these realms, it likely makes them very happy. On the other hand, you may have expressed beliefs or behaviors significantly different from those of your parents, perhaps causing them much consternation. At some point, you decided to discard a previous belief or behavior from your parents, in favor of a new idea and activity. You were no longer a fan or a follower of the previous belief, which is no longer being passed on through you. Beliefs die out when they are no longer passed on to the succeeding generations.

All these examples — Facebook, Twitter, YouTube, sports fans, following parents, and chance over choice — raise essential questions about the spread of belief systems and media usage in our culture, especially via the global networks of the internet. Let's consider another question. Does your mind hold knowledge of the world that you know to be true? Or is your mind merely the host for beliefs that have copied themselves onto your neurons as an evolutionary survival strategy? Are you master of your destiny, or merely a puppet with a mind virus?

QUESTION 2
WHY ARE QUENTIN
TARANTINO FILMS SO POPULAR?

Did you know ideas and information evolve in our culture in much the same way as the genes in your body? It makes

Are you master of your destiny, or merely a puppet with a mind virus?

sense; our minds are part of our bodies and both are the product of evolution. Understanding how ideas evolve and replicate provides a new way to understand how they spread via the media to reach your mind.

Across eons of evolutionary time, the genes in all life forms survived by successfully replicating themselves in their hosts and getting passed on to future hosts via variation and selection. Evolution is the competition for existence and survival into the future. Genes compete, but not merely by copying. Genes must also be selected from among all the other competitors in the gene pool. When genes copy themselves, occasionally the copy is imperfect, thus generating a random variation or mutation. Those variations or mutations that improve fitness or confer survival advantage — in the highly competitive gene pool — will continue to be copied, unless replaced or improved by further variations and mutations. Over millions of iterations, the surviving copies will gradually take on new qualities that increase their prospects for success in producing progeny or in competition for limited resources. In contrast, the less successful genes will eventually be unable to survive, thus disappearing from nature's game. In a nutshell, genetic evolution involves replication, variation, selection, and heredity, all for the purpose of existing and surviving into the future. Over a couple of billion years, this simple evolutionary process has produced the complexity and diversity of life on Earth.

In a purely biological sense, your body is the vessel for genes passed down from your parents and all their ancestors. If you choose to have children, your genes will be passed to them and they will become the vessels for the accumulation of genes from all their ancestors. Through the never-ending succession of generations, genes are passed down across great distances of time and have spread around the planet as humans migrated across the face of the Earth. Over the eons, simple and repetitive genetic evolution has produced the complexity that is your human body and brain.

Your brain is home to your mind — the vessel for ideas, beliefs, and worldviews. You most likely inherited many of those beliefs from your parents. You have acquired ideas from your friends, the media, and maybe even some professors. The new beliefs you acquired are the product of mutations of previous beliefs or the competitive success of new and competing ideas, which have succeeded in gaining your allegiance — especially if the new ideas or beliefs seem to better explain the world and your place in it.

To help you think about ideas and information as evolutionary beliefs in a new way, let's explore the term "meme" (rhymes with cream). "Meme" was coined by biologist Richard Dawkins in the book *The Selfish Gene*, in which he presented his explanation of genetic evolution.[1] Dawkins observed that culture evolves in many ways similar to genes and created "meme" as a term for explaining cultural evolution in new ways. Since then, the concept of memes has spread out into society to become the object of study among many thinkers, as illustrated in the various definitions provided in Richard Brodie's reading in Chapter 1.

> BIOLOGICAL DEFINITION: The *meme* is the basic unit of cultural transmission, or imitation.

> PSYCHOLOGICAL DEFINITION: A *meme* is the unit of cultural heredity analogous to the gene. It is the internal representation of knowledge.

> COGNITIVE DEFINITION: A *meme* is an idea, the kind of complex idea that forms itself into a distinct memorable unit. It is spread by *vehicles* that are physical manifestations of the meme.

> BRODIE'S DEFINITION: A *meme* is a unit of information in a mind whose existence influences events such that more copies of itself get created in other minds.[2]

These definitions and the accompanying readings provide a method for thinking about the transmission of ideas from consciousness to consciousness — via the media — in our culture. Across the millennia of *cultural* evolution, memes have survived and flourished because they managed to replicate, mutate for survival advantage, and continue to be selected within the minds of their hosts.

Some memes are simple, some are highly complex. Memes populate the environments of our minds, in the

---

1 Richard Dawkins, *The Selfish Gene* (Oxford, UK: Oxford University Press, 1976): 189–201. Meme is a hybrid term, derived and condensed from the word "mimeme," which has roots in the Greek word for imitation; Dawkins also thought meme could be related to memory and the French word *même*; p. 192.

2 Richard Brodie, *Virus of the Mind* (New York: Hay House, 2009): 5–11.

form of our beliefs and worldviews, which in turn shape our behaviors and destinies. The most complex memes — like sports or religions or worldviews or ecology or consumerism or counterculture — can be thought of as metamemes or memeplexes. A metameme is an overarching meme that contains many lesser memes, while a memeplex refers to a complexity of memes, or clusters of smaller memes that replicate together in a manner that furthers the survival of the memes, collectively and individually.[3]

It is important to understand that the popularity of a meme, metameme, or memeplex has nothing to do with truth or its true value, but rather its ability to survive by saying something about the world that ensures its replication in the host. In other words, any given meme may be true meaning, understanding, destiny, purpose, and a general place in the world.

The best place for memes to replicate is the global network of media environments. That is how many memes entered the environments of your mind. Times Square is filled with memes.[4] So are the tweets on Twitter, the spectacles of the Super Bowl, and movies at the IMAX theater. Memes are all around us, in our cities, our cultures, and circulating nonstop in the media networks — fashions, hairstyles, logos, tattoos, body piercings, hit songs, viral videos, conspiracy theories, apps on iPhones, and the Tetris mobile video game, which has exceeded 100 million downloads.

Wherever there are people and ideas, there are memes, all competing to replicate and survive in the meme pool.

While a meme could be popular because it is actually true, a meme might be unpopular precisely because it is true and challenges a widely held belief system. … Memes can be true or false, including the memes in your mind.

---

or may be false. While a meme could be popular because it is actually true, a meme might be unpopular precisely because it is true and challenges a widely held belief system. This does not mean that memes are "relative" or purely subjective, because proving the truth of memes eventually requires correlation with empirical evidence. Memes can be true or false, including the memes in your mind. This is why it is important to verify what you believe, and discard what you find to be untrue.

Memes are believed because they are assumed to be true, whether or not they are actually true. Memes are also believed because they are viewed as good or beautiful or valuable in some way, plus a host of lesser reasons. The most powerful of memes, metamemes, and memeplexes are believed because they provide a model of the world — however accurate or inaccurate — that provides a sense of meaning, a sense of understanding, and a sense of destiny and purpose. Woody Allen's film *Whatever Works* shows how ideological and behavioral memes "find" their believers through a combination of conscious choice by the believer and chance encounters in society. "Whatever works" for Allen is whatever memeplex provides you a sense of

This is no less true in politics. Politicians need voters and political parties need followers. You could think of the 2008 U.S. presidential election as a battle among three memes: "Hope and Change," "Maverick," and "Rogue." Do I even need to mention the names of the candidates associated with these memes? As with all memes, political memes can replicate regardless of whether they are true or false, right or wrong, good or bad. Memes can replicate regardless of whether the politician or political belief has any merit, anything new to offer, or anything coherent to say, as illustrated in Sarah Palin's famous television interview with Katie Couric. In fact, memes are more likely to be replicated when they are not really new, but only appear new and play well in the spectacle. Politicians, media personalities, and the "experts" may have actual merit, but nothing is guaranteed just because a meme is popular. These conditions are illustrated in the classic media films *Network* and *A Face in the Crowd*.

---

3 Susan Blackmore, *The Meme Machine* (Oxford, UK: Oxford University Press, 1999): 19.

4 In 2007, I wrote and directed an experimental film about media and memes in Times Square. It's called *Space Times Square* and it played at various festivals and conferences around the world and received the 2010 John Culkin Award for Outstanding Praxis in the Field of Media Ecology from the Media Ecology Association. The 24-minute film is a mind bender; you can check it out for free in Google Video. Just type in: Space Times Square. For more information, see www.spacetimessquare.net.

Virtually all of the films in this anthology are movie memeplexes, packed with many smaller memes that work together in a complexity to replicate their ideas on the screen and in the minds of moviegoers. Many of these films not only replicate memes, they have mutations that are transformative, resulting in a film with references to the past as well as new meanings and messages for the contemporary era.

Much of Quentin Tarantino's fame as a filmmaker is because his films are brimming with pop culture memes that are mutant in fresh, surprising, and shocking ways, from *Pulp Fiction* to *Kill Bill* to *Inglourious Basterds*. In fact, the name "Pulp Fiction" suggests memes from cheap novels or low-budget films, the very subject matter selected, copied, and transformed by Tarantino. In the famous conversation between two hitmen in *Pulp Fiction*, Tarantino plays with memes we know all too well, the Quarter Pounder and the Big Mac. Quoted on the title page of Chapter 1, this conversation unintentionally illustrates how memes get copied and passed along among humans. Vincent picked up the memes in France and is passing them to Jules, who repeats each meme — "Royale with Cheese" and "Le Big Mac" — after he hears it. Jules's repeating of the names of the burgers illustrates the copying power of memes. Yet, since Vincent did not go to Burger King, the French version of the Whopper does not get passed along.

Tarantino's memes also illustrate a key feature of postmodernity, where the proliferation of image and information fuels a culture of copying and "simulation." As Aaron C. Anderson explains in Chapter 1, Tarantino uses images (memes) from road movies as starting points for *Death Proof*, yet the film discards any reference to the economic or social reality that generated the "original" movies. Tarantino's *Death Proof* and Robert Rodriguez's *Planet Terror* are the two films in the double feature known as *Grindhouse*; both *Death Proof* and *Planet Terror* are not remakes, but are big budget simulations of low budget flicks screened in the "grindhouses" of the 1970s. Tarantino's films are filled with hybrid memes — copies and simulations of images which once referenced reality — that effect a cinematic "hyperreality" by transforming history into TV and movie images. That Tarantino is hailed as an original filmmaker, a rebel auteur, is a testament to the power of memes and the seductions of simulation and hyperreality.

Genes were the first replicators, fueling the biological evolution of life, including the evolution of the human mind. Emerging from our minds, memes are the second replicators, fueling the cultural evolution of humans around the world. In the words of Susan Blackmore, humans are "gene machines and meme machines." Blackmore also thinks that a third replicator has emerged among our memes, the replicator of technology, or what she has recently termed as "temes."[5] Many of these temes have converged in producing the technological evolution of our 24/7 media environments. And these media environments are the perfect ecosystems for the global replication of memes.

QUESTION 3
WHAT'S THE MEANING OF
"THE BRIDGE" IN *STAR TREK*?

Star Trek presents an idealized vision of our global network of media environments, circa 2009. The media environments on the Starship *Enterprise* are ambient, convergent, fluid, interactive and automated, digital and electronic, wired and wireless, social and mobile, operate and update in real time, have access to vast databases, and the information is represented on clear, flat screens throughout the ship. Wherever Captain Kirk and crew members go throughout the *Enterprise*, they are immersed in the ship's information networks at all times. The media function like a more advanced version of the 24/7, nonstop network that is all around us. That's why The Network is the second media model discussed in this anthology (Chapter 2).

Let's go a little deeper. Maybe this will help explain the potential *personal* power of the media environments. The main control room for piloting the *Enterprise* is called "the bridge" and it has a circular shape that resembles a panopticon, the circular surveillance system explained in Question 7. As the captain, Kirk is seated in the center of the bridge, with the top-ranked crew members seated before the circular array of screens. There is also a large windshield that allows them to directly perceive the portion of the cosmos in front of the ship. But there are far more screens than windshield, and the crew spends most of the time looking at the screens, not out the windshield.

That's because direct perception through the windshield is insufficient for traversing the cosmos, thus requiring sensory extension and amplification by technology. This is something humans learned with their first cave painting

---

5   Susan Blackmore, "Susan Blackmore on memes and temes," TED2008 Conference, February 2008; web site accessed March 11, 2010.

and spoken word. We looked out from our caves and realized we cannot survive very well without communication and technology.

Extending from the crew to the cosmos, from the bridge to beyond the *Enterprise*, is a vast network of media technologies, designed to gather, organize, interpret, and display a variety of images and information on the electronic screens. The images on the screens are enhanced representations of the reality beyond the windshield on the bridge. The panoptic networks of the starship illustrate the essential role of media technologies in assisting and extending human consciousness in its never-ending quest to acquire knowledge of reality and the cosmos. In many ways, our personal media technologies are our bridges to much larger universes — the cosmos that surrounds us and the cultural worlds of information, entertainment, and enlightenment. But what happens when entertainment overtakes enlightenment or information overtakes reality to create a substitute reality? These are the questions explored in the next two media models, The Spectacle (Chapter 3) and The Hyperreal (Chapter 4).

In a very real sense, when you are using your computer, you are sitting in your own captain's chair and navigating a vast electronic universe. What are you doing? Uploading pictures and downloading tunes, watching two-minute videos about celebrities and sports highlights, or perhaps texting and tweeting away about the trivia of life? Doesn't it seem like it ought to be more than that?

QUESTION 4
HOW CAN I GET MY
HEAD AROUND ALL THIS?

This a challenge for anyone the first time they are exposed to all these new memes. That is why this anthology was created with the combination of films and readings. It provides you with new memes and new models for understanding the role of media in culture and consciousness, including yours. These are not the only memes and models for thinking about the media — but they are among the best. They reveal structure in the chaos, rhythms in the torrents. These memes and models have emerged, replicated, evolved, and survived because of their ability to explain the patterns in the complexity of the media environments.

As discussed in Chapters 1–4, the four key models are: The Meme, The Network, The Spectacle, and The Hyperreal. These models can then be applied to explain and explore the remainder of the sections and topics in the book, which are organized by theme and chapter. In the combination of films and readings, you will be exposed to many new memes and media models, produced by filmmakers and thinkers who all believe they have something important to say about media and culture.

And here is your challenge. These films and anthologies cannot do the thinking inside your own mind. That is your responsibility to yourself. You will have to decide which memes and models match with the evidence from the world around you and that vast electronic realm, the 24/7, online, omnipresent, global network of media environments. Which of these memes and models, if any, will you take with you after this class?

Learning and understanding new ideas is not always easy, especially if the new ideas are unfamiliar or challenge those memes deeply embedded in your neural networks. Ultimately, you will have to decide which memes and models you want to believe, based on the ideas in the memes and the evidence of your life experiences. You have to decide which memes and models provide the best understanding, the most elegant explanation, or the most beautiful sense of destiny.

The choice is yours.

Let me provide some memes for inspiration and reflection:

MEME 1

YOU HAVE A MILKY WAY IN YOUR MIND

We know genes determine much about what comprises your body, the product of eons of evolution. But what about your mind, that self-awareness centered in your brain, that bioelectrical neural network that is also the product of evolution?

Guess what? You are very lucky, as are most humans on Earth.

The eons of evolution have bestowed your brain with almost as many neurons as there are stars in the Milky Way! And how many is that? Over 100 billion!

Technically, there are more stars in the Milky Way than neurons in your brain, but the exact match is not important. It is the metaphor that is powerful — you have a galaxy of neurons in your brain, a Milky Way in your mind! This meme is illustrated in the opening scene of *Contact*, where we see the Milky Way and the universe emerging from the eye of Ellie Arroway (played by a young Jena Malone in the opening and later by Jodie Foster).

So, what are you doing with your own personal Milky Way here on planet Earth? Is your Milky Way enlarging your galaxy of possibilities for living in this world, for understanding this world, for finding meaning in this world, for mastering your destiny? Is your mental universe getting larger or smaller? Are the neural networks glowing brighter or getting dimmer? Since you are in college, your mental universe should be getting larger and glowing brighter. If you open your mind, the films and readings in this anthology can surely expand your mental universe regarding media and culture.

Not only has *biological* evolution provided you with a Milky Way in your mind, but centuries of *technological* evolution have provided your cognitive galaxy with access to countless other galaxies of knowledge and wisdom, galaxies from across space and time, in that expanding universe we call cyberspace.

MEME 2

THE MEDIUM IS THE MESSAGE:

MEDIA ARE EXTENSIONS OF HUMAN CONSCIOUSNESS

Mark Zuckerberg, founder of Facebook, is a billionaire at 25 and James Cameron's *Avatar* is the highest grossing film of all time, even topping *Titanic*.

But the ideas of Facebook and 3-D films are not new. Both are as old as the earliest cave painting. Of course, Facebook and 3-D *technologies* are new, but not the *idea* of representing ourselves to the world and representing the world to ourselves, including imaginary worlds.

In the 1960s, pioneering media theorist Marshall McLuhan explained that media are extensions of human consciousness and the central nervous system, resulting in a global network that functions as a global consciousness and nervous system. Throughout human history, we have deployed technologies of perception upon the world to map the world. Spoken words, written and print media, cameras and electronic media — radio, movies, television, computers, and the internet — are extensions of the brain's ability to perceive, speak, think, and represent the world to itself.

You are extending your consciousness into cyberspace with your blog, with your posts on Facebook, with your videos on YouTube. But beyond your ability to put information online, there are many effects to such technological powers. That's because these media technologies also function to reorder our perceptions of the world, causing us to *model* the world in new ways. The films and readings in this anthology illustrate this profound point. The alphabet and the printing press changed the course of civilization, just as electronic media is effecting another transformation. Beginning with those cave paintings and the earliest languages, we have developed an ever more complex system of technologies for representing the world we perceive. These technologies permit the spread of memes and models — first locally, then regionally and globally, as with the internet and satellites.

Our thoughts about the world took physical form when we developed symbolic communication and spoken language, from which emerged written languages such as pictographs and alphabets, which allow communication in real time and across time. Stone tablets and papyrus were technologies for preserving the spoken word. Oral myths and storytelling were replaced by written knowledge that was passed down to later generations. That is why we can read Aristotle and Confucius thousands of years later. When you post on your blog, you are communicating across distances in time and space, precisely because either can be viewed at a later date and in another place. Will your post last a thousand years? Does it say anything of lasting value?

Written languages were exponentially amplified with the printing press in the 15th century, the first true mass media technology. In many ways, you are living in the world of the printing press. As explained in the first reading of Chapter 2, the printing press helped usher in the modern world that surrounds you, from mass media to mass production, nationalism to individualism, literacy to enlightenment, democracy to freedom of expression. More than five centuries later, the book you are now reading was born of the printing press. The e-books in Kindle have their origins in papyrus and the printing press.

In the 19th century, our perceptions of the world extended into new forms with photography and the camera, which captured and reproduced what the eye could see and

> Media technologies shape what we believe and how we think.

what the eye could not see, especially with slow motion and time-lapse photography. Humans have been doing theater for many millennia and with the motion-picture camera the stages of theater leapt into the studios of cinema. *Avatar* is pure theater, the theater in James Cameron's mind and staged with some very powerful digital technologies in the movie studio.

Our thoughts and perceptions extended into electronic forms with the telegraph and telephone, both of which went wireless with radio and digital technologies. IPhones and instant messages are the latest incarnation of communication across distances in space. Radio and motion-picture cameras combined to produce television, from which we get NBC, CNN, YouTube, and Hulu.

From the electronic and digital technologies emerged satellites and ever more powerful computers, within which we see all previous media technologies converging as they encircle the world and extend into the cosmos. Google maps and the Hubble space telescope express these technological powers. But what might be the effect of these latest electronic technologies?

Here is a way to begin considering the question: Since each medium is an extension of consciousness, each new medium becomes a container of the previous medium (or media), with the new medium amplifying the power of the older medium (or media). The printed word contains the written word, which contains the spoken word, which contains human thought. Television contains cinema and radio, with cinema containing the camera and the vision of the eye, while radio contains the telephone and the spoken word. With media convergence via digitalization, many computers now contain all previous media, all migrating into cyberspace and connected via the internet. This is why computers and cyberspace function as containers for the contents of human consciousness. Facebook and blogs are microcosms of what is happening throughout cyberspace and the internet.

But there is something that most everyone overlooks when thinking about the effect of new media technologies. When a new medium is developed, the older media become *the content* of the new medium. Thus, most everyone concentrates on the old media as content while ignoring or overlooking the *amplifying effects* of the newer medium.

This is what McLuhan meant in his famed phrase: "The medium is the message."[6] The social and personal effects of our media technologies are greater than the messages they carry. This does not mean the messages are of no importance. Of course, they are, as illustrated in many readings in this anthology. But each medium carries its own message, its own mode of perception. McLuhan also noted that "the medium is the massage," meaning that media massage our consciousness, conditioning our minds into ways of thinking and understanding the world.

Thus, our technologies have a great impact on our perceptions and how we organize societies and cultures. If we only think of media technologies as transporters of content, then we are missing the larger effects. Many of these effects are utterly unintended.

Think of the automobile, which takes us from point A to point B. In taking us places, the car generated suburbia and the highway system, which amplified tourism and transformed distribution systems (via trucking); all of this caused massive fossil-fuel consumption and carbon emissions, which have shaped America's domestic and foreign policies. The medium of the car has a much larger message than traveling from point A to point B.

Now, think of the computer, which transports information from various points. In transporting information, the computer helped generate the internet, both of which are combining to change our public policies, economy, social organization, distribution systems, the spread of knowledge, and the very way we communicate and represent ourselves to the world via art and media. Many of these effects are explored in the films and readings for these chapters:

- The Network
- The Spectacle
- The Hyperreal
- Surveillance
- Celebrity

- Social and Mobile
- Games and Virtual Reality
- Electronic Consciousness
- Spaceship Earth
- Trajectories

---

6   Marshall McLuhan, *Understanding Media: The Extensions of Man* (New York: McGraw-Hill, 1964): 7–21.

MEME 3

MEDIA TECHNOLOGIES ARE NOT NEUTRAL:
AS THEY INCREASE IN POWER, THEY CHANGE OUR
VIEW OF THE COSMOS, CULTURE, AND CONSCIOUSNESS.

This meme is an extension or application of McLuhan's idea of "the medium is the message." To explore it, let's consider the universe in *Star Trek*, the 2009 blockbuster movie. Just what *is* the universe in *Star Trek*?

Well, it is a very big universe. Otherwise, there would be no need for "warp drive" and the power to travel faster than the speed of light. Within *Star Trek*, the universe reflects some of what humans know about the size of the cosmos and phenomena such as the black hole, which was central to the plot of the movie. The universe in *Star Trek* could only be known and understood via media technologies such as cameras, computers, and various kinds of telescopes. Prior to the invention of telescopes, the universe of *Star Trek* was unknowable and unthinkable.

Media technologies are not neutral; as they increase in power they change our view of the world. Across the past five centuries, we have extended media technologies ever further out into space and time, and in so doing we have transformed our view of the cosmos, culture, and consciousness. Though media technologies have the power to accurately represent the world to us, it does not mean they are "neutral" in how we see and understand the world. We know human bias and personal subjectivity exists in how each of us views the world, yet here we are referring to something much different. Media technologies shape *what* we believe and *how* we think. Grasping this meme is crucial for understanding the most profound effects of the global media environments.

The films and readings in the following chapters illustrate the effect of media technology in three areas:

➢ Our cosmological worldview: Science and Spaceship Earth
➢ How we create and organize culture and societies: The Network, The Spectacle, and The Hyperreal, Surveillance, Celebrity, Social and Mobile, Theme Parks, Globalization
➢ How we view consciousness and form identities: Dumbed Down, Games and Virtual Reality, Electronic Consciousness, Trajectories.

MEME 4

WE ARE NOT THE CENTER OF THE UNIVERSE

What is the most profound philosophical and social effect of media technologies? Perhaps it is the discovery that we are not at the center of the universe. This profound insight is on display across four decades of the *Star Trek* memeplex, which includes the perpetual discovery of "new life forms and new civilizations."

Across the millennia, ancient peoples gathered around campfires and gazed up at the starry skies in search of patterns, meaning, and cosmic destiny. They told stories, created myths to provide meaning, and identified constellations in the random patterns of stars, glowing like diamonds on black velvet. Now most people live in electrified metropolises and rarely see the stars at night, and if they do, the few visible stars are faint and unimpressive. So, the urban dwellers turn on their substitute universe, their televisions and computers, which glow much brighter. Or maybe they go to an IMAX movie and look up at the domed screen that resembles the curvature of the night sky.

When watching the stars and moon rise and set on a clear night in a remote desert or over the vast ocean, it is easy to see how the ancients could have imagined only that the Earth was at the center of the universe. In addition, the repetition of movement across months and years seemed to coincide with seasonal changes and weather patterns. Thus, many peoples believed that the stars foretold their destinies because weather patterns were a matter of life and death for hunter-gatherers or agrarian cultures, all reliant on the accurate prediction of seasonal changes to find or grow food. Entire cultures were built around these seasonal patterns, which were seemingly predicted by the stars as they passed across the night skies of the Earth, which apparently was at the center of the universe. The idea that the Earth is at the center of the cosmos is called the geocentric model of the universe and this worldview and metameme prevailed across many millennia, forming the cosmological basis for most of the world's theologies and astrologies.

Over the past five centuries, the geocentric metameme has been shattered by the telescope, perhaps the most important media technology in human history. In 1609, Galileo used one of the earliest telescopes to verify the calculations of Copernicus and Kepler, both of whom suggested that a sun-centered universe might better explain and predict the patterns in the night skies. When Galileo was able to demonstrate that the Earth and planets orbited the sun, our view of the cosmos and Earth changed forever.

Four centuries later, only two of Galileo's telescopes remain in existence and one was featured in an exhibit that visited America in 2009. Entitled "Galileo, the Medici and the Age of Astronomy," the exhibit only came to Philadelphia's Franklin Institute, the prestigious science museum where I had the good fortune to see the telescope. Very slender and a mere three feet long, with two glass lenses for refracting the light, Galileo's telescope shows that a media technology does not have to be large to have a huge effect. Not unlike microprocessors.

Since Galileo's discovery, our understanding of the cosmos has grown exponentially, as has the size of the universe. A new metameme has emerged that explains our place in the cosmos and is supported by an ever-growing "galaxy" of evidence provided by our most advanced media technologies. This cosmological metameme is known as the "big bang" universe.

Using the most powerful telescopes on Earth and the Hubble space telescope, we now know that the our planet orbits a typical star situated in an arm of the Milky Way, a spiral galaxy with at least 100–400 billion stars and a width of 100,000 light years (100,000 x 6 trillion!). Even more amazing is that the Milky Way is just one of at least 100 billion galaxies in the known universe, each with many billions of stars. There exists the possibility of millions or billions of suns in the universe with planetary systems, perhaps even planets with life. E.T. may take many forms, phone many homes.

Our telescopes and computers have revealed that the universe emerged from a cosmological eruption almost 14 billion years ago, an explosion known as the "big bang." Since the big bang, the universe has been expanding in all directions, with vast voids of dark energy shoving the galaxies apart from one another at ever greater velocities. It is strange to imagine, but our planet, the sun, and the Milky Way are all hurtling through space at approximately 500,000 miles per hour. Yes, right now, as you read this book, you and everything on Earth are moving through space at 500,000 miles per hour!

And even more strangely, scientists estimate that the edges of the universe are expanding at 1 billion miles per hour. This model of a big bang universe is a mind-boggling metameme and offers further proof that as media technologies increase in power, they change our view of the cosmos and our place in it.

The evolution of our cosmological understanding of the universe — from flat earth and geocentric to the big bang and the expanding universe — perfectly illustrates the evolution of science and the role played in this evolution by media technologies. Like memes and metamemes, science (and our cosmology) evolve by replicating. But, and this is most important, science varies and selects based on one of two factors: 1) the correlation of a new model (or theory) with new evidence, or 2) the better correlation of a new model (or theory) with existing evidence. Much of this new evidence is gathered with the assistance of media technologies such as telescopes, microscopes, cameras, and computers. When new evidence warrants a new model or when a new model better explains existing evidence, a new meme or metameme is born.

When the new model is verified by additional evidence or additional tests, the model has survived and will be replicated. The meme or metameme is believed to be true, precisely because it has not been falsified by other tests, models, or theories. Science builds on the models that prove to be true over time by their correlation with evidence and/or other proven theories. Meanwhile, those metamemes that are proven false will fail to replicate and eventually die out, such as the geocentric and flat earth models. Sometimes a new model is so profound it creates a new metameme, a new model of life or the universe, such as Darwin's evolution, Einstein's relativity, and Hubble's big bang.

To model the big bang and the expanding universe, scientists use powerful supercomputers. Though you may not have access to those computers, for now, you can see a visual representation of some of the vastness of the universe in the opening sequences of the film *Contact*. You can also see a tiny approximation of the big bang in the movement of the icons on an iPhone, and that representation is laden with meaning about the nature and power of media technologies, including your media power.

> This model of a big bang universe is a mind-boggling metameme and offers further proof that as media technologies increase in power, they change our view of the cosmos and our place in it.

THE ELECTRONIC BIG BANG

A mere glance at our 24/7 media environments reveals that flat screens are proliferating in multiple sizes and forms, from iPods to iPads, laptops to desktops, television to Times Square. Day or night, it doesn't matter, the pixels are glowing ever more brightly and powerful. But what exists

iPhone, touch one of the icons with your finger. Here's what happens: when the icon is touched, the remaining icons quickly disappear, moving off the edge of the screen, not unlike galaxies moving toward the horizons of the expanding universe. Further, as the unselected icons slide off the screen, the realm signified by the selected icon — say Safari, the Apple Web browser — instantly emerges from

---

If you graduate at age 22, then Moore's Law indicates computer power will have doubled eleven times during your lifetime. … In the past two years, what have you done to double your power in the world of media? What will you do in the next two years to double your power?

---

behind or beyond those screens? Let's think of it in cosmic terms.

During the day, sunlight shines through the sky, illuminating the objects of the world. At night, stars shine through, too, but in a manner more like electronic screens, for the twinkling stars pixelate the dark sky, beckoning us to a world far beyond the sun. The stars signify mystery and destiny, situated in the vastness and emptiness of space beyond our solar system. Shining through the electronic screens of computers is yet another "world beyond," the cosmos of cyberspace, and it beckons to us across its vast and expanding universe, a universe experiencing an electronic big bang. As Paul Levinson observed: "The screen becomes a portal to a virtual infinity (in both senses of the word 'virtual') of possibilities beyond."[7]

You're probably wondering how the big bang is approximated on the iPhone and what this "virtual infinity" could mean for your media power. The representation of the big bang is not a clever app or video clip, but rather in the very way the icons function on the iPhone. If you own an iPhone, you probably are looking at it right now, maybe even thinking this meme is absurd. But keep an open mind because the visual metaphor is powerful. It might cause you to rethink the time you spend on Facebook or playing video games.

Even if you do not own an iPhone, you probably know what its screen looks like, with rows of icons that include Safari, Mail, Stocks, Weather, Maps, Notes, Text, Camera, Photos, iTunes, iPod, YouTube, and so on. If you have an

the center of the screen, directly from the vanishing point to encompass the entire screen, as if emerging from a singular point to become the universe on the screen.

Through this elegant imagery, Apple has unintentionally expressed the idea of an electronic big bang, the expanding media universe existing alongside the material universe, the two worlds we humans inhabit on Earth. It's a powerful metaphor once you get your mind wrapped around it. Think of it this way: It's not just that you live in a world of media environments, but within those environments is an expanding electronic universe. And your flat screens — TVs, computers, cell phones — are portals to that universe. You should make sure this universe does not become a mere television universe, with laptops and iPads serving as portable TV screens for passive or trivial consumption.

You might be saying: "Okay, so what, we have more media now than yesterday. No big deal. I use my iPhone to text my friends and play video games, not to think about 'electronic universes' and the big bang." I can't stop you from thinking that, but you are missing out on powerful memes that might change how you interact with and think about media.

MEME 6

MOORE'S LAW

Grasping the importance of the electronic universe meme requires understanding digitalization and the meme of "Moore's Law."

Digitalization means all words, images, and music in our media technologies are stored, manipulated, and

---

7   Paul Levinson, *Digital McLuhan* (London: Routledge, 1999): 102.

transmitted as tiny bits of digital and electronic information. Inside the microprocessors that power our media technologies, the electronic information is coded in a binary sequence of numeric ones (1) and zeros (0). These 1s and 0s are "bits" of information, the genes of digital DNA, the smallest elements in the electronic universe. They have no color, no size, and no weight and can travel at the speed of light. Inside the microprocessors, the bits are in the form of electrical current carried via electrons through the circuitry — when the current passes through the circuit, it is "on," and when the current does not pass through, it is "off." When these on-off states are sequenced as 1s and 0s, the strings of binary code become the content of the media, with the circuitry of computers functioning as the container for the expanding electronic universe.

That this universe is expanding, like the big bang, is the product of continual innovations in the microprocessors, innovations that follow a pattern known as "Moore's Law." In 1965, Gordon Moore, the cofounder of Intel, observed that the number of transistors that could fit on a computer chip had doubled every year since 1959, and predicted that the pattern would continue for at least 10 more years. By 1975, the pattern revealed the doubling of transistors every 18 months to two years, not the exact time frame Moore predicted, but still a radically fast expansion of processing power. Since then, this pattern has generally held true, with power doubling about every two years, while also declining in price relative to power. This remarkable pattern has come to be known as Moore's Law and is expected to hold true for the foreseeable future.[8] Moore's seemingly modest insight has, in effect, described and predicted a "big bang" of computer and media power, an expanding universe of media environments, doubling every 18–24 months.

This may sound like jargon for techno-geeks. But it is a key idea for understanding media technologies and their power. Moore's Law is an example of "period-doubling," the process by which a small system can grow enormously large by repeatedly doubling over a given period. For example, suppose you had a job offer upon graduation and the employer offered to pay you one penny on the first day, but pledged to double your pay every day for the first month. Should you take the job? Yes, then retire after day 30. Let's look at what you would earn if you began with a penny and doubled your pay every day for a month: Day

8   Ray Kurzweil, *The Age of Spiritual Machines* (New York: Viking, 1999), 20–25.

1 = 1 cent, Day 2 = 2 cents, Day 7 = 64 cents, Day 8 = $1.28, Day 15 = $164, Day 22 = $21,000, Day 29 = $2.7 million, Day 30 = $5.4 million. Your one-month total = $10.8 million. This is not a trick. Do the calculations for yourself.

The growth, power, content, and social value of our media environments are following this *exponential* pattern. And this does not even include the people linking to the network, which is exponentially increasing and now exceeds 1.6 billion.

QUESTION 5
IS THE INTERNET WORKING FOR YOU?

If you have been in college two years, the size and power of the global media environments have effectively doubled. So, what have you done to double your power in the past two years? This is not a trick question. Of course, you might reply that you are going to college so you can have the career and lifestyle you desire. That's a very good strategy. But is it enough?

If you graduate at age 22, Moore's Law indicates computer power will have doubled 11 times during your lifetime. So, think about that question again. In the past two years, what have you done to double your power in the world of media? What will you do in the next two years to double your power?

You may have spent a lot of time on Facebook or MySpace or perhaps playing video games and watching movies online. It may be entertaining and everyone likes a

---

Is Facebook working for you or are you working for Facebook?

---

little fun. But during all that time, have you increased your power? Are you more in control of your destiny because you spent a lot of time on Facebook or MySpace?

As of fall 2009, Facebook had a market value of approximately $10 billion with a population exceeding 300 million users. Simple math shows that each user had contributed an average of $33 to the market value of Facebook. Just think: all the time you have spent on Facebook, however fun, has yielded only $33 in market value for Facebook. Now imagine all the hours you spent on Facebook and ask if you would do it again for $33. This raises another question: Is Facebook working for you or are you working for Facebook? Let's extend the question further: Is the internet working for you or are you working for the internet?

Posting and texting may be fun, as are downloading music and films. Better than downloading someone else's memes, try creating your own *unique* memes — via blogs, books, music, films, podcasts, and so on — and get them copied by other people. Create a mind virus. The ideas in these readings can provide you with many, many memes, waiting to mutate and transform through your efforts in your creative projects. The more your new memes are being copied and replicated via the network, the more likely you are increasing your social and economic power.

This miniaturization also means computers and microprocessors could circulate throughout our bodies and minds (Chapter 19). That's why some people think video games will take on radical possibilities, like those depicted in *eXistenZ*. Perhaps we will upload our consciousness in cyberspace, as in *Vanilla Sky* or develop human-like robots, as in *Artificial Intelligence: AI*. These themes have been explored in countless films and essays. Will these technologies do our thinking for us? Will they provide us memes to keep us happy and content? Will these technologies make everyone more knowledgeable and wiser? Are we becoming a network of "smart mobs" or a herd of tribes replicating memes (Chapter 10)?

There is much debate about the effects of electronic

The power of media technologies is trivialized and the content of media is too often dumbed down.

QUESTION 6
ARE WE BECOMING SMART MOBS?

Though Moore's Law cannot hold true forever, Stephen Hawking thinks it could hold true until computers attain the complexity of the human brain (Chapter 1). He may be right. Innovations continue to happen throughout the computer industry. Here are just a few. Scientists report that DNA computers could deploy genetic technologies, where one gram of DNA could hold 1 trillion CDs.[9] Chemical computers could be powered by molecular-sized "transistors" that compute with exponentially greater speed and capacity, so that a 50-milligram vial would contain enough memory to store 125 million terabytes of information.[10] In whatever form, computing power seems certain to expand exponentially as miniaturization spirals downward to the quantum level. Microprocessors have been condensed to the size of a white blood cell; this means there could be 100 billion bits of information per square centimeter.[11] Imagine those floating around among your neurons!

and digital media on the dissemination of information, knowledge, and understanding in society. On one hand, we are living amid an information explosion, yet face information overload, as much of the enlightening information is overwhelmed by the entertaining information. And there is the proliferation of advertising and propaganda, spam and junk information. Intelligence and understanding confront proliferating inanity and non-understanding. The power of media technologies is trivialized and the content of media is too often dumbed down or narrowed down to please the various forces in the market, such as ignorance, intolerance, corporations, governments, theologies, naive relativism, and the unlimited supply of special-interest groups.

As Hawking explains, scientific knowledge is exploding, revealing stunningly beautiful new insights into the evolution of life on this planet and the life of the cosmos. Yet, as Chris Mooney and Sheril Kirshenbaum explain in Chapter 7, scientific illiteracy is reaching epidemic proportions in America, fueled, in part, by Hollywood and the media industries. This decline correlates with the precipitous deterioration in intellectual standards in America, as detailed by Susan Jacoby and Mark Bauerlein in Chapter 6. These declines are the product of a complex culture-wide process, but Jacoby and Bauerlein explain the likely roles of electronic and digital media in these deteriorations. Maybe there are deeper reasons why movies and TV shows

9   Leonard M. Adleman, "Computing With DNA," *Scientific American*, August 1998, 54–61.
10   Rick Overton, "Molecular Electronics Will Change Everything," *Wired*, July 2000, 243–51.
11   Kenneth Chang, "Scientists Build Memory Chip as Small as Blood Cell," *New York Times*, January 24, 2007; web site accessed January 6, 2010.

routinely feature an endless supply of ghosts, monsters, evil extraterrestrials, mad scientists, paranormal claims, pseudosciences, and so on.

Do these declines and trends correlate with shrinking worldviews? The majority of Americans reject the science of evolution but apparently not the sciences of physics, gravity, electricity, electronics, medicine, or many others. After all, Americans fly on jetliners, flip on light switches, turn on TVs and computers, and call on their dentists and doctors. So, why be picky about which science to reject and which evidence to ignore? Surely, there are many reasons for such trends, but perhaps there is a reason often overlooked.

Is the internet amplifying and entangling the cacophony of memes, making it harder to get a coherent view of the world? Scientific knowledge is expanding exponentially in quantity, yet fragmenting into hyper-specialized realms that make it difficult for science to serve as the foundation for coherent worldviews and metamemes. The same is true in arts and the humanities. The world has more artists and scientists than at any time in human history. Specialization is the norm, not the exception. And the news provides us with a barrage of "stories" and talking heads, all providing a collision of factoids, emotional appeals, and some analyses that is virtually impossible to integrate into a meaningful understanding of the world. This leaves the playing field of metamemes wide open for *The Celestine Prophecy* and *The Da Vinci Code* to pretend to make sense of the world.

Have the chaotic complexities of the memes driven many people to look for simplicity in their metamemes

---

Has the desire to be comforted overtaken the desire to be challenged, the desire to be entertained overtaken the desire to be enlightened?

---

and models of the world, even if they are based in magic and myth? Has the desire to be comforted overtaken the desire to be challenged, the desire to be entertained overtaken the desire to be enlightened? For many people, it seems that the chief function of media technologies is to produce fun, not insight — create instant gratification, not long-term happiness; effect cheap thrills, not deep learning; empower rants, not exercise critical thinking; provide a mirror for their ignorance, not an expansive worldview.

Are entanglement and entertainment overtaking enlightenment? The spectacle is seductive, powerful, and profitable, especially when it plays to the dominant forces in the market. What's true is what sells. These issues are discussed in Chapters 3, 5, 6, 7, and 10, and in *Network*, *A Face in the Crowd*, *Idiocracy*, *Quiz Show*, *Rollerball*, *The Truman Show*, and *Good Night, and Good Luck*.

If these questions seem cynical, then perhaps we should turn off the Google news reader, because these questions are implicit in the events of the world. Sure, there are lots of great things happening in the worlds of media, science, art, architecture, medicine, and other areas. Some people are getting smarter and more knowledgeable. There are lots of talented, visionary people out there and we benefit from their genius. I am grateful that some geniuses have made possible my laptop, upon which I am writing this essay while enjoying an espresso at my favorite Philadelphia coffeehouse, all while I am wirelessly connected to a vast repository of human knowledge. Yet there remains abundant human ignorance in the world. It permeates the news, it fuels fear, it creates economic meltdowns, it causes war.

QUESTION 7
IS EVERYONE WATCHING EVERYONE?

Celebrities are famous people—that much is obvious. They make lots of money and seem to live glamorous lives among "the beautiful people." Celebrities are the royalty of media culture, the aristocrats of popular culture. They star in our movies, TV shows, and sporting events. Many people like to watch celebrities talk to other celebrities on TV talk shows. Many people just like to watch celebrities, whatever they are doing, for a variety of reasons (Chapter 9).

"Celebrity" is part of the surveillance mania that has swept through our media environments, especially with digital cameras, computers, and the internet. This was happening long before 9/11, though it has since been ramped up by the U.S. government with the Patriot Act, which basically ignores the Bill of Rights. As Naomi Wolf and Jan Fernback explain in Chapter 8, many essential rights, freedoms, and privacies are in jeopardy. Will any privacy be preserved in the internet age?

The internet is a global "panopticon." Originally, panopticon referred to a prison system designed to maximize the efficiency of surveillance of the prisoners. A few guards could watch many prisoners. Here is how it worked: The guards were positioned in a tower at the center of the prison; the cells containing the prisoners formed a circle around the tower; the rows of cells were stacked several floors high, with all cells facing the tower. Just think of a circular apartment building, six floors high, with each apartment having one room and a clear front door, with all doors opening to the inside facing a tower with a guard or a surveillance camera. That's a panopticon. If you are having difficulty visualizing this, just use Google images and type "panopticon." Panoptic prisons have been built.

In the classic novel *1984*, George Orwell explained how television could be used as an electronic panopticon, making it possible for the few to control the memes of millions of people.[12] The government could perform surveillance on the populace inside their homes via "telescreens," which were televisions that could never be turned off. Just as you watch television, television could watch you. In *1984*, Orwell showed how television was a powerful force for propaganda and the ideological control of society. The novel was a warning for our democratic societies during the Cold War. Orwell described many of the implications of a 24/7 surveillance society, which included paranoia, distrust, and the conversion of everyone into potential suspects guilty of "thoughtcrimes" (thoughts deemed illegal by the government). Think of standing in line at the airport security check in, where everyone is a potential terrorist in the eyes of the TSA agents. Extend that to the entirety of society. Everyone is a potential suspect and the government has the power of fear and paranoia.

The internet is the most powerful panopticon ever built, with surveillance technologies operating on a global scale and giving governments and corporations enormous power. In *Minority Report*, Tom Cruise works for the "Pre-Crime" agency and is situated at the center of a circular array of screens, much like Captain Kirk in *Star Trek*. The array of screens illustrates the panoptic power of the surveillance network, which is seeking to prevent crimes before they happen. Throughout the film, it is obvious that Steven Spielberg is trying to update some of Orwell's memes by situating them in the internet age.

With the internet, there remains one *essential* difference from the traditional panopticon. Each computer is a node in the network and thus a center point in the network. Everyone using a computer is, in effect, at the center of the internet. Everyone can watch everyone.

12   George Orwell, *1984* (New York: Plume, 1983).

You have enormous power to access and distribute information, exponentially more than at any time in human history. Some thinkers believe this will preserve democracy and freedoms. Will it? What are you doing with your personal panopticon? Gazing at celebrities, rock stars, and your friends' party pics?

If so, that's not surprising, because the celebrity system is the flip side of the surveillance system. Celebrities exist at the center of their own personal panopticon, which radiates from them throughout the network. The paparazzi surround them, stalking their every move, hoping to get the money shot that will appear on the covers of all the celebrity magazines (*People*), gossip tabloids (*National Enquirer*), and the up-to-the-minute scandal sites (TMZ.com). Celebrities are memes, with their images replicating throughout the network. The celebrity system relies on the same panoptic system, but rather than the few watching the many, the many are watching the few. This is illustrated in the film *Quiz Show*.

And then Facebook appeared: the celebrity system for non-celebrities. Or maybe Facebook is a micro-celebrity system, with you functioning as your own personal paparazzi? No photographers stalking you? No problem. Whip out your iPhone, snap a few pics of yourself, upload to Facebook, and you can be seen all over the world by your "friends," the stand-ins for your fans. Facebook allows you to place yourself under surveillance and create a celebrity system with you at the center — a media world about you, starring you, created by you. Facebook is the most solipsistic and narcissistic technology ever invented, after the mirror, of course.

QUESTION 8
WHAT'S HAPPENING IN THE DALLAS COWBOYS' STADIUM?

Completed in 2009, the new Cowboys Stadium is a steel and glass cavern of monumental scale. It is the largest domed stadium in the world. In addition to football, there are rock concerts and other spectacles; music performances have included U2, George Strait, and Paul McCartney, whose concert was the first event in the stadium. Like all stadiums, Cowboys Stadium is panoptic and serves the celebrity system. The many (the fans) watch the few (the players, cheerleaders, and musicians). Plus, the wealthy and *nouveau riche* get to view the game and concerts from the exclusive luxury suites, just like the royalty in *Gladiator* and the corporate elite in *Rollerball*, long before luxury boxes existed in every stadium in America.

If you are attending a game in Cowboys Stadium, you can also watch it on high-definition television. Mounted above the playing field is a massive flat-screen TV, 60 yards long and shining *very* brightly with 30 million LEDs. Having taken a tour of the stadium prior to its opening for the 2009 NFL season, I can attest to the radiant brightness, even in the daytime. There are giant openings on both ends of the stadium, so natural light was pouring in, yet the screen easily outshone the rays from the sun. It's the largest and brightest screen at any athletic venue, though it is likely some team will top it in the future. Running throughout the stadium are 220 miles of cable connecting 3,000 flat screens of varying sizes, which are mounted everywhere you look. It's like attending a football game in Times Square. The architecture of the stadium is very sleek and somewhat futuristic, looking like a spacecraft (especially when aglow at night) sitting next to the original Six Flags theme park, which was built in 1961, just six years after Disneyland.

So, the new stadium features football in Times Square inside a spacecraft, all sitting next to a theme park! Welcome to hyperreality.

With a screen that is 60 percent the size of the playing field, it ought to be obvious that the map is overtaking the territory. Yet even the football field itself is a map, with lines marking the territories of each team, highlighted by the colors in the end zone, which signals not only touchdown, but the end of the "reality" that is the field. With football and many other sports, the map has far exceeded the territory.

So what's happening in Cowboys Stadium? Just take the Meme, the Spectacle, and the Hyperreal, combine them with Moore's Law and Sagan's "Monday Night Hunters," add 100,000 fans wearing team jerseys watching the game on TV while attending the game, and you've got it! That's NFL and college football. The meme of territorial conquest is simulated in a hyperreal environment, experienced as a spectacle by the tribes of fans. The map is the territory.

Still not convinced? Let's take the Super Bowl. Like all football games, the Super Bowl supposedly lasts 60 minutes, divided into two halves, each with two 15-minute

> So, the new stadium features football in Times Square inside a spacecraft, all sitting next to a theme park! Welcome to hyperreality.

"quarters." Yet, the average game exceeds three hours, which just happens to coincide with the needs of television advertising and viewers in sports bars and in their dwellings. And the telecasts last even longer. Then there are all the pregame shows, with masculine, virile men dispensing their supposedly brilliant insights into the strategies for both teams. It is likely no one bothers to check on the accuracy of their analyses or predictions, precisely because it doesn't matter; what matters is chatter. On a regular NFL Sunday, the telecasts last almost all day, with ESPN highlights running all day and night. For the Super Bowl, the hype runs nonstop for a week or two leading up to the spectacle of "Super Bowl Sunday." If that is not enough, the NFL Network runs 24/7 on cable, all year long. And, every major city has pundits and personalities chattering all day long on sports-talk radio. The "territory" of NFL football games lasts an hour, but the maps are running 24/7, nonstop, all year long.

Of course, sports can unite societies to help overcome bigotry and prejudice. Branch Rickey and Jackie Robinson changed America when Rickey signed Robinson to play baseball for the Brooklyn Dodgers. In 1947, Robinson was the first African-American to play in the major leagues. As dramatized in the film *Invictus*, Nelson Mandela changed the course of history in South Africa with his enthusiastic embrace of South Africa's nearly all-white Springboks national rugby team. Spurred on by Mandela, most of the Afrikaners united to support the Springboks as they won the 1995 Rugby World Cup, which was being hosted in South Africa. Most recently, the New Orleans Saints won their first Super Bowl in 2010, thus helping inspire the city that was devastated by Hurricane Katrina. Yet none of these positive memes is immune to the spectacle and hyperreality.

QUESTION 9
HOW CAN MAPS
OVERTAKE TERRITORIES?

Times Square, Disneyland, and Cowboys Stadium are all microcosms of the hyperreality first theorized by Jean Baudrillard. In fact, Baudrillard is sort of hyperreal himself, kind of like Plato and Marshall McLuhan on steroids, with some occasional Jean-Paul Sartre as his energy drink to wash it down. That helps explain why Baudrillard is a controversial and complex thinker, whose explanations of the hyperreal are often vague or obscure. For many people, the concept of the hyperreal might be the most difficult media model to understand.

One of Baudrillard's essential memes is that much of hyperreality is a hollow world of surfaces, facades, and replicas, a world of reproductions, of cloned realities, of mediated existence. If we think of media as maps, then the media maps have overtaken the territories of reality. Better yet, the maps are generating the territories as a substitute reality. In his more radical texts, Baudrillard suggests that the real or authentic reality is no longer accessible, no longer existing outside our mediated perceptions. The remaining "real" realities, if they exist, reside in "the desert of the real," those natural deserts that exist far outside the metropolises, or maybe in the cultural deserts that exist in the fissures within the metropolises.

This meme was *imperfectly* illustrated when Morpheus says to Neo, "Welcome to the desert of the real," and both are situated next to a rocky landscape, next to a smoldering metropolis, all inside in a TV reality. *The Matrix* is a metaphor for living in our 24/7 media environments, the hyperreality of everyday life. We do not have to be literally plugged in to a computer network and living in a gooey pod to be in "the Matrix." Spending 10 or more hours a day gazing into our electronic screens seems close enough to *The Matrix*, especially if we have little understanding of the world outside the media.

As William Irwin explains in Chapter 4, *The Matrix* is a retelling of Plato's Cave, where the prisoners were limited to viewing the shadows and images on the wall, unable to exit and discover the real reality in the sunlight outside the cave. Variations on the Cave abound in films about media and culture: *The Truman Show, American Beauty, Wag the Dog, Idiocracy, Quiz Show, eXistenZ, Fight Club, Vanilla Sky, V for Vendetta, Waking Life*, and the classics like *Ace in the Hole, A Face in the Crowd, Fahrenheit 451, Westworld,* and *Network*. In many ways, the Hyperreal model is a postmodern spin on Plato.

Since we humans first peered out of our caves, we have sought to represent the world to ourselves via art, language, symbols, architecture, metamemes, media technologies, models of the universe, and so on. Every era or age creates new methods and models to represent the world. For Baudrillard, the way we represent the world to ourselves has evolved over time, changing with the technologies of the eras and increasing exponentially in complexity, such that representations of reality have *become the reality*. Across many essays and books, Baudrillard identifies and critiques three broad eras of human culture, or what he termed three "orders" of simulation.[13] These "orders" roughly coincide with three eras of human civilizations: premodern, modern, and postmodern (or hypermodern).

In the *premodern* world, there was a simple and direct relation between representation and reality. The symbols and stories referred to the world of things that were perceived. For example, a cave painting of the deer represented the deer outside the cave. The drawing of the warrior represented the warrior. The stained-glass window in the monastery told creation myths. The symbol and the story were unquestioned "truths."

The *modern* world significantly altered how we represented reality. Not only did Galileo and Newton have a huge effect with the clockwork solar system, so did mass media technology. At the center of the emergence of modernity was the printing press, which mass produced identical copies of texts, such as the book you are now reading. The mass production of goods and images transformed civilization to produce the modern world you inhabit. Inspired by the printing press, industrial mass production begins with a prototype and generates a series of identical copies, abandoning the idea of authenticity for the goal of quantity and efficiency. Think McDonald's. Big Macs. Or Le Big Mac, as they say in Paris and *Pulp Fiction*.

The correlation between reality and its representation was replaced by a different model of "reality." The modern world expresses the drive to have everything approximate the industrial prototype or embody the mass-production model, which created a new social and cultural ideal. Think capitalism and communism, though they disagreed about ownership of production, which was key to the construction of industrial "reality." Industrial reality became the series of things mass produced as objects of needs and then desires, from our food to our clothes to our music to our furniture to our homes to our cities, from McDonald's to Levis to EMI to IKEA to McMansions to New York City. Our urban and suburban metropolises are machines, energized and electrified, and driven by the desire for material abundance and symbolic expression. You live in a machine of mass production. It is no wonder *Fight Club* resonated

---

13 Jean Baudrillard, *Simulacra and Simulation* (Ann Arbor: The University of Michigan Press, 1994): 121–27.

with so many youthful moviegoers. The well-crafted film was, in part, a quest for authenticity in the mass-produced metropolis. Some of these issues are addressed in Chapters 14 and 16. The industrial model is still very much our world; we live in the machine.

Yet from within the machine, a new kind of world is

and actual, cultural and natural. The real has become that which can be *re*-presented or *re*produced or *re*packaged, a world of events hyper-intensified, the realm of the "hyperreal."

This is why it is naive to view Disneyland and Las Vegas as escapist fantasy lands surrounded by "the real world,"

If we think of media as maps, then Disneyland, Times Square, and Las Vegas are examples of the map overtaking the territory.

---

emerging — what some thinkers call the *postmodern* world. Other thinkers refer to the era as hypermodern, or an intensification and amplification of some features of modernity.[14] This is the world of information and electronic screens, the networked technologies of television, cinema, computers, cyberspace, the internet, and the theme park — all of which are producing Baudrillard's hyperreality. The laws of the machine have been replaced by the codes of the media; the power of labor in the production of goods is superseded by the production of meanings in the proliferation of symbols and images. That's what the Super Bowl is about; that's why tattoos are proliferating, that's why there are more photos on Facebook than there are people on the planet — far more!

So, is authenticity still possible? Every "alternative" band on MySpace seems to think so. Tyler Durden thinks so. Or is that counterfeit authenticity and simulated individuality?

Mediation and simulation are the dominant energies of postmodern culture. They can be very powerful technologies, as illustrated by the discovery, modeling, and verification of the big bang universe, the breakthroughs in gene therapy, and the radical new designs in architecture, made possible by computers.[15]

In many areas of postmodern culture, it seems that media and simulation are less about producing something that is real or truly new, and more about making reproductions of the world that only *seem* real or new. This obscures the distinctions between the fictional and the authentic, virtual

when these sites are microcosms of media and simulation in everyday life. If we think of media as maps, then Disneyland, Times Square, and Las Vegas are examples of the map overtaking the territory, or generating the territory, or anticipating the territory. That surely seems strange, but this is even stranger. The New York-New York hotel in Las Vegas anticipated the future territories of New York City by not including the Twin Towers in its skyline, which was completed in 1997. In effect, New York-New York mapped New York City, post-9/11. The Empire State Building was the tallest building in the New York-New York skyline in 1997, which became reality for New York City in 2001. *weird...*

QUESTION 10
IS THERE AN OPTIMISTIC FUTURE AHEAD?

"The future begins" — so says the tagline for *Star Trek*, the 2009 blockbuster that rebooted the famed science-fiction franchise. Though most science-fiction films are set in "the future," they are usually commenting on the future of the world as understood in the era when the film was produced. This is no less true with *Star Trek*. In a review of the new movie on Salon.com, Stephanie Zacharek described the *Star Trek* memeplex as providing an "optimistic" vision of the future:

> For kids of the '60s and '70s, "Star Trek" offered a vision of the future that suggested we had something to look forward to, not just in terms of groovy space travel, but in the sense that

---

14 Gilles Lipovetsky, *Hypermodern Times* (Cambridge, UK: Polity, 2005).

15 For example, Frank Gehry's Guggenheim Museum Bilbao could only be designed and constructed with models first tested in virtual reality. You can check out this amazing building in Google video; just type: "Guggenheim Bilbao."

citizens of the coming centuries would share the same civic values.[16]

A product of space-age optimism, the original and new *Star Trek*s express a confident vision of the human world of tomorrow, both culturally and technologically. This is in distinct contrast to the never-ending parade of films that depict an apocalyptic future for humanity, caused by our wars against one another, our misuse of technology, or our disregard for nature. And there is the cosmos smashing us with comets and asteroids and angry extraterrestrial civilizations blasting us, apparently just for the fun of it.

By rebooting the "original" *Star Trek*, as represented in the TV series from the 1960s, the new *Star Trek* repackages an optimistic metameme born of American popular culture and Enlightenment cultural philosophy. This metameme is cleverly summarized by the following passages from reviews of the film by Zacharek and Manohla Dargis of the *New York Times*:

> Initially appearing in 1966, the original "Star Trek" is a utopian fantasy of the first order, a vision of the enlightened future in which whites, blacks, Asians and one poker-faced Vulcan are united by their exploratory mission ("to boldly go"), a prime directive (no intervention) and the occasional dust-up. An origin story directed with a sure touch and perfect tone by J.J. Abrams, the fully loaded film (…) turns back the narrative clock to the moment before the main characters first assembled on the deck of the U.S.S. *Enterprise*, a sleek spacecraft that invariably sails into intergalactic storms. Even utopia needs a little bang.[17]

> A bright, shiny blast from a newly imagined past, "Star Trek", the latest spinoff from the influential television show, isn't just a pleasurable rethink of your geek uncle's favorite science-fiction series. It's also a testament to television's power as mythmaker, as a source for some of the fundamental stories we tell about ourselves, who we are and where we came from. The famous

captain (William Shatner, bless his loony lights) and creator (Gene Roddenberry, rest in peace) may no longer be on board, but the spirit of adventure and embrace of rationality that define the show are in full swing, as are the chicks in minis and kicky boots.[18]

Though there is surely more to the *Star Trek* metameme, as legions of Trekkies will proclaim, these two passages get to the essence of the issue for our purposes. The original *Star Trek* presented a largely "utopian" vision of the "space-age" future, where the culturally diverse crew of the *Enterprise* meant that humans had put aside centuries of prejudice and tribal, religious, and nationalist warfare to unite as a secular and democratic civilization on planet Earth.

When the optimistic worldview of *Star Trek* is described as "utopian," it does not mean that the film represents a world of impossible perfection tainted by a flawed humanity. *Star Trek* does not present a meme of perfected humans, but rather a meme that expresses hope for human progress. The film portrays these technological and cultural environments as we wish they were, populated by people we wish we were, or at least people we would like to hang out with, all in a world we wish we could visit — the future. The metameme embraces the traditional Enlightenment view of progress and technology, meaning that the evolution of philosophy, science, and technology can serve to enlighten and improve the lives of humanity now and into the future. In *Star Trek*, this is suggested by the technology, design, and architecture throughout the film, including by the Starship *Enterprise*, the futuristic Vulcan city, and the vast and futuristic skyscraper metropolis of San Francisco, home to Starfleet Command and the Council of the United Federation of Planets.

The original and new *Star Trek*s are pop-culture derivatives of the Enlightenment metameme that accompanied the rise of the modern world.[19] *Star Trek* assumes that not only would science and technology evolve, but so would human consciousness and philosophy via the development of a more enlightened view of humanity, other life forms, and the cosmos. Such evolution is represented by the

---

16 Stephanie Zacharek, "Star Trek," *Salon*, May 8, 2009; web site accessed January 9, 2010.

17 Ibid.

18 Manohla Dargis, "A Franchise Goes Boldly Backward," *New York Times*, May 8, 2009; web site accessed January 9, 2010.

19 Since I have barely viewed any of the many other *Star Trek* spinoff films and TV shows, I do not know if any are derivatives of the Enlightenment worldview.

Prime Directive (which forbids interference in the affairs of other planets), the diversity of the crew, and the stated goal of exploring the universe in the search for knowledge and understanding. This overall optimism and confidence was expressed in the famed voice-over of the original *Star Trek*, which has been slightly modified in serving as the coda for the new *Star Trek*:

> Space: The Final Frontier. These are the voyages of the Starship *Enterprise*. Her ongoing mission: to explore strange new worlds; to seek out new life forms and new civilizations; to boldly go where no one has gone before.

No doubt the coda may sound cheesy or ridiculous to many people, maybe even you. However, the coda is an expression of a confident, committed, yet open-minded consciousness that has proven best for gaining new knowledge, for improving life, for building a better world, for understanding ourselves and the universe around us. Is this metameme very optimistic? Sure. But if this worldview does not make a better world, then whose fault is that?

QUESTION 11
OR IS IT THE END OF THE WORLD?

Roland Emmerich is perhaps the most famous director of apocalyptic and catastrophic films, most famously with the extraterrestrial assault of *Independence Day*, the climate apocalypse of *The Day After Tomorrow*, and the cosmic annihilation of *2012*. These films have become box office blockbusters. In an interview in the *New York Times*, Emmerich claimed the films were mirroring the cynicism of the culture:

> If I cannot destroy a big high-rise anymore, because terrorists blew up two of the most famous ones, the twin towers, what does this say about our world? … I think we have become more and more pessimistic about the future. … I see it in myself. In *Independence Day* the world was something worth defending. In *Day After Tomorrow*, the message was, "We'll go down if

we don't stop what we're doing," and in *2012*, "We're going down no matter what."[20]

A world worth defending, then a tomorrow not worth inhabiting, and now the future not happening, period. This is a rather astonishing claim about the future of civilization, an apocalyptic view that went unchallenged and largely unexplored in the story. So, what's happened to optimism and

---

Why can't Hollywood and the media imagine a more optimistic future?

---

enlightenment, especially in our media environments, with the endless memes of doom and destruction replicated by the news, governments, theologies, and popular films?[21]

The Enlightenment worldview was utopian and optimistic in its attitudes toward human potential in the modern world. The essential Enlightenment belief was that art, science, technology, and philosophy could transport humanity into a better world, a better future — from ignorance to enlightenment, scarcity to abundance, inequality to equality, servitude to freedom, endless war to perpetual peace. A quick browsing of the news and television programming makes this seem unbelievably idealistic. Yet it was generally believed that mass media would provide the means for enlightenment and education, machines and mass production would provide the material abundance, and representative governments would provide the equality and secure the freedom. The practical idea was that people would live better and more peaceful lives in more harmonious societies with a better understanding of themselves, one another, and the world.

This, of course, is a highly condensed summary of a complex global process that has been evolving for several centuries. Some thinkers have argued that all science and human knowledge are mere social constructs and have no

---

20 Tyler Gray, "Destroying the Earth, Over and Over Again," *New York Times*, November 6, 2009; web site accessed February 5, 2010.

21 These questions and many of the topics in the remainder of this introduction are the subject of my "Theory Zero" experimental book series: *Zero Conditions* (Philadelphia: Theory Vortex, 2008), *Crashing into the Vanishing Points* (Philadelphia: Theory Vortex, 2009), and *Starry Skies Moving Away* (Philadelphia: Theory Vortex, 2009).

external validity in the real world. This amounts to saying that what we know is all just "opinion." In my view, such intellectual relativism is mistaken and too often misguided, thus permitting superstitions and inanities to be substituted for reason, science, critical thinking, and the never-ending evolution (replication, variation, and selection) of human knowledge. If all knowledge is relative and every opinion has merit, then the profound is no more important than the profane and the Science Channel has no more insight than *The Jerry Springer Show*. As Steven Best and Douglas Kellner explain in Chapter 20, we can embrace art, science, technology, and some postmodern theory without a blanket commitment to excessive relativism or sheer irrationalism.

Of course, the imperfections of the Enlightenment process have rightfully faced criticisms and complaints about its association with imperialism and nationalistic hypocrisy, its inconsistent application in all societies, the uneven distribution of benefits to many citizens, or the unintended consequences of the machines and media. A decade into the new millennium, the most notable of these consequences include the rampant consumer society, issues of identity and authenticity, the sense of the loss of nature, pollution and environmental degradation, and the effects of fossil-fuel consumption. Plus, it seems humans just can't stop declaring wars and committing genocides. And there are those endless reality TV shows. No wonder the extraterrestrial civilizations want to wipe us out. They are tired of receiving the TV signals of our inane programs.

Perhaps all this helps explain why it seems Hollywood has set up a film factory to imagine and produce every possible end-of-the-world scenario in every kind of apocalyptic movie (Chapter 17). Since the 1950s, there have been a zillion apocalypses, catastrophes, and disasters. Here are some of the more popular end-game scenarios:

TECHNOLOGICAL APOCALYPSES: nuclear annihilation in *Dr. Strangelove* and *Planet of the Apes*; chatty computers killing humans in *2001: A Space Odyssey*; biowarfare wiping out humans in *The Omega Man*; global food and energy shortages in *Soylent Green*; global fuel shortages and punk bikers in *Mad Max*; Skynet nuking humans in *The Terminator*; rising sea levels in *Waterworld*; computer networks ruling the planet in *The Matrix*; and global ecological destruction in *WALL·E*.

BIOLOGICAL APOCALYPSES: deadly virus from outer space in *The Andromeda Strain*; genetically created dinosaurs run wild in *Jurassic Park*; monkey virus wipes out humans in *28 Days Later*; infertile humanity dying off in *Children of Men*; and flawed cancer cure kills most everyone in *I Am Legend*.

NATURAL APOCALYPSES: angry birds attacking small towns in *The Birds*; earthquakes leveling cities in *Earthquake*; tornados on steroids in *Twister*; asteroids blasting Earth in *Armageddon*; and all-out climate apocalypse in *The Day After Tomorrow*.

EXTRATERRESTRIAL CIVILIZATION APOCALYPSES: giant spaceships arrive and blast us from above in *Independence Day* while giant extraterrestrials rise from underground and blast us in *War of the Worlds*.

UNEXPLAINED APOCALYPSE: for reasons never made clear, most everyone is dead and civilization is wiped out in *The Road*.

COSMIC APOCALYPSE: The Milky Way, the sun's neutrinos, and gravity will combine to wipe us out in *2012*.

Somehow, we survived the wars and apocalypses well enough to keep making movies about us getting wiped out. So the cosmos has finally had enough and is going to wipe us out in *2012*. Despite the bogus (though clever) apocalyptic cosmology at the beginning of *2012*, director Roland Emmerich poses a most profound question. If we had to save civilization, what elements would we preserve? Those humans responsible for this task try to preserve the best of our art, our literature, our science, and even some of our utopian philosophies. The presence of all these things in our contemporary world is why it is not the end of the world.

Why can't Hollywood and the media imagine a more optimistic future? As explained in Chapter 17, there are complex reasons for the recurring cinematic catastrophes. There is also fear of accelerating change, the fear that things are escalating "out of control," be it in nature, technology, or culture. Perhaps the most important reason is the inherent challenge in imagining a cultural and media world that provides personal and shared meaning, while being grounded in our true place in the cosmos as passengers on Spaceship Earth.

QUESTION 12
WHAT KINDS OF
WORLDS ARE WE CREATING?

What kind of worlds are we creating with our media environments on Earth? The world of *Star Trek* and its science-savvy crew on the Starship *Enterprise* or *WALL·E* and its mindless consumers on the spacecraft *Axiom*? The world of ideas for the inquisitive Wiley Wiggins in *Waking Life* or the anti-intellectual world programmed by Diane in *Network* and Lonesome in *A Face in the Crowd*? The enlightened world of the rebel Ellie Arroway in *Contact* or the destructive world of terrorist Tyler Durden in *Fight Club*?

All of the films recommended in this book do what films are supposed to do: create a world to represent a worldview, use themes to convey ideas, let fiction present truths. Much like the models presented in the readings, these movie worlds provide memes and models of media and society that are meant to serve as prototypes for a *better* society or warnings about a *flawed* society.

A film is "utopian" to the extent that it provides a prototype or model for an improved, better, or more harmonious cultural and/or natural world. That's why Stephanie Zacharek referred to *Star Trek* as "utopian." In effect, utopian models are metamemes for improving society, be it models that are technological, ecological, or political. Like *Star Trek*, The Network is largely a utopian model for media. A film is "dystopian" when it presents a model that is negative, highly non-ideal, and meant to serve as a critique and warning for humans. The Spectacle is largely a dystopian model. George Orwell's *1984* is dystopian, as is *The Matrix*.

The worlds and worldviews in this anthology are a mix of utopian and dystopian models.

CHAPTER 1. THE MEME
PULP FICTION AND *WHATEVER WORKS*

➢ *Pulp Fiction* is mostly dystopian, while *Whatever Works* is more utopian.
➢ In *Pulp Fiction*, many cinematic memes are replicated and transformed, yet each meme seems

to involve personal identity and finding meaning in the world, even if there is little meaning beyond that in a movie theater.
➢ In *Whatever Works*, finding your identity and a meaningful worldview hold the keys to personal happiness and social harmony, along with cultural tolerance. Of course, those metamemes may find you, too.

CHAPTER 2. THE NETWORK
STAR TREK

➢ Mostly utopian.
➢ The ethnic diversity of the Federation crews suggests we overcame our prejudices on Earth, with the embrace of science, technology, and secular society being key to cultural progress, human understanding, personal identity, and cool starships.

CHAPTER 3. THE SPECTACLE
NETWORK

➢ Mostly dystopian.
➢ Media corporations, newscasters, programming executives, and audiences are active participants in the dumbing down of culture via the media spectacle.

CHAPTER 4. THE HYPERREAL
THE MATRIX

➢ Mostly dystopian.
➢ Computers are dominating humans, who do not know they are plugged in to a virtual reality network; the matrix is a metaphor for the view that most people's understanding of "reality" is filtered through a media spectacle or "reality" is a hyperreality structured via media content and media technologies.

Media, Memes, and Moments · 23

CHAPTER 5. NEWS
GOOD NIGHT, AND GOOD LUCK

➤ Mix of utopian and dystopian.
➤ An authoritarian political dystopia will prevail over popular democracy unless corruption is exposed and political power is checked by an inquisitive and vigorous media.

CHAPTER 6. DUMBED DOWN
A FACE IN THE CROWD

➤ Mostly dystopian.
➤ The media firms have the power to dumb down popular culture and political discourse in service to economic and political power in the spectacle; the film anticipates the rise of the rock star as messiah and adviser to politicians. Print media try to counter the power of electronic media.

CHAPTER 7. SCIENCE
CONTACT

➤ Mix of utopian and dystopian.
➤ Our most powerful media technologies have the potential for profound enlightenment about our place in the cosmos, with the support of the popular culture and political systems. Yet the media business and audiences can dumb down or trivialize the discovery to fit within their own narrow worldviews and mythologies.

CHAPTER 8. SURVEILLANCE
MINORITY REPORT

➤ Mix of utopian and dystopian.
➤ The film begins by presenting Washington, D.C., as a crime-free surveillance utopia, yet offers a dystopian warning when the flaws in the system are revealed.

CHAPTER 9. CELEBRITY
QUIZ SHOW

➤ Mostly dystopian.
➤ Insight and knowledge are simulated for the entertainment of the masses; a college professor sells his soul for fame and prestige; despite the highly publicized hearings, television and entertainment prevail in the triumph of the spectacle.

CHAPTER 10. SOCIAL AND MOBILE
HACKERS

➤ Mix of utopian and dystopian.
➤ The global network can be used for nefarious ends in effecting an ecological dystopia, but the enlightenment potential of media prevails as the computer-savvy high schoolers use the network to save the environment.

CHAPTER 11. SPORTS
ROLLERBALL AND GLADIATOR

➤ Mostly dystopian.
➤ Sports and spectacle are the weapons of mass distraction in service to royalty, both corporate and Roman. Remember, this refers to the original version of *Rollerball*, directed by Norman Jewison in 1975. Though the film is 35 years old, it remains relevant for today's sports culture.

CHAPTER 12. GAMES AND VIRTUAL REALITY
eXistenZ AND TRON

➤ Mix of utopian and dystopian.
➤ Is *eXistenZ* presenting a virtual world you'd like to visit or inhabit?
➤ In *TRON*, two models of cyberspace do battle in a video game; an open and democratic cyberspace versus the big brother of the "master-control program," with implications for privacy, autonomy, government, capitalism, and intellectual property.

CHAPTER 13. THEME PARKS
THE TRUMAN SHOW

➤ Mix of utopian and dystopian.
➤ Truman Burbank (the true man of television) lives in a theme park broadcast as a popular global TV show; the fans cheer his bid to escape as they remain glued to their TV screens. *Note*: This was filmed in Seaside, Florida, a "real" town founded in 1979 and a prototype for many urban design trends, while also being an unacknowledged derivative of Main Street in Disneyland.

CHAPTER 14. CONSUMER CULTURE
AMERICAN BEAUTY AND *WALL·E*

➤ *American Beauty* and *WALL·E* are mostly dystopian, except for the naive eco-utopian ending in *WALL·E*.
➤ In *American Beauty*, the veneer of suburban order and consumer abundance conceals the quest for personal identity and meaning.
➤ In *WALL·E*, consumers live on a spaceship in the supersized world of Buy N Large, with logos and electronic screens everywhere; meanwhile, a robot cleans up the garbage and ecological mess left behind on Earth.
➤ As the consumer-entertainment "utopia" is embraced by the consumers, the mediated screens and the *Axiom* mask the eco-dystopia caused by rampant mindless consumption.

CHAPTER 15. GLOBALIZATION
SLUMDOG MILLIONAIRE

➤ Mix of utopian and dystopian.
➤ The complex journey of the young lovers occurs against the backdrop of the spread of the modern metropolis and the positive and negative effects of globalization; the media spectacle and celebrity culture are shown in a utopian and dystopian manner.

CHAPTER 16. COUNTERCULTURE
FIGHT CLUB

➤ Dystopian.
➤ Consumer culture and the modern world must be returned to "zero" to make room for Tyler Durden's premodern utopia, a hunter-gatherer society where supposedly more authentic identities will flourish among the "space monkeys."

CHAPTER 17. CATASTROPHE
2012, INDEPENDENCE DAY
THE DAY AFTER TOMORROW, THE MATRIX

➤ *2012* is a mix of utopian and dystopian.
➤ Sure, *2012* is a bit cheesy, but it is a lot of fun, with a serious message, like the other films mentioned below. On the serious side, humans save the ideas of civilization by preserving art, literature, science, culture, and even some of our utopian philosophies. On the fun side, there is the scene of a jetliner flying through the expanding gorge of an earthquake in Las Vegas and avoiding the hotels falling into the gorge above the jet. Surely, there's a message in there about maps overtaking the territories, or territories reclaiming the maps. And the film is filled with witty images and commentary on popular culture.
➤ *The Day After Tomorrow, Independence Day*, and *The Matrix* are dystopian.
➤ *The Day After Tomorrow* and *Independence Day* feature spectacular catastrophes in New York City, each drawing upon a lengthy cinematic legacy. *The Day After Tomorrow* is a warning about global warming, while *Independence Day* depicts an apocalypse effected by extraterrestrials as a metaphor for humans destroying our planet's resources. Notably, the extraterrestrials are defeated by humans using the internet and laptops, a clever expression of the digital utopianism of the 1990s.
➤ *The Matrix* draws from a long line of technological dystopias in which computers or robots control humans; in the end, the film offers some hope for personal autonomy among the enlightened few. As discussed in Chapter 4, the film also explores postmodern hyperreality.

➤ Mix of utopian and dystopian.
➤ The future of human consciousness is uploaded as a dream in cyberspace; or is Lucid Dream a metaphor for our current media culture?

CHAPTER 19. SPACESHIP EARTH
WALL·E

➤ Mostly dystopian, except for the utopian ending.
➤ There is an environmental dystopia on Earth, while humans are dumb and supersized in the mediated mall and theme park on the *Axiom* floating in the cosmos. The electronic screens on the hoverchairs illustrate maps becoming territories.

CHAPTER 20. TRAJECTORIES
WAKING LIFE

➤ Mix of utopian and dystopian.
➤ The search for meaning and identity via a tour of philosophy in pop culture; the story is told through scenes featuring a mélange of memes and metamemes.

In many ways, we are living in these worlds. Yet we exist on one planet.

QUESTION 13
WHAT ARE WE DOING
ON SPACESHIP EARTH?

In 1968, the *Apollo 8* astronauts became the first humans to escape the gravity of Earth in their journey to the moon. Once there, astronaut Bill Anders turned on his 35mm camera to capture the image of Earth rising above the horizon of the moon, floating amid the dark cosmic void. The famed photo is called "Earthrise" and is likely the most important and most reproduced photo in human history. In Google images, just type: "Earthrise." Not only did "Earthrise" confirm Galileo's discovery, but it also jump-started the contemporary environmental movement and inspired the annual celebration of Earth Day.

"Earthrise" was featured prominently in the cosmic images that eloquently framed Al Gore's ecological concerns in the book and film *An Inconvenient Truth*; and it is the signature image in "The Power of Information" (Chapter 19), from *Our Choice: A Plan to Solve the Climate Crisis*. In this reading, Gore shows how the proliferating satellite and information technologies have revolutionized our understanding of Earth's weather and ecosystems, along with the human impact on these systems.

Visible in "Earthrise" are no borders, no nations, no signs of humanity, just its blue waters, white clouds, and brown and green continents, all on a planet floating amid the dark void, beyond which are billions of galaxies with billions of stars. The image is beautiful, the idea is sublime.

Perhaps most importantly, "Earthrise" inspired the understanding of our planet as a spaceship floating in the cosmos. We are all passengers on Spaceship Earth, with all its natural resources and magnificent beauty. Yet as Buckminster Fuller explained in Chapter 19, there is just one problem: there is no pilot and no instruction manual for guiding us through the cosmos or for living on this planet. Without a pilot, we are passengers who serve as crew, with nature and our minds and our technologies as our only guides.

In addition to the "Earthrise" photo, an estimated 1 billion people watched the *Apollo 8* telecast, held while the spacecraft orbited the moon and viewers and astronauts gazed in awe. It was as if television was poetically permitting us to contemplate our most profound existential conditions. This was surely one of the most important moments in media history and human history.

It has been more than four decades since the astronauts and their media technologies first left Earth to explore the moon, only to transform how we see our planet and our place in the cosmos. Many people believed then that "Earthrise" would inspire humans to learn to live together in building a peaceful, cooperative, and enlightened global civilization. Since *Apollo 8* and "Earthrise," we have strung a vast network of communication technologies around that planet floating in the void, a media environment growing ever more complex as it becomes home to our electronic consciousnesses. So what are we doing on that planet with that network?

➤ Do these networked consciousnesses threaten to mass produce the memes of monoculture and infotainment, operating under the imperatives of corporations, nations, governments, and theologies? Or are we seeing the emergence of a hybrid culture, fueled by the "universal solvents" of electronic media, pop music, ecological awareness, and the growing acceptance of the scientific account of the universe?

➤ Does the globalization of technology and capital signal electronic imperialism and cultural domination? Or does it signal the next phase of cultural evolution, as global consciousness evolves beyond hegemonic empire toward a cultural pluralism that mixes the cooperative with the competitive, both of which are inherent in biological and cultural evolution (Chapter 15)?

➤ Is this network of electronic consciousness evolving more toward the always-entertained mind of *Vanilla Sky*, or more toward the evolving planetary mind of *The Global Brain* (Chapter 18)? Or are the maps overtaking the territories so much that hyperreality is the now-dominant "reality" and few care to know the difference?

There are no easy answers. The readings in Chapter 20 speculate on some possibilities for the trajectories of media and culture in the new millennium. You will have to make up your own mind about these memes as you traverse the global networks and electronic consciousnesses. The media technologies are there for you and can enlighten you. These technologies can help build a more humane civilization, one that recognizes our need for global thinking and global culture, yet which also cherishes our local cultures as they mix, mingle, and evolve with other once-local cultures. In a future of increasingly complex global networks, will any culture or belief be merely local on Spaceship Earth? Isn't that one of the deepest meanings of *Pulp Fiction*, *Contact*, *Fight Club*, and *Slumdog Millionaire*?

Most people know little of science, yet have picked up enough in pop culture to realize we are living in a vast, awe-inspiring universe. Our media technologies have changed everything we know about human existence in the cosmos and life on our planet. From Galileo's telescopes to the Hubble space telescope, the past five centuries of media technologies have made us almost disappear within the grand scale of the cosmos, going from living at the center of the universe to living on the "Pale Blue Dot." That's the famed 1990 photo of Earth taken by the *Voyager* space probe from a distance of about 3.7 billion

miles away. In Google images, just type: "Pale Blue Dot." In the "Pale Blue Dot" photo, Earth is a tiny speck in the solar system, a "pale blue dot" of light floating amid the cosmic void. The significance of that photo is discussed by Carl Sagan in the final reading of this anthology. I invite you to read it. How can anyone look at the "Pale Blue Dot" and read the last five paragraphs of "You Are Here" and not view the world and life on Earth in a radi-

---

"Earthrise" and "Pale Blue Dot" are the two most important images in human history.

---

cally different manner?

"Earthrise" and "Pale Blue Dot" are the two most important images in human history. If you reflect upon those images for a while, then perhaps you can better understand the odyssey of Wiley Wiggins in *Waking Life*, realizing you face the ultimate responsibility for your beliefs and worldview, your memes and metamemes. You must make sure you are awake and not in a dream, not living someone else's memes and metamemes.

Launched in 1977, *Voyager* has now left the solar system on its voyage into the Milky Way and beyond. From our minds, we have extended a complex information and communications network around the planet, beyond the solar system, and inside our bodies. With our media technologies, we can map the movement of the most distant galaxies and the innermost regions of our neural networks. We know exponentially more about our planet than ever before, from geology to ecology to cosmology. We know more about ourselves than ever before, from philosophy to psychology to biology to neurology. To paraphrase Carl Sagan, everything on Earth and in our bodies is made of stardust left over from an exploding star, which means we are the stardust that has become aware of the universe!

Should these metamemes make you feel small and insignificant? No. Humble? Yes. Here's why: Everything on Earth, including each of us, is the end product of almost 14 billion years of cosmic evolution, which has provided us with a profoundly powerful consciousness for grasping the surrounding universe. The human mind is a very large space in a very small place. That is why you and I should feel proud that we possess the potential to grasp our cosmic conditions and that we are just beginning to understand our true place in the cosmos as passengers on Spaceship Earth.

As mentioned earlier, we can embrace science and some postmodern theory without a commitment to naive relativism or blind irrationalism. By our very nature, we are not omniscient beings. That's okay! Certainty and uncertainty are both part of our lives. Our methods of knowing have natural limits, but those limits are set only by our cognitive evolution and the physical universe. And evolution has given us a Milky Way of neurons for knowing the universe and mastering our destiny.

Our knowledge is always evolving and open ended. Some theories are proven to be true over time, such as evolution and the big bang, while others are proven false, such as the geocentric and flat-earth models. That science and theory evolve is their virtue and need not imply naive relativism.

If our knowledge and "certainty" mean the complete grasp of all facts or all possible theories, then we are left with the false alternative of being either omniscient gods or ignorant fools. That choice is a no-win scenario. From the fact that we cannot know everything, it does not follow that we do not understand anything — that we are not gods does not mean we are fools.[22]

All our knowledge and understanding should be thought of as contextual and evolutionary, not timeless or static. What we know may be subject to revision when presented with new facts, new conditions, or new theories. That is what this anthology is trying to do with media theory: present you with new theory to better explain the conditions created by our media environments. That is why I combined art (movies) with theory and science, precisely because we need a mix of the arts, sciences, and humanities to better understand the world.

In my view, humans will never fully learn to cooperate and peacefully evolve until we understand and embrace our true place in the cosmos — not the cosmos as we wish it was, but the cosmos as it is, as revealed by our media technologies. Yet like the cosmos and planet from which we emerged, evolution is our fate. The choice we have is how we evolve.

And that brings us back to the beginning, to that moment we all face, that moment between chance and choice, ignorance and knowledge, dream and destiny, past and future. That moment is now.

---

22 My thoughts on these complex issues in relation to science, media, and culture are detailed my books, *Zero Conditions*, pp. 70–91, and *Crashing Into the Vanishing Points*, pp. 85–99.

PART 1
FOUR MEDIA MODELS

Look, all I am asking is for you to have just the tiniest bit of vision, you know, to step back for one minute and look at the big picture.

— Ellie Arroway,
Contact (1997)

CHAPTER 1
The Meme

Vincent:	*You know what they call a "Quarter Pounder with Cheese" in Paris?*
Jules:	*They don't call it a "Quarter Pounder with Cheese"?*
Vincent:	*Nah, they got the metric system. They wouldn't know what the fuck a quarter pounder is.*
Jules:	*Then what do they call it?*
Vincent:	*They call it "Royale with Cheese."*
Jules:	*Royale with Cheese.*
Vincent:	*That's right.*
Jules:	*What do they call a "Big Mac?"*
Vincent:	*Big Mac's a Big Mac, but they call it "Le Big Mac."*
Jules:	*Le Big Mac (chuckling). What do they call a "Whopper?"*
Vincent:	*I don't know. I didn't go in a Burger King.*

— Vincent Vega and
Jules Winnfield,
Pulp Fiction (1994)

Chapter 1. The Meme

Recommended Films

Pulp Fiction (Quentin Tarantino 1994)
Whatever Works (Woody Allen 2009)

Chapter Summary

Douglas Rushkoff explores media environments and
media activism in terms of the "virus."

Richard Brodie explains the concept of "memes"
and how they are spread via the media.

Randall E. Auxier argues that Quentin Tarantino's
art does not imitate life, it imitates other art.

Aaron C. Anderson shows why Quentin Tarantino's
great contribution to cinema is the
"performance of the simulacrum."

The Nature of Infection

from *Media Virus*

— Douglas Rushkoff

The average American home has more media-gathering technology than a state-of-the-art newsroom did ten years ago. Satellite dishes spot the plains of Nebraska, personal computers equipped with modems are standard equipment in a teenager's bedroom, cable boxes linking families to seventy or more choices of programming are a suburban necessity, and camcorders, Xerox machines, and faxes have become as accessible and easy to operate as public pay phones. Household television-top interactive multimedia centers are already available, promising easy access to the coming "data superhighway." Like it or not, we have become an information-based society.

We live in an age when the value of data, images, and ideologies has surpassed that of material acquisitions and physical territory. Gone are the days when a person's social stature could be measured by the distance he had to walk to see smoke from his neighbor's campfire. We've finally reached the limits of our continental landmasses; we've viewed the earth from space over national broadcast television. The illusion of boundless territorial frontiers has been destroyed forever. There's simply no more room, nothing left to colonize. While this may keep real-estate prices high, it also demands that real growth — and the associated accumulation of wealth and power — occur on some other level.

The only place left for our civilization to expand — our only real frontier — is the ether itself: the media. As a result, power today has little to do with how much property a person owns or commands; it is instead determined by how many minutes of prime-time television or pages of news-media attention she can access or occupy. The ever-expanding media has become a true region — a place as real and seemingly open as the globe was five hundred years ago. This new space is called the datasphere.

The datasphere, or "media-space," is the new territory for human interaction, economic expansion, and especially social and political machination. It has become our electronic social hall: Issues that were formerly reserved for hushed conversations on walks home from church choir practice are now debated openly on afternoon talk shows, in front of live audiences composed of people "just like us." Good old-fashioned local gossip has been replaced by nationwide coverage of particularly resonant sex scandals. The mediaspace has also developed into our electronic town meeting (to use Ross Perot's expression). Traditional political debate and decisions have been absorbed by the ever-expanding forums of call-in radio and late-night variety shows. Today's most media-savvy politicians announce their candidacies on Larry King and explain their positions on Rush Limbaugh or, better yet, prime-time "infomercials."

It has become fashionable to bemoan the fact that "Saturday Night Live's" Dana Carvey's latest impersonation of a political celebrity means as much to the American voter as the candidate's official platform or that kids today can get passionate about the styles and attitudes depicted in the latest MTV video but may never have watched an evening news broadcast. We worry that our media industry has developed a generation of couch potatoes who are incapable of making an intelligent decision and too passive to act on one if they did.

That's not what is going on. True, the construction of the American media machine may have been fostered by those hoping to market products and develop a consumer mindset in our population. As media analysts from Marshall McLuhan to Noam Chomsky have shown, television and printed news cater to the corporate and political entities who created them and keep them in business. You don't need a conspiracy theory to figure out the basic operating principles of Madison or Pennsylvania Avenues. But even if the original intentions of the media were to manipulate the American psyche by deadening our senses and winning over our hearts and minds to prepackaged ideologies, this strategy has finally backfired.

Nielsen "peoplemeters" may indicate which channels we're watching, but they tell little about our relationship to the media as a whole. Just because a family is "tuned in" doesn't mean it hasn't turned on and dropped out, too. No, the media web has neither captured nor paralyzed the American individual. It has provided her with the ability to chart and control the course of her culture. She's been empowered.

The first step toward empowerment is to realize that no one takes the mainstream media any more seriously than you do. Having been raised on a diet of media manipulation, we are all becoming aware of the ingredients that go into these machinations. Children raised hearing and speaking a language always understand it better than adults who attempt to learn its rules. This is why, educators believe, our kids understand computers and their programming languages better than the people who designed them. Likewise, people weaned on media understand its set of symbols better than its creators and see through the carefully camouflaged attempts at mind control. And now Americans feel free to talk back to their TV sets with their mouths, their remote controls, their joysticks, their telephones, and even their dollars. Television has become an interactive experience.

The advent of do-it-yourself (DIY) technology makes direct feedback even more far-reaching. Today, homemade camcorder cassettes are as likely to find their way onto CNN as professionally produced segments. Tapes ranging from "America's Funniest Home Videos" to the world-famous Rodney King beating are more widely distributed through the datasphere than syndicated reruns of "I Love Lucy." Alternative media channels like the computer networks or even telephone and fax "trees" (distribution lists) permit the dissemination of information unacceptable to or censored by mainstream channels and have been heralded as the new tools of revolution in countries as "un-American" as Romania and Communist China. Pirate media, like illegal radio broadcasts and cable or satellite jamming, are even more blatant assertions of the power of individuals to hack the data network.

To appreciate the media as facilitator rather than hypnotizer, we must learn to decode the information coming into our homes through mainstream, commercial channels. We, the television audience, have already been trained as media theorists. We must acknowledge this education if we ever hope to gain command over the language being used to influence us. The first chapters of this book will examine some of our most popular cultural icons in the context of the mediaspace in which they live and the agendas they hope to promote.

In doing so, we'll come to know a new generation of media activists, whose techniques demonstrate a keen awareness of psychology, conditioning, sociology, and marketing. These children of the fifties, sixties, and seventies were willing participants in a great social experiment in which the world behind the television screen was presented as a depiction of reality — or at least a reality to which they should aspire. This was a dangerous perception to instill. Spending most of their energy trying to conform to media representations, these kids eventually determined that the easiest way to change the world is to change the television image. Now that these kids have grown up, we find our most imaginatively influential programming developed, written, and produced by people who were themselves products of the media age. They are in command of the most sophisticated techniques of thought control, pattern recognitions and neuro-linguistic programming and use them to create

> We, the television audience, have already been trained as media theorists. We must acknowledge this education if we ever hope to gain command over the language being used to influence us.

television that changes the way we view reality and thus reality itself.

This mainstream media subversion is accomplished through careful and clever packaging. Commercial television activism means hiding subversive agendas in palatable candy shells. Most of us do not suspect that children's programs like "Pee-Wee's Playhouse" or "The Ren & Stimpy Show" comment on gay lifestyles or that "The Simpsons" and "Liquid Television" express a psychedelic world-view. Children's television and MTV, in fact, are the easiest places to launch countercultural missiles. The more harmless or inane the forum, the more unsuspecting the audience.

The messages in our media come to us packaged as Trojan horses. They enter our homes in one form, but behave in a very different way than we expect once they are inside. This is not so much a conspiracy against the viewing public as it is a method for getting the mainstream media to unwittingly promote countercultural agendas that can actually empower the individuals who are exposed to them. The people who run network television or popular magazines, for example, are understandably unwilling to run stories or images that directly criticize the operating principles of the society that its sponsors are seeking to maintain. Clever young media strategists with new, usually threatening ideas need to invent new nonthreatening forms that are capable of safely housing these dangerous concepts until they have been successfully delivered to the American public as part of our daily diet of mainstream media.

This requires tremendous insight into the way media works. Today's activists understand the media as an extension of a living organism. Just as ecologists now understand the life on this planet to be part of a single biological organism, media activists see the datasphere as the circulatory system for today's information, ideas, and images. The datasphere was created over the past two or three decades as the households and businesses of America were hard-wired together through devices like cable television, telephone systems, and personal computer modems. As individuals we are each exposed to the datasphere whenever we come into contact with communications technology such as television, computer networks, magazines, video games, fax machines, radio shows, CDs, or videocassettes.

People who lack traditional political power but still seek to influence the direction of our culture do so by infusing new ideas into this ever-expanding datasphere. These information "bombs" spread throughout the entire information net in a matter of seconds. For instance, a black man is beaten by white cops in Los Angeles. The event is captured on a home camcorder and within hours the beating is replayed on the televisions of millions. Within days it's the topic of an afternoon talk show; within weeks it's a court case on the fictional "L.A. Law"; within months it's a TV movie; before the end of the year it's the basis of a new video game, a comic book, and set of trading cards. Finally, what began as a thirty-second video clip emerges as the battle cry for full-scale urban rioting. This riot, in turn, is amplified on more talk shows, radio call-ins, and new episodes of "L.A. Law"! A provocative image or idea — like Rodney King getting beaten or even Pee-Wee Herman masturbating in a porno theater — spreads like wildfire. The event attracts our attention and generates media for several seconds, minutes, or even months ... but its influence on us doesn't stop there.

Within every media sensation are ideas, issues, and agendas — often purposefully placed — that influence us less directly. A home video of police beating a black man, for example, initiates a series of responses in the viewer. Questions of racism, police brutality, the First Amendment, Los Angeles politics, drug abuse, even the power of consumer-grade electronics — to name a few — are all released by the single media image in its media context. Similarly, a media icon like Pee-Wee Herman attracts attention because he is bizarre and funny, but hidden in the image and forcing us to respond are questions about homosexuality, consumerism run amok, the supposed innocence of childhood, and the farce of "adulthood."

If we are to understand the datasphere as an extension of a planetary ecosystem, or even just the breeding ground for new ideas in our culture, then we must come to terms with the fact that the media events provoking real social change are more than simple Trojan horses. They are media viruses.

This term is not being used as a metaphor. These media events are not *like* viruses. They *are* viruses. Most of us are familiar with biological viruses like the ones that cause the flu, the common cold, and perhaps even AIDS. As they are currently understood by the medical community, viruses are unlike bacteria or germs because they are not living things; they are simply protein shells containing genetic material. The attacking virus uses its protective and sticky protein casing to latch onto a healthy cell and then inject its own genetic code, essentially genes, inside. The virus code mixes and competes for control with the cell's own genes, and, if victorious, it permanently alters the way the cell functions and reproduces. A particularly virulent strain will transform the host cell into a factory that replicates the virus.

It's really a battle for command of the cell, fought between the cell's own genetic programming (DNA) and the virus's invading code. Wherever the cell's existing codes are weak or confused, the virus will have a better chance of taking over. Further, if the host organism has a weak immune system, its susceptibility to invasion is dramatically increased, it can't recognize that it is being attacked and can't mobilize its defenses. The protein shell of a virus is the Trojan horse. The genetic codes are the soldiers hidden inside, battling our own genes in an attempt to change the way our cells operate. The only "intention" of the virus, if it can be said to have one, is to spread its own code as far and wide as possible — from cell to cell and from organism to organism.

Media viruses spread through the datasphere the same way biological ones spread through the body or a community. But instead of traveling along an organic circulatory system, a media virus travels through the networks of the mediaspace. The "protein shell" of a media virus might be an event, invention, technology, system of thought, musical riff, visual image, scientific theory, sex scandal, clothing style or even a pop hero — as long as it can catch our attention. Any one of these media virus shells will search out the receptive nooks and crannies in popular culture and stick on anywhere it is noticed. Once attached, the virus injects its more hidden agendas into the datastream in the form of *ideological code* — not genes, but a conceptual equivalent we now call "memes."[1] Like real genetic material, these memes infiltrate the way we do business, educate ourselves, interact with one another — even the way we perceive reality.

Media viruses spread rapidly if they provoke our interest, and their success is dependent on the particular strengths and weaknesses of the host organism, popular

---

Like real genetic material, these memes infiltrate the way we do business, educate ourselves, interact with one another—even the way we perceive reality.

---

culture. The more provocative an image or icon — like the videotaped police beating or a new rap lyric, for that matter — the farther and faster it will travel through the datasphere. We do not recognize the image, so we cannot respond automatically to it. Our interest and fascination is a sign that we are not culturally "immune" to the new virus. The success of the memes within the virus, on the other hand, depends on our legal, moral, and social resiliency. If our own attitudes about racism, the power of police, drug abuse, and free speech are ambiguous — meaning our societal "code" is faulty — then the invading memes within the media virus will have little trouble infiltrating our own confused command structure.

There appear to be three main kinds of media viruses. The most obvious variety, like publicity stunts or activist pranks, are constructed and launched intentionally, as a way of spreading a product or ideology. There are also what we can call co-opted or "bandwagon" viruses — the Woody Allen/Mia Farrow debacle or the AIDS epidemic — that no one necessarily launches intentionally, but which are quickly seized upon and spread by groups who hope to promote their own agendas. (Republicans used the Woody affair to criticize New York's family values; ultraright conservatives used the AIDS epidemic to equate homosexuality with evil). Finally, there are completely self-generated viruses — like the Rodney King beating, the Tonya Harding/Nancy Kerrigan affair, or even new technologies like virtual reality and scientific discoveries — that elicit interest and spread of their own accord because they hit upon a societal weakness or ideological vacuum.

Today's media activists understand the properties of media viruses. The designers of intentional viruses take into account both the aspects of the status quo they wish to criticize, as well as the kinds of packaging that will permit the distribution of their critique. Most, but certainly not all, intentional media viruses are cultivated from scratch. The "smart drugs" virus is an excellent example of such designer memes. By the late 1980s a small group of AIDS activists, pharmaceutical industry critics, and psychedelics advocates felt the need to call our current drug paradigm into questions. The AIDS activists were upset by laws limiting the domestic use of unapproved or experimental

---

1 See Dawkins, Richard, "Universal parasitism and the co-evolution of extended phenotypes," *Whole Earth Review* 62:90, Spring 1989.

drugs from overseas. The pharmaceutical industry critics were frustrated by the way that the profit motives of drug companies could limit rather than expand the number of helpful medications and nutrients available to the public. The psychedelics advocates were disturbed by the "just say no" drug abuse publicity campaign, which denies the possibility of any value to experimentation with mind-altering substances.

The virus began with the carefully conceived phrase "smart drugs." Like many of the media viruses we'll be exploring — virtual reality, techno-shamanism, ecological terrorism — smart drugs is an oxymoron. By juxtaposing two words or ideas that do not normally go together, the phrase demands thought: "Drugs are smart?" Utilizing a hypnosis technique first developed by Milton Erickson, the contradictory phrase creates its own unique conceptual slot in the minds of people who hear it. The longer the phrase demands conscious attention, the more opportunity the virus has to inject its memes. If it makes us think, then we cannot be immune to it. Like a deer in a car's headlights, we freeze in our tracks.

The term "smart drugs" is meant to refer to a group of nutrients and prescription drugs that have long been shown to enhance memory functioning in senile people. A few doctors and nutritionists began to experiment with these substances on normally functioning people to see if they could induce superior mental functioning and found some positive results in their tests. These doctors ran up against many obstacles when they tried to publicize their findings and get research dollars for further study. AIDS, pharmaceutical industry, and psychedelics activists adopted this cause as their own and came up with "smart drugs" as part of an overall media strategy.

The next task was to develop what we can call the "syringe" for the virus. The way a virus is administered is as important as the construction of the virus itself. Often the way in which a virus spreads communicates as much as the memes within the virus. The smart drugs activists decided to create "The Smart Bar," a dispensary for over-the-counter cognitive-enhancing substances, right on the dance floor of a popular nightclub.

Within minutes after The Smart Bar opened, computer bulletin boards carried news of the smart drugs. Within weeks, *Rolling Stone*, *GQ*, "Larry King Live," "Nightline," and a host of other media outlets were covering the event. Other clubs began to sell smart drugs, health stores stocked up on cognitive-enhancing nutrients, and a lot of people

and agencies became alarmed — not only because smart drugs were sweeping the nation, but because controversial memes within the smart drugs virus were spreading themselves throughout the datasphere.

While these drugs may or may not make a person smarter, their infusion into the datasphere as an idea has called our FDA laws, pharmaceutical industry, drug use policies, and medical mind-set into question. The smart drugs themselves are the Trojan horse — the sticky shell of the virus getting all the attention. As the smart drugs virus spread, one of its creators, John Morgenthaler, was asked to appear on "Larry King Live." Once safely nested on the studio set, he used the forum to explain how information about many smart substances has been ignored or even suppressed by the American pharmaceutical industry for years. The young, unassuming, and well-dressed man explained (to an audience whose appetite had already been whetted by the term "smart drugs" and video footage of the smart bars) how current FDA regulations require that millions of dollars of tests be done before these substances can be prescribed for cognitive purposes. Because the patents for many of these chemicals expired before the pharmaceutical companies realized their value, no firm today is willing to spend research dollars on a chemical it can't own.

This particular meme — we can call it the "patent law meme" within the smart drugs virus — burrows deeply into the existing medical business paradigm. As smart drugs promoters go on the air to discuss the problems caused by patent-motivated medical decisions, they convince viewers that the pharmaceutical industry is dangerous to the population it claims to serve. Along with smart drugs, says an AIDS activist friend of Morgenthaler's who appeared on "Nightline" a few weeks later, several potentially effective AIDS medications have been suppressed because they, too, cannot be patented. Whether or not smart drugs prove effective at all, the memes within the smart drugs media virus have infiltrated the existing conceptual framework for drug legalization.

The inconsistencies of our AIDS drug policies were exposed by the smart drugs virus — first on computer bulletin boards, then in magazines, then on cable television, and finally on national network news. The attraction to the idea and sound of smart drugs and smart bars opened the necessary media channels for the virus to spread. The immune response of our culture to the virus was weak because of our ambivalent attitudes toward drug use. The memes themselves were able to infiltrate because of our ambiguous laws and policies — our faulty societal code.

But not all media viruses are constructed purposefully. The Woody Allen/Mia Farrow scandal was — most probably, anyway — not created as a publicity stunt. The particularly New York story broke, however, during the Democratic Convention for Bill Clinton. The Republicans, who had already been denouncing New York as a hotbed of morally decadent and "cultural elitist" attitudes, were quick to capitalize on the Allen/Farrow media virus. Introductions for Bush's campaign speeches made reference to Woody Allen, hoping to reinterpret the memes that had already spread — child molestation, movie stars not being as they appear, New York confusion — as condemning evidence of Democratic family values.

Finally there exist what countercultural activists would consider "self-generated" viruses. These are concepts or events that arise in the media quite spontaneously, but spread widely because they strike a very resonant chord or elicit a dramatic response from those who are exposed to them. If all of civilization is to be seen as a single organism, then these self-generated viruses can be understood as self-corrective measures. They are ways for the organism to correct or modify its own code. This is what is known in evolutionary circles as "mutation."

One such self-generated virus, the theories of chaos math, come to us from deep in the computer departments of major universities, but their implications have reignited enthusiasm for ancient pagan and antiauthoritarian values. This new, highly heralded form of mathematics works without the straight lines and linear equations we have used to interpret reality for the past dozen or so centuries and instead paints a picture of our universe as a quite random, discontinuous field of natural phenomena. Chaos math is now used to analyze systems as complex as the stock market or the weather with astonishingly accurate results.

The famous phrase "a butterfly flapping its wings in China can create a hurricane in New York" means that a tiny event in one remote area can lead to huge repercussions in another. It is no wonder that those attempting to demonstrate the fall of hierarchical systems and to debunk the notion of top-down control cherish the memes of the chaos math virus, which contradict these orderly notions of natural behavior. Activists love evidence that supports their minute-man tactics.

It is the media activists, most of all, who depend on a world-view that accepts that a tiny virus, launched creatively and distributed widely, can topple systems of thought as established as organized religion and institutions as well rooted as, say, the Republican Party or even the two-party system altogether. This is why it is so important that we understand that, at least as far as media activists are concerned, viruses are not a "bad thing." True, biological viruses, when successful, can destroy the host organism. If they invade and take control of enough cells, they redirect vital functions that the host needs in order to survive. Media viruses do target a host organism, but that beast is not culture as whole; they target the systems and faulty code that have taken control of culture and inhibited the natural, chaotic flow of energy and information.

A media virus may be designed to fight a political party, a religion, an institution, an economy, a business, or even a system of thought. Just as scientists use viruses to combat certain diseases within the human body or to tag dangerous cells for destruction by the person's own antibodies, media activists use viruses to combat what they see as the enemies of our culture. Media viruses, whether intentional, co-opted, or spontaneous, lead to societal mutation and some sort of evolution. The purpose of this book is not to cast judgment on any of the issues these activists raise, but rather to examine the methods they use to promote what they see as positive, evolutionary change.

Interestingly enough, however, to come to grips with the efficacy of media viruses in our present datasphere, we must also accept, or at least acknowledge, the basic principles of the datasphere as these activists view them. To understand media viruses, we must allow ourselves to become infected.

J.J.
nipslip
2 Girls
1 Cup

"Memes" and "Cultural Viruses"

from *Virus of the Mind*

— Richard Brodie

MEMES AND MEMETICS

The meme is the secret code of human behavior, a Rosetta stone finally giving us the key to understanding religion, politics, psychology, and cultural evolution. That key, though, also unlocks Pandora's box, opening up such sophisticated new techniques for mass manipulation that we may soon look on today's manipulative TV commercials, political speeches, and televangelists as fond remembrances of the good old days.

The word *meme* was coined by Oxford biologist Richard Dawkins in his 1976 book *The Selfish Gene*. Since then it has been tossed about by Dawkins and other evolutionary biologists, psychologists such as Henry Plotkin, and cognitive scientists such as Douglas Hofstadter and Daniel Dennett in an effort to flesh out the biological, psychological, and philosophical implications of this new model of consciousness and thought.

The meme has a central place in the paradigm shift that's currently taking place in the science of life and culture. In the new paradigm, we look at cultural evolution from the point of view of the meme, rather than the point of view of an individual or society.

Why bother to look at life in this new, upsetting, inside-out way? Well, for the same reason explorers started to look at the earth as round instead of flat, and the same reason astronomers stopped looking at the universe as if it revolved around the earth: it makes a lot more sense, and you can get more exciting things accomplished when you find a better model for explaining the way the world works. Such a model is the theory of the meme, or *memetics*.

Memetics is the study of the workings of memes: how they interact, replicate, and evolve.

The science of memetics is the mind universe's analogue to *genetics*, which studies the same things about genes in the biological universe.

DEFINING THE MEME

It's not so easy to answer even the obvious question, "What is a meme?" If you ask a biologist, the answer is likely to be along the lines of Dawkins's original definition:

Biological Definition of <u>Meme</u> (from Dawkins)
The *meme* is the basic unit of cultural transmission, or imitation.

According to this definition, everything we call "culture" is composed of atomlike memes, which compete with one another. These memes spread by being passed from mind to mind in the same way genes spread by being passed down through sperm and egg. The memes that win this competition — those that are successful at penetrating the most minds — are the ones responsible for the activities and creations that constitute present-day culture.

The most interesting memes to a biologist have to do with behavior. Dawkins's original examples of memes were:

> … tunes, ideas, catch-phrases, clothes fashions, ways of making pots or of building arches.

According to the biological definition, women wear long skirts one year, then, a new short-skirt meme catches on for whatever reason, and now women wear short skirts. Popular songs compete for the Top 40, each a meme or perhaps a bundle of memes. Then people start humming the catchy tunes, spreading those memes even further. Engineers build bridges on the cantilever principle; then the suspension bridge is invented and its meme spreads quickly to become the new state of the art in bridge building.

This biological definition is kind of satisfying, because it gives us a way to reduce all of culture to manageable pieces and start to label them and see how they interact and evolve. Frustratingly, though, it doesn't lend much insight into the question of *why* certain memes spread and others don't. So let's put that definition on hold for a moment and look at some other points of view.

A PSYCHOLOGICAL DEFINITION

If a psychologist were asked what a meme is, he would give a slightly different answer, one that illuminates more the workings of the mind than the components of behavior. Here is psychologist Henry Plotkin's definition of *meme:*

Psychological Definition of <u>Meme</u> (from Plotkin)
A *meme* is the unit of cultural heredity analogous to the gene. It is the internal representation of knowledge.

This definition stresses the analogy to genes, which are tiny chemical patterns living on strands of DNA. As those tiny DNA patterns cause all kinds of external effects — eye and hair color, blood type, even whether you grow up to be a human or a golden retriever — the memes in your head cause behavioral effects. Likening your mind to a computer, memes are the software part of your programming; the brain and central nervous system, produced by your genes, are the hardware part.

The memes in this definition don't live in the external trappings of culture, but in the mind. After all, it is in each individual's mind where the competition for memes takes place. According to this definition, a woman might have in mind a meme like *It's good to be aware of the current fashion;* another meme, *Women who dress fashionably get ahead;* and a third meme, *I want to get ahead.* Wearing short skirts when they become fashionable is a behavior that results from having all these memes working together in her mind. If there are enough women who have these supporting memes in their minds, all it would take would be one more meme — *Short skirts are fashionable* — to cause a proliferation of raised hemlines.

Bridge-building methods evolve because of memes. An engineer might be programmed with memes such as *Suspension bridges are the most efficient for this kind of job; Engineers who do a good job get their bosses' approval;* and *Getting the approval of my boss is important.* Without any of these three, the engineer might not build a suspension bridge. All three memes acting together cause something to get built out in the world. Of course, the engineer works with other engineers, construction workers, teamsters, and so on, all behaving as directed by their memes.

Under this definition, memes are to a human's behavior what our genes are to our bodies: internal representations of knowledge that result in outward effects on the world. Genes are hidden, internal pieces of information stored in an embryo that *result,* with the influence of its environment, in the flesh and blood of the developed organism. Memes are hidden, internal representations of knowledge that *result,* again along with environmental influence, in external behavior and the production of cultural artifacts such as skirts and bridges. If I look around and see short skirts, that might cause the production of a meme in my mind such as *Short skirts are in fashion.* But the meme is in my mind, not on Meg Ryan's body.

If someone is having difficulties in life, a memetic psychologist might explore what memes the patient has that are producing the undesirable results. Once discovered, those memes could be changed.[1]

---

1   This is in fact close to what goes on in the practice of cognitive therapy, pioneered by psychologist Albert Ellis and psychiatrist Aaron Beck in the 1950s. Cognitive therapists theorize that unwanted mental states such as depression are the result of incorrect thinking ("cognition") about life and the world. Since the patient is living with an inaccurate model of reality, naturally he or she has difficulty succeeding in life. The cognitive therapist interviews the patient and methodically uncovers and "corrects" illogical or inaccurate beliefs, eventually leaving the patient with a better working model of how to get along in life and therefore a feeling of well-being.

This way of looking at memes is useful for understanding how people work. However, it still has some problems as a complete theory of the evolution of knowledge. It centers around the human mind, and not all knowledge in the world is stored in people's minds. As people interact with other forms of knowledge — geography, the genetic knowledge contained in each organism's DNA, the astronomical knowledge of the universe — how does that affect culture and behavior?

A COGNITIVE DEFINITION

We can eliminate ourselves from the picture entirely, then, and look at an even more abstract definition of *meme*. This one is from cognitive scientist and philosopher Daniel Dennett:

Cognitive Definition of <u>Meme</u> (from Dennett)
A *meme* is an idea, the kind of complex idea that forms itself into a distinct memorable unit. It is spread by *vehicles* that are physical manifestations of the meme.

As Dennett says:

> A wagon with spoked wheels carries not only grain or freight from place to place; it carries the brilliant idea of a wagon with spoked wheels from mind to mind.

Now *this* definition really gives you a meme's-eye view of the universe. Notice the phrase "forms itself." Well, we know ideas don't *form themselves* any more than spoons get up and dance on the table. This definition is a scientific model — and as we have seen, there are many such models possible just surrounding the term *meme*. Using the phrase "forms itself" is a trick to get us to look at things from a meme's point of view. You notice interesting things when you look at a specific meme and see what happens around it: how it spreads, mutates, or dies.

Someone whose mind carried the *spoked wheel* meme might build a wagon with spoked wheels. Someone else would see the wagon, "catch" the *spoked wheel* meme, and build another wagon. The process would then repeat itself indefinitely. Unlike the biological definition, this view of memes places them in the realm of the unseen — software of the mind, ready to produce results in the physical world that then carry their own seeds to other human beings.

The cognitive definition gives us license to take out a magnifying glass and follow around a specific meme like a private investigator — watching to see how infection with it affects people's behavior; noticing how people spread it; comparing it with competing memes, like the suspension bridge with the cantilever — to see what properties it has that make it occupy more or fewer minds than its rivals.

One potential pitfall with this definition is the use of the term *vehicles*. The distinction of a meme-carrying vehicle is not as clear-cut as in biology, where organisms are vehicles for the spread of DNA. Not all meme transmission is as simple as imitating a catchy tune or noticing a spoked wheel.

If memes are our internal programming, we can draw on decades of research in psychology to look at how we get programmed — how memes get transmitted into our minds. Once programmed, we behave in complex ways that spread memes indirectly.

So while it may sometimes be illuminating to use the term *vehicle* to describe behavior or an artifact that tends to infect people with a meme, more often the existence of a meme will trigger a Rube Goldberg-like sequence of actions that only indirectly causes spreading of the meme. The wagon wheel and the commercial advertising on TV programs are the exceptions as meme-spreading vehicles; the rule is more complex.

A WORKING DEFINITION

We want a definition of *meme* that gives us access to understanding cultural evolution, as in the biological definition. But we want to be clear that memes are internal representations, as in the psychological definition. And we want to look at memes as ideas — as our software, our own internal programming — that produce an effect on the outside world, as in the cognitive definition. The result is the definition I use in this book, a definition similar to the one Dawkins adopted in his 1982 book *The Extended Phenotype*:

Definition of <u>Meme</u>
A *meme* is a unit of information in a mind whose existence influences events such that more copies of itself get created in other minds.

Now, with this definition, we can answer the questions I asked Charles Simonyi and Greg Kusnick back at Microsoft. *Is a yawn a meme?* No, a yawn is behavior and, as far as I know, has nothing to do with an internal representation of any information. While it appears to be self-replicating, it's more like an unreliable radio relay: see a yawn, emit a yawn, maybe. It's not influencing events such that more copies of information get created. People yawn when they see others do so, but their internal state hasn't changed to make them more likely to yawn in the future, or to do anything that I am aware of.

How about *ta-ta-ta-TUM,* the famous motif from Beethoven's Fifth Symphony? As it's stored in my brain, Charles's, and Kusnick's, it is a meme. I've just infected you with a copy of it. If you hear the music, or hear anyone talk about Beethoven's Fifth in the next few days, you'll have no choice but to associate it with this discussion. If you then start up a conversation and say, "Hey, that's odd! I just read about *ta-ta-ta-TUM* in this book *Virus of the Mind,* and do you know it's a meme?" you will be spreading some of the memes from this book that you're already infected with.

* * *

CULTURAL VIRUSES

"Society everywhere is in conspiracy against the manhood of every one of its members. Society is a joint-stock company in which the members agree, for the better securing of his bread to each shareholder, to surrender the liberty and culture of the eater. The virtue in most request is conformity."
— Ralph Waldo Emerson

From the children's game of "telephone," we know that it's difficult to copy memes with 100 percent fidelity even if we want to. When replication occurs with slight changes in the replicator, and those modified replicators are selected somehow for their fitness, then we have evolution. When a concept appears that has all the properties of a virus of the mind, then as it starts spreading through the population, the memes constituting that concept evolve.

Toward what end do they evolve? We now come to the key to the paradigm shift: these memes, and the concepts

and cultural institutions they compose, care nothing for you, me, or our children except as vehicles for their own replication. They do not exist to raise our quality of life or to assist us in our pursuit of happiness. Their goal is to reproduce and spread, spread and reproduce, whatever the cost.

All cultural institutions, regardless of their initial design or intention (if any), evolve to have but one goal: to perpetuate themselves.

Cynical? Well, maybe, but it's an inescapable conclusion from everything we've just discussed. Suppose you have 100 cultural institutions — let's take nonprofit organizations, for example. They have varying degrees of effectiveness in the charitable tasks they are designed to accomplish, and they also attract funding and volunteers in varying degrees. It is their effectiveness in attracting funding and volunteers that determines whether they can stay in existence and perform their functions.

After some period of time — say, five years — half of them go out of existence due to lack of effectiveness at funding or staffing. The other half either already possessed memes that attracted funds and staff or else evolved them during those five years.

Given the limited resources in the world and the new organizations being introduced all the time, the surviving organizations must become better and better at surviving. Any use of their money or energy for anything other than surviving — *even using it for the charitable purpose for which they were created!* — provides an opening for a competing group to beat them out for resources.

A friend of mine recently stopped donating to a wildlife-preservation group. Appalled by the volume of mail he received from the group after his first donation, he did some quick calculations. He realized that the cost of the mailings they sent him to solicit donations actually exceeded the annual amount he was donating! He sent the group a letter explaining why he was ceasing to support them.

If you're designing a cultural institution these days, you've got to know memetics. If you don't design the thing with good memes that will make it self-perpetuating from day one, it will either die out quickly or evolve to become self-perpetuating. The trouble is, the way in which it evolves could do great violence to the original purpose you intended.

In this chapter, I'll describe several types of cultural viruses — institutions that have evolved away from their original purpose and become self-perpetuating. In the next chapter, I'll explore the evolution of the biggest cultural viruses of them all: religions.

TELEVISION AND ADVERTISING

Television is a particularly efficient medium for meme evolution. New shows or commercials can reach hundreds of millions of people at once. If the shows catch on — if they have good memes — the producers are rewarded with inpourings of sponsors' money, the advertising agencies are rewarded with more business, and the sponsors themselves sell more of their product. All this happens relatively quickly, perhaps in a matter of weeks or months, as opposed to the old days when culture spread mostly by countries trading with and conquering one another over the course of decades or centuries.

Scares about so-called subliminal advertising have abounded in recent years. The idea is that unscrupulous marketeers have put hidden images, voices, or symbols into their ads for the purpose of manipulating people into buying products that they otherwise wouldn't buy. The story goes that one liquor company had an artist airbrush the word *sex* into the random arrangement of ice cubes in a glass, or that a cigarette manufacturer hid the word *death* in a waterfall, or that a seemingly innocent arrangement of random objects, secretly formed a likeness of a naked and seductive woman.

This all raises a lot of questions, whether you see these images when you peer intently at the suspect ads or not.[2] But supposing subliminal images do exist, how did they get there? Are there really evil geniuses intentionally cackling over their airbrushes, manipulating and enslaving our minds? Or is the presence of these images nothing more interesting than Charlie Brown's looking up at the clouds and seeing a duckie and a horsie?

Of course I don't know. But if we get stuck on that question, we're falling into the biggest trap of all in understanding cultural evolution. It's the trap that conspiracy

theorists fall into, and the same trap that people who pooh-pooh conspiracy theories fall into. It's the mistaken belief that anything complicated must arise out of conscious intention.

Complicated things arise naturally out of the forces of evolution. No conscious intention is necessary.

Does subliminal advertising work? Sure! Ads can have parts that you don't become consciously aware of but which draw your attention unconsciously. If the ad pushes more of your buttons as a result of the subliminal content, you will pay more attention to it. Paying more attention is the first step toward paying more money. It can work in reverse, too: some fast-food restaurants paint their walls orange because they believe it creates subliminal discomfort; you'll want to spend less time lingering there, and your leaving opens up tables for new customers.

But don't think that subliminal ads are the only problem: as should be obvious to everyone who has watched the evolution of television programming for more than a few years, efforts to attract your attention are not limited to the subliminal.

The television is *screaming* at us day and night with all the greatest button-pushing memes there are: Danger! Food! Sex! Authority! We don't even have to believe it's real for it to attract our attention. Remember "I'm not a doctor, but I play one on TV"?

Not only commercials, but also programs are evolving to command a greater share of your mind, and to say they were doing it subliminally would be an almost humorous understatement. The first naked female breasts on American broadcast television appeared on the program *NYPD Blue. Baywatch,* a show with little plot but lots of bare skin, became the most watched television show in the history of the world. Female breasts, naked or otherwise, tend to command men's attention, and hence, in the very efficient evolutionary medium of television, they tend to proliferate. A casual observer will notice that the inclusion of breasts, not to mention the rest of the female anatomy, in much male-oriented advertising is far from subliminal.

Advertisers have learned to push your buttons. They also have learned a good deal about programming you with all kinds of memes. It's not the subliminal that we

---

2 Personally ever since I first read about subliminal advertising, I've seen the word *sex* in every glass of liquor on the rocks — now I've got a distinction-meme for it!

need to be concerned with—it's that they now have the knowledge to unleash full-blown designer mind viruses through their advertisements. And the effects of that are unpredictable and frightening.

THE EVOLUTION OF ADVERTISING

Imagine it's 1960. Television advertising is in its tender youth. New York and Los Angeles abound with Darrin Stephenses working for advertising agencies run by Larry Tates, all trying different strategies and campaigns to advertise their clients' products successfully. They're all running their ideas up the flagpole, but only a few get the salutes required for success, promotion, and unabashed copying by everyone else in the business. It's a dog-eat-dog world, and the days where "I feed my doggie Thrive-O / He's very much alive-o!" can compete for a share of the viewer's mind are as numbered as those of the set shot in basketball.

Some campaigns work; some don't. The ones that don't are quickly killed, as few advertisers can afford to prolong an expensive promotion that isn't paying dividends in attracting the attention of customers and therefore their money. The ones that succeed are copied, with various creative changes being made intentionally or unintentionally — because the copier didn't understand what was effective about the original ad — yielding another generation of fitter ads. It's almost the reverse of the way some animals have genetically evolved camouflage to make themselves less visible: like colorful flowers evolving to attract pollinators, these commercials have evolved in the world of memes to make themselves *more* visible and attract *you*.

After several years, and without any evil top executives scheming about the best way to manipulate the American public, most ad agencies are putting out commercials featuring the big button-pushing memes: *danger, food, and sex*. Soon they start fine-tuning them, still through the automatic and unconspiratorial process of meme evolution, to include some of the other button pushers: helping children, listening to authority, the unusual, a sense of belonging, and so on. Ads could have evolved to where they are today simply through the natural process of competition, even if there were never an awareness on the part of ad-agency executives about the button-pushing effect these memes had on people.

Of course, there *was* an awareness of the button-pushing effect. In fact, advertising runs hand in hand with politics in its calculating manipulation of the masses. It's

not clear to me that executives' awareness of the situation has much effect on the result, but it sure tends to make people think less of them. Even so, one can always give them the benefit of the doubt and still have a workable theory of meme evolution in advertising. Did the makers of Joe Camel deliberately set out to hook kids on Camel cigarettes by presenting a lovable cartoon figure smoking their instrument of death? Who knows? It does have that effect, according to at least one study, but that doesn't prove conscious intent.

It's a very, very attractive trap to start looking for who to blame for what people consider the decline of our culture. When culture evolves in the direction of more powerful memes, it does little good to single out people to blame. As you know by now, that's the natural order of things.

If we want to combat the mind viruses responsible for the decline of culture, we need to be conscious of our own programming, consciously adopting memes that take us in the direction we want to go.

THINGS GO BETTER WITH MEMES

Another effect of meme evolution on advertising is the divergence of advertising content from product content. As a kid, I remember noticing the Coca-Cola Company changing its slogan from "Drink Coca-Cola" to "Enjoy Coca-Cola" to "Things go better with Coke." Somewhere along the line, somebody realized that they didn't really have to discuss the product itself, just create a mood full of enough attractive elements that people took notice and felt good when they saw the product — they created an association-meme in the customer.

A '90s Diet Pepsi campaign featured celebrities and showgirls smiling, cavorting, and grunting "Uh-huh!" for half a minute. Not exactly a logical delineation of the product's features and benefits. The athletic shoes we used to call "sneakers" no longer get promoted by mothers swearing to the long life of the brand; now stroboscopic special effects surround famous athletes, poetic quotes, and rap music. Speaking of music, do you have a favorite song that has been ruined forever by an ad that used your enjoyment of it as a Trojan horse? Remember "I Can See Clearly Now"? I used to love that song, but now it just makes me think of Windex.

Advertisers are selling a feeling; they are using Trojan-horse techniques that hook into your feel-good buttons so they can unload their bundle of memes into your mind once they have your attention. In some cases, this transformation of commercials into direct communicators of powerful feelings has brought them full circle into the realm of art.

I'll follow up that little bit of blasphemy by pointing out that I have several friends who don't watch much TV. When we get together for the occasional viewing of some special program, it fascinates me that they are often more engrossed by the commercials than the program itself! It's as if, in order to sell products, the producers of TV commercials have made a return to the early days of television when a commercial consisted of little more than a mention of the product name. Many of today's commercials feature miniature dramas, comedies, music videos, or even experimental surrealism, completely unrelated to the products they're selling except for the mention of their name or a brief picture. It's a world within a world.

Beer commercials are notorious for this kind of treatment. "Sell the sizzle, not the steak," goes the advertising truism. Well, why not? When you're pushing a product made from rotten vegetation whose primary effects are to dull your wits, pad your paunch, and make you belch, any sizzle would be a big help. I remember a beer commercial from my childhood that sold the steak. It went:

> Schaefer is the one beer to have
> When you're having more than one!
> Schaefer's flavor just doesn't fade
> Even when your thirst is done!

What a nice ad promoting a true competitive advantage of the product. It even had a nice little tune you could hum. Now that's something that should really appeal to the connoisseur, right? Wrong.

Ever since Anheuser-Busch decided to bill its anything-but-outstanding Budweiser as the "King of Beers," the trend has been away from claims, true or not, about the product's competitive advantages and more and more toward building an image or mood.

Advertisers want to program people to feel good and pay attention when they encounter the product.

The ads that push people's buttons are the successful ones. You don't have to have a Ph.D. in media studies to notice that sex plays a big role in beer commercials. But the competition is so fierce, and the payoff so great, that beer advertising has split off into surprising niches, exploiting some of our other buttons. The agency representing Budweiser and Bud Light now have the two square off in a confabulated "Bud Bowl" football game between two teams of animated cans and bottles every year during the Super Bowl, perhaps guessing that people paying attention to the real football game have particularly sensitive competition buttons, and so will pay attention to the commercials as well.

Stroh's beer ran a series of commercials exploiting a man's relationship with his dog. Rainier Beer, a local Seattle brew, had a very funny series of commercials that seemed to engender good feelings in the populace around the product. There was actual community outrage when the commercials were canceled by the new owners of Rainier. Henry Weinhard's beer ran a series of commercials exploiting the *tradition* meme, talking about their hundred-year history in the Northwest. Another Anheuser-Busch campaign slogan, "Proud to be your Bud," attempts to hook into people's sense of belonging and identity. There are still a few exceptional campaigns that actually talk about benefits of the product, such as Miller Lite's innovative "Great taste, less filling," but by and large the beer industry is selling the suds, not the brew, as it were.

What does all this mean to you and me? It means that if we watch commercial television, we are guaranteed to be influenced in both our thinking and our behavior by the powerful memes being broadcast at us. Is that bad? I don't know. But anyone who claims television is not a great shaper of our culture is either naïve or mistaken. If television didn't have at least as great an effect on our behavior as one might suspect, advertisers would not pay billions of dollars a year to shape our buying habits. And shaped we are, both by the commercials and the program content.

The evolution of commercial television programming has been toward a combination of the memes that push viewers' buttons and the memes that people want to promote.[3] One way this shows up is in the phenomenon of the talk show.

While it might not be apparent to the casual viewer, most of the people who appear as experts or celebrities on talk shows are there in order to promote themselves or their agenda — to spread memes. To illustrate how important this is, a hardcover book generally needs to sell 5,000 copies in a week to make the *New York Times* bestseller list. A single appearance by an author on America's top talk show, *Oprah,* commonly sells 100,000 copies of a book. But you have to write a book that Oprah wants on her show. That may not necessarily be the book you want to write.[4]

There's no doubt that the visual media have influenced the publishing industry. Large advances go not to books with literary value, but to those that are promotable — they have components that will push people's buttons. Top-selling fiction writers are more and more penning novels that read like screenplays. The visual adaptation of the book is far more lucrative, and reaches far more people, than the written version.

Cynics perennially ask why life and culture, and television in particular, seem to be filling up with valueless and demeaning junk rather than artistic and thoughtful content. The answer is, of course, that the valueless and demeaning junk is a better replicator.

If you're interested in filling the airwaves with art and literature, you've got to make them better replicators.

There are two ways to make something a better replicator: make it better exploit the environment, or change the environment to its advantage.

Using the first method, you could create art and literature that presses people's buttons, such as Robert Mapplethorpe's erotic photographs or MTV's music videos.

Alternatively, you could work to change the selection process for what goes on the air — not likely anytime soon in the United States, given how fundamental the free market is to U.S. culture. The difference in program content of the noncommercial PBS versus commercial networks shows what a difference the selective environment makes in determining what cultural replicators win the battle for survival.

One controversial method of making art a better replicator is the colorization of old black-and-white movies. While the additional visual appeal of color generates more viewers — or at least the meme *Colorization generates more viewers* has spread to the right people — colorization offends traditionalists, who especially resent tampering with films without the directors' permission. The director intended black and white, they say, to convey a specific artistic message. They warn that soon we'll see colorization of the first 20 minutes of *The Wizard of Oz!*

'MY SO-CALLED LIFE' AXED OVER POOR RATINGS

PASADENA, Calif.

11-Jan-95 — Ten million viewers is not enough to save ABC's cult series "My So-Called Life," which finished ahead of only 16 other shows out of 116 in the season's first-half ratings.

The show will be pulled from the air Jan. 26, said Ted Harbert, president of ABC Entertainment, who called the critically acclaimed show "art" but said the show's ten million viewers were "a lot of people, but not so many people by our standards."

Explaining that he would be delighted to find a way to bring the show back, he said, "We're continuing to promote the hell out of it, trying to get an audience into it in these last few episodes in January."

While declining to predict whether the show would return in the fall, given the strong support of its core fans and critics, Harbert said he would make a decision in May, but that ratings were the key.

A critically acclaimed TV show can be a poor replicator if it doesn't meet the selection criterion for commercial television: ratings.

---

3   Douglas Rushkoff's book *Media Virus!* (Ballantine, 1994) illustrates this point in great detail. His use of the term *virus* is more like what I call a *Trojan horse* — that is, a bundle of memes with a sugarcoating of palatable memes and a hidden agenda underneath.

4   As if to prove my point: one of my reviewers wrote in the margin here: "Be careful — don't alienate Oprah!" I haven't, have I? ☺

The most offensive example I've seen of tampering with artistic content for the sake of increasing viewership is the practice of showing a preview of a gripping scene in the next segment of the movie at the start of each commercial break. That's right — they show a scene you haven't seen yet, out of order, in an attempt to create sufficient interest for you to stick around through the commercials! Argh!

The point is, the institution of television, while originally created as entertainment, has evolved into a self-perpetuating cultural virus with little possibility of anything but broadcasting the most gripping, button-pushing sounds and images. That's true not only of the entertainment portion of television but also of the news.

Vinnie's Very Bad Day: Twisting the Tale of Time in *Pulp Fiction*

from *Quentin Tarantino and Philosophy*

— Randall E. Auxier

FAIRE DES SINGERIES, OR MONKEY SEE, MONKEY DO

There's nothing *essentially* new in Quentin Tarantino's *Pulp Fiction*, and that's part of the point, as he often says in interviews — to use every Hollywood cliché, but to present these in combinations that the audience has not seen before. It's Hollywood with a (Jack Rabbit Slim's) twist contest.

Aristotle once insisted that the whole "poetic art" was just one big imitation of life (and that includes film, although Aristotle wasn't much of a movie-goer). For about two thousand years after Aristotle said that, everybody agreed — until one day in the late eighteenth century when some Germans and a few renegade Brits got bored with watching French soldiers kill everybody, and started insisting that the poetic art is *really* the expression of the artist's feelings, not mainly an imitation of life. They said it out of pure spite. That really pissed off the French army, because they liked Aristotle.

The French, who were the champions of "classical aesthetics," had an especially snooty way of reading Aristotle. They said you have to follow the rules in order to make worthy art, and especially you have to have three things to make a story work, the "three unities" is what we now call them: unity of (1) time, (2) place, and (3) action. You have to tell your audience, at least vaguely, *where* the characters are, and keep it constant. And they also thought you should present the events in their proper temporal sequence, so that no one gets confused. You can see where this is going,

I'll bet. In the movie industry, even in Tarantino movies, there is a dude whose job it is to assure the "continuity" of the set and props to make sure things don't move around from one cut to the next and one scene to the next. He's sort of the master of time and space in the movie universe — or perhaps he's just Aristotle's Gallic slave boy.

But really time and place are just unities of *action,* which is what all the fuss is actually about. Aristotle says: "The truth is that … imitation is of one thing, so in poetry the story, as an imitation of action, must represent one action, a complete whole, with its several incidents so closely connected that the transposal or withdrawal of any one of them will disjoin [that is the time requirement] or dislocate [that is the place requirement] the whole."[1]

The French were quite inflexible about this "requirement" back in those days. At first they had long-winded arguments with the Germans and the Brits (the French even accused Shakespeare of being a bad playwright because he liked to mess around with the three unities), but eventually it just had to become a shooting war. This was called the Battle of Classicism and Romanticism. The Germans pulled out the big guns to hold the center, like Goethe and Beethoven, and finished with a heroic charge by Wagner (commanding some Vikings and a detachment called the Light Brigade); the Brits reinforced with Byron and Shelley and Keats (all regrettably killed in action), and deployed Coleridge and Wordsworth to protect the flanks.

---

1 Aristotle, *Poetics,* translated by Ingram Bywater [god, I love that name], in *The Basic Works of Aristotle* (New York: Random House, 1941 [a very bad year]), lines 1451a30–34.

The French eventually moved on to Africa to kill people who didn't have quite so many guns. The three unities were in full retreat. People started writing whatever they damn well pleased while the Sun King turned over in his lavish rococo grave. It's amazing the things people will fight for.[2]

LE BIG MAC, OR "GARÇON MEANS 'BOY'"

Americans don't give a shit about such things. That's why we serve (bad) beer at the McDonald's in Paris and call the sandwich "Le Big Mac." We're mocking them and they just eat it up (complaining all the while). And then they pay us good money to watch our supposedly inferior movies (and that's what they are, "movies," not "films"). We're laughing all the way to the bank. That's our revenge on the French for their uppity ingratitude and hypocrisy. That and Michael Moore. They must know, I mean they *must*, that we set up that whole *Fahrenheit 9/11* thing just to see if they were really so far up their own asses as to honestly give that joker the *Palm d'Or* for that ridiculous string of pulp celluloid. They went for it, and for Le Big Mac. Idiots.[3]

Tarantino doesn't read Aristotle, and he doesn't imitate life; he imitates other art. And no one, I mean *no one,* is having more fun than our boy Tarantino. It ought to be a crime. In France it *is.* He bats around the three unities like a kitten. And he's no romantic either. If Tarantino were actually expressing his *feelings* in his movies, we would have to wonder about whether he should be locked up.

> Tarantino doesn't read Aristotle, and he doesn't imitate life; he imitates other art.

Of course, Mel Gibson should be locked up regardless of whether he's imitating or expressing.[4] Maybe we should put him in a birka and send him to *gay Paris.*

But with Tarantino, this imitation/expression thing actually makes a real difference. He is imitating other art — well, just other movies. Part of the reason he can get away with making us cringe so often is that we know he is toying with the art form, and with us, and it is thoroughly playful. Yes, we wonder about him a little bit, but not too much, once we get his game. One of the techniques discussed over and over in Tarantino interviews, reviews, and criticism, is his boyish experimentation with showing us what was *not* on the screen in some classic scene he imitates, and *not* showing us what they originally showed us. He knows we will fill in the other part ourselves. It gives us something to do. Tarantino is always playing this game — look at the classic movie (even a B or a C movie), ask yourself what you're *not* seeing that you *want* to see, reframe the scene from a new perspective, and then let everybody fill in the rest. It's great fun.

By contrast, Mel Gibson thinks something like: chain the viewer to a seat like poor Alex in *A Clockwork Orange* and administer the Ludovico Technique. Leave nothing to the imagination, and be certain your movie-goer is no longer able to think when it's over, or to get the images out of his poor brain ever afterwards. It is not fun. It is abuse. So while Tarantino is about art imitating art for the delight of us all, Gibson is about art imitating Nazi prison guards for the sake of … only God knows what. Some part of us apparently likes to be tortured (after all, we elected Bush and Cheney twice, sort of), but not our *best* part. Just say no.

But that old argument the philosophers used to have over whether art is imitation or expression can help us a little bit. No matter how hard he may try, an artist can't really imitate anything without placing an original stamp on the final product. It happens, one way or another, as decisions are made about what to leave in and what to leave out. And we love Tarantino because he lets *us* play along, participate in the movie, place our own stamp on

---

2 Some of you will say that I am gratuitously picking on the French in this essay. I may be, but I am not the one who built a cryptic critique of French cinema into *Pulp Fiction*. Watch it again, and watch for all things French, and see whether you think this was my idea or Tarantino's. Pay close attention to Fabienne's conversation with Butch about why she has not properly valued his father's watch. That's Tarantino telling you that French cinema has lost its sense of film time, and if Fabienne will ever just get on that damned chopper, she might learn a thing or two about how important time is in a movie. Otherwise she will make us all late for the train. To put it more plainly, the French have forgotten the *audience,* and are wasting their time. You may not believe me now, but watch it again and ask yourself "why, in this story, is Fabienne French?"

3 Say, you know what they call a "monkey wrench" in France? They call it "clé anglaise." "Clé" means "key," and I think you know what "anglaise" means. Sour grapes from Waterloo, I'd guess.

4 Here is a case where the Aussies pulled one over on us. Ask an Aussie if he or she likes Mel Gibson's films. See if you don't get an evasion, with just a hint of a wry grin that says "he used to be our problem, but he's your problem *now.*"

the film in all the places that he activates our imaginations with whatever he left out of the frame. On the other side, Gibson expresses himself, alone, and forbids us, with a cat-o'-nine-tails if necessary, to see *anything* but what he shows us. If Tarantino is the *enfant terrible* of contemporary directors, Gibson is surely the *rex tyrannis.* I could be wrong about this, but I would wager a Hanzo katana that not one person who truly admires and understands Tarantino also likes Gibson's films. There is a reason. Some people like to have fun, others just want to be tortured.

Stuntman Mike, Simulation, and Sadism in *Death Proof*

from *Quentin Tarantino and Philosophy*

— Aaron C. Anderson

Quentin Tarantino's *Death Proof* (2007): four female characters, four cruel deaths, four short sequences. Several rapid close-ups of the girls rocking out to a radio song, a quick point-of-view shot from the front seat of the girls' car. Stuntman Mike (Kurt Russell) pulls his headlights on. Slow motion as the vehicles collide. Slow motion as the bodies of Mike's victims tear apart in repeated collisions of metal, rubber, bone, flesh. In an instant, the human body forcibly joins with technology and pleasure fuses with pain.

Death Proof hinges on its two major car crash sequences. The first crash, repeated four times, marks a distinct shift in genre, setting, and cast. You could easily argue that *Death Proof* fuses two very different films, the first part of the film being largely a horror movie and the last part an action movie. Tarantino frontloads the structure of this film with combinations of horror with action, reality with fiction, pleasure with pain, and references with nonreferences.

The U.S. theatrical cut of *Death Proof* opens with a disclaimer from "The Management": "The following film may contain one or more missing film REELS. Sorry for the inconvenience." From the beginning, with this sort-of-comical warning, Tarantino draws attention to his film's status *as a film,* as a constructed work of fiction, and as a "simulation." Nowhere is this film's status as a fictional piece more obvious than in the countless references to other films that Tarantino plugs into *Death Proof.* Ultimately, however, Tarantino really references himself and his mental film library while constantly drawing attention to what the French theorist Jean Baudrillard calls "hyperreality."

In *Death Proof*'s case, hyperreality is sometimes an unclear mixture of images with reality and sometimes an unclear mixture of images with each other. For example, Tarantino continually references his influences, such as *Vanishing Point* (1971) and *Dirty Mary, Crazy Larry* (1974), both in dialogue and in image. These references to 1970s action flicks go on to become more "authentic" than Tarantino's "original" work in *Death Proof.* Tarantino uses the camera to interpret and moderate reality, but at the same time, he uses it to erase history by reducing it to movie and TV references.

REWRITING THE HISTORY OF CINEMA

From the opening stroll through Jungle Julia (Sydney Poitier)'s apartment (a character whose alliterative name throws back to *Vanishing Point*'s disk jockey Super Soul) to the pursuit of the "fuck-me-swingin'-balls-out" white 1970 Dodge Challenger (also of *Vanishing Point* fame), Tarantino's characters constantly explore images, simulations of cinematic history, and simulations of these simulations. In *Death Proof*, references and images become a form of "simulation" that somehow makes the "real" more "real" or authentic. Through the mixing of human bodies with machines and, by extension, the mixing of pleasure with pain, Tarantino repeatedly emphasizes the fact that simulation is at work in *Death Proof.* By combining human bodies with machines, Tarantino opens the door to the combination of the real with the artificial or simulated.

Death Proof, in many ways, is an attempt to rewrite cinematic history. Tarantino largely does away with the more grand "history" of Baudrillard. For instance, while the posters for *Death Proof* as well as Robert Rodriguez's *Planet Terror* (the other half of *Grindhouse,* the two-in-one "double feature" of which *Death Proof* is the second part) might throw back to the exploitation posters covering the grindhouses of Times Square in the 1960s and 1970s, the contents of *Death Proof* and *Planet Terror* are stripped of all traces of the historic and economic eras that produced the films that they reference. Tarantino seems to be the first to do away with this larger history as he freely mixes cell phones and text messaging, markers of the present, with pristine muscle cars, markers of the past.

The multi-million dollar collaboration of *Grindhouse* quickly erases the actual economic structure that dictated the tiny budgets of much grindhouse fare (although depending on your understanding of "exploitation cinema," you could still define Tarantino and Rodriguez as "exploiters" of their own niche markets). Similarly, in the contemporary production of *Death Proof* there is no space for the quickly disappearing open-road speed-freak freedom of the early 1970s that you find in *Vanishing Point.* The original historical and cinematic context can't help but be lost.

Death Proof throws away memory in favor of the speed of the muscle car. Moving away from memory like this is actually part of *Death Proof*'s structure: with the movement of the story from Texas to Tennessee, Tarantino practically erases the entire first half of the film, with the exception of a few passing references and the character that links them together, Stuntman Mike.

HYPERREALITY AND SIMULATION

Baudrillard, in *Simulacra and Simulation* (1999) and *America* (1994), argues that the United States, and Hollywood productions in particular, are evidence of an all-pervading "hyperreality."[1] It is in hyperreality that there is "no more fiction or reality," only a blurring of the two.[2] Hyperreality and simulation, in turn, connect directly to the hyper-speed of capital's circulation: everything moves, everything sells, everything disappears.

According to Baudrillard, "America is neither dream nor reality" (1999, p. 3). Instead, it is hyperreality through and through. The U.S. and American cultural productions must be understood "as fiction" (p. 29). And *Death Proof* always seems ready to embrace its position as fiction whether it's through countless references to other films or fictions or the self-imposed cult status of the film.

The characters of the second part of the film are in fact, simulations. As actresses playing stuntpersons (Kim [Tracie Thorns] and Zoë [Zoë Bell]), and actresses playing a make-up girl and an actress (Abernathy [Rosario Dawson] and Lee [Mary Elizabeth Winstead]), they create simulations in their fictional work. They also constantly draw attention to their occupations verbally, be it as stuntperson, make-up artist, or actress. Meanwhile, when the action shifts from the stuntperson's game of "Ship's Mast" to the actual violence on the part of Stuntman Mike, Stuntman Mike still *simulates* violence. The action consists at base of stuntpersons acting out car chases from their favorite movies.

What Baudrillard calls "the era of simulation," others more loosely dub "postmodernity." Theorists now, according to Baudrillard, must primarily concern themselves with the "question of substituting the signs of the real for the real" itself (1994, p. 2). Images and markers of reality take the place of what anyone might actually consider "reality." Simulation is essentially a representation. It is a representation, however, that bears no link to what it claims to represent (p. 6). You might think of the filmic references packed into *Death Proof*: to what extent do these references actually throw back to their originals and to what extent do they simply exist as references (that reference nothing)?

Baudrillard outlines four distinct stages of simulation. In the first stage, the image "reflects" a "profound reality." In the second, the image blurs or obscures a profound reality. In the third, the image disguises the nonexistence of a profound reality, and in the fourth, the image bears absolutely no relation to any reality at all. The fourth stage sees the simulation become a *simulacrum,* a simulation or duplicate without an original. Finally, the real begins to mimic the simulation of real images of the real become more real than the real itself (p. 6).

Baudrillard writes that simulation is a repetition of an original object or image. However, this repetition is somehow more authentic, more "real" than the real (1999, p. 41). Tarantino's car chases, in many ways, are perfect simulations, as they appear more genuine to the viewer than the car chases in, say, *Dirty Mary, Crazy Larry, Vanishing*

1   Jean Baudrillard, *America* (London: Verso, 1999), p. 28.
2   Baudrillard, *Simulacra and Simulation* (Ann Arbor: University of Michigan Press, 1994), p. 118.

Point, or *Gone in 60 Seconds* (1974). The challenge for us as viewers of *Death Proof* is to determine where simulation stops and the simulacrum starts. You can dig deeper and deeper but eventually certain images and objects that appear to be references are pure simulacra.

Could you simply call this originality? Perhaps. But there's something else. It's originality with a façade of references and referentiality. In this way, Tarantino seems to write his own cinematic history from his own cinematic library. After seeing *Death Proof,* you can't help but look differently at the female characters in Russ Meyer's *Faster, Pussycat! Kill! Kill!* (1965). Tarantino replaces that film's original historical context and meaning with his own.

Similarly, the car chase that closes *Death Proof* is a hip-hop style sampling of *Dirty Mary, Crazy Larry's* and *Vanishing Point's* chase scenes. It even includes similar automobile makes. Tarantino's car chase ultimately holds this referential significance and so might be characteristic of the third stage of simulation. However, the simulacrum emerges as Tarantino begins to self-consciously reference a sort of mythic exploitation film. Here Tarantino simulates a simulation thus producing a simulacrum.

FREEDOM, HORROR, AND THE ROAD

The road in Baudrillard functions in many of the same ways as Tarantino's road, specifically in the closing car chase and crash in *Death Proof.* The road is a way to move quickly, as quickly as possible, and to forget. It is a way to traverse the referential desert of simulated and anonymous Tennessee (a bucolic landscape harking back to the car chases of *Dirty Mary, Crazy Larry*), or the semi-rural road networks surrounding Austin, Texas (p. 5).

Similarly, in *Death Proof,* Tarantino's stuntpersons Kim and Zoë find America in the road, in the uninhibited circulation of driving, in the unqualified, *free*dom of the *free*ways. This is a freedom to traverse as much space as one wishes at the moment of one's choosing. Baudrillard observes the ability and willingness to move quickly and a parallel willingness to forget in the U.S. According to Baudrillard, Americans shake themselves free of "historical centrality" (p. 81). As postmodern Americans embark on their daily commutes, they think about only the present *now.*

Baudrillard argues that "the only truly profound pleasure" these days is "that of keeping on the move" (p. 53). Tarantino takes this pleasure one step further as he presents

the audience with the mythology of the all-powerful Detroit muscle car. With these powerful machines, Tarantino gives Kim and Zoë the practically *unlimited* speed and power of the 1970 *Vanishing Point* Challenger and gives Stuntman Mike the parallel power of the souped-up Nova and Charger. Here the apparatus of movement and speed, the automobile, becomes both a means to pleasure and a means to pain as the drivers of cars repeatedly collide, bang each other up, scrape stock paint jobs, and spin out. This is one of several moments in which pleasure and pain seem to coincide in *Death Proof.*

Bound up in the endless circulation of goods and peoples, Baudrillard also spots a bizarre interrelatedness and impersonality in American culture. In the U.S., "everything connects, without any two pairs of eyes ever meeting" (p. 60). Perhaps this is where the thrill and horror comes from in the interaction between Mike and his would-be victims: Mike's first victims, speeding along a deserted country road, are literally in the dark up until the moments of their deaths. The eyes of the victims (Jungle Julia, Butterfly [Vanessa Ferlito], Lanna-Frank [Monica Staggs], and Shanna [Jordan Ladd]) and the victimizer (Stuntman Mike) can't meet until Mike pulls on his headlights. Even then, it is unclear if their eyes meet Mike's eyes or meet the technological extensions of his eyes, his headlights. Their deaths, along with the repeated event of headlights flashing on, replay multiple times, from multiple angles, and in slow motion. Only in the most sadistic (or perhaps sadomasochistic) act can eyes meet, can the impersonality of the road become personal. That is, with the exception of Butterfly, whose eyes, immediately before impact, deliberately close rather than open.

GETTING OFF ON CAR CRASHES

While *Death Proof* fuses simulation with reality and technology with the body, it also fuses sadism with a peculiar form of masochism through the character of Stuntman Mike. Mike's first car crash is a deliberate act of violence (in which he drives his car head-on into his victims' car); the machine becomes an extension of his murdering body. It also becomes a death chamber and death-proof chamber at the same time as the crash kills one victim in Mike's car while he remains largely unharmed. This scene enacts a pairing of technology with the sadistic body. However, there is also some sort of risk to Mike and it may therefore be a genuine sadomasochistic scene.

The French philosopher Gilles Deleuze, in *Masochism* (1989), argues that a "meeting of violence and sexuality" is characteristic of both sadism, a condition characterized by a desire to inflict pain, and masochism, a condition characterized by a desire to be humiliated and to have pain inflicted.[3] Stuntman Mike might possess both of these conditions as he desires to inflict pain and gains sexual stimulation from actually experiencing pain.

According to Deleuze, sadism does not necessarily imply masochism nor does masochism necessarily imply sadism (p. 43). Stuntman Mike, however, confuses these separate entities and becomes a true sadomasochist: as Mike obtains a certain pleasure in doing, a pleasure in inflicting pain, when he collides with the car carrying Jungle Julia, Butterfly, Lanna-Frank, and Shanna, he obtains another sort of pleasure from his own injuries (a broken nose, a broken collarbone, and a shattered left index finger). Mike arrives at this pain willingly, even seeking it out as part of his sexual pleasure, and it is therefore a fusion of sadistic and masochistic pleasure (p. 38). Additionally, Mike seems almost completely to confuse technology and body as his car becomes the only way for him to gain sexual pleasure and inflict pain.

However, at the end of the second part of *Death Proof*, the sadisms of Kim, Zoë, and Abernathy turn Mike's sadomasochism on its head. Tarantino, in *Death Proof*'s somewhat abrupt climax, invites the audience to participate in these female characters' sadisms. After Kim shoots Mike in the arm he hurriedly speeds away. Down the road he screeches to a halt, wails in pain, pours alcohol on his wound, then wails in pain again, weeping "Oh why!?" Tarantino encourages the audience to laugh, to become sadists themselves.

Immediately before the final confrontation, as the girls chase Mike, Kim quite clearly becomes a sadist, and a masculine sadist at that. She also mixes technology with the body in her approach to Stuntman Mike as the rear-end of Mike's car metaphorically becomes his "ass" and Kim promises to "bust a nut up in this bitch right now," being

as she is "the horniest motherfucker on the road." This sexualized dialogue meanwhile simulates the hypersexual car and body dialogue toward the end of *Dirty Mary, Crazy Larry.*

FREEZE-FRAME ENDING

Looking back, the repeated images of car crashes are absolutely central to the structure of *Death Proof* as well as to the structures of the films that *Death Proof* pays homage to, especially *Vanishing Point.* Stuntman Mike's violent and sadistic body forces a collision between the nonviolent bodies of Jungle Julia, Butterfly, Lanna-Frank, and Shanna, and the disinterested metal of their car and Mike's death-proof car in the first car crash. Later, the final car crash finds Mike's car, an extension of his murdering body, beaten and half-destroyed by his would-be victims. Here Kim, Zoë, and Abernathy prove themselves bigger sadists than the professional sadist, Stuntman Mike. Ultimately, Mike's sadism itself might be a sort of simulation of the violence in the films he claims to have acted in.

With its postmodern sampling of 1960s and 1970s exploitation cinema, Tarantino's *Death Proof* journeys through terrain mapped by Baudrillard as it veers from simulation to simulacrum and from pleasure to pain, combining all elements in a decidedly postmodern way. Ultimately, the performance of the simulacrum, a negative effect of postmodernity according to Baudrillard, might be Tarantino's greatest contribution to the cinema. In the end such simulacra, through Tarantino, emerge as new forms of cinematic innovation.[4]

> Ultimately, the performance of the simulacrum, a negative effect of postmodernity according to Baudrillard, might be Tarantino's greatest contribution to the cinema.

3   Gilles Deleuze, "Coldness and Cruelty," In *Masochism* (Cambridge, Massachusetts: Zone, 1989), p. 17.

4   Many thanks to K. Silem Mohammad and Justine Lopez for their comments on earlier drafts of this chapter and to Alain J.-J. Cohen for his guidance through Baudrillard and Deleuze. All mistakes, however, are my own.

CHAPTER 2

The Network

These are the voyages of the Starship Enterprise. Her ongoing mission: to explore strange new worlds; to seek out new life forms and new civilizations; to boldly go where no one has gone before.

— Coda,
Star Trek (2009)

Chapter 2. The Network

Recommended Film

Star Trek (J.J. Abrams 2009)

Chapter Summary

Barry Vacker shows how the internet and World Wide Web
combine the printing press with electronic media
in a powerful and complex global network.

Kevin Kelly theorizes the "Net" as the new icon of
science and communication for the new century.

Stephen Hawking explains the meaning of *Star Trek*, the evolution
of information on Earth, and the increasing complexity
of computer technology in the future.

Global Village or World Bazaar?

from *Understanding the Web*

— Barry Vacker

While a single chapter cannot fully cover a complex issue such as the cultural impact of the Web, some patterns of cultural change are becoming evident. Without doubt, there is a broad pattern of technological convergence underway in the media. The traditional print and electronic media are converging around the computer and connecting with each other via global telecommunications networks, resulting in what is often described as an information revolution (Levinson, 1997) from which is emerging a new postindustrial economy (Tapscott, 1996). The World Wide Web does signal that an information revolution is certainly underway, but it is not the first innovation to generate a cultural revolution. Since the hypertext of the Web combines both textual and visual media, we should explore the effects of the "textual" revolution generated by the printing press and the "visual" revolution begun by the camera and electronic image. If we want to estimate the cultural impact of the Web, we should examine the effects of past media revolutions upon the individual, group, nation, and world. These past revolutions suggest cultural patterns that will be amplified and mutated by the World Wide Web.

History suggests that a media convergence occurred with Gutenberg's invention of the printing press, which generated the information revolution that ushered in modernity and industrial society. Closer analysis of both the printing press and the Web suggests that a near-complete convergence in media technology amplifies the collective informational power of the previously separate media, effecting a media revolution that subsequently generates

an information revolution. The distinction is not trivial, for when media technologies converge to create a new medium, they transform the function and content of the information they were originally designed to communicate. A technological convergence that produces a new form of media does not necessarily mean the disappearance or obsolescence of the previous media. The new media technology usually incorporates, mutates, and exponentially amplifies the information or communication power of the old technologies. The printing press did not make the alphabet obsolete; it transformed and amplified its power. The Web will not make the printing press or television obsolete, but will likely transform and amplify their power. A media revolution occurs when the new style of technology exponentially amplifies the power and information of the previous technologies, which then produces the substance of an information revolution that challenges the prevailing worldviews and forms of the existing culture. To paraphrase McLuhan (1996), convergent media create a new message.

The World Wide Web promises to be at the heart of the emerging media and information revolutions, for it is the product of the technological innovation of hypertext and a dual convergence involving the computer and the global telecommunications networks. Such media and information revolutions necessitate use of a broad, macro perspective in exploring the likely transformations of information and culture suggested by the Web. Information thus includes any kind of communication or expression that uses aural, written, printed, or visual symbols to represent things such as ideas, facts, feelings, knowledge,

Barry Vacker, "Global Village or World Bazaar?" from *Understanding the Web: Social, Political, and Economic Dimensions of the Internet,* edited by Alan B. Albarran and David H. Goff, pp. 212–237. First published by Iowa State University Press. Copyright © 2000 by Blackwell Publications. Permission to reprint granted by John Wiley & Sons.

stories, theories, worldviews, or any other item that can be communicated. Rather than information in a strict narrow sense, information here includes the forms and content of both art and science, as well as all realms of human knowledge and communication. Information and culture exist in a complex reciprocal relation. Culture is the complex tapestry that includes not only the arts and sciences, but also that which is expressed in the overall style and structure of society, from ritual to religion, production to politics, education to entertainment. As indicated by the rise of agricultural and industrial societies, culture can transcend any particular individual, group, or nation as it spreads around the globe.

The printing press served as the revolutionary media technology for the information revolution that fueled the transition from agrarian to industrial society. Similarly, the hypermedia technologies of the Web are emerging from the modern computer and telecommunications networks of industrial society, thus serving as the revolutionary media technologies for an information revolution that signals a transition to postindustrial society. Since information and culture both involve virtually every aspect of society, they exist in a complex reciprocal relation in which information and cultural revolutions shape each other. Culture can be transformed by new forms of information and transmitted by new forms of media, yet information and media themselves are the reciprocal products of culture. How the Web will impact individuals, groups, nations, and the world cannot be understood outside the reciprocal relations between culture and the revolutions of media and information, both visual and textual. (Broadly speaking, *group* is meant to include any economic or social organization.)

This chapter is divided into three basic sections, each accompanied by tabular material that illustrate the main points. The first two sections briefly review the impact of the printing press and the electronic image upon information and culture, illustrating how each transformed the individual, group, nation, and world. Section Three will then outline the impact of the Web on the production of information and the structure of the media, illustrating how it amplifies the past textual and visual revolutions. It will then discuss the impact of the Web on the production of culture and suggest how it may impact the individual, group, nation, and global levels of analysis. In conclusion, this chapter will suggest that the culture of the Web will retain elements of the Global Village as it comes to resemble a chaotic world bazaar.

When Gutenberg invented the printing press around 1450, he could not have imagined the future cultural revolutions around the world made possible by his technological innovation. The printing press brought together into a single machine that era's five most advanced media for producing, disseminating, and storing information — alphabetic language, paper, ink, the press process, and movable type. Since the printing press was the first true machine of media convergence and mass production, it represented a media revolution that was to have a significant effect on the production and dissemination of information. The printing press amplified not only the amount of information that could be created and stored, but also the velocity at which such information could be produced and disseminated over both space and time. The modularity of movable type provided the printing press with the production power of standardization and economy-of-scale, both of which reduced the cost (per unit) of information while exponentially increasing the diversity of output. At the time of the invention of the printing press, approximately 50,000 books existed in the world, most of which were under the control of the Church. By 1500, there were an estimated 10 million books and an information revolution was born which was to have enormous individual, group, national, and global consequences (see Table 1.1). We can expect these kinds of consequences to be amplified by the hypertext powers of the Web.

This amplified production power reduced the cost of information, thus making possible less expensive books and periodicals, both of which served to increase individual literacy over the following centuries. Education came to be associated with literacy, which was to be produced through the reciprocal systems of the mass media and mass education (the primary, secondary, and university systems that were reliant upon the printed books and periodicals produced by the mass media). Eventually, a citizenry of literate and informed individuals became a modern Utopian ideal, shaping the intellectual foundations of modern democratic and socialist nation-states. Despite their differences, democracy and socialism were national or international political systems which both claimed to reconcile the liberation of the literate individual with the needs of educated society (the group) through the legitimate political representation of the people.

From the beginning, with increased literacy came increased individual criticism and dissent. While some

Table 1.1. *The printing press: patterns of information and cultural revolution.*

A Media and Information Revolution	The Reciprocal Cultural Revolution
Media Convergence ➢ Brought together alphabet, paper, ink, movable type, and the press process, creating a media convergence and revolution. *Information Amplification* ➢ Increased dissemination of information across space and time, amplifying the spread of more diverse information around the world and to future eras. ➢ Textual revolution emphasizing the printed word and written communication. ➢ Standardized information increased information efficiency, amplifying (a) the amount and diversity of information which can be created and stored and (b) the velocity at which information can be disseminated. *Overall Media Structure* ➢ Reduced cost of information through standardization and economies of scale. ➢ A linear, one-to-many media system, sending information in one direction from one producer to many consumers.	*Overall Global Impact* ➢ The first machine of mass production, serving as the information technology in the emergence of modern industrial society. ➢ Worked toward decentralizing information and spreading it throughout the world. ➢ Spread modern science, philosophy, literature, and art around the world, generating an intellectual and cultural revolution. *The Individual* ➢ Gave birth to the modern notions of individualism and the rights to free speech and expression. ➢ Broke knowledge monopolies of religious and aristocratic authorities, making individual literacy and mass education possible throughout the world. ➢ Individual had significantly more access to information. *Economic-social Groups* ➢ Publishing was one of the first capitalist enterprises that sought to reach anticipated mass markets. ➢ Prototype for the linear mass production system of the industrial factory and mass labor. *Nation-state* ➢ The standardization of language and the rise of industrialism helped create the modern nation-state.

Note: While the cultural impact is broken down according to the individual, group, nation, and world, there exists a complex relationship between individual effects and group, nation, and global effects. Since society is a complex tapestry, the effects upon one segment impact other segments.

members of the Church supported the development of the printing press, its power to mass produce information broke the Church's monopoly on knowledge and helped fuel Martin Luther's Protestant Reformation. Naturally, the prevailing religious and aristocratic authorities saw unrestricted liberty for the printing press as a threat, further increasing the need for a cultural inquisition. The media revolution of the printing press produced chaotic cultural and social (group) effects by partially decentralizing information and intellectual authority, thus fragmenting centuries-old intellectual and social monopolies. The printing press was the media technology that spread both Newtonian science and Enlightenment philosophy, which were fundamental to the emergence of modernity. Eventually, individuals such as writers, journalists, philosophers, scientists, and intellectuals all became workers creating and spreading printed information across space and time. Publishing was an early form of capitalism, for some of the first capitalist entrepreneurs were printers. Often defying social and cultural authorities, printers assumed both monetary and physical risk in publishing books for anticipated markets of readers.

As the standardized and modularized style of the printing press helped spread literacy, it was accompanied by the reciprocal rise of individualism. Prior to the printing press, the group dissemination of knowledge to the populace was done primarily in the town or church via poets and theologians. The structural style of the alphabetic sentence was inherently linear, and the mass production of books helped idealize and increase the individual use of linear deductive logic that came to be seen as an expression of modern reason. While printing permitted the mass production of books for groups or markets of readers, these books were almost exclusively authored singularly by individuals, fostering the ideal of reflective and autonomous individuals employing reason and judgment about the empirical world. Reciprocally, books were read singularly by individuals, further nourishing the ideal of individual reflection.

Over the centuries, the vision of the reflective sovereign individual was to have huge social and cultural consequences in shaping the debate over the control of art, information, and the media. While the printing press was invented in 1450, there was no general theory of freedom of speech and press until the 1700s, a full three centuries later. When John Milton published *Areopagitica* in 1644, it was but a first defense against licensing of the press by the King. Eventually, a free press became synonymous with public liberty and the individual rights to criticize authority, spread knowledge, and exercise intellectual autonomy. Over the latter half of the 18th century, this view became generally accepted in the United States, contributing to the ratification of the First Amendment in 1791 (Powe, 1991). However imperfectly it has been interpreted, the First Amendment expressed a generally individualist view of the media, where individual freedom and social needs are to be reconciled through increased intellectualism and the spread of information (Levy, 1985). The United Nations now recognizes freedom of the press and access to information as universal human rights that should be upheld in every country.

The linear production style of the printing press helped spread the cognitive and social ideal of linearity, which later would be consistent with the universal Newtonianism that permeated modern culture. Employing a mass production process, the printing press became the prototype for the industrial factory and assembly line that was central to both capitalist and socialist production systems. With the spread of industrialism and mass production in the 19th and 20th centuries, the individual became a member of a new group, the industrial labor force employed in the factory. The printing press was also the prototype for the mass media, employing a one-to-many production system, where information flowed from a single producer to many consumers. Whereas the ability of the printing press to standardize information gave it power to diversify and increase knowledge, it also worked to subsume regional dialectical differences through linguistic standardization, producing one of the unifying foundations in the formation of the modern nation-state.

In sum, for the individual, the printing press initiated an information revolution that increased literacy and education, while making possible freedom of press and expression under a representative government. For social and economic groups, the printing press fragmented religious and aristocratic cultural monopolies, ushering in the science, art, and philosophy of modern industrial society. For the nation-state, the printing press spread industrial visions of production standardization, social massification, and territorial unification. For the world, this media revolution did not produce an "information age," but it did contribute to the information revolution that ushered in the new industrial culture. As McLuhan aptly observed, the modern world emerged from the cultural space-time coordinates of Newton's scientific solar system and Gutenberg's informational media galaxy.

THE ELECTRONIC IMAGE

When Daguerre invented the photograph (1839) and Morse invented the telegraph (1844), they could not have imagined the future cultural revolutions set in motion by their innovations. The electronic media essentially function as extensions of the sense organs, permitting the individual or group to record, send, and receive representations of information across space and time. The initial power of

Table 1.2. *The electronic image: patterns of visual and cultural revolution.*

A Visual Revolution	The Reciprocal Cultural Revolution
Partial Medial Convergence ➢ Mass media became both textual and visual, representing a media convergence and revolution. *Amplification of Information* ➢ Collapsed the traditional space-time limits on human communication, thus (a) increasing the velocity of information transmitted in real time and (b) signaling the emergence of global media networks that spanned borders. ➢ Extension of sense organs, retrieving visual information from around the world. ➢ The photograph increased the amount of "information" in the mass media (a picture is worth a thousand words). ➢ Cameras and screens became the new paintbrushes and canvases of culture. ➢ Immaterial "electronic" information would complement "paper" information. *Overall Media Structure* ➢ While the telephone was interactive and nonlinear, the remainder of the electronic media expressed the linear, one-to-many models of the printing press and factory.	**Overall Global Impact** ➢ Returned to the media the visuals that had been neglected by the printing press, thus increasing the importance of visual communication across culture. ➢ Suggested the emergence of the mass-mediated world — the global village. *The Individual* ➢ The individual offered significantly more access to visual and artistic information. *Economic and Social Groups* ➢ Roles of the traditional artist now assumed by photojournalists and cinematographers. ➢ Shaped cultural and individual ideals through the idealization of narrowly defined archetypes — the massification of society. ➢ Created the new mass media of cinema and television. *Nation-state* ➢ Used to disseminate visual advertising to consumers of industrial production. ➢ Used to disseminate visual propaganda to citizens of industrial political systems.

the printing press resided in the prolific production and dissemination of information to readers, whereas the initial power of the electronic media (such as television) resided in the capture and retrieval of images for viewers. The electronic media were to effect a collapse of the traditional space-time barriers that had limited more traditional forms of human communication while also amplifying the quantity of information and the speed of dissemination. For 400 years the printing press had been the sole mass media technology. However, with the birth of the camera and electronic communications, the media landscape was to begin a transformation culminating in the hypermedia systems of the Web.

During the 100 years between 1839 and 1939, six new electronic mass media had begun to spread around the globe — the telegraph, telephone, radio, still and motion pictures, sound recordings, and television. The development of these media represented incremental and partial technological convergences, which are likely to be fulfilled by the cyberspace and virtual reality of the Web. While the telephone was a nonlinear interactive medium, television and radio followed the pattern set by the printing press, in that both expressed a linear, one-to-many model of mass media in which information and entertainment flowed in one direction from broadcasters to millions of viewers. When radio and TV were combined with the technology of Sputnik and Telstar, the result was the possibility for global communication virtually in real time. Paperless media could now pour across borders of the industrial nation-state, as if they were nonexistent, spreading a new culture around the world. While television also combined with the wired phone systems to create cable television and improve picture quality, it also began to fragment the homogenous viewing audience by offering greater programming variety.

The visual power of the camera is central to understanding the cultural impact of the electronic image. Photography recorded highly realistic representations of the empirical world, capturing reality with much greater accuracy and in more detail than any work of art. The power of the camera increased the amount of information that could be disseminated by the mass media, especially since "a picture is worth a thousand words." Culturally treated as if they were exact copies of reality, photographs became the key source modeling and envisioning the empirical and cultural world. The mass production of photographs via the printing press and motion pictures amplified the spread of visual communication, much like the art of painting, but with much greater magnitude and velocity across space and time. While the printing press had made possible the mass production of information through textual representation, the camera press made possible the mass production of information through visual representation. Now that the mass media were both textual and visual, art and culture would never be the same (see Table 1.2).

The printing press was paper-reliant, whereas cinema and television were paperless, disseminating pictures around the world for the new canvas of a screen. Prior to the invention of the camera, the sole source for visual representation was the individual artist. No longer the sole source for visual representation, the visual artist completed the subjective turn inward by surrendering the surrounding empirical world to the camera and the mass media. Photojournalists took over the production of visual representations that documented and influenced world events through the power of a simultaneous empirical objectivity and individual subjectivity. This mixture of objectivism and subjectivism is what gives the electronic image such emotional and artistic power, for it represents empirical reality through the eyes of the subjective, individual human.

Photography used this power to penetrate the realms of fine art and high culture. The emergence of Hollywood signified a new art, one that combined literature and theatre with motion picture technology to create the first truly global entertainment industry.

Unfortunately, the power of the camera was used to express the allegedly scientific management techniques pioneered by Frederick Taylor (1947; Kanigel, 1947). Time-lapse and stop-action photography were used in Taylor's famed time-and-motion studies of the production efficiency of industrial laborers, thus permitting the camera to assist in the increased standardization and the maximization of output. Taylor's vision of scientific managers planning every aspect of production influenced industrial economic and social structures around the world, including not only the New Deal, but also Soviet socialism and the German centralization of industry prior to the rise of National Socialism (Merkle, 1980). While such techniques did improve efficiency, they also created a dehumanizing vision of the mechanistic mass worker vividly portrayed in Fritz Lang's Utopian masterpiece *Metropolis* (1927) and William Cameron Menzie's adaptation of H. G. Wells's *Things to Come* (1936). From cinema to television to advertising, the cultural ideal of the massified industrial society was spread around the globe by the mass media.

Cinema and television could provide images on screens that could be simultaneously and endlessly reproduced for mass audiences around the world. The required synchronicity between dissemination and audience reception suggested media determinism, especially since the role of the media producers was essentially productive and active and the role of consumers was essentially passive and reactive. This naturally made them desirable to the industrial economic and political leaders of the nation-state, assembling consumers for the advertising of industrial production systems and citizens for the propaganda of industrial political systems.

By the 1950s, mass production and mass media had become the dominant forms of production and information technology for both democratic and socialist nations (Toffler, 1980). Even though the economic structures of capitalism and communism differed with regard to the

> Electronic images poured across borders, transforming the sovereign reflective individuals into a tribal chorus living in a mass-mediated global village.

ownership and control of production and media, they were still two systems geared toward mass production for masses of consumer-citizens living in nation-states. During the Cold War, the visual battle was waged between the "capitalist realism" approved by Madison Avenue and the "socialist realism" approved by Moscow. While industrialism and mass media have provided many economic and cultural benefits, lifting individuals from destitution and illiteracy, they have also been used to create narrow visions of an idealized universal culture that spread around the globe with rise of democratic and socialist nation-states.

In sum, the electronic image returned to the media the visual realm that had been neglected by the printing press, thus replacing many functions of the traditional visual arts. For the individual, they could now see art and pictorial representations from around the world via the new mass media of cinema and television. For economic and social groups, the new electronic mass media mirrored the principles of mass production, linearity, standardization, centralization, and synchronization. This made the electronic image perfect for creating idealized visions of narrow archetypes that rejected the modern massified society. For the nation-state and the world, electronic images poured across borders, transforming the sovereign reflective individuals into a tribal chorus living in a mass-mediated global village.

AN EMERGING WORLD BAZAAR

The last two decades of the 20th century have seen the industrial mass media begin a massive technological transformation and convergence whose global cultural consequences may rival those of the printing press. The transformation of the print and electronic mass media began with the global proliferation of magazines, radio stations, television stations, cable networks, and satellite television, all made possible by improved media technologies. Toffler (1980) believed such a media proliferation signaled the permanent decline of the traditional mass media and the emergence of a demassified media landscape, resulting in a significant increase in information producers relative to consumers and a reciprocal decline in the proportional size of the audiences relative to producers. The interactivity of personal computers suggests that the simultaneous media proliferation and audience fragmentation will only be amplified by the convergence of traditional media around the Web and millions of new information producers of varying size, from Microsoft to Matt Drudge. With its

ever-increasing digital power, the Web will likely amplify and mutate the textual power of the printing press and the visual power of electronic image as it globally transforms the structure of the media. In any era of significant change, there will be numerous cultural variations, precisely because culture is a complex tapestry. The following two sections will outline the media revolution of the Web and suggest some broad patterns of cultural change involving the individual, groups, nations, and the world.

THE WEB:
MEDIA CONVERGENCE AND REVOLUTION

History has suggested that media revolutions occur when there is a nearly complete media convergence to create a new technology that amplifies the collective power of the previously singular media. The printing press signified the first such revolution, setting off the information revolution that ushered in modern industrial society. The electronic image expressed a partial convergence among the new electronic media technologies, thus beginning a visual media revolution that continues today. The reason the Web signifies a media revolution is that virtually all previous textual and visual media are converging to create a new digitized and interactive hypermedia network that will amplify the power of the previously separate media.

Two broad patterns of convergence are being fueled by the two basic media technologies of the Web — the local personal computer and global telecommunications networks. Personal computers are integrating virtually all of the previously separate media into a new interactive multimedia technology which utilizes alphabetic language, telephones, radio, cameras, motion pictures, television, and even Gutenberg's printing press. While the electronic media and telecommunications networks have evolved throughout the 20th century, we should remember that computers and the Web are still essentially embryonic media technologies. While no one knows the specific final forms of this technology, there seems no doubt that the media technologies are being incrementally integrated by the personal computer to produce a new interactive multimedia technology. Eventually, over time, the computer-based medium may deploy a mixture of traditional alphabetic keyboards, voice activation, wall screens, holograms, and retinal display in virtual reality, all made possible by improved computer power. The point here is that a new interactive multimedia technology is emerging from the computer.

Individuals, economic and social groups, and governments are forming information links by connecting computers to each other through the wired and wireless telecommunications technologies. Fueling this double convergence has been spiraling increases in computer power coupled with declines in cost, both afforded by the power of silicon microprocessors. Much like Gutenberg's movable type, silicon chips standardize information into the binary system of *1s* and *0s,* and then compress these bits to the microscopic level. This standardization and miniaturization of information is what gives computers such power, creating the possibility for endless variation, much like the alphabet of movable type and the screens of the electronic image. The power of computing promises to expand exponentially as miniaturization spirals downward to the molecular level with DNA computers (Adleman,

The printing press and the electronic media were essentially linear mass production systems in which information flowed in a single direction from relatively few producers to masses of consumers. While the Web will retain and amplify some of these features, the emerging new media structures suggest the continual erosion of the mass audience, a process that will have significant cultural consequences. The demassified media described by Toffler is transforming into a global network whose structure is nonlinear and "molecular," rather than linear and mechanistic.

Computers and the Web will be central to the postindustrial forms of production, serving as potential production, distribution, and media devices. When linked to the internet, each computer functions as a production and distribution *node,* existing simultaneously as its own *center* for production and as an *edge* for entry into, and exit from, the information networks of the Web. Hypertext functions like an amplified and nonlinear global footnote system that

---

Like the printing press 500 years ago, the computer and the Web are dramatically reducing the cost of receiving, creating, manipulating, storing, and disseminating information. These reduced costs are amplifying the production of information and the speed at which it is being retrieved and disseminated through the Web.

1998) and to the subatomic level with quantum computers (Gershenfeld and Chuang, 1998); both of these will possess power exponentially greater than current state-of-the-art supercomputers. These technological developments are important because they suggest that the computer and web-based information revolutions may have just begun.

Like the printing press 500 years ago, the computer and the Web are dramatically reducing the cost of receiving, creating, manipulating, storing, and disseminating information. These reduced costs are amplifying the production of information and the speed at which it is being retrieved and disseminated through the Web. Much like the electronic image, the Web permits electronic visual information to flow around the world, as if there were no local or national borders. Expanding data banks are making it possible for virtually unlimited customization and specialization, resulting in proliferation of textual and visual information. With millions of computers around the globe connecting to the Web, the very essence of the structure of the mass media is being transformed.

permits an individual to instantaneously access information from different information sources across the world. As more nodes are created and connected, and the technological power amplifies and diversifies, the Web simultaneously becomes more molecularized and less centralized in overall structure. While each computer is its own node and center, there is no single center among the millions of decentered centers. Computers or organizations that can serve as a network center, such as firms or libraries or museums or online servers or personal computers, also serve as nodes and edges of varying sizes and importance. In essence, no traditional production or distribution center exists across the Web, only the seeming paradox of decentering nodes that are simultaneously edges and centers. The Web is simultaneously local and global, spatial and immaterial. The molecular structure of nodes and edges is creating a production and distribution system of unparalleled complexity and ever-increasing speed. Computer interactivity and hypertext, when combined with satellites and fiber optics, suggest the emergence of a "chaotic" hypermedia system, much different than the linear systems which typified the industrial mass media. With many millions of information producers using networks comprised of an ever-increasing number of nodes, fiber optics, and satellites, the structure of the Web is beginning to resemble the complex molecular systems found in nature (Kauffman, 1995; Kellert, 1993). This molecularization, however, does not mean the complete disappearance of mass media, for pop culture events such as the World Cup, the Super Bowl, and *Titanic* will continue to draw audiences in the hundreds of millions. However, such mass events will be the exception, rather than the rule. The industrial mass media will no longer dominate; its power will be incrementally eroded by the waves of mutating molecularization being amplified around the globe throughout the unlimited spectrum of the Web.

Terms such as *information superhighway* and the *Infobahn* are outmoded industrial metaphors that suggest an ignorance of the chaotic molecular structure of the hypertextual Web. Unlike the industrial mass media, the Web permits one-to-one, one-to-many, many-to-one, and many-to-many communications in which information flows in multiple directions, in a more horizontal and non-linear manner. The Web suggests the emergence of a new hypermedia network likely to be characterized by nonlinearity, interactivity, immersion, virtualization, asynchrony, decentering, fluidity, customization, individualization, spatiality without territory, time without distance. Since the structure of media and production technologies have significantly influenced culture in the past, we can expect the Web to have a reciprocal impact on the production of culture as it undermines the dynamics of a massified global village.

CULTURAL TURBULENCE

The double convergence toward the computer and the Web suggests the emergence of a chaotic media system, whereas the electronic realms within the Web suggest the creation of a new realm of informational space-time. Together, the chaotic structure and the new realm will work to transform art, media, science, labor, and capital as it becomes the information backbone in the transition to a postindustrial society centered around biotechnology (Kelly, 1994), nanotechnology (Drexler, 1986), and media technology (Negroponte, 1995). The cultural effects will be reciprocal and turbulent (see Table 1.3).

Cyberspace and virtual reality are the culmination of the electronic image, representing a new realm of space-time that exists simultaneously in the quantum space of the computer chip and the relative space of the Web (Heim, 1993; 1998). This is an inversion of the normal relations of technology, space-time, and culture. While the technologies and cultures of agrarian and industrial society both exist within the physical realm of traditional space-time, cyberspace exists within the technological infrastructure of computer chips and networks. Space and time, the relative external, now also inhabit the quantum internal. The computer and the Web are producing a functional infrastructure and a formal exostructure for the economic and social groups of the new postindustrial production systems. This does not mean that computers and the Web are separating humans from reality, for it seems the new media are permeating reality and thus blurring the lines between representation and reality. These new realms intensify and amplify information while simultaneously fragmenting consensus by permitting real worldviews to become virtual worlds. While this transformation of information relative to space and time is crucial for a true information revolution, it seems almost as if cyberspace and the Web transform space and time relative to information. This implosion of space and time relative to information will produce an explosion of cultural effects as the Web increases in complexity and spreads around the globe, impacting individuals, groups, and nations.

THE INDIVIDUAL

In terms of sheer volume and variety, individuals will have significantly more access to textual and visual information than at any other time in human history. There will be more creators and disseminators of information than ever before, enlarging the role of the individual in the global marketplace of ideas. This process can only generate a renewed sense of individual expression and a reciprocal rise in cultural turbulence as the prevailing structures of industrial society struggle to adapt and maintain control.

Individual interactivity and reduced information costs are already producing an increase in the diversity of artistic, scientific, and political expression disseminated across the Web, from virtual museums to the Human Genome Project to global conspiracy theories. Intellectual and cultural dissent is also flourishing on the Web, with its virtually unlimited space and global distribution. Since there are

Table 1.3. *The World Wide Web: Patterns of information and cultural revolution and the different structures of the mass media and hypermedia.*

PATTERNS OF INFORMATION AND CULTURAL REVOLUTION

A MEDIA AND INFORMATION REVOLUTION

Media Convergence
- ➤ Virtually all previous media are converging around the personal computer and the global telecommunications networks.
- ➤ Information may be produced in any form — text, visual, motion picture, sound.

Information Amplification
- ➤ Digitization standardizes (1,0) information and increases efficiency, amplifying
- ➤ (a) the amount and diversity of information that can be created and stored and
- ➤ (b) the velocity at which information can be disseminated and received across space and time.
- ➤ Information may be infinitely specialized, customized, and encrypted.
- ➤ Reduced cost of information through standardization, economies of scale, and the lack of need for paper.
- ➤ Information is transformed because it is reproduced and circulates in cyberspace.

Overall Medial Structure
- ➤ A nonlinear interactive network in which information may flow from one-to-one, one-to-many, many-to-many, and many-to-one.
- ➤ Information instantaneous, real time, and global, flowing across cultures and borders, simultaneously local and global.
- ➤ The new media are highly mobile and central to postindustrial production system.

THE RECIPROCAL CULTURAL REVOLUTION

Overall Global Impact
- ➤ Undermining the mass society of industrialism.
- ➤ Creating a chaotic marketplace of cultures that prevents the construction of consensus and social unification.
- ➤ Global villagers amidst an emerging world bazaar.

The Individual
- ➤ Individuals can receive and disseminate more information than ever before, thus enlarging their role in the marketplace of ideas.
- ➤ There will be continual explosive and contentious debate among individuals.
- ➤ The volume of information, and its diversity, will place more responsibility upon individuals to determine what they believe is true and false.
- ➤ There will be increased individualism and independent thought, which undermine dogma and certainty.

Economic and Social Groups
- ➤ Progressive group adaptation will increase social and economic entrepreneurialism.
- ➤ Marginalized groups will find new outlets to express their ideas and connect with people of like mind.
- ➤ Regressive groups will seek state control and regulation of information and the new technologies.
- ➤ Virtual communities and markets will thrive, fueling nonterritorial socialization and digital commerce.
- ➤ Backbone of postindustrial production systems.

Nation-state
- ➤ As information becomes more fluid, governments likely to heighten information surveillance and censorship.
- ➤ Potential loss of individual and social privacy.
- ➤ Undermine democratic systems and socialist systems born of industrialism.

Table 1.4. *The Different Structures of the Mass Media and Hypermedia*

	THE DIFFERENT STRUCTURES OF THE MASS MEDIA AND HYPERMEDIA	
	TRADITIONAL MASS MEDIA	WEB HYPERMEDIA
Basic principle	➤ Mass production	➤ Mass customization
Key technology	➤ Printing press, Broadcasting	➤ Computers, microprocessors
Electronic signal	➤ Analog	➤ Digital
Information flow	➤ Linear, point-to-multipoint	➤ Nonlinear, point-to-multipoint, multipoint-to-point (or multipoint)
Audience goal	➤ Maximization, Homogeneity	➤ Individualized, diverse
Media usage	➤ Passive	➤ Interactive
Media device	➤ Dumb/receive information only	➤ Smart; transmit, alter information
Location	➤ Home, office, stationary	➤ Highly mobile, view anywhere
Information producers	➤ Relatively few	➤ Millions
Entry cost	➤ Very expensive	➤ Relatively cheap producers
Messages	➤ Aimed at mass audience	➤ Very specialized audiences
System	➤ Mechanistic, centralized	➤ Organic, decentralized

relatively no paper or distribution costs, we can naturally expect many more newspapers, magazines, and books to be produced and distributed at much lower costs via computers and the Web, perhaps generating a global publishing renaissance unparalleled since the printing press. In effect, the individual can be a global information pamphleteer, publisher, and producer, employing a full range of media. The point here is not whether the content of these publications or productions is accurate, or whether we agree or disagree with any of them. Rather, the cultural significance is that they can be disseminated, mutated, and endlessly replicated globally via the Web, almost instantaneously and at virtually the speed of light. The Web permits information to be created and disseminated generally outside the filtering gatekeepers of the mass media institutions of the capitalist and socialist nations. In what seems paradoxical, the convergence of the Web is producing a radical decentering of information, true and false, both of which the tra-

ditional mass media tried to centralize or control through the one-to-many model of information production.

This is culturally healthy, yet turbulent, for it undermines mass media centralization and ultimately requires individuals to increase their personal responsibility for the ideas and information they regard as true and false. Those individuals and groups more comfortable with having their truth disseminated for them via the traditional mass media may feel their worldviews threatened in the face of such information chaos. An information revolution tends to undermine cultural dogma, precisely because it amplifies the content of information. On the other hand, the unlimited storage capacity and ability to customize information will provide fertile ground for the survival of many old dogmas and the emergence of many new truths.

In the realm of cyberspace, individuals can transform their abstract worldviews into virtual worlds. Communities can be constructed to reflect any particular philosophical or ideological perspective, permitting individuals to interact with persons who share their ideas or interests. In such specialized communities, individuals can reinforce their own pre-existing worldviews within a narrow range of dialogue. If they want, they can use these communities to isolate themselves from the people and ideas on the Web with which they disagree. On the other hand, individuals can use the speed and diversity of the Web to broaden their worldviews and worlds. Together, such possibilities will likely increase the variety of individuals and groups across the globe. While some cyber utopians may dream of global unity or world democracy, the reality is that the tableau of the Web is likely to resemble a contentious and chaotic marketplace of cultures. The vision of a homogenous or universal cultural ideal can no longer dominate the media landscape. Instead of a single national or global unity, there will be many different unities within many different groups connected via the Web. We can imagine the worldwide cultural turbulence as the massified culture, idealized under industrial production, is supplanted by many subcultures populated by many different global villagers.

ECONOMIC AND SOCIAL GROUPS

Broadly speaking, there are four types of social and economic groups that will emerge with the spread of the Web. There are those that will progressively adapt to the hypermedia technologies, seeing in technological change the opportunity to create new communities and markets. In contrast, there will be groups that regressively adapt to the change by seeking to impose government controls upon information, producers, and technology. Because of the inevitable conflict between progressive and regressive adaptation, two other general types of social groups will emerge — those who want to control others' information and those who want to control their own information. These four overlapping groups and their conflicts will have a significant impact on the economies and social systems of nation-states and the world.

Progressive adapters will be those economic and social entrepreneurs who use the reduced information costs and increased power afforded by the Web to expand their opportunities in postindustrial production systems. The industrial print and electronic mass media required significant amounts of capital, as did their distribution systems of trucks, stations, satellites, bookstores, and theatres. In contrast, newspapers, books, TV sets, and movie tickets were inexpensive in relation to their cost of production.

The mass production and distribution technologies generated economies of scale, thus creating a system in which information production and distribution were expensive and information reception was inexpensive. While producing and distributing visual information such as movies is still expensive, the power of computers and the Web suggests that the relative production and distribution costs for information will decline over time. Because of the global nature of the Web and the reduced capital needs, we can expect increased economic entrepreneurship. Firms such as Amazon.com and broadcast.com have become billion dollar companies by using the Web's global distribution and low barriers to entry to sell the content of the traditional mass media (books and the retransmission of local radio stations and video, respectively). The fears of a "Microsoft world" are understandable, though likely unwarranted over time. Even though corporations and governments may try, malleable information flowing over chaotic networks will be impossible to centralize. Fluidic information, chaotic networks, and declining costs suggest heightened competition over time and the blurring of lines across the structure and content of the traditional media and production systems (Tapscott, 1996).

Similarly, social entrepreneurs will progressively adapt to the new media and production structures by creating nonterritorial virtual communities around the world. Previously marginalized groups, ranging from rights activists to political dissidents to digital artists, are connecting with each other through the Web to create meaningful social and political virtual communities (Jones, 1997). Such social possibilities are already yielding economic opportunities. With their portals to the Web, firms such as Yahoo! and Excite are making possible the emergence of thousands of virtual communities focused around special topics, ranging from vegetarianism to single parenting to expatriates from Chile (Napoli, 1998). Yahoo! and Excite are functioning like virtual real estate developers as they provide the nonterritorial proximity for communities of interest to emerge and flourish. As the Web diffuses, we can expect these communities to proliferate. On the other hand, this cultural and technological diversification will threaten the prevailing social groups and political authorities, shattering the illusion that they are the only institutions possessing truth and justice. It seems only a matter of time before these kinds of cultural conflicts begin to significantly impact the cultural and political systems of the industrial nation-state, generating progressive and regressive adaptations.

THE NATION-STATE

The chaotic, molecular, and borderless hypermedia network of the Web will function to undermine the ability of the traditional mass media and nation-state to control the production of information, assemble and manage mass political movements, and generate the consensus that justifies the massified political systems of the industrial nation-states. The doctrines of democracy, socialism, and representative government all presume the existence and moral validity of a political consensus that expresses "majoritarian" or mass opinion. Modern mass politics and representative government emerged simultaneously with the one-to-many models of mass media. Political leaders either controlled the mass media, or used the filter of the compliant corporate mass media to disseminate their social visions or propaganda for mass consumption. We are likely entering an era in which centralization and mass movements may be practically impossible. Symptomatic of this pattern is the perpetual political gridlock emerging in the democratic nation-states, signaling not the failure or corruption of their systems, but more likely the eventual irrelevance or obsolescence of the mass political systems born of the industrial age.

When a cultural or political system is being transformed or rendered obsolete, many groups and organizations will feel threatened and will desire regressive adaptation. Medieval religious authorities performed inquisitions, agrarian Luddites destroyed machines, industrial fascists burned books, and postindustrial democratic majoritarian groups employ clipper chips. In the current democratic nation-states, the political majority is comprised of average citizens that usually have little to fear from censorship and surveillance, precisely because they represent the average. This is why majoritarian, "democratic" government offers little defense against censorship. Freedom of expression has generally survived in the United States because of the First Amendment, and in spite of the democratic government (Emord, 1991). Even government attempts to monopolize information usually fail when faced with the chaotic information processes produced by freedom of expression and amplified technology. The printing press functioned in a chaotic manner in pre-Revolutionary America, eventually working to undermine the authority of King George

(Powe, 1991). Even the Soviet Union could not control the informational onslaught presented by the new electronic media technologies. While Beijing may have defeated the student protesters in Tiananmen Square, one suspects it will eventually lose the war with the World Wide Web. To the extent that a nation-state tries to control information flowing across the Web, it will become more stagnant; to the extent it permits open media networks and the free flow of information, it will become less relevant.

Since the increased amount of individual expression undermines the power of the prevailing groups and governments of industrial society, it is generating cultural fear and increased calls for censorship and information surveillance, usually in the name of cultural purity, social order, or national security. While computers and the Web can enhance individual expression, they can also be used to suppress such expression through information surveillance and invasions of individual and social privacy. There will be a battle between two groups — those who want to control others' information and those who want to control their own information. Censorship and surveillance are regressive adaptations, which are now being countered by the progressive adaptation of encryption. The first casualty of censorship is freedom of expression; the first casualty of surveillance is privacy. As Orwell (1949) illustrated, the control of information necessitates the elimination of privacy, precisely because information begins in the privacy of one's own thoughts. Free expression and privacy are reciprocal, and without their protection from centralized control the only result would be a spiraling closure of culture and technology in a surveillance society. While these battles will be ugly and produce some casualties, the war is likely to be won by freedom of expression and privacy. Since religious and aristocratic authorities could not put a few hundred printing presses back in Pandora's box, it seems unlikely that world governments will be able to put a few billion computers back in their packing boxes.

REFERENCES

Adleman, L.M. 1998, August. Computing with DNA. *Scientific American*, 279: 54–61.

Drexler, K.E. 1986. *Engines of Creation: The Coming Era of Nanotechnology*. New York: Anchor Press.

Emord, J.W. 1991. *Freedom, Technology, and the First Amendment*. San Francisco: Pacific Research Institute.

Gershenfeld, N. and Chuang, I.L. 1998, June. Quantum Computing with Molecules. *Scientific American*, 278: 66–71.

Hayashi, A.M. 1999, January. The Net Effect. *Scientific American*, 280: 21–22.

Heim, M. 1993. *The Metaphysics of Virtual Reality*. New York: Oxford University Press.

Heim, M. 1998. *Virtual Realism*. New York: Oxford University Press.

Jones, S.G., ed. 1997. *Virtual Culture*. Thousand Oaks, CA: Sage Publications.

Kanigel, R. 1997. *The One Best Way: Frederick Winslow Taylor and the Enigma of Efficiency*. New York: Viking.

Kauffman, S.A. 1995. *At Home in the Universe: The Search for the Laws of Self-organization and Complexity*. New York: Oxford University Press.

Kellert, S.H. 1993. *In the Wake of Chaos*. Chicago: The University of Chicago Press.

Kelly, K. 1994. *Out of Control: The New Biology of Machines, Social Systems, and the Economic World*. Reading, MA: Addison-Wesley Publishing Company, Inc.

Levinson, P. 1997. *The Soft Edge: A Natural History and Future of the Information Revolution*. London: Routledge.

Levy, L. 1985. *Emergence of a Free Press*. New York: Oxford University Press.

Malamud, C. 1997. *A World's Fair for the Global Village*. Cambridge: MIT Press.

McLuhan, M. 1962. *The Gutenberg Galaxy*. New York: New American Library.

McLuhan, M. 1996. *The Medium is the Massage*. San Francisco: HardWired.

McLuhan, M. 1997. *War and Peace in the Global Village*. San Francisco: HardWired.

Merkle, J.A. 1980. *Management and Ideology: The Legacy of the International Scientific Management Movement*. Berkeley: University of California Press.

Napoli, L. 1998, December 6. The Latest Internet Buzzword: Community. *The New York Times*. p. B10.

Negroponte, N. 1995. *Being Digital*. New York: Alfred A. Knopf.

Orwell, G. (1949). *1984*. New York: Harcourt Brace.

Powe, L.A., Jr. 1991. *The Fourth Estate and the Constitution*. Berkeley: University of California Press.

Tapscot, D. 1996. *The Digital Economy*. New York: McGraw-Hill.

Taylor, F.W. 1947. *Scientific Management*. New York: Harper & Row Publishers.

Toffler, A. 1970. *Future Shock*. New York: Random House.

Toffler, A. 1980. *The Third Wave*. New York: William Morrow and Company, Inc.

Hive Mind

from *Out of Control*

— Kevin Kelly

In a darkened Las Vegas conference room, a cheering audience waves cardboard wands in the air. Each wand is red on one side, green on the other. Far in back of the huge auditorium, a camera scans the frantic attendees. The video camera links the color spots of the wands to a nest of computers set up by graphics wizard Loren Carpenter. Carpenter's custom software locates each red and each green wand in the auditorium. Tonight there are just shy of 5,000 wandwavers. The computer displays the precise location of each wand (and its color) onto an immense, detailed video map of the auditorium hung on the front stage, which all can see. More importantly, the computer counts the total red or green wands and uses that value to control software. As the audience wave the wands, the display screen shows a sea of lights dancing crazily in the dark, like a candlelight parade gone punk. The viewers see themselves on the map; they are either a red or green pixel. By flipping their own wands, they can change the color of their projected pixels instantly.

Loren Carpenter boots up the ancient video game of Pong onto the immense screen. Pong was the first commercial video game to reach pop consciousness. It's a minimalist arrangement: a white dot bounces inside a square; two movable rectangles on each side act as virtual paddles. In short, electronic ping-pong. In this version, displaying the red side of your wand moves the paddle up. Green moves it down. More precisely, the Pong paddle moves as the average number of red wands in the auditorium increases or decreases. Your wand is just one vote.

Carpenter doesn't need to explain very much. Every attendee at this 1991 conference of computer graphic experts was probably once hooked on Pong. His amplified voice booms in the hall, "Okay guys. Folks on the left side of the auditorium control the left paddle. Folks on the right side control the right paddle. If you think you are on the left, then you really are. Okay? Go!"

The audience roars in delight. Without a moment's hesitation, 5,000 people are playing a reasonably good game of Pong. Each move of the paddle is the average of several thousand players' intentions. The sensation is unnerving. The paddle usually does what you intend, but not always. When it doesn't, you find yourself spending as much attention trying to anticipate the paddle as the incoming ball. One is definitely aware of another intelligence online: it's this hollering mob.

The group mind plays Pong so well that Carpenter decides to up the ante. Without warning the ball bounces faster. The participants squeal in unison. In a second or two, the mob has adjusted to the quicker pace and is playing better than before. Carpenter speeds up the game further; the mob learns instantly.

"Let's try something else," Carpenter suggests. A map of seats in the auditorium appears on the screen. He draws a wide circle in white around the center. "Can you make a green '5' in the circle?" he asks the audience. The audience stares at the rows of red pixels. The game is similar to that of holding a placard up in a stadium to make a picture, but now there are no preset orders, just a virtual mirror. Almost immediately wiggles of green pixels appear and grow haphazardly, as those who think their seat is in the path of the "5" flip their wands to green. A vague figure is materializing. The audience collectively begins to discern a "5" in the noise. Once discerned, the "5" quickly precipitates out into stark clarity. The wand-wavers on the fuzzy edge of the figure decide what side they "should" be on, and the emerging "5" sharpens up. The number assembles itself.

"Now make a four!" the voice booms. Within moments a "4" emerges. "Three." And in a blink a "3" appears. Then in rapid succession, "Two … One … Zero." The emergent thing is on a roll.

Loren Carpenter launches an airplane flight simulator on the screen. His instructions are terse: "You guys on the left are controlling roll; you on the right; pitch, if you point the plane at anything interesting, I'll fire a rocket at it." The plane is airborne. The pilot is … 5,000 novices. For once the auditorium is completely silent. Everyone studies the navigation instruments as the scene outside the windshield sinks in. The plane is headed for a landing in a pink valley among pink hills. The runway looks very tiny.

There is something both delicious and ludicrous about the notion of having the passengers of a plane collectively fly it. The brute democratic sense of it all is very appealing. As a passenger you get to vote for everything; not only where the group is headed, but when to trim the flaps.

But group mind seems to be a liability in the decisive moments of touchdown, where there is no room for averages. As the 5,000 conference participants begin to take down their plane for landing, the hush in the hall is ended by abrupt shouts, and urgent commands. The auditorium becomes a gigantic cockpit in crisis. "Green, green, green!" one faction shouts. "More red!" a moment later from the crowd. "Red, red! REEEEED!" The plane is pitching to the left in a sickening way. It is obvious that it will miss the landing strip and arrive wing first. Unlike Pong, the flight simulator entails long delays in feedback from lever to effect, from the moment you tap the aileron to the moment it banks. The latent signals confuse the group mind. It is caught in oscillations of overcompensation. The plane is lurching wildly. Yet the mob somehow aborts the landing and pulls the plane up sensibly. They turn the plane around to try again.

How did they turn around? Nobody decided whether to turn left or right, or even to turn at all. Nobody was in charge. But as if of one mind, the plane banks and turns wide. It tries landing again. Again it approaches cockeyed. The mob decides in unison, without lateral communication, like a flock of birds taking off, to pull up once more. On the way up the plane rolls a bit. And then rolls a bit more. At some magical moment, the same strong thought simultaneously infects five thousand minds: "I wonder if we can do a 360?"

Without speaking a word, the collective keeps tilting the plane. There's no undoing it. As the horizon spins dizzily, 5,000 amateur pilots roll a jet on their first solo flight. It was actually quite graceful. They give themselves a standing ovation.

The conferees did what birds do: they flocked. But they flocked self-consciously. They responded to an overview of themselves as they co-formed a "5" or steered the jet. A bird on the fly, however, has no overarching concept of the shape of its flock. "Flockness" emerges from creatures completely oblivious of their collective shape, size, or alignment. A flocking bird is blind to the grace and cohesiveness of a flock in flight.

*　　*　　*

Zen masters once instructed novice disciples to approach zen meditation with an unprejudiced "beginner's mind." The master coached students, "Undo all preconceptions." The proper awareness required to appreciate the swarm nature of complicated things might be called hive mind. The swarm master coaches, "Loosen all attachments to the sure and certain."

A contemplative swarm thought: The Atom is the icon of 20th century science.

The popular symbol of the Atom is stark: a black dot encircled by the hairline orbits of several other dots. The Atom whirls alone, the epitome of singleness. It is the metaphor for individuality: atomic. It is the irreducible seat of strength. The Atom stands for power and knowledge and certainty. It is as dependable as a circle, as regular as round.

The image of the planetary Atom is printed on toys and on baseball caps. The swirling Atom works its way into corporate logos and government seals. It appears on the back of cereal boxes, in school books, and stars in TV commercials.

The internal circles of the Atom mirror the cosmos, at once a law-abiding nucleus of energy, and at the same time the concentric heavenly spheres spinning in the galaxy. In the center is the *animus,* the It, the life force, holding all to their appropriate whirling stations. The symbolic Atoms' sure orbits and definite interstices represent the understanding of the universe made known. The Atom conveys the naked power of simplicity.

Another Zen thought: The Atom is the past. The symbol of science for the next century is the dynamical Net.

The Net icon has no center — it is a bunch of dots connected to other dots — a cobweb of arrows pouring into each other, squirming together like a nest of snakes, the restless image fading at indeterminate edges. The Net is the archetype — always the same picture — displayed to represent all circuits, all intelligence, all interdependence, all things economic and social and ecological, all communications, all democracy, all groups, all large systems. The icon is slippery, ensnaring the unwary in its paradox of no beginning, no end, no center. Or, all beginning, all end, pure center. It is related to the Knot. Buried in its apparent

The inefficiencies of a network — all that redundancy and ricocheting vectors, things going from here to there and back just to get across the street — encompasses imperfection rather than ejecting it. A network nurtures small failures in order that large failures don't happen as often. It is its capacity to hold error rather than scuttle it that makes the distributed being fertile ground for learning, adaptation, and evolution.

The only organization capable of unprejudiced growth, or unguided learning, is a network. All other topologies limit what can happen.

A network swarm is all edges and therefore open ended any way you come at it. Indeed, the network is the least structured organization that can be said to have any structure at all. It is capable of infinite rearrangements, and of

---

The Net is the archetype—always the same picture—displayed to represent all circuits, all intelligence, all interdependence, all things economic and social and ecological, all communications, all democracy, all groups, all large systems.

---

disorder is a winding truth. Unraveling it requires heroism.

When Darwin hunted for an image to end his book *Origin of Species* — a book that is one long argument about how species emerge from the conflicting interconnected self-interests of many individuals — he found the image of the tangled Net. He saw "birds singing on bushes, with various insects flitting about, with worms crawling through the damp earth"; the whole web forming "an entangled bank, dependent on each other in so complex a manner."

The Net is an emblem of multiples. Out of it comes swarm being — distributed being — spreading the self over the entire web so that no part can say, "I am the I." It is irredeemably social, unabashedly of many minds. It conveys the logic both of Computer and of Nature — which in turn convey a power beyond understanding.

Hidden in the Net is the mystery of the Invisible Hand — control without authority. Whereas the Atom represents clean simplicity, the Net channels the messy power of complexity.

The Net, as a banner, is harder to live with. It is the banner of noncontrol. Wherever the Net arises, there arises also a rebel to resist human control. The network symbol signifies the swamp of psyche, the tangle of life, the mob needed for individuality.

growing in any direction without altering the basic shape of the thing, which is really no outward shape at all. Craig Reynolds, the synthetic flocking inventor, points out the remarkable ability of networks to absorb the new without disruption: "There is no evidence that the complexity of natural flocks is bounded in any way. Flocks do not become 'full' or 'overloaded' as new birds join. When herring migrate toward their spawning grounds, they run in schools extending as long as 17 miles and containing millions of fish." How big a telephone network could we make? How many nodes can one even theoretically add to a network and still have it work? The question has hardly even been asked.

There *are* a variety of swarm topologies, but the only organization that holds a genuine plurality of shapes is the grand mesh. In fact, a plurality of truly divergent components can only remain coherent in a network. No other arrangement — chain, pyramid, tree, circle, hub — can contain true diversity working as a whole. This is why the network is nearly synonymous with democracy or the market.

A dynamic network is one of the few structures that incorporates the dimension of time. It honors internal change. We should expect to see networks wherever we see constant irregular change, and we do.

A distributed, decentralized network is more a process than a thing. In the logic of the Net there is a shift from nouns to verbs. Economists now reckon that commercial products are best treated as though they were services. It's not what you sell a customer, its what you do for them. It's not what something is, it's what it is connected to, what it does. Flows become more important than resources. Behavior counts.

Network logic is counterintuitive. Say you need to lay a telephone cable that will connect a bunch of cities; let's make that three for illustration: Kansas City, San Diego, and Seattle. The total length of the lines connecting those three cities is 3,000 miles. Common sense says that if you add a fourth city to your telephone network, the total length of your cable will have to increase. But that's not how network logic works. By adding a fourth city as a hub (let's make that Salt Lake City) and running the lines from each of the three cities through Salt Lake City, we can decrease the total mileage of cable to 2,850 or 5 percent less than the original 3,000 miles. Therefore the total unraveled length of a network can be shortened by *adding* nodes to it! Yet there is a limit to this effect. Frank Hwang and Ding Zhu Du, working at Bell Laboratories in 1990, proved that the best savings a system might enjoy from introducing new points into a network would peak at about 13 percent. More *is* different.

On the other hand, in 1968 Dietrich Braess, a German operations researcher, discovered that adding routes to an already congested network will only slow it down. Now called Braess's Paradox, scientists have found many examples of how adding capacity to a crowded network reduces its overall production. In the late 1960s the city planners of Stuttgart tried to ease downtown traffic by adding a street. When they did, traffic got worse; then they blocked it off and traffic improved. In 1992, New York City closed congested 42nd Street on Earth Day, fearing the worst, but traffic actually improved that day.

Then again, in 1990, three scientists working on networks of brain neurons reported that increasing the gain — the responsivity — of individual neurons did not increase their individual signal detection performance, but it did increase the performance of the whole network to detect signals.

Nets have their own logic, one that is out-of-kilter to our expectations. And this logic will quickly mold the culture of humans living in a networked world. What we get from heavy-duty communication networks, and the networks of parallel computing, and the networks of distributed appliances and distributed being is Network Culture.

Alan Kay, a visionary who had much to do with inventing personal computers, says that the personally owned book was one of the chief shapers of the Renaissance notion of the individual, and that pervasively networked computers will be the main shaper of humans in the future. It's not just individual books we are leaving behind, either. Global opinion polling in realtime 24 hours a day, seven days a week, ubiquitous telephones, asynchronous e-mail, 500 TV channels, video on demand: all these add up to the matrix for a glorious network culture, a remarkable hivelike being.

The tiny bees in my hive are more or less unaware of their colony. By definition their collective hive mind must transcend their small bee minds. As we wire ourselves up into a hivish network, many things will emerge that we, as mere neurons in the network, don't expect, don't understand, can't control, or don't even perceive. That's the price for any emergent hive mind.

Our Future? *Star Trek* or Not?

from *The Universe in a Nutshell*

— Stephen Hawking

HOW BIOLOGICAL AND ELECTRONIC LIFE WILL GO ON DEVELOPING IN COMPLEXITY AT AN EVER-INCREASING RATE.

The reason *Star Trek* is so popular is because it is a safe and comforting vision of the future. I'm a bit of a *Star Trek* fan myself, so I was easily persuaded to take part in an episode in which I played poker with Newton, Einstein, and Commander Data. I beat them all,

but unfortunately there was a red alert, so I never collected my winnings.

Star Trek shows a society that is far in advance of ours in science, in technology, and in political organization. (The last might not be difficult.) There must have been great changes, with their accompanying tensions and upsets, in the time between now and then, but in the period we are shown, science, technology, and the organization of society are supposed to have achieved a level of near perfection.

FIG. 6.1 *GROWTH OF POPULATION*

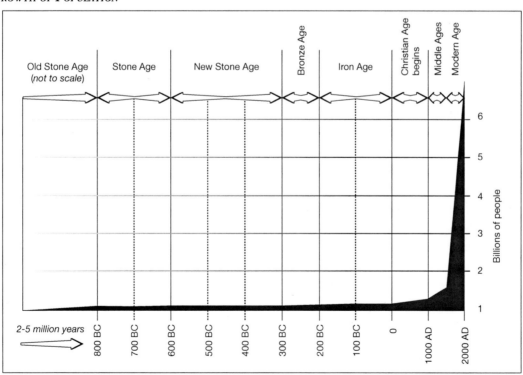

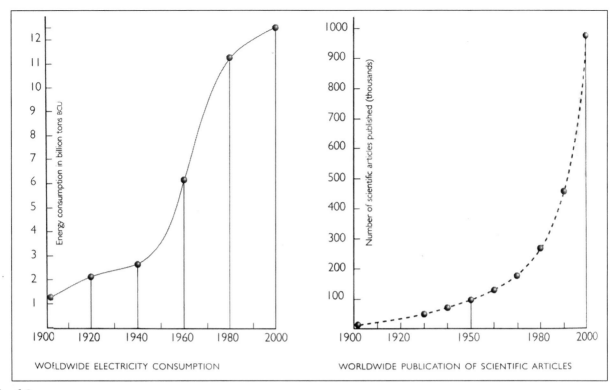

FIG 6.2

Left: The total worldwide energy consumption in billions of tons BCU, where 1 ton ~Bituminous Coal Unit = 8.13 MW-hr.

Right: The number of scientific articles published each year. The vertical scale is in thousands. In 1900 there were 9,000. By 1950 there were 90,000 and by the year 2000 there were 900,000.

I want to question this picture and ask if we will ever reach a final steady state in science and technology. At no time in the ten thousand years or so since the last ice age has the human race been in a state of constant knowledge and fixed technology. There have been a few setbacks, like the Dark Ages after the fall of the Roman Empire. But the world's population, which is a measure of our technological ability to preserve life and feed ourselves, has risen steadily, with only a few hiccups such as the Black Death (Fig. 6.1).

In the last two hundred years, population growth has become exponential, that is, the population grows by the same percentage each year. Currently, the rate is about 1.9 percent a year. That may not sound like very much, but it means that the world population doubles every forty years (Fig. 6.2).

Other measures of technological development in recent times are electricity consumption and the number of scientific articles. They too show exponential growth, with doubling times of less than forty years. There is no sign that scientific and technological development will slow down and stop in the near future — certainly not by the time of *Star Trek*, which is supposed to be not that far in the future. But if the population growth and the increase in the consumption of electricity continue at their current rates, by 2600 the world's population will be standing shoulder to shoulder, and electricity use will make the Earth glow red-hot (see illustration opposite).

If you stacked all the new books being published next to each other, you would have to move at ninety miles an hour just to keep up with the end of the line. Of course, by 2600 new artistic and scientific work will come in electronic forms, rather than as physical books and papers. Nevertheless, if the exponential growth continued, there would be ten papers a second in my kind of theoretical physics, and no time to read them.

Clearly, the present exponential growth cannot continue indefinitely. So what will happen? One possibility is that we will wipe ourselves out completely by some disaster, such as a nuclear war. There is a sick joke that the reason we have not been contacted by extraterrestrials is that when a civilization reaches our stage of development, it becomes unstable and destroys itself. However, I'm an optimist. I don't believe the human race has come so far just to snuff itself out when things are getting interesting.

The *Star Trek* vision of the future — that we achieve an advanced but essentially static level — may come true in respect of our knowledge of the basic laws that govern the universe. As I shall describe in the next chapter, there may be an ultimate theory that we will discover in the not-too-distant future. This ultimate theory, if it exists, will determine whether the *Star Trek* dream of warp drive can be realized. According to present ideas, we shall have to explore the galaxy in a slow and tedious manner, using spaceships traveling slower than light, but since we don't yet have a complete unified theory, we can't quite rule out warp drive.

On the other hand, we already know the laws that hold in all but the most extreme situations: the laws that govern the crew of the *Enterprise*, if not the spaceship itself. Yet it doesn't seem that we will ever reach a steady state in the uses we make of these laws or in the complexity of the systems that we can produce with them. It is with this complexity that the rest of this chapter will be concerned.

By far the most complex systems that we have are our own bodies. Life seems to have originated in the primordial oceans that covered the Earth four billion years ago. How this happened we don't know. It may be that random collisions between atoms built up macromolecules that could reproduce themselves and assemble themselves into more complicated structures. What we do know is that by three and a half billion years ago, the highly complicated DNA molecule had emerged.

DNA is the basis for all life on Earth. It has a double helix structure, like a spiral staircase, which was discovered by Francis Crick and James Watson in the Cavendish lab at Cambridge in 1953. The two strands of the double helix are linked by pairs of bases, like the treads in a spiral staircase. There are four bases in DNA: adenine, guanine, thymine, and cytosine. The order in which they occur along the spiral staircase carries the genetic information that enables the DNA to assemble an organism around it and reproduce itself. As it makes copies of itself, there are occasional errors in the proportion or order of the bases along the spiral. In most cases, the mistakes in copying make the DNA either unable or less likely to reproduce itself, meaning that such genetic errors, or mutations, as they are called, will die out. But in a few cases, the error or mutation will increase the chances of the DNA surviving and reproducing. Such changes in the genetic code will be favored. This is how the information contained in the sequence of DNA gradually evolves and increases in complexity (see Fig. 6.4).

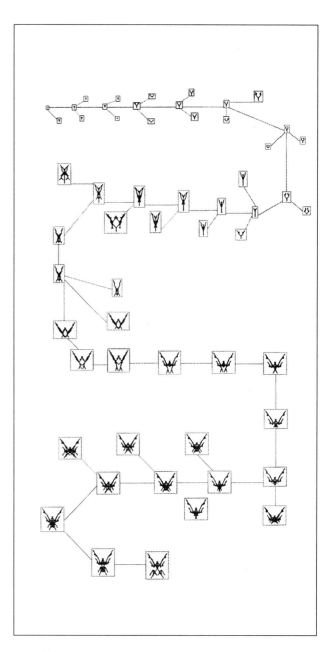

Fig. 6.4 *Evolution in Action*
On the right are computer-generated biomorphs that evolved in a program devised by the biologist Richard Dawkins.

Survival of a particular strain depended upon simple qualities like being "interesting," "different," or "insect-like."

Starting from a single pixel, the early random generations developed through a process similar to natural selection. Dawkins bred an insect-like form in a remarkable 29 generations (with a number of evolutionary dead ends).

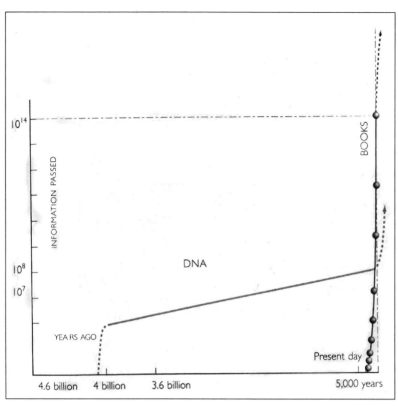

The development of complexity since the formation of the Earth
(not to scale).

Because biological evolution is basically a random walk in the space of all genetic possibilities, it has been very slow. The complexity, or number of bits of information, that is coded in DNA is roughly the number of bases in the molecule. For the first two billion years or so, the rate of increase in complexity must have been of the order of one bit of information every hundred years. The rate of increase of DNA complexity gradually rose to about one bit a year over the last few million years. But then, about six or eight thousand years ago, a major new development occurred. We developed written language. This meant that information could be passed from one generation to the next without having to wait for the very slow process of random mutations and natural selection to code it into the DNA sequence. The amount of complexity increased enormously. A single paperback romance could hold as much information as the difference in DNA between apes and humans, and a thirty-volume encyclopedia could describe the entire sequence of human DNA (Fig. 6.5).

Even more important, the information in books can be updated rapidly. The current rate at which human DNA is being updated by biological evolution is about one bit a year. But there are two hundred thousand new books published each year, a new-information rate of over a million bits a second. Of course, most of this information is garbage, but even if only one bit in a million is useful, that is still a hundred thousand times faster than biological evolution.

This transmission of data through external, nonbiological means has led the human race to dominate the world and to have an exponentially increasing population. But now we are at the beginning of a new era, in which we will be able to increase the complexity of our internal record, the DNA, without having to wait for the slow process of biological evolution. There has been no significant change in human DNA in the last ten thousand years, but it is likely that we will be able to completely redesign it in the next thousand. Of course, many people will say that genetic engineering of humans should be banned, but it is doubtful we will be able to prevent it. Genetic engineering of plants and animals will be allowed for economic reasons, and someone is bound to try it on humans. Unless we have a totalitarian world order, someone somewhere will design improved humans.

Clearly, creating improved humans will create great social and political problems with respect to unimproved

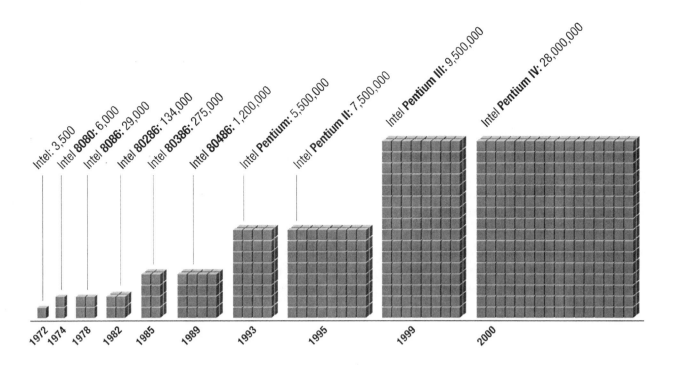

The exponential growth in computing from 1972 to a conservative estimate of 2007 by one CPU manufacturer. The figure after the actual chip gives the number of calculations per second.

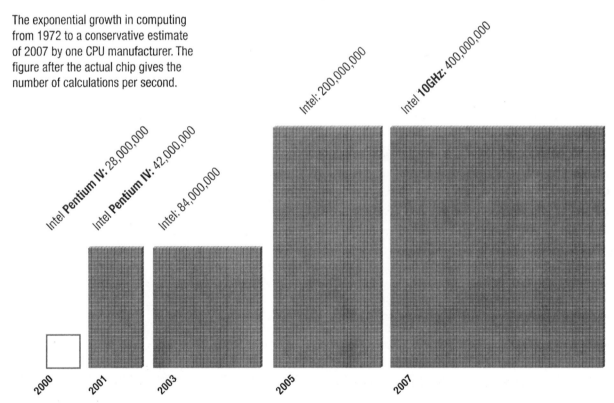

FIG. 6.6

humans. My intention is not to defend human genetic engineering as a desirable development, but just to say it is likely to happen whether we want it or not. This is the reason why I don't believe science fiction like *Star Trek*, where people four hundred years into the future are essentially the same as we are today. I think the human race, and its DNA, will increase its complexity quite rapidly. We should recognize that this is likely to happen and consider how we will deal with it.

In a way, the human race needs to improve its mental and physical qualities if it is to deal with the increasingly complex world around it and meet new challenges such as space travel. Humans also need to increase their complexity if biological systems are to keep ahead of electronic ones. At the moment, computers have the advantage of speed, but they show no sign of intelligence. This is not surprising, because our present computers are less complex than the brain of an earthworm, a species not noted for its intellectual powers.

> I think we can become a lot more intelligent than most of the people in *Star Trek*, not that that might be difficult.

But computers obey what is known as Moore's law: their speed and complexity double every eighteen months. It is one of those exponential growths that clearly cannot continue indefinitely. However, it will probably continue until computers have a complexity similar to that of the human brain. Some people say that computers can never show true intelligence, whatever that may be. But it seems to me that if very complicated chemical molecules can operate in humans to make them intelligent, then equally complicated electronic circuits can also make computers act in an intelligent way. And if they are intelligent, they can presumably design computers that have even greater complexity and intelligence.

Will this increase of biological and electronic complexity go on forever, or is there a natural limit? On the biological side, the limit on human intelligence up to now has been set by the size of the brain that will pass through the birth canal. Having watched my three children being born, I know how difficult it is for the head to get out. But within the next hundred years, I expect we will be able to grow babies outside the human body, so this limitation will be removed. Ultimately, however, increases in the size of the human brain through genetic engineering will come up against the problem that the body's chemical messengers responsible for our mental activity are relatively slow-moving. This means that further increases in the complexity of the brain will be at the expense of speed. We can be quick-witted or very intelligent, but not both. Still, I think we can become a lot more intelligent than most of the people in *Star Trek*, not that that might be difficult.

Electronic circuits have the same complexity-versus-speed problem as the human brain. In this case, however, the signals are electrical, not chemical, and travel at the speed of light, which is much higher. Nevertheless, the speed of light is already a practical limit on the design of faster computers. One can improve the situation by making

A BRIEF HISTORY OF THE UNIVERSE

EVENTS *(not to scale)*

0.00003 billion years		1 billion years	3 billion years
The big bang and a fiery, optically dense, inflationary universe.	Matter/energy decouple. The universe is transparent.	Clusters of matter form protogalaxies synthesizing heavier nuclei.	Galaxies recorded by Hubble Space Telescope in its Deep Field exploration.

(FIG. 6.7)
The human race has been in existence for only a tiny fraction of the history of the universe. (If this chart was to scale and the length that human beings have been around was 7cm, then the whole history of the universe would be over a kilometer.) Any alien life we meet is likely to be much more primitive or much more advanced than we are.

the circuits smaller, but ultimately there will be a limit set by the atomic nature of matter. Still, we have some way to go before we meet that barrier.

Another way in which electronic circuits can increase their complexity while maintaining speed is to copy the human brain. The brain does not have a single CPU — central processing unit — that processes each command in sequence. Rather, it has millions of processors working together at the same time. Such massively parallel processing will be the future for electronic intelligence as well.

Assuming we don't destroy ourselves in the next hundred years, it is likely that we will spread out first to the planets in the solar system and then to the nearby stars. But it won't be like *Star Trek* or *Babylon 5*, with a new race of nearly human beings in almost every stellar system. The human race has been in its present form for only two million years out of the fifteen billion years or so since the big bang (Fig. 6.7).

So even if life develops in other stellar systems, the chances of catching it at a recognizably human stage are very small. Any alien life we encounter will likely be either much more primitive or much more advanced. If it is more advanced, why hasn't it spread through the galaxy and visited Earth? If aliens had come here, it should have been obvious: more like the film *Independence Day* than *E.T.*

So how does one account for our lack of extraterrestrial visitors? It could be that there is an advanced race out there which is aware of our existence but is leaving us to stew in our own primitive juices. However, it is doubtful it would be so considerate to a lower life-form: do most of us worry how many insects and earthworms we squash underfoot? A more reasonable explanation is that there is a very low probability either of life developing on other planets or of that life developing intelligence. Because we claim to be intelligent, though perhaps without much ground, we tend to see intelligence as an inevitable consequence of evolution. However, one can question that. It is not clear that intelligence has much survival value. Bacteria do very well without intelligence and will survive us if our so-called intelligence causes us to wipe ourselves out in a nuclear war. So as we explore the galaxy we may find primitive life, but we are not likely to find beings like us.

The future of science won't be like the comforting picture painted in *Star Trek*: a universe populated by many humanoid races, with an advanced but essentially static science and technology. Instead, I think we will be on our own, but rapidly developing in biological and electronic complexity. Not much of this will happen in the next hundred years, which is all we can reliably predict. But by the end of the next millennium, if we get there, the difference from *Star Trek* will be fundamental.

		3.5 billion years ago	0.0005 billion years ago
New galaxies, like our own, with heavier nuclei, are formed.	Formation of our solar system with orbiting planets.	Life-forms begin to appear.	Early humans appear.

CHAPTER 3

The Spectacle

Because the only truth you know is what you get over this tube. (...) Television is not the truth. Television is a God damned amusement park. Television is a circus, a carnival, a traveling troupe of acrobats, storytellers, dancers, singers, jugglers, sideshow freaks, lion tamers, and football players. We're in the boredom killing business.

— Howard Beall,
Network (1976)

Chapter 3. The Spectacle

Recommended Film

Network (Sidney Lumet 1976)

Chapter Summary

Neil Postman argues that the nature of television technology renders it as a medium far more effective at entertainment than enlightenment.

Todd Gitlin explores some parameters of the accelerating torrent of media images produced by rapidly evolving media technologies.

Douglas Kellner conceptualizes the media spectacle as a "way of life" that has penetrated every aspect of society.

The Age of Show Business

from *Amusing Ourselves to Death*

— Neil Postman

A dedicated graduate student I know returned to his small apartment the night before a major examination only to discover that his solitary lamp was broken beyond repair. After a whiff of panic, he was able to restore both his equanimity and his chances for a satisfactory grade by turning on the television set, turning off the sound, and with his back to the set using its light to read important passages on which he was to be tested. This is one use of television — as a source of illuminating the printed page.

But the television screen is more than a light source. It is also a smooth, nearly flat surface on which the printed word may be displayed. We have all stayed at hotels in which the TV set has had a special channel for describing the day's events in letters rolled endlessly across the screen. This is another use of television — as an electronic bulletin board.

Many television sets are also large and sturdy enough to bear the weight of a small library. The top of an old-fashioned RCA console can handle as many as thirty books, and I know one woman who has securely placed her entire collection of Dickens, Flaubert, and Turgenev on the top of a 21-inch Westinghouse. Here is still another use of television — as bookcase.

I bring forward these quixotic uses of television to ridicule the hope harbored by some that television can be used to support the literate tradition. Such a hope represents exactly what Marshall McLuhan used to call "rear-view mirror" thinking: the assumption that a new medium is merely an extension or amplification of an older one;

that an automobile, for example, is only a fast horse, or an electric light a powerful candle. To make such a mistake in the matter at hand is to misconstrue entirely how television redefines the meaning of public discourse. Television does not extend or amplify literate culture. It attacks it. If television is a continuation of anything, it is of a tradition begun by the telegraph and photograph in the mid-nineteenth century, not by the printing press in the fifteenth.

What is television? What kinds of conversations does it permit? What are the intellectual tendencies it encourages? What sort of culture does it produce?

These are the questions to be addressed in the rest of this book, and to approach them with a minimum of confusion, I must begin by making a distinction between a technology and a medium. We might say that a technology is to a medium as the brain is to the mind. Like the brain, a technology is a physical apparatus. Like the mind, a medium is a use to which a physical apparatus is put. A technology becomes a medium as it employs a particular symbolic code, as it finds its place in a particular social setting, as it insinuates itself into economic and political contexts. A technology, in other words, is merely a machine. A medium is the social and intellectual environment a machine creates.

Of course, like the brain itself, every technology has an inherent bias. It has within its physical form a predisposition toward being used in certain ways and not others. Only those who know nothing of the history of technology believe that a technology is entirely neutral. There is an old joke that mocks that naive belief. Thomas Edison, it goes, would have revealed his discovery of the electric light much sooner than he did except for the fact that every time he turned it on, he held it to his mouth and said, "Hello? Hello?"

Not very likely. Each technology has an agenda of its own. It is, as I have suggested, a metaphor waiting to enfold. The printing press, for example, had a clear bias toward being used as a linguistic medium. It is *conceivable* to use it exclusively for the reproduction of pictures. And, one imagines, the Roman Catholic Church would not have objected to its being so used in the sixteenth century. Had that been the case, the Protestant Reformation might not have occurred, for as Luther contended, with the word of God on every family's kitchen table, Christians do not require the Papacy to interpret it for them. But in fact there never was much chance that the press would be used solely, or even very much, for the duplication of icons. From its beginning in the fifteenth century, the press was perceived as an extraordinary opportunity for the display and mass distribution of written language. Everything about its technical possibilities led in that direction. One might even say it was invented for that purpose.

The technology of television has a bias, as well. It is conceivable to use television as a lamp, a surface for texts, a bookcase, even as radio. But it has not been so used and will not be so used, at least in America. Thus, in answering the question, What is television?, we must understand as a first point that we are not talking about television as a technology but television as a medium. There are many places in the world where television, though the same technology as it is in America, is an entirely different medium from that which we know. I refer to places where the majority of people do not have television sets, and those who do have only one; where only one station is available; where television does not operate around the clock; where most programs have as their purpose the direct furtherance of government ideology and policy; where commercials are unknown, and "talking heads" are the principal image; where television is mostly used as if it were radio. For these reasons and more television will not have the same meaning or power as it does in America, which is to say, it is possible for a technology to be so used that its potentialities are prevented from developing and its social consequences kept to a minimum.

But in America, this has not been the case. Television has found in liberal democracy and a relatively free market economy a nurturing climate in which its full potentialities

as a technology of images could be exploited. One result of this has been that American television programs are in demand all over the world. The total estimate of U.S. television program exports is approximately 100,000 to 200,000 hours, equally divided among Latin America, Asia and Europe.[1] Over the years, programs like "Gunsmoke," "Bonanza," "Mission: Impossible," "Star Trek," "Kojak," and more recently, "Dallas" and "Dynasty" have been as popular in England, Japan, Israel and Norway as in Omaha, Nebraska. I have heard (but not verified) that some years ago the Lapps postponed for several days their annual and, one supposes, essential migratory journey so that they could find out who shot J.R. All of this has occurred simultaneously with the decline of America's moral and political prestige, worldwide. American television programs are in demand not because America is loved but because American television is loved.

We need not be detained too long in figuring out why. In watching American television, one is reminded of George Bernard Shaw's remark on his first seeing the glittering neon signs of Broadway and 42nd Street at night. It must be beautiful, he said, if you cannot read. American television is, indeed, a beautiful spectacle, a visual delight, pouring forth thousands of images on any given day. The average length of a shot on network television is only 3.5 seconds, so that the eye never rests, always has something new to see. Moreover, television offers viewers a variety of subject matter, requires minimal skills to comprehend it, and is largely aimed at emotional gratification. Even commercials, which some regard as an annoyance, are exquisitely crafted, always pleasing to the eye and accompanied by exciting music. There is no question but that the best photography in the world is presently seen on television commercials. American television, in other words, is devoted entirely to supplying its audience with entertainment.

Of course, to say that television is entertaining is merely banal. Such a fact is hardly threatening to a culture, not even worth writing a book about. It may even be a reason for rejoicing. Life, as we like to say, is not a highway strewn

---

1   On July 20, 1984, *The New York Times* reported that the Chinese National Television network had contracted with CBS to broadcast sixty-four hours of CBS programming in China. Contracts with NBC and ABC are sure to follow. One hopes that the Chinese understand that such transactions are of great political consequence. The Gang of Four is as nothing compared with the Gang of Three.

with flowers. The sight of a few blossoms here and there may make our journey a trifle more endurable. The Lapps undoubtedly thought so. We may surmise that the ninety million Americans who watch television every night also think so. But what I am claiming here is not that television is entertaining but that it has made entertainment itself the natural format for the representation of all experience. Our

I should like to illustrate this point by offering the case of the eighty-minute discussion provided by the ABC network on November 20, 1983, following its controversial movie *The Day After*. Though the memory of this telecast has receded for most, I choose this case because, clearly, here was television taking its most "serious" and "responsible" stance. Everything that made up this broadcast

---

Entertainment is the supra-ideology of all discourse on television. No matter what is depicted or from what point of view, the overarching presumption is that it is there for our amusement and pleasure.

---

television set keeps us in constant communion with the world, but it does so with a face whose smiling countenance is unalterable. The problem is not that television presents us with entertaining subject matter but that all subject matter is presented as entertaining, which is another issue altogether.

To say it still another way: Entertainment is the supra-ideology of all discourse on television. No matter what is depicted or from what point of view, the overarching presumption is that it is there for our amusement and pleasure. That is why even on news shows which provide us daily with fragments of tragedy and barbarism, we are urged by the newscasters to "join them tomorrow." What for? One would think that several minutes of murder and mayhem would suffice as material for a month of sleepless nights. We accept the newscasters' invitation because we know that the "news" is not to be taken seriously, that it is all in fun, so to say. Everything about a news show tells us this — the good looks and amiability of the cast, their pleasant banter, the exciting music that opens and closes the show, the vivid film footage, the attractive commercials — all these and more suggest that what we have just seen, is no cause for weeping. A news show, to put it plainly, is a format for entertainment, not for education, reflection or catharsis. And we must not judge too harshly those who have framed it in this way. They are not assembling the news to be read, or broadcasting it to be heard. They are televising the news to be seen. They must follow where their medium leads. There is no conspiracy here, no lack of intelligence, only a straightforward recognition that "good television" has little to do with what is "good" about exposition or other forms of verbal communication but everything to do with what the pictorial images look like.

recommended it as a critical test of television's capacity to depart from an entertainment mode and rise to the level of public instruction. In the first place, the subject was the possibility of a nuclear holocaust. Second, the film itself had been attacked by several influential bodies politic, including the Reverend Jerry Falwell's Moral Majority. Thus, it was important that the network display television's value and serious intentions as a medium of information and coherent discourse. Third, on the program itself no musical theme was used as background — a significant point since almost all television programs are embedded in music, which helps to tell the audience what emotions are to be called forth. This is a standard theatrical device, and its absence on television is always ominous. Fourth, there were no commercials during the discussion, thus elevating the tone of the event to the state of reverence usually reserved for the funerals of assassinated Presidents. And finally, the participants included Henry Kissinger, Robert McNamara, and Elie Wiesel, each of whom is a symbol of sorts of serious discourse. Although Kissinger, somewhat later, made an appearance on the hit show "Dynasty," he was then and still is a paradigm of intellectual sobriety; and Wiesel, practically a walking metaphor of social conscience. Indeed, the other members of the cast — Carl Sagan, William Buckley and General Brent Scowcroft — are, each in his way, men of intellectual bearing who are not expected to participate in trivial public matters.

The program began with Ted Koppel, master of ceremonies, so to speak, indicating that what followed was not intended to be a debate but a *discussion*. And so those who are interested in philosophies of discourse had an excellent opportunity to observe what serious television means by the word "discussion." Here is what it means: Each of six men was given approximately five minutes to say something about the subject. There was, however, no agreement on exactly what the subject was, and no one felt obliged to respond to anything anyone else said. In fact, it would have been difficult to do so, since the participants were called upon seriatim, as if they were finalists in a beauty contest, each being given his share of minutes in front of the camera. Thus, if Mr. Wiesel, who was called upon last, had a response to Mr. Buckley, who was called upon first, there would have been four commentaries in between, occupying about twenty minutes, so that the audience (if not Mr. Wiesel himself) would have had difficulty remembering the argument which prompted his response. In fact, the participants — most of whom were no strangers to television — largely avoided addressing each other's points. They used their initial minutes and then their subsequent ones to intimate their position or give an impression. Dr. Kissinger, for example, seemed intent on making viewers feel sorry that he was no longer their Secretary of State by reminding everyone of books he had once written, proposals he had once made, and negotiations he had once conducted. Mr. McNamara informed the audience that he had eaten lunch in Germany that very afternoon, and went on to say that he had at least fifteen proposals to reduce nuclear arms. One would have thought that the discussion would turn on this issue, but the others seemed about as interested in it as they were in what he had for lunch in Germany. (Later, he took the initiative to mention three of his proposals but they were not discussed.) Elie Wiesel, in a series of quasi-parables and paradoxes, stressed the tragic nature of the human condition, but because he did not have the time to provide a context for his remarks, he seemed quixotic and confused, conveying an impression of an itinerant rabbi who has wandered into a coven of Gentiles.

In other words, this was no discussion as we normally use the word. Even when the "discussion" period began, there were no arguments or counterarguments, no scrutiny of assumptions, no explanations, no elaborations, no definitions. Carl Sagan made, in my opinion, the most coherent statement — a four-minute rationale for a nuclear freeze — but it contained at least two questionable assumptions and was not carefully examined. Apparently, no one wanted to take time from his own few minutes to call attention to someone else's. Mr. Koppel, for his part, felt obliged to keep the "show" moving, and though he occasionally pursued what he discerned as a line of thought,

he was more concerned to give each man his fair allotment of time.

But it is not time constraints alone that produce such fragmented and discontinuous language. When a television show is in process, it is very nearly impermissible to say, "Let me think about that" or "I don't know" or "What do you mean when you say …?" or "From what sources does your information come?" This type of discourse not only slows down the tempo of the show but creates the impression of uncertainty or lack of finish. It tends to reveal people in the *act of thinking*, which is as disconcerting and boring on television as it is on a Las Vegas stage. Thinking does not play well on television, a fact that television directors discovered long ago. There is not much to *see* in it. It is, in a phrase, not a performing art. But television demands a performing art, and so what the ABC network gave us was a picture of men of sophisticated verbal skills and political understanding being brought to heel by a medium that requires them to fashion performances rather than ideas. Which accounts for why the eighty minutes were very entertaining, in the way of a Samuel Beckett play: The intimations of gravity hung heavy, the meaning passeth all understanding. The performances, of course, were highly professional. Sagan abjured the turtle-neck sweater in which he starred when he did "Cosmos." He even had his hair cut for the event. His part was that of the logical scientist speaking in behalf of the planet. It is to be doubted that Paul Newman could have done better in the role, although Leonard Nimoy might have. Scowcroft was suitably military in his bearing — terse and distant, the unbreakable defender of national security. Kissinger, as

> Thinking does not play well on television, a fact that television directors discovered long ago.

always, was superb in the part of the knowing world statesman, weary of the sheer responsibility of keeping disaster at bay. Koppel played to perfection the part of a moderator, pretending, as it were, that he was sorting out ideas while, in fact, he was merely directing the performances. At the end, one could only applaud those performances, which is what a good television program always aims to achieve; that is to say, applause, not reflection.

I do not say categorically that it is impossible to use television as a carrier of coherent language or thought in process. William Buckley's own program, "Firing Line," occasionally shows people in the act of thinking but who also happen to have television cameras pointed at them. There are other programs, such as "Meet the Press" or "The Open Mind," which clearly strive to maintain a sense of intellectual decorum and typographic tradition, but they are scheduled so that they do not compete with programs of great visual interest, since otherwise, they will not be watched. After all, it is not unheard of that a format will occasionally go against the bias of its medium. For example, the most popular radio program of the early 1940's featured a ventriloquist, and in those days, I heard more than once the feet of a tap dancer on the "Major Bowes' Amateur Hour." (Indeed, if I am not mistaken, he even once featured a pantomimist.) But ventriloquism, dancing and mime do not play well on radio, just as sustained, complex talk does not play well on television. It can be made to play tolerably well if only one camera is used and the visual image is kept constant — as when the President gives a speech. But this is not television at its best, and it is not television that most people will choose to watch. The single most important fact about television is that people *watch* it, which is why it is called "*television*." And what they watch, and like to watch, are moving pictures — millions of them, of short duration and dynamic variety. It is in the nature of the medium that it must suppress the content of ideas in order to accommodate the requirements of visual interest; that is to say, to accommodate the values of show business.

Film, records and radio (now that it is an adjunct of the music industry) are, of course, equally devoted to entertaining the culture, and their effects in altering the style of American discourse are not insignificant. But television is different because it encompasses all forms of discourse. No one goes to a movie to find out about government policy or the latest scientific advances. No one buys a record to find out the baseball scores or the weather or the latest murder. No one turns on radio anymore for soap operas or a presidential address (if a television set is at hand). But everyone goes to television for all these things and more, which is why television resonates so powerfully throughout the culture. Television is our culture's principal mode of knowing about itself. Therefore — and this is the critical point — how television stages the world becomes the model for how the world is properly to be staged. It is not merely that on the television screen entertainment is the metaphor for all discourse. It is that off the screen the same metaphor prevails. As typography once dictated the style of conducting politics, religion, business, education, law and other important social matters, television now takes command. In courtrooms, classrooms, operating rooms, board rooms, churches and even airplanes, Americans no longer talk to each other, they entertain each other. They do not exchange ideas; they exchange images. They do not argue with propositions; they argue with good looks, celebrities and commercials. For the message of television as metaphor is not only that all the world is a stage but that the stage is located in Las Vegas, Nevada.

> For the message of television as metaphor is not only that all the world is a stage but that the stage is located in Las Vegas, Nevada.

"Supersaturation" and "Speed and Sensibility"
from *Media Unlimited*

— Todd Gitlin

MEASURES OF MAGNITUDE

Statistics begin — but barely — to convey the sheer magnitude of this in-touchness, access, exposure, plenitude, glut, however we want to think of it.

In 1999, a television set was on in the average American household more than seven hours a day, a figure that has remained fairly steady since 1983. According to the measurements of the A. C. Nielsen Company, the standard used by advertisers and the television business itself, the average individual watched television about four hours a day, not counting the time when the set was on but the individual in question was not watching. When Americans were asked to keep diaries of how they spend their time, the time spent actually watching dropped to a still striking three hours a day — probably an undercount. In 1995, of those who watched, the percentage who watched "whatever's on," as opposed to any specific program, was 43 percent, up from 29 percent in 1979.[1] Though cross-national comparisons are elusive because of differences in measurement systems, the numbers in other industrialized nations seem to be comparable — France, for example, averaging three and a half hours per person. One survey of forty-three nations showed the United States ranking third in viewing hours, after Japan and Mexico.[2] None of this counts time spent discussing programs, reading about their stars, or thinking about either.

Overall, wrote one major researcher in 1990, "watching TV is the dominant leisure activity of Americans, consuming 40 percent of the average person's free time as a primary activity [when people give television their undivided attention].[3] Television takes up more than half of our free time if you count ... watching TV while doing something else like eating or reading ... [or] when you have the set on but you aren't paying attention to it." Sex, race, income, age, and marital status make surprisingly little difference in time spent.[4] Neither, at this writing, has the Internet diminished total media use, even if you don't count the Web as part of the media. While Internet users do watch 28 percent less television, they spend more time than nonusers playing video games and listening to the radio and recorded music — obviously a younger crowd. Long-term users (four or more years) say they go on-line for more than two hours a day, and boys and girls alike spend the bulk of their Internet time entertaining themselves with games, hobbies,

---

1   Robert D. Putnam, *Bowling Alone: The Collapse and Revival of American Community* (New York: Simon and Schuster, 2000), p. 222, citing John P. Robinson and Geoffrey Godbey, *Time for Life: The Surprising Ways Americans Use Their Time*, 2nd ed. (University Park: Pennsylvania State University Press, 1999), pp. 136–53, 340–41, 222. *France:* This April 2001 figure for individuals fifteen and older comes from Mediamat (www.mediametria.fr/television/mediamat_mensuel/2001/avril.html).

2   Putnam, *Bowling Alone*, p. 480, citing Eurodata TV (*One Television Year in the World: Audience Report*, April 1999).
3   John P. Robinson, "I Love My TV," *American Demographics*, September 1990, p. 24.
4   Robert Kubey and Mihaly Csikszentmihalyi, *Television and the Quality of Life: How Viewing Shapes Everyday Experience* (Hillsdale, N.J.: Lawrence Erlbaum Associates, 1990), pp. 71–73.

---

and the like.[5] In other words, the Internet redistributes the flow of unlimited media but does not dry it up. When one considers the overlapping and additional hours of exposure to radio, magazines, newspapers, compact discs, movies (available via a range of technologies as well as in theaters), and comic books, as well as the accompanying articles, books, and chats about what's on or was on or is coming up via all these means, it is clear that the media flow into the home — not to mention outside — has swelled into a torrent of immense force and constancy, an accompaniment *to* life that has become a central experience *of* life.

The place of media in the lives of children is worth special attention — not simply because children are uniquely impressionable but because their experience shapes everyone's future; if we today take a media-soaked environment for granted, surely one reason is that we grew up in it and can no longer see how remarkable it is. Here are some findings from a national survey of media conditions among American children aged two through eighteen. The average American child lives in a household with 2.9 televisions, 1.8 VCRs, 3.1 radios, 2.6 tape players, 2.1 CD players, 1.4 video game players, and 1 computer. Ninety-nine percent of these children live in homes with one or more TVs, 97 percent with a VCR, 97 percent with a radio, 94 percent with a tape player, 90 percent with a CD player, 70 percent with a video game player, 69 percent with a computer. Eighty-eight percent live in homes with two or more TVs, 60 percent in homes with three or more. Of the 99 percent with a TV, 74 percent have cable or satellite service.[6] And so on, and on, and on.

The uniformity of this picture is no less astounding. A great deal about the lives of children depends on their race, sex, and social class, but access to major media does not. For TV, VCR, and radio ownership, rates do not vary significantly among white, black, and Hispanic children, or between girls and boys. For television and radio, rates do not vary significantly according to the income of the community.

How accessible, then, is the media cavalcade at home? Of children eight to eighteen, 65 percent have a TV in their bedrooms, 86 percent a radio, 81 percent a tape player, 75 percent a CD player.[7] Boys and girls are not significantly different in possessing this bounty, though the relative usages do vary by medium. Researchers also asked children whether the television was "on in their homes even if no one is watching 'most of the time,' 'some of the time,' 'a little of the time,' or 'never.'" Homes in which television is on "most of the time" are termed *constant television households*. By this measure, 42 percent of all American households with children are constant television households. Blacks are more likely than whites or Hispanics to experience TV in their lives: 56 percent of black children live in constant television households (and 69 percent have a TV in their bedrooms, compared to 48 percent of whites).[8] The lower the family education and the median income of the community, the greater the chance that a household is a constant television household.

As for time, the average child spent six hours and thirty-two minutes per day exposed to media of all kinds, of which the time spent reading books and magazines — not counting schoolwork — averaged about forty-five minutes.[9] For ages two to seven, the average for total media was four hours and seventeen minutes; for ages eight to thirteen, eight hours and eight minutes, falling to seven hours and thirty-five minutes for ages fourteen to eighteen. Here, race and social class do count. Black children are most exposed, followed by Hispanics, than whites. At all age levels, the amount of exposure to all media varies inversely with class, from six hours and fifty-nine minutes a day for children in households where the median income for the zip code is under $25,000 to six hours and two minutes for children

5 UCLA Center for Communication Policy, *The UCLA Internet Report: Surveying the Digital Future*, November 2000, pp. 10, 17, 18, 14 (www.ccp.ucla.edu).

6 Donald F. Roberts, *Kids and Media @ the New Millennium* (Menlo Park, Calif.: Henry J. Kaiser Family Foundation, 1999), p. 9, table 1. There were 3,155 children in the sample, including oversamples of black and Hispanic children, to ensure that results in these minority populations would also be statistically significant. As best as a reader can discern, this was a reliable study, with a margin of error of no more than plus-or-minus five percentage points. Since the results for younger children, ages two to seven, come from parents' reports, they may well be conservative, since parents may be uninformed of the extent of their children's viewing or may be underplaying it in order not to feel ashamed before interviewers. *The uniformity:* Ibid., p. 11, tables 3-A, 3-B, 3-C.

7 Ibid., pp. 13–15, tables 4, 5-A, 5-B, 6.

8 In general, fewer western European or Israeli children than Americans have TVs in their bedrooms, but 70 percent in Great Britain do. Next highest in Europe is 64 percent in Denmark. The lows are 31 percent in Holland and 24 percent in Switzerland. Leen d'Haenens, "Old and New Media: Access and Ownership in the Home," in Sonia Livingstone and Moira Bovill, eds., *Children and Their Changing Media Environment: A European Comparative Study* (London: Lawrence Erlbaum Associates, 2001), p. 57.

9 Roberts, *Kids and Media*, pp. 21–23, tables 8-C, 8-D.

whose zip code median income is over $40,000.[10] The discrepancy for TV exposure is especially pronounced, ranging from three hours and six minutes a day for children whose zip code incomes are under $25,000 to two hours and twenty-nine minutes for children whose zip code incomes are over $40,000. Still, these differences are not vast. Given everything that divides the rich from the poor, the professional from the working class — differences in physical and mental health, infant mortality, longevity, safety, vulnerability to crime, prospects for stable employment and so on — the class differences in media access and use are surprisingly slender. So are the differences between American and western European children, the latter averaging six hours a day total, though in Europe only two and a quarter of those hours are spent with TV.[11]

All such statistics are crude, of course. Most of them register the time that people *say* they spend. They are — thankfully — not checked by total surveillance. Moreover, the meaning of *exposure* is hard to assess, since the concept encompasses rapt attention, vague awareness, oblivious coexistence, and all possible shadings in between. As the images glide by and the voices come and go, how can we assess what goes on in people's heads? Still, the figures do convey some sense of the media saturation with which we live — and so far we have counted only what can be counted at home. These numbers don't take into account the billboards, the TVs at bars and on planes, the Muzak in restaurants and shops, the magazines in the doctor's waiting room, the digital displays at the gas pump and over the urinal, the ads, insignias, and logos whizzing by on the sides of buses and taxis, climbing the walls of buildings, making announcements from caps, bags, T-shirts, and sneakers. To vary our experience, we can pay to watch stories about individuals unfold across larger-than-life-size movie screens, or visit theme parks and troop from image to image, display to display. Whenever we like, on foot or in vehicles, we can convert ourselves into movable nodes of communication, thanks to car radios, tape, CD, and game players, cell phones, beepers, Walkmen, and the latest in "personal communication systems" — and even if we ourselves refrain, we find ourselves drawn willy-nilly into the soundscape that others broadcast around us.

Crucially, who we are is how we live our time — or *spend* it, to use the term that registers its intrinsic scarcity. What we believe, or say we believe, is less important. We vote for a way of life with our time. And increasingly, when we are not at work or asleep, we are in the media torrent. (Sometimes at work, we are also there, listening to the radio or checking out sports scores, pin-ups, or headlines on the Internet.) Steadily more inhabitants of the wealthy part of the world have the means, incentives, and opportunities to seek private electronic companionship. The more money we have to spend, the more personal space each household member gets. With personal space comes solitude, but this solitude is instantly crowded with images and soundtracks. To a degree that was unthinkable in the seventeenth century, life experience has become an experience in the presence of media.

> We vote for a way of life with our time. And increasingly, when we are not at work or asleep, we are in the media torrent.

* * *

HASTE MAKES MONEY

Turn on the TV, graze around, let the tsunami of images and information wash over you. A baseball game, with stats pouring across the screen — not only batting averages, RBIs, and ERAs but the on-base percentages, the speed of the last pitch, the number of pitches and first-pitch strikes thrown, the ball and strike percentages, even a visual of the batter's "hot zone" and a

---

10   The same point applies to differences in media use throughout the prosperous world. As the economist Adair Turner writes: "European Internet penetration lags the US by 18 to 24 months. When cars or television sets were first introduced, the lag was more like 15 years. ... The shortness of the lag also suggests that social concern about a 'digital divide,' whether within or between nations, is largely misplaced. ... Time lags between different income groups in the penetration of personal computers, Internet connections or mobile phones are much shorter, once again because all these products are cheap. ... At the global level the same scepticism about a digital divide should prevail. Africa may lag 15 years or so behind US levels of PC and Internet penetration, but it lags more like a century behind in basic literacy and health care." Adair Turner, "Not the e-conomy," *Prospect* (London), April 2001 (www.prospect-magazine.co.uk/highlights/essay_turner_april01).

11   Johannes W.J. Beentjes et al., "Children's Use of Different Media: For How Long and Why?" in Livingstone and Bovill, eds., *Children and Their Changing Media Environment*, p. 96.

cutaway to the new relief pitcher, resolute, with a "scouting report" slashing across his image. Click to a basketball game — possible now that most major sports seasons overlap, often by months. Watch a slam dunk replayed, the image rotate, the picture plane flip over and peel away into oblivion. Note the stats on the Knicks' record against the Jazz over the past five seasons, and against other Western Division teams, as well as individual players' records against their match-ups at home and away.

On MSNBC an interview is in progress. An expert is discoursing on Iraq and weapons of mass destruction. At the lower right is the network logo; to its left, the current Dow Jones industrial average, next to the current temperature and a cloud graphic. Later, three bongs will sound, signaling NBC, and the interview image will shrink, while headlines burst out below. Cut to two thirty-second commercials as images flicker by at an average of more than one edit per second.

On CNN, the secretary of state speaks as a ribbon of sports scores slithers across the bottom of the screen. On CNBC, a financial news network, a man, upper right, touts his company while a swathe of text, upper left, spells out the company's products and its strategies; at the lower right are the Dow, NASDAQ, and S&P 500 indexes, with arrows indicating whether they are headed "north" or "south." On MTV, the body of the announcer occupies screen center while, to either side of her, two small pictures of singers dangle in the ether of screen space. Cut, and a music video starts, images twinkling, blurring, jump-cutting past at breakneck speed.

On the Internet, features wiggle, ads pop up or blink and flash at the edges of the screen, words in solid color fields swell, migrate, and pop like bubbles.

Remote control devices are clicked to change channels between 36 and 107 times per hour, depending on the methodology used to study such things.[12] Men and younger people, no surprise, click more than women and older people. According to a study conducted in 2000, three-quarters of Americans under thirty watched the news with a remote in hand, as did 54 percent of those over fifty. Imagining their audience fidgety, for good reason, the

information, sports, and music networks build fitfulness directly into their displays.[13]

Popular culture twitches.

* * *

THE CULTURE OF WARP SPEED

In 1916, the Futurists heralded "cinematic simultaneity and interpenetration of different times and places," and predicted that "we shall project two or three different visual episodes at the same time, one next to the other."[14] Their noisy utopia is now upon us, though the combination of commercials, promotions, weather and stock updates, sitcoms, "reality" shows, sports reports, and talking heads that radiate through the living room is blander than what the protofascist Futurists had in mind.

Tinsel ages spawn nostalgia for golden ages. Speed — whether of capital flows or imagery — ignites a longing for the good slow days that were presumably left behind in the dust.[15] Intuitively, we feel that everything moves faster today. But impressions aside, how do we really know the torrent is flowing more swiftly? Where is the hard evidence?

Examining relics is useful. Watch the recycled TV shows of a quarter century ago, and you will indeed find them sluggish. A sixty-second commercial seems interminable. Children's shows before *Sesame Street* was launched in 1969 moved at what is to today's eye a tediously languid pace; the difference is so marked, some have speculated that *Sesame Street* all by itself must be responsible for today's reputedly shrinking attention spans. Certainly, it seems unlikely that teaching the alphabet through modules patterned on advertising slogans has made anyone more patient.

Look through any video archive. Pre-MTV rock concert footage seems to sleepwalk. Jump cuts were the preserve of avant-garde cinema, not de rigueur in commercials for spectators younger than thirty. Look back fifty years, and it is hard to resist the impression that the movies were slower, newspaper and magazine articles longer, sentences longer

12 Robert V. Bellamy, Jr., and James R. Walker, *Television and the Remote Control: Grazing on a Vast Wasteland* (New York: Guilford, 2000), pp. 38–44.

13 Pew Research Center study, 2000.

14 F. T. Marinetti et al., "The Futurist Cinema," http://www. unknown.nu/futurism/cinema.html.

15 Writing about the related tendency to think that culture in general was better during a bygone age, Patrick Brantlinger has used the term *negative classicism. Bread and Circuses: Theories of Mass Culture as Social Decay* (Ithaca: Cornell University Press, 1983).

and more complex, advertising text drawn out. TV images appeared one at a time, without hyperspace peel-aways. Series episodes of an earlier era ended with the slow roll of the credits, where today the credits speed by, sharing screen space with a tease, a follow-up joke, an outtake, a promo — the screen split two or three ways — to stall that finger poised on the remote control device. The evening

again — and again — and again. The point, as in video games, is to prolong the sweet agony, complicate it with "eye candy," and stave off the inevitable reckoning.

Speed on top of speed: there is the swirling dynamic within a shot, and then the edit between one shot and the next. Montage is as relentless as the camera is restless. Just as silent film spectators learned to interpret montage

---

During the three-and-one-quarter rusty hours of *Titanic* (1997), the camera is rarely steady for more than a few seconds. If the movie ship takes longer to go under than the actual *Titanic* did, this is because time has to slow to permit Leonardo DiCaprio and Kate Winslet to career from starboard to stern and back again—and again—and again.

---

news showed a single picture, if any at all, to the side of an immobile anchorman, where today's anchor, light of foot, glides through a set swirling with clips and graphics.

Many measurements will bear out the sense that the pace of image and text alike have picked up. Compare the qualities and quantities of pictures and words in the movies. To the contemporary eye, commercial films of the 1930s, 1940s, 1950s, and even the careening 1960s are strikingly slow. In many scenes, two characters simply talk while the camera watches, unbudging. Such stationary two-shots are punctuated only by an occasional cutaway for a reaction, a slight pan to follow one character walking away, or, on special occasions, a slow pan toward a close-up. In *Mrs. Miniver*, which won the Academy Award for best picture in 1942, the lead actors, Greer Garson and Walter Pidgeon, play a scene in an English bunker during a German bombardment that goes on with barely a cutaway or camera movement for more than eight minutes — an eternity by today's standards. Mainstream audiences were moved by such scenes.

Today's camera, by contrast, cruises, glides, swoops, circles, inches, zooms, hovers, cranes, and jiggles past and around the fugitive objects of its attention. The foreground—trees, buses, pillars—goes sliding by, heightening the impression of unceasing movement. No matter how static or far-fetched the story, how leaden or cobbled-up the characters, the movie *moves*. During the three-and-one-quarter rusty hours of *Titanic* (1997), the camera is rarely steady for more than a few seconds. If the movie ship takes longer to go under than the actual *Titanic* did, this is because time has to slow to permit Leonardo DiCaprio and Kate Winslet to career from starboard to stern and back

as simultaneous action, today's spectators have learned to fill in the gaps, so that if, in the 1940s, it was necessary to show a character hailing a taxi at the train station, sitting in its backseat, getting out, beholding the front of an apartment building, getting into the elevator, ringing the doorbell of the apartment, and getting admitted, editors now cut directly from the train station to the interior of the apartment, safely assuming that the spectator will follow the narrative. In the late 1960s, directors of action scenes began to experiment with intensifying montage. In *Bonnie and Clyde* (1967), Arthur Penn deployed several cameras shooting the same murderous scene at different speeds and angles, combining quick cuts with slow motion to pump up a mingled sense of horror and excitement.[16] Freed of censorship, Penn blasted apart the integrity of the body to make a point — what he called "the shock and at the same time the ballet of death."

A movie car-chase sequence of the 1940s, 1950s, or 1960s, as George W. S. Trow has observed, "looks wonderfully realistic and old-fashioned. ... The car speeds up, and you see a cop car, and he puts on his siren, and you have a little bit of a chase"[17]; whereas Peter Yates's *Bullitt* (1968) featured "the first car-chase, car-ride sequence that went into hyperspace":

---

16 "An Interview with Arthur Penn," in John G. Cawelti, ed., *Focus on Bonnie and Clyde* (Englewood Cliffs, N.J.: Prentice Hall), 1973, p. 16.

17 *My Pilgrim's Progress* (New York: Pantheon, 1999), pp. 21, 22. (I've altered the order of some segments — my own creative editing.)

The car rocketed through the streets of San Francisco, up and down hills and past trolley cars. The screenwriters who wanted to be successful in Hollywood, watching *Bullitt*, saw that *Bullitt* was successful because of that car chase. So what if we had three car chases, what if we had four car chases, what if we had ten car chases? It's not that difficult a concept to master. Most people have a will to power that is imitative, and when they see something that works, their imitative mind says, "Well, we'll do that, but we'll do it three times better, or bigger."

This, in turn, led to "an increasing level of hyperactivity in car chases, down to *Speed* (1997)," where (perhaps half jokingly) even so lumbering a vehicle as a bus is prevented from slowing down.

Trow grasps the self-feeding dynamic of the media frenzy, the combination of competition, challenge, thrill, and pride in craft that drives hyperactivity forward in the movies, on television, in video games, and in virtual-reality simulators: "a sort of hyperactive quality, a kind of unreal, speeded-up violence, which has to do as much with the aesthetic of the people making the product as it has to do with the specific action." As Trow points out, "one wants this kind of hyperactive quality of click, click, click, click, click to hold … [the audience's] shallow attention, and the easiest way to do that is violence and the car chase." (Attention-getting dialogue requires a rare talent.) Welcome to *Star Wars* (1977), with its spaceship chases and vertiginous plunges. Welcome to digital editing, images shrinking into hyperspatial planes that peel up and away, the financial screen with its streaming tickers and multiple sectors, the animated Internet ad, the moving galactic Netscape logo, signaling that *something is happening* while we wait. Whoosh!

In a world where video games outgross movies, on-screen speed makes entertainment careers.[18] Commercials and video games are now career training grounds for movie directors. No wonder movie edits frequently work not to speed up linear consciousness but to assail it. Narrative is nothing but pretext. In action movies, chase follows chase, one vehicle after another: cars, sports utility vehicles, trucks, buses, trains, planes, helicopters, hovercrafts, ski lifts, tanks, you name it. The point is to shake, rattle, and

roll us, to keep us breathless, to delight, dragoon, and rollercoaster us into an eager suspension of disbelief. To say that the resulting plot "makes no sense" misses the point, since the goal is usually to make only enough sense to permit the senses to take over.

I do not wish to exalt the static or stately as such. Slowness can produce excellence or mediocrity. So can speed. Superior action movies — *Speed, The Matrix* — reach toward the kinetic sublime. Some of the Hong Kong action pictures directed by John Woo and Wong Kar-Wai are thrilling. Swooping around the action, the camera plunges the willing viewer into a sort of rapture. The chase exhilarates as freedom tempts fate and tests limits. The speed aesthetic can cut the spirit loose from the gravity of ordinary preoccupations. The violence that punctuates these movies, despite all the worried critics, is least important as a spur to copycat crimes; it matters far more as a drug. The rat-a-tat-tat of the editing rhymes with the violence of the action — these are two ways to rage against stasis. As cigarettes are instruments to deliver nicotine, action movies are instruments to deliver adrenaline — whiffs of the ineffable. No wonder they are rated and reviewed for their kinetic efficacy, as if they were pharmaceuticals.

Explosions, crashes, and conflagrations ignite more than one kind of pleasure. There is potency. Man uses machine to destroy machine — here lies an anarchic mastery. There is the joy of beholding the destruction of things in an overstuffed age. Conspicuous violence against property amounts to a demolition derby for material plenty. Most of all, violence pumps up the viewers. Censorious moralists who muster more energy for crusading against violent images than against guns themselves are missing the point. Violence in the movies offers a magical way out of the inertia and perplexity of everyday life — even if one that leads nowhere except the theater lobby.

* * *

HASTE MAKES FUN

The onrush of the media torrent — the speed of its images on the screen, its sentences on the page, and its talk over the air, as well as the quickness with which images move through space and the velocity of its product cycles — all these speeds depend on an overall social speed-up and are but its most visible features. A fast society produces fast

---

18 Seth Stevenson, "Why Are Video Games for Adults So Juvenile?" *Slate.com*, April 19, 2001.

people who, in all these senses, produce a fast culture. The question is, what drives the machine?

Isn't speed rational? It is natural to assume so. We are accustomed to a more or less Darwinian explanation of its economic advantages. Capitalist organizations are in the business of changeover because the environment changes and they must adapt, and because they scramble with rivals. Peasants compete for markets. Nation-states compete for wealth. Corporations compete for customers. Universities compete for students. All follow trends, trends consisting of evidently successful strategies pursued by competitors. Permanence is a drag, toast, so over — or, to use a term that is derogatory only in the United States, *history*. When novelty pays, institutions have rational grounds to search for faster techniques, to access information faster than their competitors, to devise fresh products. Aren't the fast more than the slow likely to win the great games to which we apply ourselves? From this point of view, we have a speedy society because it's rational to be speedy — to develop novelties and get them to market first. To offer a better mousetrap is perhaps not so important as to offer the *first* mousetrap, assuming that you can offer it all around town and at a sensible price.

But speed is not always rational. Speed can, in fact, backfire. If Company A is too quick to market with a new technology, it may lose out to Company B, which took its time developing a rival method — or appropriating the best of its rival's method, as Microsoft's Windows did vis-à-vis Apple. Sony was the first to develop and market a home videocassette recorder, and many aficionados believe that its Betamax technology produced clearer pictures than the rival VHS system.[19] But VHS, with its longer playback capacity, prevailed, and Betamax remains a technology for specialists. The earliest manufacturers of home computers, Altair, Osborne, Morrow, and others, were outdone by those that were slower to market with more advanced systems. For a business, as for a nation, there is such a thing as the disadvantage of going first. The culture of speed is before all else a market culture — a culture in which the prime reason to manufacture things is that they will (or so the producers believe) sell. But *will* they sell? Much of what is produced, no matter how speedily, flops. So it is more accurate to say that in a market culture, people do things because they *believe* that they will sell.

Can't it be said, then, that *on average*, speed can be counted upon to deliver practical, material, calculable advantages? Surely the search for productivity motivated massive corporate investment in computerization in the 1980s. Still, for years, economists debated whether computerization actually made for productivity gains. The Nobel economics laureate Robert M. Solow quipped in 1987, "You can see the computer age everywhere but in the productivity statistics."[20] Today, even many economists who were previously skeptical accept the claim that computerization brought productivity gains. Solow himself in 2000 amended his previous doubt: "You can now see computers in the productivity statistics." The interesting thing, however, is that the argument for productivity increases was put forward for many years before the boom time of 1995–99, when the payoff wasn't measurable.[21] In other words, when corporations made their massive investments, they had no assurances they would pay off. They acted on conventional wisdom or ideology — in short, on faith.

But there is another reason to doubt that utilitarianism explains all or even most of our culture's disposition toward speed. When we perform an action, we do not necessarily know what the results will be. In the world of the fast class (whom I am calling "we"), we speed even when it's not rational. On the road, we court danger. We invest in speedy improvements even when we were content with the previous models (at least until the new models were launched). Clearly, speed has more than dollar value. The dirty little secret is that ours is a civilization that revels in the pure experience of speed. We share a yearning for the kinetic sublime. Excepting the phobic among us, we revel in sensations of bodily speed: the sound of engines revving, the feeling of forward movement, the look of the earth passing beneath the wheels, the sensations of the wind through our hair, the blast of air — or at least air-conditioning —

19   John Nathan, *SONY: The Private Life* (Boston: Houghton Mifflin, 1999), p. 109–10.

20   But Solow adds this qualification: "I will feel better about the endurance of the productivity improvement after it survives its first recession." Louis Uchitelle, "Productivity Finally Shows the Impact of Computers," *New York Times*, March 12, 2000, Business Section, citing research by Federal Reserve economists Stephen D. Oliner and Daniel E. Sichel. Their conclusion: "Information technology has been the key factor behind the improved productivity performance."

21   See the excellent discussion of the productivity debate in Nicholas Garnham, "Information Society Theory as Ideology: A Critique," *Information, Communication, and Society* 3, no. 2 (2000).

against our skin. Upscale people jog, and working-class people throng to NASCAR races. This is — hush! — fun.

The joy of speed drives the interactivity sector of the media torrent, too. Of course, there are competitive, utilitarian motives for the Internet mania — moving capital into and out of markets, buying and selling goods and services, making deals, collecting usable information, and so on. Efficiency may turn out to be a result of all the clicking of keys and punching of numbers. Surely companies boost their efficiency when their data are entered by overstressed offshore assembly-line workers. Speed is the workers' enemy. In the poor countries, where electronic data entry has been relocating since American Airlines moved a ticket processing center to Barbados in 1981, the work is especially grueling.[22] The proprietors of Internet servers can count their employees' keystrokes per minute. These low-end workers lack the luxury of interactive distraction. But higher-end employees often enjoy a daily electronic experience that transcends — may even substitute for — calculation. What is incalculable is the emotion attached to the experience of a certain instantaneous efficiency, the fun of connection via Internet, cell phones, and the rest, the joy of making things happen *now*, the tiny, disposable, real thrill of getting a rise out of the world with your fingertips. Whatever the eventual economic outcome, you have your reward. You are wired, plugged in; you click, you transmit, you retrieve, you download — therefore you are.

Moreover, the Internet offers speed and distraction galore in addition to (or at times instead of) any promise of institutional efficiency. Chat with your buddies. Check sports scores. Gamble. See women and men cavort in interesting postures. Circulate jokes. Sign petitions. Otherwise divert yourself from the rigors of business life. At the upper end of the workforce, in the world of freelance professionals, outsourcers, ubiquitous consultants, all others who tickle their keyboards on contract, easy distraction is as close as the keyboard. According to one study, 43 million American workers access the Internet at work — many to shop.[23] Of course, in the end, distraction may be just what

they need to work more keenly — and longer hours.[24]

But whatever the eventual efficiency costs (or benefits) of playful distraction, corporations certainly believe their employees to be making unseemly use of the new gadgetry — whence surveillance and the threat of it. Managers can easily count employee minutes spent rummaging among sites where employment would not spur one to rummage. Surveillance programs can count obscene words, risqué pictures, trade secrets, whatever. The office computer is legally fair game for on-site inspection, too, as the dean of Harvard Divinity School discovered in 1999.[25] Once pornographic images were found on his university-owned computer, he resigned in disgrace.

No doubt, when managers invest in speed via computerization and electronic networks, they think they are acting rationally. In fact, they are acting culturally. Reason has its limits. They gamble. They *like* speed. Who would want to go before a board of directors and defend a decision — *any* decision — to slow down? Their technical people *love* speed. It is, for them, a devotional exercise.

---

research says that employers don't have to worry. "At home, people will surf more casually," said another researcher. "It's a much more focused initiative at work. People are squeezing this in between things."

24 As it happens, just as I was finishing this chapter, during a stupendous lightning storm in the Hudson Valley, my telephone went out, so for one working day (aside from one twenty-minute round-trip to a pay phone to call the repair office), I lacked the distractions of telephone and e-mail. I think my output improved, at least in quantity per day. The reader will have to be the judge of quality.

P.S. It is too good a coincidence to believe, but as I was writing the previous paragraph the phone repairman showed up and made the repair. I take my leave from the reader now to collect a day's worth of e-mail and voicemail messages.

25 Fox Butterfield, "Pornography Cited in Ouster at Harvard," *New York Times*, May 20, 1999. According to a 1999 survey by the market research firm Vault.com, 42 percent of employers "actively monitor their workers' Internet activity," up from 31 percent the previous year. (Pham, "E-tailers' Prime Time.") Many companies market on-line computer surveillance equipment; one Web site claims: "With Spector, you will be able to SEE what your kids and employees have been doing online and offline." (http://people.ne.mediaone.net/rizun/Spy/spy. htm.) Still more surveillance potential is built into software. According to a report in *Wired*, "any manager who purchases network-operating software is probably getting built-in snoop features. In an office hardwired with a server-based local area network managed by software such as Microsoft LAN Manager, a technically inclined boss or network administrator can turn any employee workstation into a covert surveillance post." (John Whalen, "You're Not Paranoid: They Really Are Watching You," *Wired*, March 1995.)

---

22 Barney Wurf, "Information Age Anthology," www.dodcorp. org/antch209.htm#47. The resulting company, Caribbean Data Services, the largest "informatics" employer in Barbados, opened a second office in the Dominican Republic in 1987, paying half the wages.

23 Alex Pham, "E-tailers' Prime Time Is During Office Hours," *Los Angeles Times*, December 18, 2000. On-line shopping "keeps employees at their desks," said one researcher. "They don't have to take a two-hour lunch to go out and shop." Some

In their own lives, they adore being *on*. They are *pumped*. Speed's visceral aspect is crucial. You want to cut loose from onerous calculation, to rip away from the sticky stuff of reason. Speed gives speeders a rush. It cannot be accidental that *rush* is vernacular for the burst of acceleration you experience on drugs, not least on methamphetamines, commonly known as *speed*. Surely it is no accident that as drugs spread into the middle class, the fast lane came to be prized, while activities that were not enjoyable, or speedy, came to be called a *drag* — in other words, a resistance to speed, a brake.[26]

If speed is an easy way to live, then pixels and digital data are the easiest ways to speed. Though chemical boosters are still very much in use, today's fast lane is largely licit, the torrent-soaked way of life available instantly to the professional, metropolitan, commercial classes, via laptop computers, cell phones, handheld organizers, Walkmen, pocket TVs, and the rest of our portable instruments. Educated fast-laners carry their — our — connections on their laps, clipped to belts, clutched in hands, to mountain and shore, on train and plane, detached from any fixed place, or rather, converting every fixed place, each automobile, sidewalk, theater, church, into *our* place, usable for our convenience and that of our networks; that is, into nowhere-in-particular, a noplace where we are equally accessible and in that sense equally detached. Rushing from node to node of the media torrent, in a strange town, a motel room, on the road, we are never *away*. Or rather, here *is* away. Strange as it is, the torrent becomes our home.

If time is God's way of keeping everything from happening at once, then multitasking is the antidote. Simultaneity is the goal, multitasking the means, and a *segue* — another commonplace term — the next best thing. Open envelopes while on the phone, read e-mail while on hold for "customer service," play a video game while watching a soap opera — the reader is familiar with these attempts to stretch time, to turn sequence into near-simultaneity. Bored with channel 46, switch to channel 47. We multitask because we are busy, and we are busy because we cannot multitask fast enough. No matter how many calendars we keep, how many task lists we make, how fast we clear our literal or figurative desktops, how upgraded our central processing units and modems, how many channels we get, how many Napster downloads we perform — or perhaps precisely because we have all these calendars, lists, desktops, channels, and downloads — we cannot, cannot possibly keep up.

THE DIALECTIC OF SPEED AND SLOWNESS

But the United States is not all of a piece, everyone equally speedy, equally frantic. The fast and the slow coexist. The static picture of uniform speed is painted by a class of speed freaks — journalists who rush the news, pundits who frame its significance, and marketers who wrap goods in it, almost all of whom live in the fast lane themselves, socialize with others who live (or wish to live) in the fast lane, report on and read about those who live (or wish to live) in the fast lane, and write about those whose business is to cater to and nudge still others into that same fast lane. Many of these speed freaks are driven by the fear that they may end up the roadkill of a hyperkinetic society.

With wind-tunnel vision, our chroniclers of the rush of everyday life commonly lose sight of one essential thing about the culture of speed. Harnessed to the love of speed is its contrary: resistance to speed. Speed is relational — relative to speed in the past and others' speed in the present. If, as stock market folklore has it, "The market climbs a wall of worry," then speed climbs a wall of slowness. Within a capitalist economy, the desire for speed is powered by a market imperative to overcome resistance to speed. For consumer demand to grow, increasing numbers of slow people must be brought up to speed, else they will not process the data the information machine requires, else telephones, answering machines, computers, Internet access will not be bought. What drives modern civilization is not speed by itself but the dialectic of speed and slowness.

To put it another way: a culture of speed rubs up against a culture of slowness and conquers what it can. The subsociety of the fast is the engine that pulls the whole. One of the pleasures of speed is to leave the slow behind — *eat my dust*. In the last half century, an era of vast disposable income and voluminous marketing, the consumer goods industry has recruited generation after generation of allies among each wave of children by pitting them against the style and pace of sluggish adults.

---

26   At least before the dot-com bubble burst, there were reports of growing use of cocaine, Ecstasy, and GHB among young professionals. A programmer who upped his prescribed Ritalin dosage said, "There's always been an anarchist technophile drug-use thing that seems to go together." P. J. Huffstutter and Robin Fields, "The Dirty Little Secret of the Dot-Com World," *Los Angeles Times*, Sunday, October 1, 2000.

Yet no society can long thrive on the breakneck extension of a single principle and the suppression of all others. Sooner or later, rectifications spring up. Speed brings relative sluggishness in its wake. It is also counterbalanced by routine, a slowing and channeling of human initiative. So the assembly-line production of culture has the surprising consequence of accentuating at once American restlessness and formulaic predictability. In streamlining and typecasting, speed and stasis meet.

Like many facts of popular culture, this one is best observed from outside. Having watched Armed Forces Network Television as a boy in postwar Germany, Professor Berndt Ostendorf of the University of Munich has observed how its commercial origins, its formulaic storytelling, and its stereotypical characters all fit together.[27] To make spaces for commercial breaks, and keep viewers' attention, production companies divided programs into short units — *acts*, producers still call them, hanging on to the theatrical precedent, even if they are but a few minutes long. Viewers, disposed to be fidgety, came to expect these breaks. Now, Ostendorf writes, the plot, with its traditional unities of time, place, and action, "is chopped up into short sequential bursts, each with their own simulacrum of a micro-plot. … The goal is to create an unending series of reversals, moments of ecstasy and anticipation, which then may be usurped by the commercial." Interruption was thus built into the program. Not surprisingly, in the era of television, the term *attention span* began to be heard — and worried about. Shortening attention spans led to an emphasis on formula.

To keep a fidgety audience in place, characters had to be rapidly recognizable. Since a mass audience is diverse, there had to be a variety of predictable types. In Ostendorf's words:

> This serialization of micro-plots favors roles and characters with direct audience appeal. Hence there is at least one character in each sit-com with whom any section of the audience may identify. Therefore a noticeable typecasting prevails in series such as *Bonanza*, the *Bill Cosby Show* or *General Hospital*. … Instant dramatic

effects that will entertain are more important than dramaturgical considerations of sentiment or character development. The chain of motivation is often interrupted by the logic of sensation. The overall consequence leads to a dramatization of effect and the foregrounding of character types.

A fast society grumbles about speed, and selectively cultivates some deliberate slowness. From the speediest society under the sun, the United States, came one of the slowest sports, baseball. For go-getters, the slowness industry includes golf, sailing, and hiking; for women mainly, cooking and gardening. In the age of MTV, soap operas still move at the pace of drying paint. (Observing my seventeen-year-old stepson clicking from his basketball video game to MTV to a soap opera, where he landed only now and then, I asked him how it felt. "Perfect," he said, "no danger of missing anything.") Next to the fast lane runs the slow lane, and next to the slow lane the breakdown lane. While our professional and managerial classes are commuting, multitasking, ad-scanning, channel-grazing, Web-surfing, call-waiting, cell-phoning, chat-grouping, desktop-organizing, remote-controlling, picture-in-picturing, gambling, and day-trading, they are also complaining about their hectic, lives and plotting their retreats to the country. Secretly proud of their velocity, many of them also think there is something demented about their pace. They boast of a week in the country without e-mail or the bold weekend when they leave the answering machine unplugged. They made Juliet Schor's *Overworked American* a best-seller. The men often say they would like to spend more time at home with their kids. (Some working women, beset by conflict at home, actually prefer working longer hours. The corporate environment may now offer some satisfactions more reliably than home.[28]) They practice tai chi as well as the treadmill — a sort of biathlon of modern pacing. They seek time out for golf, fishing, and yoga. Travelers to Italy are pleased to discover restaurants that proudly advertise "slow food." Storefronts offering ten-minute back rubs flourish in frantic city centers, malls, and airports. Tape and CD players and new car radios come with a pause button. Some people use a Walkman to slow themselves down, to repossess their sense of time. Enough people enjoy "easy

---

27 "Why Is American Popular Culture So Popular? A View from Europe" (Odense, Denmark: Oasis, 2000), pp. 35–36. See also Todd Gitlin, "Prime Time Ideology: The Hegemonic Process in Television Entertainment," *Social Problems*, February 1979, pp. 251–66.

28 See Arlie Hochschild, *The Time Bind* (New York: Metropolitan, 1997).

listening" and New Age music to sustain those market niches amid the more raucous alternatives.[29]

Overall, men seem to want speed more than women do. Men are more partial to action movies, women to soap operas, prizing them partly because they creep along so viscously, they seem to slow down the world. (The fact that "nothing happens" is part of what makes them attractive — they do not demand rapt attention, and leave the viewer free to attend to household tasks.) Men, more likely to graze, have itchier fingers on the remote control clicker, though the differences seem smaller among the young.[30] Men tend to surf — or hunt — the Internet; women, to stick to a small number of sites, gathering useful information.[31]

Contrary tendencies are even built into the visual culture of warp speed. Televised sports undergo their own forms of slowdown, compensating for the speed-up of the action and its entourage of surrounding commercials. The twenty-four-second clock in professional basketball sped up the game, but multiple time-outs (many imposed by networks to squeeze in more commercials) now turn the closing seconds of basketball games into endless events. In baseball, it is normal now for half a dozen pitchers or more to come into a game, each requiring time for a trot from the bullpen and then for a warm-up, each stepping off the mound after each pitch as each batter steps out of the batter's box, looks for signs, and performs mysterious rituals. Baseball's longueurs are so drawn out that the double-headers of the past are almost inconceivable. The sports seasons themselves are so drawn out that they overlap, and the playoffs seem to last almost as long as the regulation seasons themselves.

In movies, the era of the almost-subliminal cut and the hyperkinetic rush is also the era of the pause (the stop-frame) and the prolongation (slow motion). Slo-mo has become a standard feature of action sequences, stretching the moment, allowing you to admire the details — in sports, the elegance of the block that takes out the linebackers; in the movies, the bullet entering the skull, the car hurtling through the plate-glass window, the helicopter exploding in flames — all of which natural speed would otherwise force you to miss. Slo-mo prolongs suffering, permitting that ur-slo-mo film *Bonnie and Clyde*, as Pauline Kael beautifully wrote, to "put the sting back in death." It makes action look simultaneously more fateful and less inevitable — perhaps the tailback will elude the interception! Jack Ruby will miss Lee Harvey Oswald! Critic Mark Kingwell nicely observes another strange juxtaposition of slowness and speed:

> Action movies get faster, and more kinetic, all the time — a sharp acceleration of retinal-nerve stimulation from the widescreen scenes of old epics like *Spartacus*. But some movies are now, Titanically, longer than ever; and John Woo, perhaps the best action-film director alive, has a fondness for extended slow-motion sequences, protracted exercises in the instant mythologization of anti-speed, that rival, in sheer unreality, the massed, from-every-angle replays of a televised professional football game.[32]

With a productivity boost from the computer, popular books like Tom Clancy's thrillers bulk up, as if telling the reader: *On this long flight or this week's vacation, you are permitted to slow down.*

Fast people, in other words, are aware that they pay a price for speed, that after a certain point they sacrifice not only the very efficiency that was its purpose but also the physical gratification that is its by-product. Few live by speed alone. Some slowdowns of recent years descend from the counterculture of the 1960s and 1970s. "Slow down, you move too fast/You got to make the morning last," as Simon and Garfunkel sang in those years. Panicky moralists lost sight of the fact that marijuana — unlike alcohol — generally had the effect of *slowing things down*. Even suburbanites wanted to be *laid-back*. Aging boomers nap, and businesses look into the merits of furnishing employees with cots. Fast-laners need *downtime*. Slowness keeps up its fitful resistance in surprising forms. One must wonder whether it is purely coincidental that even

29 Michael Bull, *Sounding Out the City: Personal Stereos and the Management of Everyday Life* (Oxford: Berg, 2000), pp. 58–60.

30 Bellamy and Walker, *Television and the Remote Control*, pp. 126–37.

31 Jupiter Communications with Media Tetrix, "It's a Woman's World Wide Web," cited in Laurie L. Flynn, "Internet Is More Than Just Fun for Women," *New York Times*, August 14, 2000. According to one analyst of on-line behavior, "Women are interested in a more efficient experience — getting on-line and getting off. Men are more interested in technology for technology's sake, and in the more random aspects of Net surfing."

32 Mark Kingwell, "Fast Forward," *Harper's Magazine*, May 1998, p. 45.

as the rampant diagnosis of attention deficit disorder hits children, the psychiatric label du jour among young (and older) adults is *depression*, and that depression is the negation of speed, a state of mind in which the world seems to have ground to a halt.

Against the onslaught of hectic modernity, many a literary figure throughout the centuries has counseled the contemplative life and hoped to find for it a safe harbor in the gathering speed of the world. The partisans of slowness are always sure that the world is going to the fastest dogs,

in popular periodicals — *Time* with its weekly news snippets, the *New York Times Magazine* with its cheeky front-of-the-book interview fragments, Internet magazines with their punchy, semicolonless sentences.[34] Partisans of earlier film cultures likewise deplore today's jump-cutting pace. But for all their vested interest in relative slowness, the critics are not insincere when they deplore the pace of the plunging torrent or bemoan the spectacular funfest that competes with their work for public attention. Neither are they misguided in what they notice. For centuries, speed

How fast can montage go without leaving perception behind? How much shorter than seven seconds can a sound bite shrink? How much quicker can Internet access get? How much multitasking, how many advances in Palm Pilotry, can customers bear? How many channels can we surf more or less simultaneously without going mad?

and feel called upon to denounce the impoverished quality of overhasty writing and reading. The specter of the death of reading is a hardy perennial. Samuel Taylor Coleridge in 1810 feared that "'reading made easy' … would give men an aversion to words of more than two syllables, instead of drawing them through those words into the power of reading books in general."[33] Eighty years later, the London *Publishers' Circular* clucked: "The impatience of the age will not tolerate expansiveness in books. There is no leisurely browsing and chewing of the literary cud such as Charles Lamb describes with the gusto of an epicure. As a people we have lost the art of taking our ease in an inn, or anywhere else; assuredly we do not take it in the library or in a corner under the bookshelf. The world presses, and reading has to be done in snatches." In the words of literary historian Richard Altick: "The doom of the reading habit has been falsely prophesied ever since the invention of the pneumatic tire, which spelled the end of the fireside reading circle by putting the whole family on bicycles."

Now, writers who deplore speed are biased. They are invested in slowness, and good at it. As sentences get shorter, reading faster, visual competition more intense and itself speedier, how can established writers not feel the onrush of obsolescence? How can journalists fail to note the speed-up

has dragged slowness along in its wake, hastening it. None of the naysayers has been crying wolf. While the slow protest, the fast drag them along, kicking and screaming.

In recent decades, the media torrent is where speed-up is most unmistakable. The images steadily thicken, the soundscape grows noisier, montage more frenetic. This process transcends the conventional polarities of politics. It is a curiosity of our present civilization that many of those who call themselves conservatives embrace the revolutionary daemon of capitalism, the most reckless, hard-driving force in the history of the world, and celebrate Joseph Schumpeter's "gales of creative destruction" that blow through production, marketing, taste, and everyday life.[35] But among radicals, too, who will organize Students for a Slow Society? Not the rocking and rolling, post-MTV, music-downloading, raging-against-the-machine cultural left. Who is against upgrades, jump cuts, more channels, better speakers, the Sensurround pleasure dome of everyday life?

The real answer to the rhetorical question is: hardly anyone. Yet the prospect of unending, out-of-control acceleration is unnerving. Can all this clutter and haste really be good for us? Some who accept the inevitability

33 Quoted in Richard Altick, *The English Common Reader* (Chicago: University of Chicago Press, 1957), pp. 370, 369 (quoting *Publishers' Circular*, October 1, 1890, p. 1154), pp. 374–75.

34 Michael Kinsley, editor of *Slate*, has written that he programmed his computer to eliminate semicolons. E. J. Dionne, "Under Observation," *Washington Post Magazine*, November 24, 1996, p. 12.

35 *Capitalism, Socialism, and Democracy* (New York: Harper, 1942), p. 84.

of ever-increasing speed wonder whether the acceleration will someday — perhaps soon — crash against barriers of nature or psyche. How fast can montage go without leaving perception behind? How much shorter than seven seconds can a sound bite shrink? How much quicker can Internet access get? How much multitasking, how many advances in Palm Pilotry, can customers bear? How many channels can we surf more or less simultaneously without going mad? In the pilot of the inventive 1980s TV series *Max Headroom*, a network covered up the fact that some of its commercials were so compressed they caused viewers to explode. Perhaps, in the end, the ever-quickening torrent approaches some asymptotic limit that it will never quite reach, faster than which the brain cannot go. Yet in the face of such small comfort, bewilderment and dread do not disappear.

Finally, the raging torrent of images and sounds brings with it a paradox that ought to challenge any casual presumption that more is better, that the superflux of media is synonymous with progress. While our eyes and ears are taking in images and sounds in all their abundance, we are usually sitting down to receive them. The torrent speeds by, but we ourselves — despite the treadmills, the Walkmen, the sports radios — are mainly immobilized. The novelties pour forth, but the couch potato remains inert. About the human consequences of the sedentary life, some hesitancy might be called for, but it does seem improbable that fast food is the only reason why the people of the remote control clicker, cable television, and the Internet have turned out to be stunningly obese. No doubt medical researchers will be heard from on this subject in growing numbers over the years to come as reporters pound on their doors for confirmations of the intuition that inertia adds fat to the flesh, and new chemical remedies for obesity are promoted — on television, where else? In the age of the unceasing image flow, there is no social anxiety that cannot be addressed with a commodity, a craze, and a news exposé — none of which quite dispels the anxiety.

One of the worthiest remnants of Karl Marx's nineteenth-century thought is the passage in the *Communist Manifesto* where he and Friedrich Engels write that capitalism means "constant revolutionizing of production, uninterrupted disturbance of all social conditions, everlasting uncertainty and agitation. ... All fixed, fast frozen relations, with their train of ancient and venerable prejudices and opinions, are swept away, all new-formed ones become antiquated before they can ossify. All that is solid melts into air."[36] Marx and Engels thought this swirl would culminate with man "compelled to face with sober senses his real condition of life and his relations with his kind." Instead, when all that was solid melted away, what it melted into was an unceasing stream of images and sounds, an infinite promise of sensations and disposable feelings, an endless cacophony of energies and noise, the "uncertainty and agitation" of the greatest and most spectacular show on earth.

---

36   *The Communist Manifesto*. I am indebted to Marshall Berman's inspiring treatment of Marx's theme in *All That Is Solid Melts into Air* (New York: Simon and Schuster, 1982).

Media Culture and the Triumph of the Spectacle

from *Media Spectacle*

— Douglas Kellner

During the past decades, the culture industries have multiplied media spectacles in novel spaces and sites, and spectacle itself is becoming one of the organizing principles of the economy, polity, society, and everyday life. The Internet-based economy deploys spectacle as a means of promotion, reproduction, and the circulation and selling of commodities. Media culture itself proliferates ever more technologically sophisticated spectacles to seize audiences and increase the media's power and profit. The forms of entertainment permeate news and information, and a tabloidized infotainment culture is increasingly popular. New multimedia, which synthesize forms of radio, film, TV news and entertainment, and the mushrooming domain of cyberspace become extravaganzas of technoculture, generating expanding sites of information and entertainment, while intensifying the spectacle form of media culture.

Political and social life are also shaped more and more by media spectacle. Social and political conflicts are increasingly played out on the screens of media culture, which display spectacles such as sensational murder cases, terrorist bombings, celebrity and political sex scandals, and the explosive violence of everyday life. Media culture not only takes up always-expanding amounts of time and energy, but also provides ever more material for fantasy, dreaming, modeling thought and behavior, and identities.

Of course, there have been spectacles since premodern times. Classical Greece had its Olympics, thespian and poetry festivals, its public rhetorical battles, and its bloody and violent wars. Ancient Rome had its orgies, its public offerings of bread and circuses, its titanic political battles, and the spectacle of empire with parades and monuments for triumphant Caesars and their armies, extravaganzas put on display in the 2000 film *Gladiator*. And, as Dutch cultural historian Johan Huizinga (1986; 1997) reminds us, medieval life too had its important moments of display and spectacle.

In the early modern period, Machiavelli advised his modern prince of the productive use of spectacle for government and social control, and the emperors and kings of the modern states cultivated spectacles as part of their rituals of governance and power. Popular entertainment long had its roots in spectacle, while war, religion, sports, and other domains of public life were fertile fields for the propagation of spectacle for centuries. Yet with the development of new multimedia and information technologies, technospectacles have been decisively shaping the contours and trajectories of contemporary societies and cultures, at least in the advanced capitalist countries, while media spectacle has also become a defining feature of globalization.

In this opening chapter, I will provide an overview of the dissemination of media spectacle throughout the major domains of the economy, polity, society, culture, and everyday life in the contemporary era and indicate the theoretical approach that I deploy. This requires a brief presentation of the influential analysis of spectacle by Guy Debord and the Situationist International, and how I build upon this approach.

GUY DEBORD AND THE
SOCIETY OF THE SPECTACLE

The concept of the "society of the spectacle," developed by French theorist Guy Debord and his comrades in the Situationist International, has had a major impact on a variety of contemporary theories of society and culture.[1] For Debord, spectacle "unifies and explains a great diversity of apparent phenomena" (Debord 1967: Section 10). Debord's conception, first developed in the 1960s, continues to circulate through the Internet and other academic and subcultural sites today. It describes a media and consumer society organized around the production and consumption of images, commodities, and staged events.

Building on this concept, I argue that media spectacles are those phenomena of media culture that embody contemporary society's basic values, serve to initiate individuals into its way of life, and dramatize its controversies and straggles, as well as its modes of conflict resolution. They include media extravaganzas, sporting events, political happenings, and those attention-grabbing occurrences that we call news — a phenomenon that itself has been subjected to the logic of spectacle and tabloidization in the era of the media sensationalism, political scandal and contestation, seemingly unending cultural war, and the new phenomenon of Terror War. Thus, while Debord presents a rather generalized and abstract notion of spectacle, I engage specific examples of media spectacle and how they are produced, constructed, circulated, and function in the present era.

As we enter a new millennium, the media are becoming more technologically dazzling and are playing an ever-escalating role in everyday life. Under the influence of a multimedia culture, seductive spectacles fascinate the denizens of the media and consumer society and involve them in the semiotics of a new world of entertainment, information, and consumption, which deeply influences thought and action. In Debord's words: "When the real world changes into simple images, simple images become real beings and effective motivations of a hypnotic behavior. The spectacle as a tendency *to make one see the world* by means of various specialized mediations (it can no longer be grasped directly), naturally finds vision to be the privileged human sense which the sense of touch was for other epochs" (ibid.: Section 18). According to Debord, sight, "the most abstract, the most mystified sense corresponds to the generalized abstraction of present day society" (ibid.).

Experience and everyday life are thus shaped and mediated by the spectacles of media culture and the consumer society. For Debord, the spectacle is a tool of pacification and depoliticization; it is a "permanent opium war" (ibid.: Section 44), which stupefies social subjects and distracts them from the most urgent task of real life — recovering the full range of their human powers through creative practice. The concept of the spectacle is integrally connected to the concept of separation and passivity, for in submissively consuming spectacles one is estranged from actively producing one's life. Capitalist society separates workers from the products of their labor, art from life, and consumption from human needs and self-directing activity, as individuals inertly observe the spectacles of social life from within the privacy of their homes (ibid.: Sections 25 and 26). The Situationist project, by contrast, involved an overcoming of all forms of separation, in which individuals would directly produce their own life and modes of self-activity and collective practice.

The correlate of the spectacle, for Debord, is thus the spectator, the reactive viewer and consumer of a social system predicated on submission, conformity, and the cultivation of marketable difference. The concept of the spectacle therefore involves a distinction between passivity and activity, consumption and production, condemning lifeless consumption of spectacle as an alienation from human potentiality for creativity and imagination. The spectacular society spreads its wares mainly through the cultural mechanisms of leisure and consumption, services and entertainment, ruled by the dictates of advertising and a commercialized media culture. This structural shift to a society of the spectacle involves a commodification of previously non-colonized sectors of social life and the extension of bureaucratic control to the realms of leisure, desire, and everyday life. Parallel to the Frankfurt School conception of a "totally administered" or "one-dimensional" society (Marcuse 1964; Horkheimer and Adorno 1972),

---

1   Debord's *The Society of the Spectacle* (1967) was published in translation in a pirate edition by Black and Red (Detroit) in 1970 and reprinted many times; another edition appeared in 1983 and a new translation in 1994. Thus, in the following discussion, I cite references to the numbered paragraphs of Debord's text to make it easier for those with different editions to follow my reading. The key texts of the Situationists and many interesting commentaries are found on various websites, producing a curious afterlife for Situationist ideas and practices. For further discussion of the Situationists, see Best and Kellner (1997: Chapter 3); see also the discussions of spectacle culture in Best and Kellner (2001), upon which I draw in these studies.

Debord states that: "The spectacle is the moment when the consumption has attained the *total occupation* of social life" (1967: Section 42). Here, exploitation is raised to a psychological level; basic physical privation is augmented by "enriched privation" of pseudo-needs; alienation is generalized, made comfortable, and alienated consumption becomes "a duty supplementary to alienated production" (ibid.: Section 42).

Since Debord's theorization of the society of the spectacle in the 1960s and 1970s, spectacle culture has expanded in every area of life. In the culture of the spectacle, commercial enterprises have to be entertaining to prosper and, as Michael J. Wolf (1999) argues, in an "entertainment economy," business and fun fuse, so that the E-factor is becoming a major aspect of business.[2] Through the "entertainmentization" of the economy, entertainment forms such as television, film, theme parks, video games, casinos, and so forth become major sectors of the national economy. In the United States, the entertainment industry is now a $480 billion industry, and consumers spend more on having fun than on clothes or health care (Wolf 1999: 4).[3]

In a competitive business world, the "fun factor" can give one business the edge over another. Hence, corporations seek to be more entertaining in their commercials, their business environment, their commercial spaces, and their websites. Budweiser ads, for instance, feature talking frogs that tell us nothing about the beer, but which catch the viewers' attention, while Taco Bell deploys a talking dog and Pepsi uses *Star Wars* characters. Buying, shopping, and dining out are coded as an "experience," as businesses adopt a theme-park style. Places such as the Hard Rock Cafe and the House of Blues are not renowned for their food, after all; people go there for the ambience, to purchase House of Blues paraphernalia, and to view music and media memorabilia. It is no longer good enough just to have a website, it has to be an interactive spectacle, featuring not only products to buy, but music and videos to download, games to play, prizes to win, travel information, and "links to other cool sites."

To succeed in the ultracompetitive global marketplace, corporations need to circulate their image and brand name, so business and advertising combine in the promotion of corporations as media spectacles. Endless promotion circulates the McDonald's "golden arches," Nike's "swoosh," or the logos of Apple, Intel, or Microsoft. In the brand wars between commodities, corporations need to make their logos or "trademarks" a familiar signpost in contemporary culture. Corporations place their logos on their products, in ads, in the spaces of everyday life, and in the midst of media spectacles, such as important sporting events, TV shows, movie product placement, and wherever they can catch consumers' eyeballs, to impress their brand name on potential buyers. Consequently, advertising, marketing, public relations, and promotion are an essential part of commodity spectacle in the global marketplace.

Celebrity too is manufactured and managed in the world of media spectacle. Celebrities are the icons of media culture, the gods and goddesses of everyday life. To become a celebrity requires recognition as a star player in the field of media spectacle, be it sports, entertainment, fashion, or politics. Celebrities have their handlers and image managers, who make sure that their clients continue to be seen and positively perceived by the public. Just as with corporate brand names, celebrities become brands to sell their Madonna, Michael Jordan, Tom Cruise, or Jennifer Lopez product and image. In a media culture, however, celebrities are always prey to scandal and thus must have at their disposal an entire public relations apparatus to manage their spectacle fortunes and to make sure that they not only maintain high visibility but keep projecting a positive

---

2 Wolf's book is a detailed and useful celebration of the "entertainment economy," although he is a shill for the firms and tycoons that he works for and celebrates them in his book. Moreover, while entertainment is certainly an important component of the infotainment economy, it is an exaggeration to say that it drives it and is actually propelling it, as Wolf repeatedly claims. Wolf also downplays the negative aspects of the entertainment economy, such as growing consumer debt and the ups and downs of the infotainment stock market and vicissitudes of the global economy.

3 Another source notes that "the average American household spent $1,813 in 1997 on entertainment — books, TV, movies, theater, toys — almost as much as the $1,841 spent on health care per family, according to a survey by the US Labor Department." Moreover, "the price we pay to amuse ourselves has, in some cases, risen at a rate triple that of inflation over the past five years" (*USA Today*, April 2, 1999: E1). The NPD Group provided a survey that indicated that the amount of time spent on entertainment outside the home — such as going to the movies or a sporting event — was up 8 percent from the early to the late 1990s and the amount of time spent on home entertainment, such as watching television or surfing the Internet, went up 2 percent. Reports indicate that in a typical US household, people with broadband Internet connections spent 22 percent more time on all-electronic media and entertainment than the average household without broadband. See "Study: broadband in homes changes media habits" (pcworld.com, October 11, 2000).

image. Of course, within limits, "bad" and transgressions can also sell, and so media spectacle contains celebrity dramas that attract public attention and can even define an entire period, as when the O.J. Simpson murder trials and Bill Clinton sex scandals dominated the media in the mid- and late 1990s.

Entertainment has always been a prime field of the spectacle, but in today's infotainment society, entertainment and spectacle have entered into the domains of the economy, politics, society, and everyday life in important new ways.

Media spectacle is indeed a culture of celebrity which provides dominant role models and icons of fashion, look, and personality. In the world of spectacle, celebrity encompasses every major social domain from entertainment to politics to sports to business. An ever-expanding public relations industry hypes certain figures, elevating them to celebrity status, and protects their positive image in the never-ending image wars. For there is always the danger that a celebrity will fall prey to the hazards of negative image and thus lose celebrity status, or become a negative

---

Sports stadiums themselves contain electronic reproduction of the action, as well as giant advertisements for various products that rotate for maximum saturation—previewing environmental advertising, in which entire urban sites are becoming scenes to boost consumption spectacles.

Building on the tradition of spectacle, contemporary forms of entertainment from television to the stage are incorporating spectacle culture into their enterprises, transforming film, television, music, drama, and other domains of culture, as well as producing spectacular new forms of culture, such as cyberspace, multimedia, and virtual reality.

For Neil Gabler, in an era of media spectacle, life itself is becoming like a movie and we create our own lives as a genre like film, or television, in which we become "at once performance artists in, and audiences for, a grand, ongoing show" (Gabler 1998: 4). In Gabler's view, we star in our own "lifies," making our lives into entertainment acted out for audiences of our peers, following the scripts of media culture, adopting its role models and fashion types, its style and look. Seeing our lives in cinematic terms, entertainment becomes, for Gabler, "arguably the most pervasive, powerful and ineluctable force of our time — a force so overwhelming that it has metastasized into life" to such an extent that it is impossible to distinguish between the two (ibid.: 9). As Gabler sees it, Ralph Lauren is our fashion expert; Martha Stewart designs our sets; Jane Fonda models our shaping of our bodies; and Oprah Winfrey advises us on our personal problems.[4]

figure, as will some of the players and institutions of media spectacle that I examine in these studies.

Sports have long been a domain of the spectacle, with events such as the Olympics, World Series, Super Bowl, soccer World Cup, and NBA Championships attracting massive audiences while generating sky-high advertising rates. These cultural rituals celebrate society's deepest values (i.e. competition, winning, success, and money), and corporations are willing to pay top dollars to get their products associated with such events. Indeed, it appears that the logic of the commodity spectacle is inexorably permeating professional sports, which can no longer be played without the accompaniment of cheerleaders, giant mascots that clown with players and spectators, and raffles, promotions, and contests that feature the products of various sponsors.

Sports stadiums themselves contain electronic reproduction of the action, as well as giant advertisements for various products that rotate for maximum saturation — previewing environmental advertising, in which entire urban sites are becoming scenes to boost consumption spectacles. Arenas such as the United Center in Chicago,

---

4   Gabler's book is a synthesis of Daniel Boorstin, Dwight Macdonald, Neil Poster, Marshall McLuhan, and various trendy theorists of media culture, but without the brilliance of a Baudrillard, the incisive criticism of an Adorno, or the understanding of the deeper utopian attraction of media culture of a Bloch or a Jameson. Likewise, Gabler does not, à la cultural

studies, engage the politics of representation, or its ideologies and political economy. He thus ignores mergers in the culture industries, new technologies, the restructuring of capitalism, globalization, and shifts in the economy that are driving the impetus toward entertainment. Gabler also does not address how new technologies are creating new spheres of entertainment and forms of experience and in general describes rather than theorizes the trends he is engaging.

the America West Arena in Phoenix, or Enron Field in Houston are named after corporate sponsors. Of course, following major corporate scandals or collapses, such as the Enron spectacle, the ballparks must be renamed!

The Texas Rangers' Ballpark in Arlington, Texas, supplements its sports arena with a shopping mall, office buildings, and a restaurant in which, for a hefty price, one can watch the athletic events while eating and drinking.[5] The architecture of the Texas Rangers' stadium is an example of the implosion of sports and entertainment and postmodern spectacle. An artificial lake surrounds the stadium, the corridor inside is modeled after Chartres Cathedral, and the structure is made of local stone that provides the look of the Texas Capitol in Austin. Inside there are Texas longhorn cattle carvings, panels depicting Texas and baseball history, and other iconic signifiers of sports and Texas. The merging of sports, entertainment, and local spectacle is now typical in sports palaces. Tropicana Field in Tampa Bay, Florida, for instance, "has a three-level mall that includes places where 'fans can get a trim at the barber shop, do their banking and then grab a cold one at the Budweiser brew pub, whose copper kettles rise three stories. There is even a climbing wall for kids and showroom space for car dealerships'" (Ritzer 1998: 229).

Film has long been a fertile field of the spectacle, with "Hollywood" connoting a world of glamour, publicity, fashion, and excess. Hollywood has exhibited grand movie palaces, spectacular openings with searchlights and camera-popping paparazzi, glamorous Oscars, and stylish, hi-tech films. Although epic spectacle became a dominant genre of Hollywood film, from early versions of *The Ten Commandments* through *Cleopatra* and *2001* in the 1960s, contemporary film has incorporated the mechanics of

spectacle into its form, style, and special effects. Films are hyped into spectacle through advertising and trailers that are ever louder, more glitzy, and razzle-dazzling. Some of the most popular films of the late 1990s were spectacle films, including *Titanic*, *Star Wars — Phantom Menace*, *Three Kings*, and *Austin Powers*, a spoof of spectacle, which became one of the most successful films of summer 1999. During the fall of 1999, there was a cycle of spectacles, including *Topsy Turvy*, *Titus*, *Cradle Will Rock*, *Sleepy Hollow*, *The Insider*, and *Magnolia*, with the last featuring the biblical spectacle of the raining of frogs in the San Fernando Valley, in an allegory of the decadence of the entertainment industry and its deserved punishment for its excesses.

The 2000 Academy Awards were dominated by the spectacle *Gladiator*, a mediocre film that captured the best picture award and the best acting award for Russell Crowe, thus demonstrating the extent to which the logic of the spectacle now dominates Hollywood film. Some of the most critically acclaimed and popular films of 2001 were also hi-tech spectacle, such as *Moulin Rouge*, a film that itself is a delirious ode to spectacle, from cabaret and the brothel to can-can dancing, opera, musical comedy, dance, theater, popular music, and film. A postmodern pastiche of popular music styles and hits, the film uses songs and music ranging from Madonna and the Beatles to Dolly Parton and Kiss.

Other 2001 film spectacles included *Pearl Harbor*, which re-enacts the Japanese attack on the United States that propelled the country to enter World War II, and which provided a ready metaphor for the September 11 terrorist attacks. Major 2001 film spectacles ranged from David Lynch's postmodern surrealism in *Mulholland Drive* to Steven Spielberg's blending of his typically sentimental spectacle of the family with the vision of Stanley Kubrick in *AI*. And the popular 2001 military film *Black Hawk Down* provided a spectacle of US military heroism, which some critics believed sugar-coated the real problems with the US military intervention in Somalia. This created fears that future US adventures involving the Bush administration and the Pentagon would meet similar problems. There were reports, however, that in Somalian cinemas there were loud cheers as the Somalians in the film shot down the US helicopter, and pursued and killed US soldiers, attesting to growing anti-US sentiment in the Muslim world against the Bush administration's policies.

Television has been, from its introduction in the 1940s, a promoter of consumption spectacle, selling cars,

---

5 The project was designed and sold to the public in part through the efforts of the then floundering son of a former president, George W. Bush. Young Bush was bailed out of heavy losses in the Texas oil industry in the 1980s by his father's friends and used his capital gains, gleaned from what some say was illicit insider trading, to purchase part-ownership of a baseball team (the Texas Rangers). The soon-to-be Governor of Texas, and future President of the United States, sold the new stadium to local taxpayers, getting them to agree to a higher sales tax to build the stadium, which would then become the property of Bush and his partners. This deal allowed Bush to generate a healthy profit when he sold his interest in the Texas Rangers franchise to buy his Texas ranch, paid for by Texas taxpayers (for sources on the life of George W. Bush and his surprising success in politics, see Kellner (2001) and the discussion on Bush Jr. in Chapter 6).

fashion, home appliances, and other commodities along with consumer lifestyles and values. It is also the home of sports spectacles such as the Super Bowl or World Series, political spectacles such as elections, scandals, and entertainment spectacles such as the Oscars or Grammies, and its own specialties such as breaking news or special events. Following the logic of spectacle entertainment, contemporary television exhibits more hi-tech glitter, faster and glitzier editing, computer simulations, and, with cable and satellite television, a diverse array of every conceivable type of show and genre.

Television is today a medium of spectacular programs such as *The X-Files* or *Buffy, the Vampire Slayer* and spectacles of everyday life such as MTV's *The Real World* and *Road Rules*, or the globally popular *Survivor* and *Big Brother* series. Real-life events, however, took over TV spectacle in 2000–1 in, first, an intense battle for the White House in a dead-heat election that arguably constitutes the greatest political crime and scandal in US history (see Kellner 2001). After months of the Bush administration pushing the most hardright political agenda in memory and then deadlocking as the Democrats took control of the Senate in a dramatic party reaffiliation of Vermont's Jim Jeffords, the world was treated to the most horrifying spectacle of the new millennium, the September 11 terrorist attacks and unfolding Terror War. These events promise an unending series of deadly spectacles for the foreseeable future (see Kellner, forthcoming).

Theater is a fertile field of the spectacle, and thus contemporary stage has exploited its dramaturgical and musical past to create current attractions for large audiences. Plays such as *Bring in 'Da Noise, Bring in 'Da Funk, Smokey Joe's Cafe, Fosse, Swing!*, and *Contact* draw on the history of musical spectacle, bringing some of the most spectacular moments of the traditions of jazz, funk, blues, swing, country, rock, and other forms of pop entertainment to contemporary thespian audiences. Many of the most popular plays of recent years on a global scale have been musical spectacles, including *Les Misérables, Phantom of the Opera, Rent, Ragtime, The Lion King, Mama Mia*, and *The Producers*, a stunningly successful musical spectacle that mocks the Nazis and show business. These theatrical spectacles are often a pastiche of previous literature, opera, film, or theater, and reveal the lust of contemporary audiences for nostalgia and participation in all types of cultural extravaganzas.

Fashion is historically a central domain of the spectacle, and today producers and models, as well as the actual products of the industry, constitute an enticing sector of media culture. Fashion designers are celebrities, such as the late Gianni Versace, whose murder by a gay ex-lover in 1997 was a major spectacle of the era. Versace brought together the worlds of fashion, design, rock, entertainment, and royalty in his fashion shows and emporia. When Yves Saint-Laurent retired in 2002, there was a veritable media frenzy to celebrate his contributions to fashion, which included bringing in the aesthetic and images of modern art and catering for the demands of contemporary liberated women as he developed new forms of style and couture.

In fashion today, inherently a consumer spectacle, laser-light shows, top rock and pop music performers, superstar models, and endless hype publicize each new season's offerings, generating highly elaborate and spectacular clothing displays. The consumption spectacle is fundamentally interconnected with fashion, which demonstrates what is in and out, hot and cold, in the buzz world of style and vogue. The stars of the entertainment industry become fashion icons and models for imitation and emulation. In a postmodern image culture, style and look become increasingly important modes of identity and presentation of the self in everyday life, and the spectacles of media culture show and tell people how to appear and behave.

Bringing the spectacle into the world of high art, the Guggenheim Museum's Thomas Krens organized a retrospective on Giorgio Armani, the Italian fashion designer. Earlier, Krens had produced a Guggenheim show exhibiting motorcycles and showing plans to open a Guggenheim gallery in the Venetian Resort Hotel Casino in Las Vegas with a seven-story Guggenheim art museum next to it. Not to be outdone, in October 2000, the Los Angeles County Art Museum opened its largest show in history, a megaspectacle "Made in California: Art, image, and identity, 1900–2000," featuring multimedia exhibitions of everything from canonical Californian painting and photography to Jefferson Airplane album covers, surf boards, and a 1998 *Playboy* magazine with "the babes of Baywatch" on its cover. In 2001, the Los Angeles County Art Museum announced that it would become a major spectacle itself, provisionally accepting a design by Rem Koolhaas that would create a spectacular new architectural cover for the museum complex. As described by the *Los Angeles Times* architectural critic, the "design is a temple for a mobile, post-industrial age … Capped by an organic, tent-like roof, its monumental form will serve as both a vibrant public forum and a spectacular place to view art" (December 7, 2001: F1).

Contemporary architecture too is ruled by the logic of the spectacle, and critics have noticed how art museums are coming to trump the art collection by making the building and setting more spectacular than the collections.[6] The Frank Gehry Guggenheim Museum in Bilbao, Spain, the Richard Meier Getty Center in Los Angeles, the retrofitted power plant that became the Tate Modern in London, Tadao Ando's Pulitzer Foundation building in Saint Louis, and Santiago Calatrava's addition to the Milwaukee

In June 2002, the Michael Jackson spectacle took a bizarre turn when the onetime superstar called the president of Sony records a "racist," in a rally with African American activist Al Sharpton, for not releasing a September 11 single that Jackson had helped to produce and for not adequately promoting his recent album. Within days, there were reports, however, that Jackson was co-producing the September 11 fund-raising song with a child pornography producer, that McDonald's had dropped its sponsorship when it learned of this, and that Sony too had issues with the project.[7] In a culture of the spectacle, public relations and image can thus make or break its celebrities. Indeed,

---

Madonna and Michael Jackson would never have become global superstars of popular music without the spectacular production values of their music videos and concert extravaganzas. Both also performed their lives as media spectacle, generating maximum publicity and attention (not always positive!).

Museum of Art all provide superspectacle environments in which to display their art works and museum fare. Major architectural projects for corporations and cities often provide postmodern spectacles whereby the glass and steel structures of high modernism are replaced by buildings and spaces adorned with signs of the consumer society and complex structures that attest to the growing power of commerce and technocapitalism.

Popular music is also colonized by the spectacle, with music-video television (MTV) becoming a major purveyor of music, bringing spectacle into the core of musical production and distribution. Madonna and Michael Jackson would never have become global superstars of popular music without the spectacular production values of their music videos and concert extravaganzas. Both also performed their lives as media spectacle, generating maximum publicity and attention (not always positive!). Michael Jackson attracted attention in 2001 in a TV spectacle in which he reportedly paid hundreds of thousands of dollars to digitally redo the concert footage he appeared in. Jackson had his images retooled so that he would be free of sweat and appear darker than the "real" image, in order to blend in better with his family members, who were performing with him, and to appear as a cooler black to appeal to his fans.

one cannot fully grasp the Madonna phenomenon without analyzing her marketing and publicity strategies, her exploitation of spectacle, and her ability to make herself a celebrity spectacle of the highest order (Kellner 1995).

In a similar fashion, younger female pop music stars and groups, such as Mariah Carey, Britney Spears, Jennifer Lopez, or Destiny's Child, also deploy the tools of the glamour industry and media spectacle to make themselves spectacular icons of fashion, beauty, style, and sexuality, as well as purveyors of music. Male pop singers, such as Ricky Martin, could double as fashion models, and male groups, such as 'N Sync, use hi-tech stage shows, music videos, and PR to sell their wares. Moreover, hip-hop culture has cultivated a whole range of spectacle, from musical extravaganzas to lifestyle cultivation to real-life crime wars among its stars.

Musical concert extravaganzas are more and more spectacular (and expensive!) and the Internet is providing the spectacle of free music and a new realm of sound through Napster and other technologies, although the state has been battling attempts by young people to utilize P2P (peer to peer) technologies to decommodify culture. Indeed, films, DVDs, sports events, and musical spectacles have been circulating through the Internet in a gift economy that

---

6   See Nicholai Ouroussoff, "Art for architecture's sake," *Los Angeles Times*, March 31, 2002.

7   See Chuck Philips, "New spin on collapse of Jackson's charity project," *Los Angeles Times*, July 13, 2002.

has generated the spectacle of the state attacking those who violate copyright laws that some would claim to be outdated in the culture of hi-tech spectacle.

Food too is becoming a spectacle in the consumer society, with presentation as important in the better restaurants as taste and substance. Best-selling books such as Isabel Allende's *Aphrodite* and Jeffrey Steingarten's *The Man Who Ate Everything* celebrate the conjunction of eroticism and culinary delight. Magazines such as *Bon Appetite* and *Saveur* glorify the joys of good eating, and the food sections of many magazines and newspapers are among the most popular parts. Films such as *Babette's Feast, Like Water for Chocolate, Big Night,* and *Chocolat* fetishize food and eating, presenting food with the pornographic excesses usually reserved for sex.

Eroticism has frequently permeated the spectacles of Western culture, and is prominently on display in Hollywood film, as well as in advertisements, clubs, and pornography. Long a major component of advertising, eroticized sexuality has been used to sell every conceivable product. The spectacle of sex is also one of the staples of media culture, permeating all cultural forms and creating its own genres in pornography, one of the highest-grossing domains of media spectacle. In the culture of the spectacle, sex becomes shockingly exotic and diverse through the media of porn videos, DVDs, and Internet sites that make available everything from teen-animal sex to orgies of the most extravagant sort. Technologies of cultural reproduction, such as home video recorders (VCRs), DVDs, and computers, bring sex more readily into the private recesses of the home. And today the sex spectacle attains more and more exotic forms with multimedia and multisensory eroticism, as envisaged in Huxley's *Brave New World*, on the horizon.[8]

8   There is little doubt but that the emergent technologies of virtual reality, holograms, and computer implants of sensory experience (if such exotica emerge) will be heavily invested in the reproduction of sex. In a webpost by Richard Johnson, "Virtual sex is here" (www.ThePosition.com, January 4, 2001), British Professor Kevin Warwick's latest experiment is described, which involves the implanting of a computer chip, which, if successful, will make possible the communication of a wide range of sensory experience and new types of sexual stimulation. The 1995 film *Strange Days* portrayed a futuristic culture, with addictive virtual reality devices, in which spectators become hooked on videos of extreme sex and violence. *The 13th Floor* (1999) portrayed a virtual reality gadget whereby players are transported to recreations of other times, places, and identities, experiencing full bodily fears and pleasures.

The spectacle of video and computer games has been a major source of youth entertainment and industry profit. In 2001, the US video game industry hit a record $9 billion in sales and it expects to do even better in the next couple of years (*Los Angeles Times,* January 1, 2002: C1). For decades now, video and computer games have obsessed sectors of youth and provided skills needed for the hi-tech dot.com economy, as well as for fighting postmodern war. These games are highly competitive, violent, and provide allegories for life under corporate capitalism and Terror War militarism. In the game *Pacman,* as in the corporate jungle, it's eat or be eaten, just as in air and ground war games, it's kill or be killed. *Grand Theft Auto 3* and *State of Emergency* were two of the most popular games in 2002, with the former involving high-speed races through urban jungles and the latter involving political riots and state repression! While some women and game producers have tried to cultivate kinder, gentler, and more intelligent gaming, the best-selling corporate games are spectacles for predatory capitalism and macho militarism and not a more peaceful, playful, and co-operative world. Indeed, in 2002, the US military developed a highly popular and critically acclaimed computer game, freely available to anyone online for downloading and playing upon registration with the US Army (www.goarmy.com/aagame/index.htm). Promoted as "The Official Army Game," it allows the user to participate in simulated military basic training activities. The *Go Army* spectacle provides at once propaganda for the military, a recruitment tool, and participation in simulated military action. As military activity itself becomes increasingly dependent on computer simulation, the line between gaming and killing, simulation and military action, blurs, and military spectacle becomes a familiar part of everyday life.

The terrifying spectacle of fall 2001 revealed that familiar items of everyday life, such as planes or mail, could be transformed into instruments of spectacular terror. The al-Qaeda network hijacking of airplanes turned ordinary instruments of transportation into weapons as they crashed into the World Trade Center twin towers and the Pentagon on September 11. Mail delivery evoked fears of disease, terror, and death, as the anthrax scare of fall and winter 2001 made ordinary letters threatening items. And rumors spread that terrorist networks were seeking instruments of mass destruction, such as chemical, biological, and nuclear weapons, to create spectacles of terror on a hitherto unforeseen scale.

The examples just provided suggest that media spectacle is invading every field of experience, from the economy to culture and everyday life to politics and war. Moreover, spectacle culture is moving into new domains of cyberspace that will help to generate future multimedia spectacle and networked infotainment societies. My studies of media spectacle will strive to contribute to illuminating these developments and to developing a critical theory of the contemporary moment. Building on Debord's analyses of the society of spectacle, I will develop the concept in terms of salient phenomena of present-day society and culture.

But while Debord's notion of spectacle tended to be somewhat abstract and theoretical, I will attempt to make the concept concrete and contemporary. Thus, whereas Debord presents few actual examples of spectacle culture, I develop detailed analyses that strive to illuminate the present age and to update and develop Debord's notion. Moreover, although Debord's concepts of "the society of the spectacle" and of "the integrated spectacle" (1990) tended to present a picture of a quasi-totalitarian nexus of domination,[9] it is preferable to perceive a plurality and heterogeneity of contending spectacles in the contemporary moment and to see spectacle itself as a contested terrain. Accordingly, I will unfold contradictions within dominant spectacles, showing how they give rise to conflicting meanings and effects, and constitute a field of domination and resistance.

These "dialectics of the present" will disclose both novelties and discontinuities in the current epoch, as well as continuities with the development of global capitalism. The in-depth studies that follow in this book attempt to articulate defining features of the existing and emergent society, culture, and everyday life in the new millennium. Yet my studies suggest that novel and distinctive features are embedded in the trajectory of contemporary capitalism, its creation of a global economy, and ongoing "creative destruction," which has been a defining feature of capitalist modernity from the beginning. Hence, the cultural studies in this book will be rooted in critical social theory and will themselves contribute to developing a critical theory of society by illuminating key features and dynamics of the present age. The studies will illustrate, in particular, the

dynamics of media spectacle and an infotainment society in the current stage of technocapitalism.[10]

THE INFOTAINMENT SOCIETY AND TECHNOCAPITALISM

Today the society and culture of spectacle is creating a new type of information-entertainment society, or what might be called the "infotainment society." The changes in the current conjuncture are arguably as thoroughgoing and dramatic as the shift from the stage of market and the competitive and *laissez-faire* capitalism theorized by Marx to the stage of state-monopoly capitalism critically analyzed by the Frankfurt School in the 1930s. Currently, we are entering a new form of *technocapitalism* marked by a synthesis of capital and technology and the information and entertainment industries, all of which is producing an "infotainment society" and spectacle culture.[11]

In terms of political economy, the emerging postindustrial form of technocapitalism is characterized by a decline of the state and enlarged power for the market, accompanied by the growing strength of transnational corporations and governmental bodies and the decreased strength of the nation-state and its institutions. To paraphrase Max Horkheimer, whoever wants to talk about capitalism must talk about globalization, and it is impossible to theorize globalization without addressing the restructuring of capitalism. Culture and technology are increasingly important constituent parts of global capitalism and everyday life in the contemporary world and permeate major domains of life, such as the economy and polity, as well as constituting their own spheres and subcultures.

The term "infotainment" suggests the synergies of the information and entertainment sectors in the organization of contemporary societies, the ways in which information technologies and multimedia are transforming

9   For a critique of Debord, see Best and Kellner 1997: 118ff.

10   The analyses in this book are primarily cultural studies, and I explore in more detail elsewhere the consequences for social theory of the phenomena explored here. Theoretical grounding, in turn, for the investigations is found in past works, such as Kellner and Ryan (1988), Kellner (1989a, b), Best and Kellner (1991; 1997; 2001), Kellner (1995).

11   On the various stages of development of the Frankfurt School and for an earlier introduction of the concept of technocapitalism, see Kellner (1989b). For more recent reflections on the roles of new technologies in the current stage of capitalist development, see Best and Kellner (2001) and Kellner (2000a).

entertainment, and the forms in which entertainment is shaping every domain of life from the Internet to politics. It is now well documented that the knowledge and information sectors are key domains of our contemporary moment, although how to theorize the dialectics of the present is highly contested. While the theories of Harvard sociologist Daniel Bell (1976) and other postindustrial theorists are not as ideological and far off the mark as some of us once argued, the concept of "postindustrial" society is highly problematic. The concept is negative and empty, failing to articulate positively what distinguishes the alleged new stage. Hence, the discourse of the "post" can occlude the connections between industrial, manufacturing, and emergent hi-tech industries and the strong continuities between the previous and present forms of social organization, as well as covering over the continued importance of manufacturing and industry for much of the world.

Yet discourses of the "post" also serve positively to highlight the importance of significant novelties, of discontinuities with modern societies, and thus force us to rethink the original and defining features of our current social situation (see Best and Kellner 1997; 2001). Notions of the "knowledge" or "information" society rightly call attention to the role of scientific and technical knowledge in the formation of the present social order, the importance of computers and information technology, the materialization of biotechnology, genetic engineering, and the rise of new societal elites. It seems wrong, however, to characterize knowledge or information as *the* organizing or axial principles of a society still constructed around the accumulation of capital and maximization of profit. Hence, in order to avoid the technological determinism and idealism of many forms of postindustrial theory, one should theorize the information or knowledge "revolution" as part and parcel of a new form of technocapitalism. Such a perspective focuses on the interconnections between new technologies, a networked global society, and an expansion of the culture of spectacle in an emergent mode of the "infotainment society," rather than merely obsessing about "new technologies" or "globalization," without seeing the articulations of these phenomena.[12]

The limitations of earlier theories of the "knowledge society," or "postindustrial society," as well as current forms of the "information society," revolve around the extent to which they exaggerate the role of knowledge and information. Such concepts advance an idealist vision that excessively privileges the role of knowledge and information in the economy, in politics and society, and in everyday life. These optics downplay the role of capitalist relations of production, corporate ownership and control, and hegemonic configurations of corporate and state power with all their massive and momentous effects. As I argue below, while discourses of the "post" help describe key defining features of contemporary societies, at least in the overdeveloped world, they neither grasp the specificity of the current forms of global technocapitalism, nor do they sufficiently mark the continuities with previous stages of societal development.

Consequently, to grasp the dynamics of our current social situation, we need to perceive the continuities between previous forms of industrial society and the new modes of society and culture described by discourses of the "post," *and* also grasp the novelties and discontinuities (Best and Kellner 1997; 2001).[13] In the studies in this book, I argue that current conceptions of the information society and the emphasis on information technology as its demiurge are by now too limited. The new technologies are modes of information *and* entertainment that permeate work, education, play, social interaction, politics, and culture. In all of these domains, the form of spectacle is changing areas of life ranging from work and communication to entertainment and diversion.

Thus, "new technologies" are much more than solely information technology, and involve important components of entertainment, communication, and multimedia, as well as knowledge and information, in ways that are encompassing and restructuring both labor and leisure.

12 It is striking how many theories of globalization neglect the role of information technology, often falling prey to economic determinism, while many theories of information technology fail to theorize their embeddedness in the global economy, thus falling prey to technological determinism. See Kellner (2000b) and Best and Kellner (2001).

13 Frank Webster (1995: 5, *passim*) wants to draw a line between "those who endorse the idea of an information society" and "writers who place emphasis on continuities." Although he puts me in the camp of those who emphasize continuities (p. 188), I would argue that we need to grasp both continuities and discontinuities in the current societal transformation we are undergoing and that we deploy a both/and logic in this case and not an either/or logic. In other words, we need to theorize both the novelties and differences in the current social restructuring and the continuities with the previous mode of societal organization. Such a dialectical optic is, I believe, consistent with the mode of vision of Marx and neo-Marxists such as those in the Frankfurt School.

Previous forms of culture are rapidly being absorbed within the Internet, and the computer is coming to be a major household appliance and source of entertainment, information, play, communication, and connection with the outside world. To help grasp the enormity of the transformation going on, and as indicators of the syntheses of knowledge and cultural industries in the infotainment society, I would suggest reflecting on the massive mergers of the major information and entertainment conglomerates that have taken place in the United States during the past decades. This process has produced the most extensive concentration and conglomeration of these industries in history, as well as an astonishing development and expansion of technologies and media products.

During the 1980s, television networks amalgamated with other major sectors of the cultural industries and corporate capital, including mergers between CBS and Westinghouse; MCA and Seagram's; Time Warner and Turner Communications; Disney, Capital Cities, and ABC; and GE, NBC, and Microsoft. Dwarfing all previous information/entertainment corporation combinations, Time Warner and America On-Line (AOL) proposed a $163.4 billion amalgamation in January 2000, which was approved a year later. The fact that "new media" Internet service provider and portal AOL was initially the majority shareholder in the deal seemed at the time to be the triumph of the new online Internet culture over the old media culture. The merger itself called attention to escalating synergy among information and entertainment industries and old and new media in the form of the networked economy and cyberculture. But the dramatic decline of its stock price after the merger and a reorganization of the corporation in June 2002 called attention to the difficulties of merging old and new media and complexities and uncertainties within the culture industries that are producing spectacle culture.

These amalgamations bring together corporations involved in TV, film, magazines, newspapers, books, information databases, computers, and other media, suggesting a conflictual and unpredictable coming together of media and computer culture, and of entertainment and information, in a new networked and multimedia infotainment society. There have also been massive mergers in the telecommunications industry, as well as between cable and satellite industries, with major entertainment and corporate conglomerates. By 2002, ten gigantic multinational corporations, including AOL-Time Warner, Disney-ABC, GE-NBC, Viacom-CBS, News Corporation, Vivendi,

Sony, Bertelsmann, AT&T, and Liberty Media controlled most of the production of information and entertainment throughout the globe.[14] The result is less competition and diversity and more corporate control of newspapers and journalism, television, radio, film, and other media of information and entertainment.

The corporate media, communications, and information industries are frantically scrambling to provide delivery for a wealth of services. These will include increased Internet access, wireless cellular telephones, and satellite personal communication devices, which will facilitate video, film, entertainment, and information on demand, as well as Internet shopping and more unsavory services such as pornography and gambling. Consequently, the fusions of the immense infotainment conglomerates disclose a synergy between information technologies and multimedia, which combine entertainment and information, undermining the distinctions between these domains.

The constantly proliferating corporate mergers of the information and entertainment industries therefore call for an expansion of the concept of the knowledge, or information, society into concepts of technocapitalism and its networked infotainment society. In this conception, the synthesis of global corporate capitalism and information and entertainment technologies is constructing novel forms of society and culture, controlled by capital and with global reach. In this context, the concept of the *networked infotainment society* characterizes the emergent technocapitalist project in order to highlight the imbrications of information and entertainment in the wired and wireless multimedia and information/entertainment technologies of the present. Together, these corporate mergers, and the products and services that they are producing, constitute an emergent infotainment society that it is our challenge to theorize and attempt to shape to more humane and democratic purposes than the accumulation of capital and corporate/state hegemony.

The syntheses of entertainment and information in the creation of a networked infotainment society are part and parcel of a global restructuring of capital. Few theories of the information revolution and the new technologies

---

14 See the chart in *The Nation* (January 7, 2002) and the accompanying article by Mark Crispin Miller, "What's wrong with this picture?" as well as the analysis of the impact of "media unlimited" in Gitlin (2002), who discusses oversaturation, intensifying speed, and an increasingly media-mediated existence in the contemporary era.

contextualize the structuring, implementation, distribution, and use of information technologies and new media in the context of the vicissitudes of contemporary capitalism and the explosion of media spectacle and the domain of infotainment. The ideologues of the information society act as if technology were an autonomous force. They often neglect to theorize the interconnections of capital and technology, or they use the advancements of technology to legitimate market capitalism (i.e. Gilder 1989; 2000; Gates 1995; 1999). More conventional and older sociological theories, by contrast, fail to grasp the important role of entertainment and spectacle in contemporary society and culture. Likewise, other theories of the information society, such as those of Daniel Bell (1976), exaggerate the role of information and knowledge, and neglect the importance of entertainment and spectacle.

Thus, Guy Debord's concept of the "society of the spectacle" in which individuals are transfixed by the packaging, display, and consumption of commodities and the play of media events helpfully illuminates our present situation. Arguably, we are now at a stage of the spectacle at which it dominates the mediascape, politics, and more and more domains of everyday life. In a culture of the technospectacle, computers bring escalating information and multimedia extravaganzas into the home and workplace through the Internet, competing with television as the dominant medium of our time. The result is a spectacularization of politics, of culture, and of consciousness, as media multiply and new forms of culture colonize consciousness and everyday life, generating novel forms of struggle and resistance.

CHAPTER 4

The Hyperreal

You've been living in a dream world, Neo.

— Morpheus,
The Matrix (1999)

Chapter 4. The Hyperreal

Recommended Film

The Matrix (The Wachowski Brothers 1999)

Chapter Summary

Plato tells the famous story of the prisoners in the cave,
an allegory that is ever more relevant for living
in today's 24/7 media environments.

William Irwin theorizes that *The Matrix* is a
retelling of Plato's allegory of the cave.

Dino Felluga explains how *The Matrix* illustrates some features
of postmodernism and Jean Baudrillard's theory of the
media maps overtaking the territories of reality.

Andrew Gordon argues that *The Matrix* is a flawed
attempt to depict Jean Baudrillard's hyperreality
in the form of an "intellectual action film."

Allegory of the Cave

from *The Republic*

— Plato

Soc.: And now, let me show in a figure how far our nature is enlightened or unenlightened: — Behold! human beings living in an underground den, which has a mouth open towards the light and reaching all along the den; here they have been from their childhood, and have their legs and necks chained so that they can not move, and can only see before them, being prevented by the chains from turning round their heads. Above and behind them a fire is blazing at a distance, and between the fire and the prisoners there is a raised way; and you will see, if you look, a low wall built along the way, like the screen which marionette players have in front of them, over which they show the puppets.

Gl.: I see.

Soc.: And do you see men passing along the wall carrying all sorts of vessels, and statues and figures of animals made of wood and stone and various materials, which appear over the wall? Some of them are talking, others silent.

Gl.: You have shown me a strange image, and they are strange prisoners.

Soc.: Like ourselves; and they see only their own shadows, or the shadows of one another, which the fire throws on the opposite wall of the cave?

Gl.: True; how could they see anything but the shadows if they were never allowed to move their heads?

Soc.: And of the objects which are being carried in like manner they would only see the shadows?

Gl.: Yes.

Soc.: And if they were able to converse with one another, would they not suppose that they were naming what was actually before them?

Gl.: Very true.

Soc.: And suppose further that the prison had an echo which came from the other side, would they not be sure to fancy when one of the passers-by spoke that the voice which they heard came from the passing shadow?

Gl.: No question.

Soc.: To them, the truth would be literally nothing but the shadows of the images.

Gl.: That is certain.

Soc.: And now look again, and see what will naturally follow if the prisoners are released and disabused of their error. At first, when any of them is liberated and compelled suddenly to stand up and turn his neck round and walk and look towards the light, he will suffer sharp pains; the glare will distress him, and he will be unable to see the realities of which in his former state he had seen the shadows; and then conceive some one saying to him, that what he saw before was an illusion, but that now, when he is approaching nearer to being and his eye is turned towards more real existence, he has a clearer vision,—what will be his reply? And you may further imagine that his instructor is pointing to the objects as they pass and requiring him to name them,—will he not be perplexed? Will he not fancy that the shadows which he formerly saw are truer than the objects which are now shown to him?

Gl.: Far truer.

Soc.: And if he is compelled to look straight at the light, will he not have a pain in his eyes which will make him turn away to take refuge in the objects of vision which he can see, and which he will conceive to be in reality clearer than the things which are now being shown to him?

Gl.: True.

Soc.: And suppose once more, that he is reluctantly dragged up a steep and rugged ascent, and held fast until he is forced into the presence of the sun himself, is he not likely to be pained and irritated? When he approaches the light his eyes will be dazzled, and he will not be able to see anything at all of what are now called realities.

Gl.: Not all in a moment.

Soc.: He will require to grow accustomed to the sight of the upper world. And first he will see the shadows best, next the reflections of men and other objects in the water, and then the objects themselves; then he will gaze upon the light of the moon and the stars and the spangled heaven; and he will see the sky and the stars by night better than the sun or the light of the sun by day?

Gl.: Certainly.

Soc.: Last of all he will be able to see the sun, and not mere reflections of him in the water, but he will see him in his own proper place, and not in another; and he will contemplate him as he is.

Gl.: Certainly.

Soc.: He will then proceed to argue that this is he who gives the season and the years, and is the guardian of all that is in the visible world, and in a certain way the cause of all things which he and his fellows have been accustomed to behold?

Gl.: Clearly, he would first see the sun and then reason about him.

Soc.: And when he remembered his old habitation, and the wisdom of the den and his fellow-prisoners, do you not suppose that he would felicitate himself on the change, and pity them?

Gl.: Certainly, he would.

Soc.: And if they were in the habit of conferring honors among themselves on those who were quickest to observe the passing shadows and to remark which of them went before, and which followed after, and which were together; and who were therefore best able to draw conclusions as to the future, do you think that he would care for such honors and glories, or envy the possessors of them? Would he not say with Homer,

> *Better to be the poor servant of a poor master,*

and to endure anything, rather than think as they do and live after their manner?

Gl.: Yes, I think that he would rather suffer anything than entertain these false notions and live in this miserable manner.

Soc.: Imagine once more, such an one coming suddenly out of the sun to be replaced in his old situation; would he not be certain to have his eyes full of darkness?

Gl.: To be sure.

Soc.: And if there were a contest, and he had to compete in measuring the shadows with the prisoners who had never moved out of the den, while his sight was still weak, and before his eyes had become steady (and the time which would be needed to acquire this new habit of sight might be very considerable), would he not be ridiculous? Men would say of him that up he went and down he came without his eyes; and that it was better not even to think of ascending; and if any one tried to lose another and lead him up to the light, let them only catch the offender, and they would put him to death.

Gl.: No question.

Soc.: This entire allegory you may now append, dear Glaucon, to the previous argument; the prison-house is the world of sight, the light of the fire is the sun, and you will not misapprehend me if you interpret the journey upwards to be the ascent of the soul into the intellectual world according to my poor belief, which, at your desire, I have expressed—whether rightly or wrongly God knows. But, whether true or false, my opinion is that in the world of knowledge the idea of good appears last of all, and is seen only with an effort; and, when seen, is also inferred to be the universal author of all things beautiful and right, parent of light and of the lord of light in this visible world, and the immediate source of reason and truth in the intellectual; and that this is the power upon which he who would act rationally either in public or private life must have his eye fixed.

Gl.: I agree, as far as I am able to understand you.

Soc.: Moreover, you must not wonder that those who attain to this beatific vision are unwilling to descend to human affairs; for their souls are ever hastening into the upper world where they desire to dwell; which desire of theirs is very natural, if our allegory may be trusted.

Gl.: Yes, very natural.

Soc.: And is there anything surprising in one who passes from divine contemplations to the evil state of man, misbehaving himself in a ridiculous manner; if, while his eyes are blinking and before he has become accustomed to the surrounding darkness, he is compelled to fight in courts of law, or in other places, about the images or the shadows of images of justice, and is endeavoring to meet the conceptions of those who have never yet seen absolute justice?

Gl.: Anything but surprising.

Soc.: Any one who has common sense will remember that the bewilderments of the eyes are of two kinds, and arise from two causes, either from coming out of the light or from going into the light, which is true of the mind's eye, quite as much as of the bodily eye; and he who remembers this when he sees any one whose vision is perplexed and weak, will not be too ready to laugh; he will first ask whether that soul of man has come out of the brighter life, and is unable to see because unaccustomed to the dark, or having turned from darkness to the day is dazzled by excess of light. And he will count the one happy in his condition and state of being, and he will pity the other; or, if he have a mind to laugh at the soul which comes from below into the light, there will be more reason in this than in the laugh which greets him who returns from above out of the light into the den.

Gl.: That is a very just distinction.

Computers, Caves, and Oracles: Neo and Socrates

from The Matrix *and Philosophy*

— William Irwin

A TALE OF TWO CAVES

Morpheus tells Neo he was "Born into a prison for [his] mind." Even slaves, prisoners of war, and concentration camp victims sometimes manage to keep their minds free. "They may have my body but they'll never have my mind." This resistance to slavery and imprisonment has been implemented through the ages by countless heroes such as Epictetus, Fredrick Douglass, Viktor Frankl, James Bond Stockdale, Nelson Mandela, John McCain, Malcolm X, and Rubin "Hurricane" Carter, to name a few. The only thing worse than a prison for your mind would be a prison for your mind you didn't know you were in, a prison from which, therefore, you would have no urge to escape. How would a person in such a prison even recognize if he were set free?

"Suppose one of them were set free and forced suddenly to stand up, turn his head and walk with his eyes lifted to the light; all these movements would be painful, and he would be too dazzled to make out the objects whose shadows he had been used to seeing. What do you think he would say, if someone told him what he had formerly seen was meaningless illusion, but now, being somewhat nearer to reality and turned towards more real objects, he was getting a truer view? ... Would he not be perplexed and believe the objects now shown him to be not so real as what he formerly saw?" These lines are from Plato's *Republic* (514c–d) in which Plato tells a story known as the allegory of the cave (also variously called the simile, myth, or parable of the cave) (514a–521b). The account,

however, serves just as well to describe Neo's predicament upon being freed from the Matrix.

The prisoners in the cave are chained by the neck, hands, and legs. They have been this way since birth and so have no conception of any other way of life. Shadows appear on the wall in front of them, as their jailers pass animal figures before the light of a fire in the manner of a puppet show. The prisoners watch shadows on a wall, shadows not of real animals but of carved figures. The light that makes these shadows possible is firelight, not the best possible kind of light, sunlight. Yet these prisoners do not know that they are prisoners and do not suspect there is any reality but that which they experience. One day, however, one of the prisoners is set free of his chains, is dragged to the outside world, and by the light of the sun beholds things as they actually are. Rather than selfishly remaining in the outside world, the prisoner returns to tell the others, who reward his kindness with mockery and resistance, believing he has gone insane.

This story parallels the life of Plato's teacher,[1] Socrates, who was thought mad and ultimately put to death for trying to draw attention to a higher plane of reality. Of course it also parallels the story of Neo, who one day is freed from the Matrix to behold "the desert of real." Like Plato's prisoner, Neo finds himself in chains or, more precisely,

---

1 Plato uses his teacher Socrates as a character in his writings, including the allegory of the cave in *The Republic*. For a discussion of the complicated connection between Plato and Socrates see my "Jerry and Socrates: The Examined Life?" in *Seinfeld and Philosophy: A Book about Everything and Nothing* (Chicago: Open Court, 2000), pp. 3–5.

black cable wires that stimulate the illusive shadow show of the Matrix. Who frees the prisoner in Plato's allegory is unclear, though in *The Matrix* it is Morpheus (in Greek mythology the name of the God of sleep, who brings changes in shape via dreams). Like Plato's prisoner who must be dragged upward, Neo is at first horrified by the sight of the other unwitting prisoners who slumber,

the reality in which we live is the truest and highest reality there is. According to Plato, all we actually experience at the level of reality available through our five senses, are poor imitations of a higher level of reality, the Forms. We may experience beautiful sunsets, just actions, and really good noodles, but all of these things are mere imitations of the perfect Forms, copies of Beauty itself, Justice itself,

---

Like Plato's prisoner's gradual, painful period of adjustment to the world outside the cave, Neo's rehab is painful. "Why do my eyes hurt?" Neo asks. "Because you've never used them," Morpheus replies.

---

plugged in gooey pink cave-pods. Neo does not want to accept that what he now sees is real, that previously he had been living in a dream world. "Most of these people are not ready to be unplugged," Morpheus assures him. Like Plato's prisoner's gradual, painful period of adjustment to the world outside the cave, Neo's rehab is painful. "Why do my eyes hurt?" Neo asks. "Because you've never used them," Morpheus replies.

"The roots of education are bitter, but the fruit is sweet," wrote Aristotle. And we do well to keep in mind that "education" literally, etymologically, means "to lead out," as the prisoner is led out of the cave and as Neo is led out of the Matrix. The Hippocratic Oath reminds physicians that they are guardians and trustees, not owners, of medical knowledge. They must share the knowledge to help others. No solemn oath binds those who receive education in philosophy, though the duty to share is no less attendant. Plato's escaped prisoner would prefer to bask in the light of the sun, of goodness and knowledge, but he returns to help others. "Would he not feel like Homer's Achilles, that he would far sooner 'be on earth as a hired servant in the house of a landless man' or endure anything rather than go back to his old beliefs and live in the old way?" (*Republic* 515d) Neo, unlike Cypher, would similarly endure anything rather than return to a false reality.

KNOWLEDGE AND REALITY

The allegory of the cave is not only, or even most importantly, a veiled retelling of the Socrates story. Rather Plato uses it to point to, and encourage openness in the reader to, a higher level of reality, the Forms. We — all of us — are like the prisoners, for we often mistakenly suppose that

Goodness itself, and so on.

What "splinter in the mind" could rouse a person to seek the Forms? And how can they be known? Plato and Socrates teach the importance of understanding not through the senses but through the intellect alone. Morpheus tells Neo that no one can be told what the Matrix is. You have to "see it for yourself." As with the Forms, it is not a literal "seeing" but a direct knowing that brings understanding of the Matrix. This essay cannot truly teach you what the Forms are, not even reading Plato can. This is part of the challenge and frustration of Plato's dialogues. One finds oneself asking, What is Justice? What is Love? What is Goodness? What, after all, is a Form? It was asking such questions that landed Socrates in trouble. So read and proceed with caution.

Neo too learns that intellect is more important than the senses. Mind is more important than matter. As for Plato the physical is not as real as the Form, so for Neo "there is no spoon." Neo is the reincarnation of the man who freed the first humans. Plato held that the intellect and body are so alien to one another that their union at birth traumatically engenders loss of memory, a kind of amnesia. This is not the total loss of memory Cypher traitorously deals for, but rather the kind one might suffer after drinking too much of Dozer's Lethic moonshine. The details can come back with the right prompting and clues. For Plato, *déjà vu* is not evidence of a glitch in the Matrix but a recollection (*anamnesis*) of the Forms. In the time between incarnations, when the soul is free of the body, we behold the Forms. On the earthly plane all learning is actually a process of recollection in which we recall the Forms, cued in by the resemblance mundane objects bear to them. A child does not need to be taught that a flower is pretty, for example, but knows it through recollection of the Form of Beauty itself and the flower's share in it.

PHILOSOPHY: THE ROAD LESS TRAVELED

In the car, on the way to see Morpheus, Neo considers turning back, but Trinity forces the moment to its crisis. "You have been down there, Neo. You know that road. You know exactly where it ends, and I know that is not where you want to be." One cannot help but think of Robert Frost's famous lines, "I took the one less traveled by / And that has made all the difference." We must wonder just how many people this favorite yearbook quotation and valedictory allusion truly fits. After all it would have to be a super highway, and there would still be a traffic jam, if everyone who ever claimed the verse for his or her own actually lived it.

The Matrix: Paradigm of Postmodernism or Intellectual Poseur? (Part 1)

from *Taking the Red Pill*

— Dino Felluga

The Matrix has been both hailed as the first intellectual action movie and derided as a brainless action film dressed up in philosopher's clothing. So which is it? In this essay and the next, scholars of postmodernism and science fiction debate this question. In this essay Dino Felluga argues that The Matrix *successfully brings postmodernist thinking to the silver screen.*

PART I

Few films in the Hollywood canon make as clear a direct reference to postmodern theory as does *The Matrix*. In the first scene that establishes the character Neo, we find that he has hidden his hacker program inside a hollowed-out copy of Jean Baudrillard's *Simulacra and Simulation*, a work that, despite its difficulties (in both language and argument), has had a major influence in contemporary understandings of the age in which we live, an age that has, for better or worse, been given the name "postmodern." I will here take issue with those critics who dismiss *The Matrix* as a pseudo-intellectual excuse for the representation of violence (a position explored by Andrew Gordon in this collection) and will attempt to take seriously the ways the Wachowskis try to stay faithful to aspects of Baudrillard's theories, even when they appear to contradict them. In so doing, I provide here a crash course on some of the major concepts currently used to explain our contemporary postmodern age.

The relationship to Baudrillard's theories becomes especially clear in the shooting script of the film. As Morpheus informs Neo in a scene cut from the film, "You have been living inside a dreamworld, Neo. As in Baudrillard's vision, your whole life has been spent inside the map, not the territory."[1] That line of dialogue itself refers to a fable told by Jorge Luis Borges in his essay "Of Exactitude in Science." As Baudrillard describes the fable in the first sentence of his own work, "cartographers of the Empire draw up a map so detailed that it ends up covering the territory exactly." Over time, that map begins to fray until all that is left are a few "shreds … still discernible in the deserts."[2] According to Baudrillard, what has happened in postmodern culture is, to some extent, the reverse: our society has become so reliant on models and maps that we have lost all contact with the real world that preceded the map. Reality itself has begun merely to imitate the model, which now precedes and determines the real world:

> The territory no longer precedes the map, nor does it survive it. It is nevertheless the map that precedes the territory — *precession of simulacra* — that engenders the territory, and if one must return to the fable, today it is the territory whose shreds slowly rot across the extent of the map. It is the real, and not the map, whose vestiges persist here and there in the deserts that

---

1 Wachowski, p. 38.
2 Baudrillard, p. 1.

are no longer those of the Empire, but ours. *The desert of the real itself.*[3]

When Morpheus welcomes Neo "to the desert of the real" during the Construct sequence, when he informs Neo that his whole life has been an illusion generated by a computer Matrix, he is once again making a direct reference to Baudrillard's work. In so doing, Morpheus also invites the viewer to see *The Matrix* as itself an allegory for our own current postmodern condition, for, according to Baudrillard, we in the audience are already living in a "reality" generated by codes and models; we have already lost all touch with even a memory of the real.

So, what exactly is the simulacrum and how does *The Matrix* use this concept to exemplify elements of our current postmodern condition? According to Baudrillard, when it comes to postmodern simulation and simulacra, "It is no longer a question of imitation, nor duplication, nor even parody. It is a question of substituting the signs of the real for the real."[4] Baudrillard is not merely suggesting that postmodern culture is artificial, because the concept of artificiality still requires some sense of reality against which to recognize the artifice. His point, rather, is that we have lost *all* ability to make sense of the distinction between nature and artifice.

Postmodernists illustrate how in subtle ways language keeps us from accessing "reality." The very language we require to communicate and even to think is at once a product of ideology and productive of ideology (for example, the ways that gendered language instantiates stereotypical distinctions between men and women). An earlier understanding of ideology was that it hid the truth, that it represented a "false consciousness," as Marxists phrase it, keeping us from seeing the real workings of the state, of economic forces, or of the dominant groups in power. Postmodernism, on the other hand, tends to understand language and ideology as the basis for our very perception of reality. There is no way to be free of ideology, according to this view, at least no way that can be articulated in language. Because we are so reliant on language to structure our perceptions, any representation of reality is always already ideological. From this perspective, mankind cannot help but view the world through an ideological lens. The idea of truth or objective reality is

therefore meaningless. In the view of some postmodernists, this has always been true; in the view of other postmodern theorists, the period that approximately follows the Second World War represents a radical break during which various factors have contributed ever more to increase our distance from "reality," including the following:

➤ MEDIA CULTURE. Contemporary media (television, film, magazines, billboards, the Internet) are concerned not just with relaying information or stories but with interpreting our most private selves for us, making us approach each other and the world through the lens of these media images. We therefore no longer acquire goods because of real needs but because of desires that are increasingly defined by commercials and commercialized images.

➤ EXCHANGE-VALUE. According to Karl Marx, the entrance into capitalist culture meant that we ceased to think of purchased goods in terms of use-value, in terms of the real uses to which an item will be put. Instead, everything began to be translated into how much it is worth, into what it can be exchanged for (its exchange-value). Once money became a "universal equivalent," against which everything in our lives is measured, things lost their material reality (real-world uses, the sweat and tears of the laborer). We began even to think of our own lives in terms of money rather than in terms of the real things we hold in our hands: how much is my time worth? How does my conspicuous consumption define me as a person?

➤ INDUSTRIALIZATION. As the things we use are increasingly the product of complex industrial processes, we lose touch with the underlying reality of the goods we consume. A common example of this is the fact that most consumers do not know how the products they consume are related to real-life things. How many people could identify the actual plant from which is derived the coffee bean? Starbucks, by contrast, increasingly defines our urban realities.

➤ URBANIZATION. As we continue to develop available geographical locations, we lose touch with any sense of the natural world. Even natural spaces are now understood as "protected," which is to say that they are defined in contradistinction to an

---

3 Ibid.
4 Ibid., p. 2.

urban "reality," often with signs to point out just how "real" they are. Increasingly, we expect the sign (behold nature!) to precede access to nature. The *signs* of human civilization could thus be said to function like a virus, in the sense suggested not only by William Burroughs (who coined the phrase "language is a virus") but also by Agent Smith in his interrogation of Morpheus.

Because of these postmodern "conditions," Baudrillard posits that we have lost *all* sense of "reality." "Simulacra" precede our every access to the "real" and thus define our real for us, hence Baudrillard's phrase, the *"precession of simulacra." The Matrix* perfectly exemplifies this idea by literalizing it; humans plugged into this simulation program only know the facts of their culture and "reality" by way of a computer program, for the

---

The territory no longer precedes the map, nor does it survive it.

---

reality upon which that program was originally based no longer exists. In a quite literal sense, then, "the territory no longer precedes the map, nor does it survive it." Humans have only ever known the map or the model.

This insight helps to explain the importance of the mess-hall discussion about the difference between bodily requirements and taste, as well as the difference between need and desire. The scene directly follows the interview between Agent Smith and Cypher, in which Cypher states: "I know this steak doesn't exist. I know that when I put it in my mouth the Matrix is telling my brain that it is juicy and delicious. After nine years, you know what I've realized? Ignorance is bliss." The following dinner sequence on the *Nebuchadnezzar* underlines the fact that even humanity's understanding of something as apparently "real" as taste is affected by simulacra, since we cannot know for sure how individual tastes conform to their apparent referents. When Switch informs Mouse that "technically" he has never eaten Tastee Wheat and so cannot say for sure whether what he's eating tastes like Tastee Wheat, Mouse responds: "Exactly my point, because you have to wonder, how do the machines really know what Tastee Wheat tasted like? Maybe they got it wrong, maybe what I think Tastee Wheat tasted like actually tasted like oatmeal, or tuna fish. It makes you wonder about a lot of things. Take chicken, for example. Maybe they couldn't figure out what

to make chicken taste like, which is why chicken tastes like everything."

In such a world, the model replaces the real even on the level of the senses, which is also Morpheus's point when he first meets Neo face to face: "What is real? How do you define real? If you're talking about what you feel, taste, smell, or see, then real is simply electrical signals interpreted by your brain." What should be underlined is that "Tastee Wheat" itself — in our everyday world — is no more real, defined as it is by a product name: not wheat but "Tastee Wheat." The consumer product, itself defined by an involved commercial campaign, takes the place of "the real thing" (to quote Coke's effort to replace the real with its own media version of the real).

Now, if *The Matrix* merely suggested that it might be possible to escape the simulacra that run our lives, then we could say that the movie functions like a "deterrence machine set up in order to rejuvenate the fiction of the real in the opposite camp,"[5] which is how Baudrillard understands the function of, for example, Disneyland. "Disneyland is presented as imaginary in order to make us believe that the rest is real."[6] For Baudrillard, it makes perfect sense that we would find Disneyland in the most unreal, postmodern, simulacral of American cities, Los Angeles, because it allows the city that surrounds Disneyland to believe that it is real, if only by contrast. According to Baudrillard, America is desperate to reconstitute a lost sense of reality. It is for this reason, arguably, that our culture has become so fascinated with, on the one hand, narratives about the loss of distinctions between fiction and reality (*Wag the Dog, The Truman Show, Natural Born Killers, Dark City, Strange Days,* and *Fight Club,* to name but a few interesting examples) and, on the other hand, with shows about the very "reality" we may fear we have lost (from MTV's *Real World* to *Survivor,* with the most recent entry, "American Idol," being perhaps the most perverse example, since we are asked to watch real-life people competing to *become* simulacral "idols"). The first sequence of examples raises the issue of our reliance on simulacra only to suggest, in the end, that we can escape them somehow. Truman Burbank is, ultimately, able to

---

5   Ibid., p. 13.
6   Ibid., p. 12.

escape the stage set where he has lived all his life and to enter the real world. In the second set of examples, we are given the fantasy that we can reconstitute a reality principle even with the simulacra-generating medium of television.

One way of approaching *The Matrix* is to argue that a similar maneuver is at work in the film; the movie allows us to imagine a scenario whereby we can escape the simulacra that run our lives, allowing us to set up shop in the "desert of the real," or, as Neo puts it at the end of the movie, "I'm going to hang up this phone, and then I'm going to show these people what you don't want them to see. I'm going to show them a world without you, a world without rules and controls, without borders or boundaries, a world where anything is possible." In this reading, as David Lavery puts it, "The real world exists, even under the reign of Baudrillard's 'Third Order of Simulacra' and cinematic art … can represent it and tell a heroic tale of its recovery."[7] As William Gibson puts it in his foreword to the shooting script, Neo is, in this version, "a hero of the Real."[8]

However, the movie includes a number of moments that resist such an easy out. Cypher, of course, offers one alternative reading himself when he states: "I think the Matrix can be more real than this world. All I do is pull a plug here. But there, you have to watch Apoc die. <He pulls the plug and Apoc dies.> Welcome to the real world, eh baby?" This questioning of Morpheus's contention that one can still be welcomed to the real world is countered in the very next scene when a "miracle" prevents Cypher from pulling the plug on Neo (the anagrammatic *one* who is supposed to usher in a new *eon* of the real). If we look at Morpheus's original welcome, however, we find that the scene anticipates this questioning of the separation between the real world and its simulation. After all, Morpheus not only speaks those words inside simulation (the *Nebuchadnezzar*'s own loading program, "the Construct") but we access that scene by appearing to move directly through a Radiola "Deep Focus" television, which is to say that the "real world" Morpheus points to in that scene is, in fact, two orders removed from the world supposedly outside the hull of the *Nebuchadnezzar*.

The Wachowski brothers could just as easily have had Morpheus take Neo directly to the ruins of the world outside the ship. By presenting the "real" through the "Construct," they invite a number of other questions about

the choices made in filming. The ship that supposedly accesses that real is, for example, named the *Nebuchadnezzar* after the great king of Babylonia (c. 605–562 B.C.) who had troubling, prophetic dreams that eventually drove him mad. Morpheus himself, who claims to offer Neo the opportunity to wake from his dream, is named after the god of dreams in Greek mythology, a god who is described in Ovid's *Metamorphoses* (Book Eleven) as a master at simulating humans, at counterfeiting men. The heroes of the real in the film are thus made ambivalent, suggesting that all may not be right with the (real) world.

One of the longest conversations in the real world, the mess-hall sequence, similarly forces us to question the extent to which we can ever escape the Matrix. Not only has the model taken the place of our real-world referents (e.g. Tastee Wheat) but Mouse makes it clear that humans by their very nature reconstruct fantasy scenarios in order to live in the real. The conversation revolves around the unappetizing "goop" that the *Nebuchadnezzar*'s crew eats for sustenance:

> DOZER: It's a single-celled protein combined with synthetic aminos, vitamins, and minerals. Everything the body needs.
> MOUSE: It doesn't have everything the body needs. So, I understand that you've run through the agent-training program? You know, I wrote that program.
> APOC: Here it comes.
> MOUSE: So, what did you think of her?
> NEO: Of who?
> MOUSE: The woman in the red dress. I designed her. She doesn't talk much but, if you'd like to, you know, meet her, I could arrange a more personalized milieu.
> SWITCH: The digital pimp hard at work.
> MOUSE: Pay no attention to these hypocrites, Neo. To deny our own impulses is to deny the very thing that makes us human.

The scene makes clear that the human mind cannot live with the unadulterated real. This insight is perhaps what most clearly distinguishes postmodern theory from earlier understandings of ideology as "false consciousness," as that which obscures some underlying truth. For postmodernists, once again, *any* representation of reality is always already ideological.

---

7   Lavery, p. 155.
8   Wachowski, p. viii.

Morpheus falls between these two positions when he describes the Matrix to Neo during their first meeting:

MORPHEUS: Do you want to know what it is? The Matrix is every-where, it's all around us, here even in this room. You can see it out your window or on your television. You can feel it when you go to work, or go to church or when you pay your taxes. It is the world that has been pulled over your eyes to blind you from the truth.

NEO: What truth?

MORPHEUS: That you are a slave, Neo. Like everyone else, you were born into bondage, born inside a prison that you cannot smell, taste or touch. A prison for your mind.

The Matrix is analogous to ideology in the postmodern sense; it creates the very "reality" that surrounds us because of our reliance not just on rules but also on language to structure the world around us. For this reason, according to Jacques Lacan (an influential psychoanalyst among postmodern theorists), the "real is impossible." It is, by Lacan's definition, beyond language and, thus, beyond representability, though it continues to trouble the easy functioning of ideology because it reminds us of that ideology's artificiality. As Morpheus puts it, "You have come because you know something. What you know you can't explain but you feel it. You've felt it your whole life, felt that something is wrong with the world. You don't know what, but it's there like a splinter in your mind, driving you mad." According to postmodernists, that splinter of the "real" is there for everyone, causing us to question our ideologies, but it must by definition remain outside of language. Fredric Jameson refers to this postmodernist view as the "prison-house of language," which is one way to interpret Morpheus's "prison for your mind."

* * *

To what extent the film succeeds at rejecting the system is an open question. Does the self-conscious use of postmodern theory allow the Wachowskis to escape the charge of creating mere escapist drivel? Does it allow the Wachowski's to critique what Baudrillard calls capital's "instantaneous cruelty, its incomprehensible ferocity, its fundamental immorality" from within the very heart of a mass-market product? Or is the use of theories that are themselves highly critical of multinational capitalism just a way for the Wachowskis to have their cake and critique it too?

At the very least, the Wachowskis succeed at getting their audience to *think*, something that is far too uncommon in the conventional Hollywood product. They allow a mass market to enter into conversation with some of the more influential "high" theorists of our own postmodern age. They resist the audience's desire to look through the medium of film to some easy mimetic "reality" (like Cypher's ability to see not code but "blonde, brunette, and redhead"). The Wachowskis thus force us to see the matrices that structure, manipulate, and re-present that reality to us, feeding our fantasies. They remind us of their own controlling presence, and of technology's ability to create new perceptions of reality (the innovative dimensional film-making of "bullet time"). They persistently highlight the *art* of film and thus underscore, at the very least, our reliance on and manipulation by the very technology that delivers their vision to us: not just the real but the reel.

SOURCES

BOOKS

Baudrillard, Jean, *Simulacra and Simulation*, translated by Sheila Faria Glaser (Ann Arbor: University of Michigan Press, 1994).

Jameson, Fredric, *The Prison-House of Language: A Critical Account of Structuralism and Russian Formalism* (Princeton: Princeton University Press, 1972).

Wachowski, Larry and Andy Wachowski, *The Matrix: The Shooting Script* (New York: Newmarket Press, 2001).

ARTICLES

Lavery, David, "From Cinespace to Cyberspace: Zionists and Agents, Realists and Gamers in *The Matrix* and *ExistenZ*," *Journal of Popular Film and Television* 28.4 (Winter 2001): pp. 150–57.

The Matrix: Paradigm of Postmodernism or Intellectual Poseur? (Part 2)

from *Taking the Red Pill*

— Andrew Gordon

Not so fast, argues Andrew Gordon in the following essay. The Matrix *may be a great action film, but its philosophical pretensions aren't warranted.*

Early in *The Matrix* (1999), there is a scene introducing the hero, who goes by the hacker alias Neo. Neo hears a knock at the door of his apartment, answers it, and finds a client at the door. He goes to a bookshelf and takes down a volume clearly labeled *Simulacra and Simulation*, which is the title of a book by Jean Baudrillard. When he opens it, the book is a fake, hollowed out, and inside are computer disks, apparently containing illegal software. This image, with its reduplication of fakery — the title plus the fact that the book itself is fake — is an early clue foreshadowing Neo's eventual discovery of the wholly simulated, computer-generated nature of the world in which he lives. (Also, the book is fake in another way — thicker than the real book and with the "On Nihilism" chapter in the wrong place.)

In a later scene, Morpheus, the rebel leader, introduces Neo to the wasteland that is the actual, destroyed world of 2199. "Welcome to the desert of the real," he says, echoing a line from *Simulacra and Simulation*, "The desert of the real itself."[1]

In a line from the screenplay draft, which was cut from the film, Morpheus even tells Neo, "You have been living inside Baudrillard's vision, inside the map, not the territory."[2]

In an interview, Larry Wachowski, who wrote and directed *The Matrix* with his brother Andy, says, "Our main goal with *The Matrix* was to make an intellectual action movie. We like action movies, guns and kung fu, but we're tired of assembly-line action movies that are devoid of any intellectual content. We were determined to put as many ideas into the movie as we could."[3] The Wachowskis actually gave Keanu Reeves, who plays Neo, a homework assignment. Among the books he had to read to prepare for the film were Kevin Kelly's *Out of Control: The New Biology of Machines, Social Systems and the Economic World* (1994) and Jean Baudrillard's *Simulacra and Simulation*.[4]

Now, whether the Wachowskis have successfully blended the elements of the action movie — such as guns and kung fu — with intellectual content is an issue I wish to consider later. But certainly the film is heavily indebted to two central figures of contemporary science fiction and science-fiction theory. First is the novelist William Gibson, who helped found the cyberpunk subgenre in his short fiction of the early 1980s and his novel *Neuromancer* (1984). In *Neuromancer*, Gibson coined the terms "cyberspace" and "the matrix" to refer to virtual reality. Critics have claimed that *The Matrix* has helped to revive cyberpunk for the twenty-first century[5] or that it is "the first masterpiece of film c-punk."[6] The second figure is Jean Baudrillard,

---

1   Baudrillard, *Simulacra and Simulation*, p. 1
2   Matrix Unfolded

3   Probst, p. 32
4   Nichols
5   Barnett, p. 360
6   "E-Files," p. 346

one of the theoreticians of the new order of simulation or virtual reality.

"Virtual reality" is a gelatinous concept, reinterpreted anew with each telling, like "postmodern" itself. Writes Robert Markley, "What, after all, counts as a virtual space? In recent years, the term has become a catch-all for everything from e-mail to GameBoy cartridges …" Many commentators imagine virtual reality as a transcendent space, something sublime, better than ordinary reality, "as though each computer screen were a portal to a shadow universe of infinite, electronically accessible space."[7]

Yet reality that is virtual, if it ever exists, would probably not be transcendent but merely a projection or shadow of reality, missing important dimensions, just as the shadow of a three-dimensional globe is only a two-dimensional sphere. Existence in virtual reality would resemble life in Plato's Cave: a secondhand existence in a world of shadows. Someday it may be theoretically possible to write an extremely complex program that would simulate real life well enough to fool people, including not only sight and sound but also the crucial senses of touch, taste, and smell, although at present the technological obstacles are formidable. *The Matrix*, however, assumes that these obstacles have somehow been overcome.

What we are really dealing with in science fictions and other contemporary cultural concerns about virtual reality are metaphors and fantasies, projections of our fears and hopes about life inside the machine or life augmented by the machine in the cybernetic age. We are now living in a new age, not simply the postmodern but "the posthuman," in which we have to redefine what it means to be human. "In the posthuman," writes N. Katherine Hayles, "there are no essential differences or absolute demarcations between bodily existence and computer simulation."[8] As the boundary lines break down, we fear that the human may be taken over by the machine, or, at the opposite extreme, we hope that the human may be made transcendent by the machine. As David Porush says, "Virtual reality or cyberspace is … about redefining … the human within a pure … space of mechanism, and a New Jerusalem, a Promised Land."[9] Virtual reality is "a new mythology," in which the new frontier is not outer space but the "inner space" of

the computer and of the human mind and the interface between the two.[10]

Gibson's "cyberspace" or "the matrix" has as much to do with science and technology as the adventures of the wizard Don Juan in Carlos Castenada's volumes have to do with anthropology. And the same is true of virtual reality in *The Matrix*. In *Neuromancer*, cyberspace is a transcendent realm, a "consensual hallucination"[11] which, for hardcore hackers, is better than drugs or sex. *The Matrix* taps into this new mythology to invert Gibson's notion of cyberspace, creating not a New Jerusalem but a cyber-hell. In the virtual prison of the Matrix, human beings are maintained in a permanent dream state, unaware they are merely slaves of the machine.

Just as *The Matrix* plays on but inverts Gibson's notion of cyberspace, so it also plays on Baudrillard's ideas about simulation, but without Baudrillard's pessimism, because *The Matrix* offers a solution to the problem of simulation whereas Baudrillard believes there is none.

One needs first to place Baudrillard's sweeping, often hyperbolic pronouncements — that simulation, or what he calls "hyperreality," has completely taken over the contemporary world — in perspective. For example, one critic, Istvan Csicsery-Ronay Jr., has called Baudrillard "a virtuoso stylist of theory-SF," who writes theory in a lyrical mode, creating "a visionary SF poem or film."[12] Baudrillard treats "certain motifs and themes dear to utopian and scientific fiction" as "actualized phenomena."[13] Csicsery-Ronay terms Baudrillard's mode of theory "apocalyptic-dystopian-idealist."[14] In other words, we should not take Baudrillard's remarks literally but instead treat them metaphorically, as exaggerations to make a point, as we would the imagined world of a dystopian science fiction novelist such as George Orwell. Because Baudrillard writes "theory-SF" about simulation and hyperreality, because he deals in hyperbolic and apocalyptic pronouncements, and because he is creating "a visionary SF poem or film," it is not surprising then that he would appeal to science fiction filmmakers creating an apocalyptic, dystopian movie about hyperreality, such as *The Matrix*.

Ironically, although Baudrillard has been a tremendously influential critic of virtual reality, he has little knowledge

7   Markley, p. 2
8   Hayles, p. 3
9   Porush, p. 126

10   Ibid., p. 109
11   Gibson, p. 51
12   Csicsery-Ronay, pp. 392–93
13   Ibid., p. 393
14   Ibid., p. 389

of cyberculture but began his critique of hyperreality by attacking TV advertising and theme parks years before the digital revolution that brought about the Internet, the PC, and virtual reality. Baudrillard also fails to distinguish in his theorizing between the effects of television and of the computer, which are very different. Television is not interactive, unlike the computer and the Internet, nor does television constitute "virtual reality."[15] Baudrillard tends to lump theme parks, television, and virtual reality together as forms of simulation.

Baudrillard's central idea is that, in the postmodern world, the real has been almost totally displaced by the simulated. "It is a generation by models of a real without origin or reality: a hyperreal. The territory no longer precedes the map. ... It is ... the map that precedes the territory." He claims that the real survives only in vestiges "here and there in the deserts ... The desert of the real itself."[16]

Baudrillard speaks of four orders of simulation: in the first, the image reflects reality; in the second, it masks reality; in the third, "it masks the absence of a profound reality"; and in the fourth, "it has no relation to reality whatsoever; it is its own pure simulation."[17] Baudrillard is especially interested in postmodern examples of simulation of the third order, theme parks such as Disneyland. "Disneyland is presented as imaginary in order to make us believe that the rest is real, whereas all of Los Angeles and the America that surrounds it are no longer real but belong to the hyperreal order and to the order of simulation."[18] What Baudrillard means by "the hyperreal" is "the generation by models of a real without origin or reality."[19]

Baudrillard has commented elsewhere on what he calls "simulation simulacra: based on information, the model, cybernetic play. Their aim is maximum operation, hyperreality, total control."[20] He fears that the coming of the era of hyperreality marks "the end of SF" because "something like the reality principle disappears."[21] If there is no baseline

> What Baudrillard means by "the hyperreal" is "the generation by models of a real without origin or reality."

reality, then science fiction has no foundation on which to build, for how can we measure "the fantastic" except by comparison with "the real"?

How then does simulation operate in *The Matrix*? In the film, it is 2199 and the surface of the earth has been destroyed in a war with artificially intelligent machines. Deep underground, human beings are bred as a source of energy for the machines and kept in an embryonic state, dreaming that they are living in an American city in 1999. This dream world, called the Matrix, is a computer simulation intended to keep the populace docile.

A few humans remain in the real world and fight the machines. Morpheus, the rebel leader, cruises the underworld in a hovercraft, like Jules Verne's Captain Nemo. Morpheus and his crew rescue from the Matrix Thomas Anderson, by day a computer programmer for a large corporation, by night an outlaw hacker known as "Neo." Morpheus is convinced Anderson may be "The One" foretold by the Oracle: the man who can defeat the agents. Neo, whose name is an anagram of "One," is unaware he is living in a simulated reality. First he must be extracted from the Matrix, reborn in the real world, reeducated and trained.

Morpheus first explains to Neo the nature of the Matrix:

MORPHEUS: Do you want to know what it is? The Matrix is everywhere. It's all around us, even here in this room. You can see it out your window or on your television. You can feel it when you go to work, or go to church or pay your taxes. It is the world that has been pulled over your eyes to blind you from the truth.
NEO: What truth?
MORPHEUS: That you are a slave, Neo. Like everyone else you were born into bondage, kept inside a prison that you cannot smell, taste or touch. A prison for your mind.

The Matrix deals with what Baudrillard would call "the fourth order of simulation," with no relation to reality whatsoever. That is, the everyday world in which Neo exists is totally false, a dream world with no substance and no relation to 2199 (although it does strongly resemble the present-day world of the movie's audience). The machines

15   Poster, pp. 48–50
16   Baudrillard, *Simulacra and Simulation*, p. 1
17   Ibid., p. 6
18   Ibid., p. 12
19   Ibid., p. 1
20   Baudrillard, "Simulacra and Science Fiction," p. 309
21   Ibid., p. 311

have created a virtual reality simulacrum of the world of 1999, a world which no longer exists in the future. As Baudrillard writes, seeming to describe the movie, "The real is produced from miniaturized cells, matrices, and memory banks, modes of control — and it can be reproduced an indefinite number of times from these."[22]

According to Baudrillard, in the electronic era, "it is the real that has become our true utopia — but a utopia that is no longer in the realm of the possible, that can only be dreamt of as one would dream of a lost object."[23] The real, he believes, has been replaced by the electronic and other forms of simulation, by "models of a real without origin or reality."[24] The real has been irretrievably lost, and even if we wanted to, we couldn't distinguish anymore between the simulation and the real. For example, when we try to retreat to what we think of as reality, we find not nature but a nature park. The "natural" has been displaced by the artificial. Thus utopia, the realm of the real, cannot exist any longer in the future but only in the past, which creates a problem for science fiction, a literature and film about anticipating the future. "Perhaps science fiction from the cybernetic and hyperreal era can only exhaust itself, in its artificial resurrection of 'historical' worlds, can only try to reconstruct in vitro, down to the smallest details, the perimeters of a prior world, the events, the people, the ideologies of the past, emptied of meaning, of their original process, but hallucinatory with retrospective truth."[25]

Thus in *The Matrix* the world of 2199 prefers to dwell in a permanent 1999. As Baudrillard comments elsewhere, Americans live "in a perpetual simulation."[26] In other words, in Baudrillard's hyperbolic, pessimistic view, we have already replaced the real with the hyperreal, America is in the vanguard of this movement, and the future promises no recovery of the real but only more and more simulation. *The Matrix* also seems to warn that it is not just for the characters in the film but also for the film audience that 1999 is a dream world, a fourth-order simulation. According to Slavoj Žižek, *The Matrix* is not about the future but about the unreality of present-day America in the oppressive, all-enveloping world of virtual capitalism: "The material reality we all experience and see around us is a virtual one, generated and coordinated by

a gigantic computer to which we are all attached."[27] Žižek seems to share Baudrillard's pessimism and is given to making similarly sweeping, hyperbolic pronouncements about present-day reality. The dystopian metaphors of science fiction have strongly affected contemporary theory.

This virtual prison in the film is then supposed to resemble our present, a world both we and the masses within the film accept despite the fact that it is far from utopian, not only unreal but also unhappy. There is a lot of evidence for this point in the film. One can easily argue that *The Matrix* protests against our corporate cubicle lives, the sort of artificial life Neo must reject. As Agent Smith, one of the sentient programs who police the Matrix, tells Morpheus:

> "Have you ever stood and stared at it, Morpheus? Marveled at its beauty. Its genius. Billions of people just living out their lives … oblivious. Did you know that the first Matrix was designed to be a perfect human world? Where none suffered, where everyone would be happy. It was a disaster. No one would accept the program. Entire crops were lost. Some believed we lacked the programming language to describe your perfect world. But I believe that, as a species, human beings define their reality through suffering and misery. The perfect world was a dream that your primitive cerebrum kept trying to wake up from. Which is why the Matrix was redesigned to this: the peak of your civilization. I say 'your civilization' because as soon as we started thinking for you, it really became our civilization which is, of course, what this is all about."

For those in the viewing audience who have not read or heard of Baudrillard (almost everyone, I assume), *The Matrix* repeats variations on the same theme of the real versus the fantastic through references to the classic popular fantasies *Alice in Wonderland* and *The Wizard of Oz*, both of which play on the idea of two separate worlds, one real and the other dreamlike. The difference is that in those two works the protagonists begin in the real world and then move into the dream or fantasy world, whereas Neo takes a reverse journey, as the world he initially believes to be real proves to be merely a computer simulation. For example,

---

22 Baudrillard, *Simulacra and Simulation*, p. 2
23 Baudrillard, "Simulacra and Science Fiction," p. 123
24 Baudrillard, *Simulacra and Simulation*, p. 1
25 Baudrillard, "Simulacra and Science Fiction," p. 123
26 Baudrillard, *America*, pp. 76–77

27 Žižek, p. 25

among the references to *Alice* in *The Matrix*, Morpheus tells Neo to "follow the white rabbit," and later says, "I imagine, right now, you must be feeling a bit like Alice, tumbling down the rabbit hole." He offers Neo a choice of two pills, one blue and the other red, saying, "You take the red pill and you stay in Wonderland and I show you how deep the rabbit hole goes." When Neo wonders what is happening after he swallows the red pill, Cypher tells him, "Buckle up, Dorothy, 'cause Kansas is going bye-bye." As Neo stares at his image in a mirror, his reality begins to dissolve. The mirror appears to liquefy and his hand goes through it, suggesting *Through the Looking Glass*.

Like *Star Wars*, *The Matrix* is a postmodern pastiche of bits and pieces of popular culture.[28] "The Wachowski brothers have exhibited a remarkable shrewdness about their cross-cultural looting. *The Matrix* slams together a more eclectic mix of mythological excess — from the Bible to Hong Kong action films — than you're likely to find this side of … the first *Star Wars*."[29] *The Matrix* also borrows concepts, images, creatures, or costumes from a host of science fiction movies, including:

1. *2001* (1968): a malicious, sentient computer takes over and starts killing people
2. *Logan's Run* (1976): the outside world has been devastated by war and the remainder of mankind live hedonistic lives in a huge domed city but are terminated when they reach age 30
3. *Star Wars* (1977): an ordinary character discovers he has superpowers and may be the one who can save his world
4. *Alien* (1979): an alien creature invades a human body, just as Neo has a spy bug implanted in his belly
5. *Tron* (1982): the hero is trapped inside a computer and forced to fight his way out by defeating the Master Control Program
6. *Blade Runner* (1982): one cannot tell the manufactured, simulated people (the replicants) from real humans
7. *The Terminator* (1984) and *Terminator 2: Judgment Day* (1991): the machines have taken over and are wiping out the humans until the humans fight back

8. *Total Recall* (1990): the hero cannot tell the programmed dream world from the reality
9. *Men in Black* (1997): the agents dress like the Men in Black

Aside from *Alice* and *Wizard of Oz*, *The Matrix* also draws on other literary sources, including Jules Verne's *Twenty Thousand Leagues Beneath the Sea* (Morpheus in his hovercraft resembles Captain Nemo), George Orwell's *1984* (the totalitarian authorities spy on the hero, who makes contact with a rebel underground), and Harlan Ellison's story "I Have No Mouth and I Must Scream" (a mad computer starts WWIII and keeps a few survivors alive underground, to be tortured for its sadistic pleasure; at the end, the computer deprives the hero of his mouth, like Agent Smith does to Neo in the interrogation scene).

The Wachowskis have been heavily influenced as well by other media, especially comic books, graphic novels (including Japanese manga), Japanese animation, music videos, TV commercials, fashion ads, and Hong Kong action movies. "More successfully than anyone else, the Wachowskis have translated a comic-book sensibility to the movies."[30] The brothers wrote for Marvel comics and originally conceived of *The Matrix* as a comic book, and it retains a lot of the graphic punch of that medium. They hired several comic-book artists "to hand-draw the entire film as a highly graphic storyboard bible."[31] Their visual-effects supervisor John Gaeta says, "They're authentic comic book freaks, and that's where many of their cinematic ideas come from — Japanimation and deviant comics artists."[32] Their cinematographer, Bill Pope, shares their love of comics and started his career filming music videos and commercials before shooting science fiction films such as *Darkman* and *Army of Darkness*.

Like *Star Wars*, *The Matrix* also coheres as a messiah story or pastiche of a series of messiah stories, a myth of the birth of a hero.[33] *The Matrix* is filled with Christian allegory, for Neo proves to be the prophesied messiah who will free humanity from the computerized dream world. There are also names redolent of Christian symbolism, such as Trinity or Cypher (suggesting Lucifer, although he functions more like Judas). The cinematographer Bill

---

28 Gordon, pp. 314–15
29 Mitchell

30 Mitchell
31 Probst, p. 32
32 Magid, p. 46
33 Gordon, p. 315

Pope says, "It's a pretty complicated Christ story but for the Wachowskis and myself, one of the best kinds of comic book is the origin story, which outlines the beginnings of a superhero like Daredevil or Spiderman. *The Matrix* is the origin story of Neo."[34]

Baudrillard is then only one element in the many layers of intertextuality in *The Matrix*. The question remains: is *The Matrix* really an intellectual action film, or is it, as one reviewer suggested, "a muddily pretentious mixture of post-modern literary theory, slam-bang special effects and Superman heroics?"[35] And second, how profound is the Wachowskis's understanding of Baudrillard? Are they borrowing from Baudrillard to give their film an intellectual cachet which it does not deserve?

First of all, what does it mean to be an intellectual action film? And what distinguishes a true intellectual action film from a pretender? There is nothing wrong with contemporary popular media such as comic books, TV, or movies making use of current literary and cultural theory, any more than "high culture," such as the novels of Saul Bellow, Philip Roth, or Thomas Pynchon, quoting cartoons, television shows, or movies. In the postmodern, eclecticism rules and the boundaries between so-called "low" and "high" culture are fluid. In its favor, *The Matrix*, like the *Star Wars* and *Star Trek* series, has spawned dozens of articles and even a few college courses exploring its philosophical, religious, and scientific dimensions. A science-fiction film like *The Terminator*, with similar action and complex themes, did no such thing.

P. Chad Barnett praises *The Matrix* for reviving the genre of cyberpunk, bringing "a Bohemian edge and smart postmodern aesthetic back to cyberpunk."[36] Perhaps carried away by reading the contemporary neo-Marxist critic Fredric Jameson, Barnett lauds the film for its political effects as an "accurate cognitive mapping of the world space of multinational capital. It … allows those who experience it to begin to grasp their position as individual and collective subjects and regain a capacity to act and struggle …"[37] In other words, Barnett believes *The Matrix* actually has politically radical potential and may inspire some viewers to organize or to revolt against the capitalist system.

But this seems to me far too utopian a reading of the ideological effect of *The Matrix*. The film may serve in part as a warning about virtual reality, but it is far from radical in its plot. Although the Wachowskis may imagine themselves as rebels like Morpheus and Neo ("we basically reject the system")[38] they are instead, like George Lucas, inextricably part of the Hollywood system. *The Matrix* is another cinematic action franchise like *Star Wars*, dependent, like George Lucas's saga, upon the appeal of a clear-cut opposition of good-versus-evil, and promising redemption by the coming of a messiah who kicks butt. To hope for change by the intervention of a messiah discourages political thought or action. One critic objects to "the whole messianic subtext: the notion that one hero can transform a world fallen irrevocably into hyperreality."[39] I believe that it is precisely this mythological, messianic subtext, like that in *Star Wars*, that accounts for the cult status of *The Matrix*. It blends the old mythology of the coming of a messiah with the new mythology of virtual reality to create a new kind of religious hero. *The Matrix* also has the same pseudo-profundity, stilted dialogue, and religious allegorical overtones as the *Star Wars* series. Although it deals in ideas, *The Matrix* is not intellectually or philosophically profound. Again, like in *Star Wars*, almost all its ideas are borrowed. Although they may have included nods to postmodern critical theory, the Wachowski Brothers's audience is not the tiny elite that reads Baudrillard but "a generation bred on comics and computers,"[40] which demands fast and violent action. Numerous critics complained that "At times, *The Matrix* plays more like a video game than a movie"[41] or that it offers "the ultimate in cyberescapism."[42] One reviewer found "fairly glaring contradiction at work in a film that relies so heavily on digital special effects at the same time that it rails against the evil of a computer-constructed reality."[43] There is also a contradiction in a film that warns against the triumph of computers but suggests that "ultimate enlightenment can be attained through skills which have been downloaded."[44]

Moreover, the demands of the recent Hollywood action movie for spectacle and violence tend to militate against

34 Probst, p. 33
35 Hoffman
36 Ibid., p. 362
37 Ibid., p. 372

38 *The Matrix* DVD
39 "E-Files," p. 347
40 Maslin
41 Anthony
42 Maslin
43 Hoffman
44 Newman

thoughtfulness. I do not object to cinematic violence per se — great literature and film are often saturated with violence — so long as the violence is necessary and advances both story and themes. Consider, for example, the sickening "ultraviolence" of Stanley Kubrick's film *A Clockwork Orange* (1971). That film, like the novel by Anthony Burgess on which it is based, is a thoughtful meditation on the nature of free will and on individual violence versus the violence of the state.

I believe, however, that the primary pleasures of *The Matrix* are not intellectual but visceral, in the innovative visual tricks and stunts and the almost nonstop action. Larry Wachowski says, "There are many incredible and beautiful images in violence, and I think violence can be a great storytelling tool. Film makers have come up with an incredible language for violence. For example, what John Woo does with his sort of hyper-violence is brilliant. He pushes violent imagery to another level. We tried to do that with *The Matrix* as well."[45] Many viewers and reviewers enjoyed the violence: "*The Matrix* offers some of the most psychotic action scenes in American film."[46] But others objected that, at the end, "the script descends into a frightening form of nihilism … as the well-armed hero sets out to save humanity by killing as many humans as possible."[47]

Problems with violent spectacle for its own sake flaw many recent science fiction action movies, such as Verhoeven's *Total Recall* (1990), which tries for an impossible blend of Philip K. Dick's mindbending reflections on the shifty nature of reality with Arnold Schwarzenegger's philosophy of "Crack their heads like walnuts and mow them down with a machine gun." Verhoeven's *Starship Troopers* (1997) (from the Heinlein novel), attempts to satirize Heinlein's militaristic, fascistic future society but then undercuts its satire by endorsing the protagonist's gung-ho war heroics and reveling in the spectacle of mutilation and gore. Heinlein's novel did celebrate a militaristic society, although without the satire and without most of the gore. *Blade Runner* (1982) and *Minority Report* (2002), both based on Philip K. Dick's novels, are to my mind far more thoughtful science fiction action movies than *Total Recall*, *Starship Troopers*, or *The Matrix*. The violence in *Blade Runner*, for example, is deliberately awkward and pain-

ful, for the cop hero is assigned to hunt and kill escaped "replicants," manufactured people who are indistinguishable from real people and who die slowly and suffer real pain. And the murders in *Minority Report* are foreseen and replayed in fragments, so that they become traumatic, like repeated nightmares. The violence in both these films helps advance the ideas.

In *The Matrix*, in contrast, I believe that the hyperreality inoculates us against the hyperviolence. For example, because it bends reality and resembles a video game, we cannot take the slaughter of the policemen in the lobby scene seriously. This is a technically astonishing scene, exhilarating to watch, but disturbing in its implications. The policemen are like anonymous targets in a video game, who exist only to be mowed down. We momentarily forget that behind these virtual-reality policemen are real people. One reviewer found disturbing parallels between the lobby scene in *The Matrix* and the real-life massacre at Columbine High School, including the black trench coats and the high-powered weaponry.[48] As Dino Felluga asks in the previous essay: "Does the self-conscious use of postmodern theory allow the Wachowskis to escape the charge of creating mere escapist drivel?" My answer would be: "Not really."

To return to my other concern: to what extent does *The Matrix* accurately reflect Baudrillard's ideas? And how faithful is *The Matrix* to Baudrillard's conclusions? In answer to the first question, I believe that the film is clearly influenced by Baudrillard's ideas but waters them down to the point that it doesn't really reflect his thinking. And in answer to the second, *The Matrix* is not faithful to Baudrillard's conclusions, because it creates a world in which the unreal is forced on people (whereas in our contemporary world we are doing it to ourselves) and because it offers the hope of returning to the real, which Baudrillard claims is no longer possible.

In one sense, *The Matrix* offers a simplified or romanticized notion of *Simulacra and Simulation*. There are two worlds in the film — the dream world of the Matrix, which is a computer-simulated version of 1999, and the real world of the postapocalyptic Earth of 2199 — and there is a strict division between the two. The division is made very clear visually. According to the cinematographer Bill Pope, the Matrix world had digitally enhanced skies to make them white. "Additionally, since we wanted the Matrix reality

---

45   Probst, p. 33
46   Covert
47   Hoffman

48   Jones, pp. 36–37

to be unappealing … we sometimes used green filters." In contrast, "The future world is cold, dark, and riddled with lightning, so we left the lighting a bit bluer and made it dark as hell. Also, the future reality is very grimy."[49] The critic David Lavery notes that "In *The Matrix*, we know very well where the real world is. … Morpheus introduces him [Neo] to it: 'Welcome to the real world.' The real world exists, even under the reign of Baudrillard's 'Third Order of Simulacra,' and cinematic art … can represent it and tell a heroic tale of its recovery."[50]

The Matrix, then, simplifies Baudrillard. *Simulacra and Simulation* argues — rightly or wrongly — that there may be no real world left behind the simulation, no baseline reality to recover. The real is gone. "In fact, it is no longer really the real, because no imaginary envelops it anymore. It is a hyperreal."[51] Instead, the Wachowskis's concept in *The Matrix* more closely resembles nineteenth-century romantic notions of a division between two worlds: a false world of appearances that obstructs or disguises the true world. Once we clear away the illusion, we can dwell in the real world. It is the old distinction between appearance and reality.

I disagree with Dino Felluga's claim that the Wachowskis intended to blur the separation between the Matrix world and the "real world" of the movie. This would further confuse the viewer, to no real purpose, in a film which many already found confusing.

Aside from the recovery of the real in the film, the messianic subtext, it should be noted, also completely contradicts Baudrillard's pessimism about the triumph of hyperreality. There is no reason for us to elevate a thinker like Baudrillard to the status of prophet or for an artist to be slavishly devoted to the ideas of any theorist. But when a film alludes to a theorist whom it apparently misunderstands or intentionally simplifies, it loses some of its intellectual cachet. Writes one critic, "If a film marks itself out as only a spectacle, I am willing to disable my idiot-plot sensor and just go along for the ride; but when a movie pretends to have a strong cognitive/ideational component (as in citing Baudrillard) and this component is half-baked or fudged, I start to seethe."[52]

In conclusion, although *The Matrix* entertains and gives us plenty to think about, especially its potent and paranoid central metaphor about the falsity of "reality," I would have to term it a flawed attempt at an "intellectual action film," in which spectacle sometimes overrides or contradicts the ideas it proposes.

SOURCES

BOOKS

Baudrillard, Jean, *America*, translated by Chris Turner (London and New York: Verso, 1988).

——, *Simulacra and Simulation*, translated by Sheila Faria Glaser (Ann Arbor: University of Michigan Press, 1994).

Gibson, William, *Neuromancer* (New York: Ace, 1984).

Hayles, N. Katherine, *How We Became Posthuman: Virtual Bodies in Cybernetics, Literature, and Informatics* (Chicago: The University of Chicago Press, 1999).

Markley, Robert, "Introduction," *Virtual Realities and Their Discontents*, Robert Markley, ed. (Baltimore: Johns Hopkins University Press, 1996), pp. 1–10.

Poster, Mark, "Theorizing Virtual Reality: Baudrillard and Derrida," *Cyberspace Textuality: Computer Technology and Literary Theory*, Marie-Laure Ryan, ed. (Bloomington: Indiana University Press, 1999), pp. 42–60.

ARTICLES

Anthony, Ted, "At the Movies: *The Matrix*," Associated Press, March 30, 1999.

Baudrillard, Jean, "Simulacra and Science Fiction," translated by Arthur B. Evans, *Science-Fiction Studies* 18.3 (November 1991): pp. 309–13.

Barnett, P. Chad, "Reviving Cyberpunk: (Re)Constructing the Subject and Mapping Cyberspace in the Wachowski Brothers's Film *The Matrix*," *Extrapolation* 41.4 (Winter 2000): p. 359–74.

Csicsery-Ronay Jr., Istvan, "The SF of Theory: Baudrillard and Haraway," *Science-Fiction Studies* 18.3 (November 1991): pp. 387–404.

Covert, Colin, "*Matrix* mates science fiction and style," *Variety*, September 24, 1999, pp. 3E.

"E-Files, The," *Science-Fiction Studies* 26.2 (July 1999): pp. 346–49.

49 Probst, p. 33
50 Lavery, p. 155
51 Baudrillard, *Simulacra and Simulation*, p. 2
52 "The E-Files" 349

Gordon, Andrew, "*Star Wars*: A Myth for Our Time," *Literature/Film Quarterly* 6.4 (Fall 1978): pp. 314–26.

Hoffman, Adina, *"Matrix's* Shallow Profundities," *The Jerusalem Post,* July 19, 1999, Arts, p. 7.

Jones, Kent, "Hollywood et la sage du numérique: A propos de *Matrix* et de *La Menace fantome," Cahiers du Cinema* 537 (July/August 1999): pp. 36–39.

Lavery, David, "From Cinespace to Cyberspace: Zionist and Agents, Realists and Gamers in *The Matrix* and *ExistenZ," Journal of Popular Film and Television* 28.4 (Winter 2001): pp. 150–57.

Magid, Ron, "Techno Babel," *American Cinematographer* 80.4 (April 1999): pp. 46–48.

Maslin, Janet, "The Reality Is All Virtual, and Densely Complicated," *The New York Times,* March 31, 1999, p. E1.

Mitchell, Elvis, "The Wachowski Brothers," *Esquire,* March 2000: pp. 224.

Newman, Kim, "Rubber Reality," *Sight and Sound* 9.6 (June 1999): pp. 8–9.

Nichols, Peter M., "Home Video: More to Satisfy *Matrix* Mania," *The New York Times,* November 9, 2001, p. E26.

Porush, David, "Hacking the Brainstem: Postmodern Metaphysics and Stephenson's *Snow Crash," Virtual Realities and Their Discontents,* Robert Markley, ed. (Baltimore: Johns Hopkins University Press, 1996), pp. 107–41.

Probst, Christopher, "Welcome to the Machine," *American Cinematographer* 80.4 (April 1999): pp. 32–36.

Žižek, Slavoj, "The Desert of the Real," *In These Times,* October 29, 2001, pp. 25–27.

WEBSITES

Matrix Unfolded. www.suspensionofdisbelief.com/matrix/faq.html. December 14, 2001.

PART 2

ENLIGHTENMENT AND ENTERTAINMENT

Just once in a while let us exalt the importance of ideas and information.

— Edward R. Murrow,
Good Night, and Good Luck (2005)

CHAPTER 5
News

This instrument can teach. It can illuminate, and yes, it can even inspire. But it can do so only to the extent that humans are determined to use it towards those ends. Otherwise it is merely wires and lights in a box."

— Edward R. Murrow,
Good Night, and Good Luck (2005)

Chapter 5. News

Recommended Film

Good Night, and Good Luck (George Clooney 2005)

Media Models

The Meme, The Spectacle

Chapter Summary

Gerald Erion draws from Neil Postman to explain the insights of Jon Stewart and the popularity of *The Daily Show*.

Henry Jenkins critiques the evolution of news and political discourse in the age of the internet and YouTube.

Amusing Ourselves to Death with Television News: Jon Stewart, Neil Postman, and the Huxleyan Warning

from *The Daily Show and Philosophy*

—Gerald Erion

While *The Daily Show* is undoubtedly funny, it also provides an intriguing study of our contemporary media environments. Indeed, hidden within many of Jon Stewart's funniest jokes are implicit critiques of the way television tends to report its news and host its public discussions of important issues. For instance, Stewart's opening rundown of the news as television covers it doesn't merely ridicule the day's major players and events, but also makes fun of the way television gathers and presents the news. In this way, over-the-top graphics and music packages, attractive but superficial "Senior Correspondents," and all the other trappings of television newscasts become fodder for *The Daily Show*'s writing staff. More than just a "fake news" program, *The Daily Show* offers a rare brand of humor that requires its audience to recognize a deeper, more philosophical criticism of contemporary television news.

From time to time, Stewart takes these implicit critiques of contemporary media and makes them explicit. Such was the case during his October 2004 appearance on CNN's since-cancelled *Crossfire*, when Stewart begged his hosts to "stop hurting America" with their substitution of entertaining pseudo-journalism for serious reporting and debate. Through this bold, format-breaking effort, Stewart highlighted the difference between thoughtful discussion and the theater of today's vapid television punditry. As we will see, Stewart's analysis of the present state of mass communication echoes that of the celebrated New York University media theorist Neil Postman, whose discerning insights ground some of Stewart's sharpest comic bits.

AMUSING OURSELVES TO DEATH

Neil Postman's *Amusing Ourselves to Death* is a book about the many forms of human communication and how those forms influence the messages that we communicate to one another. Postman acknowledges a significant intellectual debt here to Marshall McLuhan, and sees his own thesis as something of a revised version of McLuhan's famous pronouncement that "the medium is the message".[1] However, Postman extends McLuhan's ideas in ways that are both distinctive and significant.

For example, consider Postman's discussion of smoke signals. While the medium of smoke might be an effective way to communicate relatively simple messages over intermediate distances, many other types of messages can't be transmitted this way. Philosophical arguments, for instance, would be especially difficult to conduct with smoke signals because, as Postman puts it: "Puffs of smoke are insufficiently complex to express ideas on the nature of existence [or other philosophical concepts], and even if they were not, a Cherokee philosopher would run short of either wood or blankets long before he reached his second axiom. You cannot use smoke to do philosophy. Its form excludes the content."[2] So, the medium of smoke has a significant influence on the kind of content it can be used to communicate. At a minimum, smoke signaling restricts

---

1 Marshall McLuhan, *Understanding Media: The Extensions of Man* (New York: McGraw-Hill, 1964); see especially pp. 7–21.
2 Neil Postman, *Amusing Ourselves to Death: Public Discourse in the Age of Show Business* (New York: Penguin, 1985), p.7. Subsequent citations will be made parenthetically in-text.

both the complexity and the duration of the messages it carries. Likewise, we shall see that *The Daily Show*'s comedy often reflects the restrictions placed by our contemporary electronic media (including television) upon their content.

THE HUXLEYAN WARNING

Now, as Postman sees it, *all* media influence their content, and in a multitude of different ways. He writes: "[Mine] is an argument that fixes its attention on the forms of human conversation, and postulates that how we are obliged to conduct such conversations will have the strongest possible influence on what ideas we can conveniently express" (p. 6). This goes not only for smoke signals, but also for speech and written language, and even for the electronic media that are so important in our contemporary lives.

Of particular interest here is the ubiquitous medium of television, which Postman sees as a historic extension of such earlier media as the telegraph, photography, radio, and film.[3] How does television influence its content, according to Postman? His theory is complex, but in essence it maintains that television's inherent "bias" implies a tendency to render its content — even its most important news reports, political and religious discussions, and educational lessons — more *entertaining* than they would be otherwise, and consequently less serious, less rational, less relevant, and less coherent as well (pp. 67–80, 85–98).

The fact that television provides entertainment isn't, in and of itself, a problem for Postman. He warns, however, that dire consequences can befall a culture in which the most important public discourse, conducted via television, becomes little more than irrational, irrelevant, and incoherent entertainment. Again, we shall see that this is a point often suggested by *The Daily Show*'s biting satire. In a healthy democracy, the open discussion of important issues must be serious, rational, and coherent. But such discussion is often time-consuming and unpleasant, and thus incompatible with television's drive to entertain. So, it's hardly surprising to see television serving up important news analyses in sound bites surrounded by irrelevant graphics and video footage, or substituting half-minute ad spots for substantial political debates. On television, thoughtful conversations about serious issues are reserved

for only the lowest-rated niche programs. Just as ventriloquism and mime don't play well on radio, "thinking does not play well on television" (p. 90).[4] Instead, television serves as a hospitable home for the sort of "gut"-based discourse celebrated by Stephen Colbert.[5]

When we grow comfortable with the substitution of televised entertainment for serious public discourse, we begin the process of (to use Postman's words) "amusing ourselves to death." As Postman explains, this form of cultural corrosion is like that described in Aldous Huxley's classic novel *Brave New World*, in which the citizenry is comfortably and willingly distracted by the pleasures of *soma*, Centrifugal Bumble-puppy, and the feelies (pp. vii–viii, 155–6).

POSTMAN AND TELEVISION NEWS

Postman and the writing staff of *The Daily Show* seem to agree that television's presentation of news tends to degrade its content in significant ways. Consider Postman's explanation of the ironic title of his chapter on television news, "Now … This:" "There is no murder so brutal, no earthquake so devastating, no political blunder so costly — for that matter, no ball score so tantalizing or weather report so threatening — that it cannot be erased from our minds by a newscaster saying 'Now … this'" (p. 99). Thus, Postman

---

3 Postman develops his sweeping history of American media in chapter 5 of *Amusing Ourselves to Death*, "The Peek-a-Boo World" (pp. 64–80).

4 Postman acknowledges that, in other parts of the world (pp. 85–6) or in non-commercial contexts (pp. 105–6), television may serve different purposes. However, as he sees it, this does nothing to change the way that television most typically functions in contemporary American society.

5 Colbert explained the importance of one's gut in the search for truth during his April 2006 White House Correspondents' Association Dinner performance: "Every night on my show, *The Colbert Report*, I speak straight from the gut, OK? I give people the truth, unfiltered by rational argument." On this point Colbert also compared himself to President George W. Bush, who sat at the head table just a few feet away from Colbert's podium:

> We're not so different, he and I. We both get it. Guys like us, we're not some brainiacs on the nerd patrol. We're not members of the Factinista. We go straight from the gut; right sir? That's where the truth lies, right down here in the gut.
> Do you know you have more nerve endings in your gut than you have in your head? You can look it up. Now I know some of you are going to say, "I did look it up, and that's not true." That's because you looked it up in a book. Next time, look it up in your gut. I did. My gut tells me that's how our nervous system works.

maintains that the use of "Now ... this" is a tacit admission of the incoherence of television news, and "a compact metaphor for the discontinuities in so much that passes for public discourse in present-day America" (p. 99).

Of course, Postman believes that television does more to the news than disrupt its coherence. Revisiting his general thesis about how television influences its content, Postman also claims that televised news is irrational, irrelevant, and trivial. As he explains, television presents us "not only with fragmented news but news without context, without consequences, without value, and therefore without essential seriousness; that is to say, news as pure entertainment" (p. 100). So, even weighty news subjects can become entertaining under the influence of television, as the typical American newscast showcases a company of attractive reporters skipping from dramatic local stories to dramatic international stories, to celebrity gossip, to weather forecasts, to sports scores, to a closing story about babies or puppies or kittens. Commercials are scattered throughout. Music, graphics, and captivating video footage add touches of theater to the program. Quick transitions from one segment to the next ensure that audience members don't become bored—or troubled—for long.[6] Instead of useful and important information, then, viewers are treated to the impotent but entertaining trivia that Postman calls "disinformation," which isn't necessarily false but *misleading*, creating the *illusion of knowing* and undermining one's motivation to learn more (p. 107). Consequently, Postman writes, "Americans are the best entertained and quite likely the least well-informed people in the Western world" (p. 106).

THE DAILY SHOW AND TELEVISION NEWS

Now, as far as I know, the writing staff of *The Daily Show* doesn't publicly acknowledge Postman's influence. It's even possible that they've never heard of Postman. Nonetheless, it's clear that these general ideas about television news, whatever their sources, can help us to see the significance of some of the program's wittiest and most inspired jokes. *The Daily Show* is often described as a "fake news" program, but in fact, it's more than that. Much of its humor rests on

Postman-like insights that highlight the peculiar ways in which the medium of television itself influences the news that it conveys.

For example, most episodes of *The Daily Show* begin with Stewart's rundown of the day's headlines as reported by the major television news programs. A comedy show that only does "fake news" might simply build jokes around the content of these headlines, or perhaps report fictional news stories in a humorous way. On *The Daily Show*, though, the way in which television seems destined to render its news as entertainment often serves as the basis for these opening segments. In recent years Stewart and company have often joked about the major networks' coverage of natural disasters. In many of these cases they simply replay absurd clips of television reporters standing outside during hurricanes, sitting in cars with giant thermometers during heat waves, or paddling canoes through inch-deep "flooded" city streets. Other segments mock the way hordes of television reporters cover celebrity weddings, arrests, and criminal trials. Segments like "International Pamphlet" and "The Less You Know" contain their own jokes but also poke fun at the shallowness of typical television news coverage. Exchanges between Stewart and his Senior Correspondents parody their good-looking but sometimes ill-informed network counterparts.[7] Even *The Daily Show*'s clever graphics packages ("Mess O' Potamia," "Crises in Israfghyianonanaq," and so on) offer satirical imitations of the logos, diagrams, and pictorial illustrations so essential to today's television newscasts. Moreover, Stewart himself has attacked the way television is compelled to report "breaking news" with what at times seems to be inadequate or uncorroborated information, mere speculation, and no editing whatsoever; shortly after the Washington, DC-area sniper shootings of 2002, he joked with CNN's Howard Kurtz: "By watching the 24-hour news networks, I learned that the sniper was an olive-skinned, white–black male — men — with ties to Son of Sam, Al Qaeda, and was a military kid, playing video games, white, 17, maybe 40."[8] In these kinds of segments, then, *The Daily Show* is clearly doing more than just "fake news." It's also offering deep satire that relies on its audience's appreciation of the substance of Postman's the-

---

6 As Postman writes, "While brevity does not always suggest triviality, in this case it surely does. It is simply not possible to convey a sense of seriousness about any event if its implications are exhausted in less than one minute's time" (p. 103).

7 See also "Stephen Colbert's Guide to Dressing and Expressing Like a TV Journalist", in Jon Stewart, Ben Karlin, and David Javerbaum, *America (The Book): A Citizen's Guide to Democracy Inaction* (New York: Warner Books, 2004), pp. 142–3.

8 *Reliable Sources*, CNN (November 2, 2002).

sis, that television has a significant and sometimes adverse influence on the news content it reports.

At this point, one might be tempted to suggest that *The Daily Show* simply reproduces the unfortunate transformation of reporting into entertainment, as if *The Daily Show* were itself a source of news for its audience members. For instance, Bill O'Reilly (host of the Fox News program *The O'Reilly Factor*) once famously dubbed viewers of *The Daily Show* "stoned slackers" who "get their news from Jon Stewart."[9] However, at least one prominent study by the Annenberg Public Policy Center found that viewers of *The Daily Show* were *better* informed about the positions and backgrounds of candidates in the 2004 US Presidential campaign than most others. Indeed, it's difficult to see how the deepest *Daily Show* jokes could be appreciated by an audience unaware of the relevant social, political, and other newsworthy issues. As Annenberg analyst Dannagal Goldthwaite Young put it in a press release announcing the Center's Election Survey results, "*The Daily Show* assumes a fairly high level of political knowledge on the part of its audience."[10]

CONVERSATION AND *CROSSFIRE*

Postman's ideas about television also illuminate Stewart's infamous October 15, 2004 appearance on CNN's *Crossfire*. First aired in 1982, *Crossfire* was a long-running staple of CNN's lineup that featured curt discussion by hosts and guests supposedly representing both left-wing and right-wing positions on controversial political issues. Co-hosting for Stewart's visit were the unsuspecting Paul Begala and Tucker Carlson, neither of whom seemed prepared for what would become an extraordinary exchange. Instead of simply participating in a typical *Crossfire*-style debate (described by more than one observer as a "shoutfest"), Stewart quickly launched into a Postman-like criticism of the vapid and partisan punditry that passes for serious discussion on programs like *Crossfire*.

> So, it appears that much of *The Daily Show*'s sharpest comedy requires its audience to grasp a Postmanesque criticism of television news.

In fact, this theme is one that Stewart had explored before his *Crossfire* appearance. The recurring *Daily Show* segment "Great Moments in Punditry as Read by Children" draws laughs simply by having children read from transcripts of shows like *Crossfire*. Moreover, during an interview with Bill Moyers, Stewart claimed that both *Crossfire* and its MSNBC counterpart *Hardball* were "equally dispiriting" in the way their formats degrade political discourse.[11] And in his interview with CNN's Howard Kurtz, Stewart foreshadowed his *Crossfire* appearance by chiding the news network for offering entertainers instead of "real journalists" and pleaded, "You're the news ... People need you. Help us. Help us."[12]

On the *Crossfire* set, though, Stewart offered his most sustained attack against the shallow conversational style of television. Before either Begala or Carlson could catch his balance, Stewart was already begging them to "stop, stop, stop, stop hurting America" with their "partisan hackery," which he claimed serves only politicians and corporations and does nothing to help ordinary citizens make informed decisions.[13] "We need help from the media," Stewart said, "and they're hurting us." Carlson tried to counter Stewart's charges with the allegation that Stewart himself had been too lenient during the *Daily Show* appearance of 2004 Presidential candidate John Kerry. Stewart replied that there was a fundamental difference between journalism and comedy, snapping back, "I didn't realize that ... the news organizations look to Comedy Central for their cues on integrity." And when Begala tried to defend the *Crossfire* format by claiming that it was a "debate show," Stewart pointed to Carlson's trademark bow tie as evidence that *Crossfire* is "doing theater, when you should be doing debate." Finally, Stewart charged, "You have a responsibility to the public discourse, and you fail miserably." Because of such remarks, Stewart's *Crossfire* appearance produced a rare opportunity for reflecting about the effects of television on public discourse. Indeed, the incident sparked

9   *The O'Reilly Factor*, Fox News (September 17, 2004).
10 "National Annenberg Election Survey" (press release), *Annenberg Public Policy Center* (September 21, 2004), p. 2.

11 *Now*, PBS (July 11, 2003).
12 *Reliable Sources*, CNN (November 2, 2002).
13 *Crossfire*, CNN (October 15, 2004). All quotes below are from CNN's rush transcript of this episode.

much additional discussion in, for example, the *New York Times*, *Newsweek*, and countless electronic media outlets.

Once again, we can see that these are the sorts of criticisms developed by Postman in *Amusing Ourselves to Death*. His deepest discussion of such issues concerns ABC's controversial 1983 broadcast of the film *The Day After*, which depicts the bleak effects of a nuclear strike on the American Midwest. Given the film's grave subject matter, ABC decided to follow it with a roundtable discussion moderated by Ted Koppel and featuring such notable figures as Henry Kissinger, Elie Wiesel, Carl Sagan, and William F. Buckley.[14] With a serious theme and a guest list of unquestionable distinction, Koppel proceeded to march his cast through a fragmented 80 minutes of "conversation" in which the participants rarely engaged one another on points of substance. Instead, they used their camera time to push whatever points they had decided to make before-hand, without regard to the contributions of their fellow participants. Postman writes:

> Each of the six men was given approximately five minutes to say something about the subject. There was, however, no agreement on exactly what the subject was, and no one felt obliged to respond to anything anyone else had said. In fact, it would have been difficult to do so, since the participants were called upon seriatim, as if they were finalists in a beauty contest. (p. 89)

To put it another way, this wasn't a genuine discussion, but a *pseudo-discussion* warped by television's drive to enter-tain. "There were no arguments or counterarguments, no scrutiny of assumptions, no explanations, no elaborations, no definitions" (p. 90), and yet each of these elements is essential to genuine and thoughtful dialogue.

So, how did ABC go wrong? According to Postman, the root problem remains that thoughtful conversation just isn't entertaining, and thus plays poorly on television. Televised discussions about even the most serious of subjects tend to be rendered in forms that are more amusing or dramatic

than reflective. On this both Postman and the writing staff of *The Daily Show* agree.[15] Moreover, CNN President Jonathan Klein cited Stewart's critique when he announced the cancel-lation of *Crossfire* in January 2005. In an interview with the *Washington Post*, Klein said, "I think [Stewart] made a good point about the noise level of these types of shows, which does nothing to illuminate the issues of the day."[16]

A HUXLEYAN MOMENT OF ZEN?

So, it appears that much of *The Daily Show*'s sharpest com-edy requires its audience to grasp a Postmanesque criticism of television news. In addition, Stewart himself seems to offer a more general critique of today's televised public dis-course that is reminiscent of Postman's in several significant ways. This isn't to say, however, that Postman and Stewart are in perfect agreement. For one thing, Postman argues that the transformation of serious discussion into enter-tainment is all but inevitable when this discussion takes place on television. Stewart, on the other hand, seems to believe that television can do better. As we've seen, he has even appeared on CNN and used the news network's own programs to issue his call for reform. Postman and Stewart might also disagree about the suitability of television as a vehicle for sophisticated media criticism. Postman writes, for example, that any televised critique of television would likely be "co-opted" by the medium, and thus rendered in the typical fashion as mere entertainment (pp. 161–2).[17] In his eyes, television is simply incapable of carrying serious

---

14 Postman actually cites Buckley's own legendary program *Firing Line* as a rare example of television as a "carrier of coherent language and thought in process" that "occasionally shows people in the act of thinking but who also happen to have television cameras pointed at them" (p. 91). *Firing Line* never received high ratings, though, and spent most of its 33 years on public television.

15 Postman's son Andrew sums all of this up nicely in his "Introduction" to the 20th Anniversary Edition of *Amusing Ourselves to Death*, writing: "When Jon Stewart, host of Comedy Central's *The Daily Show*, went on CNN's *Crossfire* to make this very point—that serious news and show business ought to be distinguishable, for the sake of public discourse and the republic—the hosts seemed incapable of even understand-ing the words coming out of his mouth" (pp. xiii–xiv).

16 Howard Kurtz, "Carlson & 'Crossfire:' Exit Stage Left & Right," *Washington Post* (January 6, 2005), C1.

17 In the final chapter of *Amusing Ourselves to Death*, Postman describes a then-hypothetical but subversive anti-television television program that's eerily similar to *The Daily Show*. According to Postman, this program would serve an important educational purpose by demonstrating how television recreates and degrades news, political debate, religious thought, and so on. He writes: "I imagine such demonstrations would of ne-cessity take the form of parodies, along the lines of 'Saturday Night Live' and 'Monty Python,' the idea being to induce a national horse laugh over television's control of the public discourse" (pp. 161–2). In the end, Postman rejects the idea of such a show as "nonsense," since he thinks that serious and

public discourse, including serious public discourse about mass communication itself. That Stewart has appeared on *Crossfire* and other such programs to address this issue suggests that he believes otherwise. No doubt this is a question worth further consideration, and through any medium capable of giving it a thoughtful hearing.

intelligent televised discussion could never attract an audience large enough to make a difference.

Reflections on Politics in the Age of YouTube

from *Convergence Culture*

— Henry Jenkins

Newscaster Anderson Cooper opened the Democratic CNN/YouTube debate with a warning to expect the unexpected: "Tonight is really something of an experiment. This is something we've never done before. What you're about to see is, well, it's untried. We are not exactly sure how this is going to work. The candidates on this stage don't know how it is going to work. Neither do their campaigns. And frankly we think that's a good thing."[1] The eight candidates seeking the Democratic Party's nomination for the presidency would face questions selected from more than 3,000 videos "average" citizens had submitted via YouTube. Speaking on NPR's *Talk of the Nation* a few days before, CNN executive producer David Bohrman stressed that the new format would give the American public "a seat at the table," reflecting a world where "everyone is one degree of separation away from a video camera."[2]

"Welcome to my Home, Candidates," said Chris of Portland, before demanding that the presidential hopefuls provide straight answers. Many of the questions came in the confessional form many associated with YouTube — speaking directly into a handheld camera from their own living rooms and kitchens. There were some powerful

moments — a relief camp worker asking about Darfur, a man holding a semiautomatic weapon asking about gun control, a lesbian couple wondering about the candidates' perspective on gay marriage — and some questions on topics like the government's unsatisfactory response to Katrina, the minimum wage, and reparations for slavery which hadn't surfaced in previous debates.

Afterwards, most people only wanted to talk about the Snowman.

One short segment featured a claymation snowman talking about global warming, "the single most important issue to the snowmen of this country." As the video showed Junior's frightened face, the Snowman asked, "As president, what will you do to ensure that my son will live a full and happy life?" The candidates chuckled. Cooper explained, "It's a funny video. It's a serious question," before directing the query to Dennis Kucinich. The serious-minded Kucinich drew links between "global warming" and "global warring," explaining how the military defense of oil interests increased American reliance on fossil fuels and describing his own green-friendly policies: "We don't have to have our snowmen melting, and the planet shouldn't be melting either." Follow up questions pursued other environmental policy issues.

CNN ended the broadcast by announcing a future debate involving the GOP candidates, but the status of this debate was far from resolved. By the end of the week, most of the front-runners for the Republican nomination were refusing to participate. Former Massachusetts governor Mitt Romney put a face on their discomfort: "I think the

---

1   For a video archive of the debates, see http://www.youtube.com/democraticdebate and http://www.youtube.com/republicandebate. I am indebted to Colleen Kaman and Steve Schultz for their assistance in tracking down references and materials for this study.
2   *Talk of the Nation*, "Digital Democracy: YouTube's Presidential Debates," July 18, 2007, http://www.npr.org/templates/story/story.php?storyId=12062554.

presidency ought to be held at a higher level than having to answer questions from a snowman."[3] CNN's Bohrman deflected criticism of this particular selection: "I think running for president is serious business ... but we do want to know that the president has a sense of humor."[4]

Many bloggers also argued that the Snowman demeaned citizens' participation in the debates: "By heavily moderating the questions, by deliberately choosing silly, fluffy, or offbeat videos to show the nation, CNN is reinforcing the old media idea that the Internet entertains, but does not offer real, serious discussion or insight."[5] There would be a CNN/YouTube GOP debate, but behind the scenes negotiations delayed it and substantially toned down the content.

In this afterword, I will use the Snowman controversy as a point of entry for a broader investigation into the role of Internet parody during the pre-primary season in the 2008 presidential campaign. This debate about debates raises questions about the redistribution of media power, the authenticity of grassroots media, and the appropriateness of parody as a mode of political rhetoric. Parody videos, produced both by the public and by the campaigns, played an unprecedented role in shaping public perceptions of this unusually crowded field of candidates. By studying YouTube as a site of civic discourse, I want to better understand how convergence, collective intelligence, and participatory culture are impacting the political process.

I will pick up where chapter 6, "Photoshop for Democracy," left off — with a call for us to rethink the cultural underpinnings of democracy in response to an era of profound and prolonged media change.[6] The rise of networking computing, and the social and cultural practices which have grown up around it, have expanded the ability of average citizens to express our ideas, circulate them before a larger public, and pool information in the hopes of transforming our society. To do so, however, we

have to apply skills we have acquired through our play with popular culture and direct them towards the challenges of participatory democracy. Chapter 6 showed how Howard Dean's so-called cybercampaign actually unfolded across multiple media channels, new and old, commercial and grassroots. I argued that the public was seizing control over the campaign process — for better and for worse — and speculated about new forms of political rhetoric that blurred our roles as citizens, consumers, and fans. A closer look at the role parody videos played in American politics in 2007 may help us to understand how we are or are not realizing the potentials of this new communication environment. Such videos give us an alternative perspective on what democracy might look like, though we have a long way to go before we can achieve anything like a revitalized public sphere in the online world. As Anderson Cooper suggests, none of us knows where this will take us — and for the moment, at least, that's a good thing.

TURD BLOSSOM VS. THE OBAMATAR

Debates about digital democracy have long been shaped by the fantasy of a "digital revolution," with its assumptions that old media (or in this case, the old political establishment) would be displaced by the rise of new participants, whether new media startups confronting old media conglomerates, bloggers displacing journalists, or cybercandidates overcoming political machines. The same month that CNN was hosting the debates, *Mother Jones* ran a cover story on the "Politics 2.0 Smackdown," thus linking the upcoming campaign to larger conversation about how the participatory platforms and social networks of "web 2.0" were impacting culture and commerce. The *Mother Jones* cover juxtaposes Karl Rove, dressed like an old-style politico, with Barack Obama, represented as a video game avatar. The caption reads, "Turd Blossom vs. The Obamatar," while an asterisked comment tells us that "Turd Blossom" was George W. Bush's nickname for his longtime political adviser and "The Obamatar" was a phrase the magazine coined. *Mother Jones* summed up the stakes: "Forget party bosses in smoky backrooms — netroots evangelists and web consultants predict a wave of popular democracy as fundraisers meet on MySpace, YouTubers crank out attack ads, bloggers do oppo research, and cell-phone-activated flash mobs hold miniconventions in Second Life. The halls of power will belong to whoever can tap the passions of the online masses. That kid with a laptop has Karl Rove

3   Jose Antonio Vargas, "The Trail: The GOP YouTube Debate is Back On," *Washington Post*, August 12, 2007, http://blog. washingtonpost.com/the-trail/2007/08/12/the_gop_you-tube_debate_is_back_1.html.

4   Ibid.

5   Jason Rosenbaum, "It's a Trap!," The Seminal, November 29, 2007, http://www.theseminal.com/2007/11/28/its-a-trap/. See also Micah L. Sifry, "How CNN Demeans the Internet," TechPresident, November 29, 2007, http://www.techpresident. com/blog/entry/14238/how_cnn_demeans_the_internet.

6   See Henry Jenkins, *Convergence Culture: Where Old and New Media Collide* (New York: New York University Press, 2006).

quaking in his boots. And if you believe that, we've got some leftover Pets.com stock to sell to you."[7] *Mother Jones* reproduced the logic of a "digital revolution," even as it expressed skepticism that the changes would be as dramatic as advocates predicted.

This depiction of media change as a zero-sum battle between old powerbrokers and insurgents distracts us from the real changes occurring in our media ecology. Rather than displacing old media, what I call convergence culture is shaped by increased contact and collaboration between established and emerging media institutions, expansion of the number of players producing and circulating media, and the flow of content across multiple platforms and networks. The collaboration between CNN (an icon of old media power) and YouTube (an icon of new media power) might be understood as one such attempt to work through the still unstable and "untried" relations between these different media systems. Promoters and pundits alike represented the CNN/YouTube debates as a decisive event, raising expectations that opening up a channel for public participation might broaden the political agenda, rewrite the campaign rhetoric, or reveal the candidates' authentic personalities. Yet, it also represented a temporary tactical alliance between old and new media players on the eve of an important political struggle.

YouTube has emerged as a key site for the production and distribution of grassroots media — ground zero, as it were, in the disruption in the operations of commercial mass media brought about by the emergence of new forms of participatory culture. Yet, we need to understand YouTube as part of a larger cultural economy. First, YouTube represents the meeting ground between a range of different grassroots communities, each of which has been producing indie media for some time, but are now brought together by this shared media portal. By providing a distribution channel for amateur and semiprofessional media content, YouTube incites new expressive activities — whether through formal events like the CNN/YouTube debates or on a day-to-day basis. Having a shared site means that these productions get much greater visibility than they would if distributed by separate and isolated portals. It also means that they are exposed to each other's activities, learn quickly from new developments, and often find themselves collaborating across communities in unpredictable ways. YouTube has become a simple signifier for these alternative

sites of production, creating a context for us to talk about the changes taking place.

Second, YouTube functions as a media archive where amateur curators scan the media environment, searching for meaningful bits of content, and bringing them to a larger public (through legal and illegal means). They can do this in response to mass media content, as for example they focused much more attention on Stephen Colbert's appearance at the Washington Press Club dinner, or to amateur content, as in the case of a home video record-

---

YouTube has emerged as a key site
for the production and distribution
of grassroots media.

---

ing of candidate George Allen's racist dismissal of a South Asian cameraman which effectively foreclosed his entry into the 2008 presidential race. Collectors are sharing vintage materials; fans are remixing contemporary content; and everyone has the ability to freeze a moment out of the "flow" of mass media and try to focus greater attention on what just happened.

Third, YouTube functions in relation to a range of other social networks; its content gets spread via blogs and Livejournal entries, via Facebook and MySpace, where it gets reframed for different publics and becomes the focal point for discussions. YouTube content might be described as spreadable media, a term which shares some of the connotations of "memes" or "viral video," both commonly used terms, but which carries with it a greater sense of agency on the part of the user. Metaphors from genetics or virology still carry with them notions of culture as self-replicating or infectious, whereas thinking of YouTube content as spreadable focuses attention on both properties of texts and the activities of participants. Talking about YouTube content as spreadable also enables us to talk about the importance of distribution in the creation of value and the reshaping of meaning within YouTube culture.

Participation occurs at three distinct levels here — those of production, selection, and distribution. Each of these functions and relationships plays a role in the following analysis. None of these activities is new, even in the context of digital media, but YouTube was the first to bring all three functions together into a single platform and direct so much attention on the role of everyday people in this

---

7 "Fight Different," *Mother Jones*, August 2007, p. 27.

changed media landscape. Skeptical readers of this book have argued that in focusing so much attention on fans, I remain in the borderlands of the culture. They miss two points: first, in the age of convergence culture, there may no longer be a strong mainstream but rather a range of different niche sites of media production and consumption; second, in the cultural context of YouTube, what might once have felt like fringe activities are increasingly normalized, with more and more people routinely checking out and discussing content produced by amateur media makers and with mass media institutions routinely reworking their practices to incorporate this alternative site of cultural activity. The CNN/YouTube debates might be seen as an illustration of the negotiations now occurring between these alternative models for how culture gets produced and distributed.

Romney framed his distaste for the Snowman in terms of issues of respect, asserting that there was a proper way to speak to someone who wants to be the next president of the United States. Senior newscaster Dan Rather, however, argued that behind-the-scenes negotiations reflected more generalized anxieties about questions from unexpected quarters: "Candidates do hate, genuinely hate, audience participation, because they like to control the environment."[8] For Romney, the Snowman was a haunting specter of all that worried him about the new digital culture. During his press conference, for example, he mistakenly linked YouTube to public concerns about sexual predators, confusing conservative criticisms against the multimedia portal with those concerning MySpace.[9] Yet, Romney's campaign had itself launched an effort to get his supporters to create and circulate their own political advertisements.[10] None of the candidates — Republican or Democratic — could afford to ignore any potential platform that might allow them to reach undecideds or mobilize supporters. Techniques that seemed radical when deployed by the Howard Dean campaign four years earlier were now taken for granted by the most mainstream candidates; even establishment figures were experimenting with web 2.0 tools to increase their visibility and lower costs. Candidates were adopting avatars and moving their message into Second Life and other virtual worlds; they were using social network sites like MySpace and Facebook to rally their supporters, giving them means to contact each other and organize "meetups" without having to go through the centralized campaigns; candidates were sending out regular podcasts and Webcast messages to their supporters. Romney and the other candidates might fear the disruptive impact of web 2.0, but none of them was willing to forgo its affordances, and some candidates — Ron Paul for example — thrived online even as they failed to generate any traction through traditional media channels.

Bloggers and netizens often distrusted the YouTube / CNN debates for the opposite reason: because CNN's role in selecting the final questions protected mainstream media's historical gatekeeping and agenda-setting functions. Writing in *The Huffington Post*, media reform leader Marty Kaplan dismissed what he called the "faux populism" of the "Rube-Tube" debate as an act of corporate ventriloquism: "The notion that the CNN/YouTube debate represents a grass-roots triumph of the Internet age is laughable. The 4,000+ videos are pawns; the questioners are involuntary shills, deployed by the network producers in no less deliberate, calculating and manipulative a fashion as the words and stories fed by teleprompters into anchors' mouths."[11]

THE POWER TO NEGATE AND THE POWER TO MARGINALIZE

Far from advocating digital revolution, CNN's Bohrman openly dismissed new media platforms as "immature" and questioned whether the user-moderated practices of YouTube would have been adequate to the task of determining what questions candidates should address, given how easily such processes could be "gamed." Bohrman often cited what he saw as the public's fascination with "inappropriate" questions: "If you would have taken the most-viewed questions last time, the top question would have been whether Arnold Schwarzenegger was a cyborg sent to save the planet Earth. The second-most-viewed

8   "The YouTube-ification of Politics: Candidates Losing Control," CNN.com, July 18, 2007, http://edition.cnn.com/2007/POLITICS/07/18/youtube.effect/index.html.

9   Ana Marie Cox, "Will the GOP Say No to YouTube?," Time.com, July. 27, 2007, http://www.time.com/time/politics/article/0,8599,1647805,00.html.

10   "Team Mitt: Create Your Own Ad!," http://www.jumpcut.com/groups/detail?g_id=5DD3300851A311DC8DA1000423CF381C.

11   Marty Kaplan, "The CNN/RubeTube Debate," *The Huffington Post*, November 25, 2007, http://www.huffingtonpost.com/marty-kaplan/the-cnnrubetube-debate_b_74003.html.

video question was: Will you convene a national meeting on UFOs?"[12]

Here, the CNN producer showed limited understanding of the role which parody was going to play in the buildup to this presidential campaign. Tongue-in-cheek questions about cyborgs and aliens allowed many to thumb their noses at the official gatekeepers and their anticipated dismay at being "forced" to put such content onto the public airwaves. Such gestures reflect a growing public skepticism about old media power as well as uncertainty about how far to trust emerging (though still limited and often trivial) efforts to solicit our participation. We might link this phenomenon back to the discussion of the Vote for the Worst movement among *American Idol* fans, for example. Given a toehold into mass media, the public seems to take great pleasure in its ability to negate its normal operating procedures, forcing the networks to act against their own interests if they wish to preserve the credibility of these mechanisms for popular participation.

Some such material made it into the final broadcast but only as part of an opening segment in which a smirking Cooper lectured the public about videos that did not belong on national television: "Dressing up in costume was probably not the best way to get taken seriously." Here, participatory culture's power to negate ran up against old media's power to marginalize. Old media still defines which forms of cultural expression are mainstream through its ability to amplify the impact of some user-generated content while labeling other submissions out of bounds. On YouTube, there were thousands of submissions, each equally accessible; on CNN, a corporate selection process had narrowed the field to maybe thirty questions; and the news coverage of the debates might focus on only three or four (maybe only the Snowman video). At each step along the way, the field narrowed, but those messages which survived gain greater attention.

Because the public openly submitted their videos through a participatory media channel like YouTube, the selection process leaves traces. Even if we can't know what happened within the closed-door meetings of the CNN producers, we can see which submitted questions got left out, which issues did not get addressed, and which groups did not get represented. The thousands of posted videos drew significant traffic to YouTube prior to the debates, suggesting that the promise of greater participation did generate greater public interest than more traditional debates.

Afterwards, some who felt excluded or marginalized deployed YouTube as a platform to criticize the news network. AnonymousAmerican, a rotund man in a Mexican wrestling mask who speaks with a working-class accent, posted a video labeled "Fuck You, CNN." He describes his anger over the fact that CNN deployed his masked face but not his words: "This could lead the public to imagine that my question was insulting or irrelevant. We all know that CNN would never air anything insulting such as a host asking the only Moslem member of Congress if he's a terrorist or irrelevant like a very old man spending his show interviewing people like Paris Hilton (That would be Larry King, wouldn't it?)." Links lead to the question he submitted (calling for the immediate withdrawal from Iraq) and other political videos concerning the Bush administration's crackdown on civil liberties. His mask allows him both to speak as an everyman figure and to represent visually the process of political repression; it also links his videos to the Luchador tradition, where Mexican wrestlers often used their masked personas to speak out against social injustice.[13] CNN may have taken away his voice, but YouTube offered him a way to speak back to that silencing power.

THE BIRTH OF A SNOWMAN

Writing in *The Wealth of Networks*, Harvard law professor Yochai Benkler suggests, "What institutions and decisions are considered 'legitimate' and worthy of compliance or participation; what courses of action are attractive; what forms of interaction with others are considered appropriate — these are all understandings negotiated from within a set of shared frames of meaning."[14] All involved in contemporary media recognize that our future culture will be more participatory but there is widespread disagreement

12   Sarah Lee Stirland, "CNN-YouTube Debate Producer Doubts the Wisdom of the Crowd," *Wired*, November 27, 2007, http://www.wired.com/politics/onlinerights/news/2007/11/cnn_debate#.

13   Heather Levi, "The Mask of the Luchador: Wrestling, Politics, and Identity in Mexico," in Nicholas Sammond (ed.), *Steel Chair to the Head: The Pleasures and Pain of Professional Wrestling* (Durham: Duke University Press, 2005), pp. 96–131.

14   Yochai Benkler, *The Wealth of Networks: How Social Production Transforms Markets and Freedom* (New Haven, Conn.: Yale University Press, 2006), pp. 274–275.

about the terms of our participation. A range of public controversies are erupting around the terms of our participation — struggles over intellectual property and file sharing, legal battles between media producers and fans, conflicts between web 2.0 companies and the communities they serve, or disagreements over the nature of citizen participation in televised debates. As average citizens acquire the ability to meaningfully impact the flow of ideas, these new forms of participatory culture change how we see ourselves ("through new eyes — the eyes of someone who could actually interject a thought, a criticism, or a concern into the public debate") and how we see our society (as subject to change as a consequence of our deliberations).[15] What "pissed off" anonymousAmerican at CNN was the way the debates had raised expectations of greater citizen participation and then offered up a high-tech version of *America's Funniest Home Videos*. Such heightened expectations motivated thousands to grab their camcorders or cell phones and produce videos for submission. Some were making their first videos, but many more had acquired their skills as media producers through more mundane and everyday practices, through their production of home movies or their participation in various fan communities, or through media sharing sites.

The strange history of the Snowman illustrates this process at work. The Snowman video was produced by Nathan and Greg Hamel, two brothers from Minneapolis.[16] Their debate video repurposed animations from an earlier, less-politically-oriented video showing a samurai attacking Billiam the Snowman while his young child watched in horror. The name of the Snowman, his high-pitched voice, and the video's aggressive slapstick paid homage to the Mr. Bill videos originally produced by Walter Williams for *Saturday Night Live* in the 1970s. The Mr. Bill segments represented an earlier chapter in the history of the networks' relationship to user-generated content: Williams had submitted a Super-8 reel in response to *Saturday Night Live*'s request for home movies during its first season.[17] The impressed producers hired Williams as a full-time writer, resulting in more than twenty subsequent Mr. Bill segments, all maintaining the low-tech look and feel of his original amateur productions. Williams's subsequent career might have provided

the Hamel brothers with a model for their next step—from broad slapstick towards political satire. Starting in 2004, Williams deployed Mr. Bill as a spokesperson in a series of public service announcements about environmental issues (specifically, the threat to Louisiana wetlands).[18]

The Hamel brothers were surely surprised that Billiam had become the focal point for responses to the debate. Empowered by the media attention, they produced a series of other videos confronting Romney, the man who refused to debate a snowman. While these subsequent videos were not incorporated into the GOP debate, they did attract other media attention. When interviewed by CNN about a video in which Billiam tells Romney to "lighten up slightly," the brothers used their explanation to direct attention at a growing controversy within the blogosphere. During a campaign appearance in New Hampshire, Romney had been photographed holding a supporter's sign, which read "No to Obama, Osama, and Chelsea's Mama" (part of a larger effort to play on xenophobic concerns about Barack's "foreign sounding" name).[19] Another amateur videomaker had captured a confrontation at an Iowa campaign appearance where Romney told a critic of the sign to "lighten up slightly," insisting that he has little control over what his supporters might bring to an event.[20] Bloggers were circulating the video of what they saw as a disingenuous response. This Romney video fits into a larger history of footage captured by amateur videomakers that reached greater public visibility via YouTube and sometimes found its way into mainstream coverage. For example, one popular video showed John McCain joking with supporters, singing "Bomb, Bomb, Bomb Iran" in imitation of a classic rock-and-roll tune. The Hamel brothers were using their five minutes of fame to direct the media's attention onto a brewing controversy that might further undermine Romney's credibility.

Over just a few weeks, the Hamel brothers progressed from sophomoric skit comedy to progressively more savvy interventions into media politics, demonstrating a growing understanding of how media travels through YouTube

15 Ibid.
16 See "Snowman vs. Romney — CNN Reports," http://www. youtube.com/watch?v=NmVIm_JRHH4.
17 "Walter Williams," http://www.mrbill.com/wwbio.html.

18 Cain Burdeau, "Mr. Bill Tapped to Help Save La. Swamps," Associated Press, as reprinted at http://www.mrbill.com/ LASinks.html.
19 http://www.tmz.com/2007/07/21/ mitt-catches-s-t-over-hillary-bashing-sign/.
20 http://www.tmz.com/2007/07/23/romney-on- osama-sign-lighten-up/; http://www.dailykos.com/ story/2007/7/23/31656/4987.

and how YouTube intersects broadcast media. As they did so, they formed an informal alliance with other "citizen journalists" and inspired a range of other amateur producers to create their own snowman videos, including those which included a man wearing a snowman mask, or which recycled footage from old Christmas specials, in hopes that they might get caught up in Billiam's media coverage.

CNN had urged the public to find "creative" new ways to express their concerns, yet the producers clearly saw many of the more colorful videos as the civic equivalent of *Let's Make a Deal* — as so many people in colorful costumes huckstering to get on television. Some certainly were hungry for personal fame, but others were using parody to dramatize legitimate policy concerns. In the case of the Snowman, his question about global warming was not outside the frames of the current political debate, but the use of the animated Snowman as a spokesperson broke with the rationalist discourse that typically characterizes Green politics. The Snowman parody spoofed two of American politics' most cherished rhetorical moves. Snowmen are represented here as one more identity politics group; snowmen are made to "embody" larger societal concerns. We might compare Billiam's attempt to speak about the environment on behalf of snowmen with the oft-cited image of Iron Eyes Cody weeping as a Native American over the littering of the American landscape during the Keep America Beautiful campaign produced for the 1971 Earth Day celebration, or for that matter the ways that Al Gore deployed drowning polar bears to dramatize the threat of global warming in *An Inconvenient Truth*. The video also spoofs the ways both conservative and progressive groups make policy appeals in the name of protecting innocent children from some perceived threat.[21] We might link Billiam's frightened offspring back to the famous LBJ spot depicting a little girl plucking the petals from a daisy over the soundtrack of a countdown to a nuclear bomb blast.

Presidential candidates have long deployed animations and dramatizations as part of the rhetoric of their advertising campaigns, so why should voters be prohibited from using such images in addressing candidates? What's different, perhaps, is the way such videos appropriate popular culture contents (Mr. Bill) as vehicles for their message. As Benkler notes, mass media has so dominated American culture for the past century that people are necessarily going to draw on it as a shared vocabulary as they learn how to use participatory media towards their own ends: "One cannot make new culture ex nihilo. We are, as we are today, as cultural beings, occupying a set of common symbols and stories that are heavily based on the outputs of the industrial period. If we are to make this culture our own, render it legible, and make it into a new platform for our needs and conversations today, we must find a way to cut, paste, and remix present culture."[22]

Parody represents one important mode for reworking mass media materials for alternative purposes. Television commercials, for example, often provide simple, easily recognized templates for representing ideological concerns. A group called SmallMediaXL produced a series of spoofs on the differences between Republicans and Democrats modeled on a popular Mac/PC campaign. While the Apple commercials represent the PC as a stuffed-shirt middle manager and the Mac as a free-thinking hipster, SmallMediaXL depicts Republicans as "very good at looking after the interests of big business" and the Democrats as "being better at the people stuff." Here, the Mac/PC template invites us to comparison shop for presidential candidates, creating new personas who dramatize the differences between the two major parties and the consequences of their policies. No doubt, the producers turned to advertising images and rhetoric to express their critiques, recognizing that the power of Madison Avenue had already ensured that this iconography bore deep cultural resonances and would be widely recognized by a range of potential viewers.

> Parody represents one important mode for reworking mass media materials for alternative purposes.

PARODY IN HIGH PLACES

In "The Spectacularization of Everyday Life," Denise Mann discusses the ways that early television deployed parody to signal its uncomfortable relationship to Hollywood

---

21   For more discussion, see Henry Jenkins, "Childhood Innocence and Other Modern Myths," *The Children's Culture Reader* (New York: New York University Press, 1998), pp. 1–40.

22   Benkler, *The Wealth of Networks*, p. 200.

glamour, positioning its technology — and its own stars — as closer to the public than their cinema counterparts.[23] Early television often spoofed the gap between Hollywood and reality, making fun of its overdramatic style and cliché situations, depicting television characters (such as Lucy in *I Love Lucy*) as fans who want but are denied access to film stars. In the process, these programs helped to negotiate television's emerging social status, stressing the authenticity and everydayness of its own modes of representing the world. Something similar has occurred as digital media has negotiated its own position within the media landscape. As we saw in chapter 4, amateur media makers often signal their averageness through parody, openly acknowledging their limited economic resources or technical means compared to more polished commercial entertainment.

Hollywood stars often embraced self-parody when they appeared in early television, showing that they were also in on the joke and were able to make the adjustments needed to enter our homes on television's terms. Something similar occurs when presidential candidates embrace self-parody as a campaign tactic. In one famous example, the former president and first lady reenacted the final moments of *The Sopranos*. Here, "Hillary" and "Bill" seek to become more like average Americans, tapping a YouTube trend in the aftermath of the HBO series's wrap-up. Through this video's jokes about Hillary's attempts to control her husband's diet and Chelsea's difficulty with parallel parking, the Clintons hoped to shed some of the larger-than-life aura they gained during their years in the White House and to reenter the lifeworld of the voters. A candidate who was otherwise closely associated with a culture war campaign against media violence sought to signal her own fannishness; a candidate often seen as uptight sought to show that she could take a joke.

Or take the case of a Mike Huckabee campaign commercial, originally broadcast but also widely circulated via YouTube. The spot's opening promise of a major policy announcement sets up its punchline: action-film star Chuck Norris is unveiled as the Arkansas governor's policy for securing the U.S./Mexico border. The video thus seeks to establish Huckabee's credentials as a man's man, even as it makes fun of his need to do so. The video

both publicizes — and spoofs — the role of celebrity endorsements in American politics. And the notoriously underfunded Huckabee campaign hoped its grassroots circulation would attract mainstream media attention.

MANUFACTURING DISSENT

Traditional campaign rhetoric stresses the seriousness of the choices Americans face, rather than the pleasures of participating within the political process. Both progressives and conservatives have displayed discomfort with the tone and content of popular culture. Most attempts to mobilize popular culture towards political ends are read contemptuously as efforts to dumb down civic discourse.

In a recent book, *Dream: Re-imaging Progressive Politics in an Age of Fantasy*, Stephen Duncombe offers a different perspective, arguing that politicos need to move beyond a knee-jerk critique of popular entertainment as "weapons of mass distraction" and learn strategies for "appropriating, co-opting and most important, transforming the techniques of spectacular capitalism into tools for social change."[24] Playing on a Walter Lippman phrase brought back into public awareness through Noam Chomsky's critique of propaganda (*Manufacturing Consent*), Duncombe calls on progressives to learn new strategies for "manufacturing dissent": "Given the progressive ideals of egalitarianism and a politics that values the input of everyone, our dreamscapes will not be created by media-savvy experts of the left and then handed down to the rest of us to watch, consume, and believe. Instead, our spectacles will be participatory: dreams that the public can mold and shape themselves. They will be active: spectacles that work only if the people help create them. They will be open-ended: setting stages to ask questions and leaving silences to formulate answers. And they will be transparent: dreams that one knows are dreams but which still have power to attract and inspire. And, finally, the spectacles we create will not cover over or replace reality and truth but perform and amplify it."[25]

Duncombe cites Billionaires for Bush as a primary example of this new kind of political spectacle. Billionaires for Bush used street theater to call attention to issues, such as campaign finance reform, media concentration, and tax cuts for the wealthy. Seeking to dodge attempts by

23   Denise Mann, "The Spectacularization of Everyday Life: Recycling Hollywood Stars and Fans in Early Television Variety Shows," in Lynn Spigel and Denise Mann (eds.), *Private Screenings: Television and the Female Consumer* (Minneapolis: University of Minnesota Press, 1992), pp. 41–70.

24   Stephen Duncombe, *Dream: Re-Imagining Progressive Politics in an Age of Fantasy* (New York: New Press, 2007), p. 16.

25   Ibid., p. 17.

conservative critics to paint their efforts as "class warfare," the group adopted a more playful posture, dressing up like cartoon-character versions of the wealthy, showing up at campaign stops, and chanting along with other Bush supporters. These "Groucho Marxists" encouraged supporters and bystanders alike to enter into the joking process, not simply to make fun of Bush but to see political activism as a fun activity. As we described in chapter 6, similarly playful tactics were adopted by True Majority during the 2004 campaign — including their spoof of *The Apprentice* to imagine George W. Bush being fired for incompetency.

As YouTube's cultural visibility has increased, more activists have adopted True Majority's "serious fun" approach, making parody videos as a more playful and pleasurable mode of political discourse. Consider, for example, how the HP Alliance, discussed in chapter 5, formed a partnership with Wal-Mart Watch, a group backed by the Service Employees International Union as a focal point for criticism for the retail chain's employment practices. The HP Alliance and the Boston-based comedy troupe the Late Night Players translated the union's agenda into a series of campy, over-the-top videos depicting further adventures impacting Hogwarts and the wizarding world. Harry and Hermione (who is played in drag) discover that the traditional business in Diagon Alley has been closed by "you know which superstore." If they want to keep "magic" in their community, Harry and his friends must do battle with Lord Waldemarte (whose Smiley Face exterior masks his evil intentions, such as exploiting his house elves, driving out local competitors, and refusing to provide health care to his underlings). Andrew Slack of the alliance told a *Chicago Tribune* reporter, "We don't want anyone feeling that they're being lectured at. We want to break away from that to what they're interested in, and humans tend to be interested in laughing."[26] The circulation of these spoofs, in turn, drove traffic back to the Wal-Mart Watch Website, where one could find a more straightforward discussion of their protest against the company.

BARELY POLITICAL?

Most writing about the CNN/YouTube debates gets framed in terms of amateur media makers and commercial network, overlooking how many videos were submitted by semiprofessionals or even by editorial cartoonists for various newspapers and magazines. We might better understand the videos produced for the debates as emerging from the mixed media economy Yochai Benkler describes in *The Wealth of Networks*. Media producers with different motives — governmental agencies, activist groups, educational institutions, nonprofit organizations, fan communities — operate side by side, using the same production tools and distribution networks. YouTube constitutes a shared portal through which these diverse groups come together to circulate media content and learn from each other's practices. In this shared distribution space, short-term tactical alliances between such groups are commonplace. On YouTube, it becomes increasingly difficult to distinguish between videos produced by fans as a playful tribute to a favorite media property like *Harry Potter*, those produced by average citizens seeking to shape the agenda of the campaigns, those produced by activist organizations to promote a specific political objective, and those produced by small-scale comedy groups seeking to break into the commercial mainstream. Such distinctions may not necessarily be productive, given the ways that a range of grassroots intermediaries grab content of all kinds and recirculate it through a range of blogs, discussion boards, and social network sites often without regard to the circumstances of its origin.

A case in point might be the series of Obama Girl videos. The initial video, "I Got a Crush ... on Obama," was produced by advertising executives Ben Relies and Rick Friedrick in collaboration with actress and model Amber Lee Ettinger and singer/comedian Leah Kauffman. These media professionals wanted to use their sexy and irreverent content to generate a buzz that might draw attention to a newly launched online comedy site. In the original video, the scantily clad Obama Girl describes how she fell in love with Obama during his talk to the 2004 Democratic convention, signals her growing passion for the man and his ideas through stroking his campaign posters and kissing his photograph on a Web site, and has the candidate's name printed on her panties. News commentators often reduce women's political interests to which male candidate is most attractive, reading them less as concerned citizens and more as groupies for the campaigns. The Obama Girl videos turn such representations around, transforming the candidates into beefcake embodiments of these women's erotic fantasies. The rapid-paced images and the multilayered wordplay reward careful decoding, requiring consumers to

26 Sandra M. Jones, "Wal-Mart Case as Dark Lord," *Chicago Tribune*, July 1, 2007, p. xx.

learn more about the campaigns in order to "get" the jokes. But like the other media "snacks" associated with YouTube, they may also be consumed on a more casual level, and we cannot easily account for the range of meanings which emerged as these videos were spread within different online communities, passed between friends and co-workers, or mobilized by activist groups and campaign workers.[27]

The buzz pushed the giggling Obama Girl onto the cable news circuit, where she became one more pundit commenting on the election season. The producers announced a partnership with Voter Vision, a multimedia political campaign marketing program which wanted to demonstrate the political value of "viral video." Somewhere along the way, the videos had moved from entertainment to activism, from a parody of the campaign into something that was explicitly intended for activist purposes. The slippery nature of such distinctions is suggested by the company's name — "Barely Political."

This hybrid media environment and the active circulation of content beyond its points of origin make it hard to tell where any given video is coming from—in both the literal and the metaphoric sense. Increasingly, we are seeing fake grassroots media being produced by powerful institutions or economic interests—what has become known as "Astroturf."

Al Gore's Penguin Army is perhaps the best known example of an Astroturf Internet parody. This cut-up animation spoof of *An Inconvenient Truth* was first posted by a user named Toutsmith from Beverly Hills, but further investigation revealed that it was professionally produced by the DCI Group, a commercial advertising firm whose clients included General Motors and Exxon Mobil; the firm also had historically, produced content for the Republican Party.[28]

One of the best known Internet parodies of the 2007 campaign season, a remix of Apple's "1984" commercial where Hillary Clinton stands in for Big Brother, has a similarly dubious history. The video turned out to be the work of Phil de Vellis, an employee of Blue State Digital, an Internet company that provided technology to both the Richardson and Obama presidential campaigns. As both the company and the campaigns sought to distance

themselves from his activities, de Vellis was forced to resign his job. He told the readers of *The Huffington Post*:

> I made the "Vote Different" ad because I wanted to express my feelings about the Democratic primary, and because I wanted to show that an individual citizen can affect the process. There are thousands of other people who could have made this ad, and I guarantee that more ads like it — by people of all political persuasions — will follow. This shows that the future of American politics rests in the hands of ordinary citizens. The campaigns had no idea who made it — not the Obama campaign, not the Clinton campaign, nor any other campaign. I made the ad on a Sunday afternoon in my apartment using my personal equipment (a Mac and some software), uploaded it to YouTube, and sent links around to blogs. ... This ad was not the first citizen ad, and it will not be the last. The game has changed.[29]

The game has indeed changed, but it isn't necessarily clear what game is being played here or by whom. Will we see other such videos circulated by groups or campaigns which hope to maintain a "plausible deniability" about their roles in generating their content? What parallels might be drawn between this material which circulates without an acknowledged source and the "swift boat" efforts four years earlier which similarly claimed independence from the Bush campaign?

PARODY AS PEDAGOGY

We cannot reduce the complexity of this hybrid media ecology to simple distinctions between top-down and bottom-up, professional and amateur, insider or outsider, old and new media, Astroturf and grassroots, or even "serious fun" and "barely political." In such a world, grassroots and mainstream media might pursue parallel interests, even as they act autonomously. Consider, for example, a video which TechPresident identifies as one of the top

---

27   *Wired* represented YouTube as central to a new culture of media snacks in "Snack Attack!," *Wired*, March 2007, http://www.wired.com/wired/archive/15.03/snack.html.

28   *Wall Street Journal*, August 3, 2006, http://online.wsj.com/public/article/SB115457177198425388-0TpYE6bU6EGvfSqtP8_hHjJJ77I_20060810.html?mod=blogs.

29   Phil de Vellis, aka Parkridge47, "I Made the 'Vote Different' Ad," *The Huffington Post*, March 21, 2007, http://www.huffingtonpost.coin/phil-de-vellis-aka-parkridge/i-made-the-vote-differen_b_43989.html.

"voter-generated videos" of 2007. The video starts with a clip of Joseph Biden joking during one debate appearance that every sentence Rudolph Giuliani utters includes "a noun, a verb, and 9/11," and follows with a database of clips showing the former New York mayor referencing 9/11. The video was produced and distributed by Talking Points Memo, one of the most widely read progressive political blogs. In many ways, all the parody does is amplify

institutions. Under what he calls the "engaged youth" paradigm, there is no such rigid separation between the kinds of civic engagement these young people find through their involvement in game guilds or the expressive freedom they experienced through circulating their do-it-yourself videos on YouTube and other forms of citizenly discourse. Young people are finding their voice through their play with popular culture and then deploying it through their

---

Young people have come to see YouTube as supporting individual and collective expression; they often feel excluded by the policy-wonk language of traditional politics and the inside-the-beltway focus of much campaign news coverage.

Biden's own political message, supporting his claims that Giuliani was exploiting a national tragedy for his own political gains. The ready access of digital search tools and online archives makes it easy for small scale operators, like the bloggers, to scan through vast amounts of news footage and assemble clips to illustrate their ideas in a matter of a few days. Such rapid response practices emerged late in the 2004 presidential campaign, when both Democratic and Republican supporters used amateur videos to support their competing interpretations of the presidential debates (such as a series of videos disproving Dick Cheney's claim that he had never previously met John Edwards).

Often, these playful tactics get described in terms of the need to adopt new rhetorical practices to reach the so-called *digital natives*, a generation of young people who have grown up in a world where the affordances of participatory media technologies have been commonplace. Researchers debate whether these young people are, in fact, politically engaged since their civic lives take very different forms from those of previous generations. They are, for example, more likely to get information about the world through news comedy shows and blogs than through traditional journalism. There is conflicting evidence about their willingness to vote, but most research shows that they are very concerned about issues such as the war and the environment and willing to translate their concerns into community service. W. Lance Bennett contrasts two different framings of this data: under what he calls the "disengaged youth paradigm," forms of participatory culture are seen as "distracting" emerging citizens from more serious inquiry, seducing them with the freedoms offered by virtual worlds rather than encouraging them to transform real-world

participation in public service projects or various political movements.[30]

The activist deployment of parody videos can be understood as an attempt to negotiate between these two perspectives. Young people have come to see YouTube as supporting individual and collective expression; they often feel excluded by the policy-wonk language of traditional politics and the inside-the-beltway focus of much campaign news coverage. Parody offers an alternative language through which policy debates and campaign pitches might be framed, one that, as Duncombe suggests, models itself on popular culture but responds to different ethical and political imperatives. The often "politically incorrect" style of Internet parody flies in the face of the language and assumptions by which previous generations debated public policy. Such videos may not look like "politics as usual," yet the people who produced and circulated these videos want to motivate young voters to participate in the electoral process. Such a model sees Internet parodies as springboards for larger conversations — whether through blogs and discussion forums online or face-to-face between people gathered around a water cooler.

These parody videos bring the issues down to a human scale, depicting Bush as an incompetent reality show contestant, Romney as someone who's afraid to go man-to-man with a snowman, Giuliani as obsessed with 9/11, or Edwards as a narcissist with fluffy hair. Duncombe has

---

30   W. Lance Bennett, "Changing Citizenship in a Digital Age," in W. Lance Bennett (ed.), *Civic Life Online: Learning How Digital Media Can Engage Youth* (Cambridge, Mass.: MIT Press, 2008), pp. 2–3.

argued that news comedy shows, such as *The Daily Show* or *The Colbert Report*, foster a kind of civic literacy, teaching viewers to ask skeptical questions about core political values and the rhetorical process that embodies them: "In doing this they hold out the possibility of something else, that is, they create an opening for a discussion on what sort of a political process wouldn't be a joke. In doing this they're setting the stage for a very democratic sort of dialogue: one that asks questions rather than simply asserts the definitive truth."[31] We might connect Duncombe's argument back to Benkler's larger claim that living within a more participatory culture changes how we understand our place in the world, even if we never choose to actively participate. Yet, there is also the risk, as Duncombe points out, that such parody "can, just as easily, lead into a resigned acceptance that all politics are just a joke and the best we can hope for is to get a good laugh out of it all." Here, skepticism gives way to cynicism. Nothing ensures that a politics based in parody will foster one and not the other.

THE DOWNSIDES OF DIGITAL DEMOCRACY

If this chapter can be read as a defense of the Snowman as a meaningful and valid participant in a debate about the future of American democracy, it is at best a qualified defense. I have tried to move us from an understanding of the CNN/YouTube debates through a lens of digital revolution in favor of a model based on the ever more complicated interplay of old and new media and on the hybrid media ecology that has emerged as groups with different motives and goals interact through shared media portals. I have tried to move beyond thinking of the Snowman as trivializing public policy debates towards seeing parody as a strategy which a range of different stakeholders (official and unofficial, commercial and grassroots, entertainers and activists) are deploying towards their own ends, each seeking to use YouTube as a distribution hub.

While I believe very firmly in the potential for participatory culture to serve as a catalyst for revitalizing civic life, we still fall short of the full realization of those ideals. As John McMurria has noted, the democratic promise of YouTube as a site open to everyone's participation is tempered by

the reality that participation is unevenly distributed across the culture. An open platform does not necessarily ensure diversity.[32] The mechanisms of user-moderation work well when they help us to evaluate collectively the merits of individual contributions and thus push to the top the "best" content; they work badly when they preempt the expression of minority perspectives and hide unpopular and alternative content from view.

Chuck Tyron has argued that the speed with which such videos are produced and circulated can undercut the desired pedagogical and activist goals, sparking short-lived and superficial conversations among consumers who are always looking over their shoulders for the next new thing.[33] To put it mildly, the user comments posted on YouTube fall far short of Habermasian ideals of the public sphere, as was suggested by one blogger's parody of the CNN/YouTube debates. Here, the candidates interact in ways more commonly associated with the online responses to the posted videos:

> *Sen. Christopher Dodd*: omg that video was totaly gay
>
> *Sen. Barack Obama*: Shut up Dodd thats offensive when u say gay like that.
>
> *Former Sen. Mike Gravel*: Check out my vids at youtube.com/user/gravel2008.
>
> *Rep. Dennis Kucinich*: to answre your question bush is a facist who only wants more power. hes not even the president you knopw, cheny is. i would b different because i would have a vice presidant that doesnt just try and control everything from behind the seens/
>
> *Sen. Hillary Clinton*: CHENEY CANT BE PRESIDENT BECUZ THE CONSTITUTION SAYS THE VICE PRESIDENT IS NOT THE PRESIDENT WHY DON'T U TRY READING THE CONSTITUTION SOMETIME??????!!!![34]

In this parody, YouTube is associated more with mangled syntax, poor spelling, misinformation, and fractured

31 Henry Jenkins, "Manufacturing Dissent: An Interview with Stephen Duncombe," Confessions of an Aca-Fan, July 23, 2007, http://henryjenkins.org/2007/07/manufacturing_dissent_an_inter.html.

32 John McMurria, "The YouTube Community," FlowTV, October 20, 2006, http://flowtv.org/?p=48.

33 Chuck Tyron, "Is Internet Politics Better Off Than It Was Four Years Ago?," FlowTV, September 29, 2007, http://flowtv.org/?p=797.

34 "Transcript: CNN/YouTube Democratic Debate," Defective Yeti, http://www.defectiveyeti.com/archives/002172.html.

logic than with any degree of political self-consciousness or citizenry discourse. Yet, YouTube cannot be understood in isolation from a range of other blogging and social network sites where the videos often get discussed in greater depth and substance.

The insulting tone of this depicted interaction captures something of the no-holds-barred nature of political dialogue on YouTube. In an election whose candidates include women, African Americans and Hispanics, Catholics and Mormons, groups which have historically been under-represented in American political life, online parody often embraces racist, sexist, and xenophobic humor, which further discourages minority participation or conversations across ideological differences. One popular genre of Internet parodies depicts insult matches between Hillary Clinton and Barack Obama or their supporters (typically represented as women and minorities). One prototype of this style of humor was a MADtv sketch, which drew more than half a million viewers when it was posted online. The sketch ends with a Giuliani supporter clapping as the two Democratic campaigns rip each other apart, suggesting an interpretation focused on the dangers of party infighting. But this frame figures little in the public response to the video, whether in the form of comments posted on the site (such as one person who complained about being forced "to pick between a Nigger and a woman") or videos generated by amateur media producers (which often push the original's already over-the-line humor to even nastier extremes). Here, "politically incorrect" comedy provides an opportunity for the public to laugh at the unseemly spectacle of a struggle between women and African Americans, or may offer a justification for trotting out ancient but still hurtful slurs and allegations — women are inappropriate for public office because of, haw, "that time of the month"; black men are irresponsible because they are, haha, likely to desert their families, to go to jail, or to experiment with drugs.

Another Web site posted a range of Photoshop collages about the campaign submitted by readers, including ones showing Hillary in a yellow jump suit waving a samurai sword on a mocked-up poster for *Kill Bill*, Obama depicted as Borat in a parody which plays upon his foreign sounding name, and Obama depicted as a chauffeur driving around

Mrs. Clinton in an ad for a remake of *Driving Miss Daisy*.[35] Such parodies use humor to put minority candidates and voters back in "their place," suggesting that women and blacks are inappropriate candidates for the nation's highest office. This problem may originate from the interplay between old and new media: racist and sexist assumptions structured the original MADtv segment, self-consciously playing with racial and gender stereotypes even as it reproduces them; these racist and sexist assumptions may account for why Internet fans were drawn to it in the first place; the subsequent reactions amplify its problematic aspects, though the amateur responses stoop lower than network standards and practices would allow.

In doing so, Internet parody producers fall far short of the "ethical spectacles" Duncombe advocates: "A progressive ethical spectacle will be one that is directly democratic, breaks down hierarchies, fosters community, allows for diversity, and engages with reality while asking what new realities might be possible."[36] By contrast, too many of the parody videos currently circulating on YouTube do the opposite — promoting traditional authority, preserving gender and racial hierarchies, fragmenting communities, discouraging diversity, and refusing to imagine any kind of social order other than the one which has long dominated American government. Speaking to a *Mother Jones* reporter, Lawrence Lessig explained, "If you look at the top 100 things on YouTube or Google it's not like it's compelling art. There's going to be a lot of questions about whether it's compelling politics either. We can still play ugly in lots of ways, but the traditional ways of playing ugly are sort of over."[37] All of this is to suggest that Romney would have faced things far more frightening than snowmen if he had ventured into the uncharted and untamed space of YouTube rather than the filtered and protected space provided him by CNN.

> For better and for worse, this is what democracy looks like in the era of convergence culture.

35 Each of these examples taken from images submitted to http://political humor.about.com/.

36 Duncombe, *Dream*, p. 126.

37 "Interview with Lawrence Lessig, Stanford Law Professor, Creative Commons Chair," *Mother Jones*, June 29, 2007, http://www.motherjones.com/interview/2007/07/lawrence_lessig.html.

The advent of new production tools and distribution channels have lowered barriers of entry into the marketplace of ideas. These shifts place resources for activism and social commentary into the hands of everyday citizens, resources which were once the exclusive domain of the candidates, the parties, and the mass media. These citizens have increasingly turned towards parody as a rhetorical practice which allows them to express their skepticism towards "politics as usual," to break out of the exclusionary language through which many discussions of public policy are conducted, and to find a shared language of borrowed images that mobilize what they know as consumers to reflect on the political process. Such practices blur the lines between producer and consumer, between consumers and citizens, between the commercial and the amateur, and between education, activism, and entertainment, as groups with competing and contradictory motives deploy parody to serve their own ends. These tactics are drawing many into the debates who would once have paid little or no attention to the campaign process. As they have done so, they have brought to the surface both inequalities in participation and deep-rooted hostilities between groups within American society. Democracy has always been a messy business: the politics of parody offers us no easy way out, yet it does offer us a chance to rewrite the rules and transform the language through which our civic life is conducted.

For better and for worse, this is what democracy looks like in the era of convergence culture. Those of us who care about the future of participatory culture as a mechanism for promoting diversity and enabling democracy do the world no favor if we ignore the ways that our current culture falls far short of these goals. Too often, there is a tendency to read all grassroots media as somehow "resistant" to dominant institutions rather than acknowledging that citizens sometimes deploy bottom-up means to keep others down. Too often, we have fallen into the trap of seeing democracy as an "inevitable" outcome of technological change rather than as something which we need to fight to achieve with every tool at our disposal. Too often, we have sought to deflect criticism of grassroots culture rather than trying to identify and resolve conflicts and contradictions which might prevent it from achieving its full potentials. Too often, we have celebrated those alternative voices which are being brought into the marketplace of ideas without considering which voices remain trapped outside. As this book has suggested, the current moment of media change is bringing about transformations in the way other core institutions operate. Every day we see new signs that old practices are subject to change. If we are to move towards what Pierre Lévy called an "achievable utopia," we must continue to ask hard questions about the practices and institutions which are taking their place. We need to be attentive to the ethical dimensions by which we are generating knowledge, producing culture, and engaging in politics together.

CHAPTER 6
Dumbed Down

There's nothing as trustworthy as the ordinary mind of the ordinary man.

— Political banner for
Lonesome Rhodes,
A Face in the Crowd (1957)

Chapter 6. Dumbed Down

Recommended Film

A Face In the Crowd (Elia Kazan 1957)

Media Models

The Meme, The Network, The Spectacle

Chapter Summary

Susan Jacoby explains how American society is being
"dumbed down" by the rampant anti-intellectualism
of media culture.

Mark Bauerlein argues that the proliferation of electronic
screens is not leading to increased enlightenment
among the digital youth.

The Way We Live Now: Just Us Folks

from *The Age of American Unreason*

— Susan Jacoby

The word is everywhere, a plague spread by the President of the United States, television anchors, radio talk show hosts, preachers in megachurches, self-help gurus, and anyone else attempting to demonstrate his or her identification with ordinary, presumably wholesome American values. Only a few decades ago, Americans were addressed as people or, in the more distant past, ladies and gentlemen. Now we are all folks. Television commentators, apparently confusing themselves with the clergy, routinely declare that "our prayers go out to those folks" — whether the folks are victims of drought, hurricane, flood, child molestation, corporate layoffs, identity theft, or the war in Iraq (as long as the victims are American and not Iraqi). Irony is reserved for fiction. Philip Roth, in *The Plot Against America* — a dark historical reimagining of a nation in which Charles Lindbergh defeats Franklin D. Roosevelt in the 1940 presidential election — confers the title "Just Folks" on a Lindbergh program designed to de-Judaize young urban Jews by sending them off to spend their summers in wholesome rural and Christian settings.

While the word "folks" was once a colloquialism with no political meaning, there is no escaping the political meaning of the term when it is reverently invoked by public officials in twenty-first-century America. After the terrorist bombings in London on July 7, 2005, President Bush assured Americans, "I've been in contact with our homeland security folks and I instructed them to be in touch with local and state officials about the facts of what took place here and in London and to be extra vigilant as our folks start heading to work." Bush went on to observe that "the

contrast couldn't be clearer, between the intentions of those of us who care deeply about human rights and human liberty, and those who've got such evil in their heart that they will take the lives of innocent folks." Those evil terrorists. Our innocent folks. Even homeland security officials, who — one lives in hope — are supposed to be highly trained experts, cannot escape the folkish designation. All of the 2008 presidential contenders pepper their speeches with appeals to folks, but only John Edwards, who grew up poor in North Carolina, sounds as if he was raised around people who actually used the word in everyday conversation. Every time Hillary Rodham Clinton, brought up in a conservative Republican household in an upper-middle-class suburb of Chicago, utters the word "folks," she sounds like a hovering parent trying to ingratiate herself with her children's friends by using teenage slang.

The specific political use of folks as an exclusionary and inclusionary signal designed to make the speaker sound like one of the boys or girls, is symptomatic of a debasement of public speech inseparable from a more general erosion of American cultural standards. Casual, colloquial language also conveys an implicit denial of the seriousness of whatever issue is being debated: talking about folks going off to war is the equivalent of describing rape victims as girls (unless the victims are, in fact, little girls and not grown women). Look up any important presidential speech in the history of the United States before 1980 and you will not find one patronizing appeal to folks. Imagine: *We here highly resolve that these folks shall not have died in vain ... and that government of the folks, by the folks, for the folks, shall not perish from the earth.* In the 1950s, even though there were no orators of Lincoln's eloquence on the political scene, voters still expected their leaders to employ dignified, if not necessarily erudite, speech. Adlai Stevenson may have sounded too much like an intellectual to suit the taste of average Americans, but proper grammar and respectful forms of address were mandatory for anyone seeking high office.

The gold standard of presidential oratory for adult Americans in the fifties was the memory of Roosevelt, whose patrician accent in no way detracted from his extraordinary ability to make a direct connection with ordinary people. It is impossible to read the transcripts of FDR's famous fireside chats and not mourn the passing of a civic culture that appealed to Americans to expand their knowledge and understanding instead of pandering to the lowest common denominator. Calling for sacrifice and altruism in perilous times, Roosevelt would no more have addressed his fellow citizens as folks than he would have uttered an obscenity over the radio. At the end of 1940, attempting to prepare his countrymen for the coming of war, the president spoke in characteristic terms to the public.

> Tonight, in the presence of a world crisis, my mind goes back eight years to a night in the midst of a domestic crisis. … I well remember that while I sat in my study in the White House, preparing to talk to the people of the United States, I had before my eyes the picture of all those Americans with whom I was talking. I saw the workmen in the mills, the mines, the factories; the girl behind the counter; the small shopkeeper; the farmer doing his spring plowing; the widows and the old men wondering about their life's savings. I tried to convey to the great mass of the American people what the banking crisis meant to them in their daily lives.
>
> Tonight I want to do the same thing, with the same people, in this new crisis which faces America. …
>
> We must be the great arsenal of democracy. For us this is an emergency as serious as war itself. We must apply ourselves to the task with the same resolution, the same sense of urgency, the same spirit of patriotism and sacrifice as we would show were we at war. …

> As president of the United States I call for that national effort. I call for it in the name of this nation which we love and honor and which we are privileged and proud to serve. I call upon our people with absolute confidence that our common cause will greatly succeed.[1]

Substitute folks for people, farmer, old men, and widows, and the relationship between the abandonment of dignified public speech and the degradation of the political process becomes clear. To call for resolution and a spirit of patriotism and sacrifice is to call upon people to rise above their everyday selves and to behave as true citizens. To keep telling Americans that they are just folks is to expect nothing special — a ratification and exaltation of the quotidian that is one of the distinguishing marks of anti-intellectualism in any era.

The debasement of the nation's speech is evident in virtually everything broadcast and podcast on radio, television, and the Internet. In this true, all-encompassing public square, homogenized language and homogenized thought reinforce each other in circular fashion. As George Orwell noted in 1946, "A man may take to drink because he feels himself a failure, and then fail all the more completely because he drinks. It is rather the same thing that is happening to the English language. It becomes ugly and inaccurate because our thoughts are foolish, but the slovenliness of our language makes it easier for us to have foolish thoughts."[2] In this continuous blurring of clarity and intellectual discrimination, political speech is always ahead of the curve — especially because today's media possess the power to amplify and spread error with an efficiency that might have astonished even Orwell. Consider the near-universal substitution, by the media and politicians, of "troop" and "troops" for "soldier" and "soldiers." As every dictionary makes plain, the word "troop" is always a collective noun; the "s" is added when referring to a particularly large military force. Yet each night on the television news, correspondents report that "X troops were killed in Iraq today." This is more than a grammatical error; turning a soldier — an individual with whom one may identify — into an anonymous-sounding troop encourages the public

1   Franklin Delano Roosevelt, *Fireside Chats* (New York, 1995), pp.48–49, 62–63.
2   George Orwell, "Politics and the English Language," *Horizon*, 76 (London, 1946); www.orwell.ru/library/essays/politics/english/e_polit.

to think about war and its casualties in a more abstract way. Who lays a wreath at the Tomb of the Unknown Troop? It is difficult to determine exactly how, why, or when this locution began to enter the common language. Soldiers were almost never described as troops during the Second World War, except when a large military operation (like the Allied landing on D-Day) was being discussed, and the term remained extremely uncommon throughout the Vietnam era. My guess is that some dimwits in the military and the media (perhaps the military media) decided, at some point in the 1980s, that the word "soldier" implied the masculine gender and that all soldiers, out of respect for the growing presence of women in the military, must henceforth be called troops. Like unremitting appeals to folks, the victory of troops over soldiers offers an impressive illustration of the relationship between fuzzy thinking and the debasement of everyday speech.

By debased speech, I do not mean bad grammar, although there is plenty of that on every street corner and talk show, or the prevalence of obscene language, so widespread as to be deprived of force and meaning at those rare times when only an epithet will do. Nor am I talking about Spanglish and so-called Black English, those favorite targets of cultural conservatives — although I share the conservatives' belief that public schools ought to concentrate on teaching standard English. But the standard of standard American English, and the ways in which private speech now mirrors the public speech emanating from electronic and digital media, is precisely the problem. Debased speech in the public square functions as a kind of low-level toxin, imperceptibly coarsening our concept of what is and is not acceptable until someone says something so revolting — Don Imus's notorious description of female African-American college basketball players as "nappy-headed hos" is the perfect example — that it produces a rare, and always brief, moment of public consciousness about the meaning and power of words. Predictably, the Imus affair proved to be a missed opportunity for a larger cultural conversation about the level of all American public discourse and language. People only wanted to talk about bigotry — a worthy and vital conversation, to be sure, but one that quickly degenerated into a comparative lexicon of racial and ethnic victimology. Would Imus have been fired

for calling someone a faggot or a dyke? What if he had only called the women hos, without the additional racial insult of nappy-headed? And how about Muslims? Didn't Ann Coulter denigrate them as "ragheads" (a slur of which I was blissfully unaware until an indignant multiculturalist reported it on the op-ed page of *The New York Times*).[3] The awful reality is that all of these epithets, often accompanied by the F-word, are the common currency of public and private speech in today's America. They are used not only because many Americans are infected by various degrees of bigotry but because nearly all Americans are afflicted by a poverty of language that cheapens humor and serious discourse alike. The hapless Imus unintentionally made this point when he defended his remarks on grounds that they had been made within a humorous context. "This is a comedy show," he said, "not a racial rant." Wrong on both counts. Nothing reveals a lack of comic inventiveness more reliably than the presence of reflexive epithets, eliciting snickers not because they exist within any intentional "context" but simply because they are crass words that someone is saying out loud.

Part of Imus's audience was undoubtedly composed of hard-core racists and misogynists, but many more who found his rants amusing were responding in the spirit of eight-year-olds laughing at farts. Imus's "serious" political commentary was equally pedestrian. He frequently enjoined officials who had incurred his displeasure to "just shut up," displaying approximately the same level of sophistication as Vice President Dick Cheney when he told Senator Patrick J. Leahy on the Senate floor, "Go fuck yourself." As the genuinely humorous Russell Baker observes, previous generations of politicians (even if they had felt free to issue the physically impossible Anglo-Saxon injunction in a public forum) would have been shamed by their lack of verbal inventiveness. In the 1890s, Speaker of the House Thomas Reed took care of one opponent by observing that "with a few more brains he could be a halfwit." Of another politician, Reed remarked, "He never opens his mouth without subtracting from the sum of hu-

The debasement of the nation's speech is evident in virtually everything broadcast and podcast on radio, television, and the Internet.

3   Robert Wright, "Shock Talk Without Apologies," *New York Times*, April 14, 2007.

man intelligence."[4] Americans once heard (or rather, read) such genuinely witty remarks and tried to emulate that wit. Today we parrot the witless and halfwitted language used by politicians and radio shock jocks alike.

The mirroring process extends far beyond political language, which has always existed at a certain remove from colloquial speech. The toxin of commercially standardized speech, now stocks the private vault of words and images we draw on to think about and to describe everything from the ridiculous to the sublime. One of the most frequently butchered sentences on television programs, for instance, is the incomparable Liberace's cynically funny, "I cried all the way to the bank" — a line he trotted out whenever serious critics lambasted his candelabra-lit performances as kitsch.* The witty observation has been transformed into the senseless catchphrase, "I laughed all the way to the bank" — often used as a non sequitur after news stories about lottery winners. In their dual role as creators of public language and as microphones amplifying and disseminating the language many American already use in their daily lives, the media constitute a *perpetuum mobile*, the perfect example of a machine in which cause and effect can never be separated. A sports broadcaster, speaking of an athlete who just signed a multi-year, multi-million-dollar contract, says, "He laughed all the way to the bank." A child idly listening — perhaps playing a video game, on a computer at the same time — absorbs the meaningless statement without thinking and repeats it, spreading it to others who might one day be interviewed on television and say, "I laughed all the way to the bank," thereby transmitting the virus to new listeners. It is all reminiscent of the exchange among Alice, the March Hare, and the Mad Hatter in *Alice's Adventures in Wonderland*. "Then you should say what you mean," the March Hare tells Alice. "'I do,' Alice hastily replied; 'at least — at least I mean what I say — that's the same thing, you know.'" The Hatter

chimes in, "Not the same thing a bit! Why, you might just as well say that 'I see what I eat' is the same thing as 'I eat what I see'!" In an ignorant and anti-intellectual culture, people eat mainly what they see.

It is impossible to define anti-intellectualism as a historical force, or a continuing American reality, in a manner as precise or useful as the kind of definition that might be supplied for, say, abolitionism or feminism. In Hofstadter's view, anti-intellectualism is not an independent historical or social phenomenon but the consequence of some other goal — such as the desire to extend educational opportunities to a broader population or to wrest control of religious life from ecclesiastical hierarchies. "Hardly anyone believes himself to be against thought and culture," Hofstadter writes. "Men, do not rise in the morning, grin at themselves in their mirrors, and say: 'Ah, today I shall torment an intellectual and strangle an idea!'"[5] This seems to me an overly charitable portrait of anti-intellectualism — then and now. It is surely true that few people like to consider themselves enemies of thought and culture. Bush, after all, called himself the "education president" with a straight face while simultaneously declaring, without a trace of self-consciousness or self-criticism, that he rarely read newspapers because that would expose him to "opinions."*

However, there are ways of trying to strangle ideas that do not involve straightforward attempts at censorship or intimidation. The suggestion that there is something sinister, even un-American, about intense devotion to ideas, reason, logic, evidence, and precise language is one of them. Just before the 2004 presidential election, the journalist Ron Suskind reported a chilling conversation with a senior Bush aide, who told Suskind that members of the press were part of what the Bush administration considers "the reality-based community" — those who "believe that solutions emerge from judicious study of discernible reality." But, the aide emphasized, "That's not the way the world

---

* Liberace first used this line in 1957, when he won a libel judgment against the British tabloid *Daily Mirror*, which published a column calling the entertainer a "deadly, winking, sniggering, snuggling, chromium-plated, scent-impregnated, luminous, giggling, fruit-flavored, mincing, ice-covered heap of mother love." The British court concluded that the article had libelously implied that Liberace was a homosexual (which of course he was, but there was no proof).

4   Russell Baker, "Talking It Up," *New York Review of Books*, May 11, 2006.

* On September 22, 2003, the Associated Press reported that President Bush scans headlines but rarely reads entire newspaper stories, which would expose him to nonobjective "opinions." He prefers that White House staffers provide him with a more "objective" digest of the daily news.

5   Richard Hofstadter, *Anti-Intellectualism in American Life* (New York, 1963), p. 22.

really works anymore. We're an empire now, and when we act, we create our own reality. And while you're studying that reality — judiciously, as you will — we'll act again, creating other new realities, which you can study too. … We're history's actors … and you, all of you, will be left to just study what we do."[6] The explicit distinction between those who are fit only to study and those who are history's actors not only expresses contempt for intellectuals but also denigrates anyone who requires evidence, rather than power and emotion, as justification for public policy.

Anti-intellectualism in any era can best be understood as a complex of symptoms with multiple causes, and the persistence of symptoms over time possesses the potential to turn a treatable, livable condition into a morbid disease affecting the entire body politic. It is certainly easy to point to a wide variety of causes — some old and some new — for the resurgent American anti-intellectualism of the past twenty years. First and foremost among the vectors of anti-intellectualism are the mass media. On the surface, today's media seem to offer consumers an unprecedented variety of choices — television programs on hundreds of channels; movies; video games; music; and the Internet versions of those products, available in so many portable electronic packages that it is entirely possible to go through an entire

---

First and foremost among the vectors of anti-intellectualism are the mass media.

---

day without being deprived for a second of commercial entertainment. And it should not be forgotten that all of the video entertainment is accompanied by a soundtrack, usually in the form of ear-shattering music and special effects that would obviate concentration and reflection even in the absence of visual images. Leaving aside the question of whether it is a good thing to be entertained twenty-four hours a day, the variety of the entertainment, given that all of the media outlets and programming divisions are controlled by a few major corporations, is largely an illusion.

But the absence of genuine choice is a relatively minor factor in the relationship between the mass media and the decline of intellectual life in America. It is not that

---

6   Ron Suskind, "Without a Doubt," *New York Times Magazine*, October 17, 2004.

television, or any of its successors in the world of video, was designed as an enemy of active intellectual endeavor but that the media, while they may not actually be the message, inevitably reshape content to fit a form that subordinates both the spoken and the written word to visual images. In doing so, the media restrict their audience's intellectual parameters not only by providing information in a highly condensed form but by filling time — a huge amount of time — that used to be occupied by engagement with the written word.

It is easy with hindsight to view the present saturation of our culture by video images and all-encompassing noise as an inevitable progression from the early days of television. But that is not how things looked in the early fifties, when many intellectuals had great hopes for television as an educational medium and as a general force for good. Television coverage had, after all, spelled the beginning of the end for Senator Joseph R. McCarthy in the spring of 1954, when ABC devoted 188 hours of broadcast time to live coverage of the Army-McCarthy Hearings. Seeing and hearing McCarthy, who came across as a petty thug, turned the tide of public opinion against abuses of power that had not seemed nearly as abusive when reported by the print media. The hearings pitted the bushy-browed McCarthy and his chief counsel, the vulpine Roy Cohn, against the U.S. Army and its special outside counsel, the well-mannered Joseph Welch. The most famous sound bite of the hearings came after McCarthy, reneging on an earlier agreement, accused a young lawyer at Welch's firm of being a Communist sympathizer. Welch, turning in an instant from a kindly uncle into an avenging angel, thundered at McCarthy, "Until this moment, senator, I think I never gauged your cruelty or your recklessness. … Have you no sense of decency, sir, at long last?" Although ABC televised the hearings live, the other networks provided a foretaste of the commercial priorities that now completely control network television. CBS, fearful of losing revenue through the preemption of its popular daytime soap operas, declined to cover the hearings at all. NBC opted out early on, when it became clear that there was no drama to be had in the initial sessions. In their fifteen-minute evening news programs, both CBS and NBC presented snippets of the hearings, edited from ABC's live broadcasts. But by the time the climax of the hearings came with the confrontation between McCarthy and Welch, millions of Americans had gained context by watching at least some of the live committee sessions; that context ensured that the Welch-McCarthy exchange would not become a five-second wonder.

Optimism about the civic educational value of television — at least among those who had favored the election of John Kennedy — was bolstered again by the broadcast of the first presidential debates in the fall of 1960. Yet Kennedy's victory in the initial debate was based more on his appearance than on his words or policies; the pasty-read before television entered their homes. People now in their early sixties, unless they came from the tiny minority of families affluent enough to afford a television set in the 1940s, spent the first five to seven years of their lives in much the same fashion as their parents had — playing outdoors, listening to a favorite radio program, learning their ABCs from parents and books, and not from *Sesame Street*. But adults now in their early fifties were being schooled in

---

It is sobering to reflect that during the next decade, as the oldest baby boomers enter retirement beginning in 2011, the political and cultural leadership of the nation will inevitably pass to the first generation raised on television from Day 1.

---

faced Nixon, with his five o'clock shadow, projected an image not unlike that of Joe McCarthy, while the tanned Kennedy, with his thick shock of hair, seemed the very essence of youth, energy, and virility. The potential civic danger of determining a presidential election on the basis of a telegenic appearance was largely ignored at the time. Later polls showed that those who had listened to the debate on radio thought Nixon had won, while those who saw the debate on television judged Kennedy the winner. This finding might have raised a red flag among more farsighted members of the intellectual community, but it was largely ignored — possibly because no politician, until the rise of Bush *fils*, was more despised by American intellectuals than Nixon.

In spite of the growing influence of television on public affairs, the overall power and presence of television were less pervasive throughout the fifties and the first half of the sixties than they would become by the beginning of the seventies — let alone with the rise of cable in the eighties. This was true even though the number of American households with television jumped from 9 percent in 1950 to nearly 90 percent in 1960. Although television had ceased to be a novelty by the mid-fifties, it still offered only a limited number of programs and did not broadcast around the clock. Moreover, the relatively small number of home television sets at the start of the decade meant that for older baby boomers, born before 1950, television was a treat rather than the metronome of everyday life — at least in their formative preschool years. Americans born in the late forties might well be viewed as a different cultural generation from the younger boomers, because a great many, if not most, members of the elder cohort learned to

front of the television set long before entering a real school. And boomers now in their forties, like their own children today, were exposed to television from infancy — though few parents in the 1960s were foolish enough to put television sets in front of their babies' cribs.

It is sobering to reflect that during the next decade, as the oldest baby boomers enter retirement beginning in 2011, the political and cultural leadership of the nation will inevitably pass to the first generation raised on television from Day 1. The prospect is especially depressing to those of us who doubt that any attempts at adding more "quality" programming to the video menu can ever offset the negative intellectual impact of sheer quantity. This view was first expressed by Neil Postman in his prescient 1985 jeremiad, *Amusing Ourselves to Death*. "I raise no objection to television's junk," Postman declared unequivocally. "The best things on television *are* its junk, and no one and nothing is seriously threatened by it. Besides, we do not measure a culture by its output of undisguised trivialities but by what it claims as significant. Therein is our problem, for television is at its most trivial and, therefore, most dangerous when its aspirations are high, when it presents itself as a carrier of important cultural conversations."[7]

Postman was writing at the dawn of the era of personal computers and just before various taping devices, beginning with the VCR, became a fixture in homes and made it possible for entertainment consumers to acquire a virtually limitless stock of visual images for home viewing at their leisure. Everything he had to say about the implications of

---

7   Neil Postman, *Amusing Ourselves to Death* (New York, 1985), p. 16.

the shift from a print to a video culture is valid today — only more so. Well-off professionals, including a fair number of intellectuals, have proved especially vulnerable to the bromide that there is no harm, and may be great benefit, from video consumption as a way of life — as long as the videos are "educational." But medical research does not support the comforting notion that a regular diet of videos, educational or otherwise, is good for the developing brains of infants and toddlers. A growing body of pediatric research does indicate that frequent exposure to any form of video in the early years of life produces older children with shortened attention spans. It does not matter whether the images are produced by a television network, a film studio, or a computer software company: what matters is the amount of time children spend staring at a monitor. The American Academy of Pediatrics has concluded that there is no safe level of viewing for children under age two, but whatever the Academy may recommend, the battle against videos for infants is already lost.

One of the most common statements made on blogs by anxious parents, fearful that too much viewing is bad for their children but eager for the convenience supplied by an electronic babysitter, is: "We never let our child watch TV, only videos." A comical example of this widespread rationalization is the enthusiasm of ambitious, time-starved upper-middle-class parents for the *Baby Einstein* series, which force-feeds toddlers with a series of educational films designed to introduce them to everything from Monet's water lilies to the poetry of Wordsworth. Infants are next in line. Home Box Office's *Classical Baby*, which premiered in the spring of 2005, is a perfect illustration of the genre. The half-hour film consists of musical excerpts from Tchaikovsky, Bach, Duke Ellington, and Irving Berlin, all accompanied by animated images of clowns, fairies, and animals, and irritating, flashing glimpses of famous paintings by the likes of Jackson Pollock, Vincent van Gogh, and Claude Monet. When groups opposed to marketing television programs to infants objected, Dr. Eugene Beresin, a child psychiatrist on the staff of the Harvard Medical School and a consultant to HBO, declared that "to say that this kind of TV is bad is tantamount to saying art is bad."[8]

This statement should be considered prima facie evidence of video's capacity to dull the wits of highly educated professionals as well as innocent babies. How pathetic

it is that such products now appeal to a huge market of people who do not understand that the way to introduce children to music is by playing good music, uninterrupted by video clowns, at home; the way to introduce poetry is by reciting or reading it at bedtime; and the way to instill an appreciation of beauty is not to bombard a toddler with screen images of Monet's *Giverny* but to introduce her to the real sights and scents of a garden. It is a fine thing for tired parents to gain a quiet hour for themselves by mesmerizing small children with videos — who would be stuffy enough to suggest that the occasional hour in front of animals dancing to Tchaikovsky can do a baby any real harm? — but let us not delude ourselves that education is what is going on. Or rather, education is going on — but it is the kind of education that wires young brains to focus attention on prepackaged visual stimuli, accompanied by a considerable amount of noise.

Only a Luddite would claim that the video culture, whether displayed on television screens or computer monitors, has nothing to contribute to individual intellectual development or the intellectual life of society. Certainly the promotion of anti-intellectualism is not the intent of *Baby Einstein*, which, after all, is designed to cater to both the competitive anxieties and the intellectual pretensions of upper-middle-class parents. Yet there is little question that the intrusion of video into the psyches of Americans at ever earlier ages is not only making it unnecessary for young children to entertain themselves but is also discouraging them from thinking and fantasizing outside the box, in the most literal as well as a figurative sense. Predictably, the video culture has spawned an electronic cottage industry of scholars and writers taking up the cudgels in defense of a multi-billion-dollar conglomerate and pooh-poohing old-fashioned intellectuals (a.k.a. curmudgeons) for their reservations about sucking at the video tit from cradle to grave. Only in today's America could a book titled *Everything Bad Is Good for You: How Today's Popular Culture Is Actually Making Us Smarter* have received respectful reviews. The author, Steven Johnson, writes the "Emerging Technology" column for *Discover* magazine and, by his own account, spends a fair amount of time immersed in video games. "Parents can sometimes be appalled at the hypnotic effect that television has on toddlers," Johnson writes. "They see their otherwise vibrant and active children gazing silently, mouth agape at the screen, and they assume the worst: the television is turning their child into a zombie." Not to worry, Johnson assures us. The glazed stares at the

---

8   In "HBO Criticized for Pushing TV to Infants," Associated Press, May 12, 2005.

television — and later, at video games — "are not signs of mental atrophy. They're signs of *focus*."[9]

The real point is not what children are focusing *on* but what they are screening *out* with their intense focus, most likely directed at a video already viewed scores of times. Johnson then goes on to declare that studies demonstrating the decline of reading and writing skills are deeply flawed because they "ignore the huge explosion of reading (not to mention writing) that has happened thanks to the rise of the Internet." While conceding that e-mail exchanges or Web-based dissections of the television show *The Apprentice* are "not the same as literary novels," Johnson notes approvingly that both are "equally text-driven."[10] Such self-referential codswallop is only to be expected from a self-referential digital and video culture; one might as well make the statement that kiddie porn and Titian nudes are "equally image-driven." The appeal of such rationalizations in an acquisitive, technology-dependent society is obvious: parents can rest assured, that their money is being well spent because electronic media toys all have educational value; that there is really nothing wrong with not having made time to read a book for the past six months; and that their children are actually getting smarter as they watch the action on their various monitors.

What kind of reading has exploded on the Internet? Certainly not the reading of serious books, whether fiction or nonfiction. The failure of e-books to appeal to more than a niche market is one of the worst kept secrets in publishing, in spite of the reluctance of publishers to issue specific sales figures. Even a popular mass-market novelist like Stephen King has flopped on the Web. In 2001, King attempted to serialize one of his supernatural thrillers online, with the proviso that readers pay $1 for the first three installments and $2 for subsequent portions. Those who downloaded the installments were to pay on an honor system, and King pledged to continue the serialization as long as 75 percent of readers paid for the downloads. By the fourth installment, the proportion of paid-up readers dropped to 46 percent, and King canceled the series at the end of the year. King's idea of serialization had of course been tried before, and it was a huge success — in the nineteenth century. London readers used to get up early and wait in line for the newest installment of a novel by Charles Dickens; in New York, Dickens fans would meet the boats known to be carrying copies of the tantalizing chapters. The Web, however, is all about the quickest possible gratification; it may well be that people most disposed to read online are least disposed to wait any length of time for a new chapter of a work by their favorite writer.

The tech stock analysts who predicted a limitless future for e-books have tried to explain their misjudgment in terms of the current state of technology: all that is lacking for their bright forecasts to be fulfilled is a better tool for downloading and reading. Something small, light, and easily perused while the reader is riding on a bus, eating a sandwich, or propped up against pillows. Something like … a paperback book? A much more likely explanation for the e-book fizzle is that reading for pleasure — as distinct from necessary, often work-related reading for information — is in certain respects antithetical to the whole experience of reading on computers and portable digital devices. The Internet is the perfect delivery medium for reference books and textbooks, which were never designed to be read from cover to cover. But a narrow, time-saving focus is inimical not only to reading for enjoyment but to reading that encourages the retention of knowledge. Memory, which depends on the capacity to absorb ideas and information through exposition and to connect new information to an established edifice of knowledge, is one of the first victims of video culture. Without memory, judgments are made on the unsound basis of the most recent bit of half-digested information. All mass entertainment media, and the expanding body of educational media based on the entertainment model, emphasize "stand alone" programming that does not require a prior body of knowledge. The media provide the yeast, which, when added to other American social forces and institutions, creates a fertile culture for the spread of invincible ignorance throughout the public square.

> What kind of reading has exploded on the Internet? Certainly not the reading of serious books, whether fiction or nonfiction.

9   Steven Johnson, *Everything Bad Is Good for You* (New York, 2005), p. 181.

10 Ibid., p.183.

The second major spur to anti-intellectualism during the past forty years has been the resurgence of fundamentalist religion. Modern media, with their overt and covert appeal to emotion rather than reason, are ideally suited to assist in the propagation of a form of faith that stands opposed to most of the great rationalist insights that have transformed Western civilization since the beginning of the Enlightenment. Triumphalist Christian fundamental-

does not rest on biblical literalism, but from right-wing Protestants.

Even when the entertainment media are not promoting a particular version of religion, they do promote and capitalize on widespread American credulity regarding the supernatural. In recent years, television has commissioned an unceasing stream of programs designed to appeal to a vast market of viewers who believe in ghosts, angels,

---

> The second major spur to anti-intellectualism … has been the resurgence of fundamentalist religion. Modern media, with their overt and covert appeal to emotion rather than reason, are ideally suited to assist in the propagation of a form of faith that stands opposed to most of the great rationalist insights that have transformed Western civilization since the beginning of the Enlightenment.

---

ism, mainly though not entirely Protestant, is based on the conviction that every word in the Bible is literally true and was handed down by God Himself. Public opinion polls conducted during the past four years have consistently found that more than one third of Americans believe in a literal interpretation of the Bible, while nearly six in ten believe that the bloody predictions in the Book of Revelation — which involve the massacre of everyone who has not accepted Jesus as the Messiah — will come true.[11]

Beginning with the radio evangelist Billy Sunday in the twenties, American fundamentalists, with their black-and-white view of every issue, have made effective use of each new medium of mass communication. Liberal religion, with its many shades of gray and determination to make room for secular knowledge in the house of faith, does not lend itself as readily to media packaging and is at an even greater disadvantage in the visual media than it was on radio. From the rantings of Pat Robertson on the *700 Club* to Mel Gibson's movie *The Passion of the Christ*, religion comes across most powerfully on video when it is unmodified by secular thought and learning, makes no attempt to appeal to anything but emotion, and leaves no room for doubt. Gibson's *Passion*, for instance, is rooted in a Roman Catholic brand of fundamentalism, long rejected by the Vatican itself, that takes the Gospel of Matthew literally and blames Jews for the crucifixion of Jesus. The core audience for the immensely popular movie in the United States was drawn not from mainstream Catholics, whose faith

and demons. More than half of American adults believe in ghosts, one third believe in astrology, three quarters believe in angels, and four fifths believe in miracles.[12] The American marketing of the Apocalypse is a multi-media production, capitalizing on fundamentalism and paranoid superstition. Mainstream denominations have long downplayed the predictions in Revelation, which modern biblical scholars say was written at least sixty years after the death of the historical Jesus and has only the most tenuous relationship to the Gospels. One of the many rational developments rejected by fundamentalism, however, is biblical scholarship since the mid-nineteenth century. Who cares what some pointy-headed intellectual has to say about when various parts of the Bible were actually written and what, if any, relationship the text has to real history? Americans' enthusiasm for apocalyptic fantasy probably owes more to movies like *The Exorcist* and *The Omen* than to the Bible itself.

During the past fifteen years, and especially since the terrorist attacks on the World Trade Center and the Pentagon gave substance to every sort of paranoia, the driving force behind the "end times" — meaning the end of the world — scenario has been a series of books marketed through right-wing Christian bookstores and fundamentalist Web sites. Also known as the *Left Behind* series — meaning those left behind to be slaughtered for their unbelief after Jesus returns to earth for the Last

---

11   See Nancy Gibbs, "Apocalypse Now," *Time*, July 1, 2002.

12   "The Religious and Other Beliefs of Americans 2003," Harris Interactive Poll, February 26, 2003.

Judgment — the religious horror stories for adults are accompanied by a series of children's books (*Left Behind: The Kids*); audiotapes; and last but not least, *Left Behind: The Movie*. The books are written by Jerry B. Jenkins, whose previous works consisted mainly of ghostwriting for sports celebrities, and are based on the scriptural interpretations of Tim LaHaye, a fundamentalist minister and founding member of the Moral Majority. More than 100 million copies have been sold in the United States. The saga is also known to aficionados as the Rapture with a capital "R."

Rapture is also a verb; "to rapture" means to frolic in heaven after God has dispatched every skeptic on earth, thereby fulfilling the biblical prophecy that "Eye hath not seen, nor ear heard, neither have entered into the heart of man, the things which God hath prepared for them that love him" (1 Corinthians 2:9). As for those who doubted Him, the sadistic Armageddon script spells out their unenviable fate: "And there came out of the smoke locusts upon the earth: and unto them was given power, as the scorpions of the earth have power. And it was commanded them that they should not hurt the grass of the earth, neither any green thing, neither any tree; but only those men which have not the seal of God in their foreheads. … And in those days shall men seek death, and shall not find it; and shall desire to die, and death shall flee from them." (Revelation 9:3–4:6). Another popular fundamentalist Web site, run by an Air Force mechanic in Bellevue, Nebraska, publishes a daily "Rapture Index," which its founder describes as a "Dow Jones Industrial Average of End Time Activity." The index at raptureready.com hit a high on September 24, 2001, as Armageddon enthusiasts concluded that the terrorist attacks signified the imminent end of the world.

What is most disturbing apart from the fact that millions of Americans already believe in the imminent end of days, is that the mainstream media confer respectability on such bizarre fantasies by taking them seriously. In a 2002 *Time* cover story on the Bible and the Apocalypse, the magazine soberly declared that "since September 11, people from the cooler corners of Christianity have begun asking questions about what the Bible has to say about how the world ends, and preachers have answered their questions with sermons they could not have imagined giving a year ago."[13] Notably absent from the *Time* story was any secular or rationalist analysis. The article quoted liberal Christians who said that *their* God would never behave as cruelly as a God who would

13   Gibbs, "Apocalypse Now."

obliterate millions of innocents at the Last Judgment, but it gave no space to those who dismiss the end-times scenario as a collective delusion based on pure superstition and who understand the civic danger inherent in the normalization of ideas that ought to be dismissed as the province of a lunatic fringe. Discussing Armageddon as if it were as real as the earth itself, the *Time* story was, on one level, an effort to capitalize on public fear and sell magazines. On a deeper level, though, the article exemplifies the journalistic conviction that anything "controversial" is worth covering and that both sides of an issue must always be given equal space—even if one side belongs in an abnormal psychology textbook. If enough money is involved, and enough people believe that two plus two equals five, the media will report the story with a straight face, always adding a qualifying paragraph noting that "mathematicians, however, say that two plus two still equals four." With a perverted objectivity that gives credence to nonsense, mainstream news outlets have done more to undermine logic and reason than raptureready.com could ever do.

Misguided objectivity, particularly with regard to religion, ignores the willed ignorance that is one of the defining characteristics of fundamentalism. One of the most powerful taboos in American life concerns speaking ill of anyone else's faith — an injunction rooted in confusion over the difference between freedom of religion and granting religion immunity from the critical scrutiny applied to other social institutions. Both the Constitution and the pragmatic realities of living in a pluralistic society enjoin us to respect our fellow citizens' right to believe whatever they want — as long as their belief, in Thomas Jefferson's phrase, "neither picks my pocket nor breaks my leg." But many Americans have misinterpreted this sensible laissez-faire principle to mean that respect must be accorded the beliefs themselves. This mindless tolerance, which places observable scientific facts, subject to proof, on the same level as unprovable supernatural fantasy, has played a major role in the resurgence of both anti-intellectualism and anti-rationalism. Millions of Americans are perfectly free, under the Constitution, to believe that the Lord of Hosts is coming one day to murder millions of others who do not consider him the Messiah, but the rest of the public ought to exercise its freedom to identify such beliefs as dangerous fallacies that really *do* pick pockets and break legs.

Modern American fundamentalism (the term was not widely used until the twenties) emerged as an identifiable religious and cultural movement after the First World War, and its defining issue was opposition to the teaching in public schools of Darwin's theory of evolution by means of natural selection. Intellectuals of that era, including nonfundamentalist religious believers as well as secularists, mistakenly concluded that the anti-evolutionists and fundamentalists had been dealt a decisive blow by the 1925 Scopes "monkey trial" in Dayton, Tennessee. Clarence Darrow, the nation's leading trial lawyer and a crusading

a subject in America at the dawn of the twenty-first century as it had been at the end of the nineteenth.

The perfect storm over evolution is a perfect example of the new anti-intellectualism in action, because it owes its existence not only to a renewed religious fundamentalism but to the widespread failings of American public education and the scientific illiteracy of much of the media.

The perfect storm over evolution is a perfect example of the new anti-intellectualism in action, because it owes its existence not only to a renewed religious fundamentalism but to the widespread failings of American public education and the scientific illiteracy of much of the media.

---

agnostic, took on the case of John T. Scopes, a high school teacher charged with violating Tennessee's law banning the teaching of evolution in public schools. His opponent was William Jennings Bryan, the three-time Democratic presidential candidate and hero of fundamentalists, who famously declared that he was "more interested in the Rock of Ages than in the ages of rocks." Bryan made the mistake of taking the stand as an expert witness on the Bible, and Darrow, whose skills at cross-examination were legendary, forced his onetime friend to admit that many biblical stories, such as the sun standing still for Joshua's armies, could not be taken literally in light of contemporary scientific knowledge.

Although Scopes's conviction by a fundamentalist jury was a foregone conclusion, northern journalists, scientists, and intellectuals believed that Bryan's humiliation on the stand had discredited fundamentalism once and for all. In 1931, the cultural historian Frederick Lewis Allen observed that "legislators might go on passing anti-evolution laws and in the hinterlands the pious might still keep their religion locked in a science-proof compartment of their minds; but civilized opinion everywhere had regarded the ... trial with amazement and amusement, and the slow drift away from Fundamentalist certainty continued."[14] Intellectuals like Allen, who came of age in the early decades of the twentieth century, would surely have been incredulous if anyone had predicted that evolution would be just as controversial

Usually portrayed solely as a conflict between faith and science, the evolution battle is really a microcosm of all of the cultural forces responsible for the prevalence of unreason in American society today. The persistence of anti-evolutionism, and its revival as a movement during the past twenty years, sets the United States apart from every other developed country in the world. On August 30, 2005, the Pew Forum on Religion and Public Life released the results of a public opinion poll that received almost no attention in the press because Hurricane Katrina had slammed into the Gulf Coast the day before. But the Pew findings, for those who bothered to read them, revealed an intellectual disaster as grave as the human and natural disaster unfolding in New Orleans. Nearly two thirds of Americans want both creationism, generally understood as the hard-core fundamentalist doctrine based on the story of Genesis, to be taught along with evolution in public schools. Fewer than half of Americans — 48 percent — accept any form of evolution (even guided by God), and just 26 percent accept Darwin's theory of evolution by means of natural selection. Fully 42 percent say that all living beings, including humans, have existed in their present form, since the beginning of time.[15]

This level of scientific ignorance cannot be blamed solely on religious fundamentalism, because the proportion of Americans who reject evolution in any form is higher — by 15 percentage points — than the proportion who believe in a literal interpretation of the Bible. Something

---

14   Frederick Lewis Allen, *Only Yesterday* (New York, 1931), p. 171.

15   "Public Divided on Origins of Life," August 30, 2005, Pew Forum on Religion and Public Life; www.pewforum.org.

else must be at work, and that something else is the low level of science education in American elementary and secondary schools, as well as in many community colleges. The poor quality of public science education at anything below the university level is easily inferred from the educational disparities in responses to the Pew Poll on evolution. Only 27 percent of college graduates believe that living beings have always existed in their present form although that in itself is an astonishingly high figure—but 42 percent of Americans with only a partial college education and half of high school graduates adhere to the creationist viewpoint that organic life has remained unchanged throughout the ages. A third of Americans mistakenly believe that there is substantial disagreement about evolution among scientists—a conviction reinforcing and reflecting the right-wing religious mantra that evolution is "just a theory," with no more scientific validity than any other cockamamie idea. Since evolution is just a theory, the anti-evolutionists contend, it must not and should not be viewed as scientific truth.

There are of course many scientific disagreements about the particulars of evolution, but the general theory of evolution by means of natural selection is a settled issue for the mainstream scientific community. The popular "just a theory" argument rests not only on religious faith but on our national indifference to the specific meanings of words in specific contexts. Many Americans simply do not understand the distinction between the definitions of theory in everyday life and in science. For scientists, a theory is a set of principles designed to explain natural phenomena, supported by observation, and subject to proofs and peer review; scientific theory is not static but is modified as new tools of measurement and research findings become available. In its everyday meaning, however, a theory is nothing more than a guess based on limited information or misinformation—and that is exactly how many Americans view scientific theory. To those who equate theory with uninformed guessing, Einstein's theory of relativity and Darwin's theory of evolution have no more validity than the convictions of a *Left Behind* enthusiast who declares, "My theory is that the end of the world will come after one more terrorist attack." Predictions about the end of the world are perfect examples of nonscientific theories: each time they fail to come true, the prognosticators simply set a new date for fulfillment of the prophecy. A specific set of calculations may be wrong, but the prophecy retains its status as an eternal and unverifiable supernatural truth. Who, after all, can prove that the end of the world is not just one more disaster away? In science, new information either unmasks a falsehood, as Copernicus's and Galileo's observations undermined the long-held belief that the sun revolves around the earth, or supports an earlier theory based on less complete information.

One of the most important contributors to the evolution tempest is local control of elementary and secondary schooling, an American tradition responsible for vast and persistent regional disparities in the quality of education throughout the land. In Europe, national curriculum standards prevail: Sicilians may have different cultural values from Piedmontese, but a high school graduate in either Italian region will have been taught the same facts about science. In the United States, the geographical dimension of the culture wars, with the powerful fundamentalist presence in the South and parts of the Middle West, means that teachers in those areas, even if they believe in evolution themselves, are wary of incorporating the subject into their biology classes. A turn-of-the-millennium report by the Thomas B. Fordham Foundation, an education research institute, concluded that schools in more than a third of American states, most in the South and the Midwest, are failing to acquaint students not only with the basic facts of evolution but with the importance of Darwin's theory to all modern scientific thinking.[16]

One of the most common strategies of schools kowtowing to anti-evolutionists is avoidance of the "E-word" and the substitution of bland, meaningless phrases like "change over time." Biological evolution is frequently ignored in favor of the geological history of the solar system, a phenomenon less disturbing to fundamentalists than the descent of man. Ron Bier, a biology teacher in Oberlin, Ohio—one of the states receiving a poor grade in the Fordham Report—summed up his teaching strategy for *The New York Times*. He believes in teaching evolution but tries to avoid challenges from fundamentalist parents by teaching the subject not as a "unit" but by putting out "my little bits and pieces wherever I can." Bier added, "I don't force things. I don't argue with students about it."[17] One might ask what the point of teaching is, if not to replace ignorance with knowledge—a process that generally does involve a fair amount of argument. But passivity and teacher avoidance of controversy are not the worst-case scenarios. Many teachers—products of the same inadequate public schools—do not understand evolution themselves.

16 "Good Science, Bad Science: Teaching Evolution in the States," Thomas B. Fordham Foundation, September 1, 2000, figure 1; www.edexcellence.net.
17 Cornelia Dean, "Evolution Takes a Back Seat in U.S. Classes," *New York Times*, February 1, 2005.

A 1998 survey by researchers from the University of Texas found that one out of four public school biology teachers believes that humans and dinosaurs inhabited the earth simultaneously.[18] These misconceptions do not tell us anything about the teachers' religious beliefs, but they do reveal a great deal about how poorly educated the teachers are. Any teacher who does not know that dinosaurs were extinct long before *Homo sapiens* put in an appearance is unfit to provide instruction in late nineteenth-century biology, much less, modern biology.

To add to the muddle, it seems that Americans are as ignorant and poorly educated about the particulars of religion as they are about science. A majority of adults in what

tour de force filmed in Antarctica, to avoid any mention of evolution. As it happens, the emperor penguin is literally a textbook example, cited in college-level biology courses, of evolution by means of natural selection and random mutation. The penguins march seventy miles from their usual ocean feeding grounds in order to mate in a spot that offers some shelter from the fierce Antarctic winter. By the time the birds pair off, the female is starving and must transfer her egg to be sheltered under the male's fur. Then she waddles back to water to stock up on fish so that she may return, making another seventy-mile trek, in time to feed her new offspring and trade places with the male, who by then is starving himself and must return to the sea.

The surprise hit movie of 2005, *March of the Penguins*, chronicled the bizarre reproductive cycle of the emperor penguin and managed, in a cinematic tour de force filmed in Antarctica, to avoid any mention of evolution. As it happens, the emperor penguin is literally a textbook example, cited in college-level biology courses, of evolution by means of natural selection and random mutation.

---

is supposedly the most religious nation in the developed world, cannot name the four Gospels or identify Genesis as the first book of the Bible.[19] How can citizens understand what creationism means, or make an informed decision about whether it belongs in classrooms, if they cannot even locate the source of the creation story? And how can they be expected to understand any definition of evolution if they were once among millions of children attending classes in which the word "evolution" was taboo and in which teachers suggested that dinosaurs and humans roamed the earth together?

On evolution, as in so many other vital areas of knowledge, popular infotainment culture reinforces public ignorance about both science and religion. The news media tend to cover evolution with the same bogus objectivity that they apply to other "controversies" like the Armageddon scenario. Even in nature documentaries, it is difficult to find any mention of evolution. The surprise hit movie of 2005, *March of the Penguins*, chronicled the bizarre reproductive cycle of the emperor penguin and managed, in a cinematic

A scientist looks at emperor penguins and sees a classic example of random mutation, natural selection, and adaptation to the harshest climate on earth. A believer in creationism or intelligent design, however, looks at the same facts and sees not the inefficiency but the "miracle" of the survival of the species. Exactly why an "intelligent designer" would place the breeding grounds seventy miles from the feeding grounds or, for that matter, would install any species in such an inhospitable climate, are questions never addressed by those who see God's hand at the helm. The film has been endorsed by religious conservatives not only as a demonstration of God's presence in nature but as an affirmation of "traditional norms like monogamy, sacrifice, and child-rearing."[20] These penguin family values, however, mandate monogamy for only one reproductive cycle: mama and papa penguin, once their chick is old enough to survive on its own, flop back into the ocean and never see each other or their offspring again. In the next mating cycle, they choose new partners. But why quibble? Serial monogamy, if ordained by a supreme being, is apparently good enough.

The financial wisdom of avoiding any mention of evolution was borne out at the box office: a year after its release,

18   George E. Webb, *The Evolution Controversy in America* (Lexington, Ky., 1994), p. 254.

19   George Gallup, *The Role of the Bible in American Society* (Princeton, N.J., 1990), p. 17; Genesis reference in Stephen Prothero, *Religious Literacy* (San Francisco; 2007), p. 12.

20   Michael Medved, "March of the Conservatives: Penguin Film as Political Fodder," *New York Times*, September 13, 2005.

the movie was the second highest grossing documentary of all time, exceeded at the time only by Michael Moore's *Fahrenheit 911*. There is no need to speculate about what would have happened to box office receipts in the United States if the filmmaker (National Geographic) and the distributor (Warner Independent) had used the E-word. In 2001, the Public Broadcasting Service produced an eight-part documentary, accompanied by materials designed for use in schools, boldly titled *Evolution*. The Christian right went beserk, labeling the series anti-religious, unscientific propaganda, and succeeded in keeping the supplementary educational materials out of most American schools. Furthermore, the evolution series prompted the Bush administration to begin monitoring all PBS productions for "liberal bias" and provided justification for further budget cuts in a government program already on the religious right's hit list.

In the evolution wars, the campaign on behalf of intelligent design deserves special mention because it achieved success in many communities by brilliantly employing an intellectual and scientific vocabulary to attack "elitist" scientists who reject religious attacks on Darwin's theory. The intelligent design movement is spearheaded by the Discovery Institute, a think tank based in Seattle and bankrolled by far right conservatives. The slick media-savvy right-wingers who run the Discovery Institute prefer to downplay religion and highlight the anti-Darwinist views of a handful of scientific contrarians, many with ties to the religious right. That their views are almost universally rejected by respected mainstream scientists is seen by the intelligent design crowd as evidence of a liberal establishment conspiracy to protect its Darwinist turf. Institute spokesmen constantly compare their contrarian faith-based researchers with once scorned geniuses like Copernicus and Galileo — a contention conveniently ignoring the fact that the Catholic Church, not other seekers of scientific truth, was the source of opposition to the heliocentric theory of the solar system. Intelligent design does not insist on the seven days of creation but it does rest on the nonscientific hypothesis that the complexity of life proves the existence of a designer. "If you want to call the designer God, that's entirely up to you" is the intelligent design pitch—along with "teach the controversy." The lethal inefficiencies of penguins marching across a frozen wasteland in order to reproduce, or of blood requiring the presence of numerous proteins in order to clot and prevent humans from bleeding to death, are viewed not as accidents of nature but as marvels of intention. The obvious question

of why a guiding intelligence would want to make things so difficult for his or her creations is never asked because it cannot be answered.

The proponents of intelligent design were dealt a major blow at the end of 2005, when Federal District Court Judge John E. Jones III handed down a decision prohibiting the teaching of intelligent design as an alternative to evolution in the public schools of Dover, Pennsylvania. Jones was forthright in his opinion, which states unequivocally that intelligent design is a religious, not a scientific, theory and that its teaching in schools therefore violates the establishment clause of the First Amendment. "To be sure, Darwin's theory of evolution is imperfect," Jones concluded. "However, the fact that a scientific theory cannot yet render an explanation on every point should not be used as a pretext to thrust an untestable alternative hypothesis grounded in religion into the science classroom or to misrepresent well-established scientific propositions."[21] Jones's opinion, grounded in science, will not of course be the last political word on the subject. President Bush—who must have failed to do his homework about his nominee's views of both the Constitution and science when he appointed Jones to the federal bench—has followed the anti-evolution script by vigorously advocating the teaching of both evolution and intelligent design.

When Bush endorsed the teaching of intelligent design, he was predictably cheered by the religious right and denounced by the secular and religious left, but no one pointed out how truly extraordinary it was that any American president would place himself in direct opposition to contemporary scientific thinking. Even when they have been unsympathetic to new currents in philosophical, historical, and political thought, American presidents have always wanted to be on the right side of science, and those who understood nothing about science were smart enough to keep their mouths shut. One cannot imagine Calvin Coolidge making pronouncements about the desirability of teaching alternatives to Einstein' s theory of relativity or about the theory of evolution — even though Coolidge was in the White House when the Scopes trial became the subject of major national publicity and controversy.

Unlike its predecessor in the twenties, the current anti-rationalist movement has been politicized from the bottom up and the top down, from school boards in small towns to

---

21 *Kitzmiller v. Dover School District*, U.S. District Court for the Middle District of Pennsylvania, case no. 04cv.2688.

the corridors of power in Washington. Bill Moyers, who has long been under attack from the religious and political right for the pro-science, pro-rationalist, and anti-fundamentalist content of his programs on public television described the process in a scathing speech about the end-times scenario. "One of the biggest changes in politics in my lifetime," Moyers said, "is that the delusional is no longer marginal. It has come in from the fringe, to sit in the seats of power in the Oval Office and in Congress. For the first time in our history, ideology and theology hold a monopoly of power in Washington. Theology asserts propositions that cannot be

confusing, and less dangerous world before the Great War. What Edenic past is calling out today to those who rail against experts, scientists, and intellectual "elites"? Most Americans would certainly like to return to the safety—or the perceived safety—of the world before September 11, 2001, but the rise of ideological anti-rationalism in American life antedates the terrorist attacks by several decades. Are we still arguing about evolution because we really long to return to the pre–digital revolution idyll of the seventies and early eighties? Or are we looking back on a more distant paradise, the decade in which American schoolchildren were trained to cower under

---

The United States has proved much more susceptible than other economically advanced nations to the toxic combination of forces that are the enemies of intellect, learning, and reason, from retrograde fundamentalist faith to dumbed-down media.

---

proven true; ideologues hold stoutly to a worldview despite being contradicted by what is generally accepted as reality. The offspring of ideology and theology are not always bad but they are always blind. And that is the danger: voters and politicians alike, oblivious to the facts."[22] In the land of politicized anti-rationalism, facts are whatever folks choose to believe.

The question is why now. It is much easier to understand the resurgent religious fundamentalism of the 1920s than it is to understand the politicization of anti-rationalism over the past twenty-five years. Both the fundamentalism of the early twentieth century and the anti-rationalism of the late twentieth century tapped into a broader fear of modernism and hatred of secularism that extend beyond the religious right and have always been an important component of American anti-intellectualism. But the reactionary fundamentalism of the twenties was deeply rooted in nostalgia—of which traditional religion was only one component—for a sampler time. Bryan, the leading populist and fundamentalist politician of his era, was the product of prelapsarian, late nineteenth-century small-town America, which had considered itself singularly blessed by God and in need of no further enlightenment from outside experts. It is understandable that fundamentalism and anti-rationalism would have appealed to many who longed for a return to the less exciting but also less pressured, less commercial, less

their desks in order to protect themselves against atomic attack by the Soviet Union?

An equally puzzling question is why *us*. People throughout the world must cope with social, economic, and technological changes that call traditional verities into question, and the empire of mind-numbing infotainment knows no national boundaries. Yet the United States has proved much more susceptible than other economically advanced nations to the toxic combination of forces that are the enemies of intellect, learning, and reason, from retrograde fundamentalist faith to dumbed-down media. What accounts for the powerful American attraction to values that seem so at odds not only with intellectual modernism and science but also with the old Enlightenment rationalism that made such a vital contribution to the founding of our nation? Any attempt to answer these questions must begin with the paradoxical cultural and political forces that shaped the idea of American exceptionalism even before there was an American nation and became an integral part of the American experiment during the formative decades of the young republic. Many of these forces combine a deep reverence for learning with a profound suspicion of too much learning, and they have persisted and mutated, through economic and population changes that the first generation of Americans could never have envisaged, into our current age of unreason.

---

22   Bill Moyers, "The Delusional Is No Longer Marginal," *New York Review of Books*, March 24, 2005.

Screen Time

from *The Dumbest Generation*

The Apple Store at Lenox Square is clean and bright. The portal doesn't contain any words, just two white Apple logos set in black panels flanking the entry. In the display window to the right sit two hand-size iPods on a small stand with poster-size reproductions hanging behind them, one showing on its screen Bono singing in the spotlights, another with the cast of *The Office* seated glumly around a meeting table.

Step inside and the white walls, white lights, and ash floors rouse you from the dreary escalators, potted plants, and dull metal railings in the mall promenade. Laptop and desktop screens line the sides of the room and flash pictures of canny urban youths until someone touches the mouse and icons appear bidding customers to check email and browse the Web. Halfway back, iPods, photo printers, digital cameras, and video take over, with salespersons hovering eager to demonstrate. Two modest shelves run up the middle exhibiting games and books such as *GarageBand 3: Create and Record Music on a Mac, Final Draft* (a scriptwriting program for TV and film), *The Sims 2*, and various "Brainbuilding Games for Kids." A bright red rug marks the youngsters' section, where four screens rest on a low table with chairs that look like fuzzy black basketballs. Behind it rises the Genius Bar, where three clerks in black T-shirts guide clients through digital snags as others wait on benches arranged in front of a large screen on the rear wall with a video streaming nonstop.

It's eleven o'clock on Friday morning and only 20 customers, all adults, have entered. By tomorrow afternoon, though, the Atlanta mall will overflow with teenagers, and packs of 16-year-olds and resolute young stragglers will pile into the Apple Store for an hour of sampling, surfing, and (sometimes) buying. An affable clerk with three-inch spikes in a Mohawk from forehead to nape responds with a smile when I ask him how many kids will arrive. "Oh, it'll be crazy," he chortles. On a weekday morning you can wander freely, but on Saturday afternoon with the kids in force, he says, "It takes a little bit of 'intentionality' to get around."

No other spot in the mall, at school, or at home provides so much concentrated and inviting fun and experimentation. Three doors away, Abercrombie & Fitch lures young shoppers with a 10-by-12-foot black-and-white photo of a shirtless male seen from the rear, his jeans sliding down his hips as he peers into a turbulent sky. Two floors below, the music/video shop f.y.e. stocks compact discs and movies in the standard layout, and a single bored employee nods behind the cash register. Farther down, the theaters have closed, but in the food court diners gobble pizza and cashew chicken while watching *Entertainment Tonight* on eight plasma screens hanging from the ceiling.

They sound like tepid fare set beside the joys and wonders of Apple offerings. And not only is the machinery ever-improving, ever more prosthetic. It has a special relationship to teens and 20-year-olds. More and more, it seems, the technology itself is their possession, their expression. The press release for a 2005 report by the Pew Internet & American Life Project on online usage has the grand subtitle "Youth are leading the transition to a fully wired and mobile nation." The report marvels that half

Mark Bauerlein, "Screen Time," from *The Dumbest Generation: How the Digital Age Stupefies Young Americans and Jeopardizes Our Future (Or, Don't Trust Anyone Under 30)*, pp. 71–96. Copyright © 2008 by Jeremy P. Tarcher/Penguin (USA). Permission to reprint granted by Penguin Group, Inc. (USA).

Screen Time · 187

the teenagers in the United States are not merely passive consumers. They are "content creators," making their own Web pages or posting their artwork, photos, stories, or videos online. People at Pew's Research Center call them the "Dot-Nets," director Scott Keeter says, "because of their technological savvy." They form the first generation reared on Google, never knowing a time when television meant ABC, NBC, CBS, PBS, and a local station showing reruns. They blink at the terms "LP," "station wagon," "Betamax," "IBM Selectric," "rabbit ears," and a thousand other apparatuses from their parents' time, and if they encountered them now they would hoot at the primitivism. A world with only land lines impresses them as ridiculously inconvenient. No cohort has witnessed such enabling advances in personal gadgetry. What perplexes their elders they act out as the natural thing to do, passing days and nights rapping comments into a blog, role-playing in a chat room, surfing paparazzi photos, logging onto *Facebook*, running *Madden NFL*, checking for voice messages, and uploading pictures of themselves while watching TV shows at the same rate they did before the other diversions appeared.

Keeter calls them savvy, and countless commentators recite their tech virtues with majestic phrases, as does *Get Ready: The Millennials Are Coming!*, a 2005 Forrester Research report whose Web summary announces: "The 'Millennials' — those born between 1980 and 2000 — have an innate ability to use technology, are comfortable multitasking while using a diverse range of digital media, and literally demand interactivity as they construct knowledge." Young users don't just possess good skills — they have "innate ability." They don't just tinker online; they "construct knowledge." In his *Philadelphia Inquirer* op-ed, Jonathan Fanton effuses about digital kids who've "created communities the size of nations … mastered digital tools to create new techniques for personal expression … redefined the notion of 'play'" — all through games, message boards, and social networking. As we shall see, some research questions the Millennials' digital wisdom, but nobody doubts the connectedness of their lives. Indeed, the degree of their immersion in digital technology and screen media itself sets them apart.

Political commentators often observe that blogs have altered the way campaigns and elections work, but in 2004 a little more than half of the 4.1 million blogs counted by Perseus Development Corporation were kept by 13- to 19-year-olds. A July 2007 report sponsored by the National School Boards Association ("Creating and Connecting: Research and Guidelines on Online Social — and Educational — Networking") found that 30 percent of students with online access run their own blogs, and "More than one in 10 (12 percent) say they upload music or podcasts of their own creation at least weekly." Many of them, the study affirms, "are adventurous nonconformists who set the pace for their peers." Indeed, Glenn Reynolds, pioneering host of *InstaPundit.com*, believes that blogs have produced an "army of Davids," young and inquisitive Net users who free knowledge and information from the control of mainstream media and Big Government, although in truth, few of the under-30-year-olds' blogs have much political content (Pew found in 2005 that only 7 percent of 18- to 29-year-olds go online for "political news"). And in the cell phone field, an August 2006 *Wall Street Journal* article headed "Dialing into the Youth Market: Cellphone Services and Products Become Increasingly Tailored to Teenager Users" explains that teens provide most of the growth for the industry. Furthermore, they bring new demands that steer innovations in the market: "Phone executives say a high priority is making it possible for teens to access, from their cellphones, blogs, online photo galleries and social-networking sites" (see Ricketts). Indeed, a *Wall Street Journal* story seven months later predicted that cell phones will soon be the primary medium for streaming news clips, sports, network television shows, video and photo sharing, and advertising ("What's New in Wireless"; see Sharma), and we may expect youths to be the earliest adopters.

The daunting size of Generation DotNet energizes the digital trades, and the intensity of its digital thirst never seems to wane. The Kaiser Family Foundation's ongoing research project demonstrates how steadily screen activities saturate the younger populations. As noted earlier, Kaiser's Study of Entertainment Media and Health conducts surveys of the home and leisure lives of children and families, highlighting media types and exposure. In 2003, it released *Zero-to-Six: Electronic Media in the Lives of Infants, Toddlers, and Preschoolers*, a study of children's media exposure in the first six years of life. The American Academy of Pediatrics advises parents to keep two-year-olds and under away from the television screen altogether, and to restrict older children to one to two hours of educational programming per day. But the 1,000+ subjects in the Kaiser study ranging from six months to six years old, went well beyond that. They averaged fully one hour and 58 minutes per day on screen media. That's three times the amount they devoted to reading or being read to (39 minutes per day). Children pass as many moments in front of a screen as they do playing outside (two hours and one minute), and the number of kids who let a day pass without enjoying screen images is less than the number of those who spend a day without opening a book.

The home environment supports the behaviors. One-third of the subjects (36 percent) reside in homes in which the television is on "always" or "most of the time." Half of the children occupy homes with three or more television sets in use, and 36 percent of them have one in their bedroom. Half the households have a video game player, and 49 percent of them have Internet access (since 2003, of course, that figure has climbed steadily), while only 34 percent subscribe to a newspaper.

We might assume that with children at such tender ages the screen activities follow a parent's directive. While father fights the traffic, mother must prepare dinner, and so she sets their two-year-old on the living room carpet and starts a *Sesame Street* video that the child soaks up agreeably for 30 minutes. In truth, however, most of the children have acquired enough knowledge of the screen to form preferences of their own, and they act on them. Fully 77 percent of them, the study found, turn the TV on by themselves, and two-thirds request particular shows, 71 percent a preferred video or DVD. Sixty-two percent change channels with the remote control, 36 percent install their own music CDs or tapes, 23 percent insert CD-ROMs into the computer, and 12 percent surf the Net in search of favorite Web sites. The media selection habits don't quite parallel the selection of a book from the shelf, either. Book browsing is sometimes an exploratory thing, with children finding stories and pictures they hadn't seen before. Each book is a new world, and the object itself is unique. Parents see the process unfold every time they take their four-year-olds to the public library and have to narrow down the checkouts to five books. The screen, however, is always the same, a generic object. There is nothing magical about it except its function as gateway to something else. Kids usually know exactly what they want and where they want to go, and they get there with a few mouse clicks or channel changes.

In the Kaiser study, television tops the list, but other screen habits fill ample daily minutes as well. In fact, while 73 percent of infants to six-year-olds watch TV every day, an equal percentage watches videos and DVDs. Eighteen percent use a computer and 9 percent play video games. For the four- to six-year-old group alone, the digital side of screen media jumps. One-quarter of them (27 percent) use a computer in a "typical day," and 64 percent know how to use a mouse.

For the *Zero-to-Six* report, surveyors collected data in spring 2003, and certainly the numbers have risen since then. The preschoolers in the study have almost finished elementary school by now, and they've refined their screen acumen at every grade level. Another study from Kaiser, released in March 2005, picked up the older age group and asked similar questions. Aiming to provide "reliable and objective data documenting the patterns and trends of media use among young people," *Generation M: Media in the Lives of 8–18-Year-Olds* collected information, on recreational consumption — not school or work — from 2,032 third- to twelfth-graders through questionnaires and week-long diaries. The foremost conclusion: the total amount of leisure time kids spend with media "is the equivalent of a full-time job." On average, the subjects in the study log six hours and 21 minutes a day. And because they spend many of those minutes multitasking, playing a video game while listening to the radio, for instance, eight- to 18-year-olds actually take in eight and one-half hours of media content. Here's a breakdown of the percentage of kids who consume different media in an average day and for how long:

> ➢ watch television: 84 percent (3:04 hours)
> ➢ use a computer: 54 percent (48 minutes in online usage alone)
> ➢ read a magazine: 47 percent (14 minutes)
> ➢ read a book: 46 percent (23 minutes)
> ➢ play video games: 41 percent (32 minutes at console, 17 minutes with handheld)
> ➢ watch videos/DVDs: 39 percent (32 minutes)
> ➢ watch prerecorded TV: 21 percent (14 minutes)
> ➢ go to a movie: 13 percent

Add up the television times and they reach three hours and 18 minutes, and coupled with 49 minutes with a video game and 48 minutes online, they yield a daunting screen time of 295 minutes a day, 2,065 minutes per week. Book reading came in higher than the results from studies of late teens cited in the previous chapter, suggesting, perhaps, that the lower ages, eight- to 14-year-olds, pull the average up, or that many responses included homework reading with leisure reading. If reading included class assignments, the voluntary rate looks positively negligible alongside the screen options.

Once again, the home environment supports the pattern. Here's a tally of media access in the homes and in the bedrooms of eight- to 18-year-olds.

> television: in the home (99 percent), children's bedroom (68 percent)
> VCR/DVD player: home (97 percent), bedroom (54 percent)
> computer: home (86 percent), bedroom (31 percent)
> video game console: home (83 percent), bedroom (49 percent)

The 10-year-old's bedroom has become, as Kaiser puts it, a "multimedia center." Children leave the dinner table, which is often accompanied by network news, reruns of *Seinfeld*, and other 6 P.M. fare, and head off to their rooms to turn on their own shows or crank up iTunes while poring over some homework. Bored with that, they can check a *MySpace* forum, or play *Mortal Kombat*, or look at school pictures. The long division exercises await while the computer dings a new email coming through, the cell phone buzzes with a new message, and *Toonami* comes on in a half hour. They never need exit their bedroom doors, and in most households, parents won't interrupt them. For 55 percent of the eight- to 10-year-olds, parents don't lay down any rules for TV. For older teens, only 5 percent have parents who set limits on the video games they can play. The private access continues outside the home, too, with 55 percent of eight- to 18-year-olds taking a handheld video game player with them, and 65 percent carrying a portable music player.

Cell phones provide the mobility, and they encourage more initiative on the part of the kids. In a 2004 survey by NetDay, an initiative of Project Tomorrow, a nonprofit education group, more than half (58 percent) of the students in sixth through twelfth grade carried a cell phone, and 68 percent of those students took them to school. On campus, one-fifth of them had text and video/photo capabilities, no doubt producing thousands of funny and embarrassing snapshots that got passed around the cafeteria. A year later another NetDay survey came out, the findings published as *Our Voices, Our Future: Student and Teacher Views on Science, Technology, and Education* (sponsored by Bell South and Dell). Using the Internet to collect data from 185,000 students and 15,000 teachers, NetDay concluded that "Younger students are continuing to adopt more sophisticated technologies in the footsteps of their older siblings." Researchers asked students if they use various tools in a typical week, and while computers and cell phones came up at the expected high rates, other gadgets scored big as well.

> digital camera: 25 percent of third- through sixth-graders, 43 percent of sixth- through twelfth-graders
> video camera: 16 percent of third- through twelfth-graders, 22 percent of sixth- through twelfth-graders
> DVD or CD burner: 31 percent and 59 percent
> video game player: 55 percent and 61 percent

The way children and teens use this equipment grows more individualized by the year, too, NetDay found. Thirty percent of K–3 students have their own email accounts, and one-fifth of them say they prefer email to any other medium of communication. For sixth-through twelfth-graders, though, email already appears clunky. Overwhelmingly, they prefer Instant Messaging. They like variety, too. Thirty percent report using a computer, cell phone, DVD or CD burner, *and* a video game player on a weekly basis, a 10 percent jump from a year earlier. One-third admit that they update their personal Web sites "on a regular basis."

The expansion of media options and access never stops, and one wonders how sixth-graders juggle them all. But, to return to *Generation M*, a counterintuitive drift holds steady. With leisure time finite, one would think that increased Internet and video game minutes would cut into TV and radio time, but the Kaiser study found a contrary trend. Youngsters who spend more time with computers and games also watch more television and listen to more radio. Multitasking enables it. As *Generation M* concludes, "media use begets media use," and as more connections and feeds and streams and channels enter their private space, kids assimilate them with accelerating ease, adding one without dropping another.

Forty-year-olds don't get it, the cluttered airspace, the joy in multiple input. Growing up in what appears to their offspring a sluggish and elementary sensory ambiance, they welcome the latest invention as an add-on, something else to do besides reading the newspaper or watching a movie. Kids regard it differently. They mature in and with the flashing, evolving multimedia environment, integrating each development into a new whole, a larger Gestalt. They don't experience the next technology as a distraction or as a competition with other diversions. It's an extra comfort, and it joins nicely with the rest. As one of my students just declared last week in class, "I can't concentrate on my homework without the TV on. The silence drives me crazy."

The craving for input begins in the home, and as a follow-up to *Generation M* revealed, parents understand it well from the earliest ages. In May 2006, Kaiser released *The Media Family: Electronic Media in the Lives of Infants, Toddlers, Preschoolers, and Their Parents.* The study produced similar findings of media immersion for six-month- to six-year-olds, but added observations by parents about their children's habits. Kaiser assembled fathers and mothers into focus groups that reflected rates of media consumption found in the national survey, and then posed questions about reasons and outcomes. The predictable answer quickly followed: setting kids in front of the screen frees up time for cooking, cleaning, or just plain rest. A single mother coming home from work needs a few moments to regroup, and a beloved DVD keeps the children docile and preoccupied. A mother from Columbus, Ohio, reports, "He's a good little boy. He won't bother anything. He won't get into stuff. He's glued to the TV." A Denver mother who'd recently lost her job recalls that when she arrived home that day she could say "Let's watch *Finding Nemo*, kids. Here are some chicken strips, here are sippy cups — I'll see you in about an hour and a half." Half the parents agreed that television calms their children, while only one in six noted that it pumps them up. Three in ten installed TV sets in the kids' bedrooms because it helps them fall asleep (and lets parents watch their own shows in the living room). With DVDs, video games, and computers added to television, the division of tastes between younger and older family members is handled smoothly, parents have more ways to pacify their kids, and screen minutes climb accordingly.

Some parents feel guilty about the virtual babysitting, but not as much as they would if they let the children play with blocks on the kitchen floor while mother stepped around them while washing dishes. The screen, they contend, has educational benefits. Kids learn from what they watch. One mother from Irvine, California, insisted, "Anything they are doing on the computer I think is learning." And another parent: "Out of the blue one day my son counted to five in Spanish. I knew immediately that he got that from *Dora*." And another: "My daughter knows ... her letters from *Sesame Street*. I haven't had to work with her on them at all." One parent highlighted the social lessons imparted through the screen: "I think they are exposed to a little bit more diversity. I think that it's good for them to be comfortable with that ... to know that it's okay for everyone to be different." Yes, the children play alone, but they learn, too, so that as the new technologies relieve harried parents, they also improve impressionable little minds.

Left to themselves nightly with three screen options, wired for music and podcast as they hit the treadmill, reaching in their pocket for an email between classes, stocked with 600 cell phone minutes a month, a DVD collection by age 12 ... young Americans tune in and turn on as routinely and avidly as they eat lunch. They "live" technology the way high school garage bands in the seventies lived rock 'n' roll, sporting long hair and fraying jeans, idolizing Page and Richards, and blasting *Houses of the Holy, Get Your Wings,* and *Ted Nugent* all weekend. Except that what was then a short-term fad for a sub-subgroup of juniors and seniors whom the rest of us thought were a set of cool outsiders is now a thoroughgoing lifestyle for the majority of students from kindergarten upward. "Without question," *Generation M* ends, "this generation truly *is* the media generation," and new and old media practices have settled into essential youth rituals. It starts early, with researchers finding in one study that by three months of age around 40 percent of children are regular watchers of television, DVDs, or videos, and by 24 months the rate reaches 90 percent (Zimmerman et al., "Television and DVD/Video Viewing in Children Younger than 2 Years"). In 2002, in *Media Unlimited: How the Torrent of Images and Sounds Overwhelms Our Lives,* Todd Gitlin phrased it in a simple existential axiom: "*being with media.*"

In Pew Research's 2006 survey of cell phone use, 32 percent of 18- to 29-year-olds acknowledge that "they couldn't live without their cell." A January 2007 study by Pew, *How Young People View Their Lives, Futures, and*

> As one of my students just declared last week in class, "I can't concentrate on my homework without the TV on. The silence drives me crazy."

Politics: A Portrait of "Generation Next," found that about half the 18- to 25-year-olds interviewed had sent or received a text message over the phone the previous day, and more than four in 10 "Nexters" have created a personal profile on a social networking site such as *MySpace*. In a parallel study of younger ages, Pew discovered that fully 55 percent of all 12- to 17-year-olds have created a personal profile page, and 48 percent of them visit social networking Web sites at least once a day (*Social Networking and Teens: An Overview,* 2007). A follow-up Pew study, *Teens, Privacy & Online Social Networks* (April 2007), reported that one in four online teens make friends through the Web, and their virtual social life is a genuinely multimedia exchange. Three-quarters of social networking teens post photos online, and one in five posts videos. In early 2007, Harris Interactive surveyed teens and tweens (eight- to 12-year-olds) for their video game usage and found that the average tween plays 13 hours per week, the average teen 14 hours per week. About one in 12 of them counted as clinically addicted. Their social/visual habits have so proliferated that Nielsen/Net Ratings could report in a July 2006 press release, "YouTube U.S. Web Traffic Grows 75 Percent Week over Week," ranking it the fastest-growing Web brand for the year. And a press release two months earlier from Nielsen/Net Ratings declared, "Social Networking Sites Grow 47 Percent, Year over Year, Reaching 45 Percent of Web Users." The growth rate of *MySpace* reached an astronomical 367 percent.

No wonder they associate technology with their leisure, with their distinguishing youthfulness. The newer screens become a generational hinge, allowing 68 percent of 18- to 25-year-olds (according to Pew's *Generation Next* report) to "see their generation as unique and distinct from other generations." The writers of *Generation Next* echo the opinion: "This generation's relation with technology is truly unique." And while 18- to 25-year-olds claim uniqueness for themselves, they grant it much less so (44 percent) to the previous generation. After all, their elders may have had the Sexual Revolution and Civil Rights, *The Breakfast Club* and *Less Than Zero*, but Generation Next grasps its predecessors' ideals and icons while experiencing something no youth group has before: the Digital Revolution. They play rock 'n' roll and hook up at parties just like Boomers

and X-ers did, but their parents never loaded a thousand songs into a palm-size gadget when they were 18, or sent a message to 50 friends at once with a double-click, or kept a blog. And it is the youngsters themselves discovering novel practices. "They are innovative users of technology," NetDay's 2005 report gushes, "adopting new technologies to support their learning and their lifestyles."

The digital accoutrements signify much more than a lifestyle, too, more than yet another youth cohort's rebellious social mores and personal tastes. Digital habits reach down into their brains. As kids fixate on the twenty-first-century screen, they learn to count and spell, cut and paste, manage information, relate to others, and "construct knowledge." New technologies induce new aptitudes, and bundled together in the bedroom they push consciousness to diversify its attention and multiply its communications. Through blogs and Listservs, young Americans join virtual communities, cultivating interests and voicing opinions. Video games quicken their spatial intelligence. Group endeavors such as *Wikipedia* and reality gaming nurture collaborative problem-solving skills. Individuals who've grown up surrounded by technology develop different hard-wiring, their minds adapted to information and entertainment practices and speeds that minds maturing in pre-digital habitats can barely comprehend, much less assimilate.

That's the claim. Screen time is cerebral, and it generates breakthrough intelligence. E-literacy isn't just knowing how to download music, program an iPod, create a virtual profile, and comment on a blog. It's a general deployment capacity, a particular mental flexibility. E-literacy accommodates hypermedia because e-literates possess hyperalertness. Multitasking entails a special cognitive attitude toward the world, not the orientation that enables slow concentration on one thing — a sonnet, a theorem — but a lightsome, itinerant awareness of numerous and dissimilar inputs. In a white paper entitled "Confronting the Challenges of Participatory Culture: Media Education for the 21st Century," MIT professor Henry Jenkins sketches the new media literacies in precisely such big, brainy terms: *distributed cognition* — the "ability to interact meaningfully with tools that expand mental capacities" (search engines, etc.); *collective intelligence* — the "ability to pool knowledge and compare notes with others toward a common goal"

> That's the claim. Screen time is cerebral, and it generates breakthrough intelligence.

(Listservs, etc.); *transmedia navigation* — the "ability to follow the flow of stories and information across multiple modalities"; and so on. A report from EDUCAUSE affirms, "We take it to be self-evident that college-bound digital natives are in fact *digital cognoscenti, sophisticates,* and perhaps even *digital connoisseurs*" (*ECAR Study of Undergraduate Students and Information Technology, 2006*).

Over and over, commentators stress the mental advance, the learning side over the fun and fantasy side. In describing *Second Life*, the virtual universe in which people log on as themselves or as make-believe identities; become "residents," and manufacture their own settings, the *Wikipedia* entry claims that users "learn new skills and mature socially." When reading expert Professor James Gee, author of *What Video Games Have to Teach Us about Learning and Literacy*, started to play a video game for the first time, he discovered a whole new consciousness. "Suddenly" he avows, "all my baby-boomer ways of learning and thinking, for which I had heretofore received ample rewards, did not work." At a panel on "Technology and Community" at the 2006 Aspen Institute, humanitarian activist and architect Cameron Sinclair announced, "there is a real problem with education in the U.S., and, you know what, the students know it more than the teachers do, and they're beginning to mobilize [through the Web], and they're forming their own ways of learning." In February 2007, Jonathan Fanton, president of the MacArthur Foundation, announced a new digital youth initiative by wondering, "Might it be that, for many, the richest environment for learning is no longer in the classroom, it is outside the classroom — online and after school?" The MacArthur project is called Digital Media and Learning, a five-year $50 million initiative to study how digital technologies affect young people's lives. At the same event, University of Wisconsin Professor David Williamson Shaffer, a "Game Scientist," asserted that computers alter "the way people think in the digital age," and that the invention of computers ranks with "the development of language itself" in the advancement of human intelligence. Consider that analogy: the caveman stands to the average 1950s person as the average 1950s person stands to us.

With so much money supporting digital research, and so many students going online hourly, the faith in young people's digital intelligence reaches well into the academic sphere, and the academic press has made the students' digital mentality into a topic of the day. Here's a paragraph from "The Net Generation in the Classroom," a 2005 story

in the *Chronicle of Higher Education* that explores the prospect of aligning college teaching with the entering classes' e-mindset.

> Born between roughly 1980 and 1994, the Millennials have already been pegged and defined by academics, trend spotters, and futurists: They are smart but impatient. They expect results immediately. They carry an arsenal of electronic devices — the more portable the better. Raised amid a barrage of information, they are able to juggle a conversation on Instant Messenger, a Web-surfing session, and an iTunes playlist while reading *Twelfth Night* for homework.

The author, Scott Carlson, adds a skeptical note at the end — "Whether or not they are absorbing the fine points of the play is a matter of debate" — but the main voice in the article, librarian and higher-ed consultant Richard T. Sweeney, has no doubts. Millennials "want to learn," he observes, "but they want to learn only what they have to learn, and they want to learn it in a different style that is best for them." The approach grants remarkable discretion to the kids, assuming that they know what "is best," and that their preferences mark a distinct "learning style." Another voice in the article, educator and futurist Marc Prensky, likewise insists that young people have turned learning itself into a whole different process. In 2004, Prensky stated in a paper entitled "The Death of Command and Control" that "The unprecedented changes in technology … have led to **new patterns of thinking**, especially in young people" (emphasis in original). Here in the *Chronicle* piece, in casual tones that belie the grave transformation at work, he wonders, "The things that have traditionally been done — you know, reflection and thinking and all that stuff — are in some ways too slow for the future. … Is there a way to do those things faster?"

The fervor spills freely in public discourse as well. When Steven Johnson published *Everything Bad Is Good for You: How Today's Popular Culture Is Actually Making Us Smarter* in early 2005, it sparked across-the-country newspaper reviews, radio spots, and television appearances, including one on *The Daily Show*. The appeal was overt, and as Johnson observes on his Web site, "The title says it all." As a specimen of contrary mischievousness, an anti-anti-pop culture polemic, the book offered a crisp and witty argument for the good of the mouse and the console, and also for the helpful tutelage of twenty-first-century sitcoms and next-version video games. Everyone with a stake in the rise of screen diversions or who treasured the virtual universe seized upon the thesis, and Johnson unveiled it with élan. To turn a commonsense notion on its head — "TV is good, not bad" — was a winning tactic, and Johnson added an image of himself as defender of a pop culture world disdained by widespread powers as vulgar, violent, and infantile. While Joe Lieberman railed against the "amoral pop-culture threat to public values," as *Time* magazine put it in 2000 (see Poniewozik), and as Hillary Clinton fretted "about the content [of video games] and what that's doing to my child's emotional psychological development," as she stated at the Kaiser Foundation's release of the report *Generation M*, *Everything Bad Is Good for You* turned it all around. In the last 30 years, Johnson insisted, popular culture has become "more complex and intellectually challenging … demanding more cognitive engagement … making our minds sharper." Often the content of popular culture is coarse and inane, he conceded, but the formal elements — rules, plotlines, feedback, levels, interactivity — have grown more sophisticated, making today's games and reality shows into "a kind of cognitive workout" that hones mental gifts. Screen diversions provide something more lasting and effectual than "healthy messages." They inculcate "intellectual or cognitive virtues," aptitudes for spatialization, pattern recognition, and problem solving, virtues that reflect twenty-first-century demands better, in fact, than do traditional knowledge and reading skills.

Once again, the thinking element prevails, and screens are praised for the way they shape the consciousness of users, not pass along to them ideas and values. The case for cognitive benefits begins with a fundamental feature of games: "far more than books or movies or music," Johnson asserts, "games force you to make decisions." True, books involve judgment, but they don't allow readers to determine the next chapter or decide a character's fate. Game realities, by contrast, let them steer the car, invest money, and grab weapons. The content is juvenile, yes, but "because learning how to think is ultimately about learning how to make the right decisions," game activity evokes a collateral learning that carries over to users' real lives. As Malcolm Gladwell

noted in his fawning review in *The New Yorker*, "When you play a video game, the value is in how it makes you think." The images may be flashy and jumbled, the action silly and inconsequential, but when you play the game, Johnson explains, "It's not about tolerating or aestheticizing chaos; it's about finding order and meaning in the world, and making decisions that help create that order."

The advantages continue with the progressive complexity of television shows. *Hill Street Blues* introduced multiple plotlines and character tensions, Johnson recalls. *The Simpsons* and *Seinfeld* abound with allusions and double entendres, forcing viewers to work harder to "fill in" the context in which they make sense. The pace of their delivery makes the old comedies, *Andy Griffith* et al., seem like slow motion. Reality shows are crass, but they enact "elaborately staged group psychology experiments." Johnson alludes to *The Apprentice* and says that, compared with *The Price Is Right*, it's "an intellectual masterpiece."

All of them signal an evolution in programming from the linear plots and dull patter of *Good Times* and *Starsky and Hutch*, and the more clever and modish shows activate the minds of those who watch them. When young viewers catch reruns of shows from the sixties, they chuckle at the low-tech action and fidget at the under-stimulating imagery and camera work. Pop culture hasn't plunged downward into puerile deviancy and artificial violence and general stupidity, Johnson concludes. It has fostered "a race to the top," and the moralists and doomsayers and elitists with their sky-is-falling pronouncements should cease. Audiences are smarter.

The claim is bold, and it ultimately rests not upon the structural elements of screen materials, but upon the cognitive outcomes for those who consume them. If we stick to the latter, several objections to Johnson's breezy applause stand out. For instance, buried in the depths of the Kaiser report *Generation M* is a startling finding about different media use and student achievement. It shows that leisure reading of any kind correlates more closely with a student's grades than any other media. While eight- to 18-year-olds with high and low grades differed by only one minute in TV time (186 to 187 minutes), they differed in reading time by 17 minutes, 46 to 29 — a huge discrepancy in

> As Malcolm Gladwell noted in his fawning review in *The New Yorker*, "When you play a video game, the value is in how it makes you think."

relative terms (a 36 percent drop in leisure reading for kids with low grades), one that suggests that TV doesn't have nearly the intellectual consequences that reading does. Furthermore, on Johnson's "multiple plotlines are more sophisticated" criterion, dramas that fail include not only *Dragnet* and *Kung Fu* but also *Oedipus* (Sophocles), *Medea* (Seneca), and *Phédre* (Racine). The complexity he approves lies wholly on the surface — plotlines and verbal play — while other complexities (moral, psychological, and philo-

and were the least likely to receive postsecondary education. (Johnson et al.)

Contrast that bleak assessment derived over several years with the evidence-lite enthusiasm of Johnson and other pop culture fans.

But while Johnson cites few of the knowledge/skill/habit surveys we've seen so far, he does point to one significant intellectual trend: average intelligence. In the

---

If cognitive talents rise correspondingly with the proliferation of screens and the sophistication of shows and games, why hasn't a generation of historically informed, civically active, verbally able, and mathematically talented young adults come forth and proven the cultural pessimists and aged curmudgeons wrong?

---

sophical) go unremarked. Finally, while Johnson neatly divides form from content, the act of decision-making isn't so distinct from the things decided upon. The content of screen substance — at its worst, juvenile loves and lusts, blood and guts, distortions of historical fact, petty clashes of reality contestants — is more important than he thinks.

In May 2007, another study appeared showing long-term outcomes for television viewing, and it relied on long-term observations by trained researchers. Published as "Extensive Television Viewing and the Development of Attention and Learning Difficulties During Adolescence" in *Archives of Pediatrics & Adolescent Medicine*, the research tracked children in 678 families in upstate New York at ages 14, 16, and 22 years. The article abstract summarizes:

> Frequent television viewing during adolescence was associated with elevated risk for subsequent attention and learning difficulties after family characteristics and prior cognitive difficulties were controlled. Youths who watched 1 or more hours of television per day at mean age 14 years were at elevated risk for poor homework completion, negative attitudes toward school, poor grades, and long-term academic failure. Youths who watched 3 or more hours of television per day were the most likely to experience these outcomes. In addition, youths who watched 3 or more hours of television per day were at elevated risk for subsequent attention problems

general fund of mental talent, something remarkable has happened. IQ scores have risen markedly over the century, about three points per decade since before World War II, doing so, Johnson observes, at the same time that popular culture has expanded and evolved. It's the so-called Flynn Effect, named after New Zealand political scientist James Flynn, who noted the rise (which is masked by the fact that the test is re-normed every few years). In the early 1980s, Flynn surveyed studies in which subjects took IQ tests dating from different years and disclosed the rising pattern. For instance, one experiment recorded a group scoring 103.8 on a 1978 test leaping to 111.3 on a 1953 version of the same test. Successive tests aimed to keep the average at 100 points, but to do so they had to become harder.

The question is, Why has intelligence jumped? Cognitive psychologists explain the gain variously noting improved nutrition, better early schooling, smaller families, and wider acquaintance with tests themselves. With the largest increases occurring in the area of "spatial reasoning," however, some researchers attribute them to escalating cognitive demands of an increasingly visual environment. Johnson agrees, and gives screen diversions most of the credit. With the proliferation of screens, people have grown up in a more visually challenging habitat. Brains have developed with more complex spatial stimuli than before, and teens experienced with screen technology now handle those IQ questions showing a chart of numbers with one vacant space — fill in the space with the correct number or shape — more adroitly than teens who are not.

IQ tests are controversial, of course, and questions of cultural bias, test-taking situations, and the fuzzy definition of intelligence have made them easy targets. Furthermore, research indicates that the bulk of the Flynn Effect has taken place in the lower percentiles, which have raised the average but not touched the upper tiers. Geniuses yesterday are just as smart as geniuses today. Still, the overall advances in IQ scores signify too sweeping and consistent a change to downplay, and the idea that more visual stimuli in children's lives should yield higher visual aptitudes makes intuitive sense. With IQ scores complementing it, and so many voices in academia, foundations, popular journalism, and the entertainment industries pushing the point, the connection of screen time to new learning styles, visual intelligence, media literacy, and other cognitive progressions seems sure. It is reasonable to think that media-wise youths have minds more attuned to visual information, that multitasking hours grant them a more mobile consciousness.

Maybe that's the case, but if so, then Johnson and other votaries of the screen have something else to explain. It's the question we ended with in the previous chapter. Why haven't knowledge and skill levels followed the same path? If cognitive talents rise correspondingly with the proliferation of screens and the sophistication of shows and games, why hasn't a generation of historically informed, civically active, verbally able, and mathematically talented young adults come forth and proven the cultural pessimists and aged curmudgeons wrong?

Surprisingly, the IQ issue suggests an answer, and it works against those who invoke it to promote the benefits of the screen. For, while incontestable in its data, the Flynn Effect has an extraordinary generational implication. Assuming that scores have indeed risen three points per decade, psychologist Ulric Neisser laid out the repercussions in a 1997 article in *American Scientist*:

> If a representative sample of the American children of 1997 were to take that 1932 test, their average IQ would come out to be around 120. This would put about one-quarter of the 1997 population above the 130 cutoff for "very superior" — 10 times as many as in 1932. Does that seem plausible?
>
> If we go by more recent norms instead, we arrive at an equally bizarre conclusion. Judging the American children of 1932 by today's standards — considering the scores they would

have obtained if they had somehow taken a test normalized this year — we find that their average IQ would have been only about 80! Hardly any of them would have scored "very superior," but nearly one-quarter would have appeared to be "deficient." Taking the tests at face value, we face one of two possible conclusions: Either America is now a nation of shining intellects, or it was then a nation of dolts.

Two possibilities, both extreme, yet both in accord with the notion that pop culture makes us smarter, that better tools make better minds, that more wiring and more channels yield more intelligence. Either way, we should notice momentous signs and wonders of intellect all around us.

Flynn himself recognized in 1987 that the Effect should have thrown us into an era of genius, and that we should be enjoying "a cultural renaissance too great to be overlooked." Needless to say, the 1980s fell far short, and Flynn found no evidence in Europe that mathematical or scientific discovery had increased in the preceding decades, adding as well that "no one has remarked on the superiority of contemporary schoolchildren." So, he concluded, IQ scores must measure something less than general intelligence. Observing that results for verbal and mathematical tests hadn't increased at nearly the rate that those for spatial-reasoning tests did, he characterized the intelligence measured by IQ tests as an "abstract problem-solving ability." The more tests emphasize "learned content" such as vocabulary, math techniques, and cultural knowledge, the less the Flynn Effect shows up. The more they involve "culturally reduced" material, puzzles and pictures that require no historical or verbal context, the more the gains surface. Moreover, the significance of those gains apart from the test itself diminishes. "We know people solve problems on IQ tests; we suspect those problems are so detached, or so abstracted from reality," Flynn remarked, "that the ability to solve them can diverge over time from the real-world problem-solving ability called intelligence."

Flynn's analysis explains the curious bifurcation in the intellectual lives of young adults. On one hand, they navigate the multimedia environment like pros, wielding four email accounts and two virtual identities, jumping from screen to keypad to iPod without pause, creating "content" and expressing themselves to the world. On the other hand, they know remarkably little about the wider world, about civics, history, math, science, and foreign affairs, and their reading and writing skills remain at 1970s levels. If Johnson, Richard Sweeney, Randy Bomer, and, more important, some serious cognitive researchers are right to link screen activities to higher intelligence, we may agree with them partway, but, with Flynn, limit the intelligence that screen activities produce. The screen doesn't involve learning per se, but, as Sweeney says, a particular "learning style," not literacy in general, but "viewer literacy" (Bomer's term). It promotes multitasking and discourages single-tasking, hampering the deliberate focus on a single text, a discrete problem. "Screen-mindedness" prizes using search engines and clicking 20 Web sites, not the plodding, 10-hour passage through a 300-page novel. It searches for information, fast, too impatient for the long-term acquisition of facts and stories and principles. As an elementary school principal told me last year, when the fifth-grade teachers assign a topic, the kids proceed like this: go to Google, type keywords, download three relevant sites, cut and paste passages into a new document, add transitions of their own, print it up, and turn it in. The model is information retrieval, not knowledge formation, and the material passes from Web to homework paper without lodging in the minds of the students.

Technophiles celebrate the ease and access, and teens and young adults derive a lesson from them. If you can call up a name, a date, an event, a text, a definition, a calculation, or a law in five seconds of key-punching, why fill your mind with them? With media feeds so solicitous, the slow and steady methods of learning seem like a bunch of outmoded and counterproductive exercises. In this circumstance, young people admit the next connection, the new gadget, smoothly into their waking hours, but the older "learning styles," the parents' study habits, are crowded out. Years of exposure to screens prime young Americans at a deep cognitive level to multitasking and interactivity. Perhaps we should call this a certain kind of intelligence, a novel screen literacy. It improves their visual acuity, their mental readiness for rushing images and updated information. At the same time, however, screen intelligence doesn't transfer well to non-screen experiences, especially the kinds that build knowledge and verbal skills. It conditions minds against quiet, concerted study, against imagination unassisted by visuals, against linear, sequential analysis of texts, against an idle afternoon with a detective story and nothing else.

This explains why teenagers and 20-year-olds appear at the same time so mentally agile and culturally ignorant.

Visual culture improves the abstract spatialization and problem solving, but it doesn't complement other intelligence-building activities. Smartness there parallels dumbness elsewhere. The relationship between screens and books isn't benign. As "digital natives" dive daily into three visual media and two sound sources as a matter of disposition, of deep mental compatibility, not just taste, ordinary reading, slow and uniform, strikes them as incompatible, alien. It isn't just boring and obsolete. It's irritating. A Raymond Chandler novel takes too long, an Emily Dickinson poem wears them down. A history book requires too much contextual knowledge, and science facts come quicker through the Web than through *A Brief History of Time*. Bibliophobia is the syndrome. Technophiles cast the young media-savvy sensibility as open and flexible, and it is, as long as the media come through a screen or a speaker. But faced with 100 paper pages, the digital mind turns away. The bearers of e-literacy reject books the way eBay addicts reject bricks-and-mortar stores.

Or rather, they throw them into the dustbin of history. In the video "Are Kids Different Because of Digital Media?" sponsored by the MacArthur Foundation as part of its 2006 Digital Learning project, one young person declares as a truism that "books are not the standard thing for learning anymore." Another divulges, "My parents question me why I don't have my books. ... The books are online now, so you don't really need the books." They back their dismissal up with their purchases. In 1990, according to the *Consumer Expenditure Survey* (Bureau of Labor Statistics), the average person under 25 spent $75 on reading and $344 on television, radio, and sound equipment. In 2004, reading spending dropped to a measly $51, while TV, radio, and sound climbed to $500. Imagine the proportions if computers were added to the mix.

CHAPTER 7

Science

If this discovery is confirmed it will surely be one of the most stunning insights into our universe that science has ever uncovered. Its implications are as far reaching and awe inspiring as can be imagined. Even as it promises to answer some of our oldest questions, it poses still others even more fundamental. We will continue to listen closely to what it has to say as we continue to search for answers and for knowledge that is as old as humanity itself but essential to our people's future.

— President Bill Clinton,
Contact (1997)

Chapter 7. Science

Recommended Film

Contact (Robert Zemeckis 1997)

Media Models

The Meme, The Network, The Spectacle

Chapter Summary

Chris Mooney and Sheril Kirshenbaum provide an overview of the anti-science attitudes that guide Hollywood filmmaking, with only a few notable exceptions.

Heather Keith and Steven Fesmire contrast faith with science and scientific thinking, as depicted in *Contact*.

Neil deGrasse Tyson explains the scientific meaning of the opening scene of *Contact* and what it says about how we present ourselves to the cosmos.

Hollywood and the Mad Scientists

from *Unscientific America*

— Chris Mooney and Sheril Kirshenbaum

"Reality ends here." It's the unofficial motto of the university of Southern California School of Cinematic Arts, cast in concrete at the entranceway to the Robert Zemeckis Center for Digital Arts and, in Latin, at the South entryway of a new complex building. As scientist-turned-filmmaker and USC film school graduate Randy Olson explained to us, the slogan

> is not a joke. It's a bold, challenging statement — a basic "screw you" to the outside world who thinks that accuracy and reality are important variables in storytelling, when in fact they are the dread enemy of storytelling. No storyteller wants an expert around who will question his premises. It's hard enough to tell a story without having some annoying expert sitting there correcting every detail and negating every premise.

Translated for more literal-minded scientists — who, when they think of *Star Wars*, think of the impossibility of having fire and loud explosions in space — the motto might be better rendered: Abandon All Accuracy, Ye Who Enter Here.

No wonder scientists haven't always been pleased with depictions of themselves, and the subjects they study, in the entertainment media. There's a long litany of complaints: Too many stereotypically nerdy scientists — think Rick Moranis in *Honey, I Shrunk the Kids* — and too few positive role models. Too many mad scientists trying to play God.

Too many plotlines dependent upon the supernatural and the paranormal — stories in which, as in *The X-Files*, the credulous believer is always right and the scientist-skeptic is always wrong.[1] And too many simply ridiculous "scientific" premises, epitomized by the 2003 film *The Core*, in which Earth's magnetic field begins to collapse because the planet's core stops spinning.[2]

In light of the massive influence of the American entertainment industry, both here and around the world, scientists' complaints about Hollywood deserve to be taken seriously. Successful blockbusters reach audiences numbering in the tens of millions or more, and gross in the hundreds of millions of dollars at the box office. Some become pop-culture reference points for entire generations: Even those countless Americans who can't name a living scientist probably know who "Doc" from *Back to the Future* is. Entertainment industry expert Marty Kaplan, director

---

1. William Evans, "Science and Reason in Film and Television," *Skeptical Inquirer* (January–February 1996).
2. An occurrence that, if it really did happen, would likely destroy us all and pose a vastly bigger risk than the film's alleged microwave threat from space. No, waves of the sort produced by your microwave could not destroy the Golden Gate Bridge. For critiques of the science of *The Core*, see Phil Plait's movie review, http://www.badastronomy.com/bad/movies/thecore_review. html. See also the discussion by Sidney Perkowitz in *Hollywood Science: Movies, Science, and the End of the World* (New York: Columbia University Press, 2007), pp. 85–86. Finally, see Michael Barnett, Heather Wagner, Anne Gatling, et al., "The Impact of Science Fiction Film on Student Understanding of Science," *Journal of Science Education and Technology*, Vol. 15, No. 2 (April 2006), in which the authors use *The Core* as a case study.

of the Norman Lear Center at the University of Southern California's Annenberg School for Communication, perhaps puts it best when he describes Hollywood films as the "unofficial curriculum of society."[3]

Within this curriculum, science usually gets taught through the medium of science fiction and the sometimes related disaster-movie genre, both of which have become dominant storytelling modes. From the *Star Wars* films to *The Matrix* to *Jurassic Park*, it has been estimated that sci-fi blockbusters constitute fully one-third of the top fifty biggest film moneymakers in history — and disaster movies don't do too shabbily either.[4] But the relationship between science fiction and actual science is, at best, complicated.

In the sci-fi film genre, there's a kind of unending arms race to achieve ever higher degrees of verisimilitude through ever more stunning computerized graphics and special effects. Reality — or at least the semblance of it — sells. The pursuit of filmic "realism," however, comes about to serve moneymaking goals rather than to satisfy a small, scientifically trained demographic, which may be the only audience group that sees past the veneer enough to contest aspects of it.[5] Consider the dramatic presentation of big-screen dinosaurs in 1993's *Jurassic Park*: Many aspects of their portrayal — the idea that dinosaurs were warm-blooded, for instance — were contested on a scientific level[6], but viewers thought they were watching the most "realistic" dinosaurs yet depicted. Seeing is believing, especially when the picture is worth millions of dollars.

And so sit the scientists, in the dark, struggling to suspend disbelief but feeling rather ambiguous at best. Yes, science underlies the imaginative leaps of the sci-fi genre, and whenever a big geophysical disaster movie is being made, you can bet that the producers will call on a scientist to consult and lend the film plausibility.[7] Yet scientists remain perennial Hollywood outsiders, always threatening the plot with their pesky emphasis on details. The problem was apparent as early as the 1920s, with Fritz Lang's film *Woman in the Moon (Frau im Mond)*. Lang's science

consultant, a rocket scientist named Hermann Oberth, reasonably pointed out that as the moon doesn't have any atmosphere, the characters would have to carry out their roles dressed in spacesuits. Lang replied, "How could one present a love story taking place on the Moon and have the lead characters talk to each other and hold hands through space suits?"[8] Needless to say, there were no spacesuits in the final cut of the film.

To better grasp why science can stumble in its interactions with the entertainment industry, perhaps we need only define our terms. According to Kaplan's Norman Lear Center, the word *entertaining* in its broadest sense simply means "*not boring*."[9] The entertainment drive, Kaplan adds, is "the imperative to capture and hold attention"[10]; that's how the entertainment industry makes money. To hold attention, successful entertainment requires a strong story line, character development, and high stakes, often of the life-and-death variety. Events unfold at high speed, and there must be serious action or serious drama, not to mention very attractive people.

The problem for science in this context is that the technical facts it furnishes can rarely hold the attention of non-scientists — and anyone who has watched presentations at a scientific conference knows why. That is not to say the goals of science, education, and critical thinking can't also be advanced through entertainment: They can, but only if doing so poses no apparent risk to the product and if the people who matter — writers, directors, producers — see some value in it.

In the many notorious cases where they don't, meanwhile, the most stunning factual and theoretical howlers can occur. It's not merely that you shouldn't look to *Spider-Man* or *X-Men* to learn about the process of mutation, as these films greatly exaggerate it for dramatic purposes. Some of the worst sci-fi and disaster films go much further, seizing upon entirely nonsensical "scientific" premises and then proceeding to come increasingly unhinged as the story advances. In 1997's *Volcano*, for instance, an actual volcano suddenly appears out of the ground to threaten Los Angeles (luckily for L.A., the San Andreas fault, due to its particular tectonic nature, can only produce earthquakes)[11]. Then

3   Interview with Marty Kaplan, August 28, 2008.
4   Perkowitz, *Hollywood Science*, p. 12.
5   See David Kirby, "Science Consultants, Fictional Films, and Scientific Practice," *Social Studies of Science*, Vol. 33, No. 2 (April 2003), pp. 231–268.
6   As discussed in ibid.
7   See Scott Frank, "Reel Reality: Science Consultants in Hollywood," *Science as Culture*, Vol. 12, No. 4 (December 2003).

8   This episode is related in Kirby, "Science Consultants."
9   University of Southern California Annenberg School, "Enter the Entertainment Initiative," informational materials.
10 Interview with Marty Kaplan, August 28, 2008.
11 See Perkowitz, *Hollywood Science*, p. 85.

there are the simply excessive made-for-TV disaster movies, like NBC's heavily watched four-hour miniseries *10.5* (about a scientifically impossible earthquake)[12] and CBS's *Category 7* (about a scientifically ridiculous mega-storm)[13]. And don't forget the idiotic bloopers, as when a boastful geneticist in 2000's *Red Planet*, showing off his wisdom, names the DNA bases "A, G, T, P." That's right, the actor actually says "*P.*" Didn't the filmmakers see *Gattaca*? A high school science student would have been able to catch that one.

Yet in marshaling scientific complaints against the entertainment industry, it's important to consider what really matters and what doesn't. Any specialist — a historian, say, or an anthropologist — is prone to get ticked off if a film or TV drama makes a mistake about his or her field. And films like *The Core* and *Volcano* probably don't help stu-

— just think of *Grey's Anatomy*, *House*, *Lost* (in which the main character, Jack, is a spinal surgeon), *E.R.* — and these are just prime-time dramas, not movies. These shows pride themselves on their medical realism; the directors and cast of *E.R.*, for instance, make much of the fact that they consult constantly with real doctors. Good for them, but there's much to make up for. For example, one mid-1990s study of television episodes involving CPR found that survival rates were unrealistically high and concluded that "the misrepresentation of CPR on television shows undermines trust in data and fosters trust in miracles."[16]

Perhaps more consequential than scientific inaccuracy, however, is a problem we might call scientist stereotyping. Many groups in society get exercised about how they come across in entertainment depictions, and scientists aren't necessarily the most aggrieved. Still, their complaints have

---

As science-fiction film director James Cameron (*Aliens, The Terminator, Titanic*, and much else) has observed, the movies generally "show scientists as idiosyncratic nerds or actively the villains."

---

dents or the public understand science — but then, neither are they intended to.[14] So how worried should we really be if an inaccuracy or implausibility slips into a film to serve the plot or to satisfy audience expectations — if, say, *Star Wars* shows fiery explosions in space? Probably not very.

In other realms, though, matters grow more serious. For instance, inaccuracy about medical conditions and treatments can have a real impact on people who get a little too much of their sense of reality from the screen or television. Hollywood's medical plots and subplots are legion[15]

merit. As science-fiction film director James Cameron (*Aliens, The Terminator, Titanic*, and much else) has observed, the movies generally "show scientists as idiosyncratic nerds or actively the villains."[17]

Cameron's statement finds support in a considerable body of data produced by scholars who have analyzed the treatment of science in film and on television going back several decades. A study of prime-time television programs between 1973 and 1983, for instance, found that one in six scientists was depicted as a villain[18] and that one in ten got killed[19], both results being the highest rate

---

12 For a scientific critique of *10.5*, see Sid Perkins, "What's Wrong with This Picture? Educating via Analyses of Science in Movies and TV," *Science News*, October 16, 2004.

13 For a further parsing of nonsense in such movies, see Barnett, Wagner, Gatling, et al., "The Impact of Science Fiction Film on Student Understanding of Science," May 16, 2007 lecture, http://frontrow.bc.edu/program/barnett/.

14 See ibid.

15 A 2008 analysis by the Kaiser Family Foundation and USC's Norman Lear Center found that from 2004 through 2006, out of the top ten most highly rated scripted (i.e., not "reality") shows on TV, 59 percent of episodes "had at least one health-related storyline," with "storyline" defined as three or more lines of dialogue on a health topic. See Sheila T. Murphy, Heather J. Hether, and Victoria Rideout, "How Healthy Is Prime Time? An Analysis of Health Content in Popular

Prime Time Television Programs," Kaiser Family Foundation, September 2008.

16 Susan J. Diem, John D. Lantos, and James A. Tulsky, "Cardiopulmonary Resuscitation on Television: Miracles and Misinformation," *New England Journal of Medicine*, Vol. 334, No. 24, June 13, 1996, pp. 1578–1582.

17 Quoted in Perkowitz, *Hollywood Science*, p. 172.

18 Scientist hero characters also emerge from the products of Hollywood (there are several in *Jurassic Park*, for instance). But we shouldn't confuse counterexamples with a counterargument. In the entire corpus of Hollywood film, it's undeniable there are a whole lot of freaky, geeky, and even evil scientists.

19 George Gerbner, Larry Gross, Michael Morgan, et al., "Television Entertainment and Viewers' Conceptions of Science," University of Pennsylvania Annenberg School of

---

for any occupational group on television. Such representations have consequences: Researchers who have studied the stereotypical views of scientists held by children even report that when they encounter real-life researchers who visit their classrooms[20], they think someone's pulling their leg, because the scientists aren't anything like the big-screen version—mean, male, gray-haired, and mad. As one study author explained to the magazine *Nature:* "They might say the person was too 'normal' or too good looking to be a scientist. The most heart-breaking thing is when they say, 'I didn't think he was real because he seemed to care about us.'"[21]

The uncaring scientist, unconcerned about consequences, pursuing knowledge at all costs — this is the ugliest scientist stereotype, and also the most deeply rooted. It hails from a long literary tradition[22], dating back before Mary Shelley's *Frankenstein* to Goethe's *Faust* and Greek precedents like the story of Prometheus, which depict the search for knowledge as forbidden and dangerous, and leading to disastrous consequences. In this narrative, knowledge leads the scientist to play God[23], interfere with nature, and attempt to thwart fate by determining who lives and who dies. To know is, in essence, to kill. In film, such depictions go all the way back to Fritz Lang's 1926 classic early sci-fi film *Metropolis*[24], in which the grotesque

mad scientist Rotwang builds an evil robot to resemble the woman he loves, because he can't have her in real life.[25] The paradigmatic modern example of the evil scientist trope is perhaps *E. T.*, in which the scientists, looking like astronauts in their protective gear, want to slice up the cute alien for research.[26]

As we don't see many films about evil literary critics, it's safe to infer there's something about scientists that triggers a particular kind of stereotyping, and that this reflects our society's uneasiness with the power they can sometimes wield. As we saw in the Pluto story that began this book, scientists also make enemies by taking away from people things they cherish — beliefs, settled understandings.

Communications, July 1985. In another study, surveying 100 films made through the late 1980s and examining previous research on the subject, Lehigh University's Stephen L. Goldman found that science and technology "have been depicted largely negatively in popular films of all genres." See Goldman, "Images of Technology in Popular Films: Discussion and Filmography," *Science, Technology, and Human Values*, Vol. 14, No. 3 (Summer 1989), pp. 275–301.

20 See, for example, Gayle A. Buck, Diandra Leslie-Pelecky, and Susan K. Kirby, "Bringing Female Scientists into the Elementary Classroom: Confronting the Strength of Elementary Students' Stereotypical Images of Scientists," *Journal of Elementary Science Education*, Vol. 14, No. 2 (Fall 2002), pp. 1–9.

21 Quoted in Jonathan Knight, "Hollywood or Bust: Last Month, a Handful of Scientists Who Have Toyed with the Idea of Writing for the Movies Were Given a Masterclass by Tinseltown's Finest," *Nature*, Vol. 430, August 12, 2004.

22 See Jon Turney, *Frankenstein's Footsteps: Science, Genetics, and Popular Culture* (New Haven: Yale University Press, 1998).

23 Or as Victor Frankenstein puts it in Shelley's novel: "Learn … by my example, how dangerous is the acquirement of knowledge, and how much happier that man is who believes his native town to be the world, than he who aspires to become greater than his nature will allow."

24 We can also detect the Frankenstein mythology in such late nineteenth- and early twentieth-century novels as H. G.

Wells's *The Island of Dr. Moreau* and Aldous Huxley's *Brave New World*, both of which also became films.

25 As scientist and film enthusiast Sidney Perkowitz summarizes the plot: "Boy meets girl, boy loses girl, boy builds girl." Perkowitz, *Hollywood Science*, p. 7.

26 There are many other such films, often linked to the biomedical sciences and especially to the subject of cloning. One thinks of films like 2005's *The Island* — in which the doctor running the clone complex has a "God complex" — but the same trope appears in flicks ranging from *Jurassic Park* to *Star Wars* (especially episodes 2 and 3) to 1995's *Batman Forever*, in which mad scientist Edward Nigma ("The Riddler") develops a device to extract victims' thoughts and intelligence, making him smarter but ultimately contributing to his mental breakdown. As *Slate* magazine put it after surveying nearly a century of "mad scientist" films: "What do cinematic images of scientists say about cultural attitudes toward scientific progress? They are usually about science as a source of anxiety, scientists as outsiders and oddballs, research as very likely to get into the wrong hands, and scientific institutions as dangerous places to be. Never mind that cinema depends on technological progress — this is one of the great unresolved contradictions of popular culture." Christopher Frayling, "Spawn of Frankenstein: Mad Scientists in the Movies," *Slate*, May 9, 2006, http://www.slate.com/id/2140772/.

Possibly that contradiction arises in part as the legacy of the late 1960s and 1970s, a period that instilled doubt about science and its societal benefits and costs among many intellectuals, including those in the entertainment industry. Possibly it goes back still further, descending from the battles between C. P. Snow and the "literary intellectuals" who had such a negative view of technology-dependent industrialization. *Frankenstein* was a product of the British Romantic movement.

These are undoubtedly important antecedents and influences; but with film and television we must always bear in mind that the bottom line involves not ideology, but profits — or as Stephen Colbert has so felicitously put it, getting "asses in seats." So if these depictions of scientists recur, it's likely they serve some purpose, even if it's one as narrow as predictability — giving audiences more of what they already know and have thus come to expect.

Through such actions, they can intimidate and sometimes even enrage non-scientists, and thus they play some role in the construction of their own image.

Without condoning stereotypes, then, or asking scientists to stop being scientists, we might at least suggest some reflection on this fact.

Does Hollywood hate scientists because they're mean and intimidating and spoil all the fun? Probably not. But throughout the industry, there is certainly a sense that science is inimical to storytelling, that it quashes creativity, which must be allowed to breathe. As screenwriter and ScienceDebate2008 founder Matthew Chapman explained about some of his fellow writers: "Among the less talented, there's I think a kind of inherent prejudice against science, because science means being rational, and being rational is considered the opposite of being creative — whereas fantasy, superstition, magic, all of these more childlike ways of looking at life, are somehow thought to be what the creative process is about."[27]

Not everyone in Hollywood shares such sentiments: Many filmmakers care about science, as do many writers. But unless they have serious clout within the industry, they may not be able to get their way even if they try. "The person who creates the idea for a story or screenplay is not the person who makes it generally," explains Joe Petricca, a screenwriter and executive vice dean of the American Film Institute. "The person who makes it is about money, business, filling theaters, and sales — and they will exert all the pressure they can to make changes so that it's not so, ah, threatening in that way ... threateningly intelligent."[28]

The top directors — the Ron Howards, James Camerons, Steven Spielbergs — have enough status in Hollywood to ensure the realization of their artistic visions, which may include the favorable or serious treatment of science (or math, as in Howard's *A Beautiful Mind*). And a number of films have been commended for their plausibility and scientific accuracy, ranging from Carl Sagan's *Contact* (directed by Robert Zemeckis) to the 2003 smash-hit Pixar film *Finding Nemo*, which luxuriated in its sensuous depictions of undersea life and strove, with the help of its science consultant, to achieve the maximum degree of ichthyological realism possible.[29] But when it comes to the sympathetic treatment of science in Hollywood, "the word that comes to mind is *serendipitous*," observes Martin Gunderson, a University of Southern California electrical engineer who has consulted on several films, most notably 1985's *Real Genius*.[30] In other words, it happens — but more because some individual director, writer, or producer cares than because of industry culture.

Hollywood ought to do better, but scientists also need to be realistic about what they can expect. At least at the extreme, we find in the scientists' camp a hectoring annoyance over inaccuracy[31], the unwillingness or inability to suspend disbelief, and the strange idea that serious science education — instruction about facts and theories — ought to occur through the medium of fictional film and television. These tendencies just won't help in Hollywood interactions. And some scientists will also have to get over the idea that everyone ought to be as captivated by the intricacies of science as they are. "The natural world is fascinating in its own right,"[32] Oxford's Richard Dawkins has stated. "It really doesn't need human drama to be fascinating." He even reportedly told the *New York Times* that he wondered why *Jurassic Park* required a cast that included human beings — after all, it already had dinosaurs.

Such science-centrism simply won't work for the broader, non-scientist population. It ignores their compelling need not to be bored. Successes like *March of the Penguins* notwithstanding, most of the time people need to see and hear stories about other people, or about animals that are given human attributes, as in Disney-Pixar films. Dawkins

27 Interview with Matthew Chapman, August 20, 2008.
28 Interview with Joe Petricca, September 5, 2008.
29 See Alison Abbot, "The Fabulous Fish Guy," *Nature*, Vol. 427, February 19, 2004, pp. 672–673.
30 Interview with Martin Gunderson, August 27, 2008.
31 Not every scientist is overly literal-minded or unable to grasp the exigencies of storytelling. But the generalization isn't entirely without merit. For instance, Joe Petricca describes an experiment in which the American Film Institute set up a workshop to train a group of scientists in the art of screenwriting. "They would have these incredible, fascinating, you-can't-believe-they're-true scientific ideas, stuff you can't even make up," he remembers, "but not a character in sight, not a person, no nothing." But "the granularity of science, the specificity of science, doesn't help the story," Petricca said. "The story is about honesty, the story is about emotion — even if it's a ridiculous story, or a comedy story. Those are the things that will speak to an audience." Interview with Joe Petricca, September 5, 2008.
32 Richard Dawkins quoted in Andrew Pollack, "Scientists Seek a New Movie Role: Hero, Not Villain," *New York Times*, December 1, 1998.

and some other scientists fail to grasp that in Hollywood, the story is paramount — that narrative, drama, and character development will trump mere factual accuracy every time, and by a very long shot. Either science will align itself with these overweening objectives or it will literally get flattened by the drive for profit.

The scientific method, as a process, generally does not make for great storytelling, and particularly not filmmaking. As the late novelist, screenwriter, and movie producer Michael Crichton once put it[33], there are at least four important rules of movies that don't mesh with the process of research: "(i) Movie characters must be compelled to act. (ii) Movies need villains. (iii) Movie searches are dull. (iv) Movies must move."[34] Crichton argued that real science, with its long, drawn-out intellectual processes and frequent dead ends, simply can't be reconciled with such exigencies. "The problems lie with the limitations of film as a visual storytelling medium," he concluded. "You aren't going to beat it."

But maybe scientists can join it? The entertainment industry needs science both to achieve very valuable filmic "realism" and to serve up the most intriguing ideas about the future, in order to furnish compelling sci-fi and disaster story lines. The scientific community should take advantage of this fact and seek out constructive consulting roles within the entertainment industry.[35] It should develop relationships with important players and learn how to serve them to further shared goals, rather than merely issuing criticism and denunciation. Scientists who have done so have frequently reported that the experience was a very

enjoyable one[36], and that they made a real difference.[37] For instance, science consultants working on the 1990s films Dante's Peak (about a volcanic eruption) and Twister apparently headed off attempts to cast scientific leaders or institutions in the role of out-and-out villains.[38]

Science consultants can have an impact on the scientific content in a film's script, on its set design, on its sound effects. In general, they are invited on board by those at the head of film projects — directors, producers — and their influence is proportionate to the closeness of their relationship to that leader.[39] By the time a science consultant arrives on the scene to work on a project, many things such as plotline, cast, and budget are usually already agreed upon, and a script has likely been written, at least in draft form.[40] Given all of this, any effective science consultant or adviser will be acutely aware of the realities and constraints of filmmaking and will work with them, rather than trying to overturn them.[41]

36 Frank, "Reel Reality."

37 There are risks in science consulting, such as getting used as a rubber stamp whom filmmakers can cite to show that they did indeed run things by an expert. The scientifically ludicrous Volcano, for instance, had a consultant, and The Core director Jon Amiel has boasted, "We wanted to actually put some science in the science fiction." Quoted in Cindy White, "Director Jon Amiel Spearheads a New Journey to the Center of the Earth," Sci-Fi Weekly, March 24, 2003, http://www.scifi.com/sfw/interviews/sfw9571.html. But it's also clear that those scientists who work or consult with Hollywood can learn a great deal about how to be an effective go-between, connecting two worlds and two cultures.

38 Frank, "Reel Reality."

39 Ibid.

40 Ibid.

41 As an example, consider Marty Kaplan's Norman Lear Center, whose "Hollywood Health and Society" project — funded by the Centers for Disease Control and the National Institutes of Health — focuses on medical content in television dramas. One central role played by the project is to take calls from television writers who have medical questions and quickly put them in con-tact with on-call experts: Over 200 such inquiries were answered in the year 2006. See Lauren Movius, Michael Cody, Grace Huang, et al., "Motivating Television Viewers to Become Organ Donors," Cases in Public Health Communication and Marketing (June 2007). "Without trying to wag a finger, without saying that there is a compromise between profit — which is what the entertainment industry is about — and storytelling, there are often intriguing solutions that can be both accurate and live within the parameters of the storytelling situation you're in," explains Kaplan. "We don't succeed because people want to be good guys ... We succeed because writers and producers and network executives have come to the point of view that if you can be accurate, without a cost to the entertainment value and story structure and so

---

33 Despite his late-life attacks on climate science, there can be no doubt that Michael Crichton was a great innovator and had massive influence upon the depiction of science in Hollywood and in popular culture. As Chris has argued, we shouldn't let one late-life misjudgment totally cloud our image of him. See Mooney, "The Crichton Effect: A Chief Designer of the Image of Science in America Passes," Science Progress, November 11, 2008, http://www.scienceprogress.org/2008/11/the-crichton-effect/.

34 Michael Crichton, "Ritual Abuse, Hot Air, and Missed Opportunities," 1999 AAAS annual meeting lecture, Anaheim, California, http://www.crichton-official.com/speech-scienceviewsmedia.html.

35 There's at least some evidence suggesting Hollywood science-consultant numbers are actually on the rise — or at least, they were as of 2003, according to a study published in that year by University of Manchester science-communication scholar David Kirby. Kirby, "Science Consultants."

on, it's probably a good thing to do." (Interview with Marty Kaplan, August 28, 2008.)

Sensitivity of this type is critical, because Hollywood is already massively overlobbied by scores of interest groups that monitor the depictions of all sorts of subjects, and all have their own grievances and wants. The "Hollywood Health and Society" project teaches another lesson, too, a more practical one. It is this: Although those unfamiliar with the industry tend to think first about ways of influencing blockbuster films, the truth is that it's possible to have a far greater and more immediate impact through television.

The reason is sheer numbers. Studios see tens of thousands of film-scripts and script ideas per year, and even after winnowing these down dramatically and putting some small percentage of projects into development, only one in twenty ideas that survive the first cut gets produced. By the time the call has been made to bring a particular film project all the way to production, "there have been 7 million meetings, script conferences, notes," says Kaplan. "And in at the end walks a scientist or consultant, and says, 'No, it can't work like that'? The notion of throwing out key elements of the story is not very welcome." (Interview with Marty Kaplan, August 28, 2008.)

Television is different. The audience is still very large: During the week of October 22, 2007, the ten leading network prime-time shows drew in 15 to 21 million viewers apiece. Murphy, Hether, and Rideout, "How Healthy Is Prime Time?" But these shows — like *House* and *Grey's Anatomy* — have to produce weekly episodes, often retaining for that purpose regular consultants who work intensively with the writers week in and week out to offer ideas and feedback.

Consider the successful CBS series *Numb3rs*, which features a non-nerdy mathematician (played by David Krumholtz) who helps his FBI agent brother solve crimes. Stanford University mathematician Keith Devlin, who consulted for the show during its first season, was aware that creators Ridley and Tony Scott very much wanted to have a scientist-mathematician hero character. He explains his motivation for helping out thusly: "I just knew, if it was successful as a series, it would have a huge impact on the public perception of mathematics." That certainly did occur — during the 2005–2006 season *Numb3rs* garnered an average of 13 million viewers per night. (Movius, Cody, Huang, et al., "Motivating Television Viewers to Become Organ Donors.") Devlin adds: "Once audiences get used to the fact that you can have good science intelligently portrayed, that raises the bar and the expectations." (Interview with Keith Devlin, September 5, 2008.)

USC's Norman Lear Center worked with *Numb3rs* writer J. David Harden to provide information for a January 27, 2006, episode, entitled "Harvest," which involved the subject of organ donation. (Movius, Cody, Huang, et al., "Motivating Television Viewers to Become Organ Donors.") The episode, which was viewed by 13.36 million people, ended with a kind of teachable moment in which the characters discuss how important it is to become an organ donor; afterward, in surveys posted on the show's Web site and fan sites, viewers expressed themselves as more likely to sign up to be a donor after seeing the episode. As Harden has commented: "I'm not naive — we all understand TV has a big impact. Just consider

It's worth taking a chance on collaborations of this kind because the stakes are extremely high. We're talking about perhaps the single most influential slice of the media, an arena in which a success can have a dramatic impact.

To see as much, one need only consider Al Gore's *An Inconvenient Truth*. It was a very unconventional film — a documentary centered on a PowerPoint presentation — but something in the zeitgeist just clicked, perhaps because the messenger was the man who should have been president. Thus, the film's smash success not only transformed Gore's image and influence but also helped to move the global warming debate onto a new footing. Gore's subsequent garnering of an Oscar (again bestowed by Hollywood) and a Nobel Peace Prize (not bestowed by Hollywood, but certainly very much influenced by it) only broadened the impact further. The stars aligned, and a Hollywood film had a massive impact in translating science's relevance to policymakers and the public.[42]

Hollywood can also shape and direct the pursuit of scientific careers. The success of CBS's television series *CSI: Crime Scene Investigation*, which glamorizes and dramatizes forensic science, led to a much-noted growth of student interest in the field and the proliferation of university programs to service that demand.[43] This happened despite the fact that real forensic work is hardly as exciting and dramatic as it appears on TV, and few forensic scientists are as hot.

Perhaps these examples show why we badly need more go-betweens to link the science world and the entertainment

---

the size of the audience for our show: Eleven million people and upwards watching Friday nights. You definitely live with a sense that there's some responsibility incumbent upon you in the face of that audience."

42 This isn't the only example of Hollywood depictions influencing politics. In 1998, two blockbuster films — *Armageddon* and *Deep Impact* — dramatized the risk to the planet from a collision with a so-called near-Earth object (an asteroid in one film, a comet in the other). Although one could quibble with some of the specific details in these films — the asteroid in *Armageddon* is unrealistically large, for instance — there's no doubt that both treated a scenario that doesn't merely lie within the realm of theoretical possibility but has occurred repeatedly in the past history of the planet. These treatments resulted in dramatically increased public awareness and closely coincided with (and may have helped trigger) the launch of NASA's Near-Earth Object Program, which now tracks such risks. For further details, see Kirby, "Science Consultants."

43 See Scott Smallwood, "As Seen on TV: 'CSI' and 'The X-Files' Help Build Forensics Programs," *Chronicle of Higher Education*, July 19, 2002.

industry. Luckily, the science community has begun to recognize this and work in a concerted way to promote it. The U.S. National Academy of Sciences — whose members once spurned Sagan — recently launched a project entitled the Science and Entertainment Exchange[44], which aims to

Contact didn't do badly. It earned $171 million worldwide, nearly doubling the $90-million production budget.[46] But it was also competing with two considerably more brainless alien-related sci-fi movies, 1997's *Men in Black* and 1996's *Independence Day*, both of which made

---

The success of CBS's television series *CSI: Crime Scene Investigation*, which glamorizes and dramatizes forensic science, led to a much-noted growth of student interest in the field and the proliferation of university programs to service that demand.

"facilitate a valuable connection between the two communities." This included the opening of a permanent National Academies office in Los Angeles to "make introductions, schedule briefings, and arrange for consultations to anyone developing science-based entertainment content." This is a new initiative, so one cannot yet judge its success, but it is precisely the type of outreach the scientific community should be engaging in if it wants to take advantage of the immense opportunities afforded by the mass medium of film.

a great deal more money ($589 million and $817 million, respectively).[47] And that unfavorable financial comparison, more than anything else, dramatizes the incredible challenge science faces in Hollywood. If films that strive to balance scientific plausibility with a compelling story line don't succeed at the box office, the road will be tougher for future efforts. Luckily, scientific stinkers don't necessarily make the biggest fortunes, either. When you compare two dueling 1997 volcano movies, the more plausible *Dante's Peak* and the much less scientifically serious *Volcano*, the

---

Contact didn't do badly. It earned $171 million worldwide, … But it was also competing with two considerably more brainless alien-related sci-fi movies, 1997's *Men in Black* and 1996's *Independence Day*, both of which made a great deal more money …

Sagan in fact epitomizes both the promise and the perils of scientists working with Hollywood. His 1997 film *Contact*, based on his novel of the same name, strove to preserve scientific accuracy and plot plausibility. It also depicted the main character, astrophysicist Ellie Arroway (played by Jodie Foster), as a positive role model, a visionary who overcomes numerous obstacles to pursue her quest of determining whether extraterrestrial life really does exist and is trying to reach us.[45]

former did more business ($178 million worldwide) than the latter ($122 million worldwide).[48]

Such figures provide hope that Hollywood could play a role that serves the interests of the entertainment industry, science, and society alike by helping us grapple with the future we are hurtling toward. The ideal synergy would occur if more sci-fi and disaster plots took as their basis the problems that we really need to worry about, and dramatized

---

44 See http://www.scienceandentertainmentexchange.org/index. html.

45 Still, none of this could prevent the need to construct, for the film version of *Contact*, a love interest for Arroway that doesn't exist in the novel — her semi-mechanical fling with the preacher Palmer Joss (Matthew McConnaughey). Some scientists were displeased at the compulsory affair, but, well, that's Hollywood. See Pollack, "Scientists Seek a New Movie Role."

46 *Contact* earnings figures from Box Office Mojo, http://www. boxofficemojo.com/movies/?id=contact.htm.

47 *Men in Black* earnings figures from Box Office Mojo, http:// www.boxofficemojo.com/movies/?id=meninblack.htm.
    Independence Day earnings figures from Box Office Mojo, littp://www.boxofficemojo.com/movies/?id=independenceday. htm.

48 *Dante's Peak* earnings figures from Box Office Mojo, http:// www.boxofficemojo.com/movies/?id=dantespeak.htm.
    Volcano earnings figures from Box Office Mojo, http://www. boxofficemojo.com/movies/?id=volcano.htm.

them compellingly. There have been some excellent, and successful, examples of such films in the relatively recent past, and in closing, let's survey them.

Among science-related topics, human cloning and genetic engineering — issues that are already raising ethical concerns for us now and that will likely raise a great many more in the future — seem to generate some of the very worst filmmaking (as anyone who has seen *The Sixth Day* or *Godsend* or *The Island* can affirm). But 1997's *Gattaca*, starring Ethan Hawke and Uma Thurman, represents an exception, a counterexample showing how filmmaking can help audiences contemplate the challenges that new discoveries could pose down the road.

In the futuristic film, Hawke plays Vincent Freeman, a so-called In-Valid because his parents did not opt, before his birth, to have a child whose genetic defects had been weeded out. This puts Vincent into a lower genetic caste, limiting his ability to achieve his dream of flying into space to Titan, the largest of the Saturnian moons. The film details how Vincent overcomes the obstacles posed by his genetic "limitations" — because in the end, genes aren't everything. In laying out such a story line, *Gattaca* undercuts a kind of unthinking proposition that we've been fed all too often, which one critic called "genetic determinism."[49] In many Hollywood films, the techniques of biotechnology and genetic manipulation appear all-powerful and perfect; in the Arnold Schwarzenegger film *The 6th Day*, for instance, it's no big deal to clone an exact replica of a human being. *Gattaca* challenges such questionable presumptions and constructs a far more realistic scenario in which the techniques of genetic manipulation have become unevenly distributed in society, creating considerable inequities, while at the same time, some genetically "limited" people overcome the hurdles they start out with even as some genetically "gifted" ones fail to achieve their potential.[50]

Another film that tried to prepare us for the future — the 2004 blockbuster *The Day After Tomorrow*, which grossed a very impressive $542 million worldwide — focused on global warming.[51] Unfortunately, on a scientific level the films plot is risible: It depicts climate change as the trigger for an instantaneous new ice age (huh?) and shows the world facing a massive, coordinated assault by upsidedown, freezing hurricanes that somehow travel over land. Still, the movie also features a scientist (played by Dennis Quaid) in the lead protagonist role and contains a considerable amount of accurate dialogue and even some speeches about climate science — before the improbable lunacies begin, anyway. Virtually all of the film's top characters are scientists and are treated sympathetically; and the message, inaccuracies aside, is that global warming is a problem that we can't delay addressing, lest very bad things happen — so let's listen to the scientists before it's too late.

It would surely have been possible to make a global-warming-related disaster movie with a much closer connection to the actual risks posed. Still, it appears *The Day After Tomorrow* did have an important effect on its audiences. According to one study, those who had seen it were significantly more worried about global warming than those who had not and were significantly more convinced that global warming could trigger specific weather and climatic impacts (including, unfortunately, the idea of a new ice age caused by an ocean-current shutdown).[52]

Contact, *Gattaca*, and *The Day After Tomorrow* all demonstrate the potential for collaboration between the world of science and the world of Hollywood

---

49 See David Kirby, "The New Eugenics in Cinema: Genetic Determinism and Gene Therapy in *Gattaca*," *Science Fiction Studies*, Vol. 2, Pt. 2 (2000), pp. 193–215.

50 Alas, *Gattaca* wasn't successful enough at the box office to count as a model that Hollywood would want to follow again — it only grossed $12 million domestically. *Gattaca*

earnings figures from Box Office Mojo, http://www.boxofficemojo.com/movies/?id=gattaca.htm.

51 *The Day After Tomorrow* earnings figures from Box Office Mojo, http://www.boxofficemojo.com/movies/?id=dayaftertomorrow.htm.

52 Anthony Leiserowitz, "Before and After *The Day After Tomorrow*," *Environment* 46 (2004), pp. 22–37. Leiserowitz also found that the film's U.S. viewership within a few weeks of its release was roughly 21 million, or 10 percent of the population. Yet this was not enough to significantly move total public opinion on global warming. That's a sobering consideration, especially in light of yet another of Leiserowitz's findings: The film generated over ten times as much media attention as the 2001 release of the U.N. Intergovernmental Panel on Climate Change's "Third Assessment Report," the definitive scientific study of climate change and its impact, which is released at roughly five-year intervals. In the total media arena, then, *The Day After Tomorrow* made a much

Contact, *Gattaca*, and *The Day After Tomorrow* all demonstrate the potential for collaboration between the world of science and the world of Hollywood, and suggest such interactions could be mutually beneficial, at least if those who care about science take up the challenge of connecting in a more positive way with the film and television industry.

That challenge must be met quickly, because the enemies of science certainly recognize the medium's potential as a tool of propaganda. For example, the 2008 right-wing documentary *Expelled!* features the comedian Ben Stein in a dishonest look at the evolution controversy that slanders the scientific community for intolerance toward religion and the quashing of anti-evolutionist dissent. Throwing the kitchen sink at evolution, Stein not only charges that pro–intelligent design scientists have been repressed on university campuses by dogmatic Darwinists, but even preposterously blames Charles Darwin and his work for the Holocaust.

This is all quite inaccurate, even ludicrous; but the message conveyed by *Expelled!* about the evils of the scientific community has reached a lot of people, because it debuted at 1,000 theaters across the country. It ultimately earned over $7 million, making it the fifth-highest-grossing political documentary ever.[53]

Expelled! represents a cultural warning sign that should not go unheeded. Film and television are massively powerful media and can be used as damaging weapons. Scientists must learn how to wield them as well, and for more virtuous purposes. They've been in the dark for far too long.

---

bigger splash than the release of a groundbreaking scientific report, but a much smaller one than a sustained politico-media scandal story, such as the Abu Ghraib prison saga.

53 Data from Box Office Mojo, http://www.boxofficemojo.com/genres/chart/?id=politicaldoc.htm.

Our Place in the Cosmos: Faith and Belief in *Contact*

from *Movies and the Meaning of Life*

— Heather Keith and Steven Fesmire

Some of [the experimental method's] obvious elements are willingness to hold belief in suspense, ability to doubt until evidence is obtained; willingness to go where evidence points instead of putting first a personally preferred conclusion; ability to hold ideas in solution and use them as hypotheses to be tested instead of as dogmas to be asserted; and (possibly the most distinctive of all) enjoyment of new fields for inquiry and of new problems.

> — John Dewey (American philosopher, 1859–1952), *Freedom and Culture*

It's a hot, windy evening in the middle of the desert. You're sitting alone at the base of an imposingly large satellite dish — a telescope for detecting radio waves from insanely distant objects like quasars and pulsars. Only it turns out that you're not exactly alone. Your laptop is plugged into the dish, and what before was static in your headphones forms itself into a distinct and haunting rhythm. The aliens are calling, and they want to talk to you. You feel a shiver down your spine, a blend of elation and terror. Elation, because you have spent your scientific career poised to hear some hint of order in the cosmic chaos, and your professional credibility hinges on this moment. Terror, because — well, they are aliens, after all. It's an awesome experience. But now anxiety presses itself upon you. What on earth will you do with this information? What can it possibly mean? How does it affect your place in the cosmos? How can you even be sure that what you are experiencing is real, not an illusion or hoax? How will others respond to you? Will they believe you? Why should they?

In *Contact*,[1] such is the experience of Dr. Ellie Arroway (Jodie Foster), a scientist working with S.E.T.I., the Search for Extra-Terrestrial Intelligence. Based on the 1985 science-fiction novel by the astronomer Carl Sagan,[2] *Contact* tells the story of what a first encounter between humans and intelligent extraterrestrial beings might be like. It also details the complexities of faith and belief in a world where religion and science often come into conflict — a favorite theme of Sagan's, and a major subject in the history of philosophy.

This chapter explores tangles of faith and belief through the lens of philosophy and the characters and concepts of *Contact*. We pay special attention to Sagan's mouthpiece Ellie Arroway, who embodies the practice of *doubting* as essential to living a life rich in insight and meaning. While this is far from the sole philosophic quandary raised by the film, it is perhaps the central one.

---

1 *Contact*, Directed by Robert Zemeckis, 2 hr. 30 min. Warner, 1997. Videocassette.

2 Carl Sagan, *Contact* (New York: Simon and Schuster, 1985), based on the story by Carl Sagan and Ann Druyan. Sagan gained national fame in the early 1980s as host of the PBS television series, *Cosmos*. He died in 1996. The last book he published before his death was The *Demon-Haunted World: Science as a Candle in the Dark* (New York: Random House, 1996).

Perhaps, like us, you are a bit of a geek. Not of the stereotypical techno-crazed pocket-protector-wearing klutzy misfit variety, but simply someone more often transfixed by ideas than fashions and trends. Thinking matters more to you than what's on tonight at 8:00 or whether you're a Size 8. It's okay. You're not alone.

Here's some food for thought for us geeks wondering about meaning in life: We humans have been emitting radio waves, which travel at the speed of light (186,000 miles per second), for about one hundred years. So a sort of "shell" of radio waves extends a hundred light years in a sphere around Earth. This shell is one-thousandth the distance across the Milky Way galaxy, one of hundreds of billions of galaxies. If intelligent beings were to emit powerful radio waves from the other side of our own galaxy, they and their planet might be long gone before we detected the

Now the story: Downtrodden by the loss of government funding for S.E.T.I., Ellie seeks financing in the private sector. Her passion finally persuades a corporate philanthropist, the eccentric and reclusive S.R. Hadden (John Hurt), to support her project at the Very Large Array radio telescope in New Mexico. Here, Ellie spends countless hours listening to static from space. At the last minute before her lease is revoked, she detects an encoded message emanating from the Vega star system, twenty-eight light years away. Disturbingly, the message includes a television image of Hitler at the opening of the 1936 Olympics in Berlin, the first television broadcast strong enough to be picked up in space. This prompts the President's Press Secretary (Angela Bassett) to exclaim, "Twenty million people died defeating that son of a bitch, and he's our first ambassador to outer space?" Apparently the message was an E.T. way of saying "hello, we heard you." Attached to

---

Thanks to fellow geeks like Copernicus, Darwin, and Hubble, students today can contemplate their evolving primate lives circling a medium-sized star in a galaxy with hundreds of billions of similar stars in a cosmos with hundreds of billions of galaxies clustering across fifteen billion light years.

---

signals. Or radio waves may have arrived while our distant ancestors were too busy being single-celled organisms in the primordial ooze. The most distant object visible to the unaided eye, our nearest neighbor the Andromeda galaxy, left its source around two and a half million years ago; anatomically modern humans, in comparison, evolved in Africa around 150,000 to 200,000 years ago.

It's humbling, but we historically educated geeks are used to being humbled. A few centuries ago our medieval European ancestors were safely ensconced as the central figures in the universe's drama of redemption. We're the end-all be-all of it all, they believed. Your great great grandparents were probably unchallenged in the belief that their species was specially created in an instant by a word from God. Your great grandparents' schooling probably did not include the notion that we live in one galaxy among many. Today, thanks to fellow geeks like Copernicus, Darwin, and Hubble, students today can contemplate their evolving primate lives circling a medium-sized star in a galaxy with hundreds of billions of similar stars in a cosmos with hundreds of billions of galaxies clustering across fifteen billion light years.

this is a coded message that Hadden helps Ellie to break: a blueprint for a machine that might take a passenger to meet the aliens.

In the midst of a predictable explosion of public attention, a conversation begins in various religious communities about the nature and consequences of such a discovery. From abductee fanatics to Christian fundamentalists to intergalactic Elvises, the public discourse seems to reflect more superstitious than scientific beliefs. While Ellie might want to ignore the religious buzz, it imposes itself on her world in the character of Palmer Joss (Matthew McConaughey), once her lover, and now a presidential advisor on religion and public affairs.

At first, Palmer is Ellie's foil. While she finds truth and meaning in scientific discovery based on hard evidence, his meaning comes via what he experiences as a personal relationship with God. Having read Palmer's book, Ellie quotes it back to him at a White House reception: "Ironically, the thing that people are most hungry for, meaning, is the one thing that science hasn't been able to give them." Ellie replies, "Come on, it's like you're saying science killed God

… what if science simply revealed that He never existed in the first place?"

Ellie then introduces "Ockham's Razor," a principle made famous by the medieval philosopher William of Ockham (1285–1349) which holds that all things being equal, the simplest explanation tends to be the best. That is, the best explanation isn't an extravagant one, littered by unnecessary assumptions. Using Ockham's Razor, Ellie says: "So what's more likely, an all-powerful mysterious god created the universe and decided not to give any proof of his existence, or that he simply doesn't exist at all, and that we created him so that we wouldn't have to feel so small and alone?" While Palmer — ironically, like Ockham himself — can't imagine a meaningful existence without faith in God, Ellie finds meaning through scientific practice.

Even as a child, filled with grief after her father's fatal heart attack, Ellie seeks only natural explanations. In a misguided attempt to comfort Ellie, a priest tells her that all things happen for a reason. The death, he implies, is justified as part of a supernatural plan. Ellie agrees that things happen for a reason, but using Ockham's Razor she shaves away the supernatural assumptions: She laments that she didn't place her father's heart medicine in the more accessible downstairs bathroom.

WISE FOOLS

Is there some particular way of forming beliefs that makes a meaningful life more likely? Let's assume, perhaps wrongly, that there is some correlation between living a meaningful life and sincerely pursuing truth: if ignorance is bliss, then only the timid crave bliss. Yes, we humans are all turtles carrying comfortable shells, but we engage life fully and sensuously only when facing the joys and hazards outside our shells. Is there, then, a way of forming and evaluating beliefs that can best be trusted to reveal the way things *actually* work rather than merely confirming whatever we *wish* to be true? This question is an important theme for Ellie, and also for the philosopher Charles Sanders Peirce (1839–1914), an American regarded as the father of the philosophic tradition called Pragmatism.

Peirce (pronounced "purse," like a handbag) recognized that there is no psychological difference between believing a truth and believing a falsehood; whatever we believe, we believe is true until we have some reason to doubt it. As Socrates (Plato's teacher in ancient Athens) grasped 2,300 years before Peirce, we humans are a sophomoric bunch.

A "sophomore" isn't merely an arbitrary and uninteresting designation for second-year college students. The word literally means "wise fool," someone who thinks she knows things she does not in fact know. What she mistakenly *thinks* she knows far exceeds the little she *actually* knows. To the degree that we are sophomoric, we mistake ignorance for knowledge, and we generally pay a price for this delusion. Avoiding this is one of the greatest challenges of human existence.

If only a bell would go off in our heads whenever we hit upon a true belief! Then we could escape the perils of ignorance. Our reputations would never again suffer from false claims of knowledge, our bodies would be spared the agony of false beliefs in our own abilities ("Sure, I drive better when I'm drunk," "Of course I can ski on the expert slope!"), and our social perspectives would finally be liberated from inherited prejudices about "our kind" and "their kind." An American philosopher and U.S. congressperson named Thomas Vernor Smith (1890–1964), influenced by Peirce, wisely observed that "much of the misery that men inflict upon one another is in the name of and because of their feeling so certain that they know things and that the other fellow does not."[3]

FIXING BELIEFS

In an 1877 article titled "The Fixation of Belief," Peirce explores this human predicament. He describes ways in which people's beliefs become "fixed" (in the sense of "hardened," not "repaired"). We are all too aware of how people become "*set* in their ways" just as plaster becomes fixed or set. Peirce writes as though his descriptions are neutral, but he does not hold that all approaches are created equal. To the contrary, he implies that some ways of believing are more reliable than others. This may appear controversial, but consider his descriptions in turn. We'll discuss them alongside corresponding characters in *Contact*.

According to Peirce, one very popular approach to believing is the "method of tenacity," better known as the "ostrich mentality." We are all experts at using this method. People sidestep their rational capacities and stubbornly avoid situations that might provoke doubt. In Peirce's words: "When an ostrich buries its head in the sand as danger approaches, it very likely takes the happiest

---

3 Thomas Vernor Smith, *Creative Sceptics: In Defense of The Liberal Temper* (Chicago: Willitt, Clark, and Co.,1934), p. 7.

course. It hides the danger, and then calmly says there is no danger."[4] Many people are remarkably skilled at hiding from all that could challenge their beliefs. This is the method of a religious terrorist in *Contact*. He simply

destroys the machine. Peirce evaluates the method of authority with biting sarcasm: "If it is their highest impulse to be intellectual slaves, then slaves they ought to remain."[5]

According to the eighteenth-century German phi-

Many people are remarkably skilled at hiding from all that could challenge their beliefs. This is the method of a religious terrorist in *Contact*. He simply won't — or can't — tolerate the obvious upshot of a message from outer space: the universe *doesn't* revolve around humanity!

---

won't — or can't — tolerate the obvious upshot of a message from outer space: the universe *doesn't* revolve around humanity! So he denies access to the evidence by setting off a bomb in the heart of the machine. He and many others are killed in the massive explosion (a required element for all science-fiction films!), including David Drumlin (Tom Skerritt), the scientist who edged out Ellie in the bid to represent humanity to the ETs. This is indeed a dangerous and deadly method of believing.

A second approach, the "method of authority," is to hold beliefs because institutionalized authority declares them to be true. Since new discoveries can challenge traditional beliefs, this approach often works hand-in-hand with the ostrich mentality. Those who took a literalist view of scripture were infuriated by Copernicus's 1543 *On the Revolution of Heavenly Bodies*, which proposes a Sun-centered rather than Earth-centered universe. Martin Luther quoted Joshua 10:12–14 in the Bible, in which Joshua commands the sun to stand still in the heavens. Luther reasoned that if the sun stood still, then it must first have been moving. Therefore, the sun is in motion rather than the earth. On the basis of scriptural authority, Copernicus was thus refuted, and human beings could for a few more years believe they were the literal center of the cosmos.

It is precisely this de-centering of humanity by science that leads some today to reject evolutionary biology in favor of an interpretation of religious authority. Some feel an almost primal need for humans to be the central figures on the Divine stage. In *Contact*, authority-driven fear sets the social environment within which the religious terrorist

losopher Immanuel Kant, the problem with those who follow the method of authority is not "lack of intelligence, but lack of determination and courage to use that intelligence without another's guidance. Sapere aude! Dare to know! Have the courage to use your own intelligence."[6] Recognizing the dangers of methods such as tenacity and authority, Peirce, like the philosopher John Dewey in the epigraph to this chapter, turns to science for a model of experimental, community-engaged, and error-correcting thinking. As Ellie sees it, religious believers like Palmer follow tenacious and authority-influenced methods when developing what she regards as their unquestioned and unanalyzed faith. Meanwhile, she exemplifies an approach to "fixing" her beliefs through constant questioning, probing experimentation, and hard evidence: the method of science. Ellie, Sagan, and Peirce believe this method, to be best suited to the quest for truth.[7]

SCIENCE AND THE MEANING OF LIFE

The philosopher Bertrand Russell wrote in 1903 that science reveals us alone in a hostile and purposeless universe, our loves and beliefs "the outcome of accidental collocations of atoms."[8] We must, says Russell, revolt in active defiance of this meaningless void. Like Russell, Ellie does

---

4   Charles Sanders Peirce, "The Fixation of Belief" in *Philosophical Writings of Charles Sanders Peirce*, edited by Justus Buchler (New York: Dover, 1955), p. 12.

5   Peirce, p. 14.

6   Immanuel Kant, "What Is Enlightenment?" in Marvin Perry, *et. al.,* eds., *Sources of Western Tradition* (Boston: Houghton Mifflin, 1999), pp. 54–55. Kant replaces the method of authority with an *a priori* approach that, according to Peirce, is not much better than what it replaces.

7   For more on science, pragmatism, and meaning, see Steven Fesmire, *John Dewey and Moral Imagination* (Bloomington: Indiana University Press, 2003), Chapter 2.

8   Bertrand Russell, "A Free Man's Worship," in *Why I Am Not A Christian* (London: Allen and Unwin, 1957), p. 107.

not believe science supports traditional religious beliefs about a divine cosmic plan. But in contrast with Russell's pessimism, science gives meaning to Ellie's life. By opening the doors to contemplation of the sublime vastness of the universe ("billions and billions of stars surrounded by billions and billions of galaxies," as Sagan was reputed to say), science reveals that we Earthlings may be far from alone in the universe. If not, as *Contact* tirelessly repeats, "It'd be an awful waste of space."

Yet science is not just about *conclusions*; it is a way of living and thinking that embraces intellectual suspense and constant questioning. Suspense is endured gladly in films, novels, and magic. It is not always welcomed, much less enjoyed for its own sake, in matters of real world beliefs — particularly religious, moral, and political ones. To Ellie, a scientific turn of mind spells an end to the dogmatism and fanaticism that mark the idea that beliefs can be declared true without worldly testing. Consider the feeling of absolute certainty that drove the Inquisition and that today drives terrorism, genocide, and nationalism. To whatever extent a belief is held scientifically, it is tentative and hypothetical. Through testing, we ask the world to answer back, and the answer we hear is always open to ongoing questioning.

This suggests a sort of faith that differs from the authority-driven variety. Ellie's scientific faith embraces doubt and suspense as an ally, not an adversary. She passionately wants to be the passenger transported to Vega by the machine, and she appears before a committee formed to make that decision. Seemingly betraying her, Palmer thwarts her chances by asking her if she believes in God. While it happens not to be of any great importance to Palmer (who, out of romantic interests, wants Ellie to stay on Earth), other members of the committee and the general public are put off by her answer: "As a scientist, I rely on empirical evidence, and in this matter I don't believe that there is data either way." Since, one member of the committee falsely asserts, "ninety-five percent of the world's population believes in a supreme being in one form or another,"[9] the committee, chooses Ellie's former boss and professional competitor, David Drumlin. He disingenuously seals the deal by saying what the committee wants to hear about "our most cherished beliefs."

When the machine is sabotaged (killing Drumlin), Ellie's dreams of cosmic contact seem destined to remain unfulfilled. However, the mischievous and ingenious S.R. Hadden arranges for Ellie to travel on a secret, second machine that has been built in Japan. The massive machine's arms spin to create a highly charged vortex. Her pod is dropped into the energy field. The moviegoer shares her experience, which she describes as a trip through some kind of wormhole. Ellie apparently arrives on a planet that resembles a picture of Pensacola, Florida that she drew as a child. An alien greets her in the comforting form of her late, beloved father. Contact made, culminating in promises for future small steps in developing an Earth-extraterrestrial relationship, Ellie travels safely home after an eighteen-hour adventure. A baffled mission control, relieved that she was not injured, struggles to detect the source of what seems to them an obvious malfunction: her spacecraft appears to have fallen unimpeded through the machine straight into the water below. Only a few Earth seconds have elapsed.

This makes it difficult for even Ellie's friends and colleagues to believe that she traveled light years away. In a government hearing dominated by National Security Advisor Michael Kitz (James Woods), Ellie is forced to scrutinize what she fervently believes to have been a non-subjective (that is, not a movie projection of her own mind) experience — the most awe-inspiring and meaningful one of her life. Was Ellie's adventure distinguishable from thousands of so-called "abduction" experiences, in which people faithfully and whole-heartedly believe they have been kidnapped and experimented on by aliens? She appears to have no evidence to prove that her experience was more than a vivid hallucination or nightmare. Yet Ellie has faith in her experience. Is her faith any different than the religious terrorist's absolute faith in the objective moral rightness of his suicide bombing?

In fact, one very important capacity sets Ellie's interpretation of her experience apart from the beliefs of abductees and religious fanatics: *doubt*. Rather than being mortally offended by others' lack of faith in her experience, she

> Yet science is not just about *conclusions*; it is a way of living and thinking that embraces intellectual suspense and constant questioning.

---

9   It should be underscored that this is a deeply misleading statistic, particularly in light of atheistic perspectives in Asia.

encourages doubt as the most reliable path to knowledge. In Sagan's own words: "Surely it's unfair of me to be offended at not being believed; or to criticize you for being stodgy and unimaginative — merely because you rendered the Scottish verdict of 'not proved.'"[10]

THE "BEACON OF THE WISE"

We're prone to think the opposite of belief is disbelief — that, for example, the opposite of belief in God is atheism. While accurate as far as formal logic goes, this captures nothing of any relevance to how we think. The psychological opposite of belief is doubt, uncertainty about what to believe. To doubt that we're alone in the universe is not to assert its opposite. Ellie's doubt reveals her readiness to re-open her mind to other interpretations; this is what it means to have an open, rather than an empty, mind. She is not indifferent or slacking, nor is she merely putting on an act of doubting; she is simply unwilling to make claims that outstrip her knowledge. Peirce describes this scientific spirit: it "requires a man to be at all times ready to dump his whole cartload of beliefs the moment experience is against them. The desire to learn forbids him to be perfectly cocksure that he knows already."[11]

Freedom from doubt is often purchased by those with low tolerance for bewilderment, but the price is high: such fear has always been a prelude to atrocities. The terrorist attack in *Contact* disturbingly illustrates this all-too-familiar point. Doubt is the key to learning and growth; it is essential to any passage from ignorance to knowledge. Insofar as one does not doubt one does not *grow*. For organic life, this is equivalent to death or dying. Ellie doubts her way to a meaningful and value-rich life marked by humility and tolerance.

In this spirit, the great philosopher (and ancient geek!) Socrates is reported to have said "the unexamined life is not worth living."[12] In 399 B.C.E., Socrates was put on trial by his fellow citizens for "corrupting the young," but he in fact aided young and old by showing that those who claimed to have wisdom often did not. Unlike those he daily questioned in the Athenian marketplace, Socrates was wise enough to recognize his own ignorance. Unlike his accusers, Socrates was not afraid of examining beliefs, and he encouraged such activity in others. He described himself as a "gadfly." Just as a horsefly buzzing around your hammock makes it impossible to doze, Socrates pestered his fellow citizens whenever they were sleepwalking through life. He wouldn't let them intellectually doze, resting on whatever beliefs they happened to have picked up. While most of his neighbors mistook their unexamined beliefs for knowledge, Socrates creatively disturbed himself and others.

In contrast, because of David Drumlin's willingness to say whatever he thinks will get him aboard the machine (without opening himself up to self-examination and doubt), he gives up his integrity. J.D. Salinger's Holden Caulfield would have called Drumlin a "phony." Two thousand, four hundred years ago, the unexamined beliefs of Socrates's accusers had disastrous consequences: he was executed by the state. Drumlin's life was also unjustly taken as a result of fanaticism, but he left little legacy of integrity and humility.[13]

Although Ellie's life is not on the line, her professional credibility and integrity are. In the end, it is intellectual humility that gives weight to Ellie's beliefs. Her openness to self-examination validates her experience — both to herself and to the audience — and nurtures her scientific and personal growth. As a scientist, Ellie must both trust her experience (as empirical data) and doubt it at the same time. Unfortunately, she — like us — is surrounded by people who are uncomfortable with doubt. Impatient, they have no tolerance for ambiguity. Fearful of being bewildered, they clamor for ironclad certainty. This fear drives Kitz to persecute Ellie. Like those who put Socrates on trial, Kitz probably believes that's what the public desires. Ellie, however, responds to Kitz's arrogance by expressing her own doubts rather than countering his abuse with statements of unquestioned truth. There is a vital lesson in *Contact* for our post-9/11 world. Again in the words of Thomas Vernor Smith: "The world may flee from doubt in fear; but the world will come back to the method of doubt in sanity."[14] "Modest doubt," Shakespeare adds, "is call'd the beacon of the wise."[15]

---

10 Sagan, *The Demon-Haunted World*, p. 172.
11 In Smith, p. 232.
12 Plato, "Apology" in *Five Dialogues* (Indianapolis: Hackett, 1981), p. 41.

13 Drumlin's character is much more nuanced in Sagan's novel, from which the movie is loosely adapted.
14 Smith, *Creative Sceptics*, p. 233.
15 William Shakespeare, *Troilus and Cressida*, Act. II, Scene II; in *The Complete Works of William Shakespeare*, edited by William Aldis Wright (New York: Garden City Press, 1936), p. 830.

In the hearing, Kitz ridicules Ellie's claim that she traveled in the machine through a wormhole. He hypothesizes, that either she is lying or that she is the victim of a malicious scheme of Hadden's. When Kitz asks Ellie if she expects him to take her word on faith, she replies in a way that embodies experimental thinking and open-mindedness:

ELLIE: Is it possible that it didn't happen? Yes. As a scientist, I must concede that, I must volunteer that.

KITZ: Wait a minute, let me get this straight. You admit that you have absolutely no physical evidence to back up your story?

ELLIE: Yes.

KITZ: You admit that you very well may have hallucinated this whole thing?

ELLIE: Yes.

KITZ: You admit that if you were in our position you would respond with exactly the same degree of incredulity and skepticism?

ELLIE: Yes.

But when asked why she doesn't withdraw her testimony in this case, Ellie responds:

ELLIE: Because I can't! I had an experience. … I can't prove it, I can't even explain it … but everything that I know as a human being, everything that I am tells me that it was real. I was given something wonderful, something that changed me forever. A vision of the universe that tells us undeniably how tiny and insignificant, and how rare and precious we all are. A vision that tells us that we belong to something that is greater than ourselves, that we are not, that none of us are alone. I wish I could share that. I wish that everyone, even for one moment, could feel that awe and humility and hope.

"I DON'T KNOW" (OR DOES SHE?)

Though Ellie has faith in her own experience, she tempers it with a healthy dose of doubt. This moves Palmer, who himself evinces a new temperament of openness. When asked what he thinks is true, he replies, "As a person of faith, I'm bound by a different covenant than Dr. Arroway.

But our goal is one and the same — the pursuit of truth. I for one believe her." This openness to experience is a hallmark of Peirce's method of science.

Unlike Palmer, the moviegoer doesn't have to decide whether to trust Ellie's experience. We can consider her claim skeptically, at least until the end of the film when we eavesdrop on a conversation between Kitz and the Press Secretary regarding video taken during Ellie's "trip." The video shows only static. But it shows eighteen hours of it. Although we may still be able to come up with reasons to be skeptical, this is substantial evidence for Ellie's claim. Has director Robert Zemeckis made our experience of *Contact* more, or less, meaningful? Would having to wrestle with doubt about the reality within the film be a more meaningful, provoking, and fitting way to end Ellie's story?

Rejecting blind faith, even in her own experience, Ellie finds meaning in examining her beliefs by embracing and encouraging doubt wherever possible. The end of the film finds Ellie giving a school tour of the Very Large Array. When a child asks Ellie if there are aliens, she replies with the skepticism and humility of an experimental thinker:

CHILD: Are there other people out there in the universe?

ELLIE: That's a good question. What do you think?

CHILD: I don't know.

ELLIE: That's a good answer. A skeptic, huh? The most important thing is that you all keep searching for your own answers.[16]

TO THINK ABOUT

1. Should we approach all aspects of our lives with Ellie's skepticism? Moral beliefs? Political beliefs? Religious beliefs? Scientific beliefs?

2. By including hard-to-dispute evidence of Ellie's ET encounter (the eighteen hours of static), has director Robert Zemeckis made our experience of *Contact* more, or less, meaningful? Would having to wrestle with doubt about the reality within the film

16   For viewing *Contact* and offering suggestions and insights, thanks to Tatiana Abatemarco, Joshua Bakelaar, Daniel Guentchev, Elizabeth Howe, Charlotte Norris, David Rasmussen, and Alisha Rogers.

be a more meaningful, provoking, and fitting way to end Ellie's story?

3. Some people have claimed that science has its own area of expertise and explanation, while religion occupies another. Neither account can give us the entire view of the nature of the universe. Do you think *Contact* supports such a position?

TO READ NEXT

John Dewey. *Democracy and Education*, Volume 8 of *The Collected Works of John Dewey: The Middle Works*, edited by Jo Ann Boydston. Carbondale: Southern Illinois University Press, 1985 [1916].

William James. *Pragmatism*. Indianapolis: Hackett 1997 [1907].

Charles Sanders Peirce. The Fixation of Belief. In Justus Buchler, ed., *Philosophical Writings of Charles Sanders Peirce* (New York: Dover, 1955).

Plato. Apology. In *Five Dialogues* (Indianapolis: Hackett, 2002).

Carl Sagan, *The Demon Haunted World: Science as a Candle in the Dark*. New York: Random House, 1996.

Michael Shermer. *Why People Believe Weird Things*. Second edition New York: Owl Books, 2002.

Our Radio Bubble

from *Death by Black Hole*

— Neil deGrasse Tyson

For the opening scene to the 1997 film *Contact*, a virtual camera executes a controlled, three-minute zoom from Earth to the outer reaches of the universe. For this journey, you happen to be equipped with receivers that enable you to decode Earth-based television and radio broadcasts that have escaped into space. Initially, you hear a cacophonous mixture of loud rock music, news broadcasts, and noisy static as though you were listening to dozens of radio stations simultaneously. As the journey progresses out into space, and as you overtake earlier broadcasts that have traveled farther, the signals become less cacophonous and distinctly older as they report historical events that span the broadcast era of modern civilization. Amid the noise, you hear sound bytes in reverse sequence that include: the *Challenger* shuttle disaster of January 1986; the Moon landing of July 20, 1969; Martin Luther King's famous "I Have a Dream" speech, delivered in August 28, 1963; President Kennedy's January 20, 1961, inaugural address; President Roosevelt's December 8, 1941, address to Congress, where he asked for a declaration of war; and a 1936 address by Adolf Hitler during his rise to power in Nazi Germany. Eventually, the human contribution to the signal disappears entirely, leaving a din of radio noise emanating from the cosmos itself.

Poignant. But this scroll of acoustic landmarks would not unfurl exactly as shown. If you somehow managed to violate several laws of physics and travel fast enough to overtake a radio wave, then few words would be intelligible because you'd hear everything replayed backward. Furthermore, we hear King's famous speech as we pass the planet Jupiter, implying Jupiter is as far as the broadcast has traveled. In fact, King's speech passed Jupiter 39 minutes after he delivered it.

Ignoring these facts that would render the zoom impossible, *Contact*'s opening scene was poetic and powerful, as it indelibly marked the extent to which we have presented our civilized selves to the rest of the Milky Way galaxy. This radio bubble, as it has come to be called, centers on Earth and continues to expand at the speed of light in every direction, while getting its center continuously refilled by modern broadcasts. Our bubble now extends nearly 100 light-years into space, with a leading edge that corresponds to the first artificial radio signals ever generated by Earthlings. The bubble's volume now contains about a thousand stars, including Alpha Centauri (4.3 light-years away), the nearest star system to the Sun; Sirius (10 light-years away), the brightest star in the nighttime sky; and every star around which a planet has thus far been discovered.

> *Contact*'s opening scene was poetic and powerful, as it indelibly marked the extent to which we have presented our civilized selves to the rest of the Milky Way galaxy.

Neil deGrasse Tyson, "Our Radio Bubble," from *Death by Black Hole: And Other Cosmic Quandaries*, pp. 238–242, 244–245. Copyright © 2007 by W.W. Norton & Company, Inc. Permission to reprint granted by the *Natural History Magazine*.

Not all radio signals escape our atmosphere. The plasma properties of the ionosphere, more than 50 miles up, enable it to reflect back to Earth all radio-wave frequencies less than 20 megahertz, allowing some forms of radio communication, such as the well-known "short wave" frequencies of HAM radio operators, to reach thousands of miles beyond your horizon. All the broadcast frequencies of AM radio are also reflected back to Earth, accounting for the extended range that these stations enjoy.

If you broadcast at a frequency that does not correspond to those reflected by Earth's ionosphere, or if Earth had no ionosphere, your radio signals would reach only those receivers that fell in its line of "sight." Tall buildings give significant advantage to radio transmitters mounted on their roofs. While the horizon for a 5'8" person is just 3 miles away, the horizon seen by King Kong, while climbing atop New York City's Empire State Building, is more than 50. After the filming of that 1933 classic, a broadcast antenna was installed. An equally tall receiving antenna could, in principle, be located 50 miles farther still, enabling the signal to cross their mutual 50-mile horizon, thereby extending the signal's reach to 100 miles.

The ionosphere reflects neither FM radio nor broadcast television, itself a subset of the radio spectrum. As prescribed, they each travel no farther on Earth than the farthest receiver they can see, which allows cities that are relatively near each other to broadcast their own television programs. For this reason, television's local broadcasts and FM radio cannot possibly be as influential as AM radio, which may account for its preponderance of politically acerbic talk shows. But the real influence of FM and TV may not be terrestrial. While most of the signal's strength is purposefully broadcast horizontal to the ground, some of it leaks straight up, crossing the ionosphere and traveling through the depths of space. For them, the sky is not the limit. And unlike some other bands in the electromagnetic spectrum, radio waves have excellent penetration through the gas and dust clouds of interstellar space, so the stars are not the limit either.

If you add up all factors that contribute to the strength of Earth's radio signature, such as the total number of stations, the distribution of stations across Earth's surface, the energy output of each station, and the bandwidth over which the energy is broadcast, you find that television accounts for the largest sustained flux of radio signals detectable from Earth. The anatomy of a broadcast signal displays a skinny and a wide part. The skinny, narrow-band part is the video carrier signal, through which more than half the total energy is broadcast. At a mere .10 hertz wide in frequency, it establishes the station's location on the dial (the familiar channels 2 through 13) as well as the existence of the signal in the first place. A low-intensity, broadband signal, 5 million hertz wide, surrounds the carrier at higher and lower frequencies and is imbued with modulations that contain all the program information.

As you might guess, the United States is the most significant contributor among all nations to Earth's global television profile. An eavesdropping alien civilization would first detect our strong carrier signals. If it continued to pay attention, it would notice periodic Doppler shifts in these signals (alternating from lower frequency to higher frequency) every 24 hours. It would then notice the signal get stronger and weaker over the same time interval. The aliens might first conclude that a mysterious, although naturally occurring, radio loud spot was rotating into and out of view. But if the aliens managed to decode the modulations within the surrounding broadband signal they would gain immediate access to elements of our culture.

Electromagnetic waves, including visible-light as well as radio waves, do not require a medium though which to travel. Indeed, they are happiest moving through the vacuum of space. So the time-honored flashing red sign in broadcast studios that says "On the Air" could justifiably read "Through Space," a phrase that applies especially to the escaping TV and FM frequencies.

As the signals move out into space they get weaker and weaker, becoming diluted by the growing volume of space through which it travels. Eventually, the signals get hopelessly buried by the ambient radio noise of the universe, generated by radio-emitting galaxies, the microwave background, radio-rich regions of star formation in the Milky Way, and cosmic rays. These factors, above all, will limit the likelihood of a distant civilization decoding our way of life.

At current broadcast strengths from Earth, aliens 100 light-years away would require a radio receiver that was fifteen times the collecting area of the 300-foot Arecibo telescope (the world's largest) to detect a television station's carrier signal. If they want to decode our programming information and hence our culture, they will need to compensate for the Doppler shifts caused by Earth's rotation on its axis and by its revolution around the Sun (enabling them to lock onto a particular TV station) and they must increase their detection capacity by another factor of 10,000 above that which would detect the carrier signal. In radio telescope terms, this amounts to a dish about four hundred times Arecibo's diameter, or about 20 miles across.

If technologically proficient aliens are indeed intercepting our signals (with a suitably large and sensitive telescope), and if they are managing to decode the modulations, then the basics of our culture would surely befuddle alien anthropologists. As they watch us become a radio-transmitting planet, their attention might first be flagged by early episodes of the *Howdy Doody* show. Once they knew to listen, they would then learn how typical human males and females interact with each other from episodes of Jackie Gleason's *Honeymooners* and from Lucy and Ricky in *I Love Lucy*. They might then assess our intelligence from episodes of *Gomer Pyle*, *The Beverly Hillbillies*, and then, perhaps, from *Hee Haw*. If the aliens didn't just give up at this point, and if they chose to wait a few more years, they would learn a little more about human interactions from Archie Bunker in *All in the Family*, then from George Jefferson in *The Jeffersons*. After a few more years of study, their knowledge would be further enriched from the odd characters in *Seinfeld* and, of course, the prime-time cartoon *The Simpsons*. (They would be spared the wisdom of the hit show *Beavis and Butthead* because it existed only as a nonbroadcast cable program on MTV.) These were among the most popular shows of our times, each sustaining cross-generational exposure in the form of reruns.

Mixed in among our cherished sitcoms is the extensive, decade-long news footage of bloodshed during the Vietnam war, the Gulf wars, and other military hot spots around the planet. After 50 years of television, there's no other conclusion the aliens could draw, but that most humans are neurotic, death-hungry, dysfunctional idiots.

* * *

Rather than let aliens listen to our embarrassing TV shows, why not send them a signal of our own choosing, demonstrating how intelligent and peace loving we are? This was first done in the form of gold-etched plaques affixed to the sides of the four unmanned planetary probes *Pioneer 10*

and *11* and *Voyager 1* and *2*. Each plaque contains pictograms conveying our base of scientific knowledge and our location in the Milky Way galaxy while the *Voyager* plaques also contain audio information about the kindness of our species. At 50,000 miles per hour — a speed in excess of the solar system's escape velocity — these spacecraft are traveling through interplanetary space at quite a clip. But they move ridiculously slow compared with the speed of light and won't get to the nearby stars for another 100,000 years. They represent our "spacecraft" bubble. Don't wait up for them.

A better way to communicate is to send a high-intensity radio signal to a busy place in the galaxy, like a star cluster. This was first done in 1976, when the Arecibo telescope was used in reverse, as a transmitter rather than a receiver, to send the first radio-wave signal of our own choosing out to space. That message, at the time of this writing, is now 30 light-years from Earth, headed in the direction of the spectacular globular star cluster known as M13, in the constellation Hercules. The message contains in digital form some of what appeared on the *Pioneer* and *Voyager* spacecraft. Two problems, however: The globular cluster is so chock full of stars (at least a half-million) and so tightly packed, that planetary orbits tend to be unstable as their gravitational allegiance to their host star is challenged for every pass through the cluster's center. Furthermore, the cluster has such a meager quantity of heavy elements (out of which planets are made) that planets are probably rare in the first place. These scientific points were not well known or understood at the time the signal was sent.

In any case, the leading edge of our "on-purpose" radio signals (forming a directed radio cone, instead of a bubble) is 30 light-years away and, if intercepted, may mend the aliens' image of us based on the radio bubble of our television shows. But this will happen only if the aliens can somehow determine which type of signal comes closer to the truth of who we are, and what our cosmic identity deserves to be.

What is our cosmic identity?

> After 50 years of television, there's no other conclusion the aliens could draw, but that most humans are neurotic, death-hungry, dysfunctional idiots.

PART 3

SEEING AND BEING SEEN

You don't get it, do you? I go out on the street,
and everybody knows me. Me, Herb Stempel.

— Herb Stempel,
Quiz Show (1994)

CHAPTER 8
Surveillance

We want to make absolutely certain that every American can bank on the utter infallibility of this system, and to ensure that which keeps us safe will also keep us free.

— Precrime Unit propaganda,
Minority Report (2002)

Chapter 8. Surveillance

Recommended Film

Minority Report (Steven Spielberg 2002)

Media Models

The Meme, The Network

Chapter Summary

Howard Rheingold explains the panopticon and its evolving role in power and surveillance.

Naomi Wolf critiques the U.S. government's aggressive use of surveillance and political harassment in post-9/11 America.

Jan Fernback explores some of the roles that Google plays in the emerging "surveillance environments."

David Brin describes several possible forms of surveillance societies that might emerge in the not-too-distant future.

Always-On Panopticon ... or Cooperation Amplifier?

from *Smart Mobs*

— Howard Rheingold

CAN DISCIPLINE EVOLVE?

In 2002, BBC News reported that the image of the average urbanite is caught on closed-circuit television cameras three hundred times a day.[1] In 2001, Virgin Mobile admitted that they had stored the location records of every mobile call made by each one of its 1 million customers since the service launched in 1999.[2] During Super Bowl XXXV, seven months *before* the terrorist attacks on the United States made high-tech surveillance checkpoints a part of daily American life, the face of every person who entered the stadium was captured by digital video cameras and compared computationally to a database of wanted criminals.[3] In March 2002, Motorola and Visionics, the company that created the Super Bowl facial recognition system, announced their intention to market mobile telephones that include real-time facial recognition capabilities to law enforcement personnel.[4]

Every telephone call, credit card transaction, mouse-click, email, automatic bridge toll collection, convenience market video camera, and hotel room electronic key collects and broadcasts personal information that is increasingly compiled, compared, sorted and stored by an unknown and possibly unknowable assortment of state security agencies and people who want to sell something. Context-aware, location-based, and agent-mediated services will multiply the amount of information that citizens will broadcast in the near future. The amount of information that comes back at us is multiplying at an alarming rate as well, as everyone who spends time clearing unsolicited commercial email ("spam") from their inboxes knows.

Although state-sponsored surveillance and much commercially motivated data collection is conducted for the most part without the consent or knowledge of the surveillant, issues of privacy today are complicated by the voluntary adoption of technologies that disclose private information to others. How many mobile telephone users know that they don't have to make a call for others to triangulate their location? They only need to switch on the device. Will users of mobile and pervasive technologies have the power to cloak, give away, or sell their personal data clouds — or to know who is inspecting them?

For decades, people have feared the use of surveillance technology as a tool of repressive social control by a totalitarian state — Orwell's "Big Brother."[5] Orwell didn't take into account the possibility that computing

1   Jane Wakefield, "Watching Your Every Move," *BBC News Online*, 7 February 2002, <http://news.bbc.co.uk/hi/english/sci/tech/newsid_1789000/1789157.stm> (16 March 2002).

2   Stuart Millar and Paul Kelso, "Liberties Fear Over Mobile Phone Details," *The Guardian*, 27 October 2001, <http://politics.guardian.co.uk/attacks/story/0,1320,581861,00.html> (18 March 2002).

3   Declan McCullagh, "Call It Super Bowl Face Scan 1," *Wired News*, 2 February 2001, <http://www.wired.com/news/politics/0,1283,41571,00.html> (18 March 2002).

4   Ryan Naraine, "Face Recognition, Via Cell-Phones," *Symobile*, 27 March 2002, <http://www.syniobile.com/comtex/content.cfm?transmit_id=2002086a9917> (29 March 2002).

5   George Orwell, *Nineteen Eighty-Four* (London: Martin Seeker and Warburg, 1949).

and communication technologies would seduce consumers into voluntarily trading privacy for convenience. David Lyon, an astute analyst of the surveillance society, made this observation about the effect of consumerism on contemporary surveillance:

> Things have changed since Orwell's time, and consumption, for the masses, has emerged as the new inclusionary reality. Only the minority, the so-called underclass, whose position prevents them from participating so freely in consumption, now experience the hard edge of exclusionary and punitive surveillance. Anyone wishing to grasp the nature of contemporary surveillance must reckon with this fact. Whereas the major threat, for Orwell, came from the state, today consumer surveillance poses a series of novel questions which have yet to find adequate analytical and political answers. A perfectly plausible view is that in contemporary conditions consumerism acts in its own right as a significant means of maintaining social order, leaving older forms of surveillance and control to cope with the nonconsuming residue.[6]

Remember the point of sale display at the IBM Almaden Research Center (Chapter 4) that observes consumers and tailors its message to what it learns about them? Increasingly, the most sophisticated privacy intrusions are instigated by merchants, not secret police. Merchants want personal information about people in order to tailor their products and pitches, and they are willing to spend money to gain customers. Smart mob technologies, because they sense and communicate what users/wearers transact and experience, greatly increase the chances that consumers will voluntarily trade their privacy for various enticements from merchants, from money to bargains to the latest, coolest, algorithmically recommended identity-signifiers.

If the day comes when millions of people go about their lives while wearing sensor-equipped wearable computers, the population itself could become a collective surveillant: Big Everybody. Steve Mann proposed that communities of wearable computer users will monitor, warn, and aid each other, creating virtual "safety nets" for voluntary affinity groups.[7] Steven Feiner, who has pioneered "wearable augmented reality systems" at Columbia University, has proposed a chilling counter-scenario. Feiner asks what might happen in a future world of wearable computer communities if some organization offers individuals a small payment for continuous real-time access to their digital experience-stream.[8] Individuals in Feiner's scenario would have the power to protect their own personal privacy while displaying what they see of the rest of the world. Feiner conjectures that the enabling technology for peer-to-peer journalism also enables many-to-many surveillance.

> Massively parallel image and audio processing could make it possible to reconstruct a selected person's activities from material recorded by others who have merely seen or heard that person in passing. Imagine a private two-person conversation, recorded by neither participant. That conversation might be reassembled in its entirety from information obtained from passersby, who each overheard small snippets and who willingly provided inexpensive access to their recordings. The price paid for such material, and the particular users to whom that price is offered, might even change dynamically, based on a user's proximity to events or people of interest to the buyer at that time. This could make it possible to enlist temporarily a well-situated user who may normally refuse access at the regular price, or to engage a user's wearable computer in a "bidding war" among competing organizations, performed without any need for the user's attention.[9]

The Osaka police took the first steps toward Feiner's scenario in April 2002, when they opened a call-in line for

6   David Lyon, *The Electronic Eye: The Rise of Surveillance Society* (Minneapolis: University of Minnesota Press, 1994).

7   Steve Mann, "Smart Clothing: The Wearable Computer and WearCam," *Personal Technologies* 1, 1 (March 1997), <http://wearcam.org/personaltechnologies/> (18 March 2002).

8   Steven K. Feiner, "The Importance of Being Mobile: Some Social Consequences of Wearable Augmented Reality Systems," *Proceedings of IWAR 99 (International Workshop on Augmented Reality)*, San Francisco, California, 20–21 October, 1999, 145–148, <http://www.cs.columbia.edu/graphics/publications/FEINERiwar99.pdf> (18 March 2002).

9   Ibid.

citizens with 3G phones to send video of crimes they might witness.[10]

Sociologist Gary Marx was the first to describe a "surveillance society," in which, "with computer technology, one of the final barriers to total control is crumbling."[11] Marx noted that the growing ability of computers to compile dossiers about individuals by piecing together countless tiny, otherwise harmless shards of information about transactions, medical conditions, buying habits, and demographic characteristics constituted a distinct class of "dataveillance," distinguished from traditional snooping methodologies of audio or visual recording by its ease of computer automation: "Computers qualitatively alter the nature of surveillance — routinizing, broadening, and deepening it."[12]

Surveillance technologies become a threat to liberty as well as dignity when they give one person or group power to constrain the behavior of others. Any inquiry into the relationship between social control, surveillance, power, and knowledge must contend with the historian-philosopher-psychologist-sociologist Michel Foucault, a fiercely cross-disciplinary thinker who was to surveillance what Darwin was to evolutionary biology. Foucault's fundamental insight was that power not only belongs to the powerful but permeates the social world. He wrote that power "reaches into the very grain of individuals, touches their bodies and inserts itself into their actions and attitudes, their discourses, learning processes and everyday lives."[13]

As Einstein showed that space and time could be understood only in relation to each other, Foucault revealed the reciprocal connections between knowledge and power. In Foucault's view, power is so strongly connected to knowledge that he often wrote them this way: "power/knowledge." About the relationship of the two, Foucault stated: "Knowledge, once used to regulate the conduct of others, entails constraint, regulation and the disciplining of practice. Thus, there is no power relation without the correlative constitution of a field of knowledge, nor any knowledge that does not presuppose and constitute at the same time, power relations."[14]

Examining the history of punishment, Foucault focused on a change over recent centuries in the way societies treat criminals and the mentally ill. The age-old techniques of torture and execution or consignment to dungeons were replaced by more subtle and effective methods. Rational institutions and authoritative specialists — modern prisons and police, hospitals, asylums, psychiatrists, and doctors — helped order society more effectively than the threat of physical punishment.

"Discipline" was Foucault's term for a mode of power/ knowledge that included social welfare bureaucracy, armies and police forces, public education, and other practices that impose regular patterns on behavior and relationships. Foucault uses the word "discipline" to refer both to methods of control and to different branches of knowledge, for he saw knowledge specialization and social control as part of the same power/knowledge matrix.

As an example of discipline and power/knowledge, Foucault cited the Panopticon ("all-seeing place"), an architectural design put forth by Jeremy Bentham in the mid-nineteenth century for prisons, insane asylums, schools, hospitals, and factories. Instead of employing the brutal and spectacular means used to control individuals under a monarchial state, the modern state needed a different sort of system to regulate its citizens. The Panopticon applied a form of mental, knowledge-based power through the constant observation of prisoners, each separated from the other and allowed no interaction. The Panoptic structure would allow guards to continually see inside each cell from their vantage point in a high central tower, unseen themselves. The system of unobserved observation created a kind of knowledge in the mind of the inmate that was in

> Surveillance technologies become a threat to liberty as well as dignity when they give one person or group power to constrain the behavior of others.

10 Graeme Wearden, "Can 3G Phones Capture Criminals?" *ZDNet News*, 22 March 2002, <http://zdnet.com.com/2100–1105–867005.html> (27 March 2002).

11 Gary T. Marx, "The Surveillance Society: The Threat of 1984-Style Techniques," *The Futurist*, June 1985, 21–26.

12 Gary T. Marx, *Undercover: Police Surveillance in America* (Berkeley: University of California Press, 1988).

13 Michel Foucault, *Power/Knowledge: Selected Interviews and Other Writings, 1972–1977*, ed. Colin Gordon (New York: Pantheon, 1980), 39.

14 Michel Foucault, *Discipline and Punish: The Birth of the Prison* (London: Tavistock, 1977), 27.

itself a form of power. It isn't necessary to constantly surveil people who believe they are under constant surveillance:

> The major effect of the Panopticon: to induce in the inmate a state of conscious and permanent visibility that assures the automatic functioning of power. So to arrange things that the surveillance is permanent in its effects, even if it is discontinuous in action; that the perfection of power should tend to render its actual exercise unnecessary; that this architectural apparatus should be a machine for creating and sustaining a power relation independent of the person who exercises it; in short, that the inmates should be caught up in a power situation of which they are themselves the bearers.[15]

The emergence of surveillance and social control institutions marked a historical transition to a system of disciplinary power in which every movement is supervised and all events recorded. The result of this surveillance of every part of life, by parents, teachers, employers, police, doctors, accountants, is acceptance of regulations and docility as part of the way every "normal" person thinks and behaves. Disciplinary methods systematically isolated and neutralized "the effects of counter-power that spring from [an organized group] and which form a resistance to the power that wishes to dominate it: agitations, revolts, spontaneous organizations, coalitions — anything that may establish horizontal conjunctions."[16] For Foucault, the real danger was not necessarily that individuals are repressed by this form of social order but that they are "carefully fabricated in it."[17]

Power and counter-power sometimes combine with the human talent for cooperation rituals to create significant benefits. The rule of law, governance through social contracts, protection of civil rights, expansion of political enfranchisement, and evolution of cooperative enterprises (think of the Red Cross) demonstrate how power that goes around in the right circles can work to common advantage. Social communication — what people in cities, on the Internet, in smart mobs do — is the means by which power and counter-power coevolve. Since we climbed down from the trees and started hunting together, human groups have found numerous ways to cooperate for mutual benefit. We do so in the face of significant challenges, and when we succeed, we do so with the help of mutual monitoring and sanctioning. When I encountered Foucault's attention to mutual monitoring and sanctioning as a way in which groups self-enforce conformity and suppress potential rebellion, I recalled how Ostrom and others highlighted mutual monitoring and sanctioning in communities that solve collective action dilemmas.

Every social order, not just repressive ones, requires methods of mutual social control. The key question is whether populations of users can use what we now know about cooperation to drive power/knowledge to a higher level of democracy. Isn't that exactly what happened when printing made literacy available to entire populations, not just to a tiny elite? If discipline did not include the capacity for changing itself, the cooperation and democracy that exist today would not have come into being after millennia of slavery, tyranny, and feudalism. More to the point is a question for the present generations: Can discipline change in the future? Can people use mobile communication, peer-to-peer and pervasive computing, location awareness, and social accounting systems to evolve a higher form of discipline, transforming the forces revealed by Foucault according to the principles revealed by Ostrom and Axelrod?

> The key question is whether populations of users can use what we now know about cooperation to drive power/knowledge to a higher level of democracy.

---

15 Michel Foucault, "Panopticism," in *Discipline and Punish: The Birth of the Prison*, trans. Alan Sheridan (New York: Vintage Books, 1995), 195–228.

16 Ibid.

17 Ibid.

"Surveil Ordinary Citizens" and "Infiltrate Citizens' Groups"

from *The End of America*

— Naomi Wolf

People need to watch what they say, watch what they do.

—Ari Fleischer;
former White House Press Secretary, 2001

I warn every animal on this farm to keep his eyes very wide open.

—Squealer,
in George Orwell's *Animal Farm*

According to the ACLU's Barry Steinhardt, you should assume, if you are an activist, that your e-mail may be monitored and your phone calls tracked. He says that if your communications reach a certain level of interest to the government, a human being may be tasked to read and listen in on what you are saying, and you won't know about it. The White House surveillance program is triggered by certain key words and names. (The sophisticated Stasi listening station on Brocken Mountain, which monitored ordinary citizens' calls between East and West Germany was also programmed to record conversations when a certain name or word came up.)

Even though you pose no terrorist threat to the state, there is a reason you can be placed under surveillance now. Tyrants place populations under surveillance because this is a prime means of control. The Gestapo, the NKVD, the KGB, the Stasi, and the Chinese Politburo all requisitioned private data such as medical, banking, and library records; now, with the Internet, Chinese authorities track citizens' computer use. One reason dictators demand access to such private data is that this scrutiny breaks down citizens' sense of being able to act freely against those in power. Such intrusions also erode citizens' loyalties to civil and professional groups and redirect their primary loyalty to the state.

Torture doesn't get you better information, but the Bush team wants to be able to torture — and to let you know that torture takes place. Many critics have noted that illegal wiretapping doesn't speed intelligence gatherings but the Bush administration wants to eavesdrop on your calls and e-mails without a warrant — and to let you know that there is such surveillance underway.

Why?

THE IRON TRIANGLE IN AMERICAN LIFE

The Department of Homeland Security's surveillance apparatus is certainly aimed at prosecuting the War on Terror. But it may also be aimed at us, for domestic political purposes.

As I noted, all the societies we are looking at were facing real enemies and used surveillance to seek out their enemies. But all of them also used state surveillance against ordinary citizens to make them docile. Each dictatorship defended this on national security grounds.

In July of 2002, the Bush administration rolled out Operation TIPS, the Terrorism Information and Prevention System, which sought to recruit "a million letter carriers, meter readers, cable technicians, and other workers with access to private homes as informants to report to the

Justice Department any activities they think suspicious."[1] TIPS was to begin with a pilot program in ten cities and offered citizens a toll-free number to call. The million citizens the program hoped to enlist would have worked out to one informant for every twenty-four Americans. (The ACLU notes that this pilot program alone would have doubled the Stasi's ratio of informant to citizen. In 1989, when the Stasi records were opened, the people of the former GDR were amazed to find that only a minority of citizens had actually been watched, because most had simply assumed they had open files on them.[2] That is why surveillance is effective — even cost effective: You don't have to actually monitor citizens — just let them know they might be monitored.)

Tom Ridge, then-Secretary of the Department of Homeland Security, suggested that Americans report to the hotline about their neighbors. This trial balloon was whenever you try to change your job, go abroad, or get a promotion."[4]

American citizens now have a *dangan*: Three new forms of state surveillance were initiated in 2005 and 2006. *New York Times* reporters Eric Lichtblau and James Risen exposed an e-mail and phone monitoring program that was operating without legal warrants in 2005;[5] in 2006 they revealed that U.S. treasury officials, under the auspices of a CIA program, were reviewing millions of private bank transactions without individual court-ordered warrants or subpoenas.[6] The stories ran as scoops. But were these scoops undermining the government's broader agenda or inadvertently advancing it? If you don't know you are under surveillance, you won't be intimidated. Dictatorships want citizens to know they are being watched.

The net effect of the stories, whether they were scoops or leaks (or both), was that U.S. citizens now knew that

---

TIPS was to begin with a pilot program in ten cities and offered citizens a toll-free number to call. The million citizens the program hoped to enlist would have worked out to one informant for every twenty-four Americans.

---

met with mockery: Train the cable guy to spy! Though Congress soon prohibited the administration from funding TIPS, according to the ACLU, a version of the program was simply shifted to the Pentagon's "black budget." ("I don't make this stuff up," commented Steinhardt.[3])

In China, Communist officials subject citizens to three forms of government surveillance, together called the "iron triangle." (Bush referred to three of his aides as "the iron triangle.") This consists of the residence permit, which limits where you live; the secret personnel file, which records your sins and political liability; and the work unit, which supervises every aspect of your life. The *dangan*, or secret personnel file, shadows every Chinese citizen. "The *dangan* looks like a manila envelope, and there is a special postal system for transferring them around the country. If you make a serious political mistake, your leaders put a note in your *dangan*, and it will haunt you in the future

they had an "iron triangle" of surveillance over them: phone calls — social and sexual life; e-mails — work life; and bank records — financial life. Where else does one communicate private and confidential information?

Americans understand, even if most of us feel it would be only a remote possibility, that our most intimate correspondence can now be monitored by the State.

This surveillance is chilling dissent already: Emily Whitfield notes that "people are already reluctant to sign petitions. They are saying, 'I don't want my name to go on a list.'"[7]

Many citizens have noted how relatively muted Democratic and other opposition leaders seem to be in the face of all of this. The new surveillance reality helps to explain this unusual moderation in tone. Politicians

1   Nat Hentoff, *The War on the Bill of Rights and the Gathering Resistance* (New York: Seven Stories Press, 2003), 75.
2   Barbara Miller, *The Stasi Files Unveiled: Guilt and Compliance in a Unified Germany* (New Brunswick, NJ: Transaction Publishers), 2.
3   Author interview, August 2006.

4   Nicholas B. Kristof and Sheryl WuDunn, *China Wakes: The Struggle for the Soul of a Rising Power* (New York: Vintage Books, 1995), 49.
5   Eric Lichtblau and James Risen, "Bush Lets U.S. Spy on Callers Without Courts," *New York Times*, December 16, 2005, A1.
6   James Risen and Eric Lichtblau, "Bank Data Sifted in Secret by U.S. to Block Terror," *New York Times*, June 23, 2006, A1.
7   Author interview, August 13, 2006.

understand what state surveillance means faster than ordinary people do: Political candidates assume as a matter of course that their opponents are trying to monitor them.

When I worked on the Gore 2000 campaign — working on issues of concern to women and the youth vote — staffers took it for granted that they should have sensitive conversations on landlines because cell phones were assumed to be unsecured. Before you work for the White House or for a presidential candidate, you go through a search of anything potentially embarrassing in your past or present life because everyone knows that if the opposition can find something with which to blackmail or embarrass you, they will use it. You go through your stock holdings and tax returns; review any past drug use; you have to confess to your own team any illicit affairs or mental health treatment or addiction treatment; you disclose how you pay your babysitter. You have to do this because your team needs to know what the other team can find. The National Committees devote vast amounts of money and staff time to this kind of scrutiny: it's called "opposition research," and while it's not nice, it is still playing within the rules of democracy.

But now, opposition research that used to be reserved for political leaders alone can be directed at the rest of us. Politicians are not bland and inhibited because they are naturally boring; they are bland and inhibited because they know they are being watched. So they censor themselves.

If our government's only goal were to fight terror, most Americans would have no major problem with this kind of surveillance: They would feel that the benefit of being spared another 9/11 outweighs the discomfort of being listened in upon. Whitfield says that people often remark, "If I am not doing anything wrong, why should I worry about it?"

That faith presupposes that no one can get away with using your words or actions against you unfairly. This is a good assumption in a working democracy — but disastrous naïveté in a fascist shift.

Dictatorships use citizen surveillance in a clear way: to blackmail and coerce the people, especially critics. In the 1960s and 1970s, J. Edgar Hoover's FBI amassed files on the private lives of political, union, Civil Rights, antiwar,

and other leaders and blackmailed or harassed them. The FBI's Counter Intelligence Programs (COINTELPRO) actions against civil rights workers and the left in the 1960s included planting fake evidence on them, sending bogus letters accusing them of adultery to ruin their marriages (one fake letter called Dr. King an "evil, immoral beast" and suggested he kill himself), disclosing activists' sexually transmitted diseases, tapping their phones, getting activists fired from their jobs, distributing false articles that portrayed them as drug abusers, and planting negative articles about them in newspapers.[8]

We all have things we wish to keep private: a flirtation or even an affair, a struggle with alcohol, an old brush with the law. Think about all the things you have said in a phone conversation, sent to a friend in an e-mail, or discussed with your accountant that could, if available to someone who wanted to shut you up, be used or taken out of context to blackmail or smear you. Now understand that all of these things *are* available and *can* be used against you.

The USA PATRIOT Act set the stage for booksellers, librarians, and even doctors to have to turn over to the state information about Americans that had been private up until then. The American Booksellers Foundation for Free Expression took a stand against this, and librarians spoke out as well. (National Socialists also went after the booksellers, librarians, and doctors.)

When closed societies gather information on ordinary people's lives — when people know that their book-buying and library records are open, their sexual behavior and financial decisions are no longer private, their conversations are bugged, their class lectures are taped, their protests are photographed by police, their medical records are exposed, and that all this information can be used against them — their will to challenge the regime in power falters.

> The USA PATRIOT Act set the stage for booksellers, librarians, and even doctors to have to turn over to the state information about Americans that had been private up until then.

---

8   David Cunningham, *There's Something Happening Here: The New Left, the Klan, and FBI Counterintelligence* (Berkeley: University of California Press, 2004), 2.

FASCIST AND TOTALITARIAN SURVEILLANCE

Spying is the fuel of fascism. Mussolini pioneered the use of spying as a way to control his people. After 1922, Fascists ostentatiously made lists of names of communists to be punished. By 1927, Fascists were tapping phone lines and even spying on the Pope. Mussolini tapped his own party secretary's phone to blackmail him.[9] By 1933 the secret police encouraged ordinary Italians to inform on their neighbors. People were turned in for things as commonplace as singing the wrong song after they had been drinking. Secret police also tapped business leaders, including Giovanni Agnelli. Finally, Italians at every level

which I have received from, or sent to, my New York office. I of course have known for some time that they saw all my outgoing arid incoming messages and have had no end of fun sending absurd messages to New York criticizing these officials by name or concocting something that would keep them guessing."[14] Amusing — if you're not subject to arrest.

Many people who lived through the Nazi years said in one survey that they had been spied on by neighbors, coworkers, fellow pupils, and police. People said that nannies, maids, office coworkers, and teachers were all enlisted as spies. As in the GDR, only a minority — between three and twenty-five in a hundred — were actually sure of hav-

---

The German film *The Lives of Others* brings this everyday Stasi surveillance to life: The playwrights assume there are bugs in their friends' apartments and discuss politics on outdoor walks; journalists assume their own apartments will be ransacked and hide their manuscripts under floorboards.

---

of society understood that they were being watched.[10]

SS leader Himmler used surveillance too: He "whipped the Gestapo into an organization which ... watches over almost every department of life in the country and which keeps for Hitler and the politicians a watchful eye on the army itself."[11] Most people in Germany did not at first support the Nazis. But as Nazis paired citizen surveillance with state violence, opposition stilled.

From 1930 onward, the SS spied on the Brownshirts and kept files to use against them.[12] That year, police put masses of citizens under surveillance: half a million Berliners alone. Welfare officers and medical researchers began keeping lists of "asocial" citizens: Once on "the list," it was difficult to get off, and you lost jobs and benefits.[13] By the mid-1930s, most citizens understood that their conversations were no longer private, and National Socialists were bugging the conversations of reporters and political leaders. "Amusing to note of late," wrote Shirer in 1940, "on the desks of the German officials I have business with, copies of cables

ing been spied on, but the paranoia extended to everyone.[15]

Nazi surveillance increased over the years. "You never knew who it might be when the doorbell rang," one person told the interviewers. "[W]e children were not allowed to touch the curtains. ... There was always somebody with a leather trench coat standing there in the hallway. And, especially when there were two or three people at our place, there would be several people standing outside in front of our house."[16]

Secretary of State Condoleezza Rice is an expert on at least one surveillance society, which she analyzed in a book she coauthored, *Germany Unified and Europe Transformed*. The German film *The Lives of Others* brings this everyday Stasi surveillance to life: The playwrights assume there are bugs in their friends' apartments and discuss politics on outdoor walks; journalists assume their own apartments will be ransacked and hide their manuscripts under floorboards. Neighbors had to inform against neighbors; students informed on professors; children were encouraged to turn in their parents. Information equaled control.

---

9   R. J. B. Bosworth, *Mussolini's Italy: Life under Dictatorship, 1915–1945* (New York: The Penguin Press, 2006), 233.

10   Bosworth, *Mussolini's Italy,* 310.

11   William L. Shirer, *Berlin Diary: The Journal of a Foreign Correspondent 1934–1941* (New York: Black Dog & Leventhal Publishers, 1941), 469.

12   Richard J. Evans, *The Coming of the Third Reich* (New York: The Penguin Press, 2004), 229.

13   Evans, *Coming of the Third Reich,* 143–144.

14   Shirer, *Berlin Diary,* 448.

15   Barbara Miller, *The Stasi Files Unveiled: Guilt and Compliance in Unified Germany* (New Brunswick, NJ: Transaction Publishers, 2004), 3–25.

16   Eric A. Johnson and Karl-Heinz Reuband, *What We Knew: Terror, Mass Murder, and Everyday Life in Nazi Germany* (New York: Basic Books, 2005), 181.

Czech authorities also used surveillance during the Cold War to crush prodemocracy agitation. Havel describes the anxiety that the Czech Secret Police cultivated as "that hideous spider whose invisible web runs right through society [causing] a dull, existential fear that seeped into every crack and crevice of daily life and made one think twice about everything one said and did."[17]

China too uses surveillance to crush democracy. Reporters Nicholas Kristof and Sheryl WuDunn evoke a scene similar to those played out in the GDR. A Chinese friend asks Kristof to go for a walk:

> "You know Hongjun, don't you?" she asked. "Well, you should know that he's not for real. He's a spy for State Security, and you should never, ever trust him with any information. He's been a spy for a long time, and now he's interested in you and Sheryl. He's been asking about a book he thinks you're writing, and about how you're writing it. He wants to know if you're writing it on the hard drive of the computer, or on floppy disks. If you are writing a book, you might want to be very, very careful with it."

"I was speechless," writes Kristof. "I hadn't told Hongjun about a book."[18]

With these early steps in place, people start to restrict their own activities voluntarily. They start to think twice about bulk e-mailing the "Impeach George Bush" message, or checking Amnesty International's Website to see what Iraqis with relatives held in U.S.-run prisons are saying, or sending information about the Professor Ward Churchill controversy to a friend.

In that atmosphere, dissent stifles itself before it can develop. Surveillance leads to fear, and fear leads to silence.

And silence is un-American.

* * *

Congress shall make no law … prohibiting … the right of the people peaceably to assemble, and to petition the Government for a redress of grievances.
First Amendment

The next time you meet with your antiwar group, I am afraid you have to ask yourself if everyone present really is who you think he or she is. Incredible as it sounds, you may well have undercover investigators hanging out with you.

Dictatorships and would-be dictators routinely infiltrate legal citizens' groups and report back to the group in power or seeking power. Historically, infiltrators are also directed to disrupt and harass such organizations. The goal: to make sure that it becomes too costly and nerve wracking to act out as a citizen.

In Italy, Fascist spies infiltrated groups of trade unionists. In Stalin's Russia, spies reported on the activities of intellectuals and dissidents.[19] In Germany, National Socialist agents infiltrated groups of anti-Nazi students, Communists, and labor activists; these agents were busy, even attending cabarets where jazz and other "un-German" music was being played, to denounce the musicians.[20] In the GDR, the Stasi infiltrated the usual dissident groups. In Prague in 1968, infiltrators joined in with groups of writers, theater workers, journalists, and intellectuals. In Chile, Pinochet's agents joined groups of prodemocracy students.[21] The Chinese Politburo sends state agents to infiltrate forbidden prodemocracy and banned religious groups.

Infiltration is not just an intelligence tool; like surveillance, it is also a psychological pressure point. When the state infiltrates citizens' groups, people feel vulnerable about acting in accord with one another and so are less likely to risk the assertive collective behavior that democracy requires.

In dictatorships, infiltrators are joined by *agents provocateurs* at marches and rallies. These provocateurs don't just

---

17 Vaclav Havel, *Disturbing the Peace: A Conversation with Karel Hvizdala* trans. Paul Wilson (New York: Alfred A. Knopf, 1990), xi.

18 Kristof and WuDunn, *China Wakes*, 22.

19 Roy A. Medvedev, *Let History Judge: The Origins and Consequences of Stalinism,* trans. Colleen Taylor (New York: Alfred A. Knopf, 1971), 352–54.

20 Richard J. Evans, *The Coming of the Third Reich* (New York: The Penguin Press, 2004), 403.

21 John Le Rector, *The History of Chile* (New York: Palgrave Macmillan, 2003), 202.

act and dress like the protesters: Their task is to provoke a violent situation or actually to commit a crime. One FBI infiltrator, Gary Thomas Rowe, for instance, warned his handler of an impending police attack on the Freedom Riders — then went ahead to participate energetically in the beatings that followed.[22] *Provocateurs* also serve a PR purpose: They set up protesters to look like lawless threats to society, thus providing would-be dictators with the rationale for declaring martial law as a means to "restore public order."

Since 2000, there has been a sharp increase in U.S. citizens' groups that are being harassed and infiltrated by police and federal agents, often in illegal ways.

Since 2000, there has been a sharp increase in U.S. citizens' groups that are being harassed and infiltrated by police and federal agents, often in illegal ways. A 2006 ACLU report notes that police departments in California had infiltrated antiwar protests, political rallies, and other constitutionally protected gatherings and were secretly investigating them, even though the California state constitution forbids this.[23]

But that was just the beginning. A Defense Department program called Talon created a database of "antiterror" information about peaceful U.S. citizens' groups and activists.[24] Talon included details of antiwar groups' planning meetings in churches; a church service for peace in New York City; even details of the meetings of such all-American groups as Veterans for Peace. The Defense Department even had e-mails that had been forwarded to it by people who had pretended to be members of the groups.[25] Some of the

groups were placed in this database with the rationale that while they weren't violent yet, they might become so. Jen Nessel of the Center for Constitutional Rights said, "We have absolutely moved over into a preventive detention model — you look like you could do something bad, you might do something bad, so we're going to hold you."[26]

Harassment is a more serious tactic. Before the Republican convention in New York in 2004, the police department's intelligence team sent detectives throughout the city to infiltrate groups planning to demonstrate peacefully at the convention. When the New York Civil Liberties Union asked to unseal the records of this undercover spying, lawyers for the city argued that the records should be kept secret, because the news media would "fixate upon and sensationalize them."[27]

It is in a fascist shift that the truth is recategorized as being unseemly — destructively inflammatory.

Today, if you are outspoken, you are increasingly likely to face other kinds of harassment, such as an IRS investigation: All Saints Episcopal Church in Pasadena, California, was scrutinized by the IRS after a rector gave a sermon that characterized Jesus as antiwar. (A year after the 1917 Espionage Act was passed, Rev. Clarence Waldron was sentenced to prison for fifteen years for passing out a pamphlet that said that war was un-Christian.[28])

The IRS asked for the California church's internal documents and e-mails to investigate if it had violated tax law.[29] Many conservative churches have helped Republicans: Two Ohio churches turned their facilities over to Republican groups, hosted Republican candidates, and were credited with turning out voters for Bush in 2004. But they were not investigated by the IRS.[30]

Harassment takes many forms: Peace activist Cindy Sheehan wore a T-shirt with the message, "2,245 Dead.

---

22   David Cunningham, *There's Something Happening Here: The New Left, The Klan, and FBI Counterintelligence* (Berkeley: University of California Press, 2004), 109.

23   Mark Schlosberg, "The State of Surveillance: Government Monitoring of Political Activity in Northern & Central California," ACLU of Northern California, July 2006. Available at: http://www.aclunc.org/issues/government_surveillance/the_state_of_surveillance.shtml.

24   Joe Conason, *It Can Happen Here: Authoritarian Peril in the Age of Bush* (New York: St. Martin's Press: 2007), 192–93.

25   Eric Lichtblau and Mark Mazzetti, "Military Documents Hold Tips on Antiwar Activities," *New York Times,* November 21, 2006, A18.

26   Author interview, May 9, 2007, Center for Constitutional Rights.

27   Jim Dwyer, Jim. "City Asks Court Not to Unseal Police Spy Files," *New York Times,* March 26, 2007, B1.

28   Mark Bushnell, "The Minister Was Jailed for Anti-War Beliefs," *Times Argus Sunday Magazine,* December 12, 2004. Available at: http://www.times argues.com/apps/pbsc.d11/article?AI D=2004121/NEWS/412120306/1013; Geoffrey R. Stone, *War and Liberty: An American Dilemma, 1790 to the Present* (New York: W. W. Norton, 2007), 55.

29   "Taxing an Unfriendly Church," Editorial, *New York Times,* November 22, 2005, A22.

30   Stephanie Strong "Group Seeks I.R.S. Inquiry into 2 Ohio Churches Accused of Improper Campaigning," *New York Times,* January 16, 2006, A9.

How many more?" referring to the war in Iraq, in the gallery of the House of Representatives. Capitol Police arrested her and charged her with "unlawful conduct," which could have given her a year in prison. Beverly Young, a Republican congressman's wife, wore a T-shirt in the same place that read, "Support Our Troops": she was asked to leave but was not arrested or charged with a crime.[31]

On July 25, 2006, Jim Bensman, a coordinator with Heartwood, an environmental organization, was at a public meeting in Illinois convened by the Army Corps of Engineers to discuss proposed construction of a channel on a dam in the Mississippi River. Bensman advocated a standard solution to the problem under discussion: using explosives. Dams are typically destroyed with explosives, a point that the Corps of Engineers' own presentation at the meeting noted. News coverage of the meeting included the summary that Bensman "would like to see the dam blown up."

Less than a week later, Bensman got called by an FBI agent. The agent persuaded him that the call was for real by telling Bensman about items in his FBI file. The agent also told Bensman that he wanted to visit him at home. Bensman recalls: "I was thinking, 'I need to talk to an attorney' … and he said, 'Well, O.K., I will put you down as not cooperating.'"[32]

So Americans do need to watch what they say, watch what they do. Be careful how you phrase things. Don't leave your meeting's minutes lying around. Check your gut reaction when you are talking to people in your local group. Be mindful while you pursue your activism.

Have the number of a good lawyer handy.

But most important of all, lead your friends and community to unite in a grassroots movement to restore our nation's freedom.

---

31   "Activist Sheehan Arrested in House Gallery," CNN.com. February 1, 2006. Available at: http://www.cnn.com/2006/POLITICS/01/31/Sheehan.arrest/.

32   Cornelia Dean, "A Man, a Plan, a Dam. Then, an FBI Call," *New York Times,* August 22, 2006, A15.

Surveillance Environments: Google

— Jan Fernback

For decades, the mass media have contributed to the environment of surveillance in which we exist. Communication research pioneer Harold Lasswell described how the mass media perform a surveillance function by collecting and distributing news of events, thereby allowing an individual to look over the horizon in order to know about events in the broader world. But the implication of media as devices of surveillance and voyeurism has gone far beyond Lasswell's vision.

THE EVOLUTION OF SURVEILLANCE

We form perceptions about surveillance environments through the media in novels (*Nineteen Eighty-Four*), in film (*Enemy of the State*), and online (data mining, targeted advertising). But we both perform the watching and succumb to being watched through the media (online social networking, Twitter, CCTV, interactive computer games, the television show *Big Brother*). Digital media technologies in particular are agents of surveillance because of their ubiquity in contemporary life and because they permit capable users to produce content. As our lives become more entwined with digital technologies, we must consider the nature of the surveillance environment and its ramifications, both dangerous and innocuous, for individuals and for society. This chapter focuses on the role of digital technologies in creating the surveillance environment, with emphasis on Google as the preeminent online products and services company.

Surveillance is a process of concentrated monitoring of human details — at times clandestinely and at times openly — for the purposes of control. Communication technologies serve as obvious devices for surveillance and control. George Orwell warns of the dangers of total state surveillance enabled by communication technologies. Michel Foucault's (1977) ideas about technologies as tools of discipline and regulation are articulated in his description of Jeremy Bentham's panopticon prison. In the panopticon, a prison designed for control of the mind, an unseen observer monitors all inmates simultaneously, thus assuring that inmates would assume constant surveillance and behave in a self-disciplinary manner. For Foucault, the control warranted by surveillance expanded beyond prisons to other social institutions — including workplaces, hospitals, or schools — served to dehumanize individuals.

Oscar Gandy's (1993) "panoptic sort" describes an elaborate system of information gathering, filtering, and dispersion enabled by information technologies. This system operates as a panopticon that uses accumulated personal data to assign individuals an economic value and sorts them into categories determined by that value. The "panoptic sort" is routine in Western society — for example, in the issuance of credit scores — and is thus a powerful element of social discipline. Roger Clark (1988) defines "dataveillance" as the use of individual data in tracking personal behaviors or communications. Dataveillance is so widespread, it has become the prevailing form of surveillance, according to Clark. Examples of dataveillance include radio-frequency identification

(RFID) chips embedded in consumer goods; cell phone tracking; computer surveillance software (keystroke and data capture programs); web beacons and cookies; online data mining programs; and consumer-supplied tracking (warranty cards, mp3 player registrations, and sharing of personal information in blogs).

David Lyon (1997) sees communication networks of information collection and distribution as the contemporary counterpart to Foucault's theories on control and discipline through surveillance. For Lyon, however, the panopticon is a limiting way to view surveillance; the internet and other digital technologies aid the surveillance enterprise as databases link together and expose more and more personal information, but such monitoring does not have to be as overtly visible as the panopticon. Much digital surveillance is decentralized, invisible, and even voluntary. Also, there

and its self-surveilling nature contribute to Google Inc's status as a powerful contributor to the surveillance environment. That the surveillance environment exists is understood; but what engineers this environment? How has it flourished?

Whether surveillance has protective elements or intrusive ones, its growth and vigor has resulted from the powerful interplay among military, economic, political, corporate, technological, and legal institutional bureaucracies. As surveillance tactics and modes became integrated across these bureaucracies (think ID cards and basic record-keeping), similarities emerged that allowed surveillance to become a natural part of everyday life. In Colonial America, meticulous slave records were kept, slaves were required to hold "passes" when moving about town, and slave patrols were organized to detect and capture runaways. The U.S.

The revelation of personal information on Facebook or on blogs is a type of ritualized identity formation and expression. Even the use of Google takes advantage of a type of surveillance to provide convenience. Google features such as Google Maps and Streetview provide web users with information obtained from an army of watchers.

---

are means to resist or evade some aspects of monitoring.

Not all perspectives on surveillance environments reflect its sinister intrusiveness. Lyon (2007) theorizes a type of "caring" surveillance exhibited by means such as security cameras that identify criminals, forensic scrutiny that bolsters law-enforcement efforts, and lifeguards that ensure water safety. Store-loyalty cards provide customer discounts. Reality TV shows provide entertainment around surveillance activities — what Robertson (2007) calls "engaging in the publication of privacy" (p. 410). Citizen-gathered "news" video finds its way to legitimate news organizations. Voyeurism finds an outlet in surveillance activities as amateur porn is distributed online.

Online social networking flaunts surveillance environments by embracing the watchers; users willingly succumb to surveillance to assert identities or viewpoints within the digital technological landscape. The revelation of personal information on Facebook or on blogs is a type of ritualized identity formation and expression. Even the use of Google takes advantage of a type of surveillance to provide convenience. Google features such as Google Maps and Streetview provide web users with information obtained from an army of watchers. Google's purchase of YouTube

military issued identification passes to soldiers during the Civil War and military bureaucratization led to further governmental surveillance and disciplinary measures (citizen passports, census, social security numbers), criminal surveillance, workplace surveillance for purposes of controlling immigrant labor, and ultimately, consumer surveillance (Parenti, 2003). In all of these sectors, the emergence of computers and the digital revolution made surveillance more complete, more profound, and more ubiquitous. As surveillance is catalyzed by desires for efficiency, global power consolidation, and general control and discipline in each sector, the surveillance environment expands (Lyon, 2007). Thus, computers and the digital revolution enable monitoring through interlinked IDs, swipe cards, databases, video patrols and CCTV, and through the integrated data repositories found on Google.

GOOGLE AND THE HEGEMONY OF ACCESS

Another means by which the surveillance environment is permitted to flourish is what I call the "hegemony of access" to information in contemporary culture. Hegemony is a form of naturalized dominance, engineered through consensus among powerful elites in major social institutions. Enabled by the seductive ease with which we can obtain data, this hegemony of access encourages a social mindset that all information be viewable, useable, and commoditized. The desire for total information access is hegemonic because it is an unquestioned, accepted form of dominion over all social institutions and all people.

The sheer amount of information that now exists triggers a sensibility that all data should be readily accessible.

clearing houses). Google keeps logs of user-generated content for 14–60 days. No other online service company is as innovative or as comprehensive (Conti, 2009).

Google's mission is "to organize the world's information and make it universally accessible and useful" (http://www. google.com/corporate). In order to fulfill this mission, Google uses its information web-crawler script, Googlebot, to feed its data banks. The company also gathers information through data you provide; web-browsing demograph-

---

Privacy law in the United States is partially about control over personal information, yet access to information is a democratic impulse. Thus, antagonisms exist between the concept of freedom of information in a democratic society and the impulse toward control of that information.

There is a quality of surveillance surrounding this desire for absolute access; it is about control and power. Whether surveillance is used for management, protection, influence, or discipline, elements of power that can impact individual lives are at work. Everyone wants access — consumers, governments, and corporations. We all want to monitor; we are all monitored.

The access we desire and are often granted is to everything, including our own personal information, media content, medical records, financial information, personal dossiers ("Googling" other people), crime records, sexual histories. Ways in which we enact the desire for total information access tend to invade privacy, from data mining to online social networking to Google Earth to obsessive Twitter feeds. Privacy law in the United States is partially about control over personal information, yet access to information is a democratic impulse. Thus, antagonisms exist between the concept of freedom of information in a democratic society and the impulse toward control of that information.

How does Google feed these impulses? Google is a powerful online company because of its innovative free applications, its vast information holdings and processing, and its colossal data storage. Using Google's top applications such as Gmail, the Google search engine, Streetview, YouTube, Picasa, the Chrome browser, Google Talk, Google Latitude (cell phone tracking) and Google Docs creates a large dossier of personal data stored by Google for use in marketing, data mining, the development of user profiles, and for sale to third parties (usually information

ics in Google Analytics and Google AdSense; data provided by others who use Google services (such as Google Docs); and what is acquired through third parties (such as Google business partners). Even Googlesightseeing.com, which is not run by Google but is a compendium of compelling images taken from Google applications, contributes to the company's mission of information dominance (Conti, 2009). Future applications may permit the identification of individual faces in Google's Streetview image bank. Whether or not Google is an all-encompassing surveillance device akin to Orwell's Big Brother or the panopticon, its capabilities and mission are ordained by the hegemony of access.

ANALYSIS: BENEFITIS AND HAZARDS

The impact of the surveillance environment is manifold. There are implications for individuals, for society, for privacy, and for democracy. Lyon (2007) reminds us that digital surveillance technologies can aid the storage and sorting of personal data in ways that are harmless as well as insidious to individuals and to democracy. But as technologies become more sophisticated, the dangers may increase. The capacities of monitoring devices and agencies are increasing, creating linkages among detailed data sets, including biometric data (passports, fingerprints, facial scans); locational data (GPS, cell phone tracking, RFIDs, satellite photos); medical data (records, genomic data); and criminal, consumer, military, educational, and employment data. The data flows are now global as the boundaries between nations and national policies are blurring. Thus, the bounty of data gathered via surveillance could be shunted toward so-called "data havens" — countries that do not recognize data protection laws that exist in the European Union or the United States.

LOSS OF PRIVACY

Some citizen groups and scholars worry about a surveillance state fostered by government and corporate monitoring of private citizens. For example, government investigators, litigators, corporate data brokers, or identity thieves might monitor you based on information traces left online that Google might store. In the United States, the government relies on corporate data-mining operations such as Choicepoint or Acxiom as a means to monitor individuals without adhering to the 4th Amendment to the U.S. Constitution, which prohibits law enforcement from conducting unreasonable searches of persons or property. These companies sell data to foreign and domestic government agencies, direct marketers, and law enforcement.

or Twitter as a form of voluntary "personal expression" that showcases our identities in the datasphere, but SNS's exhibitionistic tendencies open us to the downside of being watched. We expect freedom online — freedom to be me — but the surveillance impinges on that freedom. The SNS user defines her/his identity in part through consumer goods, thereby submitting to self-marketing, self-disclosure, self-surveillance (and mass-surveillance). As another example, Facebook quizzes "scrape" information gleaned from the quizzes for whomever authors the quiz so that person/company/group can view your profile, regardless of your profile's privacy rating. Ultimately we invite self-surveillance through mediated outlets like Facebook or Google.

DEHUMANIZATION

For Foucault (1977) the type of knowledge construed through the surveillance environment results in a boundless control that can be used to dehumanize individuals. This dehumanization can be seen in the impact of surveillance

---

We use Facebook, Google's Orkut, or Twitter as a form of voluntary "personal expression" that showcases our identities in the datasphere, but SNS's exhibitionistic tendencies open us to the downside of being watched.

Privacy advocates and other groups claim that surveillance is a threat to privacy because it intrudes upon our freedom, dignity, and integrity. Defined by Samuel Warren and Louis Brandeis in an 1890 *Harvard Law Review* article as the "right to be let alone," privacy encompasses the concepts of territory (environmental intrusion); information (personal data); body (physical intrusions such as drug testing); and communication (wiretapping or hacking). Our private thoughts and private lives are what make us free and dignified individuals; surveillance threatens to expose those private thoughts — our private selves — by allowing access to the bits and pieces that constitute our behaviors.

Privacy is also about controlling information about ourselves. We may attempt to control our information against corporate or governmental monitors, but we also willfully engage in providing information without recognizing that we are being surveilled. For example, online social networking (SNS) is seen as social intimacy through information sharing. We use Facebook, Google's Orkut,

on the psychology of the watchers as well as the watched. Philip Zimbardo's classic Stanford Prison study (http://www.prisonexp.org) used student volunteers to perform the roles of prison guards and prisoners. The students embodied their roles; the guards treated the prisoners with contempt and brutality; the prisoners experienced emotional trauma (crying, rage).

What parallels exist in the surveillance environment? Does being watched imply that we *should* be watched? Could that same brutality emerge when the watchers of society observe the rest of us? Do modes of surveillance encourage the emergence of a social contract of altered behavior or conformity (among the watched) and empowerment and discrimination (among the watchers)? A power divide is created between the groups as rights and privileges are questioned. Distrust, fear, and hatred can result, and the freedom to engage in social life with dignity may be lost. The more watchers are able to construct people by virtue of an electronic dossier or by ID tracking or CCTV images, the more reductive we become as entities. We become compilations of data, bodily movements, consumer purchases, and geographic location. Not only is humanity potentially sacrificed, we may also become deindividuated — a psychological term for feeling anonymous, disconnected, and overwhelmed in the crowd. Ultimately, the surveillance environment can be examined as a moral issue in addition to a political one.

TRANSPARENCY

But not all believe that surveillance threatens to produce an atmosphere of totalitarianism, either in terms of privacy, dignity, or freedom. Some view certain types of surveillance as a comfort [e.g., anti-terrorism policies, nanny cams, lifeguards, public security cameras, medical supervision, even Google Streetview], hence a movement toward a transparent society (Brin, 1998; Lyon, 2007) has developed in which information in all spheres is completely open for all to access. Transparency provides the watched with knowledge of the types, means, and purposes of surveillance. Essentially, transparency is the idea that government and corporations can watch citizens, but citizens can watch back. If we all know one another's secrets, those secrets can no longer be used as weapons.

The notion of transparency neutralizes arguments about security versus privacy. Thus the appetite for total information and the hegemony of access have cultivated the movement toward transparency in all aspects of information as a means to combat the consequences of surveillance with the motto, *Nothing to hide, nothing to fear*. Transparency is a necessity, advocates claim, because the sheer accumulation of data acquired through surveillance results in profiling and discrimination against groups and individuals. This discrimination could take the form of curtailed lending or differential pricing for consumer goods or denial of insurance to population segments deemed too risky based on "data categories" assigned to individuals under surveillance. Is transparency a tool to quash discrimination or could transparency harm oppressed groups that rely on secrecy to flourish (such as religious minorities)? Does transparency really correct power imbalances between the watchers and the watched? Is transparency a mere excuse to legitimize more-sophisticated surveillance techniques? Will transparency comfort us when Google has become *the* gateway to all things virtual?

If the surveillance environment has indeed become so entrenched into everyday life that citizens and institutions have no ability to negotiate a state of non-surveillance, then transparency seems to be the only means toward ensuring some dignity and freedom. But would transparency then become a technologically mandated solution to a technologically derived problem? Should citizens allow the march of technological development to inflict its will upon the human spirit, which needs its own private core and its own sense of dignity and freedom? David Brin (1998) argues that technological evolution will modify human behavior such that transparency is the only means of recourse. However, critics might respond that Brin assigns technology too central a role in determining the course of human freedom and equality. Might the reliance on technology for enhanced security simply encourage reliance on technology for enhanced surveillance? Might openness and transparency encourage further escalation of spying in the name of security?

RESISTANCE

There are both non-technological and technological means to resist the surveillance environment. Measures of resistance include exhibitionism, citizen protests, anonymizing or falsifying data, hacking surveillance technologies, or refusal to participate in online shopping, blogging, or loyalty clubs. Lorna Rhodes (2004) researched prisoners who mutilate themselves when subjected to the gaze of maximum security guards. She theorizes that rather than demonstrating insanity, the prisoners make themselves more visible in a subversive act of rebellion against surveillance.

Another technique of resistance is sousveillance, literally "watching from below," a type of inverse surveillance in which the public sector monitors the security sector. Examples include citizen video, keeping tabs on various authorities (government, corporations, doctors, etc.), "watchdog" web sites or blogs, or recording telephone conversations. Google itself could be a tool for sousveillance; YouTube now contains a sousveillance channel: http://www.youtube.com/user/sousveillance.

Sousveillance usually requires a response from surveillors in the form of acknowledgement, power shifting, or even the development of new, more-powerful surveillance mechanisms. For example, participants in the 1999 World Trade Organization protests in Seattle recorded their own interaction with law enforcement, which spurred security organizations to reconceive surveillance and control mechanisms (mostly in the form of increasingly sophisticated CCTV). The security sector's response to citizen resistance could ultimately change the power dynamic between the watchers and the watched.

CONCLUSION

The surveillance environment is a product of the evolution of the information society from other types of social orders based on punishment, discipline, and control. Surveillance is a socio-technical system; it is enabled by technology but defined by socio-cultural realities, and those technologies are socially shaped. Google's many products mirror those realities in contemporary culture. As we are increasingly defined by the data profiles constructed from the harvest of the surveillance machine, we must examine the nature of surveillance, its consequences, and potential responses to it. Because digital technologies progress so rapidly, and because they contribute to and enable the surveillance environment in which we live, citizens must consider the impact of this environment on identity, freedom, dignity, and democracy.

REFERENCES

Brin, D. (1998). *The Transparent Society: Will Technology Force Us to Choose Between Privacy and Freedom?* Reading, MA: Addison-Wesley.

Clarke, R. (1988). Information technology and dataveillance. *Communications of the ACM, 31*(5), 498–512.

Conti, Greg. (2009). *Googling Security: How Much Does Google Know About You?* Upper Saddle River, NJ: Addison-Wesley.

Foucault, M. (1977). *Discipline and Punish: Birth of the Prison.* Translated by A. Sheridan. New York: Pantheon.

Gandy, Oscar. (1993). *The Panoptic Sort.* Boulder, CO: Westview Press.

Lyon, David. (1997, May 22). *Surveillance Systems: Towards an Electronic Panoptical Society?* Interview with Christian Höller for Telepolis. http://www.telepolis.de/english/special/pol/8026/1.html

Lyon, David. (2007). *Surveillance Studies: An Overview.* Cambridge: Polity.

Parenti, Christian. (2003). *Soft Cage: Surveillance in America From Slavery to the War on Terror.* New York: Basic Books.

Rhodes, Lorna. (2004). *Total Confinement: Madness and Reason in the Maximum Security Prison.* Berkeley, CA: University of California Press.

Robertson, Roland. (2007). Open Societies, Closed Minds? Exploring the Ubiquity of Suspicion and Voyeurism. *Globalizations, 4*(3), 399–416.

Humility and Limits

from *The Transparent Society*

— David Brin

1. SURVEILLANCE ELITES

In the world we all fear most, the answer to that question, "Who watches and controls?" will be hierarchical power structures. Some form of oligarchic tyranny. It hardly counts whether the elite is based on inherited wealth, personal connections, public office, ideological purity, fighting prowess, demagoguery or several other standard methods by which groups organized themselves to dominate others in the past. What matters is that this despotism will be like none other, because it will know all and see all.

In 1990, [professor Gary] Marx illustrated this chilling scenario by creating a composite corporation to serve as an example, combining a spectrum of already current surveillance techniques under one roof. Job applicants underwent extensive medical and psychological screening, including detailed background questions about their parents' health. The company searched databases, credit, and police records. Employees were checked weekly by an automated health analysis of urine, blood pressure, etc. Workplace chiefs monitored more than two hundred criteria to assess productivity — including keystroke speed, errors, and time away from the job. Computer screens sent periodic productivity messages. In addition to audio and video surveillance, all telephone numbers dialed were recorded. In Marx's composite scenario, "transparency of human behavior for the purposes of total control" became habitual, addictive. Unseen managers monitored people down to the smallest detail, recording and detecting all variances in a process called "accountability through visibility."

We needn't go into the towering hypocrisy of managers refusing to let the same degree of all-penetrating scrutiny apply to them. That is simply what people in power will do, if they are allowed to get away with it — the very outcome that *reciprocal* transparency might prevent. Certainly, if left unchecked, this tendency could inexorably bring about Marx's maximum security society. A world not of glass houses, but of one-way mirrors.

In such a world, we would have just one hope — that eventually a generation of rulers might feel less frantic and driven than their fathers. Perhaps, eventually, these sons and daughters of the mighty will grow bored with watching and controlling everybody else. But this is only a slim reed to clutch if we ever find ourselves living in such an awful world. Anyway, I doubt this particular dismal future will come to pass, simply because we are already so wary of it from a relentless drumbeat in countless works of culture and fiction. Surely, the worst danger must lurk in other directions.

2. SURVEILLANCE OBSESSION

A second dark vision also fits Marx's overall scenario of a maximum security society. In this rendition of tomorrow, privacy has vanished, as in example 1. We live harried, supervised lives. Only now those doing the watching are not an elite, but *everybody*.

Remember city number two back in chapter 1? That's the metropolis where the people control the cameras. Everyone enjoys the same high level of access. As a result, citizens have more freedom. The police are supervised. Everyone is held accountable.

But this vision could go desperately wrong if folks grow *obsessed* with watching.

Here, my restaurant analogy has broken down. Instead of being deterred from staring, people become addicted to it. In their rising paranoia, the natives of city number two might get stuck in a viciously competitive cycle. Believing that any lapse in vigilance could cause them to lose out, they band together in groups of common interest, peering at their foes relentlessly, pursuing them across the cityscape and through corridors of cyberspace, suspecting that any shadow may conceal a conspiracy. And they, in turn, are just as vigorously pursued. Encryptions and illusions spread, along with tailored viruses sent to corrupt opponents' precious data stores in a war of attrition that only accentuates the desperate race to see more with gnat drone cameras, which are countered by antignats, and so on. In such a society, you might officially have plenty of freedom, and yet be so frightened and lost that life as a sovereign individual becomes impossible.

Utterly dependent on the protection of your "tribe," you will conform to every social ritual and constraint the group demands of you. Recall from chapter 6 how Philip Agre and Christine Harbs described a similar scenario: "Shorn of the ability to enter into relationships of responsibility and trust, individuals will tend to gravitate towards a safe average, suppressing their individuality and creativity in favour of a thoroughgoing orientation to the demands of an omniscient observer."[1]

In effect, such a world is ruled not by monarchs, nobility, or captains of industry, but by a new class of witch doctors, cyberpunk-style hackers whose sophisticated software hexes may offer just a little shelter against the endless swarm of eyes that fill an awful night. It is a world of accountability

> In such a society, you might officially have plenty of freedom, and yet be so frightened and lost that life as a sovereign individual becomes impossible.

gone mad, reminiscent of Dr. Seuss's children's story about the land of Hawtch-Hawtch, where citizens were so frenetically busy keeping an eye on each other ("watching") that "today all the Hawtchers who live in Hawtch-Hawtch are watching on Watch-Watcher-Watchering-Watch."[2]

Frankly, I can think of better ways our descendants might choose to spend their time.

3. SURVEILLANCE ACCEPTANCE

There is another possible "chilling" outcome to a world of universal surveillance, one that is very different from those we just looked at.

Suppose the cameras do eventually pervade everywhere, creating a society where not a single nook or cranny is left unobserved. And let us venture further that everyone has access to all the cameras (hence no overt tyranny). Now, let's add one more supposition.

The first generation to be surrounded by lenses may feel nervous under the pervasive gaze.

The next is mildly irked, though used to it.

And later generations?

Growing up with this situation, they take it completely for granted. From infancy, they have looked at a myriad strangers all over the globe, and have been looked at by just as many. Their fear levels are low, since nothing can happen to such children — either by accident or deliberate harm — without it being instantly known by those who love them. Watched over in this way, eight-year-olds feel free to wander both city and countryside, exploring as most children could not possibly be allowed to do nowadays.

The author Damon Knight described such a world in his short story "I See You," a fascinating tale about a future when all people own machines that can look through any wall.[3] Defying the hackneyed plot of abuse by some dicta-

---

1 Philip E. Agre and Christine A. Harbs, "Social Choice About Privacy: Intelligent Vehicle-Highway Systems in the United States," *Information Technology & People,* vol. 7, no. 4 (1994).

2 Dr. Seuss, *Did I Ever Tell You How Lucky You Are?* (New York: Random House, 1973).

3 In Damon Knight, *On Side Laughing* (New York: St. Martin's Press, 1991). Another science fiction tale depicting people exchanging privacy for participation in a new culture can be seen in the novel *Oath of Fealty,* by Larry Niven and Jerry Pournelle.

tor, Knight instead posited an era when everything has eerily changed. Lies and injustice have vanished, and privacy is considered a quaint, archaic concept, like phlogiston. In Knight's spooky world there are no mysteries. Moreover, people find, at first to their surprise, that they do not miss them.

Elsewhere we have envisioned transparency being all

be defined as "garbage": old postin
after they have been erased and
apparent reason; stored drafts
different from one another, th
away; "spammed" messages tha
reproducing endlessly; acres
funky Web pages that feature live

Every time humans discovered a new resource, or technique for using mass and energy, one side effect has always been pollution. *Why should the information age be any different from those of coal, petroleum, or the atom?*

---

about accountability and freedom, while preserving a curtilage of decent reserve and genuine privacy for individuals and families to retreat within, whenever they choose. In fact, I see transparency as a principal tool for *preserving* some privacy. But in Damon Knight's alternative scenario, a flood of light has effectively transmuted humanity into something new, A people as much unlike us as …

… as *we* are unlike our Cro-Magnon ancestors, who likewise saw and knew everything about one another, almost all the time.

Of course, Knight's tale is just a vivid fabulation, the sort of "what if?" that makes a reader go "huh!" and mull silently for a while, as the best science fiction is supposed to do. Personally, I doubt human nature would provide for such happy attitudes in a world so utterly transformed. In any event, I am not ready to live in a society anywhere near that transparent.

4. SURVEILLANCE OVERLOAD

A final dystopic vision of transparency is called *data smog.* It tells of a time, a few years or decades from now, when the sheer volume of information does to us what all the secret codes and ciphers never could — deafening us in a cacophony of noise, blinding us in a bitter fog of our own profligacy.

This scenario is disturbingly realistic in one way. Every time humans discovered a new resource, or technique for using mass and energy, one side effect has always been *pollution.* Why should the information age be any different from those of coal, petroleum, or the atom?

Already, those who manage the Internet have to contend with a rising fraction of bits and bytes that can only

bowl or coffee pot. Updating an old lawyer's trick, some corporations and government agencies nowadays respond to reporters' freedom-of-information demands by spewing back more raw data than any journalist could possibly sift through in a dozen lifetimes. This "fire hose" defense often proves an effective way to stymie investigators, holding accountability safely at bay and neutralizing some of society's best T-cells.

Even if encryption proves overrated — or if we somehow evade the seductive trap of secrecy fetishism — there remains a danger that the proud promise of this new age may drown in an effluvium of openness. We may lose all the advantages of candor in an acrid data smog of our own making.

Each of these four scenarios depicts a world of transparency taken to some logical extreme. Naturally, I have a reply to all four extrapolations. The answer is that *human nature rebels against oversimplification,* such as drastic social systems that limit the breadth of our ability to experiment and experience. This response will be especially true in a society whose most popular myths sermonize from the pulpit of eccentricity. For instance, our best hope against unhappy worlds 1 and 3 above may lie in the power of boredom to make the act of watching start to pall. A quid pro quo, a polite averting of eyes, could reduce the oppressiveness, if each person chose to see self-interest beyond the nose on his or her face.

In our hypothetical society plagued by data smog, there is a good chance that the problem would be solved by the development of new software agents, sophisticated autonomous servant programs designed to cull and search through the morass, adroitly sifting the information byways

...eds foremost in mind, clearing away dross and ... restoring clarity to cyberspace, the way the air of ...geles is gradually becoming breathable once again. ...As for the benighted denizens of dystopia number 2 ...urveillance Obsession), their self-made suffering will

small conspiracy will be able to meet in your sanctum or bedroom. But that's okay. People won't have much use for conspiracies in a civilization filled with well-educated amateurs and dedicated eccentrics.

Above all, citizens will be much too busy to spend time

I believe this balance of technology with common sense may result in a world where we are observed only about 80 percent of the time, and still have that personal curtilage, a sanctuary where we can relax unwatched, share intimacy, or simply be solitary for a while.

---

inevitably end in a way that they deserve, either when some clique or dictator finally takes over, or else when a computer, program, or virus finally evolves out of that fetid "darwinnowing" ferment, rising up to achieve artificial intelligence. Such a sapient program might then take over the world — a laudable situation, since the citizens of that wretched commonwealth have already exchanged sovereign judgment for paranoia. Fools forsake any right of mastery over their creations, a truth that has always held for parents, and may apply to humanity as a whole.

These four scenarios were radical extrapolations of what might happen if we are stupid and let some malign trend reach its ultimate conclusion. In fact, though, I have faith that citizens of the neo-West will notice and correct such dismal tendencies before they get that far.

Can future Vince Fosters — and all the others who find in-your-face confrontation painful — feel at home in a transparent society? While extroverted "T-cells" go careening about, challenging errors and battling threats to freedom, will there be serenity for the reticent and the shy? Throughout this book I have maintained that a culture of openness will sustain some privacy, if that is what free citizens want, and if Peeping Toms have reason to fear getting caught. Courtesy may return as an important moderating force, for the simple reason that it will make life among the cameras more bearable — and because those who don't practice it will be found out, losing their neighbors' good will.

I believe this balance of technology with common sense may result in a world where we are observed only about 80 percent of the time, and still have that personal curtilage, a sanctuary where we can relax unwatched, share intimacy, or simply be solitary for a while. Those havens may not offer enough space for a mad scientist's lab. Only a very

peering at one another. They'll have better things to do.

In contrast to these five views of a transparent society (four of them chilling and one guardedly optimistic), the chief alternative is a world filled with a different kind of blinding fog. An encrypted haze that will nonetheless completely fail to thwart the sophisticated surveillance tools of the rich and powerful, who will simply work *around* the mathematics. Most of us will live in houses with glass roofs. Our neighbors may not be able to peer at us through the surrounding murk of anonymous masks and secret codes, but those dwelling higher on the restored social pyramid will look down and know everything about our lives, even the smallest detail, while we happily imagine that the mighty are still somehow our equals.

They won't be. They never have been. Among all the human cultures yet devised, only one came close to applying the tools of accountability evenly in all directions. But if we choose secrecy as our course, we will abandon the only reliable weapon that freedom ever had.

* * *

A WITHERING AWAY?

Governments of the Industrial World, you weary giants of flesh and steel, I come from Cyberspace, the new home of Mind. On behalf of the future, I ask you of the past to leave us alone. You are not welcome among us. You have no sovereignty where we gather.

This quotation from John Perry Barlow's "A Declaration of Independence of Cyberspace" illustrates one of the essential issues that will confront us in the coming decades: a realignment of the relationship between individuals and nations. We can see signs of this process all around us: in the breakup of the old Soviet Union; in a devolution of power from the British Parliament to regional assemblies; in rising influence by nongovernmental organizations (NGOs) on the international stage; and in a reborn American "states' rights movement," whose fringe elements now eagerly spurn a flag they were brought up to revere.

"Just as during the Enlightenment the nation-state took over from 'the church' to become the dominant seat of action, so the nation-state is now receding, yielding center stage to the marketplace," says Lawrence Wilkinson, cofounder of the net-wise Global Business Network, who goes on to suggest that national patriotism may fade to the level of affection people now give sports teams, or even "brand loyalty" to their favorite companies.

Amid a spate of recent books extrapolating this trend to a stateless future, financier Walter Wriston's *The Twilight of Sovereignty* contends that, whereas geography once made history, the information revolution will make geography history. "How does a national government measure capital formation when much new capital is intellectual?" Wriston asks. "How does it track or control the money supply when financial markets create new financial instruments faster than regulators can keep track of them?" *The Sovereign Individual*, by James Dale Davidson and William Rees-Mogg, makes the same argument by pointing out that technology is reducing the ability of government to enforce its power and control. The overhead cost of the modern industrial state will no longer be supported when people find ways to escape it. Wriston has supported efforts to transform offshore banking havens into high-tech sanctuaries, masking cybercommerce from national taxing authorities. Taking a slightly different approach to the same notion, David Post and David Johnson, codirectors of the Cyberspace Law Institute, have proposed that cyberspace should be a separate legal jurisdiction with its own laws and regulations, created and enforced by the online community.

This is not a new dream. A thread of resentment toward hierarchical power structures has always gained strength from time to time, aided by some promising (usually informational) technology; for example, the printing press encouraged dissemination of vernacular bibles, breaking the rigid hold of church officials on religious thought and encouraging the rise of "individualist" Protestant alternatives. But the decline of church influence turned out to be only partial, as it adapted to changing times. Moreover, we should note that nation-states soon took advantage of the same technological innovations, replacing church authority and gaining strength from the increased information flow, rather than losing ground to it. Stephen Kern's *The Culture of Time and Space: 1880–1918* describes how the telegraph, telephone, and airplane helped prompt "a general cultural challenge to all outmoded hierarchies." But other kinds of hierarchies soon emerged, from the totalitarianism of Hitler and Stalin to the business empires of Ford and Du Pont. The tendency of humans in leadership to leverage permanent positions atop pyramids of power should never be underrated.

Despite all the transcendentalist proclamations we have heard that the Internet and new media will inevitably level social differences and empower individuals, most of the cash (and accompanying influence) seems to be passing through major corporations.

In an article in the December 1997 *Atlantic Monthly* titled "Was Democracy Just a Moment?," Robert D. Kaplan paid respect to the resiliency of authoritarians in adapting to fresh styles of technology and control, including the corporate boardroom. Picking and choosing in order to cite a few tyrannical success stories, and largely ignoring the error-prone, war-loving, and self-delusional nature of most dismal autarchies, Kaplan nevertheless did strike home by pointing out how nearly universal has been the tendency for cliques to take over during times of chaos, transition, or unaccountability. Extending this into the future, Kaplan's view is that "Corporations are like the feudal domains that evolved into nation states; they are nothing less than the vanguard of a new Darwinian organization of politics."

What can we conclude from these seemingly contradictory predictions? We seem to be surrounded by bright fellows who think they have road maps for tomorrow. Kaplan, at least, has some history he can cite to support his dour view of natural trends. The cyberanarchists have nothing but a vivid dream.

Still, the revolutionizing power of the information age *is* impressive, fostering reinvigorated utopian hopes. As discussed in the section "An Open Society's Enemies" at the end of chapter 4, many libertarians have long called for dismantling those state structures they believe hobble and corrupt a natural free market — after which poverty and oppression would presumably vanish, dissolving in a cornucopia of unleashed creativity and enterprise. While some libertarians, such as those at the prestigious Cato Institute, would define this dismantling process in cautious or moderate terms, negotiating an evolving consensus with society at large, a radical or "anarchist" wing sees nothing about the word *government* worth preserving.

The Internet's arrival has stoked this quixotic aspiration to new levels, provoking proclamations of a coming age when tyrants and bureaucrats will smolder away in a soot of their own irrelevance. While the U.S. Libertarian Party

when society finishes "forming capital." In the modern era, factory equipment becomes obsolete with ever-increasing speed, requiring rapid and agile retooling that will leave us needing innovatively competitive "capitalist" managers for any foreseeable future.

Alas, the anarcho-libertarian vision is no more realistic. Believers can cite no historical cases when following a prescription of unbridled individualism caused productivity and freedom to skyrocket in the manner they predict.

We do know that markets often respond well to a moderate and continuing easing of onerous government supervision, a self-correcting process of gradual deregulation

---

The Internet's arrival has stoked this quixotic aspiration to new levels, provoking proclamations of a coming age when tyrants and bureaucrats will smolder away in a soot of their own irrelevance.

---

polls only single digits in most elections, informal surveys indicate that up to 40 percent of the most technologically sophisticated netizens sympathize with libertarian agendas and goals.

It can be interesting to compare the vision of radical libertarian utopianism with another one that was penned more than a century ago, by Karl Marx. Both look forward to a natural and supposedly inevitable *withering away of the state*, and a resulting civilization without coercion or authority figures, where free adults deal with each other under conditions of perfect independence, gravitating to any work they desire. The chief difference between these two transcendentalist world views, one "extreme left" and the other "far right," has to do with *how* this result will be achieved.

Marx believed that it would occur once industrial societies finish constructing the means of production. After the needed capital — factories, infrastructure, and all that — is completed, there will be no further need for the specialized skills of "capitalists." Their services can then be dispensed with, along with the governments that protect their privileges.

Anarcho-libertarians project a somewhat different path to the same goal. Their ideal society of free and rich individualism awaits one prime task: assertively demolishing the oppressive and inefficient state apparatus.

In retrospect, the progression described by Marx sounds incredibly naive. For instance, there is never a point in time

that many nation-states are currently performing through their own political processes, even as we speak, and one that we have discussed several times in this book. As Jaron Lanier put it, "Of course government intervention screws up a market, but at the same time it is the existence of government that creates markets in the first place.[4] Otherwise, people would resort to violence instead of money to get things." A position that is perfectly compatible with moderate libertarian thought.

---

4 Jaron Lanier, quoted from "Karma Vertigo: Or Considering the Excessive Responsibilities Placed on Us by the Dawn of the Information Infrastructure," *Netview: Global Business Network News,* winter 1995. Although bureaucrats are often depicted as relentlessly power hungry, many officials actually share the same cautious attitude toward government's proper role, as expressed in March 1997 by Christine A. Varney of the Federal Trade Commission, at the Seventh Conference on Computers, Freedom and Privacy: "First, I believe that, in general, government should regulate only when there has been an identifiable market failure or where an important public policy goal cannot be achieved without government intervention. Second, the pace of change in the information industry is unprecedented. Government regulation, on the other hand, moves very slowly, and the predictive skills of government agencies are notoriously limited. As a result, regulatory and legislative solutions to consumer protection issues are unlikely to be either timely or sufficiently flexible with respect to the digital world at this juncture. And finally, I believe the electronic medium itself offers new opportunities for consumer education and empowerment, which in turn increases the likelihood that self-regulatory regimes will be effective."

Without a doubt, many areas of public policy merit further attention for possible deregulation, for example, numerous cases of "corporate welfare." In fact, mainstream economists believe that enhanced openness of information flows will result in gradual easing or replacement of many bureaucratic structures, as cheating is eliminated and all market players can participate with full knowledge. In other words, transparency.

Unfortunately, libertarians in general (even the moderates) have little voice in this ongoing process, because a large fraction have politically marginalized themselves through blanket contempt for gradualism. By publicly ridiculing the current consensus, worked out by a free and educated citizenry over the course of many decades, enthusiasts like Wriston emulate the followers of Marx in dismissing their fellow citizens as puppets and dupes. Hardly an effective way to elicit support.

Ironically, the dream that anarcho-libertarians and Marxists share may yet come about, though not in the manner that either group ordains. Instead of happening through some transcendent revolutionary transformation — a semiviolent or semimystical upheaval — their ideal world of true individual sovereignty might appear through a gradual combination of the pragmatic tools and skills that have been described in this book.

1. Rising wealth and education levels may extend people's horizons, encouraging them to consider alternatives to traditional tribes and empires. New affections won't necessarily banish the old.

2. The propaganda campaigns described earlier — a tsunami of films, books, and images promoting individualism and suspicion of authority — will accelerate a desire by billions to find ways of perceiving themselves as somehow unique and special. Millions will actually succeed in achieving truly creative eccentricity.

3. Where this results in a proliferation of avocations, or "hobbies," many private individuals and groups will take on tasks that formerly only state bureaucrats were thought capable of performing, such as nosing around for inefficiency and error. As shown by the example of public feedback regulation discussed in chapter 8, many paternalistic protections may prove less necessary, and even fade away, once consumers have ready access to the correlated

information they need for making truly informed choices.[5]

4. Human nature will not change (though both Marxists and anarcho-libertarians seem to expect it to). Cliques and groups of would-be oligarchs will always conspire to improve their position through cheating rather than fair competition. But in a world of free-flowing information, these efforts may prove futile. Infections of nascent tyranny will heal under liberal applications of light. Government will be an essential tool for preventing coups and criminality in the short term. But transparency may eventually reduce or eliminate the need for armies and police to safeguard our lives and property.

5. Poverty will not go away all by itself, or through some idealized magic of free markets. But when all the world seems "next door," it will be impossible for the well off to escape hearing, seeing, and ultimately feeling the pain of their neighbors. They will help. The detailed methods may range all the way from person-to-person charity to collective

---

5   Jeff Cooper, director of the Center for Information Strategy and Policy, contends that states have traditionally relied on five monopolies in order to maintain their sway: (1) legitimate use of violence, (2) promulgation of views through propaganda, (3) establishment of a firm currency and setting exchange rates, (4) access to cutting edge technology, and (5) expertise and credibility. Today we see the power of states eroding in four out of five of these categories. The new wired world offers vast alternatives to state propaganda, for instance. Private currency brokers are now more important than state bankers in establishing rates of exchange. New technologies enter the civilian realm so quickly that armed forces now buy many items straight off the shelves. And expertise is spreading to the populace at large, at unprecedented rates.

The chief questions we face are (a) Do we really want the legitimate use of coercion or violence to be "deregulated" or "privatized" along with the rest? (b) Might there be plenty of jobs left for government, even if Cooper's monopolies are broken? (c) Will the loss of state control in categories 2 through 5 be a *democratic dispersal* or simply wind up giving these powers over to the hands of other elites?

In a society that is mostly transparent, former monopolies 2 through 5 may become so widely distributed, among so many players, that accumulation of tyrannical power may never become likely again. This could result in nation-states that are less relentlessly dominant in our lives than in the past. That does not mean nations will necessarily go away, or even lose great importance in helping mediate consensus approaches to solving great problems. One role they can serve is as the centripetal centers of common loyalty that bind together all the diverse, spinning "tribes" of interest we will be joining, a core identification of citizenship that people share.

(tax-supported) efforts, but we will help. Or else we will not deserve a better world.

Again, this scenario is perfectly compatible with the views of many reasonable and mature "libertarians," who see no harm in gradualism, as long as real progress is being made. But to those we saw at the beginning of this section, gleefully rubbing hands over the imminent demise of nations, this particular sketch for a "withering away of the state" lacks one vital feature that both anarchists and Marxists adore about their ideologies — a "them versus us" resentment so well illustrated by Barlow's wonderfully vivid "Declaration of Independence."

In contrast, an empirical-gradualist approach, using transparency to slowly replace government with free will, suggests that we are already far along the path. Moreover the neo-Western liberal democracies that got us to this point will be essential tools for helping us travel the rest of the way. They have (so far) provided a benign environment in which we can stretch and explore unprecedented realms of freedom. These are balmy parks compared to the fear-drenched chiefdoms of our ancestors — peaceful commonwealths where we've been fed, clothed, and tutored, even as we dream about outgrowing them.

Centuries ago, the inventor of modern democratic theory, John Locke, replaced mystical-Platonic justifications of power with a new model: a "social contract" in which rulers were ultimately answerable to the people. Under Locke's *implicit* contract, the sole recourse of an afflicted populace was to rebel against oppressors and replace those at the top of the pyramid, a crude model, but one appropriate to an age when few could read.

Now we may be headed for an era when the social contract will become *explicit*. When each of our supereducated grandchildren may negotiate fresh trade-offs of liberty and responsibility with individuals and remnant institutions in a world of sophisticated, sovereign human beings.

If so, this utopian vision will come about only because we passed successfully through this complicated, irritating, noisy, indignant-but-hopeful era of transition. A pragmatic, gritty progression that was fostered and enabled by some of the world's states. By governments that are occasionally oppressive, but are far more often our possessions and tools.

In other words, our nations, which still deserve our rambunctious citizenship, some loyalty, and perhaps even our wary love.

CHAPTER 9
Celebrity

Toby, that box is the biggest thing since Gutenberg invented the printing press, and I'm the biggest thing on it.

— Herb Stempel,
Quiz Show (1994)

Chapter 9. Celebrity

Recommended Film

Quiz Show (Robert Redford 1994)

Media Models

The Meme, The Spectacle, The Hyperreal

Chapter Summary

Ellis Cashmore explores the complex layers
of meanings in celebrity culture.

Answering/The Big Question

from *Celebrity/Culture*

— Ellis Cashmore

WHY?

April, 2005: Reese Witherspoon says she's been chased across town from her gym by paparazzi who encircled her in the Hollywood Hills and only retreated after she appealed to a private security guard at the entrance to a gated community. A photographer is later charged with child endangerment and battery after allegedly hitting a five-year-old child with his camera and pushing away another to take pictures of Witherspoon and her children.

June, 2005: Driving her Mercedes-Benz, Lindsay Lohan is in collision with a pursuant minivan driven by a photographer who is subsequently charged with assault with a deadly weapon — the vehicle. The photographer is later cleared, though the case encourages Governor Arnold Schwarzenegger to sign legislation allowing celebrities to collect large damage awards from paparazzi who harass them.

August, 2005: Several cars follow Scarlett Johansson as she leaves her Hollywood home for Disneyland in her Mercedes. In her attempt to escape them, she bumps a Daihatsu carrying a mother and daughter to whom she apologizes. Johansson's agent tells the *Los Angeles Times*: "At least two or three of them [paparazzi] had been camping outside of her house for five days … she's left Los Angeles. You can't deal with it any more."

September, 2005: The *Daily Mirror* newspaper carries a story based on a 45-minute video that purports to show Kate Moss preparing and snorting five lines of cocaine in a London recording studio, where her boyfriend Pete Doherty — who has a well-documented history of drug dependency — was working with his band. Earlier, the *Daily Mirror*'s sister paper, the *Sunday Mirror*, had paid out "substantial damages" after publishing a story claiming that Moss had collapsed after taking coke in Barcelona in 2001.

October, 2005: After disappearing in 1993, Kate Bush re-emerges from her self-imposed exile to release a new album. She became a recluse to escape the media and to raise a family away from the glare of the kind of publicity to which she had become accustomed since her first single "Wuthering Heights" became an international hit in 1978.

When Kate Bush receded from the public view, we let her. When I say "we" I mean everybody, not just the paparazzi, the television crews, and the other members of the media, but everybody who licensed them, however unwittingly. Despite avoiding scandals, she must have sensed that it was going to be hard to slide between professional and personal lives. The membrane separating them was getting evermore permeable. She opted for the personal. By the time she decided to return to her recording career, things had changed appreciably. It's likely that had she started her recording career today, she would be pursued as vigilantly — and in Moss's case, the pursuit was downright vengeful — as any of the other female celebrities in the vignettes that opened this chapter.

It could be argued that it's a small price to pay. After all, celebrities earn serious money and, much as some deny it, they wallow in the admiration if not outright adoration. Having your home staked out and having a perpetual tail of media personnel, as they say, goes with the territory. My purpose in this book is not to put the case for or against the celebrities. Rather, it's to understand the changes that have led to the collective preoccupation with them. The vignettes are not untypical. On the contrary, they are representative illustrations of the lengths to which the media will go just to satisfy our appetites for pictures and news of, or just gossip about, people whom we don't know but feel we do know. When all's said and done, celebrities should make no lasting impact on most of our lives, apart from prompting the occasional emotion: like the joy we take in listening to their music; or the contentment in watching their acting; or the thrill of just seeing them; or maybe the ecstasy in fantasizing about them. But there's more. We spend an inordinate amount of time and money reading about them, staring at pictures of them, discussing them, and, in some cases, obsessing over them. All of which leads us to our final question. Why?

Why? is a loaded question, of course. On what grounds? Under what conditions? In what circumstances? For what reason? With what purpose? If you've read this book chapter-by-chapter rather than dipping in and out, you'll have one answer ready. But there are others, many of which I've alluded to throughout the text. In concluding, I will formalize them.

Celebrity culture has been with us just about long enough to generate a body of literature. A glance at the bibliography of this book indicates the scale of work already available. Like any other subject-based literature, there is a branch devoted to theorizing. This is where the Why? question gets answered, though, as we will see, in a number of different, sometimes contrasting ways. We shouldn't expect anything less: celebrity culture, like any other aspect of study, defies any once-and-for-all answers. Instead, there are perspectives, models, accounts, and conceptual approaches, all of which offer a way of answering questions and asking a few more.

Most of the theorists of celebrity culture have appeared earlier in the book, their one- or two-line wisdoms helping advance the overall argument. In this, the final chapter, I will consider their work again, this time with the intention of disclosing their overall designs. The perspectives are those of the twenty-first century: the influences of earlier writers such as Leo Braudy and Richard Dyer are clear enough, though my interest is in how these influences have been distilled into contemporary analysis.

THE NEW ECCLESIASTES

Religion. It enchants us. I mean this literally. We are caught in a spell we either can't break or don't want to break because we have faith. Faith replaces the need for evidence. Our belief in whatever particular complex of beliefs we call our religion dictates that we believe *in* it rather than believing it conditionally. Adherents of religions don't, for example, say: "I'm prepared to accept that there is a superhuman, controlling power such as god and that god should be worshipped, but only on the condition that, at some stage, I'll be supplied with proof of this." More typically, we devote ourselves and organize our mental outlook and conduct accordingly without ever needing even a sign. Those who do search for signs usually find them in the quotidian, that is, the common everyday things that most people take for granted.

Religion has been under threat since before the eighteenth-century Enlightenment, which used reason and individualism to challenge traditions of prejudice and superstition. Science and technology addressed many of the questions asked and answered by religion and poured them into a different mould. It reshaped them in a way that invited answers, without any recourse to faith. Science offered proof.

This occasioned a gradual decline not so much in religious belief but in the significance religion had in society, especially Western European societies. Secularization spread, though perhaps not as universally as enthusiasts of science would like. Religion has held fast and still dominates the politics and culture in some parts of the world. In others, it's retreated temporarily, only to return with renewed influence. But science meant that religion's power to bewitch had been weakened. The overall project started by the Enlightenment brought with it disenchantment. This has led some writers to conclude that celebrities have served to re-enchant a world in which deities have either been abandoned or emptied of their power, leaving a "post-God world."

"Celebrities are our myth bearers; carriers of the divine forces of good, evil, lust and redemption," declared Jill Neimark, marshaling the historical work of Leo Braudy to bolster her claim (1995: 56). Braudy's *The Frenzy of Renown: Fame and its history*, was, as its sub-title indicates, a historian's perspective on fame (1997). First published in 1986, just before the changes that animated our intense interest in celebrities, it examined the triumphs of famous figures long before the age of celebrity. In fact, Braudy identifies Alexander the Great as the first truly famous person. As long ago as the third century BCE Alexander regarded himself as no other human: more a deity or a hero of Homeric legend. With no media in the sense we understand it today, Alexander made use of an alternative apparatus for spreading news of himself and his achievements. He commissioned authors to chronicle his battles, artists to depict his likeness, and engravers to design, shields, coins, and other artifacts bearing his profile. Alexander actively encouraged worship and exaltation by fashioning himself after the gods and demigods of ancient Greece.

Alexander may be a prototype of the godlike human, but he certainly wasn't a celebrity (at least, only when played by Colin Farrell, in the movie *Alexander*). All of his efforts at immortality and indeed those of the many Roman emperors, who vaingloriously followed his example, were aimed at separating themselves from their subjects. They deliberately flouted legal and moral rules as a way of confirming their extraordinary status: rules applied to humans, not gods. In a similar way, the Pharaohs of ancient Egypt, such as Akhenaten and his wife Nefertiti, ordered the building of edifices to commemorate their existences and the European aristocracy of the Middle Ages commissioned portraits of themselves to ensure their posterity. They cultivated the popular conception that their world was not that of ordinary mortals; they were untouchable.

There are remnants of this type of behavior in today's celebrity temple. For example, Mariah Carey's famous refusal "to do stairs" assisted her elevation above both her audience and the rest of her entourage. Outlandish demands worked for the likes of Cleopatra, so presumably today's celebs think they will work for them. But, no one seriously thinks the celebrities are deities. Or do they?

"Post-God celebrity is now one of the mainstays of organizing recognition and belonging in secular society," writes Chris Rojek (2001: 58). Celebrities appear as gods in human form or simulacra of departed deities. Celebrity culture, in this view, becomes a functional equivalent of religion, with beliefs and practices associated with religion "converging" with those of celebrity culture.

As we have seen in previous chapters, what was once a vast gulf between Them and Us has been narrowed to the point where celebrities have become touchable. The likes of Lohan, Johannson, and indeed Carey appear on celluloid, but hawkish photographers make sure that most of the widely circulated images show them tracksuited on their way to the shopping mall, often bedraggled, and sometimes annoyed enough to greet their watchful media with all-too-human gestures (Cameron Diaz was famously photographed giving the finger to paparazzi). So it appears to make little sense to regard them as godlike beings rather than ordinary people who have bad hair days like everyone else. Rojek suggests that the "glut of mass-media information" which personalizes the celebrity has turned them from being distant figures, not just into ordinary people but "significant others." "They are also symbols of belonging and recognition that distract us in positive ways from the terrifying meaninglessness of life in a post-God world" (2001: 95).

This might strike some readers as decaf phenomenology, with the "terrifying meaninglessness" in fact being a resignation to the mundane monotony of everyday life, and with the "positive ways" in which celebrities distract us being retail therapy. But there is more complexity to the argument. "Celebrities offer peculiarly powerful affirmations of belonging, recognition, and meaning in the midst of the lives of their audiences" (2001: 53).

Secularization may have been overstated, but religion has certainly had to adapt in order to survive in many parts

> "Celebrities are our myth bearers; carriers of the divine forces of good, evil, lust and redemption."

of the world. In some important respects, it has reconfigured so that it can respond to the "uprooting effect of globalization." In striving to meet the needs of the rootless flock, religion has borrowed the style of celebrity culture. Its leaders are charismatic tv personalities, its sermons arrive in people's homes via television or the internet, and it elevates its showbusiness devotees into standard bearers. This is part of a convergence. The other part is celebrity culture's ability to supply experiences that, for fans, are every bit as meaningful as religious experiences. This is why fans spend more time reading tabloids than they do the Good Book. As Rabbi Shmuley Boteach put it: "MTV and Access Hollywood has supplanted Ecclesiastes and Proverbs" (2002: 1).

While Rojek describes this as a "hypothesis," other writers have put it to the test. Lynn McCutcheon and John Maltby are part of a team of psychological researchers who have explored the manner in which consumers engage with celebrities. In Chapter 5, we covered several of their research projects, many of which explore what the researchers call "celebrity worship." The term makes clear allusions to religion, though we should remain mindful that the word worship derives from the Old English *weorthescipe*, meaning, basically, worthy. To worship someone or something means to show respect or acknowledge merit. Paying reverence to deities is but one meaning of the term. Celebrity worship sounds less profound once this is borne in mind, though the research of McCutcheon *et al.* delivers a somewhat surprising conclusion: many of those who follow celebrities do so with a zeal that actually does resemble religious fervor (2002, 2003; Maltby *et al.* 2004).

Celebrity worship is measurable on a Celebrity Worship Scale, low worship describing what many of us do: watch and read about celebrities. At the other extreme, there is the level at which worshipful followers show "a mixture of empathy with the celebrity's successes and failures, over-identification with the celebrity, compulsive behaviours, as well as obsession with details of the celebrity's life" (McCutcheon *et al.* 2002: 67). This is the kind of uncompromising and extreme disposition we might regard in a different context as religious zealotry or fanaticism (remember: some trace the origins of the word fan to fanatic, which has religious connotations, as we saw in Chapter 5).

Adoring or even obsessing over celebrities as idols or role models is a "normal part of identity development in childhood and adolescence," according to McCutcheon *et al.* (2003: 309). It's a form of parasocial interaction. We may identify with cartoon characters or the fictional characters played by actors, rather than the actors themselves. But we may also idolize rock stars, movie stars, and any other kind of celeb that attracts us. It becomes a psychologically abnormal state when it continues into adulthood, perhaps leading to the worshipper's neglect of everyday duties. It may lead to the believer's having deluded conceptions about the nature of his or her relationship with one or more celebrities. Or even what the researchers call "addiction to a celebrity."

McCutcheon and her colleagues are specifically interested in the psychological origins and effects of celebrity worship on the individual, rather than its cultural sources or its wider ramifications. As such, they don't address the question of whether celebrity worship has converged with or even replaced religious worship, as Rojek suggests. Their evidence is, however, persuasive: the intensity of emotional involvement, the impact on the life of the believer, the pattern of engagement with the rest of the world (from sociability to withdrawal) are all features of celebrity worship that have religious counterparts. As I pointed out in Chapter 5, the scholars question the usual separation of stalkers from other devotees: "The distinction between pathological and nonpathological worship is somewhat tenuous" (2002: 69).

The team's findings are complemented by those of Susan Boon and Christine Lomore, also psychologists, who discovered that fans were not simply influenced by the way celebrities dressed, made up, wore their hair, or by their overall demeanor: "they took note of their attitudes and values, especially on issues of morality" (2001). Such a finding invites comparisons not only with prophets, preachers, or sages, but with priests, pastors, and ordained ministers responsible for the spiritual leadership of a church or other religious organization.

THE WORLD THROUGH A LENS

In the 1960s, when Daniel Boorstin was completing the first edition of his *The Image: A guide to pseudo-events in America*, he wondered about the effects of living in an "illusory" world of created characters. Mediated, two-dimensional images were becoming as important to us as real people: we only needed to flick a switch or open a magazine and we were in the alternative world. Compared to this, our own world must have seemed colorless and uninteresting. In Boorstin's world, people exchanged ideas and gossiped about stars and tv characters rather than learning about each other and, by implication, about themselves.

The early 1960s: the Beatles, Martin Luther King, Motown, George Best, *Cleopatra*. The names seem to be from a different age. They are. Yet we know them all. And they're all comprehensible and not just as historical entities. The media supports a vivid imagination. We may be detached observers, but we feel we know, perhaps do actually know, all about the Beatles and the story of Motown without having to delve into the history books. The media is just *there* like a Greek chorus, different voices singing different things simultaneously and continuously.

This is where our story of celebrity began, of course. The early 1960s witnessed the beginning of our new enchantment. Our senses were massaged or manipulated by a newly tenacious media that fed on the real people behind the image. Of course, what they were doing was delivering new images to replace the old.

There were potent images that lingered in the mind long after the early 1960s: the first live transatlantic television broadcast via the Telstar satellite in 1962; the assassination of John F. Kennedy in 1963; the first spacewalk in 1964; England's World Cup win in 1966 (watched by about 400 million tv viewers). These were delivered by television. The "illusory" world grew both bigger and smaller to viewers watching "live" transmissions of events 250,000 miles away.

Essentially the same media that delivered the first moon landing delivered celebrities. To be precise, images of celebrities. David Giles provides an illustration, inviting his readers to put themselves in the shoes of a famous female recording artist. After a harrowing experience with the paparazzi, she is summoned to the studios by her record company to make a second album, a single from which is going to be released ahead of the album. When the single becomes available (downloads are typically around before the cd), the press office arranges over 100 interviews and the singer is whisked around the country to make tv and radio appearances. "You are replicated furiously," Giles assures the hypothetical singer/reader. "Dozens of newspapers and glossy, full-colour magazines carry photographs of you … The video, for a start, receives heavy 'rotation' on specialist TV channels and several plays on terrestrial TV" (2000: 52).

The single sells well, prompting another few weeks of "saturation media coverage" and every time the song is played whether on radio, tv, iPod, or whatever, "you stroll into their living room … you are *there*" (2000: 52).

The singer obviously isn't physically there: Giles means that her presence is summoned by a visual or audile representation that registers in the imagination. Jessica Evans tenders a phrase to capture this: "Mediated persona is a useful term in that it reminds us how celebrity as a category is *absolutely dependent on the media* to create and disseminate a persona to an audience" (2005: 19).

Evans's emphasis reveals the colossal importance she places on the role of the media in the creation and perpetuation of celebrity. Giles is equally convinced of the media's efficacy in bringing celebrity culture into being, though his inflection is on the way in which technology has taken matters to a new level.

Braudy's history of fame alerts readers to the manner in which primitive media were used not only to circulate news but to glorify and lionize rulers, whether kings, generals, priests, or saints. "So it can be argued that there is much continuity between the representations of the famous in the past and the present," writes Evans (2005: 20).

Citing examples from history, Evans argues that even the "pseudo-events" Boorstin believed were stage-managed episodes specific to the twentieth century have much older precedents. Louis XIV (the seventeenth-century French king, not the San Diego band) was adept at making carefully designed public rejoicings appear spontaneous. The point is: public relations is not as new as we think and the media, even before the age of print, were used as promotional vehicles. Fame then has always involved some mediating agency that represents and disseminates news and images. Edited collections, such as James Monaco's 1978 *Celebrity: The media as image makers* and Lisa Lewis's 1992 *The Adoring Audience: Fan culture and popular media*, as their titles suggest, concentrated on the power of the media both in governing the depiction of celebrities and influencing the experience of consumers through the twentieth century.

While her approach accentuates historical continuity, Evans identifies the period 1890–1930 as "crucial" when "the mass media invented a particular kind of 'star' persona" (2005: 23). This is slightly later than the take-off

> Essentially the same media that delivered the first moon landing delivered celebrities.

phase identified in Chapter 4, though Evans's argument is in broad agreement: in making the private lives of entertainers a part of their overall public persona, the emerging media in concert with the film industry nurtured a new kind of relationship between the famous and their audiences. Between them, there were texts, defined by Evans's collaborator Frances Bonner as "socially constructed assemblages of items such as spoken or written words, or pictures" (2005: 59). (An "assemblage" is something made of unrelated things joined together, so the text is basically anything that's intelligible to the consumer, or the person doing the "reading.")

In Evans's model then, there are three conceptual elements: the production, text, and reception. While each contributes to making celebrity a meaningful social entity,

Hype has no object of any value: it just implies "that a phenomenon can be made to appear valuable, even when its value is non-existent" (2000: 20). While he doesn't go into the etymology of the term, note that its root is *huperbole*, Greek for excess, from which we get hyperbole, an exaggerated statement. Giles cites P. T. Barnum as the pioneer of hyping: the techniques he used for publicizing the exhibits of his shows were much the same as those used today. The Hollywood film industry's publicity machine refined and perfected what was an art for Barnum into something resembling a science. After the 1950s, domestic television became a new medium for creating celebrities *par excellence*. There had been nothing to compare with tv: it served to shrink the distance between viewers and events and the people who featured in the events; but it also began

---

Giles believes that there is a long-standing and even desperate desire for fame among human populations. Changing forms of media have effectively made it possible for more and more people to gain the kind of mass exposure that brings fame.

---

the relationship between them is variable. Culture industries may produce a particular set of images or personae of celebrities, but there is no guarantee that audiences will interpret them in the way intended: the texts may be quite different. "Reception" is perhaps a poor choice of words in that it implies passivity, whereas consumers are seen as discriminately selecting and decoding media messages in a way that resists manipulation.

Although the media and the elaborate organizations that augment them drive celebrity production and, as such, remain the engine of the model, the texts that circulate in a way have a life of their own once in the public discourse (actually "in" the public discourse isn't quite appropriate as the discourse is actually constituted or made by the public).

Giles sees less historical continuity. New media technologies rupture developments, opening up unanticipated opportunities for aspiring celebrities. They did so in the fourteenth century when the modern theater became popular, providing a "vehicle … for creating fame." Then again in the fifteenth century with the invention of the printing press; engravings were a popular way of portraying the human face before photography. "Celebrity is essentially a media production, rather than the worthy recognition of greatness," says Giles, echoing Evans and naming hype as its "purest form."

to create events of its own — shows, performances, competitions, and even news items specifically made by and for television. The video recorder pushed things further, allowing viewers to play events over and over again. As with Evans, Giles's stress is on the media as the engine that drives celebrity culture. The actual celebrities are almost incidental to the theory.

Giles believes that there is a long-standing and even desperate desire for fame among human populations. Changing forms of media have effectively made it possible for more and more people to gain the kind of mass exposure that brings fame. Myriad media around the globe rapidly and exponentially reproduce images of people. "The proliferation of media for publicizing the individual has been reflected in a proliferation of celebrated individuals," writes Giles. "As the mass media has expanded, so individuals have had to do less in order to be celebrated" (2000: 32).

The process copies itself like a replicating DNA. Technological developments in the media have enabled humans to reproduce images of themselves "on a phenomenal scale, thus providing an evolutionary rationale for the obsessive pursuit of fame" (2000: 53).

While both Evans and Giles acknowledge that other writers (and I need to include myself in this group) see something qualitatively distinctive and exceptional about contemporary celebrity culture, they highlight the continuity in the role of the media. Admittedly, Giles pinpoints the bewilderingly fast reproductive properties of today's media as crucial to the fleeting celebrities that flit across our screens today and disappear next week. But celebrity culture is continuance masquerading as uniqueness. The media were always pivotal: their forms have changed; their effects haven't.

IN THE SERVICE OF CAPITAL

The Roman poet Juvenal might have been reflecting on the way his countryman in the first century of the common era assigned celebrity status to gladiators when he coined the phrase *panem et circenses*. Translated as "bread and circuses" it describes the way in which ancient Roman leaders would provide food and entertainment to the underprivileged plebeians, allowing them access to the spectacular gladiatorial contests and chariot races at the Colosseum and other vast stadiums. Without the agreeable distractions and a full stomach, the masses might have grown discontented and started to wonder why they had little money, lived in inadequate accommodation, and, unlike their rulers, could never afford life's luxuries. Immersing themselves in the excitement of the contests and cheering on their champions diverted their attention away from more mundane matters.

Juvenal was alluding to power, specifically the uneven distribution of it and how this imbalance was maintained. The sections of the populations that had little power and no real chance of gaining the advantages that go with it had to be placated somehow. If not, they might have grown restless and begun to ask searching questions that could destabilize power arrangements. Keeping them satisfied maximized the chances that they wouldn't notice. The entertainment may have been good wholesome fun — well, as wholesome as pitching humans against lions can be — but it also served an ideological purpose. It fostered a style of popular thinking that was compatible with a particular type of political and economic system.

Critics of sports such as Paul Hoch (1972) and Jean-Marie Brohm (1978) wrote challenging polemics in the 1970s, identifying athletics events as key amusements that kept the working class preoccupied. Too preoccupied, it turned out, to oppose capitalist systems that were designed to exploit them. Drawing on Marx's opiate thesis, in which he likened religion to a drug that dulls the senses and provides a temporary sensation of well-being, critics saw sports as a kind of functional equivalent of religion, commanding the attention of millions of fans without delivering any tangible improvements to their lives. Sports and, by implication, other types of popular entertainment have ideological utility: they reinforce the status quo.

This invites the kind of images I mentioned in Chapter 1, with heads of mega-corporations gathered around a table to hatch plots designed to keep the working classes from noticing how the system works against them. Neither Hoch, Brohm, nor any of the other theorists who followed their leads pictured the scene so melodramatically. Sports and entertainment today may be overpraised and soak up too much of our time and money; but they haven't been designed to assist society's ruling power-holders. They are best viewed as convenience rather than connivance.

Celebrities do ideological work too. This is hardly profound: more a statement of the obvious. They massage our senses in a way not totally dissimilar to the gladiators. Like the citizens of ancient Rome, we are captivated, enthused, and thrilled by people we don't know and who probably don't care about us. Maybe we don't have the same deprivations from which we have to be distracted, but there are serious issues that impact on everybody: climate change, globalization, war, for instance. These and other issues already provoke widespread dissent and, often, outright protest. The prospects for even more forceful protests might be great were it not for the diverting power of celebrities. At least, that's what theorists of the bread and circuses school would argue. They'd find an ally in the comic Chris Rock who offered his own take on celebrity culture in 2004: "It's a trick to get your mind off the [Iraq] war. I think [George] Bush sent that girl to Kobe's room. Bush sent that little boy to Michael Jackson's house. Bush killed Laci Peterson [whose mysterious disappearance stirred up widespread curiosity] … all to get your mind off the war!" (quoted in *Maclean's*, June 21, 2004).

> Like the citizens of ancient Rome, we are captivated, enthused, and thrilled by people we don't know and who probably don't care about us.

Even those who are not persuaded by the basic version have converted its premise into a more sophisticated model, the engine of which is still ideology. The title of P. David Marshall's book *Celebrity and Power: Fame in contemporary culture* is a clue to his approach (1997). He sees the concept of individuality as vital to both contemporary capitalist democracy and consumerism. Celebrities are not just people; they are influential representatives. They represent "subject positions that audiences can adopt or adapt in the formation of social identities" (1997: 65). There is a "celebrity-function" which is to "organize the legitimate and illegitimate domains of the personal and the individual within the social" (ibid.: 57).

Matt Hills interprets this: "The celebrity or star appears to give rise to, and anchor their very own authenticity and individuality. But what appears as a natural property of the charismatic celebrity is actually produced by discourses of celebrity" (2005: 151). Giles pares this down to basics: "The capitalist system uses celebrities to promote individualism and illusions of democracy (the 'anyone can do it' myth) [...] capitalism retains its hold on society, by reducing all human activity to private 'personalities' and the inner life of the individual" (2000: 19 and 72).

Multiplying numbers of celebrity escapees of the *Big Brother* house and other reality television shows have appeared since the publication of Marshall's book, though he would surely use the "ordinary" celebrities as further proof of his thesis. And, despite the attempts of the previously mentioned Mariah Carey and the others who strive to keep the purdah that separates Them from Us intact, consumers have seen through the veil.

Graeme Turner has adopted Marshall's framework in his book *Understanding Celebrity*. In particular, he points to Marshall's potentially useful "spin": "His proposition [is] that the celebrity-commodity provides a very powerful form of legitimation for capitalism's models of exchange and value by demonstrating that the individual has a commercial as well as a cultural value" (2004: 25).

Celebrities then have social functions. Like the proto-celebrity gladiators, they serve political ends as well as providing pleasure for the masses. They participate, however unwittingly, in a process that entices — some might say inveigles — Us into thinking about ourselves and Them in a particular way: as freestanding individuals living in a merit-rewarding society; and one, we might add, in which the good life advertised by celebrities is open to anyone with enough money. This is, for Turner, the primary function:

"Celebrities are developed to make money" (2004: 34). In the kind of competitive market system fostered by capitalism, only ever-increasing consumption can keep the system running.

Vertical integration features in Turner's analysis. This describes the tendency of large corporations, especially media corporations, to incorporate a range of industrial processes in its portfolio. News Corp., for example, can produce the content of tv, film, and other media, market it through its agencies and distribute it to consumers through its multimedia networks. It can also promote its own films or programs through its print media and cross-promote other products. Straightforward product placement is commonplace in all media, though the movie *Tomorrow Never Dies* took it to a new level. 007 used an Ericsson JB988 phone, which was advertised using the movie as a frame, while the movie was promoted in a complementary process of brand integration — an arrangement we covered in Chapter 9.

While Turner doesn't mention this movie, nor its star Pierce Brosnan, whose own value was elevated by the cross-promotion, he seems to have something like them in mind when he writes: "The celebrity's usefulness to the cross-media expansion of the major media and entertainment industry conglomerates has translated into an enhanced value for the celebrity as a commodity" (2004: 34).

Turner would find evidence for this in the way celebrities are used to transfer brand "values." Mercedes-Benz, for example, linked up with TAGHeuer, a global brand in its own right endorsed by, among others, Brad Pitt and Tiger Woods. Figures like these may not represent Mercedes directly, but their associations with the watch company that produced the Mercedes watch were useful in establishing credibility. Turner would surely find this kind of cross-brand development complementary to the cross-media expansion he cites.

So, when we learn about the kind of situations presented at the start of this chapter and either sympathize with, abhor, or just laugh at the celebs' displeasure, we should remain mindful of how: "The expression of interest, in turn, provides them with the power to elicit an adulatory photo feature in *Hello!* or to demand approval of the writer assigned to prepare a profile on them for *Vanity Fair*" (2004: 36). (Within two months of her coke exposé, Kate Moss appeared on the cover and across eleven pages of this very publication.)

Celebrities perform important functions in a mature capitalist economy in which consumer demand is paramount. A competitive market needs ever-increasing consumption to keep the system moving. The "accelerator of consumer demand," to use the phrase we took from Zygmunt Bauman in Chapter 1, has to be kept hard down at all times. Turner himself uses a similar analogy when he writes of the constant, urgent need for new celebrities to whet the appetites of consumers: "The industrial cycle of use and disposal … does seem to have radically accelerated in response to the demand created by new media forms" (2004: 85).

Celebrities and the culture they epitomize are products themselves. They can be bought and sold, much like the merchandise they advertise. As such, they are parts of an industrial process that maintains our spending levels while keeping us pleasantly occupied. Turner doesn't dismiss other purposes the celebrities may have in, for instance, the fan's sense of self and individuality. He even quotes Rojek who believes that celebrities offer "peculiarly powerful affirmations of belonging, recognition, and meaning" (2001: 94).

Yet, with Marshall, Turner insists that any account of celebrities must be predicated on the recognition that "the interests served are first of all those of capital." Capitalism's growing dependence on what some call hyperconsumerism has led to an ethic of hedonism and health, excess and extravagance. Prudence, self-denial, deferred gratification, and all manner of frugality have been rendered old-fashioned by a culture that continually tries to develop discontents that can be salved only by buying commodities. Celebrities have to be understood in this context: they operate with the advertising industry — almost *as* an advertising industry — to persuade, cajole, and convince consumers that dependence is nothing to be ashamed of. If we depend on commodities, so what? As long as we have money enough to assuage the urge to consume, there is no problem.

None of the contemporary theorists on celebrity culture subscribes to the crude bread and circuses explanation. If that were so, celebrities would be no more that eye-catching diversions that prevent us noticing more pressing issues.

Yet, there is a sense in which both Marshall and Turner understand the utility of celebrities to the capitalist enterprise and believe that this is their *raison d'être* — the purpose that accounts for their very existence.

So, we return to a question asked by all the writers covered in this chapter: what are celebrities for? Are they new replacement gods, media-born creations, or commodity representatives of a capitalist system that thrives on consumption? This is not an either/or question, of course. The media, as we've seen in previous chapters, have become increasingly obsessed with the young and prosperous, with glamour, money, and the kind of power that they confer. We, the consumers, have become fascinated, often to the point of prurience, with their well-chronicled lives. Celebrities have become godlike objects to us and we seem to delight in their sense of self-importance, their scandalous behavior, and their eagerness to deplore the media's intrusions, while inciting their interest with any device available.

The sometimes fanatical devotion we show has tempted several writers into seeing celebrity culture as a secular religion; impulse seems to dictate the behavior of some consumers more certainly than calculation. As we've seen, there is empirical support for this perspective: as there is for the other perspectives that attribute the rise of celebrities to the media and to capitalist consumerism. Neither secularization, the media, nor capitalism can be absolved; but nor can they be burdened with the whole shebang.

Celebrity culture is guided by the logic of consumerism and the celebrities are guided by this basic message: enjoy novelty, change, excitement, and every possible stimulant that can be bought over a shop counter or an internet website. The message falls on receptive ears. Consumers thrill to the sight and sound of celebrities, not because they're dupes, suckers, airheads, or simpletons, but because they have become willing accomplices in the enterprise. They too are guided by the logic of consumerism.

Appetites that were once damned as the cause of unhappiness and instability are extolled. An expansion of demand for commodities and a continuous redefining cycle of what's luxury and what's necessity has led to the

> What are celebrities for? Are they new replacement gods, media-born creations, or commodity representatives of a capitalist system that thrives on consumption?

elevation of new groups into the sphere of consumption we know as celebrity culture.

SUPREMELY CULTIVATED

As the first wave of theories of celebrity culture arrived, much of the critical impulse concerned its democratizing effect. The pronouncement of death for the old-style stars and egalitarian promises of fame for all seemed to herald a new continuous communion in which celebrity status was available to everyone, regardless of talent, if only for short periods. Reality television, as we saw in Chapter 10 seemed to confirm the promise.

Accompanying this and integral to it was what we could call a democratization of taste. Consumer items that may once have been associated with the rich and famous became widely available. Everyone could participate in a version of the good life. The once-unbreachable wall between Them and Us was replaced by gossamer-thin gauze that was thin enough to be seen through and occasionally torn. Consumers defined themselves by the commodities they bought. As we noted before, Derek Layder alludes to this in his *Understanding Social Theory* when he observes: "The pervasive effects of consumerism link identity and social status to the market for commodities" (2006: 53). "The compulsive buying of new fashions and new products" is one manifestation of this.

In 1991, Christopher Lasch wrote of the kind of society he dreaded, one in which abundance would appear to be available to everyone, while in reality being restricted to the wealthy: "The progressive conception of history implied a society of supremely cultivated consumers" (1991: 531). We now have them. In this sense, celebrity culture has been successful: the seamless unity occasioned by the end of the traditional Them and Us has brought delirious pleasure to billions the world over. Consumers devour magazines, movies, downloads, and practically everything else bearing the image, signature, or just aura of celebrities. And celebrity culture has been even more successful than Lasch could have imagined. It thrives in painlessly easing money away from people who, in a genuine sense, feel themselves part of the communion, which is less about spiritual unity, more about market harmony.

Celebrity culture does not, of course, come with a free pullout panacea for all the problems that afflict us in the early twenty-first century. For all the well-intentioned efforts of the campaigning celebrities we discussed in Chapter 11, we have to conclude that they have prompted big questions, though without answering them. But there may still be opportunities: after all, there has probably never been a comparable time in history when so many people have held the ability to influence, inspire, and perhaps incite others to action. We've seen glimpses of this when celebrities confront particular issues, such as global warming, globalization, or debt relief. But, so far, no wide-ranging vision shapes the way in which people view the world.

This is probably asking too much: what celebrity is prepared to risk rearranging the thoughts of his or her fans in a way that will undermine their devotion? "Stop buying my cds, don't rent dvds, or go to the movies. And don't buy clothes or the jewelry just 'cause you see celebs wearing something similar. But, above all, become interested in people who say things that enlighten or do things that matter!" This would be like trying to stop a car with no brakes while driving it.

Celebrity culture has offered us a distinctive vision, a beguiling one too: one in which there are few limits, an expanding range of opportunities, and inexhaustible hope. Celebrities themselves are, as I've stressed throughout, the living proof of this. Ideas like restraint, prudence, and modesty have either been discredited or just forgotten. Celebrity culture has replaced them with impetuosity, frivolity, prodigality. Human impulses like these were once seen as vices; now they are almost virtuous.

Universal consumption, the promise of luxury for all, and an endless cycle of insatiable desire have been introduced not through political discourse but through the creation of a new cultural group. Celebrities have energized our material expectations, helping shape a culture in which demand is now a basic human experience. What were once luxuries are now regarded as necessities. What was once improvement is now replaced by upgrading. For all the fantasy and escapist tendencies it radiates, celebrity culture's most basic imperative is material: it encourages consumption at every level of society.

Celebrity culture's paradoxical feat is not in advancing a worldview in which social discontents have their causes in the scarcity of material commodities, so much as promoting an idea that we shouldn't think about this long enough to distract ourselves from what we do best — consume even more of those very commodities.

CHAPTER 10
Social and Mobile

This is our world now, the world of the electron and the switch, the beauty of the baud. We exist without nationality, skin color or religious bias.

— Special Agent Bob
Hackers (1995)

Chapter 10. Social and Mobile

Recommended Film

Hackers (Iain Softley 1995)

Media Models

The Meme, The Network

Chapter Summary

Jarice Hanson critiques some of the possible social and
personal effects of mobile phones, the internet,
and the 24/7 media environments.

Howard Rheingold theorizes the concept of the "smart mob"
and the potential "swarm intelligence" of mobile phones
and ad hoc social networks.

"24/7: Anytime Anywhere" and "Living in the Global Village"

from 24/7

— Jarice Hanson

THE CHALLENGE OF ALWAYS BEING "ON"

At first it may sound like a stretch to claim that technology has the potential to shape the way we think about other things in life. After all, many of us have been led to believe that technology has no real power in itself and that it's how people use technology that matters. Neil Postman wrote a book titled *Technopoly: The Surrender of Culture to Technology*,[1] in which he explains how using technology leads us to think of everything in technological terms. According to Postman, human beings have a need to fit the pieces of their lives into something that gives the impression of coherence, and the technologies themselves structure our interests. That's why we often seek technological solutions to technological questions and why we often reach for more technology to solve the problems caused by present technologies. We may not be consciously aware of the many ways in which technology structures our thoughts, but at the unconscious level, the same characteristics that are inherent in the technology begin to creep into our daily practices. This affects both our behavior and attitudes, but also our assumptions and expectations. Throughout the twentieth century, American society embraced the belief that technology equaled progress and that if we could get technology into the hands of more people, we could all participate in the great American Dream of consuming products and enjoying better, more comfortable lives.

Now we're waking up from that dream. There are more technologies available to a wider range of people these days, and they've become easier to use, but the quality of life issues are still a problem. Many people are finding that although the Internet works wonders for communicating with others by controlling workflow or facilitating a job, there never seems to be enough hours in the day to get things done. Cell phones are useful tools to let someone know you're running late for a meeting, but they often are used to cover poor planning or inconsiderate actions. These wonderful inventions have done so much to liberate us from traditional ways of working or communicating with friends or family, but we often are unaware of the "speed-up" in our lives. We tend to be working more, playing less, and finding that by being always connected by phone or computer to responsibilities and obligations, our stress levels increase, rather than decrease. The technologies make it easier to react in moments, but at the same time, we can speed through tasks and ignore thinking about their consequences or their quality. It's hard to relax when the constant barrage of messages demands our attention. Like Pavlov's dog, we become conditioned to respond immediately to electronic messages. Our nerves and senses become keenly attuned, we viscerally need to respond, and we therefore contribute to the constant hum of information and message flow and exchange. People who jump to grab their cell phones when one rings in a public place, even if it isn't their own phone, know about this type of conditioning. Most people answer e-mail sequentially, and if they think they'll go back to a previous

---

1 Neil Postman, *Technopoly: The Surrender of Culture to Technology* (New York: Knopf, 1992).

message, the message is easily forgotten. These people understand the way the technology is controlling them, too—especially when someone screams, "Didn't you get my e-mail?"

Cell phones, like many technologies we use in public, also confer a level of status for their users. The executive who uses a BlackBerry to answer e-mail during a business meeting, the person in the grocery store wearing a prominently displayed wireless earpiece while shopping, and the college student who balks at paying fifty dollars for a textbook but thinks nothing of spending two hundred dollars for the latest cell phone often justify their purchase of the technology by publicly displaying it and wordlessly boasting about their importance and technological sophistication.

On the surface, changes to the Internet may seem less obvious, but in reality they are even more profound. The ubiquity of accessing the Internet through a host of technologies and the growing functionality of cell phones to access the Internet is throwing the traditional media companies into a tizzy to find suitable content for delivery to the small video screen. Advertisers are fearful that they may lose their traditional revenue streams if they continue to promote products the old fashioned way. Subscription services that don't include ads or content that had been designed to catch someone's attention change the way people may be motivated to think about a purchase of a product. The biggest change, though, is how pop-up ads, animation, and design factors punctuate content on the computer screen, competing for attention and immediate action from the consumer, all of which can be seen more legibly on a large computer screen, but which suffers when reduced to a two-inch cell phone screen.

Whether people use cell phones and the Internet at work, in public, or for personal reasons also contributes to how "connected" they feel to other people and to their daily obligations. The portable features of cell phones and the ease of accessing the Internet in public places or over the cell phone influences peoples' attitudes and behaviors about where they can go and still remain productive. When people can be contacted wherever they are, the distinctions between personal time and obligations to work, family,

or friends can seem endless. We might feel that we have greater control over our time, but the urge to be constantly in touch with others can be so stressful that consciously or unconsciously, we begin to think in Luddite terms.[2] After all, people might find it more comfortable to work from home and more convenient to buy things over the Internet, and it may be more reassuring to know that we can reach a loved one at any time of day or night, but at the same time we become primed for responding to the cell phone's ring or the computer's audio cue that something just arrived, and we may feel that whatever the message, it needs immediate attention.

Many people justify the use of these technologies by claiming that the conveniences outweigh the annoyance of listening to someone else's phone ring, or overhearing a private conversation in a public place, or feeling oppressed by e-mails that need answering. Using cell phones and the Internet in different places creates competition for attention and focus. The portability and small size of a cell phone allows people to shift attention to the technology rather than paying attention in some environments that are structured to allow a person to focus on an activity. Evidence shows that when we use a cell phone in a car, our attention is not necessarily on our driving, and accidents can occur. Personal conversations are often interrupted while someone answers a cell phone call, to the annoyance of the other person in the conversation, who feels less important in the personal interaction. Technologically savvy teens are adept at text messaging, game playing, and downloading free content, but they often do this while in class or some other inappropriate place, much to the consternation of their teachers. The intersection of the positive and negative aspects of technology results in a change in values — how we think about what we do, and how we reach a feeling of satisfaction or contentment with our present lives, or not.

> When people can be contacted wherever they are, the distinctions between personal time and obligations to work, family, or friends can seem endless.

2 The Luddites were a social movement in Great Britain during the nineteenth century. Possibly named for Ned Ludd, who destroyed machinery, the Luddites smashed machines because they feared the changes that would result in social life if the industrial revolution were allowed to spread. Today, a Luddite is someone who fears or disdains technology.

TECHNOLOGICAL REVOLUTIONS AND SOCIAL CHANGE

Would we use cell phones and the Internet so readily if they didn't fit a contemporary lifestyle that attempts to pack more organizational productivity into every day? Do cell phones and the Internet really contribute to a feeling that we can control more aspects of our social environments? Few would disagree that the pace of American life has accelerated throughout the twentieth century, but how convincing is the argument that technology has contributed to this feeling of faster-paced lifestyles? It would be difficult to mount an argument that the faster pace of life is the result of cell phones and the Internet, but these technologies are undoubtedly components of the type of social change that Americans have experienced in recent years, particularly as instant communication has become more of a factor in social life. The rise of the wired communication system in the late 1800s (the long revolution) and the mobility afforded by cell phones and the Internet (the short revolution) are tied to what is specifically a question of lifestyle in the United States.

In 1991, Juliet B. Schor published an influential book titled *The Overworked American: The Unexpected Decline of Leisure*,[3] in which she demonstrated that Americans then were working more and having less leisure time than they had before World War II. While her book provided a rich understanding of how the American standard of living reached a level of material comfort that far surpassed that of every other country, she explained how the desire to acquire goods and live in a consumer society in effect drove personal attitudes and values toward working more and having less free time.

Today, we live in a society in which children's playtimes are often scheduled as "playdates." We can use online services to buy almost anything, from gifts to groceries, from home or work. We can meet others, conduct romances, and live in a different life in a fantasy world via the Internet. We can shield ourselves from unwanted phone calls by blocking calls, using caller-ID, or letting voicemail answer for us. All of these examples give witness to Schor's predictions about the decline of leisure, but they also reflect a lifestyle that increasingly embraces the use of technology to give us greater control over our busy lives. Whether the pace of American life has accelerated

as part of our more demanding consumer lifestyles or not, human beings naturally want to control their lives. As we work more, seek to gain status and consumer goods, and try to maintain the equilibrium necessary for survival in a busy world, why shouldn't we use the technologies that promise us greater control? The examples in this book provide a window on understanding the relationships among historical and contemporary forms of communication, social issues, and culture, and how they affect our lives.

CONTROLLING TIME AND SPACE

Though we don't often consciously dwell on how each new technology influences our sense of time and space, these issues have always formed a basis for understanding cultural change. Scholars have demonstrated how powerful these factors are in shaping social attitudes and values. Edison's invention of the electric light bulb was credited for changing how Americans approached activities that had formerly been structured because of available daylight. The electric light metaphorically turned night into day and brought about a culture that no longer was reliant on sunlight to provide a "productive" workday.

Lewis Mumford wrote about the impact of the clock on the fifteenth-century life of Benedictine monks, who began to regulate their prayers and dally activities in response to the bells in the clock tower.[4] Before long, other people within range of the bells also began to regulate their workday to the cues provided by the bells, and social life started to revolve around the clock and the characteristics of mechanical clock time.

The old-fashioned clock imposed arbitrary units to systematize time into sixty seconds that made up a minute, and sixty minutes in an hour. Controlling time began to influence the workday in stores, fields, and in other social organizations. As clocks became more commonplace, they regulated activities in communities and imposed a structure of thinking about time and life. During the industrial revolution, factory owners adopted the clock as the regulator of all human activity on the assembly line, and the concept that "time was money" dictated social relations in the factory. The psychologist Bernard Doray writes of the rules in the factory in 1863:

---

3   Juliet B. Schor, *The Overworked American: The Unexpected Decline of Leisure* (New York: Basic Books, 1991), 1–2.

4   Lewis Mumford, *Technics and Human Development: The Myth of the Machine* (New York: Harcourt Brace Jovanovich, 1966).

Regulations specifying starting times, and the corresponding sanctions for late arrival, are an expression of the employers' attempts to impose a rigid working day; workers who were five minutes late were often fined, and in no case could they be more than fifteen minutes late without being fined. Repeated late arrival led to heavier fines and eventually to dismissal.[5]

During the industrial revolution, the factory assembly line became synonymous with scientific management and social control. These revolutions, in using time as an agent of social change were much more gradual than today's rapid adoption of the cell phone, but the social phenomenon was similar. Doray describes how this social control alienated the workers. The point is then, that when technologies influence time, humans have to adapt, either because the institutions in which they live become affected

time[6]—that is, time that has no context to which we can relate. Not only does the appearance of the clock face influence how we "see" and experience time, but today time can be actualized by other technologies without our having to think about it at all. Now we have watches, clocks, and appliances that beep, tap us, flash, and even turn themselves on or off. Cell phones, computers, coffeemakers, thermostats, video recorders, automobiles, and garage doors, among other items, can be digitally programmed to run themselves or to monitor their own actions. When this happens, we cede a conscious awareness of the elements of time to the technology or in other words, the technologies can appear to control us.

The anthropologist Edward T. Hall writes about the cultural implications of synchronous time and observes that synchronicity contributes to a feeling that we can only do one thing at a time.[7] By contrast, asynchronous time provided by a digital watch is nonlinear, essentially void of

---

Analog time, with hands sweeping around a clock face, presented us with a sense of *synchronous* time, a visual representation of past, present, and future. The digital display presents *asynchronous* time, showing only the present moment, and therefore is decontextualized time—that is, time that has no context to which we can relate.

---

by time management or because the time characteristics of the technology with which they work get changed. And the individual is not immune to reacting psychologically to this type of control.

We are still slaves to clocks today but our concept of time has changed because of the clocks we use. If you were to ask someone with a traditional analog watch what time it is, he or she might respond, "Oh, it's about quarter to one." Someone with a digital watch might answer, "It's 12:43 and 10 seconds." We have moved from the relatively "sloppy" sense of analog time to the precision of digital time. Analog time, with hands sweeping around a clock face, presented us with a sense of *synchronous* time, a visual representation of past, present, and future. The digital display presents *asynchronous* time, showing only the present moment, and therefore is decontextualized

a sense of continuity. Digital time encourages us to think in fragments, with little connection to a sense of process. Is it any wonder, then, that younger people who have grown up knowing only digital technologies develop a sense of time that is less connected to a sense of history and look for quick answers rather than synthesizing different pools of information or engaging in complicated deliberation?

We can also see how the economy of time influences our behaviors. Mumford's writing on the impact of the clock shows how time becomes a commodity in the sense that it provides us with the means to structure our work and personal lives. But time is also a unit of measurement for using cell phones and the Internet. Use is measured in units computed by the second and millisecond — all easily measurable by digital technologies, and yet we often seem

---

5   Bernard Doray, *From Taylorism to Fordism: A Rational Madness*, trans. David Macey (London: Free Association Books, 1988).

6   Lance Strate, "Cybertime," in *Communication and Cyberspace: Social Interaction in an Electronic Environment*, ed. Lance Strate, Ron L. Jacobson, and Stephanie Gibson, 2nd ed. (Cresskill, NJ: Hampton Press, 2003), 364.

7   Edward T Hall, *The Dance of Life: The Other Dimension of Time* (Garden City, NY: Anchor, 1984).

unaware that our charges are associated with our technology use. The companies that provide us with these services know that by selling us large "packages" of use time, they distract us from thinking about its cost — the way we might have in the "old" days, when a long-distance call racked up charges. Only when something goes terribly wrong, like the teenager with her first cell phone who goes well beyond the minutes of her packaged plan to rack up exorbitant charges, does the connection between technology use and money become obvious, and the "time equals money" equation becomes painfully clear.

Jeremy Rifkin begins chapter 1 of his book *Time Wars: The Primary Conflict in Human History* with these words: "It is ironic that in a culture so committed to saving time we feel increasingly deprived of the very thing we value."[8] We've come to regard speed, as represented by today's electronic technologies, as a desirable quality. The legacy of American efficiency and centralization — the idea that "bigger is better" — has given way to the belief that "faster is better."[9] And yet, technologies that work at a speed faster than our minds can comprehend distance our bodies and minds from the process of interaction. This can condition us to be impatient, rushed, and intolerant of any time we can't control.

If some technologies, such as the cell phone and Internet, give us the illusion of controlling time, they also offer the freedom of space — to move far beyond the confines of a wired phone, the traditional office, or the stacks in a library — and still have access to information and communication. Because they are wireless and instantaneous, they render irrelevant the question of where anyone or anything we are accessing may be physically located at that moment. But the term "space" has connotations beyond the obvious. Space can be both literal and figurative, and thinking about space helps us understand the impact of cell phones and the Internet. After all, if the Internet is the "information superhighway," the metaphor is transportation, and transportation suggests both time and space in the process of moving from point A to point B.

Space has yet another figurative connotation. Cyberspace is that ephemeral concept of space, that place, where we interact with computers over the Internet. Where is the information we seek? Where are those people who write to us, or to whom we write? Knowledge of physical location becomes unimportant to anyone who uses computers and the Internet. Yet there is still a sense of space on our computer monitors, one that sometimes competes with our daily relationship to the three-dimensional world.

Joshua Meyerowitz[10] has studied electronic technology and how it divorces us from traditional notions of space. He posits that electronic technology provides a sense of "placelessness" that is very much a part of a digital world because there is no concrete, physical sense of space. We don't observe or intuit where messages come from or where they go when we push the "send" button. To elaborate on his idea, we can think of how online "communities" are formed that are not physically located in a geographic vicinity, such as traditional communities in which we might know many people by name or face. In cyberspace, there is little knowledge of what the person you're e-mailing looks like, or, if you're in a chat room, how many lurkers (people who read messages but don't post any) might be watching, but not participating.

The time/space issue is at the heart of using cell phones and the Internet. While each is available twenty-four hours a day, seven days a week, the time features give the illusion of allowing us to control our lives, but the space issues reinforce all that is good about using cell phones and the Internet. We can easily see the benefits of working from home (unless the distractions of home are too great to get anything done), but we might not easily realize that our need to feel a part of a community, socially or professionally, is satisfied more by face-to-face communication with others rather than by sitting alone at a computer, no matter where we are. At the same time, though, computers connected to the Internet and cell phones give people freedom to live in areas that might be more physically and economically suitable. Furthermore, the time and space manipulations lead us to think in different ways about what might have formerly been clear delineations between private and public behavior.

* * *

---

8   Jeremy Rifkin, *Time Wars: The Primary Conflict in Human History* (New York: Simon & Schuster, 1987), 19.

9   Ibid., 19

10   Joshua Meyerowitz, *No Sense of Place* (New York: Oxford University Press, 1985).

As discussed, some technologies have a greater impact on issues of time and space than others. The analog clock imposed a way of thinking about time that was measured in units of sixty seconds, sixty minutes, and twenty-four hours as a means of measuring one day and night. When the electric light bulb was invented, illumination in the home and in public places changed the concept of day and night. Both the clock and electric light contributed to the growth of the industrial revolution that measured workers' time and productivity and changed the economic relationship between production and consumption of goods.

Electronic technologies such as the cell phone and the Internet do much the same thing. They change a person's sense of time, because they are available twenty-four hours a day, seven days a week. They give their users an illusion of control over their own activities, while reinforcing the idea that to be good cell phone or Internet users, we must respond quickly, or risk appearing disinterested in our work or in others.

The demand to always be "on"—whether online or on call—has introduced a level of technologically induced stress in our lives that has made many people feel compelled to respond quickly, even though they may respond incompletely or very briefly, using a shorthand style of communication. For many, responding, rather than communicating, has taken a toll on the quality of their interactions with others and on their sense of satisfaction about living or working in a social environment. No matter how often we use cell phones and the Internet, the basic need for human interaction is still a part of our culture, though many people seem to reject this need or divert it to the relationships they find in cyberspace.

The placeless nature of communicating on the Internet through cyberspace or by using cell phones that allow greater mobility and control over where someone uses them results in a disassociation from geographic place. The ability to use these technologies in nontraditional places, or to connect to others over spaces that can't even be comprehended because the sense of space is irrelevant, is a powerful influence over how people think of themselves in relationship to others. The feeling a person has, along with the illusion of control, can be both liberating for those who have any type of social anxiety or for those who live in conditions that don't support their needs for some types of interactions or communities, but at the same time, the instability of the relationships in cyberspace can be fleeting or transitory. Depending on the person's needs and desires, the fragmented, disassociated relationships may be somewhat fulfilling, or they may contribute to further alienation and loneliness.

The ability to deal with the characteristics of the technologies people use depends on how these people are socialized and what other technologies they use — including the types of technologies available to them and their comfort in learning to use them. When they feel that they have mastered a technology, they feel even greater control over their environments. These illusions of control contribute to the personal relationships that people begin to feel with their technologies, and lead to further reliance on them, despite any potential drawbacks, such as system failure or forgetting to charge batteries. While cell phones are, for the most part, thought about as highly personal technologies, using the Internet by cell phone or over laptop computers or PDAs changes an individual's relationship to traditional places that had already reflected a socially constructed set of appropriate behaviors.

BLURRING PUBLIC AND PRIVATE ACTIVITIES

The sense of mobility that small, portable devices give has now resulted in a period of time in which new behaviors are being tested and negotiated. When we use these technologies for personal reasons in public places, the contrast of what had been appropriate behavior in a personal place becomes a matter of public display. A spotlight is focused on entire social relationships and expectations for appropriate behavior.

At the same time, greater reliance on technologies that are consumed personally, rather than communally, becomes a challenge for institutions that had previously based their delivery models on serving the masses, rather than the individual members of a heterogeneous audience. Former media industries that have provided the "glue" that reflects and reinforces social culture have begun to explore delivering content to consumers to guarantee their dominance in a technologized world where potentially every user can become a content provider. Public activities, from making a phone call to shopping, have been reconstructed to target individual use rather than to serve a broader "public." Targeted advertising to individuals has reinforced the ideas that individuals matter more than social groups, and traditional social practices have attempted to find new ways of maintaining relationships and encouraging participation even though technologies make it easier for individuals to be disconnected from other people in real places in real time.

All of these changes are affecting generational cohorts differently, largely because habits play such an important role in helping people negotiate new technologies and practices. Peer groups are important social networks, and social learning over time conditions people to consider how willing they are to change traditional patterns of behavior. Lifestyles that change over a lifetime are important factors for how people maintain social relationships and how they manage the tasks that they must, to get through the day. New technologies have always favored the young, because they have not yet established a pattern of behavior that is so deeply entrenched that they don't have to "unlearn" behavioral patterns. For young users, mastery over new technologies is a matter of superiority over elders, and expertise is empowering. The characteristics of digital technologies accelerate traditional concepts of time; these technologies operate faster than the human mind, and they substitute information that is separated from its source for instant, fragmented, and incomplete data that meet the needs of a fast-paced culture for speed, rather than completeness or context. For all of these reasons, cell phones and the Internet remain powerful technologies to simultaneously give people an illusion of control over their lives and to make them feel that they are responding to a social imperative to use more technology in a more technologized world.

When comparing the use of cell phones and the Internet in the United States with the cultural changes that other countries are experiencing, the cultural change in the United States may appear to be happening at a snail's pace. Many other cultures are experiencing more dramatic changes than the United States, because wireless coverage can be more effective in small regions or small countries, and low-cost cell phones can revolutionize communication patterns in places that were not encumbered by established wired telephone infrastructures.

The International Telecommunications Union (ITU) conducted a study in 1984 titled *The Missing Link,* in which it determined that at the time, there were approximately 600 million (wired) telephones in the world, but that two-thirds of the world's population had no access to a telephone at all.[11] While the growth of cell phones worldwide has not been steady or exponential, some regions have experienced very rapid diffusion of telephony in general and cell phones in particular, and in most cases, these countries are currently using 3G cell phones rather than the 2G phones that are most common in America. Access to the Internet is also changing throughout the world, largely because of the wireless systems that reduce the cost for expensive wired systems. In many regions the combination of cell phones, wireless communications, and links to Internet services has dramatically changed regional and national cultures.

In Japan, 3G phones enable full motion video, and commuters can watch entire films or television programs on their cell phones. In South Korea, where in the 1980s only one wired phone was in existence for every 600 people, 90 percent of the population now has wired phones, and three-quarters of them have 3G cell phones.[12]

In Saudi Arabia, where young males and females are kept apart, cell phones have allowed young people to have relationships with members of the opposite sex, date by phone, and even have phone sex, thus potentially changing gender relationships and religious law that is centuries old. Phones with camera features are illegal because they may be used to photograph women,[13] a violation of religious practice.

Cell phones have also been adapted in some parts of the world to reinforce cultural practices. In many Muslim countries, cell phone users have the option of using electronic reminders of when to pray and a directional service to orient them toward Mecca. In Taiwan, cell phones blessed at the Temple of Matsu are held in high regard.[14] Even some of the world's poorest people have embraced using cell phones for economic empowerment. The United Nations set a goal of having 50 percent of the poorest

---

11   "The Device That Ate Everything," *Economist*, March 12–18, 2005, 22.

12   "Behind the Digital Divide," *Economist*, March 12–18, 2005, 25.

13   "Islamic Dilemma," *National Geographic*, April 2005, 13.

14   "Technology Quarterly," *Economist*, March 12–18, 2005, 12–15.

nations connected to a form of telephony by 2015, but already, 77 percent of the world's population lives within range of a wireless network, and people in many poorer countries have organized to share cell phones.[15]

A bevy of articles in recent issues of the *Economist* predict a great future for cell phones, opining that perhaps cell phones will be the engine of creating greater economic

---

In industrialized nations, most uses of cell phones and the Internet extend social networks and serve individuals rather than the masses. In third world nations, groups tend to work together with the cell phone or the Internet as a tool for empowerment.

---

growth in the developing world: "When it comes to mobile phones, there is no need for intervention or funding from the UN: even the world's poorest people are already rushing to embrace mobile phones because their economic benefits are so apparent. Mobile phones do not rely on a permanent electricity supply and can be used by people who cannot read or write."[16]

In many third world nations that had no telephone service at all, cell phones have contributed to radically different communication practices. Many people in poor countries spend a larger proportion of their income on telecommunications than those in rich ones, because they realize what economic benefits can result from wireless communication forms. Farmers and fishermen can pool resources to use a cell phone to check official prices for their goods. In Bangladesh, the telephone ladies — those women who buy or rent a cell phone and charge others to make or receive calls — received attention when Muhammad Yunus won the 2006 Nobel Peace Prize for his system of offering "micro-loans" to poor people to empower them to engage in activities that could perhaps help lift them from poverty.

THE GLOBAL VILLAGE

The definition of a "global village" depends on the approach taken to describing what social arrangements constitute the conditions surrounding communication among individuals and groups of people. Samuel F. B. Morse, credited as

the inventor of the telegraph, used the term when he envisioned a world with telegraph wires that would allow electronic communication over distances using his electronic "language" of dots and dashes called Morse code. Guglielmo Marconi, credited as the inventor of wireless radio, thought that wireless communication would allow everyone in the world to be a broadcaster as well as a receiver of radio signals. Marshall McLuhan, considered a prophet of the electronic age, thought more philosophically of how the combination of electronic media would link every region of the world through real-time satellite distribution of images and sounds that would return us to an electronically distributed form of oral communication. All of these visionaries used the term "global village" to describe their view of the world's future, with their own preferred technology as the hub around which all social life could thrive. Each of them had a good idea, but each was limited in the way he saw the world. What they did have in common, though, was the idea that each of their technologies could radically change time and space for their users. What they didn't realize was how their technologies would be developed and how they would ultimately radically redefine families, social groups, communities, religion, and every other social institution.

Morse, Marconi, and McLuhan, the alliterative trio of prognosticators who each thought they knew what the global village would be, were thinking technologically, if not socially. What seemed to be missing in each of their scenarios of the future was a sense of who could afford to use their chosen technologies, how expensive it would be to maintain an infrastructure of support, and finally, how their technologies would change over time. The new global village that is emerging uses technologies, but situates its similarities and its differences in the social realm.

In industrialized nations, most uses of cell phones and the Internet extend social networks and serve individuals rather than the masses. In third world nations, groups tend to work together with the cell phone or the Internet as a tool for empowerment. In the new global village, there is greater access to technology, even if it has to be shared or

15   "Calling Across the Divide," *Economist*, March 12–18, 2005, 74.
16   "Technology Quarterly," 15.

creatively distributed. What happens socially determines whether someone can have the opportunity to participate in village life, though much of that life is in cyberspace. The real future, then, of increasing reliance on cell phones and the Internet may well result in a global village that is not so much separated by social difference as it is united by the tools used for the members of the new global village.

Smart Mobs: The Power of the Mobile Many

from Smart Mobs

— Howard Rheingold

NETWAR—DARK AND LIGHT

On January 20, 2001, President Joseph Estrada of the Philippines became the first head of state in history to lose power to a smart mob. More than 1 million Manila residents, mobilized and coordinated by waves of text messages, assembled at the site of the 1986 "People Power" peaceful demonstrations that had toppled the Marcos regime.[1] Tens of thousands of Filipinos converged on Epifanio de los Santas Avenue, known as "Edsa," within an hour of the first text message volleys: "Go 2EDSA, Wear blck."[2] Over four days, more than a million citizens showed up, mostly dressed in black. Estrada fell. The legend of "Generation Txt" was born.

Bringing down a government without firing a shot was a momentous early eruption of smart mob behavior. It wasn't, however, the only one.

> On November 30, 1999, autonomous but internetworked squads of demonstrators protesting the meeting of the World Trade Organization used "swarming" tactics, mobile phones, Web sites, laptops, and handheld computers to win the "Battle of Seattle."[3]

> In September 2000, thousands of citizens in Britain, outraged by a sudden rise in gasoline prices, used mobile phones, SMS, email from laptop PCs, and CB radios in taxicabs to coordinate dispersed groups that blocked fuel delivery at selected service stations in a wildcat political protest.[4]

> A violent political demonstration in Toronto in the spring of 2000 was chronicled by a group of roving journalist-researchers who webcast digital video of everything they saw.[5]

> Since 1992, thousands of bicycle activists have assembled monthly for "Critical Mass" moving demonstrations, weaving through San Francisco streets en masse. Critical Mass operates through loosely linked networks, alerted by mobile phone and email trees, and breaks up into smaller, tele-coordinated groups when appropriate.[6]

Filipinos were veteran texters long before they toppled Estrada. Short Message Service (SMS) messaging was

---

1   Michael Bociurkiw, "Revolution by Cell Phone," *Forbes,* 10 September 2001, <http://www.forbes.com/asap/2001/0910/028.html> (1 March 2002).

2   Ibid.

3   Paul de Armond, "Black Flag Over Seattle," *Albion Monitor* 72, March 2000, <http://www.monitor.net/monitor/seattlewto/index.html> (1 March 2002).

4   Alexander MacLeod, "Call to Picket Finds New Ring in Britain's Fuel Crisis," *Christian Science Monitor,* 19 September 2000. See also: Chris Marsden, "Britain's Labour Government and Trade Union Leaders Unite to Crush Fuel Tax Protest," *World Socialist Web Site,* 15 September 2000, <http://www.wsws.org/articles/2000/sep2000/fuel-s15.shtml> (1 March 2002).

5   Steve Mann and Hal Niedzviecki, *Cyborg: Digital Destiny and Human Possibility in the Age of the Wearable Computer* (Mississauga: Doubleday Canada, 2001), 177–178.

6   Critical Mass, <http://www.critical-mass.org/> (6 March 2002).

introduced in 1995 as a promotional gimmick.[7] SMS messaging, free at first, remained inexpensive. Wireline telephone service is more costly than mobile service, and in a country where 40 percent of the population lives on one dollar a day, the fact that text messages are one-tenth the price of a voice call is significant.[8] A personal computer costs twenty times as much as a mobile telephone; only 1 percent of the Philippines' population own PCs, although many more use them in Internet cafés.[9] By 2001, however, 5 million Filipinos owned cell phones out of a total population of 70 million.[10]

Filipinos took to SMS messaging with a uniquely intense fervor. By 2001, more than 70 million text messages were being transmitted among Filipinos every day.[11] The word "mania" was used in the Manila press. The *New York Times* reported in 2001:

> Malls are infested with shoppers who appear to be navigating by cellular compass. Groups of diners sit ignoring one another, staring down at their phones as if fumbling with rosaries. Commuters, jaywalkers, even mourners — everyone in the Philippines seems to be texting over the phone. … Faye Slytangco, a 23-year-old airline sales representative, was not surprised when at the wake for a friend's father she saw people bowing their heads and gazing toward folded hands. But when their hands started beeping and their thumbs began to move, she realized to her astonishment that they were not in fact praying. "People were actually sitting there and texting," Slytangco said. "Filipinos don't see it as rude any more."[12]

Like the thumb tribes of Tokyo and youth cultures in Scandinavia, Filipino texters took advantage of one of the unique features of texting technology — the ease of forwarding jokes, rumors, and chain letters. Although it requires effort to compose messages on mobile telephone keypads, only a few thumb strokes are required to forward a message to four friends or everybody in your telephone's address book. Filipino texting culture led to a national panic when a false rumor claimed that Pope John Paul II had died.[13]

Many Filipino text message jokes and rumors were political. Vicente Rafael, professor at the University of California, San Diego, sees Filipino texting culture as inherently subversive:

> Like many third world countries recently opened to more liberal trade policies, the Philippines shares in the paradox of being awash in the latest technologies of communication such as the cell phone while mired in deteriorating infrastructures such as roads, postal services, railroads, power generators and land lines. With the cell phone, one appears to be able to pass beyond these obstacles. And inasmuch as such infrastructures are state run so that their breakdown and inefficiencies are a direct function of governmental ineptitude, passing beyond them also feels like overcoming the state, which to begin with is already overcome by corruption. It is small wonder then that cell phones could prove literally handy in spreading rumors, jokes, and information that steadily eroded whatever legitimacy President Estrada still had.[14]

The "People Power II" demonstrations of 2001 broke out when the impeachment trial of President Estrada was suddenly ended by senators linked to Estrada. Opposition leaders broadcast text messages, and within seventy-five minutes of the abrupt halt of the impeachment proceedings, 20,000 people converged on Edsa.[15] Over four days, more than a million people showed up. The military withdrew support from the regime; the Estrada government fell, as the Marcos regime had fallen a decade previously, largely as a result of massive nonviolent demonstrations.[16] The rapid assembly of the anti-Estrada crowd was a hallmark of early smart mob technology, and the millions of text

7 Anne Torres, "4 SME, Txtng is Lyf," *TheFeature.com,* 18 April 2001, <http://www.thefeature.com> (1 March 2002).
8 Bociurkiw, "Revolution by Cell Phone."
9 Rafael, "The Cell Phone and the Crowd."
10 Ibid.
11 Arturo Bariuad, "Text Messaging Becomes a Menace in the Philippines," *Straits Times,* 3 March 2001.
12 Wayne Arnold, "Manila's Talk of the Town Is Text Messaging," *New York Times,* 5 July 2000, C1.

13 Bariuad, "Text Messaging Becomes a Menace."
14 Rafael, "The Cell Phone and the Crowd."
15 Ibid.
16 Richard Lloyd Parry, "The TXT MSG Revolution," *Independent Digital,* 23 January 2001, <http://www.independent.co.uk/story.jsp?story=51748> (1 March 2002).

messages exchanged by the demonstrators in 2001 was, by all accounts, a key to the crowd's esprit de corps.

Professor Rafael sees the SMS-linked crowd that assembled in Manila as the manifestation of a phenomenon that was enabled by a technical infrastructure but that is best understood as a social instrument:

> The power of the crowd thus comes across in its capacity to overwhelm the physical constraints of urban planning in the same way that it tends to blur social distinctions by provoking a sense of estrangement. Its authority rests on its ability to promote restlessness and movement, thereby undermining the pressure from state technocrats, church authorities and corporate interests to regulate and contain such movements. In this sense, the crowd is a sort of medium if by that word one means the means for gathering and transforming elements, objects, people and things. As a medium, the crowd is also the site for the generation of expectations and the

The Battle of Seattle saw a more deliberate and tactically focused use of wireless communications and mobile social networks in urban political conflict, more than a year before texting mobs assembled in Manila. A broad coalition of demonstrators who represented different interests but were united in opposition to the views of the World Trade Organization planned to disrupt the WTO's 1999 meeting in Seattle. The demonstrators included a wide range of different "affinity groups" who loosely coordinated their actions around their shared objective. The Direct Action Network enabled autonomous groups to choose which levels of action to participate in, from nonviolent support to civil disobedience to joining mass arrests — a land of dynamic ad hoc alliance that wouldn't have been possible without a mobile, many-to-many, real-time communication network. According to a report dramatically titled, "Black Flag Over Seattle," by Paul de Armond:

> The cohesion of the Direct Action Network was partly due to their improvised communications network assembled out of cell phones,

---

The Battle of Seattle saw a more deliberate and tactically focused use of wireless communications and mobile social networks in urban political conflict, more than a year before texting mobs assembled in Manila.

---

circulation of messages. It is in this sense that we might also think of the crowd not merely as an effect of technological devices, but as a kind of technology itself. ... Centralized urban planning and technologies of policing seek to routinize the sense of contingency generated in crowding. But at moments and in areas where such planning chronically fails, routine can at times give way to the epochal. At such moments, the crowd ... takes on a land of telecommunicative power, serving up channels for sending messages at a distance and bringing distances up close. Enmeshed in a crowd, one feels the potential for reaching out across social space and temporal divides.[17]

radios, police scanners and portable computers. Protesters in the street with wireless Palm Pilots were able to link into continuously updated web pages giving reports from the streets. Police scanners monitored transmissions and provided some warning of changing police tactics. Cell phones were widely used.

Kelly Quirke, Executive Director of the Rainforest Action Network, reports that early Tuesday, "the authorities had successfully squashed DAN's communications system." The solution to the infrastructure attack was quickly resolved by purchasing new Nextel cell phones. According to Han Shan, the Ruckus Society's WTO action coordinator, his organization and other protest groups that formed the Direct Action Network used the Nextel system to create a cellular grid over the city. They broke into talk groups of eight people each. One of the eight

---

17 Rafael, "The Cell Phone and the Crowd."

overlapped with another talk group, helping to quickly communicate through the ranks.

In addition to the organizers' all-points network, protest communications were leavened with individual protesters using cell phones, direct transmissions from roving independent media feeding directly onto the Internet, personal computers with wireless modems broadcasting live video, and a variety of other networked communications. Floating above the tear gas was a pulsing infosphere of enormous bandwidth, reaching around the planet via the Internet.[18]

From Seattle to Manila, the first "netwars" have already broken out. The term "netwar" was coined by John Arquilla and David Ronfeldt, two analysts for the RAND corporation (birthplace of game theory and experimental economics), who noticed that the same combination of social networks, sophisticated communication technologies, and decentralized organizational structure was surfacing as an effective force in very different kinds of political conflict:

Netwar is an emerging mode of conflict in which the protagonists — ranging from terrorist and criminal organizations on the dark side, to militant social activists on the bright side — use network forms of organization, doctrine, strategy, and technology attuned to the information age. The practice of net-war is well ahead of theory, as both civil and uncivil society actors are increasingly engaging in this new way of fighting.

From the Battle of Seattle to the "attack on America," these networks are proving very hard to deal with; some are winning. What all have in common is that they operate in small, dispersed units that can deploy nimbly — anywhere, anytime. All feature network forms of organization, doctrine, strategy, and technology attuned to the information age. They know how to swarm and disperse, penetrate and disrupt, as well as elude and evade. The tactics they use range from

battles of ideas to acts of sabotage — and many tactics involve the Internet.[19]

The "swarming" strategies noted by Arquilla and Ronfeldt rely on many small units like the affinity groups in the Battle of Seattle. Individual members of each group remained dispersed until mobile communications drew them to converge on a specific location, from all directions simultaneously, in coordination with other groups. Manila, Seattle, San Francisco, Senegal, and Britain were sites of nonviolent political swarming. Arquilla and Ronfeldt cited the nongovernmental organizations associated with the Zapatista movement in Mexico, which mobilized world opinion in support of Indian peasants, and the Nobel Prize–winning effort to enact an anti-landmine treaty as examples of nonviolent netwar actions. Armed and violent swarms are another matter.

The Chechen rebels in Russia, soccer hooligans in Britain, and the FARC guerrillas in Colombia also have used netwar strategy and swarming tactics.[20] The U.S. military is in the forefront of smart mob technology development. The Land Warrior experiment is scheduled to field-test wearable computers with GPS and wireless communications by 2003.[21] The Joint Expeditionary Digital Information (JEDI) program links troops on the ground directly to satellite communications. JEDI handheld devices combine laser range-finding, GPS location awareness, direct satellite telephone, and encrypted text messaging.[22] Remember the DARPA-funded startup MeshNetworks from Chapter 6, the company whose technology enables military swarms to parachute onto a battlefield and self-organize an ad hoc peer-to-peer wireless network? Small teams of special forces, wirelessly networked and capable of calling in aircraft or missile strikes with increasing accuracy, were introduced by the United States and its allies in Afghanistan: netwar.

18   de Armond, "Black Flag Over Seattle."

19   David Ronfeldt and John Arquilla, "Networks, Netwars, and the Fight for the Future," *First Monday* 6, 10 (October 2001), <http://firstmonday.org/issues/issue6_10/ronfeldt/index.html> (1 March 2002).

20   John Arquilla and David Ronfeldt, eds., *Networks and Netwars: The Future of Terror, Crime, and Militancy* (Santa Monica, Calif.: RAND, 2001).

21   Jim Lai, "The Future of Infantry," *Mindjack* 28, January 2002, <http://www.mindjack.com/feature/landwarrior.html> (1 March 2002).

22   Ian Sample, "Military Palmtop to Cut Collateral Damage," *New Scientist,* 9 March 2002, <http://www.newscientist.com/news/news.jsp?id=ns99992005> (29 March 2002).

Examples later in this chapter demonstrate that smart mobs engaging in either violent or nonviolent netwar represent only a few of the many possible varieties of smart mob. Netwars do share similar technical infrastructure

hierarchical form matured through the institutionalization of states, empires, and professional administrative and bureaucratic systems. In like manner, the early spread of the market form,

---

Social network means that every individual in a smart mob is a "node" in the jargon of social network analysis, with social "links" (channels of communication and social bonds) to other individuals.

---

with other smart mobs. More importantly, however, they are both animated by a new form of social organization, the network. Networks include nodes and links, use many possible paths to distribute information from any link to any other, and are self-regulated through flat governance hierarchies and distributed power. Arquilla and Ronfeldt are among many who believe networks constitute the newest major social organizational form, after tribes, hierarchies, and markets. Although network-structured communications hold real potential for enabling democratic forms of decision-making and beneficial instances of collective action, that doesn't mean that the transition to networked forms of social organization will be a pleasant one with uniformly benevolent outcomes. Arquilla and Ronfeldt note the potential for cooperation in examples like the nongovernmental organizations that use netwar tactics for public benefit, but they also articulated a strong caution, worth keeping in mind when contemplating the future of smart mobs:

> Most people might hope for the emergence of a new form of organization to be led by "good guys" who do "the right thing" and grow stronger because of it. But history does not support this contention. The cutting edge in the early rise of a new form may be found equally among malcontents, ne'er-do-wells, and clever opportunists eager to take advantage of new ways to maneuver, exploit, and dominate. Many centuries ago, for example, the rise of hierarchical forms of organization, which displaced traditional, consultative, tribal forms, was initially attended, in parts of the world, by the appearance of ferocious chieftains bent on military conquest and of violent secret societies run according to rank — long before the

only a few centuries ago, was accompanied by a spawn of usurers, pirates, smugglers, and monopolists, all seeking to elude state controls over their earnings and enterprises.[23]

In light of the military applications of netwar tactics, it would be foolish to presume that only benign outcomes should be expected from smart mobs. But any observer who focuses exclusively on the potential for violence would miss evidence of perhaps an even more profoundly disruptive potential — for beneficial as well as malign purposes — of smart mob technologies and techniques. Could cooperation epidemics break out if smart mob media spread beyond warriors — to citizens, journalists, scientists, people looking for fun, friends, mates, customers, or trading partners?

Substitute the word "computers" for the words "smart mobs" in the previous paragraph, and you'll recapitulate the history of computation since its birth in World War II.

* * *

MOBILE AD HOC SOCIAL NETWORKS

Imagine my excitement, many months into my smart mob odyssey; when I came across a research report titled "When Peer-to-Peer Comes Face-to-Face: Collaborative Peer-to-Peer Computing in Mobile Ad Hoc Networks," from the "Wearable Computing Group" at the University of Oregon.[24] The Oregon group, assembled by Professor Zary Segall and led by Gerd Kortuem, had designed a test bed

---

23 Arquilla and Ronfeldt, eds., *Networks and Netwars*, 310–313.
24 Gerd Kortuem et al., "When Peer-to-Peer Comes Face-to-Face: Collaborative Peer-to-Peer Computing in Mobile Ad Hoc Networks," 2001 International Conference on Peer-to-Peer Computing (P2P2001), 27–29 August 2001, Linköping,

for smart mobs around the same time I began to believe such a development was possible.

"Mobile ad hoc social network" is a longer, more technical term than "smart mob." Both terms describe the new social form made possible by the combination of computation, communication, reputation, and location awareness. The *mobile* aspect is already self-evident to urbanites who see the early effects of mobile phones and SMS. *Ad hoc* means that the organizing among people and their devices is done informally and on the fly, the way texting youth everywhere coordinate meetings after school. *Social network* means that every individual in a smart mob is a "node" in the jargon of social network analysis, with social "links" (channels of communication and social bonds) to other individuals. Nodes and links, the elements of social networks made by humans, are also the fundamental elements of communication networks constructed from optical cables and wireless devices — one reason why new communication technologies make possible profound social changes.

The Wearable Computing Group specializes in exploring the community aspects of wireless, wearable, and peer-to-peer technologies. Kortuem agreed with my assessment when I called him to talk about the research at the University of Oregon. "When I talk about community," he told me, "I mean both the users who form social networks when they interact personally and communities of developers, like the open source community, where each member shares ideas and contributes to building something larger."[25] In Oregon, Toronto, Pittsburgh, Atlanta, Palo Alto, and Tokyo, small bands of researchers are beginning to walk around the same geographic neighborhoods while wearing intercommunicating computers.

Kortuem and colleagues realized that p2p computing and wireless networking technologies made it possible to design ad hoc networks of mobile devices to support the ad hoc social networks of the people who wear them. The fundamental technical unit cited by Kortuem and other wearable computing researchers has come to be known as the "personal area network," an interconnected network of devices worn or carried by the user. The concept was first described by Tom Zimmerman, now at IBM's Almaden Research Center, who had invented the VR "dataglove" while he was an MIT student.[26]

Kortuem and colleagues treat the personal area networks as building blocks of a dynamic community of networks with emergent capabilities of its own. The research is as much behavioral as it is computational, beginning with simple experiments matching properties of mobile computing networks with the needs of social networks. The community of personal area network users within geographic proximity, for example, could serve as a wireless mesh network, dynamically self-organizing a cloud of broadband connectivity as nodes came in and out of physical proximity, providing always-on Internet connections to members. Using Bluetooth and other short-range wireless technologies such as very-low-power wideband radio, individual members of the community could engage in more intimate and timely information exchanges when face to face, whereas WiFi technologies could provide the infrastructure for neighborhood-wide and Internet-wide communication:

> Mobile ad hoc systems provide opportunities for ad hoc meetings, mobile patient monitoring, distributed command and control systems and ubiquitous computing. In particular, personal area networks enable the creation of proximity-aware applications in support of face-to-face collaboration.
>
> Mobile devices like cell phones, PDAs and wearable computers have become our constant companions and are available wherever we go. … Personal area networks open the opportunity for these devices to take part in our everyday social interactions with people. Their ability to establish communication links among devices during face-to-face encounters can be used to facilitate, augment or even promote human social interactions.
>
> In some sense, an ad hoc mobile information system is the ultimate peer-to-peer system. It is self-organizing, fully decentralized, and highly dynamic.[27]

Sweden, <http://www.cs.uoregon.edu/research/wearables/Papers/p2p2001.pdf> (6 March 2002).

25 Gerd Kortuem, telephone interview by author, 27 February 2002.

26 T. G. Zimmerman, "Personal Area Networks: Near-Field Intrabody Communication," *IBM Systems Journal* 35, 3&4 (1996), <http://www.research. ibm.com/journal/sj/mit/sectione/zimmerman.html> (6 March 2002).

27 Kortuem et al., "When Peer-to-Peer Comes."

Short-range radio frequency links such as those used by Bluetooth chips and wearable computers create a sphere of connectivity within the immediate vicinity of the wearer. Paul Rankin, at Philips Research laboratory in England, wrote about the need for intermediary agents to negotiate transactions between the "aura" of one person and radio beacons in the environment, or another person's aura.[28] "Auranet" is what Jay Schneider, Kortuem, and colleagues named their "framework for structuring encounters in social space based on reputations and trust."[29] The wireless instantiation of a 12-foot information bubble around wearable computer users is a physical model of what sociologist Erving Goffman calls the "Interaction Order," the part of social life where face-to-face and spoken interactions occur.[30] Goffman claimed that the mundane world of everyday interactions involves complex symbolic exchanges, visible but rarely consciously noticed, which enable groups to negotiate movement through public spaces. Although people use the ways they present themselves to "give" information they want others to believe about themselves, Goffman noted that people also "give off" information, leaking true but uncontrolled information along with their more deliberate performance.

One form of information that people give off, called "stigma" by Goffman, is markings or behaviors that locate individuals in a particular social status. Although many stigma can have negative connotations, stigma can also mark positive social status. The information we give off by the way we behave and dress helps us coordinate social interaction and identify likely interaction partners. When the Interaction Order is formalized and modeled automatically in an Auranet, the social network and the technological network meet in a way that makes possible new capabilities such as automated webs of trust for ad hoc interactions — for example, assembling a carpool of trustworthy strangers when you drive downtown or seek a ride.

Kortuem et al., noting the lack of fully embodied "human moments" in purely virtual worlds, concentrated on ways to enhance the most basic sphere of human social behavior, the face-to-face encounters of everyday life. Indeed, the primary question asked by the Oregon researchers is the primary question regarding smart mobs: What can communities of wearable computer users do in their face-to-face encounters? At a technical level, the wearable devices can share bandwidth by acting as nodes in an ad hoc wireless network. The devices could exchange media and messages, similar to the way Napster and Usenet use links between individual nodes to pass data around. However, as soon as the members of the community allow their computers to exchange data automatically, without human intervention, complex issues of trust and privacy intervene — the unspoken norms of the interaction order. Kortuem et al. explored the social and technical implications of personal agent software, which filters, shields, and acts as a go-between for their users.

A number of social and technical barriers must be overcome in order for mobile ad hoc communities to self-organize cooperatively. Nobody is going to contribute their personal area network to a community internetwork unless they feel secure about privacy and trust — who snoops whom, and who can be counted on to deal honestly? Privacy requires data security, and security is complicated by wireless communications. Encryption techniques make secure wearable community infrastructure possible, but someone has to figure out how to build them. Trust means a distributed reputation system, which the Oregon group has prototyped. When you break down the interesting idea of mobile, ad hoc social networks into the elements needed to make it work in practice, a rich and largely undeveloped field for research opens.

Another experiment by the Eugene group mediates social encounters by comparing personal profiles automatically and alerting participants in a face-to-face encounter of mutual interests or common friends that they might not know about (a recommendation system for strangers).[31] Each social encounter of wearable computer users involving automatic exchanges of personal data, sharing of bandwidth, or passing of messages from others would necessarily involve individual computations of where each participant's self-interest lies in relation to a computation of the other party's trustworthiness. Kortuem et al. recognized

28 Paul Rankin, "Context-Aware Mobile Phones: The Difference Between Pull and Push, Restoring the Importance of Place," Philips Research Laboratories, Redhill, Surrey, U.K.

29 Jay Schneider et al., "Auranet: Trust and Face-to-Face Interactions in a Wearable Community," Technical Report WCL-TR15, July 2001, <http://www.cs.uoregon.edu/research/wearables/Papers/auranet.pdf> (6 March 2002).

30 Erving Goffman, *The Presentation of Self in Everyday Life* (Garden City, N.Y.: Doubleday, 1959).

31 Jay Schneider et al., "Disseminating Trust Information in Wearable Communities," 2nd International Symposium on Handheld and Ubiquitous Computing (HUC2K), 25–27 September 2000, Bristol, England, <http://www.cs.uoregon.edu/research/wearables/Papers/HUC2K.pdf> (6 March 2002).

this complex weighing of trust versus self-interest as an example of our old friend, the Prisoner's Dilemma, and designed an experimental system called WALID to test some of these issues, taking advantage of the fact that the Oregon wearable computing researchers lived and worked in the same general neighborhood in Eugene, Oregon:

> WALID implements a digitized version of the timeworn tradition of borrowing butter from your neighbor. You do a favor for others because you know that one day they will do it for you.
>
> With WALID two individuals use their mobile devices to negotiate about and to exchange real world tasks: dropping off someone's dry cleaning, buying a book of stamps at the post office, or returning a book to the local library.
>
> WALID employs personal agent software to find close-by community members and to negotiate the exchange of tasks. The agents maintain a user's task list, become fully aware of the locations and activities involved. When an encounter occurs, the agents produce a negotiation. If both users approve, a deal is struck.
>
> The role of the agent in a negotiation is to evaluate the value of favors and to keep scores. Having to run across town just to drop off someone's mail compares unfavorably with buying milk for someone if the grocery store is just a block away. Agents employ ideas from game theory to ensure that results of negotiations are mutually beneficial; they cooperate only if there is the opportunity to enhance the user's goals.[32]

In our telephone conversation, Kortuem noted that at the beginning of wearable computing research, the main goals involved either creating tools for professionals, such as maintenance and repair specialists, or creating tools to augment individuals, in the manner promoted by Steve Mann. "I came to realize," Kortuem told me, "that what is really interesting is not the technology of a specialized application at a job site, but what happens if ordinary people are empowered to use this technology and what effects might emerge when technology penetrates society."[33] These words will be worth remembering when millions of people carry devices that invisibly probe and cloak, reach out, evaluate, interconnect, negotiate, exchange, and coordinate invisible acts of ad hoc cooperation that create wealth, democracy, education, surveillance, and weaponry from pure mind-stuff, the way the alchemy of inscribing ever-tinier patterns on purified sand invokes the same forces from the same place.

SWARM INTELLIGENCE AND THE SOCIAL MIND

Massive outbreaks of cooperation precipitated the collapse of communism. In city after city, huge crowds assembled in nonviolent street demonstrations, despite decades of well-founded fear of political assembly. Although common sense leads to the conclusion that unanimity of opinion among the demonstrators explained the change of behavior, Natalie Glance and Bernardo Huberman, Xerox PARC researchers who have studied the dynamics of social systems, noted that a *diversity* of cooperation thresholds among the individuals can tip a crowd into a sudden epidemic of cooperation. Glance and Huberman pointed out that a minority of extremists can choose to act first, and if the conditions are right, their actions can trigger actions by others who needed to see somebody make the first move before acting themselves — at which point the bandwagon-jumpers follow the early adopters who followed the first actors:

> Those transitions can trigger a cascade of further cooperation until the whole group is cooperating.
>
> The events that led to the mass protests in Leipzig and Berlin and to the subsequent downfall of the East German government in November 1989 vividly illustrate the impact of such diversity on the resolution of social dilemmas. ... The citizens of Leipzig who desired a change of government faced a dilemma. They could stay home in safety or demonstrate against the government and risk arrest — knowing that as the number of demonstrators rose, the risk

---

32 Gerd Kortuem et al., "When Cyborgs Meet: Building Communities of Cooperating Wearable Agents," *Proceedings Third International Symposium on Wearable Computers,* 18–19 October 1999, San Francisco, California, <http://www.computer.org/proceedings/iswc/0428/04280124abs.htm> (6 March 2002).

33 Kortuem, telephone interview by author.

declined and the potential for overthrowing the regime increased.

A conservative person would demonstrate against the government only if thousands were already committed; a revolutionary might join at the slightest sign of unrest. That variation in threshold is one form of diversity. People also differed in their estimates of the duration of a demonstration as well as in the amount of risk they were willing to take. Bernhardt Prosch and Martin Abram, two sociologists from Erlangen University who studied the Leipzig demonstrations, claim that the diversity in thresholds was important in triggering the mass demonstrations.[34]

Sudden epidemics of cooperation aren't necessarily pleasant experiences. Lynch mobs and entire nations co-operate to perpetrate atrocities. Decades before the fall of communism, sociologist Mark Granovetter examined radical collective behavior of both positive and negative kinds and proposed a "threshold model of collective behavior." I recognized Granovetter's model as a crucial conceptual bridge that connects intelligent (smart mob) cooperation with "emergent" behaviors of unintelligent actors, such as hives, flocks, and swarms.

Granovetter studied situations in which individuals were faced with either-or decisions regarding their relationship to a group — whether or not to join a riot or strike, adopt an innovation, spread a rumor, sell a stock, leave a social gathering, migrate to a different country. He identified the pivotal statistic as the proportion of *other* people who have to act before an individual decides to join them. Thresholds appear to be an individual reaction to the dynamics of a group.

One of Granovetter's statements yielded a clue to smart mob dynamics: "By explaining paradoxical outcomes as the result of aggregation processes, threshold models take the 'strangeness' often associated with collective behavior out of the heads of actors and put it into the dynamics of situations."[35] Smart mobs might also involve yet-unknown properties deriving from the dynamics of situations, not the heads of actors. Goffman's Interaction Order, the social sphere in which complex verbal and nonverbal communications are exchanged among individuals in real time, is precisely where individual actions can influence the action thresholds of crowds. Mobile media that can augment the informal, mostly unconscious information exchanges that take place within the Interaction Order, or affect the size or location of the audience for these exchanges, have the potential to change the threshold for collective action.

I started looking for ways to connect these congruent ideas operationally. How would they map onto an ad hoc social network of wearable computer users, for example? When my idea hunting brought me to "the coordination problem," a social dilemma that is *not* a Prisoner's Dilemma, separate ideas began to fit together into a larger pattern.

A coordination problem does not involve the Prisoner's Dilemma zero-sum game between self-interest and common resources but instead represents the quandary that confronts individuals who are ready to cooperate, but whose cooperation is contingent on the prior cooperation of others. Monitoring and sanctioning are important not simply as a way of punishing rule breakers but also as a way of assuring members that others are using common resources wisely. That is, many people are contingent cooperators, willing to cooperate as long as most others do (what Ostrom referred to as a "commitment problem"). Thus, monitoring and sanctioning serve the important function of providing information about others' actions and levels of commitment.

In *Rational Ritual: Culture, Coordination, and Common Knowledge,* Michael Suk-Young Chwe claims that public rituals are "social practices that generate common knowledge," which enables groups to solve coordination problems. Suk-Young Chwe writes: "A public ritual is not just about the transmission of meaning from a central source to each member of an audience; it is also about letting audience members know what other audience members know."[36] Everyone in a group has to know who else is contributing, free riding, and sanctioning in order to solve both free rider and coordination problems on the fly with maximum trust and minimum friction. This is the key to

---

34 Natalie S. Glance and Bernardo A. Huberman, "The Dynamics of Social Dilemmas," *Scientific American,* March 1994, 76–81.

35 Mark Granovetter, "Threshold Models of Collective Behavior," *American Journal of Sociology* 83, 6 (1978): 1420–1443.

36 Michael Suk-Young Chwe, *Rational Ritual: Culture, Coordination, and Common Knowledge* (Princeton: Princeton University Press, 2001), <http://www.chwe.net/michael/r.pdf> (6 March 2002).

the group-cooperation leverage bestowed by reputation systems and many-to-many communications media.

Threshold models of collective action and the role of the Interaction Order are both about media for exchange of co-ordinating knowledge. Understanding this made it possible to see something I had not noticed clearly enough before—a possible connection between computer-wearing social networks of thinking, communicating humans and the swarm intelligence of unthinking (but also communicating) ants, bees, fish, and birds. Individual ants leave chemical trail markers, and the entire nest calculates the most efficient route to a food source from a hundred aggregated trails without direction from any central brain. Individual fish and birds (and tight-formation fighter pilots) school and flock simply by paying attention to what their nearest neighbors do. The coordinated movements of schools and flocks is a dynamically shifting aggregation of individual decisions. Even if there were a central tuna or pigeon who could issue orders, no system of propagating orders from a central source can operate swiftly enough to avoid being eaten by sharks or slamming into trees. When it comes to hives and swarms, the emergent capabilities of decentralized self-organization can be surprisingly intelligent.

What happens when the individuals in a tightly coordinated group are more highly intelligent creatures rather than simpler organisms like insects or birds? How do humans exhibit emergent behavior? As soon as this question occurred to me, I immediately recalled the story Kevin Kelly told at the beginning of *Out of Control,* his 1994 book about the emergent behaviors in biology, machinery, and human affairs.[37] He described an event at an annual film show for computer graphics professionals. A small paddle was attached to each seat in the auditorium, with reflective material of contrasting colors on each side of the paddle. The screen in the auditorium displayed a high-contrast, real-time video view of the audience. The person leading the exercise, computer graphics wizard Loren Carpenter, asked those on one side of the auditorium aisle to hold the paddles with one color showing and asked the other half of the audience to hold up the opposite color. Then, following Carpenter's suggestions, the audience self-organized a dot that moved around the screen, added a couple of paddles on the screen, and began to play

a giant game of self-organized video Pong, finally creating a graphical representation of an airplane and flying it around the screen. Like flocks, there was no central control of the

---

When it comes to hives and swarms, the emergent capabilities of decentralized self-organization can be surprisingly intelligent.

---

exercise after Carpenter made a suggestion. Members of the audience paid attention to what their neighbors were doing and what was happening on the screen. Kelly used this as an example of a self-conscious version of flocking behavior.[38]

Musician and cognitive scientist William Benzon believes that the graphical coordination exercise led by Carpenter and described by Kelly is similar to what happens when musicians "jam" and that it involves a yet unexplored synchronization of brain processes among the people involved:[39]

> The group in Carpenter's story is controlling what appears on the screen. Everyone can see it all, but each can directly affect only the part of the display they control with his or her paddle. In jamming, everyone hears everything but can affect only that part of the collective sound that they create (or withhold).
>
> Now consider a different example. One of the standard scenes in prison movies goes like this: We're in a cell block or in the mess hall. One prisoner starts banging his cup on the table (or on one of the bars to his cell). Another joins in, then another, and another, until everyone's banging away and shouting some slogan in unison. This is a simple example of emergent behavior. But it's one that you won't find in chimpanzees. Yes, you will find them involved in group displays where they're all hooting and hollering and stomping. But the synchrony isn't as precise as it is in the human case.

37   Kevin Kelly, *Out of Control* (Reading, Mass.: Addison-Wesley, 1994), <http://www.kk.org/outofcontrol/index.html> (6 March 2002).

38   Ibid.
39   William Benzon, *Beethoven's Anvil: Music in Mind and Culture* (New York: Basic Books, 2001).

And that precision is critical to my argument. That precision allows me to treat the human group as a collection of coupled oscillators. Oscillation is one of the standard and simplest emergent phenomena. Once a group has become coupled in oscillation, we can treat the group as a single entity. To be sure, there's more to music than simple oscillation. But oscillation is the foundation, the starting point, and all the elaboration and complexities take place within this framework.

In effect, in musical performance (and in dance), communication between individuals is pretty much the same as communication between components of a single nervous system. It's continuous and two-way, and it does not involve symbolic mediation. Think of Goffman's interaction order, but drop verbal communication from it. It is a public space that is physically external to the brains of participating individuals, but it is functionally internal to those brains.[40]

Kevin Kelly traced back the new theories regarding emergent properties to William Morton Wheeler, an expert in the behavior of ants.[41] Wheeler called insect colonies "superorganisms" and defined the ability of the hive to accomplish tasks that no individual ant or bee is intelligent enough to do on its own as "emergent properties" of the superorganism. Kelly drew parallels between the ways both biological and artificial "vivi-systems" exhibit the same four characteristics of what he called "swarm systems":

- ➤ the absence of imposed centralized control
- ➤ the autonomous nature of subunits
- ➤ the high connectivity between the subunits
- ➤ the webby nonlinear causality of peers influencing peers[42]

Steven Johnson's 2001 book, *Emergence,* shows how the principles that Kelly extrapolated from biological to technological networks also apply to cities and Amazon.

com's recommendation system: "In these systems, agents residing on one scale start producing behavior that lies on one scale above them: ants create colonies; urbanites create neighborhoods; simple pattern-recognition software learns how to recommend new books. The movement from low-level rules to higher level sophistication is what we call emergence."[43] In the case of cities, although the emergent intelligence resembles the ant-mind, the individual units, humans, possess extraordinary onboard intelligence — or at least the capacity for it.

At this point, connections between the behavior of smart mobs and the behavior of swarm systems must be tentative, yet several of the earliest investigations have shown that the right kinds of online social networks know more than the sum of their parts: Connected and communicating in the right ways, populations of humans can exhibit a kind of "collective intelligence." In the summer between my smart mob inquiries in Scandinavia and my expedition to Tokyo, my inquiries brought me to a fellow who seems to have discovered the underpinnings of group intelligence. Bernardo Huberman, formerly at Xerox PARC, now scientific director of Hewlett-Packard's Information Dynamics research laboratory, was doing intriguing research on the emergence of primitive forms of collective intelligence.

I visited Huberman in his office, located in the same Palo Alto complex as the CoolTown laboratory. Huberman is a master of thinking of new ways of looking at familiar phenomena, seeing computer networks as ecologies, markets as social computers, and online communities as social minds. Originally a physicist, Huberman presents his findings in pages of mathematical equations. When I visited him in his office, he seriously agreed that "the Internet enables us to building collective intelligence."[44] At PARC, he had directed investigations of "the ecology of computation." As soon as I told him about smart mobs, he jumped up and exclaimed, "The social mind!" And he dug out a chapter on "The Social Mind" that he had published in 1995. Huberman thought it useful to think of emergent intelligence as a social computation:

Intelligence is not restricted to single brains; it also appears in groups, such as insect colonies,

---

40 William Benzon, email interview by author.
41 William Morton Wheeler, *Emergent Evolution and the Development of Societies* (New York: W. W. Norton, 1928).
42 Ibid.

43 Steven Johnson, *Emergence: The Connected Lives of Ants, Brains, Cities, and Software* (New York: Scribner, 2001).
44 Bernardo Huberman, interview by author, October 2001, Palo Alto, California.

social and economic behavior in human societies, and scientific and professional communities. In all these cases, large numbers of agents capable of local tasks that can be conceived of as computations, engage in collective behavior which successfully deals with a number of problems that transcend the capacity of any individual to solve. ... When large numbers of agents capable of symbolic-processing interact with each other, new universal regularities in their overall behavior appear. Furthermore, these regularities are quantifiable and can be experimentally tested.[45]

The interesting statement is the last one. There have been varieties of theories about the Internet as the nervous

predictive performance of participants in information markets and create weighting schemes that will predict future events, even if they are not the same event on which the performance was measured."[47]

Decades ago, computer scientists thought that someday there would be forms of "artificial intelligence," but with the exception of a few visionaries, they never thought in terms of computer-equipped humans as a kind of social intelligence. Although everyone who understands the use of statistical techniques to make predictions hastens to add the disclaimer that surprises are inevitable, and one of the fundamental characteristics of complex adaptive systems is their unpredictability, the initial findings that internetworked groups of humans can exhibit emergent prediction capabilities are potentially profound.

The knowledge and technologies that triggered the jump from clan to tribe to nation to market to network all shared one characteristic: They each amplified the way individual humans think and communicate, and magnified their ability to share what they know.

---

system of a global brain, but Huberman and colleagues have made clever use of markets and game simulations as computational test beds for experiments with emergent group intelligence. The fall that I visited Huberman, he and his colleagues had used "information markets" to perform experiments in emergent social intelligence and found that group forecasts were more accurate than those of any of the individual participants' forecasts.[46] In information markets, members trade symbolic currency representing predictions of public information. The Hollywood Stock Exchange, for example, uses the market that emerges from the trading of symbolic shares to predict box office revenues and Oscar winners. The HP research team makes the extraordinary claim that they have created a mathematically verifiable methodology for extracting emergent intelligence from a group and using the group's knowledge to predict the future in a limited but useful realm: "One can take past

Another research group that takes emergent group intelligence seriously is the laboratory at Los Alamos, where a group of "artificial life" researchers issued a report in 1998, "Symbiotic Intelligence: Self-Organizing Knowledge on Distributed Networks, Driven by Human Interaction."[48] The premise of this interdisciplinary team is based on the view proposed by some in recent years that human society is an adaptive collective organism and that social evolution parallels and unfolds according to the same dynamics as biological evolution.[49] According to this theory, which I will revisit in the next chapter, new knowledge and new technologies have made possible the evolution of the maximum size of the functioning social group from tribes to nations to global coalitions. The knowledge and technologies that triggered the jump from clan to tribe to nation to market to network all shared one characteristic: They each amplified the way individual humans think and

45 Bernardo A. Huberman, "The Social Mind," in *Origins of the Human Brain,* ed. Jean-Pierre Changeux and Jean Chavaillon (Oxford: Clarendon Press, 1995), 250.

46 Kay-Yut Chen, Leslie R. Fine, and Bernardo Huberman, "Forecasting Uncertain Events with Small Groups," HP Laboratories, Palo Alto, California, 3 August 2001, <http://papers.ssrn.com/sol3/papers.cfm?abstract_id=278601> (6 March 2002).

47 Ibid.

48 Norman Johnson et al., "Symbiotic Intelligence: Self-Organizing Knowledge on Distributed Networks, Driven by Human Interaction," in *Artificial Life VI: Proceedings of the Sixth International Conference on Artificial Life (Complex Adaptive Systems,* No. 6), ed. C. Adami, R. Belew, H. Kitano, and C. Taylor (Cambridge: Bradford Books/MIT Press, 1998)

49 George Dyson, *Darwin Among the Machines: The Evolution of Global Intelligence* (Reading, Mass.: Addison-Wesley, 1997).

communicate, and magnified their ability to share what they know.

The Los Alamos team, looking at some of the same characteristics of the Internet that Huberman and his colleagues investigated and citing a range of research that has only recently begun to emerge as a discipline, claim that "self-organizing social dynamics has been an unappreciated positive force in our social development and has been significantly extended, at least in scope, by new technologies."[50] The Los Alamos group cited evidence for their hypothesis that the self-organizing social systems that have driven human social evolution will be enhanced by self-organized, distributed, information and communication systems. The research conducted directly by the Los Alamos researchers reinforced Huberman et al.'s claim that groups of humans, linked through online networks, can make collective decisions that prove more accurate than the performance of the best individual predictors in the group. If it isn't a dead end, the lines of research opened by Huberman's team, the Los Alamos researchers, and others could amplify the powers of smart mobs into entirely new dimensions of possibility, the way Moore's Law amplified the powers of computer users.

Will self-organized, ad hoc networks of computer wearers, mediated by privacy-protecting agents, blossom into a renaissance of new wealth, knowledge, and revitalized civil society, or will the same technological-social regime provide nothing more than yet another revenue stream for Disinfotainment, Inc?

Or is that the wrong question? Given the direction of the technological, economic, and political changes I have touched on so far, I propose the following questions:

> What do we know now about the emergent properties of ad hoc mobile computing networks, and what do we need to know in the future?
> What are the central issues for individuals in a world pervaded by surveillance devices — in terms of what we can *do* about it?
> What are the long-term consequences of near-term political decisions on the way we'll use and be affected by mobile, pervasive, always-on media?

I hope that the understandings I've shared from my investigations of the past two years make it clear that smart mobs aren't a "thing" that you can point to with one finger or describe with two words, any more than "the Internet" was a "thing" you could point to. The Internet is what happened when a lot of computers started communicating. The computer and the Internet were designed, but the ways people used them were not designed into either technology, nor were the most world-shifting uses of these tools anticipated by their designers or vendors. Word processing and virtual communities, eBay and e-commerce, Google and weblogs and reputation systems *emerged*. Smart mobs are an unpredictable but at least partly describable emergent property that I see surfacing as more people use mobile telephones, more chips communicate with each other, more computers know where they are located, more technology becomes wearable, more people start using these new media to invent new forms of sex, commerce, entertainment, communion, and, as always, conflict.

50   Johnson et al., "Symbiotic Intelligence."

PART 4
REALITY OR SIMULATION

Mike (TV host):	*Christoph, let me ask you. Why do you think that Truman has never come close to discovering the true nature of his world until now?*
Christoph:	*We accept the reality of the world with which we're presented. It's as simple as that.*

— The Truman Show (1998)

CHAPTER 11
Sports

You know how a game serves us, it's a definite social purpose.

— Bartholomew,
Rollerball (1975)

Are you not entertained? Is this not why you are here?

— Maximus,
Gladiator (2000)

Chapter 11. Sports

Recommended Films

Rollerball (Norman Jewison 1975)
Gladiator (Ridley Scott 2000)

Media Models

The Meme, The Spectacle, The Hyperreal

Chapter Summary

Carl Sagan explains why the roots of football
and competitive team sports reside in
humanity's hunter-gatherer past.

Douglas Kellner illustrates the role of the media spectacle
in sports and Michael Jordan's global fame as
a basketball legend and advertising icon.

Monday-Night Hunters

from *Billions and Billions*

— Carl Sagan

We can't help ourselves. On Sunday afternoons and Monday nights in the fall of each year, we abandon everything to watch small moving images of 22 men — running into one another, falling down, picking themselves up, and kicking an elongated object made from the skin of an animal. Every now and then, both the players and the sedentary spectators are moved to rapture or despair by the progress of the play. All over America, people (almost exclusively men), transfixed before glass screens, cheer or mutter in unison. Put this way, it sounds stupid. But once you get the hang of it, it's hard to resist, and I speak from experience.

Athletes run, jump, hit, slide, throw, kick, tackle — and there's a thrill in seeing humans do it so well. They wrestle each other to the ground. They're keen on grabbing or clubbing or kicking a fast-moving brown or white thing. In some games, they try to herd the thing toward what's called a "goal"; in other games, the players run away and then return "home." Teamwork is almost everything, and we admire how the parts fit together to make a jubilant whole.

But these are not the skills by which most of us earn our daily bread. Why should we feel compelled to watch people run or hit? Why is this need transcultural? (Ancient Egyptians, Persians, Greeks, Romans, Mayans, and Aztecs also played ball. Polo is Tibetan.)

There are sports stars who make 50 times the annual salary of the President; some who are themselves, after retirement, elected to high office. They are national heroes. Why, exactly? There is something here transcending the diversity of political, social, and economic systems. Something ancient is calling.

Most major sports are associated with a nation or a city, and they carry with them elements of patriotism and civic pride. Our team represents *us* — where we live, our people — against those other guys, from some different place, populated by unfamiliar, maybe hostile people. (True, most of "our" players are not *really* from here. They're mercenaries and with clear conscience regularly defect from opposing cities for suitable emolument: A Pittsburgh Pirate is reformed into a California Angel; a San Diego Padre is raised to a St. Louis Cardinal; a Golden State Warrior is crowned a Sacramento King. Occasionally, a whole team picks up and migrates to another city.)

Competitive sports are symbolic conflicts, thinly disguised. This is hardly a new insight. The Cherokees called their ancient form of lacrosse "the little brother of war." Or here is Max Rafferty, former California Superintendent of Public Instruction, who, after denouncing critics of college football as "kooks, crumbums, commies, hairy loudmouthed beatniks," goes on to state, "Football players … possess a clear, bright, fighting spirit which is America itself." (That's worth mulling over.) An often-quoted sentiment of the late professional football coach Vince Lombardi is that the only thing that counts is winning. Former Washington Redskins' coach George Allen put it this way: "Losing is like death."

Indeed, we talk of winning and losing a war as naturally as we do of winning and losing a game. In a televised U.S. Army recruitment ad, we see the aftermath of an armored warfare exercise in which one tank destroys another; in the tag line, the victorious tank commander says, "When we win, the whole team wins — not one person." The connection between sports and combat is made quite clear. Sports fans (the word is short for "fanatics") have been known to commit assault and battery and sometimes murder, when taunted about a losing team; or when prevented from cheering on a winning team; or when they feel an injustice has been committed by the referees.

The British Prime Minister was obliged in 1985 to denounce the rowdy, drunken behavior of British soccer fans

becomes clear. (When there is a succession of losing seasons, fan loyalties tend to drift elsewhere.) What we are looking for is victory without effort. We want to be swept up into something like a small, safe, successful war.

In 1996, Mahmoud Abdul-Rauf, then a guard for the Denver Nuggets, was suspended by the National Basketball Association. Why? Because Abdul-Rauf refused to stand for the compulsory playing of the National Anthem. The American flag represented to him a "symbol of oppression" offensive to his Muslim beliefs. Most other players, while not sharing Abdul-Rauf's beliefs, supported

---

Team sports are not just stylized echoes of ancient wars. They also satisfy an almost-forgotten craving for the hunt. Since our passions for sports run so deep and are so broadly distributed, they are likely to be hardwired into us—not in our brains but in our genes.

---

who attacked an Italian contingent for having the effrontery to root for their own team. Dozens were killed when the stands collapsed. In 1969, after three hard-fought soccer games, Salvadoran tanks crossed the Honduran border, and Salvadoran bombers attacked Honduran ports and military bases. In this "Soccer War," the casualties numbered in the thousands.

Afghan tribesmen played polo with the severed heads of former adversaries. And 600 years ago, in what is now Mexico City, there was a ball court where gorgeously attired nobles watched uniformed teams compete. The captain of the losing team was beheaded, and the skulls of earlier losing captains were displayed on racks — an inducement possibly even more compelling than winning one for the Gipper.

Suppose you're idly flipping the dial on your television set, and you come upon some competition in which you have no particular emotional investment — say off-season volleyball between Myanmar and Thailand. How do you decide which team to root for? But wait a minute: Why root for either? Why not just enjoy the game? Most of us have trouble with this detached posture. We want to take part in the contest, to feel ourselves a member of a team. The feeling simply sweeps us away, and there we are rooting, "Go, Myanmar!" Initially our loyalties may oscillate, first urging on one team and then the other. Sometimes we root for the underdog. Other times, shamefully, we even switch our allegiance from loser to winner as the outcome

his right to express them. Harvey Araton, a distinguished sports writer for the *New York Times,* was puzzled. Playing the anthem at a sporting event "is, let's face it, a tradition that is absolutely idiotic in today's world," he explains, "as opposed to when it began, before baseball games during World War II. Nobody goes to a sporting event to make an expression of patriotism." On the contrary, I would argue that a kind of patrotism and nationalism is very much what sporting events are about.[1]

The earliest known organized athletic events date back 3,500 years to preclassical Greece. During the original Olympic Games, an armistice put all wars among Greek city-states on hold. The games were more important than the wars. The men performed nude: No women spectators were allowed. By the eighth century B.C., the Olympic Games consisted of running (*lots* of running), jumping, throwing things (including javelins), and wrestling (sometimes to the death). While none of these events was a team sport, they are clearly central to modern team sports.

They were also central to low-technology hunting. Hunting is traditionally considered a sport, as long as you don't eat what you catch — a proviso much easier for the rich to comply with than the poor. From the earliest pharaohs, hunting has been associated with military aristocracies. Oscar Wilde's aphorism about English fox hunting,

---

1 The crisis was resolved when Mr. Abdul-Rauf agreed to stand during the anthem, but pray instead of sing.

"the unspeakable in full pursuit of the uneatable," makes a similar dual point. The forerunners of football, soccer, hockey, and kindred sports were disdainfully called "rabble games," recognized as substitutes for hunting — because young men who worked for a living were barred from the hunt.

The weapons of the earliest wars must have been hunting implements. Team sports are not just stylized echoes of ancient wars. They also satisfy an almost-forgotten craving for the hunt. Since our passions for sports run so deep and are so broadly distributed, they are likely to be hardwired into us — not in our brains but in our genes. The 10,000 years since the invention of agriculture is not nearly enough time for such predispositions to have evolved away and disappeared. If we want to understand them, we must go much further back.

The human species is hundreds of thousands of years old (the human family several millions of years old). We have led a sedentary existence — based on farming and domestication of animals — for only the last 3 percent of that period, during which is all our recorded history. In the first 97 percent of our tenure on Earth, almost everything that is characteristically human came into being. So a little arithmetic about our history suggests we can learn something about those times from the few surviving hunter-gatherer communities uncorrupted by civilization.

—

We wander. With our little ones and all our belongings on our backs, we wander — following the game, seeking the water holes. We set up camp for a time, then move on. In providing food for the group, the men mainly hunt, the women mainly gather. Meat and potatoes. A typical itinerant band, mainly an extended family of relatives and in-laws, numbers a few dozen; although annually many hundreds of us, with the same language and culture, gather — for religious ceremonies, to trade, to arrange marriages, to tell stories. There are many stories about the hunt.

I'm focusing here on the hunters, who are men. But the women have significant social, economic, and cultural power. They gather the essential staples — nuts, fruits, tubers, roots — as well as medicinal herbs, hunt small animals, and provide strategic intelligence on large animal movements. Men do some gathering as well, and considerable "housework" (even though there are no houses). But hunting — only for food, never for sport — is the lifelong occupation of every able-bodied male.

Preadolescent boys stalk birds and small mammals with bows and arrows. By adulthood they have become experts in weapons procurement; in stalking, killing, and butchering the prey; and in carrying the cuts of meat back to camp. The first successful kill of a large mammal marks a young man's coming of age. In his initiation, ceremonial incisions are made on his chest or arms and an herb is rubbed into the cuts so that, when healed, a patterned tattoo results. It's like campaign ribbons — one look at his chest, and you know something of his combat experience.

From a jumble of hoofprints, we can accurately tell how many animals passed; the specks, sexes, and ages; whether any are lame; how long ago they passed; how far away they are. Some young animals can be caught by open-field tackles; others with slingshots or boomerangs, or just by throwing rocks accurately and hard. Animals that have not yet learned to fear men can be approached boldly and clubbed to death. At greater distances, for warier prey, we hurl spears or shoot poisoned arrows. Sometimes we're lucky and, by a skillful rush, drive a herd of animals into an ambush or off a cliff.

Teamwork among the hunters is essential. If we are not to frighten the quarry, we must communicate by sign language. For the same reason, we need to have our emotions under control; both fear and exultation are dangerous. We are ambivalent about the prey. We respect the animals, recognize our kinship, identify with them. But if we reflect too closely on their intelligence or devotion to their young, if we feel pity for them, if we too deeply recognize them as relatives, our dedication to the hunt will slacken; we will bring home less food, and again our band may be endangered. We are obliged to put an emotional distance between us and them.

—

So contemplate this: For millions of years, our male ancestors are scampering about, throwing rocks at pigeons, running after baby antelopes and wrestling them to the ground, forming a single line of shouting, running hunters and trying to terrify a herd of startled warthogs upwind. Imagine that their lives depend on hunting skills and teamwork. Much of their culture is woven on the loom of the hunt. Good hunters are also good warriors. Then, after a long while — a few thousand centuries, say — a natural predisposition for both hunting and teamwork will inhabit many newborn boys. Why? Because incompetent or unenthusiastic hunters leave fewer offspring. I don't think how to chip a spearpoint out of stone or how to feather an arrow is in our genes. That's taught or figured out. But a zest for the chase — I bet that *is* hardwired. Natural selection helped mold our ancestors into superb hunters.

The clearest evidence of the success of the hunter-gatherer lifestyle is the simple fact that it extended to six

---

I worry that Monday-night football is insufficient outlet for the modern hunter, decked out in his overalls or jeans or three-piece suit.

---

continents and lasted millions of years (to say nothing of the hunting proclivities of nonhuman primates). Those big numbers speak profoundly. After 10,000 generations in which the killing of animals was our hedge against starvation, those inclinations must still be in us. We hunger to put them to use, even vicariously. Team sports provide one way.

Some part of our beings longs to join a small band of brothers on a daring and intrepid quest. We can even see this in role-playing and computer games popular with prepubescent and adolescent boys. The traditional manly virtues — taciturnity, resourcefulness, modesty; accuracy consistency; deep knowledge of animals, teamwork, love of the outdoors — were all adaptive behavior in hunter-gatherer times. We still admire these traits, although we've almost forgotten why.

Besides sports, there are few outlets available. In our adolescent males, we can still recognize the young hunter, the aspirant warrior — leaping across apartment rooftops; riding, helmetless, on a motorcycle; making trouble for the winning team at a postgame celebration. In the absence of a steadying hand, those old instincts may go a little askew (although our murder rate is about the same as among the surviving hunter-gatherers). We try to ensure that any residual zest for killing does not spill over onto humans. We don't always succeed.

I think of how powerful those hunting instincts are, and I worry. I worry that Monday-night football is insufficient outlet for the modern hunter, decked out in his overalls or jeans or three-piece suit. I think of that ancient legacy about not expressing our feelings, about keeping an emotional distance from those we kill, and it takes some of the fun out of the game.

Hunter-gatherers generally posed no danger to themselves: because their economies tended to be healthy (many

had more free time than we do); because, as nomads, they had few possessions, almost no theft and little envy; because greed and arrogance were considered not only social evils but also pretty close to mental illnesses; because women had real political power and tended to be a stabilizing and mitigating influence before the boys started going for their poisoned arrows; and because, when serious crimes were committed — murder, say — the band collectively rendered judgment and punishment. Many hunter-gatherers organized egalitarian democracies. They had no chiefs. There was no political corporate hierarchy to dream of climbing. There was no one to revolt against.

So, if we're stranded a few hundred centuries from when we long to be — if (through no fault of our own) we find ourselves, in an age of environmental pollution, social hierarchy, economic inequality, nuclear weapons, and declining prospects, with Pleistocene emotions but without Pleistocene social safeguards — perhaps we can be excused for a little Monday-night football.

The Sports Spectacle, Michael Jordan, and Nike*

from *Media Spectacle*

— Douglas Kellner

ichael Jordan is widely acclaimed as the greatest athlete who ever lived, named "Athlete of the Century" by the TV network ESPN. Yet he is also a major media spectacle on a global scale, combining his athletic prowess with skill as an endorser of global commodities and as a self-promoter, which has enabled him to become a commodity superstar and celebrity of the first rank. In Michael Jordan, globalization, commodification, sports, entertainment, and media come together to produce a figure who serves as an emblematic totem of athletic achievement, business success, and celebrity in the contemporary era. His sensational basketball prowess has made him one of the most successful African American sports figures and businessmen, combining spectacles of race, sports glory, and business success. Yet Jordan's participation in a series of scandals and periods of bad press, mixed with his usually laudatory media presentation, captures the contradictions of spectacle culture, illustrating that those who live by media spectacle can also be brought down by its cruel omnipresent power and eye of surveillance.

As the millennium came to a close, Jordan reigned as one of the most popular and widely known sports icons throughout the world. The announcement of his retirement from basketball in January 1999 after leading the Chicago Bulls to six NBA championships unleashed unparalleled hyperbole describing his superlative athletic accomplishments. In China, the Beijing *Morning Post* ran a front-page story entitled "Flying Man Jordan is Coming Back to Earth," and in Bosnia Jordan's statement declaring his retirement was the lead story on the evening TV news, pushing aside the war in Kosovo.[1] An icon of global popularity, Jordan is "a kind of new world prince," in the

---

* Earlier versions of my Michael Jordan study have appeared as "Sports, media culture, and race — some reflections on Michael Jordan," *Sociology of Sports Journal,* 13 (1996): 458–67, and "The sports spectacle, Michael Jordan and Nike: Unholy alliance?" in Andrews, D. (ed.), *Michael Jordan, Inc. Corporate Sport, Media Culture, and Late Modern America*, Albany, NY: State University of New York Press, 2001, pp. 37–64. Thanks to David Andrews for providing material and comments that have helped with the production of this study, as well as to Richard Kahn for helpful critical comments and suggestions.

1   On the China and Bosnia references, see Dan McGraw and Mike Tharp, "Going out on top" (*US News and World Report,* January 25, 1999: 55). Summing up Jordan's achievements, Jerry Crowe writes: "His resume includes five most-valuable-player awards, 12 All-Star appearances, two Olympic gold medals and a worldwide popularity that filled arenas and boosted the stock of the companies with which he was affiliated" (*Los Angeles Times,* January 13, 1999: D1). In addition, Jordan garnered six NBA championship rings, ten NBA scoring titles (a record), a 31.5 regular-season scoring average (best of all times), a record sixty-three points in a playoff game, 5,987 career playoff points (best all-time), and made the game-winning shot a record twenty-six times during his NBA career. Tributes were numerous: Indiana coach Bob Knight, who mentored the budding superstar in the 1984 Los Angeles Olympics, called Jordan "the greatest basketball player ever … the best player involved in a team sport of any kind"; coach Pat Riley of the Miami Heat described him as "the greatest influence that sports has ever had"; Jerry West, former NBA superstar and executive vice president of the Los Angeles Lakers, labeled Jordan "the modern day Babe Ruth"; and Chicago Bulls Chairman Jerry Reinsdorf enthused: "Michael is simply the best player who ever put on a basketball uniform. He has defined

---

words of Pulitzer prize-winning author David Halberstam, who has published a biography of the basketball legend (1999): "You hear time and again about people being in Borneo or somewhere and coming across a kid in a tattered Michael Jordan T-shirt. He's the most famous American in the world."[2]

Not only has Jordan been acclaimed as a global superstar, he is also frequently characterized in terms of deity. The Boston Celtics great Larry Bird marveled that he had encountered "God disguised as Michael Jordan" after Jordan scored sixty-three points against the Celtics in a 1986 playoff game. Jason Williams of the New Jersey Nets sanctified him as "Jesus in tennis shoes" and many referred to him as a "Black Jesus." At a 1992 Olympic press conference, Jordan was embarrassed to be asked if he were a "god" (LeFeber 1999: 15) and *France Soir* headlined: "Michael Jordan in France. That's better than the Pope. It's God in person." (cited in Halberstam 1999: 4).

Jordan's acclaim and popularity results in part because he is a perfect embodiment of the sports spectacle in which media culture uses hi-tech wizardry to magically transform sports into a media extravaganza of the highest order. Images of Jordan's windmill dunking, blazing baseline heroics, and flying through the air to net key shots "thrilled sports spectators throughout the world, as did his controlled fade-away jump shooting and uncanny ability often to bag the decisive game-winning shot in his best years. Moreover, Jordan provides the spectacle of intense competition and the thrills of winning, perhaps *the* US passion play, leading the Chicago Bulls to the NBA Championships during six

of his eight seasons in the 1990s (the two seasons that the Bulls failed to win were during Jordan's quixotic retirement in 1993–95, in which he tried to become a baseball star). Jordan thus embodies the success ethic and the quintessential capitalist ideal of competition and winning.

In addition to being perhaps the greatest basketball player of all time, Jordan is one of the most successfully managed idols and icons of media culture. Parlaying his athletic triumphs into commercial product endorsements, Jordan became the highest paid celebrity advertising figure ever, endorsing a multitude of products for multimillion-dollar fees, promoting his own line of athletic shoes, cologne, and clothing. Jordan also participated in film spectacle, starring with Bugs Bunny in the movie *Space Jam*, (1996) and serving as the subject of a popular Imax film, *Michael Jordan to the Max* (2000), as well as a series of documentaries, now available in a 2002 DVD *Ultimate Jordan.*

Michael Jordan is thus an icon of media spectacle, combining extraordinary athletic achievement, an unrivaled record of success and winning, high entertainment value, and an ability to exploit his image into highly impressive business success. In a commercial culture that bleeds celebrity, product, and image, it is only natural that the sports shoe transnational Nike — as well as many other corporations — would purchase Jordan's star power to promote its products. Accordingly, I argue that the Michael Jordan/Nike connection calls attention to the extent to which media culture is transforming sports into a spectacle that sells the values, products, celebrities, and institutions of the media and consumer society. The Jordan-Nike nexus calls attention to the *sports entertainment colossus* that has become a major feature of media culture in the new millennium. The Nike-Jordan alliance discloses the extent to which contemporary global culture is constituted by image and spectacle and mediated by the institutions of the media, advertising, public relations, and image management. In this chapter I will show how Jordan embodies the increasing commercialization of the sports spectacle as well as its contradictions and problems. The following study will thus use the Nike-Jordan sports spectacle to uncover the central dynamics of contemporary media and consumer culture and the implosion between sports, entertainment, celebrity, and commerce in contemporary global culture.

---

the Bulls, the city and the NBA for more than a decade. He will always represent the state of excellence."

2 Halberstam, quoted in *People* (January 25, 1999: 56). In its front-page story on Jordan's retirement, *USA Today* employed three "greats," five "greatests," one "greatness," two "marvelouses," three "extraordinarys," one "unbelievable," one "unmatched," two "awe-inspirings," two "staggerings," one "superstar," and a hyperhyperbolic "great superstar" (*Sports Illustrated,* January 25, 1999: 32). Television talking heads commenting on Jordan's retirement speculated over whether he would run for president or "compete with Bill Gates in the business arena" (ibid.), while in a completely earnest front-page story the *Chicago Tribune* suggested that Jordan could be an astronaut (cited in *Time,* January 25, 1999: 68). But the winner in the Michael Jordan Retirement Hyperbole Contest is Bill Plaschke: "Hearing that you'll never see Michael Jordan play competitive basketball again is hearing that sunsets have been canceled. That star-filled skies have been revoked. That babies are no longer allowed to smile" (*Los Angeles Times,* January 12, 1999: D1).

Professional sports are one of the major spectacles of media culture. From the original Olympics in Ancient Greece and the chariot races and gladiator fights in Ancient Rome, sports have long been a major site of entertainment and spectacle. Yet contemporary sports are a largely untheorized and neglected aspect of the society of the spectacle whereby sports celebrate and reproduce dominant societal values, products, and corporations in an unholy alliance between sports, commercialism, and media spectacle. Moreover, in the current era, sports articulate spectacles of race and nationalism, celebrity and star power, and transgression and scandal, elevating its icons to godlike status, and then

themselves. Sports players were thus taught to gain recognition and success by hard work and individual skill *and* to be good team players, thus training workers for productive industrial labor.

Crucially, sports celebrated the values of competition and success, and were thus part of the reproduction of the capitalist ethic. Sports helped successive generations of immigrants in the United States to assimilate into US life, teaching them distinctly US values and providing access to success. In the early twentieth century, immigrants took to basketball, football, and baseball, helping to make them increasingly important pastimes. Later, sports became a major field of integration and cultural assimilation of

---

Postindustrial sports, by contrast, merge sports into media spectacle, collapse boundaries between professional achievement and commercialization, and attest to the commodification of all aspects of life in the media and consumer society.

---

sometimes bringing them down into the depths of scandal and disgrace.

Today, sports are a major part of the consumer society whereby individuals learn the values and behavior of a competitive and success-driven society. Sports heroes are among the best paid and wealthiest denizens of the consumer society and thus serve as embodiments of fantasy aspirations to the good life. Sports fans also learn the art of consumption of sports spectacle and inserting themselves into fandom and celebration of sports virtue and achievement. Whereas the activity of participating in sports involves an active engagement in creative practice, spectator sports involve passive consumption of images of the sports spectacle, which mobilizes spectator energies into deification of players and teams and the celebration of the values of competition and winning. Yet there is also an active dimension in fandom, in which sports consumers learn tremendous amounts of folklore, become experts and critics, and actively participate in sports communities.

One of the characteristic features of contemporary postindustrial societies is the extent to which sports have become commercialized and transformed into a spectacle. During the industrial era, actually playing sports was an adjunct to labor and production. Sports helped create strong and skillful bodies for industrial labor and taught individuals both how to play as part of a collective, to fit into a team, and how to display initiative and distinguish

people of color into mainstream US society and the glories of the American dream — for those who played by the rules and distinguished themselves within the system.

Modern sports were organized around the principles of the division of labor and professionalism, celebrating the capitalist values of competition and winning. Sports in the modern era replicated the structure of the workplace, in which both individual initiative and teamwork were necessary, and sports celebrated at once both competing values. Sports became an increasingly important social concern and realm with its own professional ethic, carefully regulated rules, and highly organized corporate structure. Postindustrial sports, by contrast, merge sports into media spectacle, collapse boundaries between professional achievement and commercialization, and attest to the commodification of all aspects of life in the media and consumer society.

Although sports were an important mode of participation in, and assimilation into, modern societies, during the postindustrial era spectator sports have emerged as the correlative to a society that is replacing manual labor with automation and machines, and requires consumption and appropriation of spectacles to reproduce the consumer society. The present-day era also sees the expansion of a service sector and highly differentiated entertainment industry, of which sports are a key part. Thus, significant resources are currently devoted to the augmentation and promotion of the sports spectacle. Athletes such as Michael Jordan accordingly have the potential to amass high salaries from the profits generated by the sports/entertainment colossus, while spectators are taught to idolize icons like Jordan, making them the deities of everyday life.

There are many ways in which contemporary sports are subject to the laws of the spectacle and are becoming totally commercialized, serving to help reproduce the consumer society. For starters, sports are ever more subject to market logic and commodification, with professional athletes

individual accomplishments during a highly entrepreneurial and competitive era of capitalist development, which celebrated individual achievement, distinction, and success.

Football is organized on a mass-production industrial model, which was appropriate to the era of factory production, and which reached its highest stage of development in the first half of the twentieth century. Football is a team sport that exemplifies arduous collective physical labor mated with individual achievement. Although the star running backs, quarterbacks, and touchdown scorers

---

Professional basketball is the ideal TV sport, fast paced, full of action, and resplendent with spectacle. Hard-charging full-court action, balletic shots, and ubiquitous instant replays make basketball the right sport for the era of MTV and ESPN.

---

making millions of dollars. Furthermore, sports events such as basketball games are hypercommodified, with the "Bud player of the game," "Miller Lite genuine moments," the "Reebok half-time report," the "AT&T Time Out," and "Dutch Boy in the Paint," along with ads featuring the star players promoting merchandise. TV networks bid astronomical sums for the rights to broadcast live professional sports events, and major spectacles, such as the Super Bowl and NBA Championship games, command some of the highest advertising rates in television.

Recent years have exhibited a dramatic implosion of the sports spectacle, commerce, and entertainment, with massive salaries and marketing contracts for the superstar players/celebrities. The major media conglomerates are becoming increasingly interested in sports channels and franchises, and the most marketable athletes earn enormous multimillion-dollar salaries. Moreover, sports stars are able to secure even more lucrative marketing deals to endorse products, star in films or TV programs, and even, in the case of Michael Jordan, to promote their own product lines.

Competing with baseball and football as the US sports of choice in the contemporary era, professional basketball has emerged during the Jordan era as the game that best symbolizes the contemporary sports/entertainment colossus. To some extent, the three major US sports encapsulate different periods of socioeconomic development. Baseball represents the challenge to a highly individualist country of uniting individual aspirations and talents with teamwork and spirit. Emerging in the nineteenth century, baseball disciplined individuals to fit into teams, but still rewarded

often get the credit and headlines, it is disciplined collective labor that provides the infrastructure for football accomplishments and victory. Without a strong defense and well-co-ordinated offense, even the most spectacular players cannot function adequately and their team cannot win consistently.

NBA basketball, by contrast, has increasingly featured superstar feats of individual brilliance, especially during the heyday of the Michael Jordan spectacle. Professional basketball is the ideal TV sport, fast paced, full of action, and resplendent with spectacle. Hard-charging full-court action, balletic shots, and ubiquitous instant replays make basketball the right sport for the era of MTV and ESPN. NBA commissioner David Stern remarked in a 2000 Museum of Broadcasting lecture that sports are "the most important programming on television" because they are original, exciting, dramatic, entertaining, and highly compelling. Sports present a primal form of live television with immediacy, action, and drama built into the event. Sports, Stern argued, drove cable penetration, creating the demand for the new technology that allowed it to succeed brilliantly, and in time sports became the United States' major export, the cultural ambassador of choice for US games, heroes, values, and products.

In 1989, the ESPN network began broadcasting sports full-time on cable and soon became a powerhouse. ESPN originally signified Entertainment Sports Programming Network, an instructive abbreviation that called attention to the nexus between sports and entertainment in the age of television. "ESPN" also signaled the way that the sports/

entertainment colossus was programming the nation to become one of sports addicts and to idolize its celebrities, values, and dramas, so as to become networked into a sports/entertainment/consumer society.[3] By the 1980s, ESPN began applying MTV-type techniques to sports events and broadcasting celebrity sports shows, which helped to elevate athletic stars such as Jordan to super-icon status. Initially aimed at a male audience, the network targeted female viewers by adding more entertainment features and women commentators. It also cultivated audiences of color, adding black sportscasters such as Stuart Scott, who combined ethnic street talk and attitude with cutting-edge flashy suits and an idiosyncratic style, as with his signature "Boo-ya!" salutation, which itself became part of the contemporary sports idiom, signaling especially spectacular moves and plays.

Basketball is a high-speed game that moves rapidly down the court, and television made a spectacle of velocity, totally appropriate for an ever faster-paced society, intensifying motion and action with quick cuts, close-ups, and zooms. Helping to speed up the game for television,

shorts. Compared with the gladiator-like body armor of football players and the nineteenth-century full-body attire of baseball, basketball presents a mode of male beefcake, especially with TV close-ups capturing the hard and agile bodies of NBA hunks.

Thus, NBA basketball became a powerful media spectacle, and television helped the sport to gain popularity and importance in the 1980s by broadcasting more games and heavily promoting basketball as it became ever more fashionable and attracted a greater and greater following. Completely embodying the fragmentary postmodern aesthetics, razzle-dazzle technical effects, and accelerating pace of today's television, basketball has emerged as a major arena of the spectacle, the ultimate game for the sports/entertainment society. Once a primarily US game, by the 1990s it had become globally popular.

Consequently, although the NBA was once the ne'er-do-well stepchild of the more successful professional baseball and football franchises, in recent years it has become one of the most popular of the US sports industries on a global scale (Andrews 1997; 2002; LeFeber 1999).

Compared with the gladiator-like body armor of football players and the nineteenth-century full-body attire of baseball, basketball presents a mode of male beefcake, especially with TV close-ups capturing the hard and agile bodies of NBA hunks.

---

the NBA instituted a twenty-four-second "shot clock," forcing teams to accelerate the pace of the game. In addition, playbacks highlighted the mechanics of brilliant plays, while the intimacy of television caught the sweat and concentration, anger and exultation, and other moments of physical and emotional intensity. Furthermore, basketball is sexy, showing glistening and well-honed male bodies in a state of semi-undress, clad in skimpy jerseys and

Whereas the NBA fed only thirty-five weekly telecasts to foreign companies in the mid-1980s at the beginning of Jordan's basketball career, by 1996 the roster had swelled to 175 foreign broadcasts in forty languages to 600 million households. By 2000, the NBA was broadcasting to 205 countries in forty-two languages with a total worldwide audience of over 750 million fans.

By 2000, NBA basketball was big business as well as megaspectacle. The average player's salary was over $2.5 million, cumulative NBA player salaries were over $1 billion, and Michael Jordan had made over $40 million in 1999 and cumulatively had collected more than $150 million from Nike over the course of his career (Halberstam 1999: 410, 412).

Many credit Michael Jordan with being one of the chief figures in promoting NBA basketball to become globally popular, recognized and beloved throughout the world. Certainly, Jordan emerged as global basketball's premiere superstar, immediately identifiable everywhere. David

---

3 ABC bought ESPN in 1985, and its official website states that ESPN now "doesn't stand for anything, but the story is this ... When ESPN started in 1979 we were the Entertainment and Sports Programming Network (thus, ESPN). However, the full name was dropped in February 1985 when the company adopted a new corporate name — ESPN, Inc. — and a new logo. We are a subsidiary of ABC, Inc., which is a wholly owned subsidiary of The Walt Disney Co. The Hearst Corporation has a 20 percent interest in ESPN." The connection with Disney and Hearst signifies how sports have become absorbed into the infotainment society and are a crucial part of a globalized entertainment/sports colossus.

Halberstam described him as "the first great athlete of the wired world" (in Coplon 1996: 35), and "arguably the most famous American in the world, more famous in many distant parts of the globe than the President of the United States or any movie or rock star" (Halberstam 1999: 7).

In his book *Michael Jordan and the New Global Capitalism* (1999), Walter LeFeber describes the process whereby Jordan, NBA basketball, and US global corporations such as Nike all attained a global reach, transnationalizing US sports, products, and idols. The globalization of Michael Jordan and Nike was made possible by a global network of cable and satellite television that broadcasts US

The dramatic evolution of the sports spectacle thus has a global dimension, with the major players now becoming international figures, marketed in global sports extravaganzas, advertising campaigns, product promotions, films, websites, and other venue of media culture. As Michael Jordan's highly successful and respected agent, David Falk, puts it: "Michael has transcended sport. He's an international icon" (in Hirschberg 1996: 46).[4] Indeed, in 1996–97, Falk put together deals that netted Jordan a record-breaking $30 million contract for the next season. Moreover, Falk's deals continued the lucrative connections with Nike and other corporations to promote their

---

In sports events, fans become part of something greater than themselves, the participation provides meaning and significance, and a higher communal self, fused with the multitudes of believers and the spirit of joy in triumph and suffering in tribulation.

---

media, sports, and advertising throughout the world, and a global economy that distributes its products, services, sports, and images. The Internet, too, contributed to the globalization of sports and culture and, as we will see later, played an ambiguous role in Michael Jordan's own personal saga.

Sports have previously often promoted nationalism, and the intensification of global sports events through omnipresent media continues to do so, although a phenomenon such as Michael Jordan and the Chicago Bulls helps produce a transnational popular sports culture. Whereas global events like the World Cup or Olympics (which I examined in Chapter 1) clearly generate nationalism and national identities and passions, in the US the major sports of baseball, football, and basketball generally engender competition between cities, and thus more communal identities. While Michael Jordan and the Bulls have given a tremendous boost on the national scale to Chicago pride and identity, and helped promote NBA basketball as a major national sport, on the global level Michael Jordan has more of a universalizing iconic effect as a global popular who represents a fusion of sports culture and starpower, commodity culture, and an Americanized globalization. That is, the Jordan effect and his deification as a global popular makes him an iconic figure of Americana, as do the global circulation of Nike shoes, Chicago Bulls hats or T-shirts, and the proliferation of NBA basketball to different countries.

products to the estimated tune of $40 million. Jordan was also able to introduce his own cologne, Eau de Michael Jordan, and negotiated a contract to star in a hi-tech film, *Space Jam,* which paired him with other NBA superstars, Bugs Bunny, and assorted cartoon characters. Including accompanying product lines, estimates circulated that Jordan could conceivably earn $20 million from his commercial projects (*USA Today*, October 14,1996: 6B), pointing to a growing convergence between the sports spectacle, entertainment, and business.

Moreover, the sports spectacle is at the center of an almost religious fetishism in which sports become a surrogate religion and its stars demigods. For many, sports are the object of ultimate concern (Paul Tillich's definition of religion), providing transcendence from the banality and suffering of everyday life. Sports stars constitute its saints and deities, while sports events often have a religious aura of ritual. Sports fans are like a congregation and their cheers and boos are a form of liturgy. In sports events, fans become part of something greater than themselves, the participation provides meaning and significance, and a higher communal self, fused with the multitudes of believers and the spirit of joy in triumph and suffering in

---

4 On Falk's role in promoting the Jordan spectacle, see Halberstam (1999: 136ff. and *passim*). Following Jordan, basketball players began to be promoted as entertainment stars and were becoming top dog icons of the spectacle and major corporate endorsers.

tribulation. Sports are a break from average everydayness, providing participation in ritual, mystery, and spiritual aura (although, as my discussion is suggesting, sports also celebrate dominant social values such as individuality, winning, teamwork, and, increasingly, commercialism). In the pantheon of sports deity, Michael Jordan is one of the reigning gods, and in the next section I will accordingly engage his iconography and celebrity.

THE SPECTACLE OF MICHAEL JORDAN

Among the spectacles of media culture, Michael Jordan is a pre-eminent figure. As an NBA superstar, Jordan is the very picture of grace, co-ordination, virtuosity, and all-round skill — adeptly marketed to earn a record salary and endorsements. Jordan received $30 million to play for the Chicago Bulls in 1997 (*Time*, July 29, 1996: 61) and $33 million in 1998. He earned over $40 million in endorsements and promotions in 1995, making him the highest paid athlete in the world (*Guardian*, June 11, 1996: 6), and reaped over $45 million in endorsements in 1996, maintaining his position as the world's highest paid athlete. In June 1998, *Fortune* magazine estimated that Jordan had generated over $10 billion during his spectacular professional career, in terms of increased ticket sales, television advertising revenue, increased profits from products endorsed, the exploitation of his name by basketball merchandising, and his own films, businesses, and product lines. Jordan *is* big business and has accelerated the trend toward the implosion of business, entertainment, and sports.

"His Airness," along with "Air Jordan," a popular nickname for "the man that flies," thus epitomizes the postmodern sports spectacle both on the playing field and in advertisements and media spectacles. The Michael Jordan spectacle implodes athletic achievement with commercialization, merging his sports image with corporate products and celebrity superstardom, making Jordan one of the highest paid and most fecund generators of social meaning and capital in the history of media culture. He is the iconic exemplar of the media/sports spectacle, obsession with winning and success, and quest for unimaginable wealth and popularity, which are defining cultural features of the last two decades of the twentieth century into the present.

Jordan first appeared as a rookie with the Chicago Bulls in 1984 and, although he was not yet a fully fledged superstar, his agent signed him to what turned out to be an incredibly influential and lucrative contract with the Nike Corporation. Nike is the Greek personification of victory, represented as a figure with wings who could run and fly at great speed — a mythological image made to order for a shoe company and Michael Jordan. A constant companion of Athena, Nike was also connected in Greek mythology with intelligence. Curiously, the US military had earlier, in the 1950s, appropriated the Nike symbol for a guided missile system, and the World Wide Web is full of pages celebrating the missile system, shut down by the SALT Treaties, as well as Nike shoe pages.

The Nike figure's connotations thus combine spirituality, speed, intelligence, and power in a potent figure. Initially, the Nike Corporation assimilated the Nike winged victory symbol from Greek mythology with images of a basketball flanked with wings, presenting an almost angelic symbol of sports mixed with divinity. Eventually, the Nike symbol mutated into its famous "swoosh," and presented a more abstract image of the wing, a distinctive corporate logo that became instantly associated with the Nike brand. In an era of branding, in which name and image are all-important, Nike thus possessed an extremely resonant media image, and bringing in Michael Jordan and other superstar athletes to enrich the symbolism of the Nike spectacle and to attract audiences to its products was a winning combination in the commodity spectacle and the competition to sell shoes and athletic ware.

Hence, the Michael Jordan mythology was articulated with a Nike figure that connoted speed, intelligence, and victory, as well as the military symbolism of the guided missile system, an apt metaphor for Jordan's basketball heroics. With Jordan and a new marketing agency, Weiden & Kennedy, the Air Jordan product line and Nike's "swoosh" symbol became icons of US and then global culture. At the same time, Michael Jordan became an authentic American hero, generally acknowledged as one of the greatest

> The Nike symbol mutated into its famous "swoosh," and presented a more abstract image of the wing, a distinctive corporate logo that became instantly associated with the Nike brand.

basketball players of all time, one of the most popular and well-known celebrities of media culture, and, since 1988, the sports celebrity most desired to market corporate products. During the era of Nike-Jordan's ascendancy, cable and satellite television and the aggressive promotion of the NBA by its commissioner, David Stern, increased tremendously the visibility and popularity of professional basketball. The Jordan-Nike era had arrived.

There seemed to be nothing that Jordan could not do on the basketball court. His slam-dunk is legendary and he seems to defy gravity as he flies through the air toward the Holy Grail of the basket. His "hang-time" is fabled and as C.H. Cole (1996) points out, designations such as "Rare Air" "render him extraordinary ... and even godlike," a figure of transcendence. Nike developed a product line of Air Jordan sports shoes around the flying mythology, and a 1989 NBA Entertainment documentary entitled *Michael Jordan: Come Fly with Me* describes the player as "the man who was truly destined to fly," and celebrates him as the very embodiment of professional excellence, morality, and US values. The published collection of photographs of Michael Jordan as sports icon, media celebrity, and down-home good guy, entitled *Rare Air*, highlights the efficacy of the Michael Jordan publicity machine in fine-tuning his image as a transcendent figure, a god of media culture.

Sports writers, too, participate in the canonization of Michael Jordan, regularly describing him as "the best player ever," "the greatest basketball player who has ever lived," and even the "greatest athlete of all time." The phrase "there is nothing he cannot do" is recurrently used to inscribe Jordan's sign value as superstar sports deity, and in Nike ads that star Jordan the corporate logo "Just Do It" signifies that you, too, can be like Michael and do what you want to do. The Gatorade "Be Like Mike" commercial also highlights Jordan's status as a role model and embodiment of iconic values and high aspiration.

Not surprisingly, McDonald's hired Jordan to promote its wares and named a McJordan burger after him. Once, after an NBA Championship game, a McDonald's advertising crew was on hand to film a commercial. A voice-over said, "Michael, you've just won your third straight NBA Championship. Are you hungry for a fourth?" The sweating and smiling Jordan answered, "I'm hungry for a Big Mac" (cited in LeFeber 1999: 117–18). Film footage from the game was added and McDonald's had an ad ready to circulate on the cable and satellite networks within 24 hours.

There have been, to be sure, some glitches in the Michael Jordan success story. After dropping out of professional basketball to pursue a baseball career,[5] Jordan returned to the Chicago Bulls in 1995 and led the team to three straight NBA Championships. In the process, he reinvented himself as a superstar player, moving from his patented flying air shots to become one of the great jump shot scorers of all time. In the words of one analyst:

> At 33, Jordan is a half-step slower than he once was. He is more beholden to gravity, less nuclear in his liftoff. He can still take wing and be *Air* when he needs to, still shift into turbo and batter the rim, but he chooses his spots now, waits for clear paths. He no longer hurls himself into walls of elbows and forearms, giving the other side's behemoths free shots at his kidneys. He has traded risk for feel, nerve for guile, spectacle for efficiency ... and because he is Jordan, even his efficiency can seem spectacular.
>
> (Coplon 1996: 37).

During the 1996–98 seasons, the Bulls emerged as a media culture spectacle of the highest order, setting records for attendance and winning regular season games and three straight NBA Championships (Halberstam 1999). With Jordan, bad guy extraordinary Dennis Rodman, all-round star Scottie Pippen, and Zen-inspired coach Phil Jackson, the Bulls earned unparalleled media attention and adulation. The Jordan spectacle helped make NBA basketball globally popular and Michael Jordan a superstar of extraordinary resonance. Jordan henceforth was identified with ardent competition and winning, embodying the values of hard drive, success, and coming out on top; his shots repeatedly won key games and he became fabled for the magnitude of his competitiveness and drive to win.

Thus, Michael Jordan is both a great player and represents a highly successful marketing phenomenon,

---

5   For the complex events that led Jordan to this seemingly bizarre decision, see Smith (1995) and Halberstam (1999). During 1993, Jordan's gambling habits were criticized and increasingly the subject of inquiry, and when his father was mysteriously murdered there were speculations that the murder was related to gambling debts. The NBA and media intensified its scrutiny of Jordan, and he abruptly quit basketball to pursue a quixotic and failed minor-league baseball career, returning to professional basketball 18 months later to achieve his greatest athletic triumphs.

which draws attention to the construction of the media/ sports spectacle by corporations, public relations, and the techniques of advertising. Just as Jordan marketed Nike, Wheaties, and other products, so did these corporations help produce the Jordan image and spectacle. Likewise, Jordan was used to market the NBA and in turn its publicity machine and success helped promote Jordan.

In the sports/entertainment colossus, a vast marketing apparatus of television, radio, magazines, and other media help to promote and manufacture the stars of sports and entertainment, attesting to an implosion between media and sports culture, and thus sports and commerce. Indeed, Jordan himself is an entire sports franchise with special pitches geared toward kids [i.e., an 800 (free) phone number for ordering Nikes that Jordan gives them "permission" to call], toward urban teens, and targeting young adults, in this case with his fragrance products. And as Cole (1996) has documented, Jordan was part of a Nike PLAY program ("Participate in the Lives of America's Youth"), designed to present a positive corporate image and promote its products to a youth audience. Then, in 1999, he began his own Jordan Fundamentals Grant Program, to provide funds to schools with outstanding youth programs.

Michael Jordan is thus a dazzling sports spectacle, who promotes both commercial sports and the products of the corporations that sell their goods to sports audiences. His distinctive image is often noted, and Jordan's look and style are truly striking. His shaved head, extremely long shorts, and short socks are often cited as defining features, which are highlighted in a Spike Lee Nike ad that, in a brilliant effort to get the Nike message across, repeatedly insists, *"It's gotta be the shoes!"* (i.e., that make Jordan the greatest). In addition, his wrist band, jersey number 23, and tongue wagging and hanging as he concentrates on a play are all distinctive of the Jordan trademark image. In fact, Jordan is so handsome that he has often been employed as a model, and his good looks and superstar status have won him countless advertising endorsements for products such as Nike, McDonald's, Gatorade, Coca Cola, Wheaties, Haines shorts, and numerous others. A Gatorade ad tells the audience to "Be like Mike," establishing Jordan as a role model, as the very icon of excellence and aspiration. In anti-drug ads, Jordan tells the nation to, "Just say no," to avoid drugs, to do the right thing, and to be all you can be, mobilizing the very stereotypes of the conservative postindustrial United States in one figure. Michael Jordan is also the paradigmatic figure of the "hard body" (Jeffords

1994), which was the ideal male image of the Reaganite 1980s, a model of the powerful bodies needed to resurrect US power after the flabbiness of the 1960s and 1970s.

Jordan is a fashion spectacle as well, nattily dressed in expensive clothes, drenched in his own cologne, and exhibiting the trademark well-oiled and shiny bald head. He is a connoisseur of fine wine and gourmet food and an upscale lifestyle. He is also willing to promote almost anything from sporting gear to underwear. As such, he was the perfect sports icon to market Nike shoes, combining tremendous athletic ability with a well-honed fashion image. Thus unfolded the fateful marriage of Michael Jordan and Nike, which I will interrogate after an analysis of the contradictory nexus between Jordan, race, and the sports spectacle.

CHAPTER 12
Games and Virtual Reality

*The world of games is in a kind of a trance.
People are programmed to accept so little,
but the possibilities are so great.*

— Allegra Geller,
eXistenZ (1999)

*All that is visible must grow beyond itself,
and extend into the realm of the invisible.*

— Dumont,
TRON (1982)

Chapter 12. Games and Virtual Reality

Recommended Films

eXistenZ (David Cronenberg 1999)
TRON (Steve Lisberger 1982)

Media Models

The Network, The Hyperreal

Chapter Summary

Edward Castronova suggests that virtual reality and
video games represent a "fun revolution" that
could transform society in the "real world."

"Dreams Fashioned in Silicon" and "The Fun Revolution"

from *Exodus to the Virtual World*

— Edward Castronova

THE HOLODECK IS HERE

A holodeck is a perfect simulation room, a science fiction fantasy from the TV show *Star Trek: The Next Generation*. As conceived there, the holodeck allows users to enter into a deeply accurate simulation of any environment, from the Wild West to the surface of Pluto. Moreover, the holodeck can be populated with simulated people who are just as realistic as their virtual environments. On the TV show, these holodecks are for training and occasional entertainment: Characters use them to practice Klingon fighting moves, or to solve Agatha Christie mysteries. According to the scripts, when the training (and fun) is over, the real people go back to their "real" work of maintaining and operating a starship. The writers, no doubt catering to their sense of what the audience expects, apparently believe that if a holodeck existed, it would be used like a super-duper but serious TV: Mostly for mild entertainment, but occasionally for working on mental and physical skills; the same mix of sitcoms, training videos, and exercise programs, but super-duper.

As an economist, I have always been puzzled by this mild conception of the holodeck's effect on the Star Trek crew. Economists generally argue that people will pursue as long as possible activities that please them. If Activity A is more pleasant than Activity B, but has the same cost in terms of money and time, Activity A will be chosen first. A person only switches to Activity B when Activity A gets too boring or too expensive. This is the basic economic theory of time allocation, described first by Nobel Laureate Gary

Becker almost a half century ago and since confirmed by reams of empirical evidence. And according to this theory, the crew's use of the holodeck is going to be driven by how entertaining the holodeck is, relative to other activities, and how expensive it is to use. It seems to me that a holodeck, on the Starship *Enterprise* or anywhere else, would be an almost infinitely entertaining toy. Remember, it is said to be programmable to produce *any scene desired*, including other people. The holodeck seems available to every crew member, free of charge. An infinitely pleasing toy, for free. Considering such an object, the question is not why people spend time with it, but rather why people spend time doing anything else. Why isn't every single crewmember in the holodeck, all the time? If the technology truly existed as described, economics clearly predicts that all crew members would program the holodeck to produce their most desired fantasy existence, and then disappear into it.

But if all crew members are in the holodeck, no one will be running the ship. If you put a holodeck on every starship, no starship would ever report back to base; indeed, *no starship would do anything at all*.

Now imagine what the world would look like if someone invented and marketed a holodeck not for starships, but for every home. This scenario has moved from the realm of nerdy speculation to that of practical policy. A new technology has emerged, in just the last five years, that is shockingly close to a holodeck. Already today, a person with a reasonably well-equipped personal computer and an Internet connection can disappear for hours and hours into vast realms of fantasy. These computer generated virtual worlds are unquestionably the holodeck's predecessor. This technology will draw in millions and millions and millions of people, and many of them will indeed dramatically reduce the amount of time they spend doing things in the real world. These developments, which will take place over the next one or two generations, will probably not bring our "starships" to a grinding halt, but they will alter patterns of daily life in a significant way.

This technology is known as *virtual worlds* (or more precisely, *synthetic worlds*): massive multiuser online environments where millions of people live out a collective fantasy existence.[1] It is not hard to do. Right now, you could put down this book, go to your local store, and buy *Lord of the Rings Online* by the game development company Turbine, Inc. After setting up the software (including agreeing to a monthly fee of about $10 to $15), the character you've created, an *avatar*, will enter a synthetic rendition of J.R.R. Tolkien's Middle Earth. Looking around, you'll see a beautiful landscape with trees, grass, birds, rabbits, lakes, and little cottages. You'll also see lots of other characters, some being run by the system's artificial intelligence engines, others by people just like you. Press the "Enter" key and type a sentence; what you wrote is transmitted to everyone else in your vicinity just as if you were in a crowded room and had spoken the sentence aloud. The people in the world will now react to you as well, asking you what you meant, what you want, where you are going. That quickly, you are virtual worlding. You've gone off to the virtual frontier.[2]

> People who own gold pieces and other forms of play money inside virtual worlds are selling them for real money, and the amount of real money being used in this way adds up to several hundred million dollars per year. This trade too is growing exponentially.

Access to these experiences is growing rapidly. *World of Warcraft*, by Blizzard Entertainment, launched in 2004 and quickly acquired one million subscribers, a first for a North American game. By 2007, the subscriber base was eight million. *Lineage*, by NCSoft, had over two million subscribers. The teen hangout world *Gaia Online*, by Gaia Interactive, does not charge a subscription fee and had grown from nothing to over two million unique monthly logins in just one year. The social world *Second Life* boasted several hundred thousand registered accounts in early 2006; by mid-2007 it had over five million. At these growth rates, a currently conservative estimate of 30 million synthetic world users will be quite low by early 2008. Already, the use of holodeck-like systems is spreading in the population. That may not seem very serious at first, or likely to affect how any of the *rest* of us live. But the fact is, so many people are becoming immersed in these synthetic environments, and spending so much time and energy there, that the combined effect is like the emergence of a new country. People buy and sell things in these worlds, and the amount of stuff being bought and sold is enormous.[3] Moreover, each virtual world spawns a large and robust exchange rate market where people trade the currency of the game — gold pieces, usually — for real dollars. Economically, that's just an ordinary foreign exchange market. What's shocking is that this market is not only robust and stable, but huge. It is worth restating: people who own gold pieces and other forms of play money inside virtual worlds are selling them for real money, and the amount of real money being used in this way adds up to several hundred million dollars per year. This trade too is growing exponentially. Whether or not this development seems interesting or "real" or fun to us on the outside, the fact, is, it is there. It is getting bigger and bigger. At some scale, at some size, it begins to have effects on other parts of the economy. When the number of virtual-world users

---

1   While most scholars and pundits in this area use "virtual world," "synthetic world" more clearly captures what these places are: worlds inside computers, completely designed and constructed by human beings. Are they "virtual"? It's hard to say, because the word "virtual" has such an ambiguous meaning. Are they "synthetic," that is, crafted, constructed, artificial? Absolutely. Nonetheless, I will use the terms interchangeably. Also, as yet there's no generally accepted term for people who spend a lot of time in these places; we might call them *synthrims* for "synthetic pilgrims." Other suggestions have been "players" (since most are playing a game), "deckers" (from the holodeck), "gaters" (from the concept of dimensional gates), or "vitizens."

2   This is not the place for an exhaustive introduction to synthetic worlds and how they operate. For that, readers should refer to

my first book, *Synthetic Worlds*. Even better: Readers who want to understand this phenomenon should just play. Practical virtual reality has to be experienced in order to be appreciated.

3   Edward Castronova, "On Virtual Economies," *Game Studies* 3(2) (2003), http://www.gamestudies.org/0302/castronova/.

expands to one hundred million or two hundred million or one billion, the economic activity generated within and around these games will be big enough that everyone will have to pay attention. Whether you play these games or not, gold pieces will mean something to you.

Despite the fact that the virtual world and the real world intersect with and impact one another, it seems best to use language that points out the contrasts: Worlds that are created completely by design and live only within computers are *synthetic*, and the world of earth, air, fire, water, and blood that we've inherited from our forebears is *real*. These are useful labels for two domains that are equally significant but distinct. I sense that these two domains are in competition with one another. An exodus is under way. Time and attention are migrating from the real world into the virtual world. The exodus will strengthen I believe. Improvements in technology will make virtual worlds into veritable dreamlands. They will be more fun, for more people. Simple economic theory predicts that in

The policy changes I have predicted will begin to hit home within a generation, but there's little awareness of them today. Current political debates make no mention of virtual worlds and show little or no understanding of what video games in general are about to do to society. It is fair to say that the policy issues relating to video games today can be summarized in one sentence: "Video games are harmful to children." This argument has become the premise for numerous pieces of legislation around the globe. The perceptual vapidity that lies behind such a sentence reveals how far we must go to get the world of policymakers up to speed with the emergence of the new technology. First we have to make them understand that video games raise far greater issues than they realize. Then we have to make them understand that virtual worlds raise even bigger issues. If only the core issue were

---

Improvements in technology will make virtual worlds into veritable dreamlands. They will be more fun, for more people. Simple economic theory predicts that in this competition, the real world is going to lose.

---

this competition, the real world is going to lose. This loss will put pressure on the real world to adapt. The broad outlines of what that adaptation must be are surprising but not hard to see. If it is to survive unchallenged, the real world is going to have to offer experiences similar to those available in virtual worlds. In short, the real world will have to become more fun. A severe shock to business as usual; a revolution.

The changes this "fun revolution" will unleash can already be seen at the level of individuals, those who have become immersed in synthetic worlds. To introduce what these changes might look like, consider a hypothetical story, typical of the people who now negotiate the boundary between the synthetic and the real. Though this probably isn't the story of any actual human being, it does illustrate the kinds of experiences that many actual human beings are already having; it predicts the kinds of experiences that many millions will have in the decades to come.

* * *

whether or not kids should be playing these games — that we could handle. But instead we face a change in the social order. A fair assessment of contemporary politics suggests primarily that our society is really not prepared for what is happening.

That is consistent with the tone of these anti-game legal efforts. I suspect that such efforts are driven by fear of unknown technology, a powerful motivator that seems to be growing in leaps and bounds. This fear is about video games in general; fear of virtual worlds will be even more intense. If the technology of synthetic worlds takes root more rapidly than people become accustomed to it, it will stir up incredible emotions and cause heated debates. If so, contemporary debates about violence in video games will quickly be overshadowed by a much more thorough, and quite possibly bitter, dispute about the immersive worlds as a whole.

Among gamers, I sense a complete and utter dismissal of the concerns voiced by game-regulation advocates. In response to objections to violence, gamers roll their eyes. A similar reaction is given to the sentence "Games are addictive." Gamers generally have no respect whatsoever for such statements. They do not perceive them as fair and well-informed commentary. Rather, they consider anyone who says such a thing thoroughly out of touch — not because gamers are addicted themselves, but because the term "addiction" does not begin to capture the nature of the compulsion many feel toward games and virtual worlds. Consider a sentence like "A mother's love is addictive." You bet it is. No one can get enough of it. Anyone who isn't addicted to mother's love is a fool, or extremely damaged in some way. Not to be addicted to a mother's love is a bad, bad thing. I think these sentiments are similar to those felt by people who have experiences inside virtual worlds that are so rich, so deep, so meaningful that their experiences in the real world pale in comparison. A person who has

---

It will become increasingly difficult to run a classroom or a boardroom in a way that is not fun; no one will pay attention.

---

had the experience of both worlds and found the virtual one so much better *ought* to return. In such a case, our complaints should be levied on the real world, for providing such a poor experience. People who love virtual worlds react to those who don't understand their attraction the way lovers of architecture react to the boors who consider the Cathedral of Rheims "some big old church." In a building like the Cathedral of Rheims, something indescribably sublime pervades the atmosphere. Something ethereal, transcendant, divine. Though intangible, it is real. Most people feel it. Some feel it very, very strongly. Others don't feel it at all. But it is there. A sentence like "Some people are addicted to these big old churches" reveals deep ignorance of a cathedral's impact on a visitor. Virtual worlds are not cathedrals, but they do transport people to another plane. They have a compelling positive effect on visitors, an effect dramatically misunderstood by many of those who have never spent time there.

This disconnect in the assessment of virtual worlds between gamers and everyone else is a concern because of the way the gaming population is growing, and also because the gaming population has universal and immediate access to an alternative social order where the politics pursued by "clueless" outsiders have no representative and

no purchase. If real-world politics turn against the gamers, they will simply leave. Unless we try to stop them. But then regulating access to games would become the cyberspace equivalent of a Berlin Wall: a glaring wound in the social fabric that does nothing but heighten tension and lower well-being so long as it is allowed to fester. Rather than prevent the inmates from escaping, the gamers will argue, make conditions in the jail better.

LONGER-RUN IMPACTS

In the long run, the ascent of virtual worlds will have the effect of a mass migration, impacting both regions. Comparisons of lifestyles in different regions will be unavoidable. Even absent any serious policy debate, the contrasts in lifestyles will change expectations. People on both sides will ask: Why is it this way here and not there?

Leaders of the real world will have to decide whether to respond to these questions. We may simply insist on no change whatsoever. Or we may try to adopt some of what the synthetic worlds have done: Make the economic game fairer, open access to more people, provide meaningful activity for everyone, and so on. Different entities may make different choices. Some companies may rewrite themselves as large-scale virtual worlds, with leveling systems, earnings points, and ad-hoc group dynamics. Others may retain a top-down corporate structure. All we know is that virtual-world users are accustomed to choosing environments based on how much fun they offer. It will become increasingly difficult to run a classroom or a boardroom in a way that is not fun; no one will pay attention.

WHAT ABOUT FAMILIES?

Throughout this book, I have been consistently positive about games, to a fault. I take that stance because I believe a social order focused on fun offers us a better future than the social order under which we suffer now. There is one area, though, where virtual worlds make me worry: the family.

Games and virtual worlds make us happy; they paint the pleasure gloss on our sensations. But the pleasure gloss is not the same thing neurologically as mood. Mood is a longer-run state of mind. Depression, for example, is a mood disorder. You can make a depressed person happy, but this does not change the overall depressive mood she is in.

Our overall emotional temperament — joy, anxiety, depression, rage — depends critically on the nature of our emotional relationships with caregivers in childhood. Weak, disrupted, or pathological ties in the family system cause lifelong emotional and behavioral problems. The social order bears responsibility, too, because its norms and structures have a critical effect on the expectations and behaviors of all family members.

In other words, parenting is really important. Yet research by happiness psychologists has indicated that parenting is not fun. As a parent of two boys in diapers, I understand these findings. The joy in parenting comes in momentary bursts, randomly allocated within a long sequence of dreary admonitions, back-breaking pursuits, and the handling of human waste.

Here then is a very deep conundrum: Happiness requires that all people have loving caregivers in childhood. But when people are doing the caregiving, it is hard for them to be happy. If everyone comes to expect constant fun in their lives, who will give that up to be a good parent?

Things have evolved in virtual worlds that touch on these problems already. There are, for example, characters that seem to serve as replacements for parents. Most players will regularly encounter mentoring figures in these games: older men and women, nonplayer characters (NPCs), whose programming makes them tell players about important quests and send them off to complete them. As a cleric (a kind of priest) in *Dark Age of Camelot*, I would regularly be called back to a huge cathedral in the middle of Camelot City, where I would meet with Lady Fridwulf. She would give my character various quests to complete, and then reward him with increases in skills and new spells. It was something of a regular ritual: Return "home" to the cathedral and check in with the good Lady, who seemed to be closely monitoring my progress. Such an interaction is far from loving care, but for some players it is probably emotionally better than the care they have received from their real-world caregivers. At least it is reliable: The NPCs always do the same thing. And you can trust them: If they say they will give you 20 silver pieces for Gorgol's head, they will indeed give you 20 silver pieces for Gorgol's head. Whereas parents, being human, change their minds and break their promises.

Fun policy has another response, far more troubling. It gets rid of kids. Virtual worlds do not have children in them. In *World of Warcraft*, there are a couple of orphanages with waifs running around in them. The ladies who

run the orphanage even give out little quests from time to time. But the little kids don't. They don't do anything if you talk to them, and you certainly can't play as a child. In most games you have this wide range of options of character types — humans, elves, lizards, cats, demons — and sometimes there's even an "age" slider bar that you can use to make your character old or young. However there are no child types and the "young" side of these age scales doesn't go below 20 or so. However strong our motivation to raise children may be, no virtual world of any measurable success has implemented a system for creating and then taking care of progeny. I have heard the notion of virtual families discussed many times, of course. Designers are well aware of the possibility. But they say it "wouldn't work." That judgment should be read as "there is no way to implement a child-rearing system so that it allows all participants to have fun with it." I do not know of any attempt at family-building within a large-scale virtual world. New characters are not born or raised, they are created by pressing a few buttons. Voilà, a person.

Thus for all my pollyannish proclamations as to the good virtual worlds will do, I remain concerned about their focus on the immediate provision of fun. The most important job many of us have to do in life involves little moment-to-moment happiness but rather a more or less constant flow of work. That work eventually leads to positive hedonic states of satisfaction, contentment, peace. But in the immediate term, it is just work. Without that work, children will have a harder time achieving happiness. Thus a work ethic in parenting — a willingness to do a good job, regardless of whether or not it is immediately fun is essential to the overall project of promoting happiness for everybody. Therefore there's a conflict between fun and satisfaction. Fun policy tells how to make people happy for a moment and how to make those happiness moments continue in an almost never-ending stream. It does not tell us how to make people achieve lifelong satisfaction. Nor does it tell us what we must do so that our children can be happy. The claims of fun must be set aside so that satisfaction and good parenting can go on. The pursuit of fun must be accompanied by the pursuit of deeper satisfaction, of a moral nature, produced primarily by things like the commitment of a parent to the well-being of his children.

But perhaps even here in this life-morals problem, we could say that fun policy provides an interesting set of guidelines. Suppose we say that our vocation is to start life as a player but end it as a designer, that is, a designer of the hedonic environment in which future generations, and most specifically our own children will live. Designing games is not playing them — it is work, plain and simple:

> One of the most difficult tasks men can perform, however much others may despise it, is the invention of good games.
> —Carl Gustav Jung[4]

If we think that the job of crafting policy — for your family or society — is basically an act of game design, Jung's dictum calls us to consider it the hardest and most important thing we do for others. We are called not to solve the problems of others, but rather to create for them problem spaces within which they can realize their full potential as happy, healthy human beings. It is neither giving a poor man, or your own son, a fish, nor is it teaching him to fish. It is the act of creating a river environment in which the man, your son, would find so much joy in the act of fishing that he would teach it to himself. That is a tough assignment indeed.

If parenting and policymaking is game design, and game design is tough to do, then we have to wonder how we will motivate people to do the designing. If the fun revolution is to improve life in general, it must improve future lives, and that means that the broader lessons of hedonic design (which involve more than mere fun) must influence how we nurture. The focus on the immediate hedonics of fun must not distract us from the job of setting policies for our children and our society. Someone has to *build* the games.

Yet how do we convince people to stay in the real world and do design work? What keeps a father in his own home, if the fun-filled virtual world sits there a mouse-click away? All we can hope is that a new social order will arise that not only takes advantage of the policies of happiness from games and virtual worlds, but also encourages parents to parent well, and legislators to govern well, and not abandon the real world for the joys of dragon hunting.

The social orders dreamed up and implemented by virtual-world designers are different from the social order of the real world. Why? The response that designing societies in a game is very different from designing societies in real life may or may not make sense, depending on how you interpret it. It makes no sense if the claim is that working within a synthetic environment filled with dungeons and dragons makes all the difference. It does not; it cannot. Surely it should be clear by now that the dungeons and the dragons are ephemera, icons, a mere skein over the workings of society. Replace the dungeons with office buildings and the dragons with bosses and you are back in the real world. Another interpretation is sensible, though. Perhaps it is the *perspective* afforded by the task of game design that allows a designer to be so socially creative. The virtual-world designer, as Richard Bartle tells us, has great ethical power when he designs his world:

> When all's said and done, the ethics of a virtual world reflect those of its designers. If *you* don't think about how to behave, about what's right and wrong, about responsibility, about rights, then why should your players? If *you* think ethics are other people's responsibility so will your players. *Your* beliefs, *your* attitudes, *your* personality — they're all reflected in your virtual world. *You* have to take responsibility because (at least initially) *you* are the world.[5]

Any of us who have worked in the area of public policy analysis can only dream of having this kind of power to translate our personal ethics into the ethical structure of an entire society. Yet this task is not even chosen by game designers, it is thrust upon them. Bartle is reminding his readers — inexperienced designers — that even if they try to ignore their role as creators of public ethics, a public ethics will emerge anyway, of which they, the designers, will be the only author. Game designers are necessarily responsible for the social orders they create.

With that great power, the tasks game designers have set for themselves have not been to create the City on the Hill, the New World Order, the Dominance of the Master Race, the Workers and Soldiers Commune, or any

---

4   Apparently quoted in Laurens van der Post, *Jung and the Story of Time*. See Charles Cameron, "Carl Gustav Jung on Game Design," observed January 2007 at http://home.earthlink.net/-hipbone/IDTWeb/Why Game.html.

5   Richard Bartle, *Designing Virtual Worlds* (Indianapolis: New Riders, 2003) p. 702.

of the utopic nightmares that have haunted humanity's overwrought imagination in the past two hundred years. They remained admirably humble and asked, merely, What kind of social order would allow people to have fun? By and large, game designers have eschewed any temptation to remake humanity and have focused steadfastly on the task of remaking humanity's sense of well-being.

In so doing, game design has spawned this new science of fun policy: a set of practical policy norms that, when applied to a society of real people, give every one of them a more or less lengthy stream of experiences that they would label as "fun."

We have guessed that the cause of this good time is a set of specific game structures: a play environment with challenges and rewards clearly labeled so that they appeal to survival drives, all of it embedded within a texture of meaning. Such structures appeal to the very nature of fun as I have defined it. If challenge is dynamically adjusted and altered for freshness, from time to time, the fun becomes intense and long-lasting. If the fun persists uninterrupted for long enough, self-consciousness shuts down and the player enters a flow state.

Game designers have figured out how to make environments through which people easily find their way into fun-induced flow states; virtual-world designers have figured out how to make environments where flow emerges in an active social context. The core principles involve open access to experiences, along with constant employment opportunities, self-management with frequent ad hoc team-building, law in the code, and a level playing field.

These policy principles, if applied to the real world, offer a dramatic challenge to business as usual. They do not match up with contemporary policy. They do not match up with contemporary politics either. They appeal in parts to both the radical right and the radical left. A fun revolution would not only cause policy change, it would realign politics. But perhaps this is the time. The politics that structured the years in which I grew up — the cold war, the welfare state, flower power vs. the establishment — died in 1989. Those debates are gone. The new debate will be about the pursuit of happiness within the social order. What's the most important objective for society — to make everyone richer (the current objective in most nations) or to make them happier?

Our all-too-new experience with virtual worlds argues strongly for the latter. Why indeed are the policies of the virtual world so very different from business as usual in the real world? Even as we accept the answer — because virtual-world designers focus on human happiness while real-world policy designers focus on other things — that answer boggles the mind. Why in heaven's name has public policy ever focused on anything other than happiness? When did we decide that human well-being was not the most important thing?

Perhaps we have ignored happiness because we believe policy should pursue something more important. I have been careful throughout this book to avoid referring to proponents of fun policy as "hedonists." Hedonists by definition care only about pleasure, and we tend to associate them with pursuit of base pleasures at that. A hedonist is thought to be irresponsible and immoral. I would argue, though, that in a country where there is plenty to eat but suicide is a common cause of death, in a country where fewer and fewer children enter maturity possessing solid emotional relationships with caregivers, it is time to refocus on happiness. Money can't buy happiness or love. Keeping up with the Jones' is a shell game, a rip-off. The career ladder is a treadmill. The source of happiness lies elsewhere. On his deathbed, no man wishes he had spent more time at the office. In fact, dying people, I am told, speak exclusively of their relationships, of the regrets and fond memories left to them by their lifetime of being with others.[6] Our public policy should reflect that wisdom and help people live a life with fewer regrets about time wasted in pursuit of things that don't matter. A life of joyful sociality, playing games together if need be, would be much, much better. Virtual worlds are already allowing people to test-drive a world that's designed for fun rather than wealth.

Virtual worlds succeed in these comparisons because they are far more focused on hedonics than the real world is.

> Virtual worlds are already allowing people to test-drive a world that's designed for fun rather than wealth.

---

6 My therapist John Ebling, M.S.W., served for 12 years as an emergency room social worker. He had, as he describes it, the "terrible privilege" of being with hundreds of people in their final hours. It would be interesting to see what sort of social order those people would collectively build if they had the chance in those last moments. I doubt that it would look much like the social order we live in today.

That focus is a responsible and mature approach at this stage in history. Plenty of people attempt to be "hedonists" — pleasure-pursuers — without success. They usually learn that a life of dissolution, of casual sex and heavy eating, is hazardous for your health. "Hedonists" operating in that mode die quickly and in sorrow. Whoever told them that indulgence was the road to happiness was a liar. Those who focus on genuine human happiness, including those who design virtual worlds, advocate that lusts be tempered with love, that friendship become the cornerstone of activity, and that appetites be tempered with challenges. Happiness researcher Stefan Klein advocates a public policy based on "The Magic Triangle of Well-Being": civic sense, social equality, and control over our own lives.[7] Virtual-world societies today look as though they used Klein's triangle as a blueprint for construction: They encourage people to form communities, they make the opportunities for fun equal for all, and, being interactive, they guarantee a player's sense of control. No wonder virtual worlds make people happy. Their designers have apparently discovered through trial and error exactly what psychologists have discovered through research: that people are happy when their society is a community of fair play. On both practical and theoretical fronts, hedonics has become a serious field.

The happy lives that practical hedonics promises will also be *good* lives in every sense of the word, including being morally praiseworthy. Stanford psychologists Zeno Franco and Philip Zimbardo have studied ordinary people who do heroic things, and found that one key distinction between heroes and those who remain bystanders is that the heroes have actively imagined heroic actions in the past. This implies that if we foster a heroic imagination among people, we can expect more of them to do heroic things. Franco and Zimbardo say that video games are probably an excellent source of heroic imaginings, since they provide choice situations laden with ethically relevant consequences.[8] Those are the same things that allow video games to provide meaning, and in the context of virtual worlds, that meaning has the power of an entire society behind it. Not only that, but choice with consequence makes people feel good, and emotional well-being is probably the single most

important resource for a person who is trying to make the right choices consistently. Happiness enables moral action. We have learned through virtual worlds, however, that causality runs the other way too: Morality is a key to feeling happy. A moral fabric, a "lore," has been found to be integral to the operation of a fun society. Perhaps here is where we find the incentive to parent well: in honor of our own desire to be loved and cared for as children, we will love and care for our own children, and the moral order will state clearly and with a loud, *shared* voice that that is the most noble action we will ever undertake. Perhaps parenting is the highest expression of a heroic imagination.

Through the revitalization of myth in the fun revolution, we will once again know that our choices have meaning. We will sense that our actions are relevant. That relevance can be applied to proper choices, such as the choice to love one another, to parent, to give. A map of good and evil causes our actions to matter, and that makes them fun.

RESURRECTING GOOD AND EVIL

In reintroducing good and evil to the social order, and doing so in a way that is acceptable to all, virtual worlds may be offering a deep and thoroughly laudable transformation of human life. Consider the story of a fictional person, Bob, whose interaction with virtual worlds is filled with meaning.

BOB: *MYSTIC*

Bob's real life is so boring it isn't worthy of being called a story. He's just Bob. Bob is 25 years old and he is a high-school graduate, an assistant manager in an office-supply store. But as soon as Bob gets home from work every day he throws the cheeseburger bag down on his desk and fires up his machine, loads a virtual world, and transforms himself into Abelaard the Paladin. This night, Abelaard will join an army of 47 other people, the realm's most powerful warriors, wizards, clerics, and rogues, in pursuit of Azengoth, the Demon of the Underworld, who has burst from his fetid lair to terrorize the game characters of hundreds of people much less powerful than Bob's Abelaard. As he flies his golden griffon through the blue skies to join with his army, Bob starts to feel so good. This. Is. Fun. Indeed this is the first moment of the day when Bob has actually felt alive. For Robert Montgomery Jones is at heart a noble young man yearning to make a difference, but his efforts to do so in the real world have been consistently and subtly shut

7   Stefan Klein, *The Science of Happiness* (New York: Marlowe and Company, 2006/2002).

8   Zeno Franco and Philip Zimbardo, "The Banality of Heroism" *Greater Good* (Fall/Winter) (2007), observed May 2007 at http://greatergood. berkeley.edu/greatergood/current_issue/ francozimbardo.html.

down. He was too peaceful for sports and was taught to think of military and public service as fraudulent activities. His religious upbringing stressed passivity and acceptance over the fight against evil. His teachers kept stressing that there were no hard and fast truths, while simultaneously informing him through mandatory standardized tests that he wasn't as smart as other people. When it came to his career, Bob's mentors all scared the heck out of him, filling him with an unconscious dread of income failures. A job with benefits — that was the only acceptable real-world choice. But as Abelaard the Paladin, this night, Bob is going to bring down Azengoth or die trying, and thereby he will make a real, clear, and positive difference in the lives of hundreds of people. For Bob, the virtual world contains a map of meaning that he cannot find in the real world.

Bob's story, or actually his utter lack of story in the real world, points to the depth of the transformation that virtual worlds will cause. In part, this is a well-known story; Bob is exploring aspects of the self that the real world represses.[9] But virtual worlds offer more than mere personality exploration; they offer a mythical cosmos in which a personality can find a reason to exist.

This aspect of virtual worlds may be their most powerful force for social transformation. In virtual worlds, we are consciously resurrecting the notion of myth and directly embedding it in human societies. In thinking about what this might mean for happiness, I return again and again to the notion of a coming "Age of Wonder." Wonder, in the sense of miracle, mysticism, and faith, may well be the single most important contribution of virtual worlds to human experience. After the "death of God" in the nineteenth century, the meaning of life for many became something of an untended flower, socially speaking; individuals were left to find it on their own. It is a difficult task. What, after all, is the point of Bob's existence? In the real world, the answer is muddy, unspecific, and fraught with tension; something to avoid in polite conversation, a fart at the dinner table of modernist sensibilities. In the virtual world, the answer is crystal clear: There are evil creatures, labeled as Evil with a capital E, and the point of Abelaard's existence is to be a weapon against them. His life is thereby noble. By extension, the life of Robert Montgomery Jones is noble too.

You may object and say that fighting evil in a childish game is morally empty. I disagree. First, merely stating

> Merely stating that good and evil exist, and are not the same thing, is an advance over the current state of affairs in the real world.

that good and evil exist, and are not the same thing, is an advance over the current state of affairs in the real world. In the real world, most well-mannered people, people who wish to appear moderate and sensible, shy away from even speaking in such terms, leaving articulation of right and wrong in the hands of fundamentalists and sectarians. These days, far too many sensible and well-intentioned people have difficulty carrying on a sophisticated moral discussion. It's unfamiliar territory. Immersing Bob in an environment where right and wrong and good and evil are common terms at least gives him practice at thinking in such categories. But perhaps you feel that thinking in terms of good and evil is actually damaging to a person, that a more nuanced sense of the rightness of things is needed. Maybe; but the human mind does not seem very comfortable when it has nothing clear to care about. This is, of course, a Jungian insight. It is perhaps striking in this context to reread Jung's opinion of game design, along with an additional comment that he made:

> One of the most difficult tasks men can perform, however much others may despise it, is the invention of good games *and it cannot be done by men out of touch with their instinctive values* [emphasis added].[10]

"The theme that fantasy provides meaning, meaning that is essential for human life, has appeared frequently. Bruno Bettelheim argues in *The Uses of Enchantment* that fairy tales—precursors of virtual worlds—serve very deep psychological purposes, and that efforts to sanitize them or inject nuance into their categories can only rob them of

9 These issues have been explored by many others. See, e.g., Sherry Turkle, *Life on the Screen: Identity in the Age of the Internet* (New York: Simon and Shuster, 1995), note 4.

10 See note 4.

their validity.[11] In fairy tales, the stepmother is evil, pure and simple. More recently, psychologist Jordan Peterson has argued that myth is a fundamental category of human consciousness.[12] The core myth is that there is a state of bliss and a state of chaos, the former to be pursued but never won, the latter to be feared, loathed, and fled from. Only through an encounter with both can the self-conscious organism motivate itself to do anything at all. By this argument, dread of evil and love of goodness accompany the human condition and cannot be removed from it. Yet the real world has become uncomfortable speaking in such black-and-white terms, fearful of the dire consequences that result from morally laden conflicts. But the problem there is not moral vision, it is the fact that we use guns and knives to fight one another. Thus perhaps if we move to an environment where fighting can happen but nobody gets killed, we may more freely speak of right and wrong. In virtual worlds, as in fairy tales, good and evil are labeled with bright, glowing letters. If nothing else, the labeling provides an environment in which those who feel the natural human need to encounter myth may do so safely.

The restoration of myth within virtual worlds goes deeper than mere labeling. Recall that Abelaard's quest involved killing a monster that was terrorizing others. In virtual worlds, those others are real people. They are running their little characters around, trying to do whatever it is they want to do, and here comes Azengoth, breathing fire on them and eating their cows. Stopping that kind of thing is clearly good. You don't need a myth to support this decision — everybody believes that if a bully is being mean to someone weaker, and someone stops the bully, that that is a good thing. The joy of the people at their deliverance gives the act meaning, even if you don't buy into the labeling of the monster as evil. Virtual worlds don't need the labeling to deliver meaning; they are ethical constructor kits where designers can create monsters that do things that everybody agrees are bad. The real world does not regularly produce settings in which someone, a monster, has clearly done something wrong, *and* another person is encouraged and enabled to do something about it. Virtual worlds produce such situations constantly — situations

that engage the moral sense and encourage moral action, labeled as such or not.

Virtual worlds produce meaning in a third way, through sociality. The labeling of action creates meaning, the design of action creates meaning, and the embedding of action in a social context creates meaning. Maybe at first the rampages of Azengoth mean nothing to Robert Montgomery Jones, but as he spends time in this society, where people cry and rage when Azengoth burns their homes and eats their cows, he gradually comes to feel as they do. Sympathy for the pain of others is natural, and even if the pain stems from an abstract situation, we will still approach the people feeling the pain carefully, and with sympathy. Regardless of the source of pain, we treat pain with reverence, and naturally so. If you live long enough in a tribe where touching your hair is taboo, you will find yourself becoming quite uncomfortable with that act, and angry at your newly arrived friend for scratching his head all the time. The escape of Azengoth from his pens predicts a season of wailing in all the lands; dreading that wailing, Bob is motivated to become Abelaard, join with others, and do something about it. It is worth stressing that all of Bob's actions in the virtual world are *with other people*. The stereotype of the loner sitting at his computer still looks right — the guy is still sitting at this computer — but today he is not alone at all. He is in constant communication and collaboration with other people from around the globe. And all of those people spend a lot of time joining together to fight Bad Things, as a *group*. What a contrast this is to the real-world, where isolated action has become the norm. Political scientist Robert Putnam has traced the gradual decline of social groupings as an element of daily life.[13] We still bowl, apparently, but not in leagues. The real world does not encourage people to band together. This must leave a yearning for a community of meaning, a yearning that can be satisfied in the community of myth-making found in most virtual worlds.

Still, in the end we might think of Abelaard's nobility as something pretty trivial. It's just a set of game-world myths, isn't it? How deep can they be? How much motivation, really and truly, can be wrought from a world where bashing orcs on the head is the main activity? Surely there cannot be any significant depth of moral meaning in dungeons and dragons. Or can there? These worlds owe much to Dungeons and

---

11 Bruno Bettelheim, *The Uses of Enchantment* (New York: Vintage, 1977).

12 Jordan Peterson, *Maps of Meaning: The Architecture of Belief* (New York: Routledge, 1999).

13 Robert D. Putnam, *Bowling Alone: The Collapse and Revival of American Community* (New York: Simon and Schuster 2000).

Dragons and other role-playing games of the 1970s, which in turn owe much to the work of J. R. R. Tolkien. Few people know that Tolkien was a faithful Roman Catholic. He was also an apologist, a person who felt comfortable trying to get others to adopt his religious views. He was a long-time friend of C. S. Lewis, and was instrumental in converting him to Christianity in middle age. Lewis went on to build a dramatically public and successful career as an apologist

---

Virtual worlds are on the path to becoming the most powerful source of personal meaning in the contemporary world.

---

himself, writing books, giving speeches, broadcasting radio addresses. He wrote the *Chronicles of Narnia*, a collection of unabashedly Christian fairy tales. In this he was emulating Tolkien, whose *Lord of the Rings*, nearing completion as Narnia was beginning, might be described as an abashedly Christian fairy tale. Earlier I suggested that Tolkien's purpose in writing his tales was to restore myth to the modern world. There is, in fact, substantial evidence to this effect in his life and writings.[14] As an orphan who witnessed the horrors of World War I firsthand, Tolkien loathed modernity for having carelessly tossed mythical meaning out the window. In a 1939 address to students and faculty at the University of Edinburgh he said that the creation of "Secondary Worlds," something he devoted his entire life to, was divinely inspired no matter who was doing it.[15] He would have called today's game designers "subcreators," and as such, agents of the king of heaven. Yet despite a clear sense of religious meaning, Tolkien did not take Lewis' approach of explicitly making his stories Christian. Rather, he set his tale in the mists of time and made it a simple conflict between evil and good. Middle Earth was not an effort to restore a specific lost myth, it was an effort to build a new myth that was consistent with the old myths that humanity had forgotten. As a new myth, separated but not divorced from its Christian roots, the lore of J. R. R. Tolkien has been dramatically successful. The vast majority of rights and wrongs one finds

in contemporary virtual worlds have their roots in Tolkien. Elves are everywhere, and everywhere, they love trees. Orcs are equally omnipresent, and they perpetually love to crack skulls. Whatever we might think about this on an individual level, there's no question that Tolkien's constructed myth has succeeded in an incredibly wide variety of cultures. His synthetic map of meaning, expressed in games and virtual worlds, resonates around the world, from Japan to America to Russia. Something deeply Jungian is at work. People around the world love fantasy video games, and no matter who designs them, these games almost always involve hobbits, elves, orcs, and humans. What players and outsider observers don't realize is how very ancient these moral maps are, tracing their roots through Tolkien quite consciously all the way back to Abraham. Video games and virtual worlds are often subjected to scorn. Yet today, they are the most vibrant of vessels, carrying revered moral traditions into the future. The myths one finds in virtual worlds deserve not scorn but reverence. Through single-player games, players encounter our most hallowed traditions; through virtual worlds, they can once again live them.

Virtual worlds are on the path to becoming the most powerful source of personal meaning in the contemporary world. The changes that result might well be compared to the ones unleashed by Luther's 95 Theses: not just a fun *revolution*, but a fun *reformation*.

BEYOND FRUSTRATION, BOREDOM, AND EMPTINESS

I've argued that fun will become a core objective of our society, that we will eventually integrate the lessons of social-level game design in the way we organize education, business, and government. Change will be traumatic. It might well be resisted. I doubt, however, that any resistance will make a difference. We are not really going to have any choice in the matter. The exodus into virtual worlds may seem like a distraction today, but it will grow from a distraction into an amusement, from there into a challenge, and from there into a revolution.

While I am concerned about the trauma of change, I think the direction in which virtual worlds are pointing society is a good one. For too long, our society has been paying attention to things that don't matter — such as wealth — and ignoring things that do matter — such as emotional well-being. The evidence has grown over the last 50 years that the focus on things like money has put us

---

14   Humphrey Carpenter, *J.R.R. Tolkien: A Biography* (London: George Allen and Unwin, 1977).
15   J. R. R. Tolkien, "On Fairy Stories," Andrew Lang Lecture, University of Edinburgh 1939; available in *Tree and Leaf* (New York: Harper Collins, 2001).

off track. Hedonic psychologists and economists have had trouble connecting happiness to incomes and shiny cars. Researchers in social policy have found that money has a very small effect on a kid's lifetime prospects; in comparison, the family's relationships have a massive effect.[16] John Kenneth Galbraith wondered in 1958 why we didn't use all of our riches to eliminate poverty, but our social programs of the 1960s showed that distributing money doesn't make poverty go away. We've generally assumed that because people avidly pursue money (and associated ephemera, like fame and power), a social order focused on getting money would make everyone happy. It didn't. It's been making everyone unhappy, as a matter of fact. The game is too frustrating for some people, too boring for others, and completely empty and devoid of meaning for most. We didn't see that society was a game design problem all along, that the solution was not to constantly put more money into the game but to improve the way the game plays. Instead, we have ignored the game design problems that confront us, focusing instead on the scores of this old, outmoded, money-hunting game.

The coming exodus into virtual worlds will force us to change. The society that emerges in the real world will have to become more fun than the society we have now. Because games and virtual worlds have learned how to help people learn and work and socialize while having fun, the new society will also probably be better educated, more productive, and more civically engaged. I hope we will parent as well or better. Our task is to prepare for the revolution by further developing the new science of fun policy, seeing what we can accomplish with the tools that virtual-world designers have created. Doing so, we will improve our understanding of the world to come. More important, though, we may well discover some new, exciting, and beneficial things about how our society works, and how it can make every one of us happier.

---

16 Susan E. Mayer, *What Money Can't Buy: Family Income and Children's Life Chances* (Cambridge: Harvard University Press, 1998).

CHAPTER 13
Theme Parks

Listen to me, Truman, there is no more truth out there than there is in the world I created for you. Same lies, same deceit. But, in my world, you having nothing to fear.

— Christoph,
The Truman Show (1998)

Chapter 13. Theme Parks

Recommended Film

The Truman Show (Peter Weir 1998)

Media Models

The Meme, The Spectacle, The Hyperreal

Chapter Summary

Jean Baudrillard theorizes on the deeper meanings
of Disneyland, a fantasyland that masks the fact
that America already exists in hyperreality.

Oliver Herwig and Florian Holzherr view the "entertainment architecture"
of Las Vegas as representing a synthesis of Disney,
Hollywood, and the "codes of the media."

The Precession of Simulacra

from *Simulacra and Simulation*

— Jean Baudrillard *translated by Sheila Faria Glaser*

> The simulacrum is never what hides the truth — it is truth that hides the fact that there is none.
>
> The simulacrum is true.
>
> — Ecclesiastes

If once we were able to view the Borges fable in which, the cartographers of the Empire draw up a map so detailed that it ends up covering the territory exactly (the decline of the Empire witnesses the fraying of this map, little by little, and its fall into ruins, though some shreds are still discernible in the deserts — the metaphysical beauty of this ruined abstraction testifying to a pride equal to the Empire and rotting like a carcass, returning to the substance of the soil, a bit as the double ends by being confused with the real through aging) — as the most beautiful allegory of simulation, this fable has now come full circle for us, and possesses nothing but the discrete charm of second-order simulacra.[1]

Today abstraction is no longer that of the map, the double, the mirror, or the concept. Simulation is no longer that of a territory, a referential being, or a substance. It is the generation by models, of a real without origin or reality: a hyperreal. The territory no longer precedes the map, nor does it survive it. It is nevertheless the map that precedes the territory — *precession of simulacra* — that engenders the territory, and if one must return to the fable, today it is the territory whose shreds slowly rot across the extent of the map. It is the real, and not the map, whose vestiges persist here and there in the deserts that are no longer those of the Empire, but ours. *The desert of the real itself.*

In fact, even inverted, Borges's fable is unusable. Only the allegory of the Empire, perhaps, remains. Because it is with this same imperialism that present-day simulators attempt to make the real, all of the real, coincide with their models of simulation. But it is no longer a question of either maps or territories. Something has disappeared: the sovereign difference, between one and the other, that constituted the charm of abstraction. Because it is difference that constitutes the poetry of the map and the charm of the territory the magic of the concept and the charm of the real. This imaginary of representation, which simultaneously culminates in and is engulfed by the cartographer's mad project of the ideal coextensivity of map and territory, disappears in the simulation whose operation is nuclear and genetic, no longer at all specular or discursive. It is all of metaphysics that is lost. No more mirror of being and appearances, of the real and its concept. No more imaginary coextensivity: it is genetic miniaturization that is the dimension of simulation. The real is produced from miniaturized cells, matrices, and memory banks, models of control — and it can be reproduced an indefinite number of times from these. It no longer needs to be rational, because it no longer measures itself against either an ideal or negative instance. It is no longer anything but operational. In fact, it is no longer really the real, because no imaginary envelops it anymore. It is a hyperreal, produced from a

---

1 Cf. J. Baudrillard, "L'ordre des simulacres" (The order of simulacra), in *L'échange symbolique et la mort* (Symbolic exchange and death) (Paris: Gallimard, 1976).

radiating synthesis of combinatory models in a hyperspace without atmosphere.

By crossing into a space whose curvature is no longer that of the real, nor that of truth, the era of simulation is inaugurated by a liquidation of all referentials—worse: with their artificial resurrection in the systems of signs, a material more malleable than meaning, in that it lends itself to all systems of equivalences, to all binary oppositions, to all combinatory algebra. It is no longer a question of imitation, nor duplication, nor even parody. It is a question

veritable concentration camp — is total. Or, rather: inside, a whole panoply of gadgets magnetizes the crowd in directed flows — outside, solitude is directed at a single gadget: the automobile. By an extraordinary coincidence (but this derives without a doubt from the enchantment inherent to this universe), this frozen, childlike world is found to have been conceived and realized by a man who is himself now cryogenized: Walt Disney, who awaits his resurrection through an increase of 180 degrees centigrade.

Thus, everywhere in Disneyland the objective profile of

> Disneyland is presented as imaginary in order to make us believe that the rest is real, whereas all of Los Angeles and the America that surrounds it are no longer real, but belong to the hyperreal order and to the order of simulation.

---

of substituting the signs of the real for the real, that is to say of an operation of deterring every real process via its operational double, a programmatic, metastable, perfectly descriptive machine that offers all the signs of the real and short-circuits all its vicissitudes. Never again will the real have the chance to produce itself—such is the vital function of the model in a system of death, or rather of anticipated resurrection, that no longer even gives the event of death a chance. A hyperreal henceforth sheltered from the imaginary, and from any distinction between the real and the imaginary, leaving room only for the orbital recurrence of models and for the simulated generation of differences.

* * *

THE HYPERREAL AND THE IMAGINARY

Disneyland is a perfect model of all the entangled orders of simulacra. It is first of all a play of illusions and phantasms: the Pirates, the Frontier, the Future Worlds, etc. This imaginary world is supposed to ensure the success of the operation. But what attracts the crowds the most is without a doubt the social microcosm, the *religious,* miniaturized pleasure of real America, of its constraints and joys. One parks outside and stands in line inside, one is altogether abandoned at the exit. The only phantasmagoria in this imaginary world lies in the tenderness and warmth of the crowd, and in the sufficient and excessive number of gadgets necessary to create the multitudinous effect. The contrast with the absolute solitude of the parking lot — a

America, down to the morphology of individuals and of the crowd, is drawn. All its values are exalted by the miniature and the comic strip. Embalmed and pacified. Whence the possibility of an ideological analysis of Disneyland (L. Marin did it very well in *Utopiques, jeux d'espace* [Utopias, play of space]): digest of the American way of life, panegyric of American values, idealized transposition of a contradictory reality. Certainly. But this masks something else and this "ideological" blanket functions as a cover for a *simulation of the third order:* Disneyland exists in order to hide that it is the "real" country, all of "real" America that *is* Disneyland (a bit like prisons are there to hide that it is the social in its entirety in its banal omnipresence, that is carceral). Disneyland is presented as imaginary in order to make us believe that the rest is real, whereas all of Los Angeles and the America that surrounds it are no longer real, but belong to the hyperreal order and to the order of simulation. It is no longer a question of a false representation of reality (ideology) but of concealing the fact that the real is no longer real, and thus of saving the reality principle.

The imaginary of Disneyland is neither true nor false, it is a deterrence machine set up in order to rejuvenate the fiction of the real in the opposite camp. Whence the debility of this imaginary, its infantile degeneration. This world wants to be childish in order to make us believe that the adults are elsewhere, in the "real" world, and to conceal the fact that true childishness is everywhere — that it is that of the adults themselves who come here to act the child in order to foster illusions as to their real childishness.

Disneyland is not the only one, however. Enchanted Village, Magic Mountain, Marine World: Los Angeles is surrounded by these imaginary stations that feed reality, the energy of the real to a city whose mystery is precisely that of no longer being anything but a network of incessant, unreal circulation — a city of incredible proportions but without space, without dimension. As much as electrical and atomic power stations, as much as cinema studios, this city which is no longer anything but an immense scenario and a perpetual pan shot, needs this old imaginary like a sympathetic nervous system made up of childhood signals and faked phantasms.

Disneyland: a space of the regeneration of the imaginary as waste-treatment plants are elsewhere, and even here. Everywhere today one must recycle waste, and the dreams, the phantasms, the historical, fairylike, legendary imaginary of children and adults is a waste product, the first great toxic excrement of a hyperreal civilization. On a mental level, Disneyland is the prototype of this new function. But all the sexual, psychic, somatic recycling institutes, which proliferate in California, belong to the same order. People no longer look at each other, but there are institutes for that. They no longer touch each other, but there is contactotherapy. They no longer walk, but they go jogging, etc. Everywhere one recycles lost faculties, or lost bodies, or lost sociality, or the lost taste for food. One reinvents penury, asceticism, vanished savage naturalness: natural food, health food, yoga. Marshall Sahlins's idea that it is the economy of the market, and not of nature at all, that secretes penury, is verified, but at a secondary level: here, in the sophisticated confines of a triumphal market economy is reinvented a penury/sign, a penury/simulacrum, a simulated behavior of the underdeveloped (including the adoption of Marxist tenets) that, in the guise of ecology, of energy crises and the critique of capital, adds a final esoteric aureole to the triumph of an esoteric culture. Nevertheless, maybe a mental catastrophe, a mental implosion and involution without precedent lies in wait for a system of this kind, whose visible signs would be those of this strange obesity, or the incredible coexistence of the most bizarre theories and practices, which correspond to the improbable coalition of luxury, heaven, and money, to the improbable luxurious materialization of life and to undiscoverable contradictions.

Las Vegas: The First Mediafied Dream World

from *Dream Worlds*

— Oliver Herwig and Florian Holzherr

"Rental car return?" The woman behind the cash desk looks up briefly as she runs the credit card through the machine. She's in her mid-forties, dyed strands of hair poke out from under her blue baseball cap. "Left across Las Vegas Boulevard, then first left onto Sunset and right onto Bermuda." And because she isn't too busy at the moment she takes a Western Pacific Kraft bag and writes down the directions on it: "Left L.V. Blvd; Left Sunset; Right Bermuda." It reads like a knowing invitation to lose oneself in what Tom Wolfe described as "The Versailles of Pop Culture." Lost in Las Vegas, something Jean Baudrillard dreamed about: "To vanish, in the middle of a motel, in one or other of Nevada's gambling halls."[1]

Everyday life comes with a bang: lines at the check-in counter, endless waiting, and security checks. There is nothing about this airport different from any other mass transportation building — with a single exception: up until final boarding you can hear the slot machines ringing in an environment of air conditioning and tinted glass. A last-minute gamble before the most successful American creation of the twentieth century melts like butter in the sun of the Nevada desert: streets, junctions, condominiums, warehouses, endless highways, and dormitory suburbs stretch as far as the horizon. The greater Las Vegas area, which includes downtown Las Vegas, Henderson, North Las Vegas, and Boulder City, has a population of one and a half million, almost six times as large as in 1970. In addition, there are the thirty million visitors who leave billions of dollars behind them in the casinos and guarantee hotel occupancy rates of around 85 percent. Las Vegas, which has transformed itself from a pit of vice into a destination for family vacations, is at the top of the list of tourist attractions, ahead of New York City or Paris, whose own silhouettes gleam along the Strip like the windows of a boutique.

If America is movement, then Las Vegas is permanent acceleration. The Boulevard revolves to the rhythm of roulette wheels, computer gaming, and one-arm bandits; even the architecture vibrates in the glow of millions of lightbulbs that transform facades into signs and surfaces into moving pictures. Las Vegas is like a vast *tableau vivant*, an installation piece on the American Way of Life, fast-paced and always on the go, a place, with its gaze firmly concentrated on maximizing profit, that constantly reinvents itself. Architecture functions here as a container for histories and a shell that can be remodeled at any time to suit the performances offered by the entertainment industry. Stage sets, theaters, and Potemkin villages plunder the warehouse of building styles and present them anew. Architecture forms a chapter in the great narrative of a new El Dorado, facades are part of the theme-casinos' cinematic method of presentation that is geared towards the perspective of motorists and pedestrians — something Robert Venturi, Denise Scott Brown, and Steven Izenour commented on in their classic book, *Learning from Las Vegas*:

1 As quoted in Ralph Eue: "Las Vegas im Film: Die Wirklichkeit ist ganz anders" (Las Vegas in film: the reality is completely different), *StadtBauwelt* 143, 1999/36: 2008–2013, p. 2013.

Oliver Herwig and Florian Holzherr, "Las Vegas: The First Mediafied Dream World," from *Dream Worlds: Architecture And Entertainment*, pp. 98, 100–119. Published in 2006 by Prestel Publishing.

"A single shot of the Strip is less spectacular; its enormous spaces must be seen as moving sequences."[2]

Las Vegas is the first completely mediafied city in history, where buildings become signs, facades are information screens that could just as easily be film sets, and the entire metropolis is the crystallization point of a media hype based

---

Las Vegas is like a vast *tableau vivant*, an installation piece on the American Way of Life

---

on glittering surfaces and (disappointed) dreams. Las Vegas owes its rapid rise to its proximity to Hollywood and the mass media, and cleverly increased its fame through films such as *Ocean's Eleven* (1960), *Diamonds Are Forever*, *One from the Heart*, *Bugsy Malone*, *Leaving Las Vegas*, *Casino*, *Showgirls*, and the recent remake of *Ocean's Eleven* (2001); cult books such as Hunter S. Thompson's *Fear and Loathing in Las Vegas* with its descriptive subtitle, *A Savage Journey to the Heart of the American Dream*; and innumerable reports in magazines and newspapers. This city leaves nobody cold; in some people it awakens glowing admiration while in others it provokes complete rejection — Michael Herr called it "Helldorado," "Neonatlantis" was Mimi Zeiger's description, and "Zeropolis" Bruce Bégout's. Red or black, all or nothing — there is no in-between in this city of illusions and sleights of hand, where appearances don't last long and seem to change in front of the viewer's eyes. Las Vegas produces material and images as extravagantly as it consumes them; in fact, even the events surrounding its founding could have been taken from a film script full of false trails and Mafia myths. This was where the Rat Pack appeared, where Elvis drank himself to death, and where Britney Spears got married. Las Vegas is sometimes a stage set, sometimes a protagonist, and at other times a catalyst for further chapters in the eternal pursuit of fortune.

DEGREE OF CONTROL

Sadly enough, nothing about Las Vegas surprises any more: everybody knows the town before they arrive. The degree of control is amazing. Everything seems perfectly arranged in this city of illusions that works with focused perspectives and landscapes of staggered backdrops, neon signs, and labyrinthine casino interiors. For a long time now, Las Vegas has ceased to live from the Mob or from games of chance, but rather from its ability to embody a dream world distinct from the run-of-the-mill, puritanical variety. Las Vegas has become a trademark, a label representing perfect entertainment of every kind and a showpiece of the post-industrial service industry. The key to its success is perfect logistics. Tourists are dropped here in much the same way as parts in the production process are delivered to factories — just on time — and during their visit they are moved vertically and horizontally from attraction to attraction by monorail, travelator, and elevator. The best way to arrive at such a place is to float in by airplane, where all that remains is to whisk your suitcase from the baggage claim to a waiting taxi or rental car. "Welcome to Fabulous Las Vegas" now blinks where the dreams of yesteryear — rundown gaming halls and dilapidated hotels — await new investors. From here the Strip, renamed Las Vegas Boulevard, reaches northwards like an extended runway. To the right and left casino hotels blend to form a collage of "sampled" and "covered" facades, a mega-soundtrack of the pop architecture of the last few decades. Mandalay Bay paints golden stripes across the sky; behind it the 350-foot-high (106 m) Luxor pyramid of dark glass shoots lasers into the air; and New York New York, a gigantic mini-Manhattan, awaits opposite the green cube of the MGM Grand. These are followed by the gamblers' palaces: Paris Las Vegas, the Bellagio, the Venetian, Caesars Palace, Treasure Island, and the landmark Stratosphere Tower. This 1,149-foot-high (350 m) tower marks the fault line between the classic downtown casinos and the more modern hotel-casino theme resorts on the Strip that epitomize the Disneyfication of Las Vegas.

TRUE HEART OF THE CITY

What started as a speculative land purchase in the Nevada desert has long since put the old town center around Fremont Street in the shade. Today the Strip forms the true heart of the city while the downtown area is now only a rundown appendage. Whereas initially the speed of the motorized guest dictated the emblematic size of the signs along the road to Los Angeles and of the huge neon advertisements of the

---

2 Robert Venturi, Denise Scott Brown, and Steven Izenour, *Learning from Las Vegas: The Forgotten Symbolism of Architectural Form*. Revised Edition. (Cambridge MA, 1977), p.35.

casinos — "The big sign and the little building is the rule,"[3] as Robert Venturi and Denise Scott Brown recognized in 1972 — the situation now is completely different. The Strip has transformed into a boulevard for strolling guests; the billboards that entice motorists are now to be found only on the parallel highway and, thanks to their presentation, the mega-hotels can even afford to move back somewhat from the Strip and create a seemingly public space — that in fact remains completely private. The "vulgar extravaganza" of the signs and the "modest necessity"[4] of the buildings behind them have recently morphed into a family-friendly stage and show surface, followed by thematically embellished casino hotels. Behind their facades (generally decorated with historical elements) these hotels are in fact a series of high-rise buildings with a splayed, star-shaped plan, arranged one after the other along the Strip. The Mirage, which was the first mega-hotel to open in 1991, launched a new cycle of investment. Treasure Island and the Bellagio followed in 1994 and 1998, respectively. Today eighteen of the twenty largest hotels in the United States are located here. There are over 130,000 rooms for mere mortals, and a number of high-roller suites for the so-called "whales" that gamble up to several hundred thousand dollars in a single day. Whereas for Venturi and Scott Brown the Strip still represented a tripartite harmony of "large open space, big scale, and high speed,"[5] in recent decades not only has the speed of traffic along this former main exit road been reduced, but also the entire feeling has changed dramatically. The Strip has become more urban, at least in regards to the density and the sequence of the casino hotels. Each hotel occupies an entire block and they are connected and networked by bridges and catwalks. Even on the sidewalk there is a lively, southern ease late into the night. Urban qualities have been created by the succession of theme hotels, yet entirely without the services of town planners: the impression is one of a lavishly dimensioned boulevard that you can drive along in comfort or — something increasingly rare in America — can even explore on foot.

> Las Vegas does not just borrow images; it cements the perception of the world, our visual repertoire. Entertainment architecture resembles film stills in that it must be instantly recognizable.

ILLUSIONISTS, EMPERORS, AND STAGE MANAGERS

In the open gallery that it calls the Strip, Las Vegas collects images of cities like so many historical landscapes. Bellagio, Monte Carlo, Paris, Venice, and even New York City are lined one after the other to create a *via triumphalis*. But in contrast to the emperors of antiquity the stagecraft in the media age has no need of real trophies: quotations appropriate to the theme of each hotel casino suffice. A sphinx of sprayed concrete and wood stands guard like a gigantic doorman in front of the Luxor while the Eiffel Tower, reduced by half to 492 feet (150 m), stands like Godzilla astride the Hôtel de Ville. XXL and XS — Las Vegas plays with dimensions and styles. With Paris Las Vegas the architects from Bergman, Walls & Youngblood celebrate their total control of image worlds with leaps in scale and dramatic perspectives, embellishing — or reducing — at will typical Parisian facades, monuments, or urban spaces. Las Vegas architects liquefy scale — Paris is reduced to just a block and Manhattan to a composite incorporating the Empire State and Chrysler Buildings. Urban silhouettes mark the location. Las Vegas does not just borrow images; it cements the perception of the world, our visual repertoire. Entertainment architecture resembles film stills in that it must be instantly recognizable. Complexity is required only if it is ornamental and does not generate any feelings of discomfort. The media city mutates into a chameleon-like meta-metropolis that exploits clichés and develops them even further. Precisely those scenes that flash through your mind when you think of Paris or Venice are arranged in Las Vegas to form a hyper-realistic distillation made up of the true-to-scale Rialto Bridge right beside St. Mark's Square, and the Hôtel de Ville directly under the Eiffel Tower.

Whereas once illuminated signs attempted to entice people from the Strip into the casinos, this role is now played by three-dimensional surfaces that open onto the boulevard like film sets, enriching the optimally detailed

---

3   Ibid., p. 13.
4   Ibid.
5   Ibid., p. 18.

landscapes with active elements. The 1,203 water jets of the *Bellagio* water ballet perform to the sound of dramatic music, a few blocks away actors stage pirate battles straight out of Stevenson's *Treasure Island*, or a volcano erupts at regular intervals. Attractions slow down visitors, entice them to stop at determined spots, and increase the likelihood they will enter the casino. Las Vegas is convenient. Why travel half way around the world when in one place you can experience the Chrysler Building as well as the Arc de Triomphe, see a part of the Paris Opéra and take a

the gamblers' city attracted the stars and starlets, and used successful films as inspiration for its casinos, the relationship has long since been reversed. Now Hollywood draws its material from the city of gambling and thus mediafies the setting yet further still. Casinos project and develop Hollywood's image worlds into the future. Every box-office success can become a theme casino, such as Melvin Grossman's Caesars Palace — an homage to the 1962 epic film *Cleopatra* starring Richard Burton as Mark Anthony and Elizabeth Taylor in the title role. And what already ex-

---

Entertainment architects know the codes of the media society and, under their direction, spaces become surfaces, and facades become consumable signs that can be recalled at any time.

---

snapshot of a singing gondolier? And to top it all off, a romantic candlelight dinner in the Piazza San Marco — in a space that darkens atmospherically to replicate the evening several times during the course of the day — to the strains of a violin beside your table.

It is hardly surprising that the world's most famous illusionists appear in Las Vegas, as the city itself is like a *fata morgana* in the desert. It is often wrongly asserted that architects and designers in Las Vegas create copies — they do not, they instead quote and amalgamate. In this, they resemble fashion designers, or DJs that sample, remix, and cover songs. Ultimately, the constructed illusion surpasses the original, as it eliminates the possibility of annoyances such as the damp moldiness of Venice's side streets, or locals that don't understand English. Here everything functions and everything is controlled: controlled color, controlled music, and controlled emotion. Entertainment architects know the codes of the media society and, under their direction, spaces become surfaces, and facades become consumable signs that can be recalled at any time. Las Vegas demonstrates how easily urban images can be recycled, reconstructed, and activated as backdrops. It is precisely the nonidentity of this place somewhere in the desert that makes Las Vegas the ideal location to create this "everywhere, immediately" quality. Ennobled by the use of plasterboard and sprayed concrete, the desert serves as a screen for the leisure and amusement society.

This sophisticated strategy would be unimaginable without the close proximity of the dream factory; Hollywood and Las Vegas live in a symbiotic relationship. While at first

ists can easily be changed. Las Vegas is perpetual change, a purposeful and permanent building site: Norman M. Klein speaks in this context of "junking up" the interior as "a useful method of suggesting that the casino is not completely finished […] the incomplete building stimulates a desire to gamble and perhaps awakens a desire to come back a few months later."[6]

DISPLAY OF WONDERS

The city changes the images in its shop window (the Strip) as you would the displays in a boutique. "Exit closed while we rebuild Rome," reads a posted notice in Caesars Palace, as workers screw on cornices and erect columns. Las Vegas resembles an open warehouse for monumental film sets with competing presentations and layers that at times penetrate each other and at others remain isolated, held together only by the traffic stripes of the street. Over here the elegant world of Monte Carlo, over there escapism and Robinson Crusoe escapades with Aladdin and Treasure Island, and further on Old Europe in the form of the Bellagio, Venetian, and Paris Las Vegas. Those major narratives whose end was celebrated by postmodernism experience a contemporary recycling in the desert of Nevada. Or their definitive end! For this city lives fast: anything

---

6   Norman M. Klein, "Scripting Las Vegas: Noir Naifs, Junking Up, and the New Strip," in *The Grit Beneath the Glitter: Tales from the Real Las Vegas*, ed. Mike Davis and Hal Rothman (Berkeley, 2002): 17–29.

that fails to bring profit is rebuilt or torn down. Las Vegas cannibalizes yesterday's dreams. On October 27, 1993, the Dunes vanished in a cloud of dust, followed on November 7, 1995, by the Landmark Hotel. Bellagio now occupies the site of the old Dunes, one of the first-generation casinos. Because the miles-long Strip offers good locations and even better sites, it never takes long before gaps are filled. Bellagio and Caesars Palace are expanding; the level of investment is rising. New York New York, with its 2,000 hotel rooms, 4,000 parking spaces, and roller coaster which winds its way around a group of Manhattan skyscrapers shrunk to 30 percent of their original size, swallowed 460 million dollars.

* * *

WHAT FACADES PROMISE

On the other hand, the gaming casinos still work according to the principle: get them in, keep them there, and suck them dry. Anyone walking along Las Vegas Boulevard today notices, with some amazement, that there are very few cars driving by. It's as if they had been swallowed up by the presentation of the casinos. If there were not, now and then, a few motorists racing their engines between stop lights you would hardly notice the traffic at all. Why should you, after all? Your gaze goes right through it to the other side where it scans, weighs up, and evaluates what the facades there promise. You try to imagine which of these promises could be kept. The street is at best a barrier that prevents tourists from rushing over spontaneously. While the traffic appears to move slower than it actually does, visitors, as they move from one attraction to the next, experience a real deceleration in their pace.

Distance, space, and luxury are the new magic words of the show, and no other casino plays this game with such mastery as the Bellagio when, for instance, the water ballet starts up to the theme from the Pink Panther. The building is concealed, piece-by-piece behind a liquid veil until, in a final orgiastic eruption, compressed-air canons shoot water 250 feet (80 m) into the air, shrouding the entire facade in a curtain of mist. Gradually the casino emerges again.

The air is still fresh, strips of vapor, as if from an oversized perfume atomizer, float across the lake and along the railing where the crowd of spectators gradually dissolves, some moving slowly along, others entering the casino. The spectacle, the trademark of the luxury casino, has fulfilled

its function. Draw their attention, keep them there, and then get them inside along travelators. There is also a different method: no electrically operated doors, no easy entry. To enter the MGM Grand you have to push open doors — twice in fact. Entering the casino is a conscious choice. Heroic Atlas-themed statues greet you, and after a short look from the balustrade to the kidney-shaped show bar you go down the escalator and past the Rainforest Café, where a voluminous rainforest frog with red eyes is intended to interest you in enjoying a cocktail, coffee, or juice under the lianas; you continue past the Grand Buffet, a kind of canteen for gamblers, and then the slot machine hall stands in front of you. These machines apparently provide about 70 percent of the gambling profits, cost around $10,000 each, and have a lifespan of about ten years.[7] The space hums, peeps, and rings like an electronic orchestra warming up. A protective, secret cave that looks like it came straight out of Aladdin's treasure trove opens up before you: dimmed lighting, winding corridors, and abruptly angled spaces whose ends are out of sight. Main aisles in harmonizing colors meander through the gambling zone. Visitors are subtly directed by lighting design and clever transitions in the shape of the space. Casinos are like modern labyrinths that leave gamblers little chance of quickly finding their way around. Las Vegas architecture has mastered the art of transition. Service areas around the gaming tables and slot machines permit the gamblers to regain their strength by drinking a coffee or eating a sandwich; they can also dine, take in a show, or shop. And then return to the gaming table. "The madness goes on and on, but nobody seems to notice. The gambling action runs twenty-four hours a day on the main floor, and the circus never ends,[8] — Hunter S. Thompson's diagnosis a generation ago. Taking a break in the Grand Buffet, Janice smiles enquiringly: "Smoking or non-smoking?" With just this simple question the brunette makes one thing perfectly clear: this is not a café in Manhattan, nor a corner bar in Orlando with a "No Smoking Please" sign at the entrance. No, this is Nevada where smoking is accepted and the only thing prohibited is doing nothing. Even the casual stroller with the greatest endurance will eventually enter somewhere and spend some money. Here there is no longer any difference between Las Vegas and Venice — the labyrinth works: get them in, keep them there, and suck them dry.

---

7   Klein, "Scripting Las Vegas," pp. 17–29.
8   Thompson, *Fear and Loathing in Las Vegas*, p. 46.

DESERT, PILGRIMAGE, OASIS

The oasis in the desert lives thanks to logistics, a constant supply of energy and water. "Sex, air conditioning and traffic planning,"[9] form the basis of urbanity here. Energy is supplied by the Hoover Dam that was built in the 1930s and offers electricity in abundance. The gigantic building site also supplies another resource: workers looking forward to the weekend for distraction of any kind, which is just what Las Vegas has to offer. In 1940, the first neon signs blazed above Fremont Street; in 1941, El Rancho opened; and shortly after World War II, the Flamingo. Similar hotel casino complexes based on the same model followed along the Strip, which at the time was still outside the city limits. In 1958, the Stardust casino created an uproar. An illuminated sign transformed a mediocre building into something else: built advertising.[10] What Venturi and Brown, over twenty years later, were to describe as a "decorated shed" — a simple box with an ornamental facade — offered a visual miracle: Kermit Wayne from YESCO (Young Electric Sign Company) magically positioned a metal panel — measuring 238 feet long and 30 feet high (72 x 9 m) and dotted with light bulbs and neon tubes — in the sky above Nevada. The number and size of neon signs exploded in the 1960s: 787 brilliantly illuminated feet (240 m) in front of the Stardust, 138 feet (42 m) high in front of the Sahara, and 197 feet (60 m) high in front of the Dunes. The Dunes was demolished in 1993 to make room for a new kind of entertainment: the mega-casino theme hotel, which, since the early 1990s, has advanced the concept behind the first theme casino (Melvin Grossman's Caesars Palace from the 1960s) and has completely altered the appearance of the Strip. Las Vegas, created out of nothing, became the center of the entertainment world in a single generation. One generation after that, it liberated itself from the reputation as a Mafia-run gambling town and rose to its position as entertainment metropolis of the world. The Strip-city, the very definition of an artificial leisuretime paradise and model of postmodernism, is so successful that it already

mourns its former reputation as Sin City. The new, family-friendly "Sim City" places its bets on congresses, exclusive boutiques, and shows featuring past-their-prime musicians; and now millions of tourists sit beside the pool and gaze at the 76,000 palm trees and bushes that were planted on the Siegfried and Roy Plaza in 1996.

As "a place of pilgrimage Mecca is the only real competition," Peter Cachola Schmal wrote ironically.[11] Las Vegas and Mecca, the cities in the desert, do in fact have something in common: they both need a great deal of water. Anyone who witnesses the greenness of the lawns along the Strip, and the extravagance of the mystery play in front of the Bellagio, believes that, in Nevada, the desert is alive. Water supplied by the Colorado River is the key to the rapid growth of Las Vegas, but in 1900, the city was nothing more than a watering hole with some grazing land. The railway came in 1905: on May 16, 1905, a special train brought speculators to a real estate auction in a no-mans land and a city was created. Gambling was legalized in 1933, attracting the first soldiers of fortune from Los Angeles, only 270 miles (435 km) away.

ELECTRICITY AND CRIMINAL ENERGY

Just how vulnerable this city in the desert actually remains — whose air conditioning systems run at full speed, elevators and ice machines hum, and light bulbs make night into day — is demonstrated in *Ocean's Eleven*, Stephen Soderbergh's remake of the 1960 original. In the film, criminal energy succeeds in paralyzing the city: an electromagnetic pulse and the electrical supply fails. Block by block the Strip sinks into darkness, panic prevails, and for a moment Las Vegas seems to be back at the beginning of its meteoric career, a black hole in the Nevada desert. Then the emergency generators spring into life and the eleven casino thieves use the momentary loss of control to carry out their plan, an illusion in the city of illusions. They trick the guards and escape. It is well-made and entertaining cinema — zero risk. The climatic change enters your consciousness rather more dramatically. Traveling across the Hoover Dam today, you see areas of white cliff face left behind by the receding water level of the Colorado River. "The period since 1999 is now officially the driest in 98 years of recorded history," wrote the *New York Times* on

---

9   Eue, "Las Vegas im Film," p. 2009.

10   Alan Hess, *Eine kurze Geschichte von Las Vegas* (A short history of Las Vegas), *StadtBauwelt* 143, 1999/36: 1980–1987, p. 1982.

11   Peter Cachola Schmal, "Learning from Las Vegas," *deutsche bauzeitung* 11/99, p. 12.

May 2, 2004, signaling a substantial drought that makes the twentieth century, with its abundance of water, seem like a major aberration. The western United States is drying up, and even the gambling city where everything seems possible is forced to respond to nature's call. "In Las Vegas the regional water authority is already removing the equivalent of a football field of grass every day from front lawns, playgrounds and golf courses to save on outdoor watering."[12] The Las Vegas of the future will be bigger but in no way greener than the city today. The Garden of Eden might even revert back into a desert.

ARCHITECTURE ON THE FAULT LINE BETWEEN TIME AND SPACE

Las Vegas is neon letters that have become a city. Electric noise dominates the architecture as if somebody had forgotten to turn off a gigantic television without reception. Hunter S. Thompson described this flickering as a mix of electricity and drugs that penetrates every crevice. Even the hotel room itself dissolves into a charged aura: "The room

couple of recent years are Steve Wynn and Jon Jerde — the creators of the Fremont Experience and Bellagio; they have propagated the Disney-fication of the Strip and the nostalgic reminiscence of Downtown, earning a pretty penny in the process. In 1995, Jerde Partnership erected a glass barrel vault over Fremont Street, the old heart of Downtown Las Vegas, under which the old neon signs of the early days such as "Vegas Vic," the symbol of the Pioneer Casino from Fremont Street, stand like exhibits in a gleaming display case of 2.1 million light bulbs: architecture cast from the same mold, yet at the same time a negation of everything built, as the structures dissolve in cascades of light. Where building is only interior design turned inside out, the real innovations take place behind the scenes, in the technical transmission and refinement of the imagery, the logistics, and the control of visitors. Like every successful business, Las Vegas operates conservatively. This capital of mass culture does not invent trends, but uses them once they begin to appeal to popular taste, inflating them to increasingly new dimensions.

Las Vegas, the real-life movie, created a process that

Las Vegas is no longer just a gambling city in the desert and an escape for dreamers, it is a sociological necessity that has developed in the gaps of American society, and that now serves the entire world as a condensed version of all our clichés.

---

was full of powerful electric noise. The TV set, hissing at top volume on a nonexistent channel."[13] The interiors of the casinos attempt to achieve this quality of dematerialization, this detachment of the gamblers from the outside world. In semi-darkness, the eye follows the shimmering colors and carpet patterns, and must constantly refocus. Stimuli rain down on the senses like visual pin pricks.

Although Las Vegas functioned in analog until now, the digital revolution has arrived. Thousands of neon tubes hum and millions of light bulbs warm the entrances, but already architecture and screens blend to form pixel facades. Digital images are wrapped arbitrarily around random facades. Las Vegas has become a stage set crafted under the orders of generations of scriptwriters. The dream

advances as a never-ending remake of itself, but each time with different costumes and new backdrops. It is therefore not surprising that it has absorbed Hollywood's store of images and strategies in its search for stars and starlets, glamour and tragedies, sets and backdrops, myths and visions. It is also no surprise that the architecture itself is mediafied, as a medium for narratives and a vehicle for expansive feudal dreams of happiness. According to Norman N. Klein: "Leisure time goals for middle-class families must look feudal. They are based on a close connection between cinema, commerce and tourism that was invented in the 1990s."[14] Public space shrinks, existing only between the gutter and the curb of the boulevard — everything else is private. You are tolerated, as long as you don't misbehave. It is said that 90 percent of Downtown and the Strip are under constant video surveillance.

---

12   Kirk Johnson and Dean E. Murphy, "Drought Settles In, Lake Shrinks and West's Worries Grow," *New York Times*, May 2, 2004, sec. 1, p. 1.

13   Thompson, *Fear and Loathing in Las Vegas*, p.181.

14   Klein, "Scripting Las Vegas," pp. 17–29.

Las Vegas celebrates total control — not only in the form of the obvious surveillance by means of cameras, security guards, and motion detectors, but also man's control over the whims of nature. Casinos have abolished both time and space. Only the moment counts. Las Vegas functions as the first city to completely embrace the total marketing of popular taste, where consumption needs no context, but rather only an infrastructure of airports and highways connecting it to the world. Las Vegas works as a highly-specialized entertainment machine that identifies popular taste in various images, places, and stories — and then uses them. It doesn't incorporate unique or original elements in its universe; instead, it uses repetition, the platitudes that everyone understands, recognize immediately, and thus, in a way, make one feel at home. Las Vegas has served as the short-term memory of the pop age. Construction and demolition follow each other rapidly. Norman N. Klein estimates the life expectancy of major projects, such as the Luxor that was built in 1993, at around twenty years.[15] The visitors, for their part, respond to the richness of the presentation and switch back and forth between the individual theme casinos, surfing through Las Vegas as they do TV channels. Las Vegas is and has for a long time been part of the global market of images, a cliché of the pre-fabricated dream. In this sense it has left the traditional city far behind. Las Vegas operates visually and acoustically — and no longer with the tools of traditional urban planning.

It is therefore little wonder that there is hardly any public space. Only the traffic infrastructure — airports and streets — has a certain autonomy, everything else is incorporated in the label "Las Vegas." What counts is opulence, an aesthetic that overpowers the eye and the ear. As in a Baroque performance, the two-dimensional replaces the three-dimensional and painted surfaces are substituted for architecture. Where once artificial marble was used, Styrofoam is employed today — a material that gives the impression of being something else. Nobody is surprised by the fact that facades sound hollow, that carpeted floors comfort the feet, and warm colors govern interiors. The profit motive determines the appearance and half-life value of everything that is new.

Size without irony? Presentation without any subtle twist? This is something that can work only in Las Vegas: the capital of illumination, the oasis of illusions. The city determinedly resists the subversion that is a part of the retro cult. Cracks in the illusion occur only by chance when, for instance, mighty facades stand directly opposite vacant lots. Whereas big budget cinema prepares and presents history with detailed precision but in the process often fails to harmonize technology and emotion, Las Vegas seems to possess the formula for creating tangible worlds from fleeting elements; possible only by means of meta-architecture, the mobile stage sets of a city that is completely mediafied. Thanks to Hollywood, everyone has been here once and has seen Downtown, strolled along the Strip, and forgotten themselves in front of the fountains of Bellagio — seen a thousand times and touched just as often. Las Vegas is no longer just a gambling city in the desert and an escape for dreamers, it is a sociological necessity that has developed in the gaps of American society, and that now serves the entire world as a condensed version of all our clichés.

---

15 Ibid.

PART 5
BUYING IN AND SELLING OUT

I will sell this house today.
I will sell this house today.
I will sell this house today!

— Carolyn Burnham,
American Beauty (1999)

CHAPTER 14

Consumer Culture

This isn't life. This is just stuff, and it's become more important to you than living. Well honey, that's just nuts.

— Lester Burnham,
American Beauty (1999)

Chapter 14. Consumer Culture

Recommended Films

American Beauty (Sam Mendes 1999)
WALL·E (Andrew Stanton 2008)

Media Models

The Meme, The Spectacle

Chapter Summary

George T. Hole examines the deeper meanings of beauty, rebellion, and suburban consumerism in *American Beauty*.

Naomi Klein critiques the power of logos, brands, and advertising images in consumer culture.

American Beauty: Look Closer

from *Movies and the Meaning of Life*

— George T. Hole

... beauty's nothing but the start of that terror
We can hardly bear; still we love
The serene scorn it could kill us with.
— RAINER MARIA RILKE, Duino Elegies

Good movies give us opportunities to imagine into the drama of other lives and, indirectly, allow us to fantasize about our own. As a result we might gain insights into how to live our own lives better. Lester Burnham, the main character of *American Beauty* played brilliantly by Oscar-winning actor Kevin Spacey, has a revelation — and he acts on it. "It's a great thing to realize you still have the ability to surprise yourself. Makes you wonder what else you can do that you've forgotten about." Can we appreciate this and his end-of-life-insight, which involves a mysterious sense of beauty that freshens and redeems life more radically than surprise?

With comic and tragic overtones, *American Beauty* allows us to witness two seemingly normal families, the Burnhams (Lester, Carolyn, and Jane) and the Fittses (Frank, Barbara, and Ricky), caught in suburban angst, breaking apart at the seams. The movie does more than entertain us with yet another story of a man going through a mid-life crisis. It offers us a philosophical challenge, not simply to intellectualize about the meaning of the movie, but to examine our assumptions about the meaning of our own lives.

LIFE POST-MORTEM

As the movie opens, a voice (we will learn is Lester's) introduces us to his daughter Jane (Thora Birch): "Janie is a pretty typical teenager. Angry, insecure, confused. I wish I could tell her all that's going to pass. But I don't want to lie to her." Janie is also highly critical of her father: "I need a father who's a role model, not some horny geek-boy who's gonna spray his shorts whenever I bring a girlfriend home from school. Like he'd ever have a chance with her. What a lame-o. Somebody should put him out of his misery." A voice off-screen asks "Want me to kill him for you?" Later, replaying this conversation, she tells her boyfriend Ricky that she would pay for his murder with the baby-sitting money that she has been saving to get "a boob job."

In the next scene, as the camera pans Robin Hood Trail, Any Town, U.S.A., a well-laid-out suburban neighborhood, we hear the same off-screen voice of Lester telling us prophetically, "In a year I will be dead. I am dead already." Lester's wife and daughter think he is a "great loser." Lester agrees: "And they are right. I've lost something very important. I'm not exactly sure what it is, but I know I didn't always feel this ... sedated." When his wife Carolyn reintroduces him to Buddy Kane, the regional real estate "king" (with whom she will later have an affair), Lester replies self-mockingly, "I would not remember me either." The voice off-screen continues, "[I]t is never too late to get it [my life] back."

Ricky Fitts (Wes Bentley), the new kid next door who has the odd habit of constantly videotaping whatever he finds curious, will become Lester's personal hero after he

George T. Hole, "*American Beauty*: Look Closer," from *Movies and the Meaning of Life: Philosophers Take on Hollywood*, edited by Kimberly A. Blessing and Paul J. Tudico, pp. 153–168. Copyright © 2005 by the Open Court Publishing Company. Permission to reprint granted by Carus Publishing Company.

"American Beauty" · 341

witnesses Ricky telling his catering boss, "I quit. Leave me alone." Lester too, quits — he quits playing his customary, un-dramatic roles as father, husband, employee and neighbor. The event that triggers Lester's journey of self-discovery takes place when he is introduced to Angela Hayes (Mena Suvari), the beautiful blonde and sexually promiscuous cheerleader friend of his daughter, Jane. Middle-aged Lester is determined to impress and seduce her, much to the disgust of his daughter and oblivion of his wife.

Following Ricky's lead, Lester quits his job and rebels against his adult responsibilities. (His rebellion leads to complications, humorous for us, as it leads to the exposure of self-deceptions in other characters.) He buys a 1972 cherry red Pontiac GTO convertible and devotes his days to lifting weights, jogging with his homosexual neighbors Jim and Jim ("I want to look good naked"), smoking pot, and listening to Bob Dylan tunes in his well-appointed up-scale, two-car garage. Lester's sexual fantasy almost becomes real. On the evening of his murder, when he is about to have sex with Angela she tells him that she has been lying about her sexual experience; this is her first time. Instead of laughing at her or even himself, he responds with compassion: "You have nothing to be sorry about." And Lester realizes that he has nothing to be sorry about either. *American Beauty* ends with us hearing Lester's disembodied voice expressing his gratitude "for every single moment of my stupid little life." The voice continues: "You won't understand. Don't worry. You will someday."

A LIFE BEHIND THINGS

What is it that we do not understand? What we need to understand is another line from Lester's concluding soliloquy: "It is hard to stay mad when there is so much beauty in the world." In fact, beauty pervades the movie and seems most enigmatic in the scene in which Ricky, Lester's personal drug-dealing hero, shows a video he recorded. In it a plastic bag is held captive in a wind for fifteen minutes, gliding aimlessly in the air in front of a non-descript red-brick wall. Ricky, the son of a stern, homophobic, retired military officer father and a mother who never speaks except to apologize, explains:

> It was one of those days when it's a minute away from snowing and there's this electricity in the air, you can almost hear it, right? And this bag was like, dancing with me. Like a little kid begging me to play with it. For fifteen minutes. And that's the day I knew there was this entire life behind things, and … this incredibly benevolent force, that wanted me to know that there was no reason to be afraid. Ever.

Ricky sees "an entire life behind things." Anticipating Lester's end-of-life insight, which he announces in his post-mortem soliloquy, Ricky exclaims, "Sometimes there is so much beauty I can't take it. Like my heart is going to cave in."

The dominant theme of *American Beauty* is the exposure, sometimes humorously, sometimes tragically, of different versions of transcendence, getting to some supposedly better place or state beyond where we are now. Instead of transcendence as a strategy for meaning in life, the movie suggests a redemptive possibility in beauty, here, in this life as it is. What is this view of beauty, so pervasive and powerful, that it will redeem a stupid life?

The ancient Greek philosopher Plato (around 428–348 B.C.E.) and the German philosopher Immanuel Kant (1724–1804) offer theories about transcendence and beauty. For Plato, we might reach some stage of transcendence by climbing out of our cave and attaining beauty by climbing the ladder of love. For his modern counterpart Kant, the transcendent realm of god, freedom, and immortality, while it must be postulated, is beyond the reach of our knowledge and experience. His theory of beauty resting on the paradoxical idea of "purposiveness without purpose"[1] comes close to Ricky's sense of beauty in the aimless movements of the paper in the wind. The Eastern Sage Buddha (560–480 B.C.E.) will be an instructive guide to help us figure out what we do not understand and what is alive in the core of beauty. But first let's consider the first movie theater ever constructed, as found in Plato's famous "Allegory of the Cave."[2]

THE URGE FOR SOMETHING BEYOND

Plato in his famous Allegory of the Cave constructs the first movie theater, figuratively, in order to answer a speculative

---

1 "Beauty is the form of the purposiveness of an object, so far as this is perceived in it without any representation of a purpose" — the concluding statement of *Third Movement of the Judgment of Taste*, article 17, Immanuel Kant, Critique of Judgment (New York: Hafner, 1951).
2 See Book VII of Plato's *Republic*.

question about us, namely, to what degree can humans be enlightened? We are to imagine an underground cave in which people seated in darkness are watching images flicker on the cave wall in front of them, much like we are seated in the movie theater—with a crucial difference; they are chained from birth to their place. Plato imagines what it would be like for a person to be unchained, turned around and face the fire, the puppets, and puppeteers who are producing the shadow-show. After an initial experience of blindness and confusion, Plato suggests that the freed person would comprehend the nature and cause of the shadow-show. Plato has us follow the prisoner through two more stages, emerging from the cave into full sunlight and then returning back into the cave, returning to his original seat alongside his friends, still engaged in their pastime of naming the shadows. At each stage the freed person suffers blindness and confusion, before gaining sight and understanding.

The sun represents what Plato calls the "form of the Good." Forms are ideal models or prototypes for all particular things that exist in the world that we experience through our senses. Furthermore, forms are unchanging and have an existence more real for Plato than the sensory things in which the forms inhere. Take for example a few of the many striking appearances of the color red in *American Beauty*: rose petals, rose bouquets, the front door of the Burnham house, and Lester's blood on the white tile and white kitchen table. For Plato, all these examples are manifestations of the form of redness (and the form of beauty) which must exist independent of its examples if we are to have any stable knowledge of our world. So, when the prisoner finally sees the sun it is like being able to comprehend Goodness itself, independent of any specifically good things. Moreover, just as the sun is the source of light in our sensory world, Goodness is the source of intelligible light by which we can truly apprehend good things. Since the Good is the highest form, it is last and most essential to know on the journey toward enlightenment. And, the Good is like the sun; it is the source of the intelligible light by which we know particularly good things — But like the sun, we cannot look

directly into the Good without being permanently blinded. Finally, just as the sun is the source of life and nourishment in the sensory, physical world, knowledge of the form of the Good is the source of vitality and meaning in what Plato characterizes as the intelligible world.

In Plato's allegory, we notice that only one person apprehends the Good and thus becomes enlightened. When he returns to the cave, the transformed prisoner is eager to tell of his remarkable journey and discoveries. In dismay, the other prisoners threaten to take his life if he persists in interrupting their entertainment.[3] For those who are ignorant of their chains, his talk about some strange place outside the cave, along with his wild idea about knowledge of the Good, has no practical value. They are deeply fascinated by the flickers of shadows and the voices of puppeteers, so they know perfectly well what is good for them; don't they? And, as Plato suggests by analogy, we know too; don't we? But recall what Lester advised at the outset of *American Beauty*: There is a truth — one that will redeem even a stupid life — we do not understand yet.

Plato's "Allegory of the Cave" — essential and exciting reading for any student of philosophy — captures a fundamental assumption that is central to most religions and, to a lesser degree, animates contemporary American culture. The assumption begins with a distinction between appearances and reality. The world of appearances — the common, everyday world that we accept based on tradition and unexamined experience — is represented by images that constitute the "reality" of the allegorical cave dwellers. Even their dreams of some better life outside the cave, are shaped by the puppeteers.[4] By contrast, the "real-reality" lies in the knowledge of the Good, which is to be learned last of all, and, at least for Plato, is realized only by a few individuals. Christianity embraces this dualism in its fundamental distinctions between the body — Caesar's world — and the soul — God's world. The notion of "transcendence," which is found in both Plato and Christianity, captures the idea of

---

3 Likely Plato is alluding to the fate of his teacher and friend, Socrates, who was put to death by his fellow Athenians for the crime of practicing philosophy. While Socrates did not claim to be enlightened, he dedicated his life to philosophy as the love of wisdom. Thus, Plato suggests that, in addition to a method of questioning, a person needs a deep love of wisdom to be free of the chains of popular belief and begin the journey toward enlightenment.

4 Lester echoes this idea of appearance: "Our marriage is for show, a commercial." But, in contrast to Plato, he suggests at this point that there is no more substantial reality in marriage.

a higher reality, or other world, vastly superior to the lower, inferior existence we experience in our everyday lives.

For Plato and Christians it is this higher realm of existence that one should seek to obtain in order to have a meaningful life. Both endorse special means that one must practice in order to transcend this inferior life of ignorance or sin, to attain a truly worthwhile existence of knowledge of the Good or God's eternal salvation. *American Beauty* satirizes a materialistic version of transcendence and portrays a different possibility: Goodness and redemption are possible through the realization of the everyday beauty pervading even the most mundane things and the most stupid and smallest lives. A prominent sign on Lester's desk issues the simple command: "Look closer."[5] This is a clue for understanding the nature of beauty, as well as Lester's final declaration — there is something we do not understand, something that presumably will make a decisive difference in the experience of the meaning of our lives.

WHEN IS A ROSE NOT A ROSE AND MUCH MORE?

American Beauty pokes fun at many of the idealizations of beauty held dear by many Americans: the beautiful house, the beautiful yard, the beautiful $4,000 Italian silk couch, the beautiful wife, the beautiful body, and so forth. One of the initial scenes of the movie, in which we are introduced to Lester's wife, brilliantly parodies this aspect of the American dream. We find Carolyn Burnham (Annette Bening) in her rose garden in front of the house, cutting flowers and placing them in a basket, with a determined, humorless look on her face. She is perfectly put together and has lots of useful, and apparently new, expensive gardening tools. Lester remarks sardonically: "That's my wife Carolyn. See the way the handle on those pruning shears matches her gardening clogs. That's not an accident." We then see two well-groomed, model-like men, Jim and Jim, who are leaving their home for work. One Jim gets into a Ford Taurus while the other Jim crosses the street to greet Carolyn:

> JIM: Morning Carolyn.
> CAROLYN (*overly friendly and dramatic*): Good morning, Jim!
> I just love your tie!

JIM: And I just love your roses. How do you get them to flourish like that?
CAROLYN: Well, I'll tell you. Egg shells and Miracle Grow.
The camera returns to Lester dressed in his bathrobe, drying his hair as he looks down on them.
LESTER: Man, I get exhausted just watching her. She wasn't always like this. She used to be happy. We used to be happy. ... But she doesn't have much use for me anymore. About the only thing that gets her excited now is money.

What is Lester's response to their mutual unhappiness? He has accepted the coma-like state of his life: He mumbles complaints to himself and he stumbles over his efforts to get into his wife's car on schedule and to be a friend to his daughter. When he eventually rebels, he exposes the shallowness of his stultified American dream.

Flowers, in particular roses, conventional things of beauty, appear prominently throughout the movie. In fact, "American Beauty" is the name of a kind of rose. In one striking scene (used in the movie's trailer) Lester fantasizes that Angela is lying in a white porcelain bathtub filled with red rose petals: As he reaches into the tub to touch her, Angela slowly spreads open her thighs. In reality, Lester's sexual encounter with Angela will prove much less idyllic, and much more beautiful. Other character's confrontation with disillusionment will be more comic and far more shattering.

REBELLION AND EXPOSURE

The adult ladder Lester has been climbing to achieve the American dream has led only to the discovery that with success he is unhappy. He now deliberately descends, breaking rungs on the way down. He quits his job. In the process, he exposes the (cowardly) double talk of his boss, Brad, self-proclaimed as "one of the good guys," who requests a job profile as a prelude for firing Lester. Exposing Brad's mean business ethic, Lester extorts a severance package by threatening Brad with a homosexual harassment charge. Empowered by his freedom from the traditional American work ethic of transcendence, Lester proclaims at home, "I rule."

Lester's choice of a new life, responsibility-free and coma-free, contrasts with the upward grasping of other characters for some idealized state of transcendence — one

---

5 Sam Mendes, in his directional debut, likely is directing us to look closer into the movie we're watching.

that is vulnerable to failure and comic exposure. We watch Carolyn psyching herself by repeating a mantra "I will sell this house today." She strips to her undergarments to spic and span the empty house. The contrast between the deadpan responses of potential buyers to her inflated enthusiasm for the house is humorous.

One woman complains with a tinge of outrage: "The ad said this pool was 'lagoon-like.' But there's nothing 'lagoon-like' about it. Except for maybe the bugs [as she slaps her arm]. There are not even any plants out here." Carolyn, ever ready to please in order to sell, replies, "I have an excellent landscape architect." The woman states bluntly what she means: "I mean, I think 'lagoon,' and I think waterfall, I think tropical. This is just a cement hole." She seems righteously angry for being disillusioned by the ad — the danger in believing in something transcendent.

greeted by two neighbors, Jim and Jim, who introduce themselves as partners. They are offering the Fitts family a welcome-to-the-neighborhood basket. Colonel Fitts, hearing "partners," thinks that they must be trying to sell him something. Slowly it dawns on him that they are men living together as partners and his disgust for homosexuality surfaces. Later, to avoid his father's hostility Ricky pretends to share his father's disgust. Much later, in an incidental comment to Lester, Ricky says with a laugh, "My dad thinks I paid for all this [expensive video equipment] with catering jobs." He adds a statement that may be true not only for his father: "Never underestimate the power of denial."

Like others in the movie, Colonel Fitts misinterprets something he sees, which leads to two cruel actions. When he thinks he sees his son commit a homosexual act with

---

American Beauty pokes fun at many of the idealizations of beauty held dear by many Americans: the beautiful house, the beautiful yard, the beautiful $4,000 Italian silk couch, the beautiful wife, the beautiful body, and so forth.

We are amused. The scene ends with Carolyn clearly disappointed that she has not satisfied her ambition to sell the house today. Her disappointment, first expressed as a pout, turns suddenly violent: She slaps herself repeatedly in the face.

Another comic scene of exposure takes place in line at the fast-food drive-through. Carolyn and Buddy are groping each other in her Mercedes SUV, after their earlier sexual "explosion" in a motel. (Later, Carolyn will follow Buddy's suggestion for power-after-sex, to shoot a pistol.) They are unaware that Lester, now the food dispatcher, is watching them. Exposed, they try to compose themselves and utter an unconvincing story. Lester is amused, giving them their two "smiley" orders and giving himself several more degrees freedom from responsibility. However, because he has witnessed their sexual tryst, their exposed fantasy completely deflates.

The chronically disillusioned character in the film is Barbara, Ricky's mother. Whenever she appears, she seems catatonic. Her mantra is "I'm sorry." His father, Colonel Fitts, is the person most dramatically exposed. When his doorbell rings, it seems as if he hears an alarm and suspiciously questions his wife and son whether they expect anyone. It is comic to watch him open the door and be

Lester, the Colonel beats his son mercilessly. Ironically, the Colonel's own homosexual desires surface when he kisses Lester, only to be gently rebuffed. Later, the Colonel kills Lester. Presumably when he discovered a shameful reality beneath his own shadow-show sense of identity, murder, not a struggle to enlightenment, is his only face-saving necessity. (We might ponder Socrates's famous assertion, "The unexamined life is not worth living" and add a caution: Never underestimate the suffering from exposure and more authentic self-knowledge.)

Angela is another character whose fantasy, in her case of self-importance, gets exposed. Nothing is worse for her than being ordinary. So, to prove otherwise, she tells stories about being the object of men's sexual attention and boy's masturbation fantasies. Ricky, who is escaping home after his father has beaten him, has asked Jane to join him. Angela protests. Ricky challenges her friendship with Jane, "She's not your friend. She's somebody you use to feel good about yourself." Angela calls him a freak and then asserts in her defense, "Oh, yeah? Well, at least I'm not ugly." Ricky challenges her deceptive sense of self, "You are totally ordinary. And you know it." Minutes later as Lester is slowly and sensually undressing Angela, finally acting out his sexual fantasy, she confesses, "This is my first time." His aroused illusion of her is shattered. Exposure no longer is comic; it is painful to watch. The only more painful exposure would be to watch some dimly recognized vulnerability of our own laid bare.

AMERICAN BEAUTY

Beyond our conventional understanding, beauty itself might be what we cannot understand. We have standard conceptions of what is beautiful: a red rose, a blonde cheerleader with a voluptuous body, a well-manicured lawn. Correspondingly, we have standard representations of what is ugly: a dead bird, a useless plastic bag, a loveless marriage. Not unlike the cave-dwellers who name the different images of the shadow-show, we do not even have to look at these particular things to know that they are beautiful or ugly — we have been taught these judgments as cultural truths. But, can we look for ourselves, as if seeing for the first time? Can we have an insight similar to the one Edna St. Vincent Millay (1892–1950) expressed in her poem, "Euclid alone has looked on beauty bare." The poem is dense and suggests a sympathy for Plato's idea of form:

> It seems as if the beautiful object has some purpose, some final objective, beyond simply being what it is. Yet, it is just what it is, a gift, a bag blowing in the wind, for our imagination and experience.

Euclid alone has looked on Beauty bare.
Let all who prate of Beauty hold their peace,
And lay them prone upon the earth and cease
To ponder on themselves, the while they stare
At nothing, intricately drawn nowhere
In shapes of shifting lineage; let geese
Gabble and hiss, but heroes seek release
From dusty bondage into luminous air.

O blinding hour. O holy, terrible day,
When first the shaft into his vision shone
Of light anatomized! Euclid alone
Has looked on Beauty bare. Fortunate they
Who, though once only and then but far away
Have heard her massive sandal set on stone.

The poem speaks of something blinding, holy and even terrible in the experience of looking on beauty bare. Beauty is bare when our minds are bare, free of pre-conceptions of beauty. At that moment, something profound happens. Ricky has experienced it: "Sometimes there's so much beauty in the world I feel like I can't take it, like my heart's going to cave in." Lester has a similar experience of beauty bare, "Sometimes I feel like I'm seeing it all at once and it's too much, my heart fills up like a balloon that's about to burst."

As Lester discovers, the experience of beauty has redemptive powers. Beauty can heal. It can heal the disappointment and anger at a life not lived as one would have hoped. Lester states what other characters and we might express, "I guess I could be pretty pissed off about what happened to me." But he adds this remarkable and rare realization, "But it's hard to stay mad, when there's so much beauty in the world." Ricky, too, could have been pissed off, when his parents sent him to a mental institution. Hearing this, Lester responds in an obvious way, "Yeah, but you lost two whole years of your life." Ricky has a different perspective, one that may be the eye-opener to beauty bare: "I didn't lose them. It taught me how to step back and just watch, and not take everything so personally. And that's something I needed to learn. That's something everybody needs to learn."

"Step back and just watch" might not seem like a hard lesson to learn. But it depends on how we understand its meaning. Philosophers attempt to "step back and watch;" in order to explain beauty; some of them focus attention on a particular kind of attitude that is necessary to experience it. Immanuel Kant, for one, emphasizes disinterestedness as an essential aspect of the aesthetic attitude.[6] Disinterestedness marks a boundary where we separate from our usual attitudes, practical, cognitive and moral, so that we are free to contemplate beauty bare, for its own sake.

Kant notes that our repertoire of concepts is not adequate to account for the beauty we behold. Matching concepts to objects — for example applying the concept of a freshly opening rose to our experience of this richly particular rose, in this unique setting — gives us, at best,

---

6 Kant, *ibid.*, article 2

conventional beauty and thin experience. Once free of our conventional matching of concepts to objects, we can enjoy the free play of imagination, an aspect of being creative with our experience that Kant describes paradoxically as "purposiveness without purpose." It seems as if the beautiful object has some purpose, some final objective, beyond simply being what it is. Yet, it is just what it is, a gift, a bag blowing in the wind, for our imagination and experience.

Ricky has a similar insight when he watches the bag blowing aimlessly in the wind: "And this bag was like, dancing with me. Like a little kid begging me to play with it. For fifteen minutes. And that's the day I knew there was this entire life behind things, and this incredibly benevolent force, that wanted me to know there was no reason to be afraid. Ever."

Lester, too, learns to be more fearless. Ricky had an earlier experience of a "life behind things": "When you see something like that [a dead bird] it's like God is looking right at you, just for a second. And if you're careful, you can look right back." Does he actually know there is a benevolent force or a God behind things? Ricky gives no evidence of belief in God (nor does any other character in the movie), or much else of traditional value. Ricky does seem to share Kant's intuition, that inherent in beauty there exists some greater purpose, which connects with transcendent ideas of God, freedom and immortality. For Lester, it was this intuition in beauty, which he optimistically believes we will understand someday for ourselves — an intuition that has the power to redeem "every single moment of [his] stupid little life."

In addition to "step back and watch," it is far harder to learn "not to take everything personally." Lester learns not to take everything personally, while all the other characters, except for Ricky, do take so much personally. Carolyn is not able to step back from her disappointing day: She takes it personally that she did not fulfill her self-imposed command to sell the house today. She continues to take it personally as she punishes herself, from a critic-like position, because she was not able to act and direct other characters and herself according to her script for the day. At this point she is a failed author, a failed actor, and a failed stage director. She can only satisfy her role as critic and punish herself.

Plato describes for us a path to the greatest apprehension of beauty. In the *Symposium*, Socrates is given instructions on love. If he maintains a sense of honor and reverence for a beloved, not indulging in wanton desires, he will ascend, as if on a ladder, to higher forms of beauty, from the beauty of one person to many, from the beauty of persons to the beauty of laws. He will come "to understand that the beauty of them all is of one family, and that personal beauty is a trifle."[7] At the highest rung of this famous ladder of love Socrates will behold, in its awesome splendor, "the vast sea of beauty." As a result, "he will create many fair and noble thoughts and notions in boundless love of wisdom; until on that shore he grows and waxes strong, and at last the vision is revealed to him of a single science, which is the science of beauty everywhere."[8]

For Plato, this climb is as arduous a challenge as the prisoner's struggle to find the way outside the cave, to behold knowledge of the Good. Nothing short of beholding this final revelation is adequate for Plato: "He who has been instructed thus far in the things of love, and who has learned to see the beautiful in due order and succession, when he comes toward the end will suddenly perceive a nature of wondrous beauty (and this, Socrates, is the final cause of all our former toils) — a nature which in the first place is everlasting, not growing and decaying, or waxing and waning."[9]

Ricky and Lester have found a shortcut to the top of Plato's ladder: Look closer, without taking anything personally. They both realize that beauty is already here, waiting for one to let go of personal stuff, open "beginner's eyes"[10] and behold beauty bare wholeheartedly. Rather than being pissed off at not attaining the life he thought it was supposed to be, Lester appreciates his life as it is, with gratitude.

THE BUDDHA ON BEAUTY

Maybe we can understand Ricky's seeming obsession with videotaping as his attempt to capture and record beautiful images for later viewing. But, can he capture and replay his

---

7   Plato's *Symposium*, translated by Benjamin Jowett, found online at http://classics.mit.edu/Plato/symposium.1b.txt.

8   *Ibid.*

9   *Ibid.*, 211b.

10   The phrase is a variation on the title of a Zen Buddhist book: *Zen Mind; Beginner's Mind*, which teaches the importance of seeing as if for the first time.

experience, much less beauty itself? Buddha offers a profound insight in regard to any experience, especially those great ones we try to hold onto and duplicate. About his long-sought and life-transforming enlightenment he states: "I obtained not the least thing from unexcelled, complete awakening; and for this very reason it is called 'unexcelled, complete awakening'."[11] He did not make his own enlight-

---

American Beauty shows a comic
and tragic side to more mundane,
competitive transcendence: To get
somewhere and be somebody in
America.

---

enment something personal, as if by holding onto it he would be special and entitled to claim for himself some privileged center of existence. In his concluding revelation, Lester offers a similar bit of advice that is applicable when we are tempted to grasp or hold on to what we cherish in experience: "And then I remember to relax, and stop trying to hold on to it, and then it flows through me like rain."

Plato, in contrast with the Buddha, will not be satisfied until the enlightened one is free of all particulars and has a secure hold on the never changing, eternal form of beauty. Plato and Christianity share a similar vision of transcendence: By special practices — climbing the ladder of love or loving God, neighbor and self — a person can attain entry and status in a higher reality, the intelligible realm or after-life salvation. *American Beauty* shows a comic and tragic side to more mundane, competitive transcendence: To get somewhere and be somebody in America. While the movie exposes the life of grasping after "good" things, and pushing away or avoiding seeing "bad," it affirms and offers us the choice to transcend transcendence: Beauty is present even in a stupid life if a person takes a closer look and lets go of the personal stuff. What then is difficult to understand? We typically are seeking big meaning, a meaning that rests on an image of how our lives are supposed to be, if we do the right things. Consequently, we are like Plato's cave-dwellers in the sense that we have an image of how life would be if we broke free and could live outside our imprisoning cave. When life does not match our image and

---

11 Alan Watts, *Zen Buddhism* (New York: Random House, 1957), p. 45.

---

expectations we righteously get pissed off. *American Beauty* offers a glimpse of a more satisfying option: Meaning, like beauty, is always accessible in our lives, if we take a closer look, with beginner's eyes, and experience our lives with deep gratitude.

TO THINK ABOUT

1. Make a list of five things you find beautiful and five you find ugly. For one item from your beautiful list, do the following:

    Look at it again, this particular object, in this particular setting; look as closely as possible taking it in fully. This includes looking at it with sympathy for what it is, and without any cognitive, practical, or personal interest in it. Relax; take your time looking. Consider at some point that the object is looking back at you with gratitude. Note any difference from previous looking at it. Note any thoughts that make it difficult to contemplate the object simply for its own sake. Note (and better yet, write down) your experience.

2. Do you participate fully in your life as it is? In other words, is there some condition such that if it is not met you will not fully participate? For example, if you have been, or are likely to be "pissed off" by some person or activity, do you hold back from experiencing that person or activity fully? Or, if life is not fair, do you not try as hard to secure what you most want?

3. What does the movie say about our responsibility for our own happiness? Is our happiness completely with our control?

TO READ NEXT

Edmund Burke. *A Philosophical Enquiry into the Origin of Our Ideas of the Sublime and Beautiful.* Edited with an introduction and notes by James T. Boulton. Notre Dame: University of Notre Dame Press, 1968.

Joseph H. Kupfer. *Experience as Art: Aesthetics in Everyday Life.* Albany: State University of New York Press, 1983.

Immanuel Kant. *Observations on the Feeling of the Beautiful and Sublime.* Translated by John T. Goldthwait. Berkeley: University of California Press, 1960.

Mary Mothersill. *Beauty Restored.* Oxford: Clarendon, 1984.

Plato. *Symposium*. Translated by Alexander Nehamas and Paul Woodruff. Indianapolis: Hackett, 1989.

Alan Watts. *The Way of Zen*. New York: Vintage, 1957.

The Brand Expands

from *No Logo*

— Naomi Klein

HOW THE LOGO GRABBED CENTER STAGE

Since the crocodile is the symbol of Lacoste, we thought they might be interested in sponsoring our crocodiles.
> — Silvino Gomes, commercial director of the Lisbon Zoo, on the institution's creative corporate sponsorship program, March 1998

I was in Grade 4 when skintight designer jeans were the be-all and end-all, and my friends and I spent a lot of time checking out each other's butt for logos. "Nothing comes between me and my Calvins," Brooke Shields assured us, and as we lay back on our beds Ophelia-style and yanked up the zippers on our Jordache jeans with wire hangers, we knew she was telling no word of a lie. At around the same time, Romi, our school's own pint-sized Farrah Fawcett, used to make her rounds up and down the rows of desks turning back the collars on our sweaters and polo shirts. It wasn't enough for her to see an alligator or a leaping horseman — it could have been a knockoff. She wanted to see the label behind the logo. We were only eight years old but the reign of logo terror had begun.

About nine years later, I had a job folding sweaters at an Esprit clothing store in Montreal. Mothers would come in with their six-year-old daughters and ask to see only the shirts that said "Esprit" in the company's trademark bold block lettering. "She won't wear anything without a name," the moms would confide apologetically as we chatted by the change rooms. It's no secret that branding has become far more ubiquitous and intrusive by now. Labels like Baby Gap and Gap Newborn imprint brand awareness on toddlers and turn babies into mini-billboards. My friend Monica tells me that her seven-year-old son marks his homework not with check marks but with little red Nike swooshes.

Until the early seventies, logos on clothes were generally hidden from view, discreetly placed on the inside of the collar. Small designer emblems did appear on the outside of shirts in the first half of the century, but such sporty attire was pretty much restricted to the golf courses and tennis courts of the rich. In the late seventies, when the fashion world rebelled against Aquarian flamboyance, the country-club wear of the fifties became mass style for newly conservative parents and their preppy kids. Ralph Lauren's Polo horseman and Izod Lacoste's alligator escaped from the golf course and scurried into the streets, dragging the logo decisively onto the outside of the shirt. These logos served the same social function as keeping the clothing's price tag on: everyone knew precisely what premium the wearer was willing to pay for style. By the mid-eighties, Lacoste and Ralph Lauren were joined by Calvin Klein, Esprit and, in Canada, Roots; gradually, the logo was transformed from an ostentatious affectation to an active fashion accessory. "Most significantly, the logo itself was growing in size, ballooning from a three-quarter-inch emblem into a chest-sized marquee. This process of logo inflation is still progressing, and none is more bloated than Tommy Hilfiger, who has managed to pioneer a clothing style that transforms its faithful adherents into walking, talking, life-sized Tommy dolls, mummified in fully branded Tommy worlds.

This scaling-up of the logo's role has been so dramatic that it has become a change in substance. Over the past decade and a half, logos have grown so dominant that they have essentially transformed the clothing on which they appear into empty carriers for the brands they represent. The metaphorical alligator, in other words, has risen up and swallowed the literal shirt.

This trajectory mirrors the larger transformation our culture has undergone since Marlboro Friday, sparked by a stampede of manufacturers looking to replace their cumbersome product-production apparatus with transcendent brand names and to infuse their brands with deep, meaningful messages. By the mid-nineties, companies like Nike, Polo and Tommy Hilfiger were ready to take branding to the next level: no longer simply branding their own products, but branding the outside culture as well — by

films, community events, magazines, sports and schools. This ambitious project makes the logo the central focus of everything it touches — not an add-on or a happy association, but the main attraction.

Advertising and sponsorship have always been about using imagery to equate products with positive cultural or social experiences. What makes nineties-style branding different is that it increasingly seeks to take these associations out of the representational realm and make them a lived reality. So the goal is not merely to have child actors drinking Coke in a TV commercial, but for students to brainstorm concepts for Coke's next ad campaign in English class. It transcends logo-festooned Roots clothing designed to conjure memories of summer camp and reaches out to build an actual Roots country lodge that becomes a 3-D manifestation of the Roots brand concept. Disney transcends its sports network ESPN, a channel for guys who like to sit around in sports bars screaming at the TV, and launches a line of ESPN Sports Bars, complete with giant-

---

> Over the past decade and a half, logos have grown so dominant that they have essentially transformed the clothing on which they appear into empty carriers for the brands they represent.

---

sponsoring cultural events, they could go out into the world and claim bits of it as brand-name outposts. For these companies, branding was not just a matter of adding value to a product. It was about thirstily soaking up cultural ideas and iconography that their brands could reflect, by projecting these ideas and images back on the culture as "extensions" of their brands. Culture, in other words, would add value to their brands. For example, Onute Miller, senior brand manager for Tequila Sauza, explains that her company sponsored a risqué photography exhibit by George Holz because "art was a natural synergy with our product."[1]

Branding's current state of cultural expansionism is about much more than traditional corporate sponsorships: the classic arrangement in which a company donates money to an event in exchange for seeing its logo on a banner or in a program. Rather, this is the Tommy Hilfiger approach of full-frontal branding, applied now to cityscapes, music, art,

screen TVs. The branding process reaches beyond heavily marketed Swatch watches and launches "Internet time," a new venture for the Swatch Group, which divides the day into one thousand "Swatch beats." The Swiss company is now attempting to convince the on-line world to abandon the traditional clock and switch to its time-zone-free, branded time.

The effect, if not always the original intent, of advanced branding is to nudge the hosting culture into the background and make the brand the star. It is not to sponsor culture but to *be* the culture. And why shouldn't it be? If brands are not products but ideas, attitudes, values and experiences, why can't they be culture too? As we will see later in the chapter, this project has been so successful that the lines between corporate sponsors and sponsored culture have entirely disappeared. But this conflation has not been a oneway process, with passive artists allowing themselves to be shoved into the background by aggressive multinational corporations. Rather, many artists, media personalities, film directors and sports stars have been racing to meet the corporations halfway in the branding

---

1 *Business Week*, 24 May 1999, and *Wall Street Journal*, 12 February 1999.

game. Michael Jordan, Puff Daddy, Martha Stewart, Austin Powers, Brandy and *Star Wars* now mirror the corporate structure of corporations like Nike and the Gap, and they are just as captivated by the prospect of developing and leveraging their own branding potential as the product-based manufacturers. So what was once a process of selling culture to a sponsor for a price has been supplanted by the logic of "co-branding" — a fluid partnership between celebrity people and celebrity brands.

The project of transforming culture into little more than a collection of brand-extensions-in-waiting would not have been possible without the deregulation and privatization policies of the past three decades. In Canada under Brian Mulroney, in the U.S. under Ronald Reagan and in Britain under Margaret Thatcher (and in many other parts of the world as well), corporate taxes were dramatically lowered, a move that eroded the tax base and gradually starved out the public sector. (See Table 2.1) As government spending dwindled, schools, museums and broadcasters were desperate to make up their budget shortfalls and thus ripe for partnerships with private corporations. It also didn't hurt that the political climate during this time ensured that there was almost no vocabulary to speak passionately about the value of a non-commercialized public sphere. This was the time of the Big Government bogeyman and deficit hysteria, when any political move that was not overtly designed to increase the freedom of corporations

was vilified as an endorsement of national bankruptcy. It was against this backdrop that, in rapid order, sponsorship went from being a rare occurrence (in the 1970s) to an exploding growth industry (by the mid-eighties), picking up momentum in 1984 at the Los Angeles Olympics (see Table 2.2).

At first, these arrangements seemed win-win: the cultural or educational institution in question received much-needed funds and the sponsoring corporation was compensated with some modest form of public acknowledgment and a tax break. And, in fact, many of these new public-private arrangements were just that simple, successfully retaining a balance between the cultural event or institution's independence and the sponsor's desire for credit, often helping to foster a revival of arts accessible to the general public. Successes like these are frequently overlooked by critics of commercialization, among whom there is an unfortunate tendency to tar all sponsorship with the same brush, as if any contact with a corporate logo infects the natural integrity of an otherwise pristine public event or cause. Writing in *The Commercialization of American Culture*, advertising critic Matthew McAllister labels corporate sponsorship "control behind a philanthropic façade."[2] He writes:

2   Matthew P. McAllister, *The Commercialization of American Culture* (Thousand Oaks: Sage, 1996), 177.

Table 2.1. *Corporate Tax as a percentage of Total Federal Revenue in the U.S., 1952, 1975, and 1998*

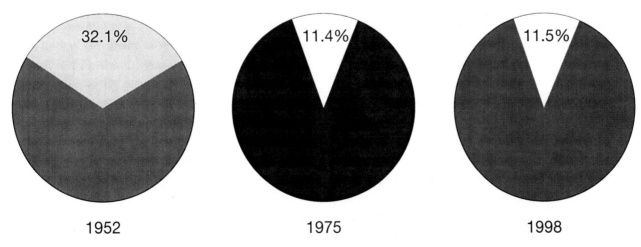

Source: *Time*, March 20, 1987: U.S. Office of Management and Budget; *Revenue Statistics 1965–1996* (1997 edition), OECD; 1999 Federal Budget.

Table 2.2. *Increase in U.S. Corporate Sponsorship Spending since 1985*

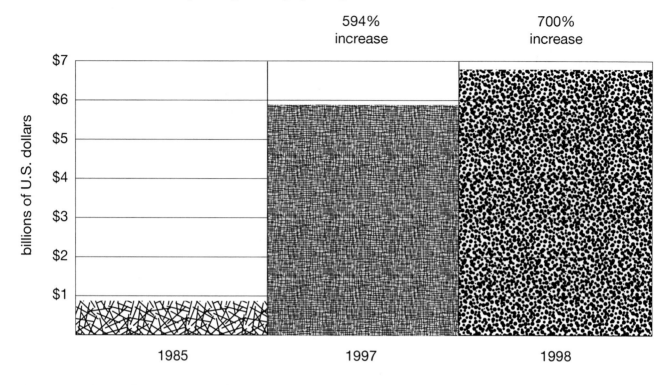

Source: *IEG Sponsorship Report*, December 22, 1997, and December 21, 1998

While elevating the corporate, sponsorship simultaneously devalues what it sponsors. ... The sporting event, the play, the concert and the public television program become subordinate to promotion because, in the sponsor's mind and in the symbolism of the event, they exist to promote. It is not Art for Art's Sake as much as Art for Ad's Sake. In the public's eye, art is yanked from its own separate and theoretically autonomous domain and squarely placed in the commercial. ... Every time the commercial intrudes on the cultural, the integrity of the public sphere is weakened because of the obvious encroachment of corporate promotion.[3]

This picture of our culture's lost innocence is mostly romantic fiction. Though there have always been artists who have fought fiercely to protect the integrity of their work, neither the arts, sports nor the media have ever, even theoretically, been the protected sovereign states that McAllister imagines. Cultural products are the all-time favorite playthings of the powerful, tossed from wealthy

statesmen such as Gaius Cilnius Maecenas, who set up the poet Horace in a writing estate in 33 B.C., and from rulers like Francis I and the Medici family, whose love of the arts bolstered the status of Renaissance painters in the sixteenth century. Though the degree of meddling varies, our culture was built on compromises between notions of public good and the personal, political and financial ambitions of the rich and powerful.

Of course there are some forms of corporate sponsorship that are inherently insidious — the tobacco industry's corralling of the arts springs to mind. But not all sponsorship deals should be so easily dismissed. Not only are such broad strokes unfair to worthy projects but, perhaps more important, they can prevent us from seeing changes in the field. If all corporate sponsorship arrangements are regarded as equally compromised, it becomes easy not to notice when the role of the corporate sponsor begins to expand and change — which is precisely what has been happening over the past decade as global corporate sponsorship has ballooned from a $7-billion-a-year industry in 1991 to a $19.2 billion one in 1999.

When sponsorship took off as a stand-in for public funds in the mid-eighties, many corporations that had been experimenting with the practice ceased to see sponsorship

---

3   Ibid., 221.

as a hybrid of philanthropy and image promotion and began to treat it more purely as a marketing tool, and a highly effective one at that. As its promotional value grew — and as dependency on sponsorship revenue increased in the cultural industries — the delicate dynamic between sponsors and the sponsored began to shift, with many corporations becoming more ambitious in their demands for grander acknowledgments and control, even buying events outright. Molson and Miller beer, as we will see further on in this chapter, are no longer satisfied with having their logos on banners at rock concerts. Instead, they have pioneered a new kind of sponsored concert in which the blue-chip stars who perform are entirely upstaged by their hosting brand. And while corporate sponsorship has long been a mainstay in museums and galleries, when Philip Morris-owned Altoids mints decided in January 1999 that it wanted to get into the game, it cut out the middleman. Rather than sponsoring an existing show, the company spent $250,000 to buy works by twenty emerging artists and launch its own *Curiously Strong Collection*, a traveling art exhibition that plays on the Altoids marketing slogan, "Curiously strong mints." Chris Peddy, Altoids brand manager, said, "We decided to take it to the next level."[4]

These companies are part of a larger phenomenon explained by Lesa Ukman, executive editor of the *International Events Group Sponsorship Report,* the industry's bible: "From MasterCard and Dannon to Phoenix Home Life and LaSalle Bank, companies are buying properties and creating their own events. This is not because they want to get into the business. It's because proposals sponsors receive don't fit their requirements or because they've had negative experiences buying into someone else's gig."[5] There is a certain logic to this progression: first, a select group of manufacturers transcend their connection to their earthbound products, then, with marketing elevated as the pinnacle of their businesses, they attempt to alter marketing's social status as a commercial interruption and replace it with seamless integration.

The most insidious effect of this shift is that after a few years of Molson concerts, Pepsi-sponsored papal visits, Izod zoos and Nike after-school basketball programs, everything from small community events to large religious gatherings are believed to "need a sponsor" to get off the ground;

August 1999, for instance, saw the first-ever private wedding with corporate sponsorship. This is what Leslie Savan, author of *The Sponsored Life*, describes as symptom number one of the sponsored mindset: we become collectively convinced not that corporations are hitching a ride on our cultural and communal activities, but that creativity and congregation would be impossible without their generosity.

THE BRANDING OF THE CITYSCAPE

The expansive trajectory of branding revealed itself to Londoners in a 1997 holiday season morality play. It began when the Regent Street Association found itself without enough money to replace the dimming Christmas lights that normally adorned the street during the season. Yves Saint Laurent stepped in and generously offered to split the cost of new decorations in exchange for seeing its logo up in lights. But when the time came to hang the Christmas lights, it seemed that the YSL logos were much larger than the agreed-upon size. Every few steps, shoppers were reminded by illuminated signs 5.5 meters high just who had brought them Christmas. The logos were eventually replaced with smaller ones, but the lesson remained: the role of the sponsor, like that of advertising in general, has a tendency to expand.

While yesterday's corporate sponsors may have been satisfied merely propping up community events, the meaning-seeking brand builders will never accept this role for long. Branding is, at its core, a deeply competitive undertaking in which brands are up against not only their immediate rivals (Nike vs. Reebok, Coke vs. Pepsi, McDonald's vs. Burger King, for example) but all other brands in the mediascape, including the events and people they are sponsoring. This is perhaps branding's crudest irony: most manufacturers and retailers begin by seeking out authentic scenes, important causes and cherished public events so that these things will infuse their brands with meaning. Such gestures are frequently motivated by genuine admiration and generosity. Too often, however, the expansive nature of the branding process ends up causing the event to be usurped, creating the quintessential lose-lose situation. Not only do fans begin to feel a sense of alienation from (if not outright resentment toward) once-cherished cultural events, but the sponsors lose what they need most: a feeling of authenticity with which to associate their brands.

---

4   *Wall Street Journal*, 12 February 1999.
5   Lesa Ukman, "Assertions," *IEG Sponsorship Report,* 22 December 1997, 2.

That's certainly what happened to Michael Chesney, the hip-hop adman who painted Canadian billboards into the branding era. He loved Toronto's Queen Street West — the funky clothing stores, the artists on all the patios, and, most of all, the graffiti art that figured large on the walls in that part of town. For Chesney, it was a short step from the public's growing interest in the cultural value of graffiti to the commercial takeover of that pocket of marginal space — a space used and reused by the disenfranchised for political and cultural expression in every city in the world.

From the start, Chesney considered himself a distant relative of the graffiti kids — though less a cousin than a rich uncle. The way he saw it, as a commercial artist and billboard salesman he was also a creature of the streets, because even if he was painting for corporate clients, he, like the graffiti artists, left his mark on walls. It was in this context that Chesney pioneered the advertising practice of the "building take-over." In the late eighties, Chesney's company Murad began painting directly onto building walls, letting the size of each structure dictate the dimensions of the ad. The idea harked back to 1920s Coca-Cola murals on corner grocery stores and to early-industrial urban factories and department stores that painted their names and logos in giant block lettering on their buildings' façades. The walls Chesney rented to Coke, Warner Brothers and Calvin Klein were a little bit bigger, however, reaching their pinnacle at a colossal 20,000-square-foot billboard overlooking one of Toronto's busiest intersections. Gradually, the ads wrapped around the corners of the buildings so that they covered not just one wall, but all of them: the ad as edifice.

In the summer of 1996, when Levi Strauss chose Toronto to test-market its new SilverTab jeans line, Chesney put on his most daring show yet: he called it "The Queen Street Takeover." Between 1996 and 1997, Levi's increased its spending on billboard advertisements by a startling 301 percent — and Toronto saw much of that windfall.[6] For one year, as the centerpiece of the most expensive outdoor ad campaign in Canadian history, Chesney painted his beloved strip silver. He bought up the façades of almost every building on the busiest stretch of

Queen and turned them into Levi's billboards, upping the ante of the ad extravaganza even further with 3-D extensions, mirrors and neon. It was Murad's greatest triumph, but the takeover presented some problems for Michael Chesney. When I spent a day with him at the tail end of the SilverTab bonanza, he could barely walk down Queen Street without running into somebody who was furious about the invasion. After ducking a few bullets, he told me a story of bumping into an acquaintance: "she said, 'You took over Queen Street.' She was really almost crying and I just, my heart sank, and she was really bummed out. But, hey, what can you do? It's the future, it's not Queen anymore."

Nearly every major city has seen some variation of the 3-D ad takeover, if not on entire buildings, then on buses, streetcars or taxis. It is sometimes difficult, however, to express dissatisfaction with this brand expansion — after all, most of these venues and vehicles have been carrying some form of advertising for decades. But somewhere along the line, the order flipped. Now buses, streetcars and taxis, with the help of digital imaging and large pieces of adhesive vinyl, have become ads on wheels, shepherding passengers around in giant chocolate bars and gum wrappers, just as Hilfiger and Polo turned clothing into wearable brand billboards.

If this creeping ad expansion seems a mere matter of semantics when applied to taxis and T-shirts, its implications are much more serious when looked at in the context of another marketing trend: the branding of entire neighborhoods and cities. In March 1999, Los Angeles mayor Richard Riordan unveiled a plan to revitalize poor inner-city areas, many of them still scarred from the 1992 riots after the Rodney King verdict: corporations would adopt a run-down part of town and brand its redevelopment. For the time being, the sponsors of Genesis L.A., as the project is called — among them Bank-America and Wells Fargo & Co. — only have the option of seeing these sites named after them, much like a sponsored sports arena. But if the initiative follows the expansive branding trajectory seen elsewhere, the sponsoring companies could well wield more politically powerful roles in these communities soon.

The idea of a fully privatized, branded town or neighborhood is not nearly as far-fetched today as it was only a few

> Nearly every major city has seen some variation of the 3-D ad takeover, if not on entire buildings, then on buses, streetcars or taxis.

---

6 *Advertising Age,* 28 September 1998.

years ago, as the inhabitants of Disney's town Celebration, Florida, can attest — and as the citizens of Cashmere, Washington, have quickly learned. A sleepy town of 2,500 people, Cashmere has as its major industry the Liberty Orchard candy factory, which has been making Aplets and Cotlets chewy sweets since it was founded in 1918. It was all very quaint until Liberty Orchard announced in September 1997 that it would leave for greener pastures unless the town agreed to transform itself into a 3-D tourist attraction for the Aplets and Cotlets all-American brand, complete with signs along the highway and a downtown turned into a corporate gift shop. *The Wall Street Journal* reported the company's ransom demands:

> They want all road signs and official correspondence by the city to say "Cashmere, Home of Aplets and Cotlets." They have asked that one of the two main streets in town be changed to Cotlets Avenue, and the other one be renamed Aplets Avenue. The candymaker also wants the Mayor and Council to sell City Mall to them, build new parking lots and possibly go to the bond market to start a tourism campaign on behalf of the worldwide headquarters of a company that says its story is "America in a nutshell."[7]

THE BRANDING OF MEDIA

I appeal to every producer not to release "sponsored" moving pictures. … Believe me, if you jam advertising down their throats and pack their eyes and ears with it, you will build up a resentment that will in time damn your business.
— Carl Laemmle of Universal Pictures, 1931

Although there is a clear trajectory in all of these stories, there is little point, at this stage in our sponsored history, in pining for either a mythic brand-free past or some Utopian commercial-free future. Branding becomes troubling — as it did in the cases just discussed — when the balance tips dramatically in favor of the sponsoring brand, stripping the hosting culture of its inherent value and treating it as little more than a promotional tool. It is possible, however, for

a more balanced relationship to unfold — one in which both sponsor and sponsored hold on to their power and in which clear boundaries are drawn and protected. As a working journalist, I know that critical, independent — even anti-corporate — coverage does appear in corporate-owned media, sandwiched, no less, between the car and tobacco ads. Are these articles tainted by this impure context? No doubt. But if balance (as opposed to purity) is the goal, then maybe print media, where the first mass-market advertising campaigns began, can hold some important lessons for how to cope with the expansionist agenda of branding.

It is common knowledge that many advertisers rail at controversial content, pull their ads when they are criticized even slightly and perpetually angle for so-called value-addeds — plugs for their wares in shopping guides and fashion spreads. For example, S.C. Johnson & Co. stipulates that its ads in women's magazines "should not be opposite extremely controversial features or material antithetical to the nature/copy of the advertised product" while De Beers diamonds demands that their ads be far from any "hard news or anti/love-romance themed editorial."[8] And up until 1997, when Chrysler placed an ad it demanded that it be "alerted in advance of any and all editorial content that encompasses sexual, political, social issues or any editorial that might be construed as provocative or offensive."[9] But the advertisers don't always get their way: controversial stories make it to print and to air, even ones critical of major advertisers. At its most daring and uncompromised, the news media can provide workable models for the protection of the public interest even under heavy corporate pressure, though these battles are often won behind closed doors. On the other hand, at their worst, these same media show how deeply distorting the effects of branding can be on our public discourse — particularly since journalism, like every other part of our culture, is under constantly increasing pressure to merge with the brands.

Part of this stepped-up pressure is coming from the explosion of sponsored media projects: magazines, Web sites and television programs that invite corporate sponsors to become involved at the development stage of a venture.

---

7 "Old-fashioned Town Sours on Candymaker's New Pitch," *Wall Street Journal,* 6 October 1997, A1.

8 Gloria Steinem, "Sex, Lies & Advertising," *Ms.*, July/August 1990.

9 "Chrysler Drops Its Demand for Early Look at Magazines," *Wall Street Journal,* 15 October 1997.

That's the role Heineken played in the British music and youth culture show *Hotel Babylon*, which aired on ITV. In an embarrassing incident in January 1996, a memo from a Heineken executive was leaked to the press that berated the producers for insufficiently "Heineken-izing" the as-yet-unaired program. Specifically, Justus Kos objected to male audience members drinking wine as opposed to "masculine drinks like beer, whisky," noted that "more evidence of beer is not just requested but needed" and complained that the show's host "shouldn't stand in the way of the beer columns when introducing guests." Most inflammatory of all was the executive's complaint that there was "too high a proportion of negroes in the audience."[10] After the controversy made its way into the press, Heineken CEO Karel Vuursteen issued a public apology.

Another sponsor scandal erupted during the 1998 Winter Olympics in Nagano, Japan, when CBS investigative journalist Roberta Baskin saw her CBS Sports department colleagues reporting on the games in jackets adorned with bold Nike logos. Nike was the official sponsor of the network's Olympic coverage and it provided news and sports reporters with the swooshed gear because, according to Nike spokesman Lee Weinstein, it "helps us build awareness about our products." Baskin was "dismayed and embarrassed" that CBS reporters seemed to be endorsing Nike products, not only because it represented a further dissolution of the line between editorial and advertising, but because two years earlier, Baskin had broken a news story about physical abuse of workers at a Nike shoe factory in Vietnam. She accused the station of refusing to allow her to pursue a follow-up and of yanking the original story from a scheduled rerun because of its sponsorship deal with Nike. CBS News president Andrew Heyward strenuously denied bowing to sponsor pressure, calling Baskin's allegations "truly preposterous." He did pull the Nike jackets off the news reporters midway through the games, though the sports department kept theirs on.

In some ways, these stories are simply pumped-up versions of the same old tug-of-war between editorial and advertising that journalists have faced for a century and a quarter. Increasingly, however, corporations aren't just asking editors and producers to become their de facto ad agencies by dreaming up ways to plug their wares in articles and photo shoots, they are also asking magazines to become their actual ad agencies, by helping them to create the ads that run in their magazines. More and more magazines are turning their offices into market-research firms and their readers into focus groups in an effort to provide the most cherished "value added" they can offer their clients: highly detailed demographic information about their readership, amassed through-extensive surveys and questionnaires.

In many cases, the magazines then use the readership information to design closely targeted advertisements for their clients. *Details* magazine, for instance, designed a twenty-four-page comic/advertisement strip in October 1997, with products like Hugo Boss cologne and Lee jeans woven into a story line about the daily adventures of a professional in-line skater. On the page following each product's extreme cameo, the company's real ad appeared.

The irony of these branding experiments, of course, is that they only seem to make brands more resentful of the media that host them. Inevitably, the lifestyle brands begin to ask why they need to attach themselves to someone else's media project in the first place. Why, even after proving they can integrate into the most stylish and trendiest of magazines, should they be kept at arm's length or, worse, branded with the word "Advertisement," like the health warnings on packs of cigarettes? So, with lifestyle magazines looking more and more like catalogs for designers, designer catalogs have begun to look more and more like magazines: Abercrombie & Fitch, J. Crew, Harry Rosen and Diesel have all shifted to a storybook format, where characters frolic along sketchily drawn plotlines.

The merger between media and catalog reached a new high with the launch of the teen TV drama *Dawson's Creek* in January of 1998. Not only did the characters all wear J. Crew clothes, not only did the windswept, nautical set make them look as if they had stepped off the pages of a J. Crew catalog, and not only did the characters spout

> The merger between media and catalog reached a new high with the launch of the teen TV drama *Dawson's Creek* in January of 1998.

10   *Independent,* 5 January 1996, 1, and *Evening Standard,* 5 January 1996, 12; and Andrew Blake, "Listen to Britain," in *Buy This Book,* edited by Mica Nava, Andrew Blake, Iain MacRury and Barry Richards (London: Routledge; 1997), 224.

dialogue like "He looks like he stepped out of a J. Crew catalog," but the cast was also featured on the cover of the January J. Crew catalog. Inside the new "freestyle magalog," the young actors are pictured in rowboats and on docks — looking as if they just stepped off the set of a *Dawson's Creek* episode.

To see the birthplace of this kind of brand ambition, you have to go online, where there was never really any pretense of a wall existing between editorial and advertisement. On the Web, marketing language reached its nirvana: the ad-free ad. For the most part, the on-line versions of media outlets feature straightforward banner ads similar to their paper or broadcast versions, but many media outlets have also used the Net to blur the line between editorial and advertising much more aggressively than they could in the non-virtual world. For instance, on the *Teen People* site, readers can click and order cosmetics and clothing as they read about them. On the *Entertainment Weekly* site, visitors can click and order the books and CDs being reviewed. In Canada, *The Globe and Mail* has attracted the ire of independent booksellers for the on-line version of its book review section, ChaptersGLOBE.com. After reading *Globe* reviews, readers can click to order books directly from the Chapters chain — a reviewer/retailer partnership that formed "Canada's largest online bookstore." *The New York Times*' on-line partnership with Barnes and Noble has caused similar controversies in the U.S.

These sites are relatively tame examples of the branding-content integration taking place on the Net, however. Sites are increasingly created by "content developers," whose role is to produce editorial that will make an ad-cozy home for the developers' brand-name clients. One such on-line venture is Parent Soup, invented by content developer "i-Village" for Fisher-Price, Starbucks, Procter and Gamble and Polaroid. It calls itself a "parents' community" and attempts to imitate a user-driven newsgroup, but when parents go to Parent Soup to get peer advice, they receive such branded wisdom as: the way to improve your child's self-esteem is by taking Polaroids of her. No need to bully or buy off editors — just publish do-it-yourself content, with ads pre-integrated.

Absolut Vodka's 1997 Absolut Kelly Internet site provided an early preview of the direction in which branded media are headed. The distiller had long since solicited original, brand-centered creations from visual artists, fashion designers and novelists to use in its advertisements — but this was different. On Absolut Kelly, only the name of the site advertised the product; the rest was an illustrated excerpt from *Wired* magazine editor Kevin Kelly's book *Out of Control*. This, it seemed, was what the brand managers had aspired to all along: for their brands to become quietly integrated into the heart of the culture. Sure, manufacturers will launch noisy interruptions if they are locked on the wrong side of the commerce/culture divide, but what they really want is for their brand to earn the right to be accepted, not just as advertising art but simply as art. Off-line, Absolut is still a major advertiser in *Wired*, but on-line, it is Absolut that is the host, and a *Wired* editor the supporting act.

Rather than merely bankrolling someone else's content, all over the Net, corporations are experimenting with the much-coveted role of being "content providers": Gap's site offers travel tips, Volkswagen provides free music samples, Pepsi urges visitors to download video games, and Starbucks offers an on-line version of its magazine, *Joe*. Every brand with a Web site has its own virtual, branded media outlet — a beachhead from which to expand into other non-virtual media. What has become clear is that corporations aren't just selling their products on-line, they're selling a new model for the media's relationship with corporate sponsors and backers. The Internet, because of its anarchic nature, has created the space for this model to be realized swiftly, but the results are clearly made for off-line export. For instance, about a year after the launch of Absolut Kelly, the company reached full editorial integration in *Saturday Night* magazine when the final page of a nine-page excerpt from Mordecai Richler's novel *Barney's Version* was wrapped around the silhouette of an Absolut bottle. This was not an ad, it was part of the story, yet at the bottom of the page were the words "Absolut Mordecai."[11] Although magazines and individual television shows are beginning to see the branded light, it is a network, MTV, that is the model for fully branded media integration. MTV started out sponsored, as a joint venture between Warner Communications and American Express. From the beginning, MTV has not been just a marketing machine for the products it advertises around the clock (whether those products are skin cleansers or the albums it moves with its music videos); it has also been a twenty-four-hour advertisement for MTV itself: the first truly branded network. Though there have been dozens of imitators since, the original genius of MTV, as every marketer will

---

11 *Saturday Night,* July/August 1997, 43–51.

tell you, is that viewers didn't watch individual shows, they simply watched MTV. "As far as we were concerned, MTV was the star," says Tom Preston, network founder.[12] And so advertisers didn't want to just advertise on MTV, they wanted to co-brand with the station in ways that are

---

We are hoping to take the attitude and lifestyle of Fox Sports off the TV and onto men's backs, creating a nation of walking billboards.

---

still unimaginable on most other networks: giveaways, contests, movies, concerts, awards ceremonies, clothing, countdowns, listings, credit cards and more.

The model of the medium-as-brand that MTV perfected has since been adopted by almost every other major media outlet, whether magazines, film studios, television networks or individual shows. The hip-hop magazine *Vibe* has extended into television, fashion shows and music seminars. Fox Sports has announced that it wants its new line of men's clothing to be on par with Nike: "We are hoping to take the attitude and lifestyle of Fox Sports off the TV and onto men's backs, creating a nation of walking billboards," said David Hill, CEO of Fox Broadcasting.

The rush to branding has been most dramatic in the film industry. At the same time that brand-name product placement in films has become an indispensable marketing vehicle for companies like Nike, Macintosh and Starbucks, films themselves are increasingly being conceptualized as "branded media properties." Newly merged entertainment conglomerates are always looking for threads to sew together their disparate holdings in cross-promotional webs and, for the most part, that thread is the celebrity generated by Hollywood blockbusters. Films create stars to cross-promote in books, magazines and TV, and they also provide prime vehicles for sports, television and music stars to "extend" their own brands.

I'll explore the cultural legacy of this type of synergy-driven production in Chapter 9, but there is a more immediate impact as well, one that has much to do with the phenomenon of disappearing unmarketed cultural "space" with which this section is concerned. With brand managers

envisioning themselves as sensitive culture makers, and culture makers adopting the hard-nosed business tactics of brand builders, a dramatic change in mindset has occurred. Whatever desire might exist to protect a television show from too much sponsor interference, an emerging musical genre from crass commercialism or a magazine from overt advertiser control has been trampled by the manic branding imperative: to disseminate one's own brand "meaning" through whatever means necessary, often in partnership with other powerful brands. In this context, the *Dawson's Creek* brand actively benefits from its exposure in the J. Crew catalog, the Kelly brand grows stronger from its association with the Absolut brand, the *People* magazine brand draws cachet from a close association with Tommy Hilfiger, and the *Phantom Menace* tie-ins with Pizza Hut, Kentucky Fried Chicken and Pepsi are invaluable *Star Wars* brand promotion. When brand awareness is the goal shared by all, repetition and visibility are the only true measures of success. The journey to this point of full integration between ad and art, brand and culture, has taken most of this century to achieve, but the point of no return, when it arrived, was unmistakable: April 1998, the launch of the Gap Khakis campaign.

THE BRANDING OF MUSIC

In 1993, the Gap launched its "Who wore khakis?" ads, featuring old photographs of such counterculture figures as James Dean and Jack Kerouac in beige pants. The campaign was in the cookie-cutter co-optation formula: take a cool artist, associate that mystique with your brand, hope it wears off and makes you cool too. It sparked the usual debates about the mass marketing of rebellion, just as William Burroughs's presence in a Nike ad did at around the same time.

Fast forward to 1998. The Gap launches its breakthrough Khakis Swing ads: a simple, exuberant miniature music video set to "Jump, Jive 'n' Wail" — and a great video at that. The question of whether these ads were "co-opting" the artistic integrity of the music was entirely meaningless. The Gap's commercials didn't capitalize on the retro swing revival — a solid argument can be made that they *caused* the swing revival. A few months later, when singer-songwriter Rufus Wainwright appeared in a Christmas-themed Gap ad, his sales soared, so much so that his record company began promoting him as "the guy in the Gap ads." Macy Gray, the new R&B "It Girl," also got her big break in a

---

12 "MTV Man Warns about Branding," *Globe and Mail,* 19 June 1998, B21.

Baby Gap ad. And rather than the Gap Khaki ads looking like rip-offs of MTV videos, it seemed that overnight, every video on MTV — from Brandy to Britney Spears and the Backstreet Boys — looked like a Gap ad; the company has

During this same period, the Rolling Stones made music history by ushering in the era of the sponsored rock tour — and fittingly, sixteen years later, it is still the Stones who are leading the charge into the latest in-

---

It wasn't until January 1999, however—when Hilfiger launched the ad campaign for the Stones' No Security Tour—that full brand-culture integration was achieved. In the ads, young, glowing Tommy models were pictured in full-page frame "watching" a Rolling Stones concert taking place on the opposite page.

---

pioneered its own aesthetic, which spilled out into music, other advertisements, even films like *The Matrix*. After five years of intense lifestyle branding, the Gap, it has become clear, is as much in the culture-creation business as the artists in its ads.

For their part, many artists now treat companies like the Gap less as deep-pocketed pariahs trying to feed off their cachet than as just another medium they can exploit in order to promote their own brands, alongside radio, video and magazines. "We have to be everywhere. We can't afford to be too precious in our marketing," explains Ron Shapiro, executive vice president of Atlantic Records. Besides, a major ad campaign from Nike or the Gap penetrates more nooks and crannies of the culture than a video in heavy rotation on MTV or a cover article in *Rolling Stone*. Which is why piggybacking on these campaign blitzes — Fat Boy Slim in Nike ads, Brandy in Cover Girl commercials, Lil' Kim rapping for Candies — has become, *Business Week* announced with much glee, "today's top 40 radio."[13]

Of course the branding of music is not a story of in-nocence lost. Musicians have been singing ad jingles and signing sponsorship deals since radio's early days, as well as having their songs played on commercial radio stations and signing deals with multinational record companies. Throughout the eighties — music's decade of the straight-up shill — rock stars like Eric Clapton sang in beer ads, and the pop stars, appropriately enough, crooned for pop: George Michael, Robert Plant, Whitney Houston, Run-DMC, Madonna, Robert Palmer, David Bowie, Tina Turner, Lionel Richie and Ray Charles all did Pepsi or Coke ads, while sixties anthems like the Beatles' "Revolution" became background music for Nike commercials.

novation in corporate rock: the band as brand extension. In 1981, Jovan — a distinctly un-rock-and-roll perfume company — sponsored a Rolling Stones stadium tour, the first arrangement of its kind, though tame by today's standards. Though the company got its logos on a few ads and banners, there was a clear distinction between the band that had chosen to "sell out" and the corporation that had paid a huge sum to associate itself with the inherent rebel-liousness of rock. This subordinate status might have been fine for a company out merely to move products, but when designer Tommy Hilfiger decided that the energy of rock and rap would become his "brand essence," he was looking for an integrated experience, one more in tune with his own transcendent identity quest. The results were evident in the Stones' Tommy-sponsored Bridges to Babylon tour in 1997. Not only did Hilfiger have a contract to clothe Mick Jagger, he also had the same arrangement with the Stones' opening act, Sheryl Crow — on stage, both mod-eled items from Tommy's newly launched "Rock 'n' Roll Collection."

It wasn't until January 1999, however — when Hilfiger launched the ad campaign for the Stones' No Security Tour — that full brand-culture integration was achieved. In the ads, young, glowing Tommy models were pictured in full-page frame "watching" a Rolling Stones concert taking place on the opposite page. The photographs of the band members were a quarter of the size of those of the models. In some of the ads, the Stones were nowhere to be found and the Tommy models alone were seen posing with their own guitars. In all cases, the ads featured a hybrid logo of the Stones' famous red tongue over Tommy's trademarked red-white-and-blue flag. The tagline was "Tommy Hilfiger Presents the Rolling Stones No Security Tour" — though there were no dates or locations for any tour stops, only the addresses of flagship Tommy stores.

---

13   "Sing a Song of Selling," *Business Week*, 24 May 1999.

In other words, this wasn't rock sponsorship, it was "live-action advertising," as media consultant Michael J. Wolf describes the ads.[14] It's clear from the campaign's design that Hilfiger isn't interested in buying a piece of someone else's act, even if they are the Rolling Stones. The act is a background set, powerfully showcasing the true rock-and-roll essence of the Tommy brand; just one piece of Hilfiger's larger project of carving out a place in the music world, not as a sponsor but as a player — much as Nike has achieved in the sports world.

The Hilfiger/Stones branding is only the highest-profile example of the new relationship between bands and sponsors that is sweeping the music industry. For instance, it was a short step for Volkswagen — after using cutting-edge electronic music in its ads for the new Beetle — to launch DriversFest '99, a VW branded music festival in Long Island, New York. DriversFest competes for ticket sales with the Mentos Freshmaker Tour, a two-year-old traveling music festival owned and branded by a breath-mint manufacturer — on the Mentos Web site, visitors are invited to vote for which bands they want to play the venue. As with the Absolut Kelly Web site and the Altoids' Curiously Strong art exhibition, these are not sponsored events: the brand is the event's infrastructure; the artists are its filler, a reversal in the power dynamic that makes any discussion of the need to protect unmarketed artistic space appear hopelessly naive.

This emerging dynamic is clearest in the branded festivals being developed by the large beer companies. Instead of merely playing in beer ads, as they likely would have in the eighties, acts like Hole, Soundgarden, David Bowie and the Chemical Brothers now play beer-company gigs. Molson Breweries, which owns 50 percent of Canada's only national concert promoter, Universal Concerts, already has its name promoted almost every time a rock or pop star gets up on stage in Canada — either through its Molson Canadian Rocks promotional arm or its myriad venues: Molson Stage, Molson Park, Molson Amphitheatre. For the first decade or so, this was a fine arrangement, but by the mid-nineties, Molson was tired of being upstaged. Rock stars had an annoying tendency to hog the spotlight and, worse, sometimes they even insulted their sponsors from the stage.

Clearly fed up, in 1996 Molson held its first Blind Date Concert. The concept, which has since been exported to the U.S. by sister company Miller Beer, is simple: hold a contest in which winners get to attend an exclusive concert staged by Molson and Miller in a small club — much smaller than the venues where one would otherwise see these megastars. And here's the clincher: keep the name of the band secret until it steps on stage. Anticipation mounts about the concert (helped along by national ad campaigns building up said anticipation), but the name on everyone's lips isn't David Bowie, the Rolling Stones, Soundgarden, INXS or any of the other bands that have played the dates, it's Molson and Miller. No one, after all, knows who is going to play, but they know who is putting on the show. With Blind Date, Molson and Miller invented a way to equate their brands with extremely popular musicians, while still maintaining their competitive edge over the stars. "In a funny way," says Universal Concerts' Steve Herman, "the beer is bigger than the band."[15]

The rock stars, turned into high-priced hired guns at Molson's bar mitzvah party, continued to find sad little ways to rebel. Almost every musician who played a Blind Date acted out: Courtney Love told a reporter, "God bless Molson … I douche with it."[16] The Sex Pistols' Johnny Lydon screamed "Thank you for the money" from the stage, and Soundgarden's Chris Cornell told the crowd, "Yeah, we're here because of some fucking beer company … Labatt's." But the tantrums were all incidental to the main event, in which Molson and Miller were the real rock stars and it didn't really matter how those petulant rent-a-bands behaved.

Jack Rooney, Miller's vice president of marketing, explains that his $200 million promotion budget goes toward devising creative new ways to distinguish the Miller brand from the plethora of other brands in the marketplace. "We're competing not just against Coors and Corona," he says, "but Coke, Nike and Microsoft."[17] Only he isn't telling the whole story. In *Advertising Age*'s annual "Top Marketing 100" list of 1997's best brands there was a new arrival: the Spice Girls (fittingly enough, since Posh Spice did once tell a reporter, "We wanted to be a 'household

14   Michael J. Wolf, *The Entertainment Economy* (New York: Times Books, 1999), 66.

15   Interview aired on Citytv's *New Music* "Smokes and Booze" special on 22 February 1997.

16   Interview aired on Citytv's *New Music* on 9 September 1995.

17   Kyle Stone, "Promotion Commotion," *Report on Business Magazine*, December 1997, 102.

name.' Like Ajax.")[18] And the Spice Girls ranked number six in *Forbes* magazine's inaugural "Celebrity Power 100," in May 1999, a new ranking based not on fame or fortune but on stars' brand "franchise." The list was a watershed moment in corporate history, marking the fact that, as Michael J. Wolf says, "Brands and stars have become the same thing."[19]

But when brands and stars are the same thing, they are also, at times, competitors in the high-stakes tussle for brand awareness, a fact more consumer companies have become ready to admit Canadian clothing company Club Monaco, for instance, has never used celebrities in its campaigns. "We've thought about it," says vice president Christine Ralphs, "but whenever we go there, it always becomes more about the personality than the brand, and for us, we're just not willing to share that."[20]

There is good reason to be protective: though more and more clothing and candy companies seem intent on turning musicians into their opening acts, bands and their record labels are launching their own challenges to the demoted status. After seeing the enormous profits that the Gap and Tommy Hilfiger have made through their association with the music world, record labels are barreling into the branding business themselves. Not only are they placing highly sophisticated cross-branding apparatus behind working musicians, but bands are increasingly being conceived — and test-marketed — as brands first: the Spice Girls, the Backstreet Boys, N' Sync, All Saints and so on. Prefab bands aren't new to the music industry, and neither are bands with their own merchandising lines, but the phenomenon has never dominated pop culture as it has at the end of the nineties, and musicians have never before competed so aggressively with consumer brands. Sean "Puffy" Combs has leveraged his celebrity as a rapper and record producer into a magazine, several restaurants, a clothing label and a line of frozen foods. And Raekwon, of the rap group Wu-Tang Clan, explains that "the music, movies, the clothing, it is all part of the pie we're making. In the year 2005 we might have Wu-Tang furniture for sale at Nordstrom."[21] Whether it's the Gap or Wu-Tang Clan, the only remaining relevant question in the sponsorship debate seems to be, Where do you have the guts to draw the borders around your brand?

18 Ann Powers, "Everything and the Girl," *Spin,* November 1997, 74.
19 Wolf, *The Entertainment Economy,* 29.
20 "And the Brand Played On," *Elm Street,* April 1999.
21 "Star Power, Star Brands," *Forbes,* 22 March 1999.

CHAPTER 15
Globalization

On an American $100 bill, there's a portrait of which American statesman?

— Prem Kumar,
Slumdog Millionaire (2008)

Chapter 15. Globalization

Recommended Film

Slumdog Millionaire (Danny Boyle 2008)

Media Models

The Meme, The Network, The Spectacle

Chapter Summary

Steven Best and Douglas Kellner explain globalization and the flow of information and entertainment across a globally networked society, fueled by techno-capitalism and techno-consciousness.

Frederick Turner sees a hybrid, intercultural globalization emerging from "universal solvents" that include global telecommunications, rock music, and the scientific account of the universe.

Globalization and the Restructuring of Capital

from *The Postmodern Adventure*

— Steven Best and Douglas Kellner

TECHNOCAPITALISM, GLOBALIZATION, AND THE INFOTAINMENT SOCIETY

Globalization is not something new under the sun, but is a particular form of capitalism, an expansion of capitalist relationships both in breadth (geographically) and in depth (penetrating ever-increasing aspects of human life).

— PETER MARCUSE

The information technology revolution has been instrumental in allowing the implementation of a fundamental process of the restructuring of the capitalist system from the 1980s onwards.

— MANUEL CASTELLS

"Globalization" was the buzzword of the 1990s and continues to serve in the new millennium as a primary attractor of books, articles, and heated debate, just as postmodernism was the most fashionable and disputed topic of the 1980s. A wide and diverse range of social theorists argue that today's world is organized by expanding globalization, which is strengthening the dominance of a world capitalist economic system, supplanting the primacy of the nation-state with transnational corporations and organizations, and generating a new global culture that is eroding all local cultures and traditions.[1] Marxists, worlds systems theorists, functionalists, Weberians, and other contemporary school of theorists agree that globalization is a distinguishing trend of the present moment. It is also becoming a hot and contested political arena as new social movements militantly oppose globalization throughout the world.

For some, globalization serves as a cover concept for imperialism. They condemn it as just another imposition of capital logic and the market on ever more regions of the world and spheres of life. For others, it is the continuation of modernization and a force of progress, bringing about expanded wealth, freedom, democracy, and happiness. Some perceive it as beneficial, creating new economic opportunities, political democratization, and cultural diversity and vitality. Others see it as harmful, engendering increased domination and control by the wealthier overdeveloped nations over the poor underdeveloped countries, thus strengthening the hegemony of the haves over the have-nots. In addition, in the negative view, globalization undermines democracy, homogenizes culture, and accelerates destruction of species and the environment.

---

1 Attempts to chart the globalization of capital, decline of the nation-state, and rise of a new global culture include the essays in Featherstone (1990), Giddens (1990), Robertson (1991), King (1991), Bird et al. (1993), Gilroy (1993), Arrighi (1994), Lash and Urry (1994), Grewal and Kaplan (1994), Wark (1994), Featherstone et al. (1995), Axford (1995), Held (1995), Waters (1995), Hirst and Thompson (1996), Wilson and Dissayanake (1996), Albrow (1996), Cvetkovich and Kellner (1997), Kellner (1998), Dyer-Witheford (1999), Friedman (1999), Held et al. (1999), Schiller (1999), Robins and Webster (1999), and Lechner and Boli eds. (2000).

Some conceive the globalization project — whether viewed positively or negatively — as inevitable and beyond human control, whereas others view it as generating new conflicts and new spaces for struggle.[2] Moreover, advocates of a postmodern break in history argue that developments in transnational capitalism are producing a novel configuration of post-Fordism (Harvey 1989), or that postmodernism is the cultural logic of capitalism (Jameson 1991). Others define the prevailing system as a "network society" grounded in globalized communications and information technology (Castells 1996, 1997, 1998). Indeed, the new global economy, society, and culture is increasingly digitized and interactive, with rapidly expanding wireless networks supplementing the wired society and producing new forms of connectivity. These technologies engender ubiquitous communication and interaction, and innovative forms of culture and everyday life (on the emergence of new broadband, multimedia, and interactive networks, see Gates 1995, 1999, and the more critical perspectives of Schiller 1999).

The new global networked society, however, is highly contested. Apologists such as Friedman (1999) regard globalization as positive, while critics such as Mander and Goldsmith (1996) and Robins and Webster (1999) view it as negative. Just as technophobic theories denounce the new technologies (see Chapter 4), so too do globophobic theories attack globalization as a novel form of imperialism, domination of the world by corporate capitalism, and destruction of the environment, local cultures, and tradition. On the other hand, globophiliacs celebrate it for producing fresh sources and escalating levels of wealth, growing democratization, and exciting forms of culture and technology. Hence, in many contemporary modern and postmodern social theories, globalization is taken as a salient feature of our times, yet is sharply contested regarding its nature, effects, and future.

In our view, globalization is extremely complex and ambiguous. It involves the flow of capital, goods, information, culture and entertainment, and people across a new networked economy, society and culture. Like the new technologies, it is an overdetermined and complex phenomenon that entails costs and benefits, an up and a down side. As with technology (see Chapter 4), we advocate development of a *critical theory of globalization* that would dialectically appraise its positive and negative features. This theory would be sharply critical of the harmful effects of globalization and skeptical of legitimating ideological discourse. It would recognize the centrality of the phenomenon in the present and embrace its beneficial features (such as the Internet, which, as we document below, makes possible a reconstruction of education and democratic technopolitics), while promoting a progressive and democratizing globalization in opposition to capitalist globalization.

Within this context, the concept of the postmodern helps to articulate what is new and different in the emergent social formation. It calls attention to breaks and discontinuities with the past, and highlights what is innovative, different, exciting, frightening, and often extremely ambiguous in the contemporary era.[3] Hence, while there is admittedly much mystification in postmodern discourse, we think that it emphatically signals the shifts and ruptures of the present age and underscores the novelties and the mutations in culture, subjectivities, and theory that many critics of globalization or the information society gloss over. Yet unless the concept of the postmodern is linked with analysis of the scientific, technological, and socioeconomic transformations of our time, the term is empty and without significant historical and analytic substance.

It is our contention that adequately theorizing globalization, scientific and technological revolution, and the genesis and effects of the postmodern requires perceiving the connections among these phenomena. Hence,

2   Negative critiques of globalization include Mander and Goldsmith (1996), Hirst and Thompson (1996), Schiller (1999), and Robins and Webster (1999). Positive takes on globalization include Friedman (1999).

3   Hence, although Manuel Castells (1996, 1997, 1998) has the most detailed theory of the new technologies and the rise of what he calls a "networked society," by refusing to link his analyses with the problematic of the postmodern, he does not adequately articulate the new — that is, what is different from the previous mode of social organization. Castells claims that Harvey (1989) and Lash (1990) say about as much about the postmodern as needs to be said (1996: 26ff.). With due respect to their excellent work, we believe that no two theorists or books exhaust the problematic of the postmodern, which involves transformations in theory, culture, society, politics, science, philosophy, and almost every other domain of experience, and is thus inexhaustible. Hence, although Castells has three weighty volumes that describes multiple dimensions of the network society, he does not engage the postmodern problematic, roots his analysis mostly in sociological literature, and does not have the theoretical and critical resources to analyze the full dimensions of the turbulent transformations that we are undergoing or to provide adequate critical perspectives on it.

we maintain that theories of globalization that do not conceptualize the transformation of capitalism and the world economy in conjunction with the coevolution of science and technology fail to adequately illuminate the key elements of the contemporary era. Many theories, by contrast, engage in economic reductionism that perceives globalization primarily as a function of the economy (e.g., Marxist-inspired theories). Or globalization is interpreted as a result of technological revolution alone, as by the

or "postFordism," in which production is fragmented and spread around the globe, rather than taking place in one big factory or plant. PostFordist production is "just in time," bringing parts or products to subcontractors or consumers quickly when needed, thus overcoming the negative drag of stockpiling and overproduction (Harvey 1989). For postmodern theorists such as Baudrillard (1993), technologies of information and simulation have permeated every aspect of society and have created a new

---

Globalization is extremely complex and ambiguous. It involves the flow of capital, goods, information, culture and entertainment, and people across a new networked economy, society and culture.

---

technodeterminists and apologists who ignore the vicissitudes of capitalism. Hence, one needs to consider the crucial constituents of the present moment dialectically, grasp their interconnections and coevolution, and dissect the conflicts and mutations they are producing.[4] One also needs to appraise both the positive and the negative effects of these phenomena on humans and society in order to identify the openings and possibilities for progressive social transformation, as well as the novel forces of domination and dangers for the human species.

Technological determinists frequently use the language of postindustrial, or postmodern, society to describe current developments. This discourse often develops an ideal-type distinction beginning with description of the previous Fordist mode of industrial production characterized by heavy industry, mass production and mass consumption, bureaucratic organization, and social conformity. Fordist industrial society is then contrasted with the new post-industrial society marked by "flexible production,"

social environment (see Chapter 2). On this view, we have left "reality" and the world of modernity behind, as we shift to a society of simulation and hyperreality, and undergo an implosion of technology and the human. Other, less extravagant, theorists of the vicissitudes of technology and society claim that we are evolving into a new postindustrial technosociety, culture, and condition in which technology, knowledge, and information are the axial or organizing principles (Bell 1976; Kelly 1994, 1998).

The postindustrial society is sometimes referred to as the "knowledge society" or the "information society," in which knowledge and information are given roles more predominant than in earlier eras (see the survey in Webster 1995). It is now clear that the knowledge, information, and service sectors are ever more important domains of our contemporary moment and that the arguments of Daniel Bell (1976) and others regarding the coming of postindustrial society were partially on target. But many theorists of the allegedly new economy and new society typically exaggerate the role of knowledge and information (see the critique in Webster 1995). They advance an idealist vision that excessively privileges knowledge and information in the economy, in politics, in society, and in everyday life; and downplays the force of capitalist relations of production, corporate ownership and control, and hegemonic modes of economic and state power. Such theorists ignore the extent to which technoscience itself has become a major productive force and has evolved within corporate capitalism and its military-technological-entertainment complex, so that today science and technology are potentially forces

---

4   Champions of technological revolution and the new economy like Toffler (1971) and Kelly (1994, 1999), as well as blatant apologists for capitalism such as Bill Gates (1995) and Thomas Friedman (1999), all ignore the continuing force of the logic of capital accumulation and the exploitation, conflict, and crises that it continues to generate. Instead, they sing praises to the wonders of the new technology and the new global economy and the wealth and benefits it will bring. Many critics of globalization, however, ignore the new technologies and interpret globalization in narrow economic terms as merely the imposition of the logic of capital upon ever more sectors of the world. For criticisms of technological determinism and "autonomous technology," see Winner (1977) and Feenberg (1991, 1995, 1999).

of destruction as well as instruments of knowledge and progress (see Chapter 2).

There is also a debate between those who claim that the emerging global networked society and culture is an entirely new phenomenon and those who stress its continuities with earlier formations (see Robins and Webster 1999, who argue the latter position). We propose a mediating position that articulates both the continuities with previous forms of industrial society and the new modes of society and culture described by concepts of the "post-" that emphasize the novelties and discontinuities. Taking this stance requires the deployment of a "both/and" logic, and not an "either/or" discourse. Hence, we wish to develop a dialectical optic that sees multiple forces of causation, connections, and breaks with the past, as well as a nexus of positive and/or negative effects, often inseparably intertwined.

We also believe that dominant conceptions of the information society and the focus on information technology as its foundation are too limited; the new technologies are modes of information *and* of entertainment and it is becoming harder and harder to separate the two. Indeed, the new technologies are much more than solely information technology; they are also forces of entertainment, communication, and play, encompassing and restructuring both labor and leisure. Previous forms of entertainment are rapidly being absorbed within the Internet. The computer is becoming a major household appliance, one that serves as a source of entertainment, information, communication, and connection with the outside world. At the same time, "post-PC" developments are advancing rapidly, linking all technologies, from computers to hand-held wireless devices to cell phones, moving from the "wired world" into a wireless, digitized, multimedia and interactive culture that allows access to e-mail, information, and entertainment, and social connections.

The mergers of major information and entertainment conglomerates that have taken place in the United States during the past several years provide clues to the immensity of the transformation going on and indicators of the syntheses of information and entertainment in the network society. We have witnessed the most extensive concentration of information and entertainment industries in history, including a $7.5 billion merger of Time Warner and Turner Broadcasting, a $19 billion deal between Disney/Capital Cities/ABC, a $20 billion conglomeration of NBC and Microsoft, and a $37 billion merger of Viacom and CBS.

Dwarfing all previous information/entertainment corporation mergers, Time Warner and America On-Line (AOL) proposed a $163.4 billion amalgamation in January 2000, which was approved in January 2001. This union brings together two huge corporations involved in TV, film, magazines, newspapers, books, information databases, computers, and other media, suggesting a coming synthesis of media and computer culture, of entertainment and information in a new infotainment society. The fact that "new media" Internet service provider and portal AOL is the majority shareholder in the deal points to the triumph of the new online Internet culture over the old media culture, while the merger points to escalating synergy among information and entertainment industries and old and new media in the form of the networked economy and cyberculture.

There have also been massive mergers in the telecommunications industry in the United States between Southwest Bell and California Bell and between New York and Atlantic Bell (on the significance of telecommunications mergers and market deregulation for the new mode of digital capitalism, see Schiller 1999). In 1999, MCI negotiated a $37 billion amalgamation with WorldCom, and then bought Sprint for $115 billion. In a $72 billion union of two regional telephone companies, SBC Communications Inc. and Ameritech formed the largest Bell operating company. The German telecommunications firm Mannesmann bought Orange for $33 billion; shortly thereafter Vodafone Airtouch, the world's leading mobile phone company, announced a hostile bid for Mannesmann, initially for a record $117 billion, and eventually for an amazing $178.7 billion when the merger was sealed in February 2000 (earlier in the year Vodafone also absorbed Airtouch Communications for $60 billion). In addition, telecommunications companies have been buying cable television systems — for example, AT&T purchased TCI in 1998 for $60.9 billion and then acquired MediaOne in 1999 for $63.1 billon.[5]

5 For an overview of these media mergers, see McChesney (1999). In an article on "Oligopoly," (*New York Times,* June 11, 2000: A1), Stephen Labaton writes: "During the 12 years of the Reagan and Bush administrations, an era widely remembered for frenzied merger activity and devotion to a laissez-faire regulatory approach, there were 44,518 mergers and acquisitions in the United States, with a combined value of $2.12 trillion according to Thomson Financial Securities Data. By contrast, the seven-and-a-half years of the Clinton administration have witnessed 71,811 corporate deals valued at $6.6 trillion."

The corporate media, communications, and information industries are frantically scrambling to provide delivery for the wealth of information, entertainment, and other services that will include expanded Internet access, cellular telephones, hand-held communication devices, and computerized video, film, and information on demand, as well as Internet shopping and more unsavory services like pornography and gambling. These developments require the concepts of the "information revolution" or "information society" to be expanded to include entertainment, multimedia, and an exploding array of technologies. Accordingly, we use the notion of the networked infotainment society to accent the imbrications of information, entertainment, and interactive media in the new digitized and global economy.

In addition, theories of the information society neglect the rise of biotechnology and the emergence of new forms of genetic engineering, nanotechnology, drugs and pharmaceuticals, and the tremendous capital realization and developments in these arenas. In November 1999, Pfizer made a hostile $82.4 billion offer for Warner-Lambert, outbidding American Home Products, which had already bid $62.1 billion, and eventually closing the deal with a $90 billion takeover bid.[6] In the world of biotechnology, chemical and seed corporations are merging to form powerful global combines that are taking control of the world's food supply. According to the Organic Consumers Association, "The top five seed companies — AstraZeneca, Du Pont, Monsanto, Novartis, and Aventis — account for nearly two-thirds of the global pesticide market (60%), almost one-quarter (23%) of the commercial seed market, and virtually 100% of the transgenic ... seed market."[7] Many of these corporations are the results of takeovers and consolidation — for example, Astra and Zeneca formed AstraZeneca in a $31.8 billion merger. In addition, Rhone Poulenc and Hoechst united with Aventis, Ciba Gelgy, and Sandoz, creating Novartis, while Du Pont absorbed Pioneer Hi-Bred early in 1999. In recent years, trying to fulfill its goal of dominating world agriculture, Monsanto has spent $8 billion buying out numerous U.S. seed companies. In 1998, Monsanto purchased Cargill's International Seed Operations and bid to acquire Delta & Pine Land Seed

Co., which co-owns the Terminator seed patent with the USDA. And in December, 1999, Monsanto and Pharmacia & Upjohn Inc. announced plans for a merger that would solidify one of the world's largest pharmaceutical and biotechnology companies, yielding a combined market value of $52 billon.

Together, these corporate consolidations and their products and services in the information, communications, entertainment, and biotech industries constitute a new networked and interactive infotainment society, and herald a coming genetic revolution, all producing fateful implosions of technology and human beings. One result is the emergence of the infrastructure of a new mode of global technocapitalism.

* * *

TECHNOCULTURE, TECHNOBODIES, AND CYBERIDENTITIES

We are here at the controls of a micro-satellite, in orbit, living no longer as an actor or dramaturge but as a terminal of multiple networks.

— Jean Baudrillard

Technoculture ... is located as much in the work of everyday fantasies and actions as at the level of corporate or military decision making.

— Constance Penley and Andrew Ross

The digerati and ideologues of today's cyberculture and new technologies advance visions of a posthumanist world where the (humanist) Subject is dethroned and overpowered by the (technological) Object — Hegelianism in reverse (see Chapter 4). The new technoculture is one of the major creations of the technological revolutions and the restructuring of capitalism. Yet human culture — a reflective product of language and intellect — has been spawned from the womb of technology since the beginning of history. As many anthropologists argue, the use of tools was crucial in stimulating human intelligence and linguistic capacities, and therefore for nurturing culture. Consequently, human beings and their technologies have co-constructed one another throughout the odyssey of human evolution.

6 See *New York Times,* November 5, 1999: A1 and C19; Associated Press, February 7, 2000.

7 www.organic consumers.org, Vol. 1, No. 14, September 28, 1999.

All human cultures have their technological components, but no culture until the 20th century has been as dominated by technology and technological thinking as ours. A technoculture arises when culture is defined more by science and technology than by religion, social norms, ethics, or the humanities; when face-to-face, concrete relations rooted in the family and neighborhood become globe are comparable, sharing high-rise buildings, traffic congestion, extreme contrasts between wealth and poverty, and similar commodities and cultural forms. As Castells demonstrates (1996), in a network society, technology structures more and more domains of everyday life and the technification of the world, feared by philosophers like Heidegger, Ellul, and Marcuse, becomes a palpable reality.

The first feature of technoculture is that technology increasingly pervades human lives through the spread of new gadgets and machines, thereby mediating our relation to nature, the social environment, and other beings.

---

electronically and digitally mediated; and when technology, shaped by distinct social and economic relations, becomes a driving source of change that overturns all stable traditions so rapidly that it impedes any attempt to control it, understand its nature, and discern its consequences. At the same time, it must be admitted that new technologies are providing exciting possibilities for accessing information, increasing communication, and creating novel cultural forms and communities.

The first feature of technoculture is that technology increasingly pervades human lives through the spread of new gadgets and machines, thereby mediating our relation to nature, the social environment, and other beings. With the shift to a consumer society, people are surrounded by a sea of commodities, services, and objects. Today, the average home in the developed countries has more technologies than ever before. Automobiles, central heating and cooling systems, telephones, beepers, cell phones, microwave ovens, stereos, color televisions, home entertainment centers, satellite dishes, personal computers, Sony Walkmans, exercise machines, digital cameras, and other gadgets weave the technological fabric of everyday life. Virtually no human activity today occurs without the mediation of these and other technologies. Consequently, we now live in a new habitat, a technoworld, qualitatively different from the processes, rhythms, and experiences of the largely natural setting in which humanity resided for millennia.

To be sure, much of the world continues to live in premodern circumstances, or rather in an overlapping state of premodern, modern, and postmodern conditions. But with the steady expansion of the global economy and culture, the same technologies, media, ideas, and images are circulating throughout the world. Major cities all over the

Second, with the escalating automation of society and everyday life, tasks that were once done by human beings are now being executed by machines. Thanks to factory assembly techniques, robotics, and computers, automated systems are increasingly running the work world. Machines are managing machines and computers are "talking" to each other, as when robots control factory production or airplanes run on computer-driven autopilot. Soon, futurists tell us, the home will be completely automated thanks to a central computer system that will manage various microtechnologies from cooking to lighting (see Gates 1995; Gerschenfeld 1999). When these technologies and systems work, they will provide us with power and pleasure, but when they break down or malfunction, they will make all too apparent our reliance on technology and our lack of real control over our environment. In this context, although the Y2K phenomenon seemed to have little effect, it pointed to human overdependence on technology and fears of disaster.

Automation and the robotization of work are accompanied by post-Fordism which multiplies service industries and shifts manufacturing labor from the unionized and regulated developed countries to sites where lower wages and more intense exploitation are the norm (Harvey 1987). A new technoservice and "net-slave" class is also emerging to service the high-tech society and culture under poor working conditions, without job security, and with varying and unstable pay rates (Lessard and Baldwin 2000). Moreover, the prospect of machines taking over manual labor is itself fraught with ambiguity. While the automation of labor could provide workers with more leisure for freedom and creativity, it also might make individuals more reliant on machines and could be accompanied by leisure forms that induce dependency, stupification, and alienation (e.g., drug addiction, escapist forms of media and virtual reality, etc.). Moreover, rather than liberating people from the drudgery or work to spend the bulk of their time in creative leisure and self-actualization activities, as Marx envisioned, automated labor has been used to intensify work, profits, the extraction of surplus value, and has led to increasing unemployment as workers are thrown onto the scrap heap of social waste (Rifkin 1995). A challenge for the future will be to creatively reconstruct the worlds of both work and leisure to maximize human creativity, freedom, and self-valorization, rather than to submit to domination by capital, the state, technology, and media culture and spectacle.

Third, a technoculture is distinguished by the hegemony of techno-consciousness, a form of thought governed largely by mathematical, analytic, means — end reasoning — a mode of rationality that Frankfurt School theorists termed *instrumental reason*. Within technoculture, information replaces knowledge, and what Marcuse (1964) called "one-dimensional thought" supplants critical and dialectical reason. Technocrats and technical workers become new social elites, the "golden geeks" and extravagantly paid instrumental aristocracy of a triumphant technocapitalism.

It appears that in a techno-culture the passion for wisdom and learning as intrinsic goods often gives way to anxious desires for a career and success. The differences between universities and high-tech trade schools are blurring, as college students choose their majors to advance their career plans and seek to minimize all courses that do not immediately "relate" to their desired financial ends. Disturbingly, pursuit of philosophy, literature, and humanities is being displaced by business, accounting, computer science, engineering, and agriculture. Many colleges and universities are threatened with stiff competition from community colleges, technical/business schools, and Internet "distance learning." On the plus side, technological mediation of all disciplines is bringing together fields once separated by disparate methods, technologies, and practices, as individuals in more disciplines communicate through digitized words and images and seek information in databases and on the Internet in similar fashions (see Lanham 1993; Landow 1995).

Fourth, technoculture replaces social life with commercially and technologically mediated communities. Some shopping malls, for example, map out different areas as "neighborhoods" and indeed become new sites of human congregation, especially for teenagers and the elderly (who take daily "mall walks"). Real communities of people interacting face to face often give way to the virtual communities of the web. In some universities, "student life" is disappearing as students interact primarily through e-mail and chat rooms.[8] The virtualization of community can also occur in cybercafes where, instead of mingling at convivial tables, people sit separated at isolated computer stalls, each interacting with their virtual partners rather than their embodied neighbor.

Yet people isolated and alienated from their real-life communities may find like-minded people in the cyber-world that can lead to new friendships, significant relationships, and even marriages. Internet chat rooms allow people to meet, explore mutual interests, and create communities without long-distance phone charges. Websites focusing on everything from the sciences through philosophy and the classics offer a wealth of material and expand possibilities for self-education. Individuals who did not formerly have access to good libraries or other sources of information can find a cornucopia of databases and educational material free of cost on the Internet. New hypertext and multimedia forms provide exciting cultural matrices. On the whole, cyber-culture is significantly more interactive and involving than the earlier dominant form: TV culture. People from the entire world can thus share in information, discussion, and cultural forms from which they were earlier excluded. The possibilities of working at home provide potential space for more freedom and creativity and open economic opportunities to those not able (or wanting) to commute to

> Technoculture replaces social life with commercially and technologically mediated communities.

---

8 Articles started appearing in the mid-1990s on the ubiquity of e-mail, chat rooms, listserves, MOOs, and MUDs; see Turkle (1995). One of the early advocates of virtual communities, Howard Rheingold (2000), had "second thoughts" that he disseminated through the Internet (see his website at www.rheingold.com). Books on "internet addiction" are starting to appear (see Young 1998); studies are also appearing on student gambling, stock market daytrading, and other addictive net activities; see *The Chronicle of Higher Education*, April 7, 2000.

work, although this can also lead to feelings of isolation and depression.

Life online, the emergent forms of the technoculture, and the novel identities and communities it is shaping have been explored in ongoing studies by Sherry Turkle (1984, 1995). In the mode of ethnographic social science, Turkle describes the emergence of personal computer (PC) technologies and the novel forms of interaction, identities, and experiences they are producing. She interprets the transition from big computers to personal computers as symptomatic of a postmodern shift from a Big Machine and Bureaucracy Age to an innovative type of computer technology and novel forms of subjectivity and culture. For Turkle, giant IBM mainframe computers are bound up with centralization, massification, hierarchy, and big government or corporations, and are thus a figure for modernity itself. Further, modern computers are connected with mechanistic science that is universalist, rationalist (there is one way to do it), and top-down, with a cult of experts and hierarchy; it is also for Turkle rooted in hard masculine science, which is logical and abstract.

By contrast, Turkle claims that PCs are compatible with a postmodern logic and aesthetics. On her account, postmodern PC technologies are "soft" and "feminine" (i.e., more concrete and ductile), subject to tinkering, more graphic and multimedia, and more expressive, merging art and technology. Whereas modern mainframe computers required highly specialized knowledge and were only accessible to a techno-elite, postmodern PCs are "user-friendly," lend themselves to experimental activity, and promote creative and multifaceted selves. PCs thus nourish a postmodern culture of the iconic surface, for while old modern computers required depth-oriented thinking and technological know-how to get behind the screen, current PCs operate on the surface, requiring only that one point and click to navigate cyberspace.

Furthermore, on Turkle's analysis PCs enable a more decentralized, individualist, and variegated culture that can generate postmodern selves: multiple, fragmented, constructed and provisional, subject to experiment and change. "Windows" for Turkle is the privileged metaphor for postmodern subjectivity: dispersed, decentered, mobile, and constructed. Computer software windows open the subject not only to the work world of texts and word processing, but also to the emerging realms of simulation, cyberspace, and interactive multimedia culture. The result is self-awareness regarding the variety of roles we play and the many dimensions to our subjectivity. So, for example, in one window the user John does word processing and expresses his professional or academic self. In another, he does e-mail and articulates his private self, although he can go back and forth from professional to personal or mix them together at will. In Internet chat rooms, John can assume whatever identity he wants and can take on multiple identities: he can "be" a young black lesbian in the morning, a liberal male politico in the afternoon, and a transgendered literary critic at night. Switching to a multimedia window, another user, Sandy, can express her more ludic and aesthetic self by playing music and downloading tunes from Napster or Gnutella, looking at film or video clips, accessing aesthetic images from art galleries and museums, or engaging new computer art forms. In surfing the web, she can be a flaneur or a slacker self, cruising, browsing, and navigating (these are interesting metaphors themselves worthy of scrutiny). Or, in her Internet web window, she might be doing serious research, enhancing her professional and scholarly subjectivity and cultural capital.

From this perspective, what those in the cyberculture call "RL" is just one more window, one more perspective or domain of interaction, one more mode of subjectivity and identity. For Turkle and Mark Poster (1990, 1996), computer technologies create novel identities, subjectivities, and realms of experience and interaction such as cyberspace, as well as original forms of communication and social relations within the emergent technoculture. Such theories, however, exaggerate the rupture with the past, and fail to note continuities and the ways that such novelties are rooted in the structures of modernity (i.e., technoculture is a part of a new stage of capitalism and integrally connected with globalization).[9]

Finally, technoculture invades not only society and culture, but also biology and nature, importing ecological models into technology as it engineers life and creates technobodies (see Chapter 4). Canadian filmmaker David Cronenberg, a prophet and poet of the posthuman

---

9   Poster (1990) argues that the mode of production is now transcended in importance by the mode of information as a fundamental principle of organizing society. We would argue, however, that the modes of production and information are intertwined as a new stage of capitalism. In "Postmodern Virtualities" (1996), Poster highlights the importance of perceiving the connection of postmodernity with the new media and the new subjectivity, but does not link these phenomena with the restructuring of capital and globalization.

condition, has explored the dynamics of the new techno-culture, the implosion between technology and humans, and the challenges and paradoxes of living in a new high-tech world. It is to his imaginative cinematic mappings of the emerging technoculture that we now turn.

* * *

DEBORD, CYBERSITUATIONS, AND THE INTERACTIVE SPECTACLE

The coincidence of the changing of circum-stances and of human activity can be conceived and rationally understood only as revolution-izing practice.

— KARL MARX

If it seems somewhat ridiculous to talk of revolution, this is obviously because the orga-nized revolutionary movement has long since disappeared from the modern countries where the possibilities of a decisive transformation of society are concentrated. But everything else is even more ridiculous, since it implies accepting the existing order in one way or another.

— SITUATIONIST INTERNATIONAL

We thus read David Cronenberg as a cineaste of the emer-gent technoculture who offers alarming and prescient vi-sions of the "new flesh" and fifth discontinuity in a rapidly approaching posthumanist world. Cronenberg dramatizes how the technoculture is constantly evolving, engaging the latest innovations in technology such as VR. Working in an epoch just before Cronenberg, combining both artistic and theoretical mapping, French writer and artist Guy Debord theorized the emergent technoculture as the "society of the spectacle" which he interpreted as the prevailing form of consumer capitalism. In fact, the influence of the ideas of Debord and the Situationist International is quite strik-ing. Contemporary society and culture are still permeated with the sort of spectacle described in classical situationist works. The notion of "spectacle" has almost become nor-malized, emerging as part-and-parcel of both theoretical and popular media discourse.

In addition, situationist texts are reaching new and ever expanding audiences through the proliferation of 'zines and websites, some of which embody situationist practice. The past decade has been marked by cultural activism that uses new communications technology to spread radi-cal social critique and alternative culture. Many of these 'zines pay homage to Debord and the situationists, as do a profusion of websites that publish their texts with diverse commentary.[10] Situationist ideas thus play an important part in contemporary cultural theory and activism, and may continue to inspire cultural and political opposition as the society of the spectacle enters cyberspace and new realms of culture and experience emerge.

Hence, we will update Debord's ideas in formulating what we see as the advent of a new stage of the spectacle, grounded in new technologies and requiring fresh map-pings and innovative forms of oppositional practice. Reflections on the prevailing globalized capitalist system suggest that contemporary overdeveloped societies are still marked by Debordian spectacle in every realm of social life. Indeed, the advent of "megaspectacles," a term we have coined by drawing on Debord, involve a significant escalation of the spectacle in size, scope, and intensity. They range from superhyped films like the *Star Wars* series (with their high-powered sound and special effects and unparalleled mega-promotion), to theme parks that create intense and thrilling technologically mediated experiences, to media-generated passion plays like the O. J. Simpson trial or the Clinton sex and impeachment scandals that are marked by such saturation coverage, repeated day after day, that they define an era of spectacle.

The capitalist economy thrives on megaspectacles of consumption, including department stores, malls, theme parks, and the booming and busting virtual cybermalls of the Internet. In the economy, more money is spent each year on advertising and packaging, which today in the United States constitutes 4% of the gross national product (see Kellner 1996). The Global Consumer Village exhibits not only a sparkling array of goods and services but also high-tech entertainment, postmodern architecture, and, increasingly simulations of famous sites past and present

---

10 On the history of the situationists, see Marcus (1989), Plant (1992), Wollen (1993), and the material in Substance 90 (1999). The key texts of the situationists and many interesting commentaries are found on various websites, such as www. nothingness.org/SituationistInternational/journal.html; www. ccwf.cc.utexas/~panicbuy/HaTeMaiL/situationist.html; and www.slip.net/~knabb. For our earlier reflections on the contributions and limitations of situationist thought, see Best and Kellner (1997, Ch. 3).

(Gottdiener 1997; Gottdiener et al. 1999). The Edmonton Mall in Canada, for example, combines an amusement park, a replica of Columbus's *Santa Maria,* a simulation of New Orleans's Bourbon Street, a casino, and a theme

that changed humans' view of our place in the cosmos, expanded the realm of human possibility, and displayed the victory of U.S. space technology. Missions to outer space have since become routine. Negative spectacles and cau-

---

Thanks to "environmental advertising," whole urban areas, like Las Vegas or the Sunset Strip in Los Angeles, are illuminated by lasers that flash commercials upon buildings and into the sky, taking the megaspectacle to new spaces and new heights.

---

hotel, and hundreds of shops, so that there is currently a 60/40 percent split between retail sales and entertainment (Ritzer 1998). Not to be outdone, Las Vegas now has on display an elaborate simulation of New York City, complete with 42nd Street, the Statue of Liberty, and rooftop roller-coasters.

Entire environments have been permeated by advertising and spectacle. Taxis and buses are now wrapped with giant and glowing graphics, thus becoming rolling billboards.[11] Thanks to "environmental advertising," whole urban areas, like Las Vegas or the Sunset Strip in Los Angeles, are illuminated by lasers that flash commercials upon buildings and into the sky, taking the megaspectacle to new spaces and new heights.[12]

Indeed, outer space has been a fertile ground for the spectacle since the Moon landing of 1969, an epochal event

tionary warnings about the limits of technology appeared with the explosion of the *Challenger* space shuttle in 1987, errors in positioning space telescopes, and many failures in the NASA space program, including the December 1999 loss of a Mars spacecraft intended to explore the surface of the planet.

Yet, no doubt, there will be more space spectacles in the future, with possibilities for outer space advertising, tourism, space colonies, and continued scientific exploration of the cosmos.[13] The successful 1998 landing of the *Explorer* on Mars and its subsequent broadcast of live pictures back to Earth was enthusiastically followed on the Internet throughout the world. Hence, there is reason to believe that explorations and representations of outer space and its territories will be one of the major spectacles of the next millennium, along with speculation concerning alien species, life on other planets, possible global and cosmic catastrophe, and controversy over the origin of life and the nature of the universe.

But it is probably the field of entertainment that today is the privileged site of the spectacle. Entertainment is a dominant mode of technoculture and is itself big business. Moreover, in the society of the spectacle, business has to be entertaining to prosper. Via the "entertainmentization" of the economy, television, film, theme parks, video games,

---

11 See Gromer, "It's a Wrap," *Popular Mechanics,* June 1998: 112–115.

12 Las Vegas is, of course, at the forefront of environmental art and advertising. Indeed, much of the city is a spectacle geared to lure consumers of the commodity spectacle to its pleasure palaces and gambling establishments:

A 190-foot obelisk, from which lasers flash, is the equivalent of the traditional Las Vegas neon sign (Promoters claim that only two man-made objects can be seen from outer space: The Great Wall of China and Luxor's laser light). The entire Luxor setup is animated and computerized. A light show in front of the hotel focuses on a 60-foot screen of weather. As the sun goes down, the shimmering and luminescent face of King Tut appears in the air, projected against a screen of raindrops from the fountains in front of the sphinx. Through the translucent face of the pharaoh, you can read a distant sign down the strip "Prime Rib Buffet."

Even the great beam and its reach skyward, consuming $1 million worth of electricity annually, suggest wider urban applications. Its designer, Zachary Taylor, foresees using this technology for forming "a new kind of skyline created by lasers." (Phil Patton, "Now Playing in the Virtual World," *Popular Science,* April 1994: 82)

13 Advertising has become a new way to raise funds to offset the dwindling resources of space travel. Seizing the initiative to bolster their cash-strapped program, Russia painted a 30-foot-high Pizza Hut logo on a rocket destined for the international Space Station in January 2000 in exchange for $2.5 million. Various groups are raising funds for privatized space exploration and colonies. Aerospace entrepreneur Peter Diamandis began a competition with a $10 million prize for the best designed spaceship that can make space travel an affordable journey in the megaspectacle for the near future (*CBS News,* November 5, 1999). Other entrepreneurs are already investing in space hotels; see "Space Tourism — Hot Ticket" *Los Angeles Times* (May 22, 2000).

casinos, and so forth become a key sector of the national economy. In the United States, the entertainment industry is now a $480 billion industry, and consumers spend more on having fun than on clothes or health care (Wolf 1999: 4).[14] in Texas, once known as a wheat state, the estimated market value of the Dallas Cowboys and the Houston Oilers in 1999 was greater ($735 million) than the total value of the wheat that the state harvested ($600 million).[15] Further, a corporate entertainment complex is rapidly advancing in Bangkok, Australia, China, India, Japan, and elsewhere, forming a crucial aspect of the global restructuring of capitalism and disseminating modernization and postmodernization processes simultaneously.

In a competitive business world, the "fun factor" can give one business the edge over another. So corporations seek to be more entertaining in their commercials, their business environment, and their websites. Hence,

---

In Texas, once known as a wheat state, the estimated market value of the Dallas Cowboys and the Houston Oilers in 1999 was greater ($735 million) than the total value of the wheat that the state harvested ($600 million).

Budweiser commercials feature talking frogs who tell us nothing about beer, but who catch the viewers' attention, while Taco Bell deploys a talking dog, and Pepsi uses *Star Wars* characters. Buying, shopping, and dining out are coded as an "experience" as businesses adopt a theme-park style. Places like the Hard Rock Cafe are not renowned for their food, after all; people go there for the ambience, to buy clothing, and to view music and media memorabilia. It is no longer good enough just to have a website, it has to be an interactive spectacle, featuring not only products to buy,

but music and videos to download, games to play, prizes to win, travel information, and "links to other cool sites."

The infotainment society reduces everything to the logic of the commodity spectacle. Always a major scene of the spectacle and a source of capital, religion itself is now packaged as a commodity with TV religion, religion websites, and the proliferation of religious artifacts ranging from Bibles on biblical stories on DVD to Christian rock music videos and CDs. Since the rise of televangelism in the 1980s, religion has been relentlessly commodified, with TV evangelists exploiting it to rake in millions of dollars from gullible contributors. Jesus2000.com advertises itself as "The Holy Lands Largest Shopping Mall on the Internet," claiming over one million "Virtual Pilgrim" visits since its December 1998 launch. *Feed* reports that

> Jesus2000.com faces stiff competition, though— and not just from Crosswalk.com, the Internet's No. 1 Christian portal. The Chosen People have developed a number of innovative Web applications including Virtualjerusalem.com, a site that lets users send e-mail directly to God. VJ Webmaster Avi Moskowitz prints and carries a batch of e-mail prayers to the Western Wall daily. Meanwhile, Taliban Online has been providing a small but faithful Muslim audience with "news and articles on Islam and Jihad" for more than a year now. The site is selling cars, stereos and other earthly delights as part of a Web banner ad network.[16]

Even the pope has become a commodity machine, a global superstar whose image the Roman Catholic Church recently licensed to sell official papal souvenirs, ranging from books and posters to watches, sweatshirts, CDs and videos featuring the pope, and bottled (holy?) water — with a papal webpage to boost the Vatican's image and to sell its merchandise. A papal visit takes on the form of megaspectacle, as when the pope's trip to St. Louis was awarded the headline "Pope Gets Rock-Star Greeting in U.S."[17]

Megaspectacles also include sports events like the World Series, the Superbowl, World Soccer Cup, and NBA championships, which attract massive audiences, are hyped to

---

14 Another source notes that "the average American household spent $1,813 in 1997 on entertainment — books, TV, movies, theater, toys — almost as much as the $1,841 spent on health care-per family, according to a survey by the US Labor Department." Moreover, "the price we pay to amuse ourselves has, in some cases, risen at a rate triple that of inflation over the past five years" (*USA Today*, April 2, 1999: E1).

15 Environmental News Network, May 12, 1999.

16 feedmag.com/daily/dyo20499.html.

17 As reported in www.suck.com/fish/99/02/02.

the maximum, and generate accelerating record advertising rates. These cultural rituals celebrate U.S. society's deepest values (e.g., competition, winning, success, and money) and corporations are willing to pay top dollar to get their products associated with such events. Indeed, it appears that the logic of the commodity spectacle is increasingly permeating professional sports which can no longer be played without the accompaniment of cheerleaders, giant mascots who clown with players and spectators, and raffles, promotions, and contests that feature the products of various sponsors.

Sports stadiums themselves contain electronic reproduction of the action, as well, as giant advertisements for various products that rotate for maximum saturation — previewing environmental advertising in which entire urban sites are becoming scenes to boost commodity spectacles. Arenas, like the United Center in Chicago, or America West Arena in Phoenix, are named after corporate sponsors. The Texas Rangers stadium in Arlington, Texas, supplements its sports arena with a shopping mall, office buildings, and a restaurant in which for a hefty price one can watch athletic events while eating and drinking. Tropicana Field in Tampa Bay, Florida, "has a three-level mall that includes places where 'fans can get a trim at the barber shop, do their banking and then grab a cold one at the Budweiser brew pub, whose copper kettles rise three stories. There is even a climbing wall for kids and showroom space for car dealerships'" (Ritzer 1998: 229).

Furthermore, the uniforms of professional sports players are becoming as littered with advertisements as racing cars. In the globally popular sport of soccer, companies such as Canon, Sharp, and Carlsberg sponsor teams and expect these teams to promote their products via logos on team shirts, thus making the players epiphenomena of transnational capital. In auto racing events, like Indianapolis 500, or professional bicycling events, like the Tour de France, entire teams are sponsored by major corporations. In summer 1999, there were discussions about putting corporate logos on the uniforms of professional baseball players, although so far this idea has been resisted by Major League Baseball officials. Top sports heros make astronomical sums endorsing products, thus imploding sports, commerce, and advertising into dazzling spectacles that celebrate the products and values of corporate America.

In fashion, inherently a consumer spectacle, laser-light shows, top rock and pop music performers, superstar mod-

els, and endless hype publicize each new season's offerings, generating ever more elaborate clothing displays:

> In the same way that movies are being judged by the size of their grosses, not whether they make any sense, couture shows are now judged by the size of the spectacle. … Keep your eye on the three-story waterfall at Givenchy, and wait for the train at Christian Dior. … At huge expense, a spice-filled Souk was recreated, and the lost luggage room had trunks tagged with names like Bing Crosby, Cleopatra and Brad Pitt.[18]

Here the logics of spectacle and simulation combine in a megaorgy of lights, music, dazzling image, and constructed environments that glorify the commodity and celebrity culture, and fetishize its idols. One of the world's most fashionable and glamorous women, Princess Diana, became a commodified spectacle in life, and continues to be commodified after her death, with an intense global marketing of her image on postage stamps, coins, portrait plates, porcelain dolls, and other wares of "Dianabilia."[19] Similarly, the days following the summer 1999 disappearance and death of John F. Kennedy Jr. were marked by wall-to-wall media coverage, instant TV documentaries,

---

A papal visit takes on the form of megaspectacle, as when the pope's trip to St. Louis was awarded the headline "Pope Gets Rock-Star Greeting in U.S."

---

and commemorative magazine issues, as media corporations capitalized on the Kennedy mystique.

Such celebrity icons provide people with deities to worship from afar and inspire individuals to enter the world of image and spectacle, becoming part of the action. The society of the spectacle attempts to make it appear that a life of luxury and happiness is open to all, that anyone can buy the sparkling objects on display and consume the spectacles of entertainment and information. But in reality

---

18   "In Paris Couture, the Spectacles the Thing" *New York Times*, July 21, 1998: C24.
19   *New York Times*, December 28, 1995: C1.

only those with sufficient wealth can fully enjoy the benefits of the capitalist spectacle, whose opulence is extracted out of the lives and dreams of the exploited. The poor souls who cannot afford to live out their commodity fantasies in full are motivated to work harder and harder, until they are trapped in the squirrel cage of working and spending, spending and working — while borrowing money at high interest rates. In fact, consumer credit card debt in the United States has skyrocketed 47% in recent years. By the mid-1990s, the average debt per household was over $3,000, up from barely $1,000 per household in 1985.[20] Near the end of the decade credit indebtedness reached $1.2 trillion, growing at a 9% annual rate and generating negative saving rates 2 months in a row for the first time on record.[21]

New forms of megaspectacle are emerging through the tourism and leisure industries. Theme parks like the Disney Worlds re-create entire spectacular simulated environments for family consumption. IMAX movies feature gigantic screens of erupting volcanoes, cascading avalanches, arduous climbs to Mount Everest, voyages to the Moon, undersea exploration, and the like, which allow simulation of the wonders of nature, or the euphoric experience of Michael Jordan's slam dunks. In the Universal Studios Islands of Adventure theme park, built for $3 billion, you can island-hop around five different sites, including Seuss Landing, Jurassic Park, The Lost Continent, Toon Lagoon, and Marvel Super Hero Island. This homage to the megaspectacle features high-tech rides, with 12-story-high roller-coasters, sophisticated animatronics, and 3-D special effects. Designed as pure escapism for the entire family, the Islands of Adventure advertisement bids, "Give Us Three Days and Nights. We'll Give You a Whole New Universe."

Cyberdigerati proclaim that VR will be the next stage in theme-park-like experiences, so that spectators can stay home, just don a helmet or visor, and have all the experiences — sights, sounds, and smells — that one would have in a "real" experience in a "real" park or site. Entrepreneurs

> Theme parks like the Disney Worlds re-create entire spectacular simulated environments for family consumption.

claim that such experiences will be designed as an interactive spectacle wherein the "visitor" will have some input about what she or he will experience — for example, what dinosaurs will appear, whether to be washed over a waterfall or to parachute out of a crashing airplane, and so on. Perhaps such spectacles will become as addictive as the VR drug in the 1995 film *Strange Days* in which spectators become hooked on videos of extreme sex and violence, or the simulated worlds of *The 13th Floor* (1999) where players are transported to re-creations of other times and places, take on new identities, and experience full bodily fears and pleasures.

Megaspectacles also include another form of mass-mediated experience: political occurrences. Media events like the Gulf War, the O. J. Simpson trial, the Clinton sex and impeachment scandal, the Elián González saga, and the battle for the White House in the aftermath of Election 2000 (see Kellner forthcoming) colonize everyday life, distracting individuals from their own and society's decisive problems as they get lost in the trivia of tabloid infotainment. In the summer of 1999, the fourth of the *Star Wars* films, *The Phantom Menace*, became the megaspectacle of the moment with saturation media coverage of spectators camped out waiting for the film to open, often dressed in the costumes of the film's characters. The phenomenon was featured on the covers of many magazines, was heavily reported by TV and other media, and was the subject of high-density Internet coverage and discussion.

Against the passivity of the spectator, Debord and the situationists espouse active, creative, and imaginative practice, whereby individuals create their own "situations" and passionate existential events, fully participating in the production of everyday life, individuality, and, ultimately, a new society. In the previous stage of the spectacle, the media and technology were seen as powerful control mechanisms keeping individuals numb, fragmented, and docile, watching and consuming, rather than acting and doing. Yet the spectacle was not always as monolithic, determining, and powerful as some believed, nor were spectators always mere dupes or conduits of manipulation. For the last several decades, work in media theory and cultural studies has challenged simplistic "hypodermic needle" models that assume individuals are merely injected

---

20 *New York Times,* August 26, 1998: C1 and C3.
21 *Los Angeles Times,* December 8, 1998: C3. For an examination of the incredible level of debt in the United States and its impact on people, see Schor (1997).

with ideology, and has analyzed the ways viewers read texts critically and against the grain, and subvert or challenge power relations in their everyday life. However, the subject was arguably not as self-constituting as later advocates of the "active audience" within British cultural studies and

and some ideas about how activist intervention might help shape a better future. Throughout the society of the interactive spectacle, we find objects communicating with other objects in densely interlinked digital networks; humans interacting with objects and information through a myriad

---

Thus, our challenge is to theorize forms of domination and manipulation *and* agency and resistance in the previous and current phases of the spectacle.

---

elsewhere would maintain in the 1980s (see the critique of the latter in Kellner 1995a, and of the situationist concepts in Best and Kellner 1997, Ch. 3).

Thus, our challenge is to theorize forms of domination and manipulation *and* agency and resistance in the previous and current phases of the spectacle. We do so with the realization that the spectacle itself has today evolved into a new stage of interactivity, which comprises new technologies (unforeseen by Debord) that allow a more active participation of the subject in (what remains) the spectacle. Individuals within the new stage of spectacle are more engaged because interactive technologies like the computer, multimedia, and VR make possible enhanced participation, albeit of limited and ambivalent types. Accordingly, we contrast a more dynamic and creative construction of cyber-situations with manipulative and pacifying modes of the interactive spectacle.

CYBERSITUATIONS AGAINST THE SPECTACLE

Today the revolutionary project stands accused before the tribunal of history — accused of having failed, of having engendered a new alienation. This amounts to recognizing that the ruling society has proved capable of defending itself, on all levels of reality, much better than revolutionaries expected. Not that it has become more tolerable. Revolution has to be reinvented, that's all.

— *INTERNATIONALE SITUATIONNISTE* #6
(August 1991)

The development and effects of new multimedia and interactive spectacle are far from clear. We can therefore offer here but a few thoughts on a condition still unfolding

of communication technologies and channels; and humans interacting with each other through the mediation of electronic media and computers. While forms of interaction are intensifying, and while computer users are more active than TV viewers, we believe that the interaction between individuals and technology, celebrated by cybertheorists like Sherry Turkle (1996) and others, exaggerates the degree and significance of interactivity and the break with previous forms of culture and subjectivity.

On the one hand, the previous stage was not as passive as Debord claimed. On the other hand, contemporary forms of the interactive spectacle are not as emancipatory and creative as many cyberdigerati argue. We concede a more interactive dimension to the present stage of the spectacle and a more energetic role for the subject, but we also see an erosion of the distinction between subject and object occurring that has disturbing implications, as individuals implode into an ever denser technological network. While we would not go as far as Baudrillard in postulating the triumph of the object in contemporary postmodern culture (see the discussion in Kellner 1989b: 153ff.), we recognize that the cyberspectacle, like its predecessors in media culture, is intensely seductive and may foster new forms of alienation and domination.

Many forms of cyberculture currently being boosted do not advance genuine interaction and instead wrap subjects more insidiously within the tentacles of the consumer society. Today, instead of merely watching TV, with beer in hand, someone may participate in public discussion, take part in polls, or respond to the hosts of talk shows and their guests by phone, fax, or e-mail. Rather than drift into the beta-wave stupor induced by TV, the cybersubject can voice an opinion. In a vividly literal application of interactive technology, video cameras can project your image into the screen to allow you to "interact" with virtual characters (as you also become one). The Media Lab at MIT developed an interactive system that allows the viewer of a cartoon called *Swamped!* to direct the movement and actions of the animal characters.

Yet one should not exaggerate the significance of such activity. Much Internet "interactivity" is limited to repetitive pointing and clicking at endless pictures of stars and celebrities, or to downloading video or sound clips at entertainment sites. Information and education sites often involve clicking on images or superficial infobites that reduce complex subjects to trivial simplifications. The culture industry thus greatly exaggerates the significance of its mode of interaction. A Pepsi commercial on MTV publicizing the 1998 MTV Music Video Awards show emphasized the fact that the video of the year award would be selected by the viewers via the Internet and live phone calls during the show. The commercial celebrated "the power of choice" and reminded viewers that "you are in charge of your destiny," equating the ability to vote for an MTV music video award with personal and social power. In such fashion, the interactive spectacle attempts to seduce viewers into playing its game and equates virtual participation with empowerment and destiny.

Moreover, typically the protocols of interaction on computer networks are structured, and websites that solicit viewer opinions through e-mail are monitored and manipulated. That is, often "wizards" or list-serve administrators can take people off lists, censor postings, and limit the type and extent of interaction. Interactive mainstream media such as CNN discussion programs that solicit viewers to e-mail or fax comments for instant dissemination are also monitored and controlled — as are websites that incorporate live viewer input. While these are interesting developments in the history of the media, they do not constitute a democratizing, empowering, or genuinely interactive culture per se. In fact, they are continuous in some ways with the media spectacles of the previous stage, although they integrate the consumer and audience into the spectacle in more engaging ways.

"Interactive TV" is not only an oxymoron, it is an ideological concealment of the fact that the stage and props of discussion are already in place and corporately controlled (e.g., a producer screens calls, the host can instantly cut off a radical perspective that may seep through). Further, individuals are still isolated in private homes. "Interactive TV" is therefore an alibi that functions in the same way that the "open hallways" of Congress (threatened by the summer 1998 shootings of two Capitol police officers) masks the fact that, open or blocked, the citizens still do not get behind the closed doors of establishment power politics.

Web TV is already providing an interactive spectacle combining the television industry and the Internet, allowing one to access databases, websites, virtual shopping, e-mail, and chat rooms, while watching TV. To simulate the more active nature of the Internet, TV networks are planning programs that allow the viewer to click on menus that will give them options for more information related to what they are looking at. Viewers watching Julia Child cook, for example, will be able to print the recipe she is making and even order necessary ingredients on the spot. Advertisers are excited about the prospects for selling clothes and fashion accessories exhibited on interactive TV, or selling objects on display in programs that individuals will be able to purchase simply by clicking on their screens. Thus, the future of TV appears to be interactive, as it seeks to emulate its Internet rival, while Internet pioneers and entrepreneurs claim that their medium will absorb and trump all others. In fact, the media are imploding into each other as they coevolve into comprehensive information, entertainment, and communications media, linked by both wired and wireless interactive networks.

In addition, Internet technology enables ordinary individuals to make their everyday life a spectacle. For example, they can offer themselves having sex live via webcams or on tape on the Internet (usually for a fee). On June 16, 1998, a woman offered a live birth on the Internet (she had a felony record for various scams). "Webcams" record and send live over the Internet the daily activities of webstars like JenniCam whose site receives some 60,000 visitors a day to watch her go through mundane activities. The "star" of AnaCam can be seen "on her couch (she has no bed), looking bored, eating a pizza, having kinky sex with her boyfriend — sometimes all at the same time."[22] Throughout the world, individuals are setting up webcam sites, sometimes charging for access. The sites are often run by sex professionals who offer nude women and round-the-clock full penetration spycams. The enterprising Gay Frat House Voyeur Cam offers 12 hidden camera angles including "butt cam," "dick cam," and "tan-line cam," not to forget the "toilet cam."[23]

---

22 *Newsweek,* June 1, 1998: 64.
23 See the description in www.suck.com/fish/99/01/21.

Webcam sites are also posting advertising. DotComGuy ran an interactive spectacle featuring himself as the subject of a 365-day 24-hour-a-day surveillance in a North Dallas house. He never left home and for a year subsisted entirely on items purchased from the web — or contributed by companies, whose products received free "advertising" (*Salon*, August 1, 2000). Many of the sites feature tedious transmissions of individuals driving their cars or even the interior of refrigerators, suggesting many people have no clue concerning how to productively use the new technologies.

Another form of Internet spectacle consists of videos of naked young people in showers or dressing room, whose images were being sold on commercial Internet sites (*CBS Evening News*, July 29, 1999). Some people, however, choose to exploit themselves. In a wildly successful Dutch TV series, *Big Brother*, a group of volunteers lived in a house under unrelenting surveillance by TV cameras, unable to have any contact with the outside world. Over time, viewers voted on which characters should stay or go, until only one was left to claim a cash prize. CBS bought rights to air a U.S. version of the show and broadcast the show in summer 2000.[24] As with the Dutch show, each week viewers voted on which contestant would be eliminated; the "winner" took home a half-million-dollar bonanza. The sight of dozens of microphones and cameras everywhere, including the CBS logo of an open eye, recalls the Orwellian nightmare, transmuted into fluff entertainment in the society of the spectacle. Quite possibly *Big Brother* helps acclimate people to surveillance, such as is exercised by the FBI "Carnivore" program that can intercept private e-mail, and to round-the-clock video surveillance at work, in public spaces, and perhaps even at home.

Another reality-based show, *Survivor*, involved a dangerous endurance contest among 16 contestants on a deserted island off Borneo. It was also broadcast by CBS in summer 2000, becoming a major ratings success. On this show, contenders voted each other off each week, with the winner receiving a million dollars. The competition elicited complex alliances and Machiavellian strategies in a social Darwinian passion play. The *CBS Morning News* show, which has a long history of merging news and entertainment, interviewed the contestants the morning after the nation watched the contestants' expulsion and the news show saw its ratings skyrocket.

Demonstrating the psychopathology of the spectacle, contestants on these "reality" shows are driven by a lust for money and perhaps even more by the 15 minutes of fame and celebrity promised to them by Andy Warhol. Buffeted by the machines of publicity, there appear to be no losers, as those voted off return to instant renown and receive offers to become TV guest hosts, VJs (video diskjockeys), or even to appear in *Playboy* (though one contestant on the Swedish *Big Brother* committed suicide after his exile, and it is not clear what the long-term effects of celebrity withdrawal on participants in these experiments may be).

Hence, whereas Truman Burbank, in the summer 1998 hit film *The Truman Show*, discovered to his horror that his life was being televised and sought to escape the video panopticon, many individuals in the cyberworld choose to make televisual spectacles of their everyday life, such as the webcam "stars" or the participants in the MTV "reality" series *Real World* and *Road Rules*. Even PBS got in the act in summer 2000 with its reality-based show *The 1900 House* which features another survival endurance trial, this time involving a family suffering without the amenities of the consumer society and techno-culture in a Victorian-era British middle-class house. "Reality television" continued to proliferate in 2001 with a *Survivor* series located in the Australian outback, *Temptation Island* that lured couples into compromising situations with attractive potential sexual counterparts, and stamina contests such as *Eco-Challenge: Borneo* and *Boot Camp*, which prepare individuals from the soft U.S. public for hand-to-hand conflict with possible Chinese, Russian, North Korean, or other "enemies" that the Bush administration is manufacturing. These shows replicate the same basic formula of putting ordinary people in extraordinary situations and promote competitive, survivalist, and militarist values.

These series and their websites seem to be highly addictive, pointing to deep-seated voyeurism and narcissism in the society of the interactive spectacle, in which individuals

---

24 See Brian Lowry, "'Big Brother's Watchers See Everything But Privacy,'" *Los Angeles Times*, February 12, 2000: Al and A50 and "The Electronic Fishbowl," *New York Times*, May 21, 2000. The new reality shows exhibit the confluence of television and Internet entertainment. The Dutch show *Big Brother*, which featured a live website with four video streams that one could check out, attracted 52 million hits; the CBS series deployed roughly the same setup. It is interesting from the perspective of globalization that recent hit TV formulas have come from Europe to the United States. The 1999–2000 ABC sensation *Do You Want to Be a Millionaire?* was closely based on a hit British TV series, as was *Survivor*. Apparently, the crassest and most commercial aspects of globalization crosses borders the most easily.

have a seemingly insatiable lust to become part of the spectacle and to involve themselves in it more intimately and to peer into the personal lives of others. Moreover, they exemplify what Daniel Boorstin (1961) referred to as "pseudoevents," in which people pay more attention to media-produced spectacles than to pressing concerns in the sociopolitical world and everyday life. As Baudrillard astutely observed (1933), postmodern media society devolves around an "obscenity" that implodes public and private spheres and puts on display the most banal and intimate aspects of everyday life — be it the sex games of Bill Clinton or the melodramas of ordinary "reality TV" drama participants.

have never fired an actual weapon. In December 1997, for example, Michael Carneal, a 14-year-old computer geek and war game freak, walked into the lobby of Heath High School in Paducah, Kentucky, and opened fire into a prayer circle, handling the gun like a pro and killing three of his classmates.[25]

VR devices promise to take individuals into an even higher and more powerful realm of spectacle in which participants may think that they are interacting with a real environment, rather than a projected simulation, be it a war game or a pornographic fantasy. The "intensor chair" provides various sensations and stimulations, as the viewer sits within the midst of a virtual environment,

---

We suggest that producing cybersituations involves engaging individuals in activities that fulfill their own potential, further their interests, and promote oppositional activity aimed at progressive change and alternative cultural and social forms.

To be sure, there are extremely valuable websites on the Internet which is potentially an excellent research tool, mode of communication, forum for debate, and site for cultural experimentation and creativity. The danger is that it is being colonized by corporate forces that are turning it into another domain of capitalist spectacle and commodification. The likelihood of this has greatly increased with the AOL-Time Warner merger in 2000–2001 that signaled the desire of megacorporations to colonize the Internet. In addition, as the April 1999 Columbine High School shooting demonstrated, there is also a dark and potentially dangerous side to the interactive spectacle in the form of brutal video games, hate sites, and the circulation of the culture of violence. While we by no means intend to reduce the complicated array of causes underlying the epidemic of teen killings in the last few years to the leisure activities of youth, it cannot be denied that a steady feast of media and interactive violence will have an impact on many impressionable minds that at the very least desensitizes them to violence in society. Interactive video games like *Doom* are particularly alarming in that they implicate young people in gory images and actions in a far deeper way than passively viewing violence on TV; moreover, they blur the boundaries between reality and unreality. The "reality effect" of some games is such that they include weapons that give a strong "kick" like a real gun. There are even examples of teen killers going on a shooting rampage, although they

playing war and action games. So far VR devices have been limited to games like *Dactyl Nightmare,* where one dons a head-mounted display to fight other characters and avoid destruction by large winged creatures in a Darwinian battle for survival, or one enters a high-tech virtual "movie ride," often based on film characters like *RoboCop.* Some of these experiences make possible a new level of multisensorium spectacles that deploy giant movie screens, 3-D images, and vibrating chairs, something like the "feelies" envisioned by Huxley in *Brave New World.*

Indeed, to capture the olfactory quality of the feelies, California-based DigiScents has developed an interactive technology that adds scents to multimedia CD-ROMs and websites. Shoppers clicking onto a scent-enhanced cosmetics website could smell the latest products. Thinking about a trip to the Caribbean? Check out the dazzling images of white sand and clear blue water, and breathe deeply the aroma of exotic beauty. In the mood for an interactive murder mystery game? You can sniff out the dastardly criminal by following scents presented as olfactory clues.

While more interesting and engaging than plain-old TV, such virtual and "interactive" technology can seduce the viewer into an even deeper tie to the spectacle. In fact, there is no substitute for getting off one's ass and becoming

---

25 www.nytimes.com/Ubraiy/magazine/home/19990523mag-keegan.html.

involved in genuinely interactive citizenship and democracy. Advocates of the superiority of cyberworlds denigrate the body as mere "meat" and "RL" as a boring intrusion into the pleasures of the media and computer worlds of cyberspace. We would avoid, however, demonizing cyberspace as a fallen realm of alienation and dehumanization, as do many of its technophobic philosophical critics (e.g., Virilio 1998a; Borgmann 1994, 1999), just as we would refrain from celebrating it as a new realm of emancipation, democracy, and creative activity.

We distinguish therefore between a more inventive and self-valorizing construction of cybersituations contrasted to the pseudointeraction of the corporate-produced interactive spectacle. Extending Debord's conception of the construction of situations into the spheres of new technologies, we suggest that producing cybersituations involves engaging individuals in activities that fulfill their own potential, further their interests, and promote oppositional activity aimed at progressive change and alternative cultural and social forms. This could consist of using cyberspace to advance struggles, such as to promote political demonstrations, actions, and organizations. It might include the construction of a website, computer-mediated space such as chat rooms, or discussion groups that provide alternative information and culture. Such cybersituations could engage individuals who are usually excluded from public discussions and could enlarge the sphere of democratic participation. In these self- or group-constructed environments, people can develop both form and content, using new technologies to advance their own projects, to express their own views and visions, and to interact in ways that they themselves decide.

Constructing cybersituations involves the appropriation, use, and reconstruction of technologies against the capitalist spectacle and other forms of domination, alienation, and oppression. The aesthetic strategies of the situationists included *détournement,* a means of deconstructing the images of bourgeois society by exposing their hidden manipulation or repressive logic (e.g., by changing the wording of a billboard); the *dérive,* an imaginative, hallucinatory "drift" through the urban environment (an urban variation on the surrealist stroll through the countryside); and the *constructed situation,* designed to unfetter, create, and experiment with desires (see the texts in Knabb 1981: 5–13, 43–47, 50–59).

There are conspicuous cyberequivalents of these categories. Hacking comprises a *détournement* within cyberspace,

whereby computer activists break into government or corporate websites, using the tools of the interactive spectacle itself against institutions deemed to be pernicious. After the bombing of the Chinese embassy in Belgrade by NATO forces in May 1999. For instance, hackers broke into the NATO website to protest the action. There have been several examples of hackers invading Pentagon and Defense Department websites to deface them or to post critical messages. Hacker campaigns have also been organized against the governments of Mexico, Indonesia, and other countries.

In general, hackers protest against unpopular policies by defacing official websites or bombarding government servers with spam or logic bombs, attempting to shut them down.[26] One of the more spectacular hacker attacks against commercial e-business sites occurred in February 2000. Hackers temporarily blocked access to the popular Internet sites Yahoo (a web portal), Amazon.com (an Internet book company), CNN (a news site), and Buy.com (an e-business retail site). Attacks followed on the news site ZDNet and the online brokerage site E-Trade. This demonstration of the ease with which commercial Internet sites can be disabled sent jitters through the stock market, put the FBI and law enforcement agencies in motion, and set off a flurry of discussions of the need for better cybersecurity.[27]

---

26 The most spectacular stories of hackers are collected in Levy (1984), Hafner and Markoff (1991), and Sterling (1992). Note that "hackers" was initially a positive term for the creators of computer networks and systems, and later became a negative term describing illicit entry and vandalism in cyberspace. On the whole, while we are against posting computer viruses and bombs that infect entire servers and networks, and that constitute a form of cyberterrorism and wanton destructiveness, we believe that creative hacking can constitute examples of Debordian *détournement* and the construction of cybersituations.

27 During the same period, the cyberhacker site RTMark claims that attacks against Internet toy giant eToys led the firm to withdraw a lawsuit against the popular art site etoy.com (see http://rtmark.com/autodesk.html). But the hacker whose program is believed to have enabled the recent e-commerce web assaults, a 20-year-old German computer whiz who goes by the name "Mixter," has denounced the attacks, calling the culprits "pretty clueless people who misuse powerful resources" (*Los Angeles Times,* February 12, 2000: A1). In fact, a 15-year-old Canadian boy using the netname "niafiaboy" was arrested for allegedly carrying out some of the February strikes against e-commerce sites, though there was speculation that his activity was exaggerated and that he was probably just a "script-kiddie" using existing hacker programs.

Surfing the web can exemplify the Debordian *dérive*, in which one abstracts oneself from the cares of everyday life and seeks adventure, novelty, and the unexpected on the Internet. Such "cruising" is equivalent to the activity of the urban flaneur, celebrated by Walter Benjamin, in which one drifts though the hypertexts of the cyberworld, clicking from one destination and curiosity to another,

---

As Aldous Huxley put it, people exchange freedom for "fun."

---

sometimes merely observing and sometimes participating in more interactive endeavors. Such activities constitute novel forms of postmodern pleasure and help cultivate new subjectivities, interpersonal relationships, and communities — although, as we signal below, there are limitations and dangers to such activity.

Constructing cybersituations includes the creation of an anti-McDonald's website against the junk food corporation and then distributing the material through digital and print media. This site was developed by supporters of two British activists, Helen Steel and Dave Morris, who were sued by McDonalds for distributing leaflets denouncing the corporation's low wages, false advertising practices, involvement in deforestation, cruel treatment of animals, and promotion of an unhealthy diet. The activists counterattacked. With help from supporters, they organized a "McLibel" campaign, assembled a "McSpotlight" website with a tremendous amount of information criticizing the corporation, and mobilized experts to testify about and confirm their criticisms. A 3-year civil trial, Britain's longest ever, ended ambiguously on June 19, 1997, with the judge defending some of McDonald's claims against the activists, while substantiating some of the activists' criticisms (Vidal 1997: 299–315). The case created unprecedented bad publicity for McDonald's which was disseminated throughout the world via Internet websites, mailing lists, and discussion groups. The McLibel/McSpotlight group claims that their website was accessed over 15 million times and was visited over two million times in the month of the verdict alone (Vidal 1997: 326). The *Guardian* (February 22, 1996) reported that the site "claimed to be the most comprehensive source of information on a multinational corporation ever assembled" and characterized it as one of the more successful anticorporate campaigns.[28]

Of course, one can get sucked into the tentacles of the Internet spectacle, trapped in the interstices of the web, seduced by images, games, and consumption of goods and unable to connect with the outside world. The distinction between creative and empowering cybersituations versus (pseudo)interactive and disempowering spectacle is often difficult to make, but we believe that some such distinction is necessary in order to provide critical perspectives on and alternatives to the forms of interactive spectacle now evolving. While pseudointeraction provides escape into an ersatz (virtual) reality, activist use of technology enables individuals to create and interact more productively with others in their everyday lives and to strive to transform culture and society by generating new spaces of connection, freedom, and creativity. Constructing cybersituations thus provides potential articulations between cyberspace and the real world, while pseudointeraction merely entangles one ever deeper in the matrices of escapism and corporate entertainment.

Hence, "constructing a situation" in cyberspace involves producing an interactive realm that allows individuals to articulate their needs and interests, and to connect with people of similar outlooks and desires. It can also involve a refunctioning of technology, as when members of the French public recast the Minitel from a centralized source of official government information to an interactive space of connection and discourse from below (see Feenberg 1995). In the case of innovative MP3 and other music distribution technologies, both well-known and unknown artists can directly release their music to a listening audience without the mediation of the record industries that exploit artists, control artistic expression, and often enforce a bland homogeneity of music choices. MP3 and Napster, Gnutella, Netbrilliant, and various netcasting technologies also allow any person with a computer, the right software, and a little technical savvy to be their own DJ and radio station (even if sometimes distributing music illegally), thereby engendering more diversity of production, distribution, and consumption of music.[29]

---

28 For the anti-McDonald's site, see www.mcspotlight.org.

29 MP3 allows computer users to compress music digitally into files that have near-CD quality. Napster has programs that search for MP3 files online and then download them to one's own computer — thus making possible the sharing of music libraries (see *New York Times,* "Powerful Music Software

Programs like *Freeware* and *Scour* make it possible to access and store programs ranging from music to text and video. Likewise, cheap digital-video cameras make possible the production of new types of low-cost film. *The Blair Witch Project,* a mockumentary about the supposed mysterious disappearance of a young documentary-film crew in the countryside of Maryland — was the film sensation of summer 1999.[30] Made on an extremely low budget, it exploited new video technologies and the Internet, which fostered tremendous subcultural Interest in the phenomenon. Indeed, the Internet itself is becoming a venue for low-budget film, using digital film technologies to expand the possibilities for new voices and alternative cultures to contest the corporate hegemony and provide new forms of political and interactive culture.

To be sure, distinctions between empowering and creative activity versus disempowering and alienating activity are ideal types, since each individual is constructed in some way or another by the social environment in which he or she lives. But even the most controlled and structured interactive cyberspace allows more participation and involvement than the passive consumption of television or film images in the solitude of one's own subjectivity. One is never totally free of social influence. In cyberspace all technologically mediated communication is structured to some extent by computer protocols, codes, and programs. Moreover, we are not against the fun and pleasure offered by the interactive and media spectacles that we have been describing. Rather, we are criticizing the organization of

an entire society structured around amusement, commodification, and consumption. Where commercial interests dominate the forms of culture, decisive issues are often not taken seriously, individuals are isolated in solipsistic activity and cut off from social practice, and, as Aldous Huxley put it, people exchange freedom for "fun."

In any case, the new forms of interactive spectacle are very ambiguous. On the one hand, they can provide more creative interaction with media and culture than viewing television or film and can promote social transformation rather than passivity. On the other hand, they ensnare individuals into technological systems that abstract them from their everyday life in favor of novel virtual worlds, the types and effects of which are difficult to conceptualize and evaluate. Yet while the form of technologically mediated interaction is always structured, limited, and coded, new technologies allow for the construction of alternative spaces that can attack and subvert the established culture. In this emergent site, one can express views and encourage alternatives hitherto excluded from mainstream media, and engage in innovative forms of democratic communication and political discussion. Consequently, the new cultural forums have many more voices and individuals participating than during the Era of Big Mainstream Media in which giant corporations controlled both form and the content of what could be spoken and shown. Cyberdemocracy and technopolitics are too recent for us to adequately appraise their possibilities, limitations, and effects, but we believe they provide the promise of the sort of subversive politics against the capitalist spectacle that Debord encouraged.

Has Industry Worried" [March 7, 2000] and *Salon,* "MP3 free-for-all" [February 3, 2000]). Yet well-publicized court rulings against Napster in May 2000 and February 2001 have rendered the future of net-music questionable, generating an impassioned debate about Internet distribution, ownership rights, and popular music. If Napster is suppressed, no doubt other technologies will emerge, assuring that new forms of production, distribution, and consumption of media culture continue to proliferate.

30   The film made the cover stories of both *Time* and *Newsweek;* for a discussion of the digital revolution in Hollywood filmmaking, see *Wired,* 1.06 (1993) and 8.05 (2000); on how "New Digital Cameras Poised to Jolt World of Filmmaking," see *New York Times,* November 19,1999: A1 and C5. Other independent filmmakers have been making their product available on the web, gaining the attention of Hollywood producers and financers for their projects. The next logical move is to make an interactive film online on the web; a German filmmaker has begun such a project. In May 2000, Mike Figgis released *Time Code,* a film shot in digital video the previous fall with four-frame real-time simultaneous juxtapositions of overlapping stories.

The Universal Solvent: Meditations on the Marriage of World Cultures

from *Tempest, Flute and Oz*

— Frederick Turner

Anyone who walks the streets or campuses of the new tier of world-cities will be struck by the fantastic combinations of races in friendship, marriage, work, and study. My son, born in America, is half British and half Chinese; he plays baseball with a Slav from Poland and an Arab from Algeria; I eat at French/Lebanese, Thai, Salvadorean, and Israeli/Chinese restaurants, buy software from emigrant South Africans, celebrate the Zoroastrian New Year with Farsi friends from Iran, and collaborate on artistic and intellectual projects with a Macedonian Yugoslav, a Greek, a Hungarian Jew, a Japanese, a Latin American, and several Germans. Yet in a strange way the place I live in does not cease at all to be Texas to the core. Cultural information not only has the property of being transferable without loss, but also of being almost infinitely superimposable. Many cultures can occupy the same place or brain without loss; there seems to be no cultural equivalent of the Pauli Exclusion Principle, which forbids two particles from existing in the same energy state and place at the same time.

What is the meaning of this unparalleled mixing that has been going on in recent years among the world's cultures? Interculturalism itself comes in a bewildering variety of genres, each with its own pressing and highly ambiguous set of moral and epistemological questions. Consider this brief and incomplete list of intercultural genres: tourism, international charity, evangelism, colonial administration anthropology, true trade (as opposed to mercantile colonialism), political and military contacts, academic consultation and exchange, artistic collaboration, artistic influence, political asylum, statelessness, refugeeism, education abroad, intermarriage, and emigration.

Of course any celebration of a new era of tolerance and ethnic harmony would be premature. The collapse in our century of the great empires — the Austrian, the Turkish, the British, the Soviet, and soon the Chinese — has left large areas of the world in a state of Balkanized tribalism and nationalist hostility, and it well may appear that we are further away than ever from the interculturalism we anticipate. It may even seem a decadent luxury to trouble our conscience with the problems of cultural mixing when such a foul-tempered resurgence of racism and ethnocentrism is under way.

But from another perspective these horrible events are belated but inevitable consequences of world forces that will eventually lead to a more comfortably intercultural world. The great empires held those tensions in an artificial stasis, and now they are playing themselves out naturally. In this view the eventual result of the enormous mobility of persons and information will be something like the condition of the United States or the European Common Market; or like those countries which, having once possessed colonial empires, now have had their homelands peacefully invaded by their erstwhile subjects and find that together with the inevitable stress, there is also a surge of cultural revitalization that is not unwelcome.

Perhaps the most remarkable fact of the modern world is that for the first time — in just the last two decades — all the member cultures of the human race have finally come to know of each other, and have, more or less, met. There

Frederick Turner, "The Universal Solvent: Meditations on the Marriage of World Cultures," from *Tempest, Flute and Oz: Essays on the Future*, pp. 6–12, 18–26, 27–33. Copyright © 1991 by Persea Books. Permission to reprint granted by the publisher.

really is no human Other now. Clearly, the ethnocentrism of the old right and of political conservatism in general cannot survive the enormous influx of information from the rest of the world. Of course, our urge to demonize the Other has not gone away, whether the other is black or white, female or male, left-wing or right-wing; it has even sometimes been artificially displaced to other species and even to some of our more human-like machines. But the urge must now contend with the logic of history, technology, and economics.

The formal complexity of interculturalism has not prevented some of our bolder, and paradoxically, more conventional, intellectuals from seeking to cut the gordian knot of the problem with the sword of neoleftist analysis.

Some kind of plausibility might be constructed for the economic/cultural exploitation argument. But a few further examples serve to show how flimsy it is. Consider Japan's success in exporting its products, including much of its material and spiritual culture, to the United States. The expropriation model, to be consistent, would imply that the United States was expropriating the cultural property of Japan. More absurd still, the enormous penetration of American music, movies, television, soft drinks, sports activities, and consumer goods into many of the poorer Asian, African, and Latin American countries would have to be interpreted as the expropriation on a huge scale of American cultural property by Third World cultural colonists.

Recently, the singer David Byrne was attacked by *Rolling Stone* magazine for "ripping off" Hispanic music in his new album. Critics of contemporary culture are thus claiming that cultural exchange is a form of economic exploitation.

A very crude reduction of their position might go like this: the rich are bad, and the poor are good. The rich got rich by exploiting the poor, and then by rigging the cultural value system to justify their privileges. The same goes for nations as well as for individuals. Nowadays, the old form of international expropriation, colonialism, has been partly replaced by a new form, whereby the bad (rich, powerful, white, male, etc.) expropriate the cultural property of the good (poor, weak, etc.). This theory attacks anthropologists, collectors of tribal art, tourists, Western followers of Oriental religions, white jazz enthusiasts, performance artists who use foreign traditional artistic and ritual techniques, and even male collectors of quilts and women's arts, as expropriators of the cultural goods of others. Recently, the singer David Byrne was attacked by *Rolling Stone* magazine for "ripping off" Hispanic music in his new album. Critics of contemporary culture are thus claiming that cultural exchange is a form of economic exploitation.

But at least implicitly the left now recognizes culture as having real economic value of its own, rather than simply being a smokescreen to conceal the true, economic, facts of coercion, power, and control; for otherwise the parallel between economic exploitation and cultural appropriation would have no meaning. If culture is a kind of goods that can be stolen by the powerful, then it is a goods.

Ah, but that's different, the determined neo-Leninist might say. But how is it different? Every answer leads to greater and greater betrayals of socialist articles of faith, some of them shared by all people of good will. Is it that the poor benighted natives (or poor benighted Americans) are in an unequal cultural contest and ought to be protected for their own good from our (or Japan's) potent and corrupting forms of cultural firewater? Besides being rather condescending, this argument is virtually identical to that of the supporters of apartheid in South Africa. Or is it that the terms of the exchange are unfair — that the Third World does not get a fair price for its cultural goods, while we gouge them for ours? This argument assumes either that there is some ultimate authority that decides which cultural goods are more valuable, ours or theirs, and does not trust either our valuation of relative value or theirs; or that there might be such a thing as a *fair* trade (and thus the possibility of a free market, entrepreneurism, and the whole capitalist ensemble). And if we use the Japan-U.S. example, it is the cheapness, not the clearness, of Japanese goods that is the problem. When it comes down to it, the only difference between being culturally expropriated, and conducting cultural imperialism is who we thought in the first place were the good guys and the bad guys.

The whole argument is based on a misleading analogy between cultural goods and industrial goods; which in turn is based on ignorance of the difference between information and matter. If matter is transferred to another location it ceases to exist at its first location. Moreover, it takes work to make the transfer, and if work is paid for out of the matter that is being transferred, one ends up with less matter at the point of arrival than at the point of origin. A steamship gets to its destination lighter than when it left its home port. However, if information is transferred, it not only remains where it started, but it is not necessarily diminished by its travels. The sender of information by radio does not cease to know what she knew when she sent it off in the message; and the message can be made redundant enough to include an arbitrarily diminishing amount of error.

In the mysterious realm of physics which deals with the thermodynamics of information, the energy cost to a computational system — that is, a system which does work by creating and/or transferring information — is in theory incurred only when it comes time to destroy the excess information that has built up in the system. Thus, one could in theory design a process for mass-producing pieces of information, whose only expense would be erasing the tape afterwards. If information is a kind of goods, then it is one which costs the maker nothing to make but which obliges its consumer to find an expensive waste-disposal system for the purchase once it is used. The logic and justice of such a transaction are almost unknown to contemporary economics, and the laws of intellectual property lag woefully behind the astonishing expansion of information-space that is now taking place in the world.

Yet do we not recognize in these goods, which it costs virtually nothing to buy but which clutter up the house and alarm environmentalists when we try to dispose of them, an increasing proportion. And if we are cultural workers, do we not recognize — though unwillingly, because it concedes how much fun our work is — those goods we create but cost us nothing to do so? And is not cultural property much more the kind that costs nothing to make or buy, that does not decay but is hard to get rid of, than the old kind, dear to Marxists and Capitalists alike, that costs the groaning labor of workers to produce, which they lose by giving to us and must be compensated for, and which wears out only too swiftly as we consume it?

It is the "expropriators" of cultural goods, then, not their creators, who are exploited. And thus the expropriation explanation collapses in absurdity.

But this meditation has already generated issues — or created information! — which it would be interesting to pursue. For instance, if it costs cultural creators nothing to produce their goods, why should they be paid? This question is not as trivial as it might appear; for as automation performs more and more repetitive and mechanical work that used to be done by humans, all workers will approach the economic condition of artists. And a theory that bases value on labor will be totally inadequate. An artist, for instance, may labor very hard at versification, draughtsmanship, secretarial detail, athletic training, or musical technique; but what we value most highly in the productions of artists is precisely that which transforms their labor into an addictive joy, which they would seek out whether they were paid or not. We do not pay artists for their *labor*: a bad artist may labor more tenaciously than a good one, but produce worthless results, as Peter Schaffer eloquently demonstrated in his play *Amadeus*. Yet if they were not paid, we would not have cultural producers, which would be a pity; even artists have to eat. Somehow there must be a medium and a method of exchange between cultural goods and the material goods which, as we say, keep body and soul together.

Another problem: If it is the audience for cultural goods that is doing the work — erasing the tape — then shouldn't they, too, be paid? Do we not already pay them, in fact, by subsidizing out of the public purse the cost of using the library, the museum, the symphony, the university, the theater? The poorest persons in our society have cheap access to a larger part of it than would an ancient emperor or Renaissance duke. And if we pay both cultural producers and cultural consumers, who foots the bill? Can money itself, in such an economy, "grow on trees" the way information clearly can? But can we retain our traditional respect for artists and other cultural producers if we pay them *despite* the fact that, as artists (rather than draughtsmen, clerks, or athletes) they do no work; and that we pay audiences to go and see them, *and to selectively forget what they have seen and heard?* Can we replace the matter-based, or industrially-based, model of respect with another more suited to the new age that is coming? Obviously, artists do indeed do something like what we used to call work, and their audience receives the most valuable goods of all; but the many jokes and tragic stories about working parents who do not want their children to grow up to be layabout artists also have a grain of truth.

* * *

What universal solvents will ensure the liquidity and translatability of cultural value? What new problems and dangers will be spawned by our very success? How do we preserve the cultural differences that we value?

The first of these questions, about universal solvents, requires some explanation. The human mind, and human culture in general, has admirable powers of compartmentalization. As any teacher knows who has experienced the coexistence in a students' mind of contradictory information (for instance, astronomical, biological, and geological book-learning together with a belief in the literal Biblical account of creation), "cut and dried" knowledge can leave

---

What are those solvents?
Most obvious, perhaps, is the
instantaneous medium provided
by worldwide telecommunications,
especially television.

---

the mind virtually unscathed. Contradictions do not even consciously arise; such knowledge has its own cocoon of insulation. To change the metaphor, the mixing of colors, or the metabolism of a ferment, or chemical reactions, or cookery, cannot take place without a liquid medium that presents the dissolved or suspended elements intimately and extensively against one another. Dry paints cannot mix.

The ready availability of multicultural information is not enough in itself to initiate the mysterious alchemy of interculturalism, whether that alchemy is the change in an individual's value system, or a transformation in the economic system and its underpinning of copyright law. All past bigotries and ethnocentrisms have coexisted with some, even much, information about other cultures. What is needed, and what our age has supplied, is a group of solvents that can serve as a common medium for all kinds of cultural information and insure that whatever processes of transformation they can engender in each other will actually happen. What are those solvents?

Most obvious, perhaps, is the instantaneous medium provided by worldwide telecommunications, especially television. There is a peculiar difference, between radio and television in this respect, which has been ignored by the critics of television. Curiously enough, it was the age of radio which saw the last great spasmodic surge in

nationalism, ethnocentrism, dictatorship, and mass ideology. It was radio that broadcast the mystagogic rant of Hitler, the brutal rhetoric of Stalin, the tirades of Franco and Mussolini. In a sense, the Allied Powers in the Second World War were lucky in getting as leaders Roosevelt, Churchill, and de Gaulle, who had a patrician loyalty to democracy, because the power that radio and its associated technologies provided them might well have been a temptation to dictatorship.

Even though television, like radio, is a broadcast medium, and thus would seem to favor the domination of a passive mass audience by a great authoritative voice, the nature of the visual medium subtly undermines the power and impressiveness of those who would use it. Somehow, if we can see the man live, see the play of expression on his face, his mortal human body taking up space in the world, turning its back, stumbling on the helicopter steps like Gerald Ford's, or dropping the banquet morsel from its chopsticks as Deng Xiaoping's did recently on television, then we cannot take his speeches very seriously. Part of it is that we can see how old he is. If he is old, we see the signs of decrepitude; if young, we feel superior to the fellow. I use the masculine pronoun here because, very significantly, female leaders do not seem to be afflicted by the television feet of clay. The great warlords of the recent past have often been women: Golda Meir, Indira Gandhi, Chiang Ching, Margaret Thatcher. In the film medium, as Leni Riefenstahl knew, the visual awkwardness can be more or less edited out, but live television is fatal to a demagogue. The only U.S. president to use television well was, significantly, a film actor. Knowing the medium, Ronald Reagan could use its deficiencies for his own purposes, and sympathy by playing subtly against his own mortal infirmities. His enemies did not realize this, and the more they attacked his apparent deafness, inattention, and wandering memory, the more affection he got. But it was affection, not obeisance.

Television is a humanizing medium, and a leveler. It also transcends, as radio does not, the barriers of language. That was why the students in Tienanmen square put up their statue to Democracy: as a visual symbol that would speak across the variety of languages both in the world at large and in China itself, where dozens of different languages are spoken. The man who stopped the tanks was making an utterance that is universally human. Television is thus a solvent for all cultural differences.

In the long run, other telecommunication media may be even more potent as solvents. Though the telephone is language-bound, it is not a broadcast medium, and thus, while enabling diverse populations within a language community to exchange ideas, cannot be used for domination of populations. Wiretapping is not a commensurate compensation for the authorities, as the Polish government tacitly admitted eight years ago when, after declaring martial law and outlawing solidarity, it closed down the telephone exchanges, thus foregoing the potentially valuable intelligence it might have got by listening in. The facsimile or fax machine, as the Chinese students found, is becoming another strong solvent, especially when there is a language problem. Here a picture is worth a million words. Computer logic and computer languages have begun to erode the acoustic language barrier, and perhaps eventually artificial intelligence may make possible the cybernetic translation of natural languages. In any case, the growth of telecommunications has tended to reinforce the development of the English language itself as a lingua franca and thus as a universal solvent. The expansion of English by the addition of hundreds of thousands of international scientific and technical words (themselves based on the old lingua francas of Latin and Greek) is part of this trend. We will deal later with the explosion of devices for recording and playing music, and the effect this has had on cultural liquidity.

> Another universal solvent is the global ecological crisis and the increasing awareness that it cannot be resolved by purely national means.

Related to the cultural solvent of telecommunications and technically based on it, has been the emergence of international financial markets, and the multinational corporations. Through new kinds of financial and investment instruments, ownership by union and pension funds of foreign securities, and the worldwide accessibility of government bonds issued by many nations, large numbers of ordinary people now own substantial property in other countries. In fact there already exists a loose and tacit world currency composed of a combination of the old petrodollar the U.S. budget deficit, and Third World debt. The world as a whole has discovered what Britain and America found in the late eighteenth century: the virtues of debt as a means of capital formation, its tendency to liquefy fixed assets and to put to work unused capital tied up in the real property of nations and, more intangibly, in the talents and education of their peoples and even in the probable political stability of their future.

> One of the most creative and positive solvents in world culture is the almost universal acceptance among the world's elites of the emerging scientific account of the universe.

Out of this world liquidity of value has come new institutions, especially the multinational corporations. These entities constitute the first examples of the true world citizen. This is not to say that they are especially virtuous; but for them there is no escape, the world itself being their field of action. They cannot emigrate, and thus their loyalty must be to the world as a whole. The welfare of a citizen of a nation is partly bound up with the welfare of that nation, and thus that citizen's vote will be motivated partly toward the national benefit, a motivation that mitigates his or her special interests. When citizens of the world are numerous and powerful enough, there will emerge a political quality akin to patriotism, an identification of one's own interests with those of the whole globe.

Another universal solvent is the global ecological crisis and the increasing awareness that it cannot be resolved by purely national means. Such threats as nuclear accidents like the one at Chernobyl, acid rain, the depletion of the ozone layer, species extinctions, and the greenhouse effect (with the accompaniment of global warming or a new ice age, depending on whose theories you accept) are world problems and require the liquefaction of different legal, industrial, and agricultural traditions in order to produce cooperative action. Related to this perceived crisis is the global danger of nuclear war and nuclear winter (or nuclear summer, according to some theorists). It is perhaps a blessing in disguise that the feedback mechanisms by which such changes might actually change the environment are as yet poorly understood. Even if alarm is misdirected, it is at least shared.

One of the most creative and positive solvents in world culture is the almost universal acceptance among the world's elites of the emerging scientific account of the universe. Here, though, there are dismaying counterforces: on both the right and the left there has been a backlash against the challenge and the cognitive expansion demanded by new developments in science. Evolution, for instance, is under attack by religious fundamentalists on one side, and by leftwing social determinists on the other, both anxious to avoid the responsibilities of creative and moral action demanded by the relationship between human nature and nature in general. The relaxation of social discipline brought about by cultural pluralism has itself been partly responsible for the new anti-science atmosphere. The hard discipline of logic and mathematics, and the self-restraint and self-criticism required by scientific method, are now out of reach of many who, in a stricter academic climate, might have acquired the rudiments of them and so been liberated.

Nevertheless, science will surely win the race between enlightenment and reaction, because those societies and groups within society which have mastered science will generally be more effective, inventive, and moral than those which have not, and will thus have greater powers of cultural survival. "More moral," by the way, because more capable of self-examination.

The last, and in some ways the most intriguing, of the great solvents is the rhythm of contemporary popular music, specifically "rock music." Originating in a fertile combination of the sophisticated African musical tradition with European and Latin American elements, a new musical medium emerged in the Sixties which is perhaps the most potent, because the most fundamental, of all forces for change. For many years jazz and blues coexisted with classical and folk music; but gradually a mutual translation took place. The names of Scott Joplin, the Gershwins, Leonard Bernstein, Bob Dylan, the Beatles, and now David Byrne and Philip Glass, chart the process of development. One recalls moments of musical insight in it: "West Side Story," Procul Harum's "A Whiter Shade of Pale," which was simultaneously real Bach and the most psychedelic pop, George Harrison's adaptations of Indian sitar music, Paul Simon's work with South Africa's Ladysmith Black Mombaso, Glass's "Satyagraha" and "Koyannisqaatsi."

> The last, and in some ways the most intriguing, of the great solvents is the rhythm of contemporary popular music, specifically "rock music."

Essentially what happened was that a very simple, pan-human rhythmic beat was discovered, of no musical merit in itself, to which the music of all world cultures could be set and which served as a liquid medium that would enable musical syncretism to take place. What has followed has been a worldwide musical revolution, where a record made in London by a talented Indian singer using a reggae base and Brazilian arrangements will influence young Nigerian, Czech, and Japanese rock groups, and perhaps form part of the raw material for a new classical opera. The extraordinary phenomena of glasnost and democracy in Eastern Europe and the Far East may have as much to do with the universality of rock and roll music as with anything else. This is not a praise of rock in itself, which is a rather insipid form of sound; but rock has been like alcohol, which can serve as the base for the most exquisite blends of perfume, the most delicate liqueurs.

The world of Homer and his Odysseus is one united by a liquid medium, literally that universal solvent that we call the ocean, that Homer called the *polyphloishoiou thalasses,* the multitudinously-flowing sea. The ambivalent and two-faced god of that medium, Poseidon, is the key problem of the *Odyssey.* The poem is about oars, about how to use the destructive element, as Stein calls it in *Lord Jim,* to do creative work and to get home with the story of Troy. The trouble with a universal solvent is what to use as a containment vessel. If the solvent is truly universal, it will melt through any walls which try to hold it in. The solution to this riddle is the solution to the problems of our times. It is, essentially, the one barrier which stands in the way of those scientists attempting to achieve nuclear fusion, and thus a cheap, inexhaustible, and clean source of energy for all humankind. In physics, the universal solvent is a plasma. What bottle can contain this genie? Uncontained, it is the principle of the greatest threat to humanity, the hydrogen bomb. Contained, it is the potential hearth of us all.

Interestingly enough, the best solutions suggested so far for the containment of this Thunderer, this Poseidonic universal solvent, is to use it as its own container, either by allowing it to power and to control an electromagnetic field that will constrain it, or by using it as an inertial jet-propulsion force to collapse it into a state of such great density that it begins to produce more energy than it consumes. If we accept this answer to the riddle as having mythic force for the containment of the intercultural plasma, we must look for ways in which interculturalism will be self-controlling or can be induced to enter turbulent but stable feedback states that maintain themselves. But first we must look more carefully at the dangers and diseases of the new informational economy that is emerging.

What are the main problems of interculturalism? One is immediately obvious: the issue of authenticity. It arises most clearly, perhaps, in the experience of tourism for both the tourist and the local population which serves and is photographed by the tourist. More subtly, but more disturbingly to the intellectual and artist, are such questions as: How authentic is my claim as an anthropologist to speak for the autochthones? Can I justify my ethnodramatic performance of their rituals? This haiku or Noh play I have written, or in which I am performing — is it genuine? Is my Buddhism authentic? Or again, how am I to feel about the modern factories on the outskirts of Athens, or the Kentucky Fried Chicken on Tienanmen Square? Or Japanese baseball and squaredancing? Or Zimbabwean rock and roll? Or my Vietnamese student's appreciation of the novels of Jane Austen?

The problem is fundamentally connected to the characteristic reproducibility of cultural (informational) goods: the fact that, unlike material objects, they are not destroyed at the point of origin when they are transferred to another place. When our fundamental model of the nature of cultural goods is pieces of matter, there can only be one original of anything. In other words, we can only worry about authenticity if we are materialists. A materialist knows that if there are two copies of something, at least one of them must be a fake. (Similarly, if two things apparently occupy the same place, at least one of them must be an illusion.)

The same suspicion can be found among materialist lovers of nature. For them, a restored or artificial prairie can never be a real prairie. What they ignore is that all living things are by nature copies: reproduction is part of the definition of life. Nor does nature even bother to copy correctly. Evolution can only take place because the copies are incorrect, and thus there is variation in a species, upon which natural selection can work. According to a materialist definition of nature, all life is inauthentic.

But suppose one understood culture to be, like nature, in its very essence a process of not-quite-correct copying, of transfer, of sexual and asexual recombination, of merging, mixing, miscegenation, and the mutual appropriation of information? Those who are nostalgic for the certainty of being they imagine among *les tristes tropiques* propose models of authenticity that are essentially closed semantic systems, hermeneutic circles impenetrable to any stranger. What they fail to take into account is that such systems must be as impenetrable and closed to their own younger generation as to any anthropological outsider. To put it another way, culture must always reproduce itself by indoctrinating its children, who start off as strangers; and irreversible slippage will happen in the process. The indoctrinators will be compelled to develop a subversive meta-consciousness of their own cultural material if only in deploying, enumerating, and organizing it so as to teach it and leave nothing out. The human child, as we know from the rapid change in all living languages, delights in creative misreadings and playful inversions; and the human adolescent is hormonally programmed to question and subvert the wisdom of the elders.

* * *

How do we get from cultural ethnocentrism to true interculturalism? The first step in the process usually involves institutions of which many now disapprove: empire, religious evangelism, and colonialism. Curiously enough, in order to break out of the bounds of their cultural limitations most peoples have had to pass through one of two morally evil experiences — of being dominated by a foreign cultural hegemony, or of being the hegemonic dominator. India and England are good examples. It is hard to say which experience is the more damaging in the long run, but the damage is necessary. It is the trauma suffered by any structure when it first encounters its corrosive, Poseidonic solvent. Very occasionally this first step can be accomplished when a group of refugees or emigrants which shares a common alienation from its parent cultures is able to band together to form a union, as did the American settlers; but even here a common hegemonic culture, embodied in the Enlightenment reasoning of the Constitution, was required. In effect, the hegemonic culture must *be* the solvent, and the experience of one's own worldview as solvent is a profoundly unsettling one, manifested eventually in a kind of collective guilt, inertia, and anomie.

What follows the first stage, of hegemony, is what we might call naive relativism. Just like a child who discovers one exception to a rule, and who in a kind of cynical dudgeon dismisses the validity of all rules, so a culture at this stage, having found that its own rules are not universal, assumes a total cultural relativity of all rules. This phase actually comes from a generous impulse, itself the product of the colonial administrator's or anthropologist's need to develop an ethic of impartiality and self-criticism (or of an

---

Though superficially attractive, relativism is not a coherent intellectual position.

---

equally generous recognition by members of an oppressed colonial people that their oppressor's culture has its own sense and beauty). The effect is that the primary stance of the anthropologist, of respect for other cultures, becomes partly disseminated throughout the population.

Sometimes this stance is adopted strategically, for the worst of reasons: as an excuse for hedonism and a relaxation of the demands and duties of adult human life. Margaret Mead's Samoa and the photographs of the naked tribespeople in *National Geographic* became in this way justifications for the "playboy philosophy." The Huichol peyote cult served a similar function a few years later. Difference is interpreted as licence, as permission; the very strict moral and ritual rules of traditional societies are ignored. Another use for cultural relativism is in its guise as cultural determinism. If a person's success in life is the result of overriding cultural forces, usually perceived as oppressive, then those who perceive themselves as unsuccessful have the advantage of being able to claim that it was not their own efforts that were at fault, but society; and that society owes them, regardless of their personal character or contribution, a handsome restitution.

Though superficially attractive, relativism is not a coherent intellectual position. Either it is uniquely, absolutely, and exclusively true, and thus the shattering exception to its own rule that all truth is relative; or it is no more true than any other intellectual position, in which case the absolutism of, say, Hitler's Germany or Khomeini's Iran is just as intellectually acceptable as is relativism. Interestingly enough, it was on these grounds that Derrida was unable to condemn apartheid as roundly as his critics wish, and there were some intellectuals who found it difficult, for similar reasons, to condemn the Ayatollah's death sentence against Salman Rushdie.

Naive relativism is still a reigning ideology in the American academy, enshrined in what some have called "oppression studies" or "victimology." The general population, though, has to some extent moved on to a more mature perspective. One of the oddities of our time is how in many humanistic and social-science fields the academy has ceased to lead the national consciousness, and has begun to drag behind it; rather as the Anglican clergy moved from being in the forefront of consciousness in the seventeenth and eighteenth centuries (witness Donne, Herbert, Herrick, and Swift) to being the butt of literary jokes in the nineteenth and twentieth.

The more mature perspective — the third phase in the intellectual passage — is what we might call pluralism: the acceptance and recognition of cultural difference and a commitment to coexistence and to a worldview that is not unified but diverse and disseminated. If it is objected that the general population, is not as sophisticated as this, we may point to the values embodied in the most popular and even vulgar TV shows — "Donahue," "All in the Family," "Perfect Strangers," "Night Court," and so on — in which pluralism and tolerance have become not just one of a number of important ethical norms, but the supreme, even the exclusive one. In such programs the ideal end result is always the uncritical acceptance of different lifestyles and of relative morality. This ideal of tolerance is indeed rather noble, and contrasts tellingly with the sometimes vicious exclusivism of academic factions, which one would suppose to be providing intellectual and moral leadership. The sheep, alas, are well in advance of the shepherds.

But pluralism itself has certain profound problems. One is that we are not neutrally organized to perceive the world in a fundamentally pluralistic way. Even if, say, we were to prove to our satisfaction that the vision of the compound insect eye gave a more accurate picture of things than the single eye of a human being, there is not much one could do about it. In actual fact, of course, a large part of an insect's brain is devoted to integrating all of its different views into a single program of action; and in another sense we humans do indeed have compound eyes, made of millions of retinal neurons, but again integrated into a single worldview by the visual cortex. The universe itself has, by overwhelming selective pressure, evolved us as unifying and integrating animals. The strong inference is that a unifying perspective is, as much as anything can be said to be, more likely to be true than a pluralistic one: if it were not more accurate, we would not have survived.

Despite its claims, "pluralism" is itself, paradoxically, a unifying perspective, but a rather procrustean one. What it does is reduce all cultural differences to a sort of grid of equal cultural black boxes laid out over an infinite plane, boxes whose external form is safely measurable but whose contents are incommensurable and thus unknowable, and which are, as it were, the fundamental monads or quanta of reality. Geometrically it resembles the characteristic grid-design of the American city, or the relationship between departments in an American multiversity. Though pluralism forbids any attempt to perceive one cultural box as containing another, and thus revealing a comparable and measurable internal structure, it is itself a sort of gigantic box containing all other boxes as its subordinate material. Thus, like relativism, it contains a subtle hegemonic ambition of its own.

discontent with the limits of mere pluralism. We might give it various names: syncretism, evolutionary epistemology, natural classicism, dramatistic ontology, the informational or Homeric/cybernetic economy.

Beneath all cultural differences certain fundamental human powers and capacities are emerging, that require cultural triggers to express themselves. These powers and capacities include language, the fundamental genres of the arts (musical tonality, the dramatic/performative ability, poetic meter, visual representation, dance, and so on), fundamental moral instincts, a religious/mystical ability, and the scientific rationality by which we learn to speak the other languages of nature. These powers and capacities are genetic endowments, created by evolution and embedded in our neural structure. Thus, true collaboration between cultures, and even a unifying syncretism of them, is pos-

---

All cultures and all worldviews will be seen as competing or cooperating together in a single evolutionary drama, in a dynamic ecology of thought that is the continuation by swifter means of the universal process of evolution.

One way of describing what is the problem with pluralism is to say that if the universe is curved, even a simple sphere, no grid of equal rectilinear blocks can cover (or "tile") it without overlap. Specialization, and the definition of smaller and smaller cultural units, might be seen as the desperate resource of an intellectual culture trying to resolve exactly this problem. If the squares are small enough, perhaps the distortions of the world's curvature will somehow go away. Pluralism is like a sort of oil, a liquid medium that merely holds its contents in suspension, and does not allow them to transform each other chemically.

Mere pluralism requires no change in one's own or one's neighbor's perspective; indeed, it is threatened by change, especially by any attempt to understand and imagine, and thus incorporate, the contents of another cultural box. It so fears hierarchy — one possible result of such an incorporation — that it would prefer ignorance. Its tolerance of other worldviews could well be described as neglect or even as a kind of intellectual cowardice. At its worst one could describe it as an abdication or shirking of the great human enterprise of mutual knowledge, communication (literally, "making one together"), and mutual transformation.

The final stage in the intellectual passage into a new world is beginning to emerge, prompted by an instinctive

sible on this shared biological basis. In this work ancient wisdom and traditional lore will join hands with the most sophisticated studies of genetics, paleoanthropology, cognitive science, cultural anthropology, ethology, sociobiology, the oral tradition, and performance theory. The word that describes our historical experience of the joining of old and new is Renaissance.

All cultures and all worldviews will be seen as competing or cooperating together in a single evolutionary drama, in a dynamic ecology of thought that is the continuation by swifter means of the universal process of evolution. The relationship between cultural worldviews will not be that between black boxes, but between characters in an ongoing drama, who can change each other, marry, and beget mutual offspring. It is not simply that this drama establishes the truth of things; it is the truth of things.

In other words, we can have faith that once the bonds that hold human ideas and cultures locked into a solid configuration are loosed by the powerful solvents of our time, the elements of culture, being basically human, will have the hooks and valencies to permit them to build up new, coherent systems not limited to one ethnic tradition. Moreover, the new systems can be very flexible and need not purchase survival by a paranoid vigilance and rigidity.

The conflict and miscegenation between and within such systems as they emerge is not a horrifying defilement or pollution, but the normal and healthy operation of an evolutionary ecology of ideas. Information will become the basis of a gift exchanges economy, the inexhaustible currency of a new order of economics. The hard, the tragic, and the inflexible will not disappear, but will be valued aesthetically and treasured for its contribution to the richness of the world. Nor will it be turned into a tyrannical fetish and a standard of conformity. As the human race recognizes itself more and more as a "we," it will paradoxically be more and more surprised by the otherness of what was once considered familiar. How strange, how exotic, how attractive our own culture is! Is not this the strangest and most interesting of worlds?

Eventually, perhaps, that greatest of all Others, Nature itself, will be recognized also as part of the "we." This is a mystical idea: it is prefigured in the lyre of Orpheus, that could make animals, trees, and rocks listen with delight, or the ring of Solomon, which gave him understanding of the languages of birds and beasts; the magic flute, the staff of Prospero, the double-helix caduceus or metatron of Hermes and Moses. We will, having learned to command Nature, find that it is sweeter to converse with it, and bury the staff certain fathoms in the earth; and that we are Nature, and Nature is ourselves.

CHAPTER 16
Counterculture

With insomnia, nothing is real. Everything's far away. Everything's a copy of a copy of a copy.

— Jack,
Fight Club (1999)

Chapter 16. Counterculture

Recommended Film

Fight Club (David Fincher 1999)

Media Models

The Meme, The Spectacle, The Hyperreal

Chapter Summary

Joseph Heath and Andrew Potter question the true meaning of the proliferating
countercultural movements that are celebrated in media and popular culture.

Barry Vacker shows how *Fight Club* reflects an existential angst toward
the postmillennial and technological futures, which is why
Tyler Durden is yearning for a rebirth of premodern culture
amid the ruins of the modern and postmodern worlds.

"Introduction" and
"The Birth of Counterculture"

from Nation of Rebels

— Joseph Heath and Andrew Potter

INTRODUCTION

September 2003 marked a turning point in the development of Western civilization. It was the month that *Adbusters* magazine started accepting orders for the Black Spot Sneaker, its own signature brand of "subversive" running shoes. After that day, no rational person could possibly believe that there is any tension between "mainstream" and "alternative" culture. After that day, it became obvious to everyone that cultural rebellion, of the type epitomized by *Adbusters* magazine, is not a threat to the system — it *is* the system.

Founded in 1989, *Adbusters* is the flagship publication of the culture-jamming movement. In their view, society has become so thoroughly permeated with propaganda and lies, largely as a consequence of advertising, that the culture as a whole has become an enormous system of ideology — all designed to reproduce faith in "the system." The goal of the culture jammers is quite literally to "jam" the culture, by subverting the messages used to reproduce this faith and blocking the channels through which it is propagated. This in turn is thought to have radical political consequences. In 1999, *Adbusters* editor Kalle Lasn argued that culture jamming "will become to our era what civil rights was to the '60s, what feminism was to the '70s, what environmental activism was to the '80s."[1]

Five years later, he's using the *Adbusters* brand to flog his own trademark line of running shoes. What happened? Did *Adbusters* sell out?

Absolutely not. It is essential that we all see and understand this. *Adbusters* did not sell out, because there was nothing to sell out in the first place. *Adbusters* never had a revolutionary doctrine. What they had was simply a warmed-over version of the countercultural thinking that has dominated leftist politics since the '60s. And this type of countercultural politics, far from being a revolutionary doctrine, has been one of the primary forces driving consumer capitalism for the past forty years.

In other words, what we see on display in *Adbusters* magazine is, and always has been, the true spirit of capitalism. The episode with the running shoes just serves to prove the point.

Lasn describes the sneaker project as "a ground-breaking marketing scheme to uncool Nike.[2] If it succeeds, it will set a precedent that will revolutionize capitalism." Yet how exactly is it supposed to revolutionize capitalism? Reebok, Adidas, Puma, Vans and a half-dozen other companies have been trying to "uncool" Nike for decades. That's called marketplace competition. It is, in fact, the whole *point* of capitalism.

Lasn defends the sneaker project against critics, pointing out that his shoes, unlike those of his rivals, will not be manufactured in "sweatshops" — although they will still be imported from Asia. This is nice. But "fair trade"

1 Kalle Lasn, *Culture Jam: How to Reverse America's Suicidal Consumer Binge — And Why We Must* (New York: William Morrow, 1999), xi.

2 Martin Patriquin, "The Running Shoe Fits for Adbusters," *The Globe and Mail*, August 20, 2003, B9.

and "ethical marketing" are hardly revolutionary ideas, and they certainly represent no threat to the capitalist system. If consumers are willing to pay more for shoes made by happy workers — or for eggs laid by happy chickens — then there is money to be made in bringing these goods to market. It's a business model that has already been successfully exploited to great effect by The Body Shop and Starbucks, among others.

Culture jammers are not the first to try to break the system through consumer revolt. Countercultural rebels have been playing the same game for over forty years, and it obviously doesn't work. With the hippies, nothing symbolized their rejection of the "consumerism" of American society more than love beads, Birkenstocks and the VW Beetle. Yet during the '80s, the same generation that had "tuned in, turned on and dropped out" presided over the most significant resurgence of conspicuous consumption in American history. The hippies became yuppies. And nothing symbolized the yuppie worldview more than the SUV — the vehicle that one commentator aptly described as "a gated community on wheels."[3] So how does one get from a VW Beetle to a Ford Explorer? It turns out to be not so difficult.

The crucial point is that (contrary to rumor) the hippies did not sell out. Hippie ideology and yuppie ideology are one and the same. There simply never was any tension between the countercultural ideas that informed the '60s rebellion and the ideological requirements of the capitalist system. While there is no doubt that a *cultural* conflict developed between the members of the counterculture and the defenders of the older American Protestant establishment, there never was any tension between the *values* of the counterculture and the functional requirements of the capitalist economic system. The counterculture was, from its very inception, intensely entrepreneurial. It reflected, as does *Adbusters*, the most authentic spirit of capitalism.

Hippies bought VW Beetles for one primary reason — to show that they rejected mass society. The big three Detroit automakers had been the target of withering social criticism for well over a decade, accused of promoting "planned obsolescence" in their vehicles. They were chastised above all for changing their models and designs so that consumers would be forced to buy a new car every few years in order to keep up with the Joneses. The tail fin was held up by many as an object of special scorn — as both embodiment and symbol of the wastefulness of American consumer culture.[4] Against this backdrop, Volkswagen

---

Culture jammers are not the first to try to break the system through consumer revolt. Countercultural rebels have been playing the same game for over forty years, and it obviously doesn't work.

---

entered the U.S. consumer market with a very simple pitch: Wanna show people that you're not just a cog in the machine? Buy our car!

When the boomers started having children, the old VW obviously was no longer sufficient. Yet there was no question of buying a wood-paneled station wagon, the kind that their parents used to drive. They may have had kids, but they were still rebels at heart. And no vehicle appealed to this desire for rebel chic more perfectly than the SUV. Off-road capability was the major selling point — even the Grateful Dead sang the praises of four-wheel drive. "The system" tells you that you have to drive in a straight line, down some "road" that The Man has built for you. The rebel can't be tied down like that; he yearns for freedom. He needs to be able to veer off at any time and start following his *own* road.

What a perfect vehicle! To anyone who passes by, it says, "I'm not one of those losers with kids, living in the suburbs. My life is an adventure." It tells them that you're not a square, not a cog in the machine.

If the boomers were obsessed with cars, Generation Xers seem to have had a special preoccupation with shoes. Shoes were an essential element of the punk aesthetic from the beginning, from army boots and Converse sneakers to Doc Martens and Blundstones. And instead of the big

---

3 Trevor Hutchinson, *This Magazine* July/Aug. 1998, Page 4 (vol 32, no 1). The quote in context is: "The SUV is not just a method of escape. It's a lifestyle. It's social Darwinism with some horsepower. A line of defence in the coming class war of whatever exotic events await the coming millennium. A fully loaded SUV isn't simply a mode of transportation, it's a gated community on wheels."

4 John Kenneth Galbraith, *The Affluent Society* (Boston: Houghton Mifflin, 1984). On Volkswagen, see Thomas Frank, *The Conquest of Cool: Business Culture, Counterculture, and the Rise of Hip Consumerism* (Chicago: University of Chicago Press, 1997), 11.

three automakers to play the villain, there were the shoe companies: first and foremost, Nike. For antiglobalization demonstrators, Nike came to symbolize everything that was wrong with the emerging capitalist world order.

Yet this animus toward Nike did create occasional moments of embarrassment. During the famous Seattle riots of 1999, the downtown Niketown was trashed by protestors, but videotape recorded at the scene showed several protestors kicking in the front window *wearing Nike shoes*. It occurred to many people that if you think Nike is the root of all evil, you really shouldn't be wearing their shoes. Yet if thousands of young people refuse to wear Nike, that creates an obvious market for "alternative" footwear. Vans and Airwalk were both able to leverage some of the rebel chic associated with skateboarding into millions of dollars of sneaker sales. It's the same story all over again, and *Adbusters* is just trying to get a piece of the action.

The question is, why would anyone think that selling running shoes could be subversive? To understand the answer, it is useful to take a closer look at the first film in the *Matrix* trilogy. Lots has been written about the "philosophy of the Matrix," most of it wrong. To understand the first film, one must look very carefully at the scene in which Neo sees the white rabbit. He hands a book to his friend, and on the spine of that book we can see the title: *Simulacra and Simulation* by Jean Baudrillard.

Many commentators on the film saw the core idea of *The Matrix* — that the world we live in might be an elaborate illusion, that our brains are simply being fed sensory input by machines, input that tricks us into thinking that we live and interact with a world of physical objects — as simply an updated version of René Descartes's skeptical "How do you know that you're not dreaming?" thought experiment. This is a misinterpretation. *The Matrix* is not intended as a representation of an epistemological dilemma. It is a metaphor for a political idea, one that traces its origins back to the '60s. It is an idea that found its highest expression in the work of Guy Debord, unofficial leader of the Situationist International, and his later disciple Jean Baudrillard.

Debord was a radical Marxist, author of *The Society of the Spectacle* and one of the prime movers behind the Paris 1968 uprising. His thesis was simple. The world that we live in is not real. Consumer capitalism has taken every authentic human experience, transformed it into a commodity and then sold it back to us through advertising and the mass media. Thus every part of human life has been drawn into "the spectacle," which itself is nothing but a system of symbols and representations, governed by its own internal logic. "The spectacle is *capital* to such a degree of accumulation that it becomes an image," Debord wrote.[5] Thus we live in a world of total ideology, in which we are completely alienated from our essential nature. The spectacle is a dream that has become necessary, "the nightmare of imprisoned modern society, which ultimately expresses nothing more than its desire to sleep."[6]

In such a world, the old-fashioned concern for social justice and the abolition of class-based society becomes outmoded. In the society of the spectacle, the new revolutionary must seek two things: "consciousness of desire and the desire for consciousness."[7] In other words, we must try to discover our own sources of pleasure, independent of the needs that are imposed upon us by the system, and we must try to wake up from the nightmare of "the spectacle." Like Neo, we must choose the red pill.

In other words, when it comes to rebellion and political activism, there is no point trying to change little details in the system. What does it matter who is rich and who is poor? Or who has the right to vote and who doesn't? Or who has access to jobs and opportunities? These are all just ephemera, illusions. If commodities are just images, who cares if some people have more of them, others less? What we need to do is recognize that the entire culture, the entire society, is a waking dream — one we must reject in its entirety.

Of course, this idea is hardly original. It is one of the oldest themes in Western civilization. In *The Republic*, Plato compared life on earth to a cave, in which prisoners are shackled to the floor, seeing only shadows flickering across the wall from the light of a fire. When one prisoner escapes and makes his way to the surface, he discovers that the world he had been living in was nothing but a web of illusions. He returns to the cave bearing the news, yet finds that his former companions are still embroiled in petty disputes and bickering. He finds it difficult to take these "politics" seriously.

Centuries later, early Christians would appeal to this story as a way of explaining away the execution of Jesus by the Romans. Prior to this event, it had been assumed

---

5 Guy Debord, *The Society of the Spectacle* (Detroit: Black & Red, 1977), 34.
6 Ibid., 21.
7 Ibid., 53.

that the arrival of the Messiah would herald the creation of the kingdom of God here on earth. The death of Jesus obviously put an end to these expectations. Some of his followers therefore chose to reinterpret these events as a sign that the real kingdom of God would be not on this earth, but in the afterlife. They claimed that Jesus had been resurrected in order to convey this news — like Plato's prisoner returning to the cave.

Thus the idea that the world we live in is a veil of illusion is not new. What does change, however, is the popular understanding of what it takes to throw off this illusion. For Plato, there was no question that breaking free would require decades of disciplined study and philosophical reflection. Christians thought that it would be even harder — that death was the only way to gain access to the "real" world beyond. For Debord and the Situationists, on the other hand, the veil of illusion could be pierced much more easily. All that it takes is some slight cognitive dissonance, a sign that something's not right in the world around us. This can be provoked by a work of art, an act of protest or even an article of clothing. In Debord's view, "disturbances with the lowliest and most ephemeral of origins have eventually disrupted the order of the world."[8]

This is the origin of the idea of culture jamming. Traditional political activism is useless. It's like trying to reform political institutions inside the Matrix. What's the point? What we really need to do is wake people up, unplug them, free them from the grip of the spectacle. And the way to do that is by producing cognitive dissonance, through symbolic acts of resistance to suggest that something is not right in the world.

Like the Black Spot Sneaker.

Since the entire culture is nothing but a system of ideology, the only way to liberate oneself and others is to resist the culture in its entirety. This is where the idea of counterculture comes from. The inhabitants of Zion, in *The Matrix*, are a concrete embodiment of how countercultural rebels since the '60s have conceived of themselves. They are the ones who have been awakened, the ones who are free from the tyranny of the machines. And the enemy, in this view, is those who refuse to be awakened, those who insist on conforming to the culture. The enemy, in other words, is *mainstream society*.

Morpheus sums up the countercultural analysis perfectly when describing the Matrix: "The Matrix is a system, Neo. That system is our enemy. But when you're inside, you look around, what do you see? Businessmen, teachers, lawyers, carpenters. The very minds of the people we are trying to save. But until we do, these people are still a part of that system and that makes them our enemy. You have to understand, most of these people are not ready to be unplugged. And many of them are so inured, so hopelessly dependent on the system, that they will fight to protect it."[9]

In the '60s, the baby boomers declared their implacable opposition to "the system." They renounced materialism and greed, rejected the discipline and uniformity of the McCarthy era, and set out to build a new world based on individual freedom. What ever happened to this project? Forty years later, "the system" does not appear to have changed very much. If anything, consumer capitalism has emerged from decades of countercultural rebellion much stronger than it was before. If Debord thought that the world was saturated with advertising and media in the early '60s, what would he have made of the 21st century?

In this book, we argue that decades of countercultural rebellion have failed to change anything because the theory of society on which the countercultural idea rests is false. We do not live in the Matrix, nor do we live in the spectacle. The world that we live in is in fact much more prosaic. It consists of billions of human beings, each pursuing some more or less plausible conception of the good, trying to cooperate with one another, and doing so with varying degrees of success. There is no single, overarching system that integrates it all. The culture cannot be jammed because there *is* no such thing as "the culture" or "the system." There is only a hodgepodge of social institutions, most tentatively thrown together, which distribute the benefits and burdens of social cooperation in ways that sometimes we recognize to be just, but that are usually manifestly inequitable. In a world of this type, countercultural rebellion is not just unhelpful, it is positively counterproductive. Not only does it distract energy and effort away from the sort of initiatives that lead to concrete improvements in people's lives, but it encourages wholesale contempt for such incremental changes.

8   Guy Debord, "Ingirum imus nocte et consumimur igni," *Œuvres cinématographiques complètes: 1952–1978* (Paris: Éditions Champ libre, 1978), 242.

9   Larry Wachowski and Andy Wachowski, *The Matrix: The Shooting Script* (New York: Newmarket, 2002).

According to the countercultural theory, "the system" achieves order only through the repression of the individual. Pleasure is inherently anarchic, unruly, wild. To keep the workers under control, the system must instill manufactured needs and mass-produced desires, which can in turn be satisfied within the framework of the technocratic order. Order is achieved, but at the expense of promoting widespread unhappiness, alienation and neurosis. The solution must therefore lie in reclaiming our capacity for spontaneous pleasure — through polymorphous perversity, or performance art, or modern primitivism, or mind-expanding drugs, or whatever else turns your crank. In the countercultural analysis, simply having fun comes to be seen as the ultimate subversive act. Hedonism is transformed into a revolutionary doctrine.

Is it any wonder then that this sort of countercultural rebellion has reinvigorated consumer capitalism? It's time for a reality check. Having fun is not subversive, and it doesn't undermine any system. In fact, widespread hedonism makes it more difficult to organize social movements,

Early on the morning of April 8, 1994, the electrician arrived to start work on a new security system being installed at an upscale home overlooking Lake Washington, just north of Seattle. In the greenhouse, he found the owner of the cottage, Kurt Cobain, lying dead on the floor in a pool of blood. Cobain had taken a lethal overdose of heroin, but, for good measure, had decided to finish the job by blowing off the left side of his head with a Remington 20-gauge shotgun.

When the news of Cobain's death spread, very few were surprised. This was the man, after all, who had recorded a song called "I Hate Myself and Want to Die." As frontman of Nirvana, arguably the most important band of the 1990s, his every move was followed by the media. His previous suicide attempts were a matter of public record. The note lying beside his body didn't leave much room for interpretation: "Better to burn out than fade away," he wrote. Nevertheless, his death generated a small cottage industry of conspiracy theories. Who killed Kurt Cobain?

In one sense, the answer is obvious. Kurt Cobain killed Kurt Cobain. Yet he was also a victim. He was the victim of a false idea—the idea of counterculture.

---

and much more difficult to persuade anyone to make a sacrifice in the name of social justice. In our view, what the progressive left needs to do is disentangle the concern over questions of social justice from the countercultural critique — and to jettison the latter, while continuing to pursue the former.

From the standpoint of social justice, the big gains that have been achieved in our society over the past half-century have all come from measured reform within the system. The civil rights movement and the feminist movement have both achieved tangible gains in the welfare of disadvantaged groups, while the social safety net provided by the welfare state has vastly improved the condition of all citizens. But these gains have not been achieved by "unplugging" people from the web of illusions that governs their lives. They have been achieved through the laborious process of democratic political action — through people making arguments, conducting studies, assembling coalitions and legislating change. We would like to see more of this.

Less fun perhaps, but potentially much more useful.

* * *

In one sense, the answer is obvious. Kurt Cobain killed Kurt Cobain. Yet he was also a victim. He was the victim of a false idea — the idea of counterculture. While he thought of himself as a punk rocker, a man in the business of making "alternative" music, his records sold in the millions. Thanks in large part to Cobain, the music that used to be called "hardcore" was rebranded and sold to the masses as "grunge." But rather than serving as a source of pride to him, this popularity was a constant embarrassment. It fed the nagging doubts in the back of his mind, which suggested that he had "sold out" the scene, gone "mainstream."

After Nirvana's breakthrough album, *Nevermind*, began to outsell Michael Jackson, the band made a concerted effort to lose fans. Their follow-up album, *In Utero*, was obviously intended to be difficult, inaccessible music. But the effort failed. The album went on to reach number one in the Billboard charts.

Cobain was never able to reconcile his commitment to alternative music with the popular success of Nirvana. In the end, his suicide was a way out of the impasse. Better to stop it now, before the last scrap of integrity is gone, and avoid the total sellout. That way he could hold fast to his conviction that "punk rock is freedom." What he failed to consider was the possibility that it was all an illusion; that there is no alternative, no mainstream, no relationship between music and freedom, and no such thing as selling out. There are just people who make music, and people who listen to music. And if you make great music, people will want to listen to it.

So where did the idea of "alternative" come from? The idea that you had to be unpopular in order to be authentic?

Cobain was a graduate of what he called the "Punk Rock 101" school of life. Much of the punk ethos was based on a rejection of what the hippies had stood for. If they listened to the Lovin' Spoonful, we punks would listen to Grievous Bodily Harm. They had the Rolling Stones, we had the Violent Femmes, the Circle Jerks and Dead On Arrival. If they had long hair, we would have mohawks. If they wore sandals, we would wear army boots. If they were into *satyagraha*, we were into direct action. We were the "un-hippies."

Why this animus toward hippies? It wasn't because they were too radical. It was because they were not radical enough. They had sold out. They were, as Cobain put it, the "hippiecrits." *The Big Chill* told you everything you needed to know. The hippies had become yuppies. "The only way I would wear a tie-dyed T-shirt," Cobain liked to say, "would be if it were soaked in the blood of Jerry Garcia."

By the beginning of the '80s, rock and roll had been transformed into a bloated, pale imitation of its former self. It had become arena rock. *Rolling Stone* magazine had become a complacent corporate sales rag, dedicated to flogging crappy albums. Given his attitude, one can only imagine Cobain's embarrassment when he was asked to appear on the cover of *Rolling Stone*. His compromise: to do the shoot in a T-shirt that read "Corporate rock magazines still suck." Cobain persuaded himself that, in so doing, he was not selling out, he was simply going undercover: "We can pose as the enemy to infiltrate the mechanics of the system to start its rot from the inside. Sabotage the

empire by pretending to play their game, compromise just enough to call their bluff. And the hairy, sweaty, macho, sexist dickheads will soon drown in a pool of razor blades and semen, stemmed from the uprising of their children, the armed and deprogrammed crusade, littering the floors of Wall Street with revolutionary debris."[10]

One can see here quite clearly that, while Cobain and the rest of us punks may have rejected most of the ideas

---

People talk about the "assassination" of Tupac Shakur, as though he actually posed a threat to the system. Eminem claims his arrest for possession of a concealed weapon was "all political," designed to get him off the streets. It's the same thing all over again.

---

that came out of the hippie counterculture, there is one element of the movement that we swallowed hook, line and sinker. This was the idea of counterculture itself. In other words, we saw ourselves as doing exactly the same thing that the hippies saw themselves doing. The difference, we assumed, is that, unlike them, *we* would never sell out. We would do it right.

Some myths die hard. One can see the same cycle repeating itself in hip-hop. The countercultural idea here takes the form of a romantic view of ghetto life and gang culture. Successful rappers must fight hard to retain their street cred, to "keep it real." They'll pack guns, do time, even get shot up, just to prove that they're not just "studio gangstas." So instead of just dead punks and hippies, we now also have a steadily growing pantheon of dead rappers. People talk about the "assassination" of Tupac Shakur, as though he actually posed a threat to the system. Eminem claims his arrest for possession of a concealed weapon was "all political," designed to get him off the streets. It's the same thing all over again.

This wouldn't be so important if it were confined to the world of music. Unfortunately, the idea of counterculture has become so deeply embedded in our understanding of society that it influences every aspect of social and political life. Most importantly, it has become the conceptual template for all contemporary leftist politics. Counterculture has almost completely replaced socialism as the basis of radical political thought. So if counterculture is a myth,

---

10   Kurt Cobain, *Journals* (New York: Penguin Putnam, 2002), 168.

nice

then it is one that has misled an enormous number of people, with untold political consequences.

The idea that artists must take an oppositional stance toward mainstream society is hardly new. It has its origins in 18th-century Romanticism, a movement that went on to dominate the artistic imagination throughout the 19th century. It found its highest expression — and most enduring commercial success — in Giacomo Puccini's *La Bohème*, a celebration of alternative "bohemian" lifestyles in Paris. In those days, "real" artists had to die of consumption (tuberculosis, that is), not heroin overdoses or drive-bys. But you get the idea.

The key to understanding early Romanticism is to appreciate the impact that the discovery of the New World, and in particular the Pacific Islands, had upon European consciousness. Before these encounters, Europeans simply assumed that humans had lived, throughout all of history, in hierarchically organized class societies. Kingship, aristocracy and class domination were simply a part of the natural order. St. Thomas Aquinas summed up the received wisdom when he wrote, back in the 13th century,

Everything that happens in nature is good, because nature always does what is best. The standard form of government in nature is the rule of one. If we consider the parts of the body, we see that there is one part that moves all the rest, namely the heart. If we look at the parts of the soul, we find that there is one faculty that rules the rest — reason. The same is true of bees, who have but one queen, and of the universe as a whole, which has only one God, who has created and governs all things. This is not without reason, since a plurality is always derived from a unity. Since the products of art imitate the works of nature, and since a work of art is the more perfect, the more closely it resembles the works of nature, the best government for a people is necessarily the government of one.[11]

Five hundred years later, Jean-Jacques Rousseau could agree with the first line of this passage — that everything in nature is good — but disagree with all the rest. Thanks

to the discovery of the New World, thinkers like Rousseau knew that there were people who lived without social hierarchy, without landed aristocracy or monarchy, and sometimes even without settlements or cities. It didn't take long to infer that this was in fact the "natural" condition of mankind, and that the major world civilizations, with their elaborate social hierarchies and systems of privilege, represented a terrible distortion of the natural order.

Thus Rousseau concluded that all of society was a giant fraud, a system of exploitation imposed upon the weak by the strong. The emergence of civilization, he argued, "gave new fetters to the weak and new forces to the rich, irretrievably destroyed natural liberty, established forever the law of property and of inequality, changed straightforward usurpation into an irrevocable right, and for the profit of a few ambitious men henceforth subjected the entire human race to labor, servility and misery."[12]

As far as sweeping indictments of society go, this one is right up there. After reading it, Voltaire was moved to write to Rousseau: "I have received your new book against the human race, and thank you for it. Never has such cleverness been used to show that we are all stupid. One longs, upon reading your book, to walk on all fours. But as I have lost that habit for more than sixty years, I feel

---

Thus Rousseau concluded that all of society was a giant fraud, a system of exploitation imposed upon the weak by the strong.

---

unhappily the impossibility of resuming it. Nor can I go off in search of the savages of Canada, because the illnesses to which I am condemned render a European doctor necessary to me."[13]

Yet despite the broad scope of his claim, Rousseau's intention was not actually to condemn "the human race" or to recommend a return to savagery. As his work on the social contract made clear, he was not opposed to social order itself, or to the rule of law. He was opposed to the specifically hierarchical form that this order had taken on

---

11   St. Thomas Aquinas, *On the Governance of Rulers*, trans. Gerald B. Phelan (Toronto: St. Michael's College, 1935), 39.

12   Jean-Jacques Rousseau, "Discourse on Inequality," *The First and Second Discourses*, ed. Roger D. Masters, trans. Judith R. Masters (New York: St. Martin's Press, 1964), 160.

13   Voltaire, *Voltaire's Correspondence*, ed. Theodore Besterman (Geneva: Institut et Musée Voltaire, 1957), 230.

in his own society. It was the perversion of the natural order into class domination that angered him.

In other words, despite the sweeping nature of his indictment, Rousseau's critique was directed against a specific class enemy — the aristocracy. Furthermore, he regarded the general population — the masses — as a natural ally in the struggle. The social upheavals that his thought inspired, up to and including the French Revolution, were not anarchic uprisings against society at large. They were aimed quite specifically at the ruling classes. (Which is why, by the end of the 18th century, almost the entire French aristocracy was either dead or in hiding.)

Even 19th-century anarchists were not really anarchists in the modern sense of the term. They were not opposed to social order, nor were they individualists. In many cases, they did not even want to smash the state. They simply opposed the coercive imposition of social order and the militarism of the early modern European nation–state. Mikhail Bakunin's "Revolutionary Catechism," one of the founding documents of political anarchism, calls for nothing more radical than voluntary federalism as the principle of national organization, along with universal suffrage of both sexes. Bakunin, the famed anarchist, was actually one of the first to call for the creation of a "United States of Europe."[14]

So while society may have been roundly condemned as a rigged game, no one was in doubt about who had rigged it against whom. The goal of radical political activists and thinkers in the 18th and 19th centuries was not to eliminate the game, but to level the playing field. As a result, radical politics throughout the early modern period had an overwhelmingly populist character. The goal was to turn the people against their rulers.

But in the second half of the 20th century, radical politics took a significant turn away from this pattern of thought. Instead of treating the masses as an ally, the people began to be regarded, to an ever-increasing degree, as an object of suspicion. Before long, the people — that is, "mainstream" society — came to be seen as the problem, not the solution. Whereas the great philosophers of the Enlightenment had railed against "obedience," as a slavish disposition that promoted tyranny, radicals began to view "conformity" as a far greater vice. The story of this remark-

able reversal provides the key to understanding the origins of the myth of counterculture.

With the so-called bourgeois revolutions of the 18th century, there was a gradual elimination of aristocratic privilege in Europe and, above all, in the United States. But rather than abolishing class domination altogether, the effect of these revolutions was primarily to replace one ruling class with another. Instead of being peasants, ruled by an aristocracy that had control of all the land, the masses were gradually transformed into workers, ruled by capitalists who controlled the factories and machines. As the nascent market economy began producing wealth on an unparalleled scale, money quickly became more important than either land or lineage as the basis for privilege.

There could be no mistake about the hierarchical nature of this emerging society. In the 19th century, capitalism seemed to be clearly in the process of dividing society into two antagonistic classes. The division between rich and poor was as stark as it is in many underdeveloped countries today. Most people had to work for a living. This meant a life of dangerous toil under unbearable conditions in the factory combined with grinding poverty at home. Then there were those who lived off the work of others, enjoying fabulous returns on their invested capital. There was not much in between.

Yet while it seemed obvious to contemporary observers that the masses had traded one form of exploitation for another, there was one key difference between the form of class domination that emerged out of the bourgeois revolutions and the aristocratic hierarchy that preceded it. Unlike the peasants, who were literally coerced into staying on the land and working for its lord, the working classes were formally free to do whatever they wanted. They were no longer tied to the land; they were free to move as they liked, to live where they liked and to take any job that was available or that appealed to them. Thus the class domination that existed in capitalist societies appeared to have an entirely voluntary character. When workers were injured at the factory or in the mine, the owner could evade responsibility by saying, "Nobody forced them to take the job. They knew the risks when they signed up."

There was no shortage of critics lining up to condemn the exploitation and suffering caused by early capitalism. But these critics were forced to confront a fundamental problem. If conditions were so terrible, why did the working classes tolerate them? Revolutionary socialists

---

14   Mikhail Bakunin, *Bakunin on Anarchism*, ed. and trans. Sam Dolgoff (Montreal: Black Rose Books, 1980), 104.

began arguing that workers should simply seize control of the factories where they worked. Yet the working classes were surprisingly reluctant to do so. This required some explanation. After all, since it seemed to be clearly in the *interest* of the working classes to take control of the means of production, what was stopping them?

This is where Karl Marx stepped in, with his famous critique of "ideology." The problem, Marx argued, was that the working class was the victim of an illusion, which he referred to as "commodity fetishism." Rather than perceiv-

Communists and socialists were often greeted with suspicion on the factory floor. The workers needed to be "radicalized" before they could be organized — through the cultivation of class consciousness. This meant freeing them from the grip of bourgeois ideology. The mindset of the workers needed to be changed, *so that they could come to see where their own interests lay*. Only when freed from the mental cage in which they were imprisoned could they begin to saw away at the bars of the real cage that society had constructed around them.

Marx argued that the working classes were unwilling to engage in revolutionary politics because they were completely caught up in this nexus of false ideas. Commodity fetishism and alienated labor provided the ideology of capitalism. All of this was wrapped up in a bow by traditional Christian religious doctrine, which promised workers paradise in the afterlife, on the condition that they behaved themselves here and now. Thus, religion was the "opiate" that kept the imposed suffering from becoming unendurable.

---

ing the economy as a set of essentially social relationships between individuals, the market gave it the appearance of a system of natural laws. Prices and wages moved up and down, seemingly at random. Losing your job seemed to be a matter of bad luck, like getting caught in a rainstorm. The ups and downs of the market were determined by forces completely outside anyone's control. So if wages dropped or the price of bread went up, there appeared to be no one to blame.

In Marx's view, this objectification of social relationships had gone so far that workers had become alienated from their own activity. They saw their own labor as merely a means to the attainment of other ends. Capitalism had created a nation of clock-watchers. Marx argued that the working classes were unwilling to engage in revolutionary politics because they were completely caught up in this nexus of false ideas. Commodity fetishism and alienated labor provided the ideology of capitalism. All of this was wrapped up in a bow by traditional Christian religious doctrine, which promised workers paradise in the afterlife, on the condition that they behaved themselves here and now. Thus, religion was the "opiate" that kept the imposed suffering from becoming unendurable.

Given this diagnosis of the problem, the role of the Marxian social critic was not necessarily to get directly involved in the organization of the working class.

The working class, unfortunately, turned out to be a terrible disappointment. Rather than agitating for the revolutionary overthrow of capitalism, workers tended to focus more on incremental gains, such as higher wages and medical benefits. From the Marxist perspective, this sort of "reformism" didn't address any of the fundamental issues; the workers were just redecorating the cage in which they were imprisoned. But once they came to see their situation more clearly, they would inevitably rise up.

Yet as the 20th century wore on, this diagnosis of the problem became increasingly unpersuasive. For example, the initial reluctance to give workers the vote was based upon the assumption, universally shared among the ruling classes in Europe and America, that if you let the people vote, the first thing they would vote for would be the dispossession of the propertied classes. In other words, they would use the vote to seize the property of the wealthy. Yet this is not what happened. Workers voted for reform, not revolution.

After the Russian Revolution, it became increasingly difficult to dismiss this peculiarly altruistic behavior on the part of workers as the effect of "commodity fetishism." How could the workers possibly believe that capitalism was natural and unalterable when the development of the Soviet Union showed quite clearly that it was optional? The Russians had proved that workers, if they wanted, could get rid of the capitalist system and replace it with one of their choosing. Furthermore, until the '60s it was still very much unclear which economic system would prove to be more efficient. The early history of the Soviet Union convinced many people that communism might produce more wealth than capitalism. So what could explain the passivity of the European and American working classes?

Capitalism had proved to be a much tougher nut to crack than many on the left had suspected. In order to avoid the conclusion that workers might actually *like* capitalism, Marxist theorists began to retool the theory of ideology. In the '20s, for instance, Antonio Gramsci began arguing that capitalism created false consciousness in the working classes not by inspiring particular false beliefs about the operations of the economy, but by establishing a complete cultural "hegemony," which in turn reinforced the system. He suggested, in effect, that the entire culture — books, music, painting — reflected a form of bourgeois ideology, and so needed to be discarded before the working class could achieve emancipation. He argued therefore for the "necessity of creating a new culture."[15]

Initially this argument fell upon deaf ears. Marx's claim that the state was merely the "executive committee of the bourgeoisie" already smacked of paranoia. The idea that the bourgeoisie could be controlling the entire culture seemed even more far-fetched. How could the whole culture be nothing but a scam? It seemed hard to believe that a fraud could be perpetrated on such a scale.

* * *

In order to see how the media can facilitate the mass contagion of sentiment, one need only turn on the television or listen to some talk radio. The classic sitcom has a laugh track, and talk shows have a studio audience, precisely because hearing other people laugh itself provokes laughter. The effect works in the same way regardless of whether people are in the same room or the laughter is simply being broadcast through the media. Similarly talk-radio stations employ a well-known formula for cultivating anger or outrage. The pattern of exchange between the host and the callers is especially effective at generating and sustaining the shared emotional response.

Nazism, of course, presented a rather extreme variant of the genre. But in the Soviet Union, Stalin demonstrated quite clearly how propaganda techniques could be used in the service of a different ideology. In *1984*, George Orwell sketched out a somewhat gentler version of this totalitarian nightmare — suggesting that a society might use more psychological control, and much less overt violence, in order to indoctrinate the masses. Many others thought that totalitarianism would insinuate itself into daily life in even more subtle ways.

These concerns were dramatically amplified by the anti-communist hysteria of the '50s. In 1951, after the defection of twenty-one American POWs to the North Korean side, journalist Edward Hunter coined the phrase "brainwashing" to describe the processes of mind control and "reeducation" supposedly imposed by communist regimes.[16] The concept proved extremely popular, and was extended back "retroactively" to describe the techniques used by the Nazis in Germany. Thus William Sargant, in his 1957 classic *Battle for the Mind*, argued that Hitler had used "organized excitement and mass hypnotism" to rally the masses.[17]

It was not long before the U.S. military and the CIA got interested. CIA director Allen Dulles took a particular interest in the subject, commissioning a special report on Chinese and Soviet brainwashing techniques. The CIA also began to conduct experiments — using both Korean POWs and unsuspecting volunteers — in order to perfect brainwashing techniques of their own. Since it was common knowledge that this sort of research was being conducted, it was not long before critics of American society began to suspect that these techniques were being used against the domestic population as well as the enemy. Vance Packard's 1957 attack on the advertising industry, *The Hidden Persuaders*, was rooted in precisely this culture of paranoia.[18] Packard's assertion that consumers were being exposed to "subliminal advertising" fed into popular

15 Antonio Gramsci, *Selections from the Prison Notebooks*, ed. and trans. Quintin Hoare and Geoffrey Nowell Smith (New York: International Publishers, 1971), 276.

16 Edward Hunter, *Brain-washing in Red China* (New York: Vanguard, 1962).

17 William Sargant, *Battle for the Mind: A Physiology of Conversion and Brain-Washing* (London: Pan Books, 1957), 142.

18 Vance Packard, *The Hidden Persuaders* (New York: Pocket Books, 1957). The subliminal scare was resurrected in 1973 by Brian Wilson Key in *Subliminal Seduction: Ad Media's Manipulation of a Not So Innocent America* (New York: New American Library, 1973). It is Key who is responsible for the idea that one can find hidden images in the ice cubes of liquor ads.

fear of mind control. People were so disturbed by the suggestion, it took more than three decades for the myth to be finally debunked.

Thus the net effect of anticommunist hysteria was to make people in the victorious Allied nations even more anxious about the possibility of creeping totalitarianism. It is easy for us to look back and claim that these concerns were overwrought. There was certainly no long-term erosion of basic liberties in these nations. But at the time, it was very far from obvious that this would be the outcome.

a steady diet of soma, a drug that dulls their senses, creates a diffuse sense of well-being and prevents them from asking too many questions. Individuality is suppressed both literally and figuratively: everyone in the society is a clone.

In the postwar era, it seemed to many people on the left that an explanation for the lack of revolutionary agitation on the part of the working classes was to be found in manipulation of this type. Unlike religion, which promised paradise after death, advertising promised paradise right around the next corner: through purchase of a new car,

---

Mass society is indelibly associated, in the popular imagination, with the United States of the 1950s. It is a world of perfect families, white picket fences, shiny new Buicks and teenagers "going steady," yet it is also a world of complete conformity, where happiness is achieved at the expense of individuality, creativity and freedom. … The movie *Pleasantville* dramatizes this critique of mass society through a rather quaint cinematic affectation.

In particular, the fear of propaganda, and of the psychological manipulation that it was thought to make possible, was easily translated into a fear of advertising and the mass media. Even setting aside television, the incorporation of visual elements, such as drawing, photography, logos and design, into print advertising appeared to be intended, just as Hitler's propaganda had been, to bypass the reader's rational faculties and appeal to him directly on an emotional level. The potential for manipulation and control seemed ominous.

Many people therefore saw a continuum between modern capitalism and fascism. (After all, Nazism was the "demon child" of European culture and society. It was hardly outrageous to suggest that the same forces that had led to the emergence of fascism in Germany and Italy might also be exercising more subtle effects in England, France and the United States.) Many people came to see Western democracies as simply more subtle variants of the basic fascist state apparatus.

The outline of this critique was already in place well before the war. In 1932, Aldous Huxley published *Brave New World*, which sketched out a dystopian society in which perfect happiness had been achieved through total manipulation. Set in 632 AF (After Ford), Huxley imagined a world in which genetic manipulation ensures that the working classes are perfectly satisfied with the menial tasks to which they are consigned. The idle upper classes are fed

a suburban home or a labor-saving appliance. Consumer goods had become the new opiate of the people — real-life "soma." To Marxists, it seemed that advertising was not just promotion for specific goods, it was propaganda for the capitalist system. It created what came to be known as "consumerism" — a kind of conformist groupthink transmitted through the mass media. Consumerism produced a simulacrum of happiness, but only by enslaving individuality and the imagination, making it impossible for the working classes to see how much more there could be to life, or to imagine a better world.

The emergence of advertising in the '50s thus gave a new lease on life to the Gramscian theory of "hegemony." Prior to the war, the claim that culture was entirely orchestrated and planned by the bourgeoisie had the whiff of a conspiracy theory. How exactly does the bourgeoisie accomplish all this? But now the answer seemed clear: by bombarding the working classes with advertising, brainwashing them into thinking that cheap consumer goods could make them happy. Suddenly, the idea that the whole culture might be a system of ideology began to seem more plausible. After all, the Germans had been completely brainwashed by the Nazis. Why not us? And if we *were* the victims of total brainwashing, how would we know?

Mass society is indelibly associated, in the popular imagination, with the United States of the 1950s. It is a world of perfect families, white picket fences, shiny new Buicks and teenagers "going steady," yet it is also a world of complete conformity, where happiness is achieved at the expense of individuality, creativity and freedom. It is a world in which, as the Dead Kennedys put it, the comfort you have demanded is now mandatory.

The movie *Pleasantville* dramatizes this critique of mass society through a rather quaint cinematic affectation. In the film, two teenagers from the present are magically transported into the world of a '50s television show. On the surface, everything is perfect: the sun always shines, the home team never loses and there is no poverty, crime or corruption. Everything is pleasant, all of the time. Yet this happiness is achieved at the expense of total uniformity. Inhabitants of the town are blissfully unaware of the existence of a world beyond their city limits. The books in the library are all blank. Everyone eats meatloaf for dinner, every night. Nothing ever changes; the entire world is in stasis.

The Giver

The film depicts the compromise at the heart of Pleasantville by filming the entire '50s world in black and white. Yet as the teenagers from the present inevitably "contaminate" the peace and harmony of Pleasantville, by introducing new ideas and new forms of behavior to the inhabitants, bursts of color begin to show up in that world: a red rose, a green car, a brightly colored painting. One by one the inhabitants of Pleasantville themselves begin to change into full color, as they free themselves from their mental shackles. They become liberated from an existence that is, quite literally, dull and gray.

Here we can see the idea of counterculture in its fully developed form. What people need to be liberated from is not a specific class that oppresses them or a system of exploitation that imposes poverty upon them. People have become trapped in a gilded cage, and have been taught to love their own enslavement. "Society" controls them by limiting the imagination and suppressing their deepest needs. What they need to escape from is conformity. And to do so, they must reject the culture in its entirety. They must form a counterculture — one based on freedom and individuality.

According to Theodore Roszak (whose 1969 book *The Making of a Counter Culture* introduced the term "counter-culture" into general usage), society as a whole has become a system of complete manipulation, a "technocracy." The discipline of the machine and the factory floor has been extended to encompass every dimension of human life. In such a society, "politics, education, leisure, entertainment, culture as a whole, the unconscious drives, and even … protest against the technocracy itself: all these become the subjects of purely technical scrutiny and of purely technical manipulation."[19] Under such circumstances, nothing short of a total rejection of the entire culture and society will suffice. In Roszak's view, traditional leftist parties, not to mention communists and trade unionists, have become the stooges of technocracy: "This brand of politics finishes with merely redesigning the turrets and towers of the technocratic citadel. It is the foundations of the edifice that must be sought."[20]

It is important to see what a profound reorientation of radical politics this critique represents. Traditional leftist concerns, such as poverty, living standards and access to medical care, come to be seen as "superficial," in that they aim only at institutional reform. The counterculture, by contrast, is interested in what Roszak calls "the psychic liberation of the oppressed."[21] Thus the hipster, cooling his heels in a jazz club, comes to be seen as a more profound critic of modern society than the civil rights activist working to enlist voters or the feminist politician campaigning for a constitutional amendment.

Stepping back for a moment, it should be obvious that there is something strange about this form of counter-cultural critique. After all, the traditional objection to capitalism — certainly Marx's primary objection — was that it exploited the working classes, creating poverty and suffering. In other words, the problem with capitalism was that it deprived workers of material goods. "The immiseration of the proletariat" was what Marx called it.

In this context, it is somewhat odd to turn around and say that the workers have sold out and that the abundance of consumer goods is merely an opiate that pacifies them, preventing them from seeing where their true interests lie. It's like saying that when you give a child something to eat, it doesn't really feed him, it merely "placates" him so that he forgets that he is hungry. It was precisely the failure of the capitalist system to provide the workers with goods that gave them the reason to overthrow the system in the first

---

19   Theodore Roszak, *The Making of a Counter Culture: Reflections on the Technocratic Society and Its Youthful Opposition* (Berkeley: University of California Press, 1996), 6. All citations used by kind permission of the University of California Press.

20   Ibid., 55.

21   Ibid., 65.

place. Thus the critique of consumerism comes perilously close to criticizing capitalism for satisfying the workers *too much*. They're so stuffed, they can't be bothered to go out and overthrow the system anymore. But this poses the question: why would they want to?

Roszak in fact criticizes the students in the Paris 1968 uprising for having tried to form an alliance with French workers. The workers, he claims, are an unreliable ally, since they have a vested interest in the system of industrial

students had simply mistaken their own class interests for the general interest — assuming that "good for me" is the same as "good for society." (They would certainly not have been the first to do so!)

The sneaking suspicion that the public might be genuinely satisfied by capitalism is reinforced by the observation that countercultural rebellion didn't seem to do anything. Unlike *Pleasantville*, where the transformation of society is instantaneous, radical and highly visible, in the real world

---

In other words, "the system" seemed to regard the hippies less as a threat to the established order than as a marketing opportunity. Punk rock was received in exactly the same way. Designer safety pins were on sale in fancy London shops long before the Sex Pistols even broke up.

---

production. "The touchstone of the matter would be," he argues, "how ready are the workers to disband whole sectors of the industrial apparatus where this proves necessary to achieve ends other than efficiency, productivity and high consumption? How willing are they to set aside technocratic priorities in favor of a new simplicity of life, a decelerating social pace, a vital leisure?"[22]

One can see here how the traditional interests of the working class have been downgraded to the status of a "technocratic priority." Yet Roszak is in danger of simply taking the class interests of intellectuals and students — freeing the imagination, finding a "new simplicity of life" — and imposing them upon the rest of the population (on the grounds that anyone who disagrees is a victim of the technocracy). The problem with assuming that everyone is the victim of a total ideology is that it becomes impossible to state what would count as evidence for or against this thesis.

In the end, workers didn't seem all that interested in having their imaginations freed. Rather than flocking to art galleries and poetry recitals when given the chance, they continued to show an unhealthy interest in sports, broadcast television and malt beverages. This naturally fed the nagging suspicion that the public at large might actually *like* capitalism, that they might genuinely *want* consumer goods. It suggested that the failure of capitalism to satisfy the "deeper needs" of the people might not be a problem, simply because *the people have no deeper needs*. Perhaps the

"freeing the imagination" doesn't seem to galvanize the proletariat, much less cure injustice, eliminate poverty or stop war. Furthermore, the ideological system that sustains capitalism did not seem to be too troubled by acts of countercultural rebellion. The sort of conformist mass culture caricatured in *Pleasantville* is supposed to be very rigid — such that the slightest display of individuality represents a mortal threat. Nonconformity must be stamped out, we were told, or it would destabilize the entire system.

So the first-generation hippies did everything they could to violate the dress code of '50s society: men grew their hair long and wore beards, refused to wear suits and ties; women adopted miniskirts, threw away their bras, stopped wearing makeup — and so on. But it wasn't long before these items and clothing styles started showing up in advertisements and on mannequins in shop windows. Soon department stores were selling peace medallions and love beads. In other words, "the system" seemed to regard the hippies less as a threat to the established order than as a marketing opportunity. Punk rock was received in exactly the same way. Designer safety pins were on sale in fancy London shops long before the Sex Pistols even broke up.

How to explain this? The countercultural rebels believed that what they were doing was genuinely radical, that it represented a profound challenge to society. Their rebellion was felt to be an especially potent threat to capitalism, which relied upon an army of docile, pacified workers, willing to submit themselves to the soul-destroying discipline of the machine. And yet "the system" seemed to take this form of rebellion in stride. This lack of discernible impact

---

22   Ibid., 68.

presented a serious threat to the countercultural idea. After all, according to the countercultural rebels, the problem with traditional leftist politics was that it was superficial. It aimed at "merely" institutional change. Countercultural rebels, on the other hand, were supposedly attacking oppression at a deeper level. Yet despite the radicalism of their interventions, it was difficult to see any concrete effects.

At this point the countercultural idea might have been in serious trouble had it not been for a singular stroke of genius: the theory of "co-optation." According to this idea, the "repression" imposed by the system turns out to be more subtle than, say, the Spanish Inquisition. At first, the system tries merely to *assimilate* resistance by appropriating its symbols, evacuating their "revolutionary" content and then selling them back to the masses as commodities. It thereby seeks to neutralize the counterculture by piling on substitute gratifications so high that people ignore the revolutionary kernel of these new ideas. It is only when this initial attempt at co-optation has failed that overt repression must be employed, and "the violence inherent in the system" is revealed.

With this theory of co-optation in place, the counterculture itself becomes a "total ideology," a completely closed system of thought, immune to falsification, in which every apparent exception simply confirms the rule. For generations now, countercultural rebels have been pumping out "subversive" music, "subversive" art, "subversive" literature, "subversive" clothing, while universities have been packed full of professors disseminating "subversive" ideas to their students. So much subversion, and yet the system seems to tolerate it quite well. Does this suggest that the system is perhaps not so repressive after all? "On the contrary," says the countercultural rebel. "It shows that the system is even more repressive than we thought — look at how skillfully it co-opts all of this subversion!"

[handwritten note: This is his main idea]

[handwritten note: from a counter cultural rebel]

Slugging Nothing

from *You Do Not Talk About Fight Club*

— Barry Vacker

Nothingness haunts being.

— Jean-Paul Sartre

FIGHT THE FUTURE

"Three Minutes. This is it: Ground Zero."

So declares Tyler Durden in the first and last scenes of the film *Fight Club*. During the apocalyptic ending of the film, these words are followed by several skyscrapers collapsing to the ground, imploded by Durden's terrorist organization, Project Mayhem. In the novel *Fight Club*, only one skyscraper is detonated, yet it is described as "the world's tallest building." These words and images offered a strange anticipation of the fate of the Twin Towers in New York City, which had once been the tallest buildings in the world.[1] The reference to Ground Zero is instructive, for the novel and film contain many references to zeros, nothings, holes, emptinesses, which is perfectly expressed in Tyler Durden's ultimate ambition in the film — to get humanity to "go all back to zero." For Durden, toppling the skyscrapers inhabited by credit card companies would not only erase the world's plastic debt, but the zero would signal planetary chaos and destruction for modernity.

"It's Project Mayhem that's going to save the world. A cultural ice age. A prematurely induced dark age."

With these words, Tyler Durden summarizes the purposes of Project Mayhem, the terrorist network created to bring about the "destruction of civilization." By toppling skyscrapers and destroying museums, Project Mayhem seeks to create cultural "chaos" and "anarchy," and thus hasten the entropy of modernity. The aim is not merely to save the world by destroying it, but to effect a reversal, toward a cultural ice age and dark age. The destination is a retreat to Tyler Durden's premodern utopia, where a hunter–gatherer society would forage for food amidst empty skyscrapers and abandoned superhighways.

"Nothing is static. Even the *Mona Lisa* is falling apart."

Here Jack is describing the existential conditions of the universe, the conditions being embraced and enhanced by Project Mayhem. The first and second rules of fight club are famous: "You do not talk about fight club!" The first and second laws of fight club are also well known: "The Second Law of Thermodynamics." In theoretical physics, the Second Law holds that all physical systems have a tendency toward increasing entropy and disorder. Though not explicitly mentioned in *Fight Club*, the Second Law of Thermodynamics is operative throughout the book and film, with numerous descriptions and depictions of disorder, dissolution, destruction, and degeneration.

"With insomnia, nothing is real. Everything's far away. Everything's a copy of a copy of a copy."

In the film *Fight Club*, Jack offers this lament while standing at a copy machine, on top of which is a Starbucks coffee cup. The copy machine methodically cranks out the copies, in a room full of identical workers also sipping

---

1 The Twin Towers were surpassed by the Sears Tower (1974) and the Petronas Towers (1998).

Starbucks and making copies. Jack expresses angst over the loss of authenticity and individuality in a world of malls packed with mass-produced goods and a mass media that never sleep, running 24/7, expanding in all directions with an explosion of image and information. The real and authentic seem ever farther away, disappearing beyond the horizons of the mediated and simulated, the realms of the replica and the reproduction. The idea that "everything's far away" also echoes the fate of the Big Bang universe, expanding in all directions, with galaxies being shoved apart by expanding voids of nothingness, apparently destined to disappear beyond all horizons.

These four quotes express the existential conditions of *Fight Club*. The novel and film captured the millennial angst felt toward modernity and technology — which revealed an ever-expanding universe of vast voids with a void of meaning — and toward a *philosophy of the future* for living in such a universe. Entering the millennium, the zeros and nothings symbolize the difficulty in imagining a positive or meaningful future, or at least a future not already lived, or not already lost.

In exploring the meanings of the zeros and nothings, this essay will draw upon Jean-Paul Sartre's *Being and Nothingness*, Marshall McLuhan's *Through the Vanishing Point*, Theodore Kaczynski's *The Unabomber Manifesto*, and Brian Greene's *The Fabric of the Cosmos*. Perhaps the most radical implication for *Fight Club* will be found in Sartre's theorization of the future as a "nothingness," the nothingness of possibilities facing and shaping humanity. *Fight Club* depicts a heavyweight title fight because the philosophical bout is the fight with the future, the precise space-time parameters for *slugging nothing*.

THE ZERO CONDITION

Time is no longer counted progressively, by addition, starting from an origin — but by subtraction, starting from the end. This is what happens with rocket launches and time bombs. And that end is no longer symbolic of an endpoint of a history but the mark of a zero sum, of a potential exhaustion.

— Jean Baudrillard

To explore the significance of the nothings and zeros in *Fight Club* requires situating the novel and film within a larger pattern of events entering the millennium, where the number zero was repeatedly associated with the future. The novel and film versions of *Fight Club* were released in 1995 and 1999, respectively, precisely as culture was speeding toward the millennium. Tyler Durden sought to make humanity "go all back to zero" by effecting a "ground zero." Zero was central to the Millennium Clock, Y2K, the Millennium Dome, the Twin Towers, *Naqoyqatsi*, *The Matrix*, Coke Zero, and even the fate of the universe. The year 2000 had long been associated with the arrival of "the future," yet the recurring pattern of zeros suggested something was awry in the spirit and philosophy of that future.

The countdown to zero began at the Centre Pompidou in Paris, where the Millennium Clock ticked toward to the end of the millennium, with electronic digits showing the many millions of seconds until the arrival of 2000. Inspired by a 1980 *Le Monde* article about the end of the millennium, the Millennium Clock in Paris was the first clock to begin the countdown. Throughout 1999, the ticking surely seemed to accelerate, with the zeros increasing on the left side and eventually cascading in the final minutes and seconds to all zeros. There was climax and completion in the cascade of zeros, heralding not only the end of the millennium, but perhaps the end of the future. For Jean Baudrillard, the Millennium Clock suggested that modernity was running down, or out of time, becoming entropic in the exhaustion of all future possibilities — the project of modernity had become the "final illusion of history," for its vision of perpetual progress and industrial technology no longer existed as utopian models of the future (*The Vital Illusion*).

As the Millennium Clock was ticking toward zero, a pair of zeros appeared on the digital horizon, known as Y2K, the non-event that masked and mapped real events. Many feared that computers would not properly recognize the arrival of the year 2000, which would be recorded as "00" at 00:00:00 between December 31, 1999, and January 1, 2000. To save scarce and expensive computer space during the 1950s, calendar years were recorded by the last two numbers — "57" instead of "1957." It was thought that computers would record 2000 as "00" and conclude that the new year was 1900, thus triggering one of two possibilities — computers might make enormous financial miscalculations and wreak havoc in the world banking systems, or the computers might crash, and thus effect a technological crisis as the crash rippled through all the media and energy networks around the world. Businesses and governments enlisted programmers to "correct" the code, combining to spend an estimated \$300–600 billion around the world. Though there were some minor glitches, the corrections apparently worked, for the computer networks did not crash at 00:00:00 on January 1, 2000.

As with the Cold War, the technological apocalypse was avoided with Y2K, thus masking the virtual apocalypse of mediation and simulation occurring around the world, where "reality" disappears beyond its representations in the proliferating territories of postmodern media. The new millennium finally arrived in 2001, though without "the future" as once imagined. Computers were reprogrammed for the future precisely as reality was being deprogrammed from the future, retreating behind the horizons of image and information, clones and copies, replicas and reproductions. Though computers did not crash in 2000, the future itself seems to have crashed into its own vanishing point, the very condition on display at the Millennium Dome.

The Millennium Dome was intended to be an architectural icon for celebrating the new millennium, symbolically situated on the Greenwich Peninsula, at 0° longitude on the prime meridian, which functions as the beginning and end point in the standardization of world time. Made from a translucent glass-fiber fabric, the Millennium Dome is the largest dome in the world, spanning three hundred and twenty meters and supported by twelve towering masts protruding through the roof. Inside the Millennium Dome was the Millennium Experience, a series of Zones designed to be educational and entertaining, each dedicated to some aspect of the human condition at the millennium. Functioning like a synthesis of world's fair and theme park, the Millennium Dome and Millennium Experience opened on December 31, 1999, and closed on December 31, 2000. Promotional literature described the Zones as "windows to the future," with the Millennium Dome being "the most forward-looking place in the world to celebrate the year 2000 and our voyage into the next thousand years."

The most popular Zone was the Body, where visitors walked inside a giant human body (the size of the Statue of Liberty) that featured a pumping heart, brain activities, and other bodily functions. The Mind depicted the functions and neural networks of the brain. The Home Planet offered a multimedia presentation about nature around the world, with an exterior made of TV screens showing various images of nature. The Living Island explored the human impact on the environment, effected through a simulation of a British seaside port, complete with a beach and the sea. Other Zones included Work, Play, Money, Faith, Learning, and Journey (transportation), each experienced much like a theme park attraction.

What can be made of this future displayed at 0°? The Planet was a multimedia experience, and the Living Island simulated ecology. Looking much like the Internet, the networks of the Mind were mapped and the "windows to the future" opened on a Disney-like vision of tomorrow. After the Millennium Experience closed, the exhibits and everything inside were dismantled and sold via an auction — a fire sale of "the future." By the end of 2001, the Millennium Dome was an empty cavern, containing nothing more than dust and debris. In less than a year, the Millennium Dome had gone from a world full of the future to a world of technological nothingness.

The Twin Towers were like binary digits, the 1s turned on, towering monoliths waiting for the countdown to (ground) zero.

If the Millennium Dome was about the future, then it seems we have entered a disposable future, or an empty future, or perhaps a future dead on arrival. Perhaps this future is suggested by the fate of the Body, for which there were no bidders, apparently because the giant human form was too unwieldy or just plain useless. After being dismembered, the Body was buried in a nearby hole. The only full-time resident of the Dome is already dead, the Body now decaying in its graveyard. The Body entered the future at 0° and was buried shortly after at 0°, at the beginning and end of world time.

Dedicated to celebrating the "future" of the space and information ages, the 1964 New York World's Fair included the debut of the Twin Towers, which were featured in a model of New York City. Originally conceived as a vertical world's fair, the Twin Towers were the first skyscrapers wired for global telecommunications. The World Trade Center was completed in 1973, and when Tower 2 was finished, it became the mirror of Tower 1, thus making the monoliths into icons for the copy, the clone, the replay of the event that had already occurred, the arrival at a destination that already had been reached. The Twin Towers were like binary digits, the 1s turned on, towering monoliths waiting for the countdown to (ground) zero. The people killed in the collapse of the Twin Towers were disintegrated and buried at a zero, not unlike the Body dismembered and buried at 0°L near the Millennium Dome. Conceived like world's fairs to celebrate the future, the Millennium Dome and the Twin Towers both met unexpected fates — burials at two zeros, two funerals for a new future, now apparently dead on arrival.

The events at Ground Zero in New York City were anticipated in Las Vegas, at the hotel New York–New York. Opened in 1997, New York–New York embraced the metaphysics of the clone and the copy, for the hotel is a giant simulation of various icons in New York City — a half-size Statue of Liberty, forty-seven-story Empire State Building, Chrysler Building, Seagram Building, Grand

an ever-accelerating journey into virtuality, into the vanishing point, the zero, nothingness.

This journey into end-of-the-millennium nothingness parallels some of the insights offered by cutting-edge cosmological theory, especially the superstring theory. Superstring theory posits that the smallest constituents of the universe are not particles of matter but loops of energy, in the form of submicroscopic strings, which are linked together like a complex web or membrane. The smallest of these loops are called "zero-branes," and, like strings on a guitar, the loops of energy vibrate to generate the matter of the universe. Though not yet empirically verified, the equations suggest the strings make up a sprawling cosmic fabric upon which

---

Like a copy of a copy of a copy, Coke Zero is the soft drink simulacrum, the virtual beverage. Once promoted as "the real thing," Coca-Cola has cloned a near nothing, marketed as nothing, a zero, in Coke Zero.

Central Station, three-hundred-foot-long Brooklyn Bridge, and many others. Within New York–New York, tourists can dine in Greenwich Village or stroll along Times Square and Broadway. However, visitors have never been able to visit the World Trade Center, for the Twin Towers were not included in the skyline of New York–New York. Like a map prophesying the *absence* of territories, the future of New York City was presaged in the Xerox of New York–New York. While the Twin Towers disappeared in Vegas before Manhattan, skyscrapers and the Superdome towered above swamps in flooded New Orleans, the site for yet another Ground Zero in the American metropolis, and perhaps a test run for the coastal effects of global warming.

The zero condition was extended to the universe in *Naqoyqatsi* (2002) by Godfrey Reggio and *The Matrix* trilogy (1999, 2003) by the Wachowski brothers. In the first film, after the word "NAQOYQATSI" is shown at the beginning, a burst of stars accelerates toward us, expanding in all directions. A zero emerges from around the four sides of the screen and then recedes into the vanishing point, while the stars accelerate ever faster, becoming a blur of white light. The zero reemerges from behind the expanding stars, accompanied by a horizontal stream of 1s and 0s that dissolve into exploding stars. Similar imagery was depicted in *The Matrix* trilogy, especially in the opening scenes of all three films. *Naqoyqatsi* and *The Matrix* vividly theorize the existential conditions of the information age,

exists the matter of the universe. Since the Big Bang, the universe has been expanding in all directions, with the galaxies hurtling away from each other with increasing velocity. Propelling the universe apart are the expanding voids in between the galaxies. Almost completely empty, these voids are like intergalactic nothingnesses, always expanding, apparently spreading the universe toward a final state of zero density and "zero curvature," or toward a flat universe that has disappeared beyond all horizons. Physicist Brian Greene likens the shape of the universe to a flat-screen TV and a hologram on a plastic card, where reality exists on a thin surface illuminated to reveal "the holographic illusions of daily life." If the Second Law of Thermodynamics and superstring theory are correct, then the ultimate trajectory of the universe is from infinite energy and density toward zero energy and zero density.

Offering the promise of zero energy and zero density, Coke Zero may be the ultimate cosmic soft drink. Introduced in 2005, Coke Zero's "zero formula" contains zero calories, zero carbohydrates, zero sugar, zero protein — apparently meaning that the drink offers nothing to increase energy and nothing to increase the density of body fat, though apparently it still contains caffeine for a quick hit. From Coke to Diet Coke to Coke Zero, the trajectory of the original Coca-Cola is to disappear, to have its flavor simulated and function emptied, to reach its vanishing point on the horizons of the global marketplace.

Like a copy of a copy of a copy, Coke Zero is the soft drink simulacrum, the virtual beverage. Once promoted as "the real thing," Coca-Cola has cloned a near nothing, marketed as nothing, a zero, in Coke Zero.

On the five-year anniversary of September 11th, the *New York Times* published a special section called "Broken Ground: The Hole in the City's Heart." On the first page was a circular photograph of New York City with Ground Zero at the center of the image and the rest of the city and world warping away toward the vanishing points. Wittingly or unwittingly, the *New York Times* depicted New York City as a zero, for what else is a circle with a hole in it — especially a hole called Ground Zero — but the site and symbol for both nothingness and singularity? In the book and film *An Inconvenient Truth*, Al Gore argues that humanity faces the moment of singularity for confronting global warming, which can only be reversed by a "zero-carbon" tomorrow.

In 2007, the zero appeared on a global scale, hovering above the clouds against a blue sky. On either side of the zero was a capital *S*, spelling out "SOS," the famed letters signaling distress or emergency. The zero was the centerpiece of the logo for Live Earth, the global "concerts for a climate in crisis." Upon arriving at the Live Earth Web site, visitors viewed each *S* disappearing behind the *O*, the center of which was black. Beside the *O* were the words "Live Earth" and if one scrolled over the two words, "Live Earth" disappeared against the black background, leaving only the *O*, the circle that became a zero, signaling countdown to the ecological apocalypse or blastoff for a zero-carbon tomorrow.

In the television documentary *Aftermath: Population Zero* (2008), special effects depicted what would happen on Earth if humans instantly vanished from the planet. Within seconds, cars are crashing; within minutes, planes are dropping from the sky. Within hours, the unattended power grid is shutting down and the entire planet is dark at night. Within ten years, roads are cracked and being covered with weeds; nature is beginning to green the cities. Within thirty years, satellites are crashing to Earth, pulled down by gravity. Within two hundred years, many skyscrapers and bridges begin to collapse because of rust and decay. Within one thousand years, the Eiffel Tower and Statue of Liberty collapse, falling beneath the green canopy, the urban rainforest of Tyler Durden, to be followed by a global ice age. Within twenty-five thousand to one hundred thousand years, the next ice age will send glaciers grinding across the collapsed cities and erasing any last remnants of the human species; on Earth, all traces of humanity have reached the vanishing point, the zero condition.

The fascination with zeros and nothingness reached art galleries and the ivory towers. There were two art exhibits on nothingness — "Nothing" opened in 2001 at the Northern Gallery for Contemporary Art in Sunderland, UK, before continuing at galleries in Lithuania and Sweden; "The Big Nothing" exhibit was held during 2004 at the Institute for Contemporary Art, located on the University of Pennsylvania campus in Philadelphia. Other than images of zeros and holes, the works in these exhibits scarcely provided interesting or insightful visualizations of nothingness, perhaps unintentionally suggesting the contemporary art world's own intellectual emptiness qua nothingness. However, some essays in the companion book for "Nothing" offered insights into the connections between nothingness in art and science, and suggested a few symbolic connections between "nothing, apocalypse, and utopia," the themes implicit in the zero conditions. More comprehensive scientific accounts appeared in three books published about the science of nothingness and three books about the history and science of zero — Robert Kaplan's *The Nothing That Is: A Natural History of Zero* (1999), Charles Seife's *Zero: The Biography of a Dangerous Idea* (2000), and Chet Raymo's *Walking Zero: Discovering Cosmic Space and Time Along the PRIME MERIDIAN* (2006). The post–September 11th cultural critique of Paul Virilio was entitled *Ground Zero*.

So, what do these zeros signify? As first suggested by the Millennium Clock, the zeros suggest that modernity is running down, becoming entropic in its exhaustion as a model of the future. The year 2000 once symbolized the arrival of "the future," yet as humanity approached the millennium, there seemed to be a declining confidence in the future, even a fear of the future. Born in an era of glowing technological confidence, the twentieth century ended in an age of growing technological skepticism, caused by fears of various apocalypses, from nuclear war to global warming to worldwide computer crashes. For many, it seemed difficult to imagine an optimistic technological future. The zeros suggest not only the entropy of modernity, but also the emergence of postmodernity, the future of mass-mediation and mass-reproductions, the future of copies, clones, replicas, reproductions, simulations, nothings, and zeros. Modernity and postmodernity: these are the two futures fought in *Fight Club*. The hipster terrorists in *Fight Club* were confronting the zero condition.

PROJECT MAYHEM VS. PROJECT MODERNITY

The Parker-Morris building will go over, all one hundred and ninety-one floors, slow as a tree falling in the forest.

— Jack

While there are many themes in *Fight Club*, the trajectory of the plot follows the emergence of a violent rebellion against the modern world, centered around brutal fistfights among gangs of men in an underground network of fight clubs. Project Mayhem and the fight clubs are organized by an alienated corporate drone named Jack, under the inspiration of his alter ego, Tyler Durden, who takes the physical form of a Luddite hipster terrorist, clad in urban grunge anti-fashion fashions. Like any bureaucratic organization, Project Mayhem had its various divisions and committees, which included the Bureaucracy of Anarchy, Organized Chaos, the Misinformation Committee, the Arson Committee, and the Assault Committee. From the fistfights, Project Mayhem soon expanded its scope and ambition to include anything from detonating computers to destroying sculptures to demolishing skyscrapers. Over the course of the novel and film, it becomes apparent that Tyler Durden is an urban Unabomber, not theorizing in the forest and mail-bombing scientists, but taking action in the metropolis and bombing skyscrapers, to get us to "go all back to zero."

So, how does *Fight Club* fit within the pattern of zeros? And how does this reflect a crisis in philosophies of the future?

The most explicit parallel is the toppling of skyscrapers in New York City. Like the New York–New York hotel, Tyler Durden offered the apocalyptic prophesy of "Ground Zero" before events of September 11th in New York City. In the book *Fight Club*, the toppled skyscraper was the fictional Parker-Morris tower, described as "the world's tallest building," which was true of the World Trade Center upon its completion in 1973. In the final scene of the film *Fight Club*, several skyscrapers are toppled, with the monoliths collapsing in a manner strikingly similar to the collapse of the Twin Towers two years later. Project Mayhem waged war on modernity and globalization, not unlike the Unabomber, the professor-turned-terrorist who mail-bombed scientists, and the terrorists who piloted planes into the Twin Towers. Project Mayhem was an army of urban Unabombers, though operating with much more powerful explosives than mere mail bombs.

The Millennium Clock thus seems prophetic, for countdowns are used when launching rockets and detonating bombs. The book *Fight Club* begins with a similar countdown — "ten minutes," "nine minutes," "eight minutes" and eventually down to "three minutes." Then follows the book's Ground Zero, the detonation of the bombs and the toppling of the skyscraper. Ground Zero was the zero to begin the cultural apocalypse. And Y2K was imagined to be the zeros that would trigger the technological apocalypse, precisely at the end of the century and millennium. At Ground Zero, Project Mayhem hoped to effect a Y2K, what many in 1999 feared would be a technological and cultural apocalypse in 2000.

However, Y2K was the non-apocalypse that masked the virtual apocalypse, for advancing technology has not caused the end of the world, but has hastened the end of "the real" in the cultural worlds. In the film *Fight Club*, Jack references this condition while making copies at a machine: "With insomnia, nothing is real. Everything's far away. Everything's a copy of a copy of a copy." In Jack's IKEA-furnished apartment, the furniture was all mass-produced derivatives of derivatives of modernism, seemingly made more real and authentic with the designer names — Johanneshov armchair, Rislampa/Har paper lamps, Alle cutlery, Vild hall clock, Steg nesting tables, and so on. The age of mass production is being overtaken by the age of mass customization and mass reproduction, where simulation is becoming the dominant operating principle.

If modernity sought to produce "the best of all possible worlds," then postmodernity seeks less to produce than to *re*produce, to recreate and replicate all previous worlds. The real is that which can be reproduced, where the real and fictional converge in models of simulation. These are the conditions symbolized by Las Vegas, perfected in the real virtualities of New York–New York and Paris, Las Vegas. Perhaps this is the destiny of the information age, the future of replication and reproduction, cloning and copying. Thus it is no surprise that the new millennium was celebrated in the Millennium Dome, with its Zones offering simulations — simulations not only of the future, but simulations *as* the future. As a first home for the millennium, the Millennium Dome soon stood empty and in disrepair, while the Body was rendered useless and buried in a hole at 0°L — the ground zero for the future. As one of Tyler Durden's "space monkeys" explains to another space monkey: "You are the same decaying organic matter as everyone else, and we are all part of the same compost pile."

The fight clubs are held in abandoned basements and empty parking garages, featuring brutal fistfights and violent assaults on the body. The fights end when one man can no longer continue, symbolically dying in a hole. As Jack declares in the film *Fight Club*: "On a long enough time line, the survival rate for everyone drops to zero." This is the condition symbolized by the fights, for everyone eventually loses a fight at fight club, just as everyone eventually dies and has no more future. Eventually, we all become part of the past. Fight club sought to hasten our arrival.

In another sense, the fights symbolized the reality we all inhabit, the ultimate reality: our bodies. In an age of fast food, fat people, and fad diets, all existing in a metrosexual media landscape of six-pack abs, hair transplants, and Viagra, there is ever more cultural pressure to improve the male body to lose weight, grow hair, get ripped, and stay hard — just like Tyler Durden (Brad Pitt) in the film version of *Fight Club*. Yet, ultimately, the fights weren't

black shirts, two black pants." One space monkey reads from Tyler's manifesto to an assembly of space monkeys: "Our culture has made us all the same. No one is truly white or black or rich, anymore. We all want the same. Individually, we are nothing."

Fight Club is the latest in a long line of attempts to resist modern mass society, or consumer society, and the desire for authenticity and autonomy. Beginning with the beatniks of the 1950s, there have been continual efforts to resist mass culture and consumer society, to create a revolutionary counterculture, including hippies and leftists, punks and fundamentalists, goths and gangstas, Luddites and antiglobalization protestors, and so on. The new struggle is less a war on poverty than it is a war on homogeneity, seeking authenticity in a culture of mass production, seeking identity in a culture of mass mediation, seeking roots in a culture of rapid acceleration. While all these countercultural groups claim to have escaped the mass mind, their efforts to resist or revolt seem to have provided more markets for capitalism, be it corporate or entrepreneurial capitalism, apparently ever ready to create and manufacture the lifestyles of the proliferating countercultures. To satisfy these new markets of "resistance,"

In another sense, the fights symbolized the reality we all inhabit, the ultimate reality: our bodies. In an age of fast food, fat people, and fad diets, all existing in a metrosexual media landscape of six-pack abs, hair transplants, and Viagra, there is ever more cultural pressure to improve the male body to lose weight, grow hair, get ripped, and stay hard—just like Tyler Durden (Brad Pitt) in the film version of *Fight Club*.

---

about improved toughness, living more fully, or being more authentic. They were brutal battles aimed at the destruction of reality, of self, of improvement, of the future. "Self-improvement is masturbation; now self-destruction, that's improvement," says Tyler, in response to Jack's comment about a Calvin Klein underwear ad and guys in gyms trying to look like guys in ads. In the end, the fights are about burying the cultural body and resurrecting the brainless body, the vessels of the unthinking true believer, the follower, the conformist, the drone, the space monkey. In *Fight Club*, the narcissist metrosexuals are countered by the conformist space monkeys, consumers of Calvin Klein are countered by clones of Tyler Durden. Like the latest urban hipsters, all the "space monkeys" dressed in black — "two

capitalism has evolved from mass production to mass customization to mass simulation, cloning and copying all possible lifestyles for experiential consumption. With communism imploded and capitalism imperial, there are no competing economic systems on the world stage, only competing lifestyles within a global village. Fueled by counterfeit individualism and simulated authenticity, rebellion is now a consumer lifestyle, and revolution is a market niche — the Coke Zero of revolution.

As it is in *Fight Club*, so it is around the world. Fundamentalists and terrorists of all stripes — from theological to ecological to ideological — are waging wars with the perceived ills of the modern project, especially environmental harm and the imperatives of secularism and consumerism, which are spread through technological and cultural globalization. By the end of the century, modernity was charged with delivering too much material abundance, filling up the cultural world with machines and metropolises, skyscrapers and suburbs, cars and computers, and so on. Modern production filled the cultural universe with material things, but modern science revealed a cosmic universe of vast voids and no self-evident meaning. Precisely as science and technology reveal a complex and expanding

between being and nothingness, to create a culture for an imagined future, the future that shapes the present.

Sartre viewed existence as everything, the entirety of the universe, seeing consciousness as part of existence and so naturally oriented to apprehending that existential universe. Existence is "being-in-itself," the universe as it is, always completely full and utterly indifferent to the fate of humanity. As with all living things, consciousness is "being-for-itself," always in a state of lack, forever seeking

---

As it is in *Fight Club*, so it is around the world. Fundamentalists and terrorists of all stripes—from theological to ecological to ideological—are waging wars with the perceived ills of the modern project, especially environmental harm and the imperatives of secularism and consumerism, which are spread through technological and cultural globalization.

---

universe, fundamentalists and terrorists seek a return to technological simplicity and spiritual purity in a shrinking cultural world, sort of like the Big Bang being countered by the Big Crunch. At a deeper level, Project Mayhem and fight club were not merely battling modernity, but were waging war against one of the key space-time parameters of the modern project — the idea of an optimistic and enlightened future. Tyler Durden and the space monkeys were fighting the future, struggling to hasten the end of the future, to effect a reversal of the trajectory of tomorrow, symbolized by getting humanity to "go all back to zero."

FROM NOTHINGNESS TO CULTURE TO DETONATING IKEA

Nothingness lies coiled in the heart of being.
— Jean-Paul Sartre

If *Fight Club* depicts wars with modernity and postmodernity, a fight with two futures, then exactly how does that equate with "slugging nothing"?

To explore this question, we should turn to Jean-Paul Sartre and the existential ontology theorized in *Being and Nothingness*. Sartre believed that all human culture mediates between two realms — existence and consciousness. Simply put, culture emerges from the inherent need for humanity to mediate between existence and consciousness,

the fullness and completeness that motivate all thought and action. To have a lack or be incomplete is to not have something, or to have a nothing that needs to be filled with something. For Sartre, a lack or incompleteness is a *nothingness* that exists in contrast to *being*. If humans were completely full of being and without some kind of nothingness, then there would be no reason to engage in any thought or action directed toward the future. In sum, nothingness exists and humans strive to improve or complete ourselves by filling nothingness with being. Just as zero is a real number, nothingness is a real thing.

This empirical nothingness is the ground for two other nothingnesses central to *Fight Club* — the nothingness of consciousness and the nothingness of the future.

Sartre theorized consciousness as the nothingness through which we experience all being, the center for the subjective experience of existence and the things of the empirical world. To be aware of any empirical thing, consciousness must not be that thing, much like seeing is separate from what is seen. Since all things are potential objects of consciousness, consciousness must be a non-thing, or a nothingness. In effect, Sartre saw consciousness functioning much like a flashlight scanning a dark room — a beam of light illuminating existence. Consciousness illuminates existence as it is, as being-in-itself. Since consciousness is being-for-itself, it can also illuminate existence as it is not, but could be, revealing nothingnesses to be filled.

Nothingness exists — in both existence and consciousness — and such nothingness is the existential discontinuity in a deterministic universe, the starting point for all human freedom and cultural possibility, collectively and individually, from past to present to future. Thus it is no surprise that the film *Fight Club* opens with a journey through the neural networks of Jack's brain, the seat for consciousness, the site for cognitive nothingness and all cultural possibility. From the neural networks, the journey exits the brain between Jack's eyebrows, where he stares down the barrel of a gun, stuck in his mouth by Tyler Durden. From the nothingness of all possibility, Jack faced his two alternatives — blow out his brains or blow up the world.

In its evolutionary and existential incompleteness, humanity is always striving for fullness and completeness, always seeking to fill nothingness with being. Humanity will always confront a double-sided existence, the world as it is and as it could be, a Möbius existence of being and nothingness. Only through experiencing existence can human consciousness begin to fill the nothingnesses of consciousness with the ideas, knowledge, philosophies, and the systems of thought that produce culture. To fill the nothingnesses of existence and consciousness, humans can either adapt to existence or adapt existence to themselves. The adaptation to existence has occurred through biological evolution across the eons, while the adaptation of existence to consciousness has occurred through cultural evolution across the millennia, from the past to the present to the future, from premodern to modern to postmodern societies, from hunter–gatherer to agrarian to industrial to information societies. These societies emerged from the identification of existence as it is not (a nothingness) and as it could be (a possibility), which produced what it is (being, reality).

Humanity rarely experiences existence directly, in sheer and unmitigated forms. Virtually all humans spend their entire lives inhabiting some form of technological mode of existence, from premodern (agrarian) to modern (industrial) to postmodern (information, media). Seeking to fill nothingnesses, these societies emerged from the evolving technology deployed in the drive toward completeness, in the desire to overcome material and informational scarcities in culture and consciousness. The ambition of agrarian culture was to fill a lack — to overcome the scarcity of food in society through the plow and improved methods of farming. The ambition of mass production was also to fill a lack — to overcome material scarcity, to use factories to fill nothingnesses with an abundance of goods. A similar ambition exists with mass media, where the original goal was to fill a lack in consciousness, to use media technologies to fill a nothingness in knowledge with information and representations of the world. Filling these nothingnesses was at the heart of modernity and the enlightenment — it represented progress into a better future. In fact, the very nature of progress was to fill the future!

Modernity and mass production offered a domestic fullness and completeness that Jack explicitly rejected in *Fight Club*. To blow up the world required an older form of consciousness, a consciousness destined to be emptied of scientific and technological knowledge, the intellectual devolution from modern to premodern. With the rise of industrial culture, it was believed that mass-produced abundance would eliminate scarcity to satisfy the needs and wants of the masses, thus liberating them from centuries of poverty and domestic squalor. Industrialization was able to fill the lives of the masses with a quantity of goods previously unimaginable, yet it was in response to mass production that the desire for authenticity and individuality appeared as a cultural force. The system of

---

Nothingness exists and humans strive to improve or complete ourselves by filling nothingness with being. Just as zero is a real number, nothingness is a real thing.

---

mass production led to the culture of mass consumption, with homes filled and fashioned with designer goods and designer clothing, illustrating the transition from use-value to symbolic-value and status-value.

The furniture in Jack's IKEA-filled apartment was mass-produced, yet was seemingly customized to his personal needs via a simulated authenticity, as implied by the many designer items. Though Jack's apartment was *filled*, it was empty of meaning to him. Feeling trapped in a life too full of goods, Jack sought liberation from the mass-produced abundance, from the artworks and material goods of the IKEA lifestyle — "Then you're trapped in your lovely nest and the things you used to own, now they own you." Jack begged Tyler for deliverance:

Deliver me from Swedish furniture.
Deliver me from clever art. …

May I never be complete.

May I never be content.

May I never be perfect.

Deliver me, Tyler, from being perfect and complete.

The deliverance is realized when the apartment and the IKEA goods are detonated — the apartment went from fullness to emptiness, from being to nothingness. In conditions of complete fullness, no action is possible, which is why Tyler had to detonate the apartment, to create Jack's nothingness that makes possible truly free actions. The destruction of consumer fullness is a microcosm of Project Mayhem's overall plan, whereupon the mass-produced fullness of culture must be destroyed to create the nothingnesses from which an old freedom emerges, a savage freedom bent upon cultural destruction. As Tyler explains: "It's only after you've lost everything that you're free to do anything."

Jack's detonation of the IKEA lifestyle suggests more than a battle against consumer society, for the goods destroyed were distant derivatives of designs born of modernity. After all, that is the specialty of IKEA, a derivative modernism, a modernism made cozy and comfy. For furniture consumers, the simulacra of IKEA is the closest they will ever get to sitting in designs by the real modernists, such as Le Corbusier, Mies van der Rohe, Frank Lloyd Wright, or Buckminster Fuller. The conceptual understanding of *modern* furniture and architectural design is largely absent in the cities around the world, leaving millions of people unable to distinguish between intellectual appreciation for modernism and the simulation of taste that fuels shallow and trendy consumerism — the very intellectual condition facing Jack. In this domestic void, we find chains like IKEA offering low-cost simulacra, which look cheap and feel spiritually empty — like copies of derivatives of knock-offs of originals. The overwhelming majority of consumers have rejected domestic modernism anyway, opting for the mass-produced crafts and simulated authenticity of Home Depot or the mass-produced styles of Martha Stewart, where devolutionary traditionalism is masked as domestic perfectionism. IKEA, Home Depot, and Martha Stewart are the three design concepts that fill the American home, and only one is a distant derivative of modernism, the one detonated in *Fight Club*.

That Jack detonates IKEA is instructive, for no matter how derivative, IKEA is the retail chain most closely associated with mass-produced modernism, the design associated with progress and the future. While Jack's IKEA goods were spread all over the street below, there is one description that is most suggestive: "My Audi was still parked in the lot, but a Dakapo halogen torchiere was speared through the windshield." With a halogen-tipped spear in its windshield, mechanized modernity faced the non-illuminated dark age, existing no longer as a vision of the future. And, since modernism was always about the future, Jack was detonating the future, creating a nothingness to confront nothingness.

FROM NOTHINGNESS TO THE FUTURE TO DESTROYING SKYSCRAPERS

The Future is the continual possibilization of all possibles.

— Jean-Paul Sartre

Sartre theorized the future as another nothingness, a nothingness that shapes the past and present. Humans are always negotiating between existence and consciousness, between being and nothingness, through actions based on plans for the future. The future is the ultimate target for slugging nothing in *Fight Club*.

Since the future has not happened yet, it is an existential nothingness of possibilities facing and *shaping* humanity. The future is made present and made real through the plans produced by human consciousness, the nothingness that seeks to fill the being of the future. Of course, these plans have intended and unintended consequences, such as nuclear power (intended) and nuclear meltdowns (unintended) or fossil fuels producing energy (intended) and fossil fuel carbons producing global warming (unintended). In any event, when we develop a plan for the future, it functions to shape our present actions, which are predicated on the possible future we have imagined. When the present happens, it immediately becomes the past, which is being-in-itself, precisely because it is full and complete and cannot be changed. The present world is always situated upon two trajectories, at once retreating into the past and on a perpetual flight toward the future.

The theory of the future as a nothingness applies to human actions, collectively and individually, for the cultural worlds emerging from our choices and actions are predicated on a possible future we have imagined. That this essay exists now, in the present, was predicated on the fact of its non-existence, a nothingness in the future that I filled with the ideas and words you are now reading. The existence of my Macintosh laptop is predicated on it first having non-existence, a nothingness in the future filled by the technologists and designers at Apple. Similarly, the existence of agrarian, industrial, and information societies were predicated on their non-existence, as nothingnesses of the future imagined as possible. Collectively and individually, we transcend ourselves in imagining the future, in planning ahead, and projecting ourselves into the plan, into our possibilities.

At any given moment, humans are astride a nothingness, a discontinuity between past and future, yesterday and tomorrow. Within finite existence, the nothingness of consciousness provides "infinite" possibilities (*Being and Nothingness*). The nothingnesses in existence, consciousness, and the future provide the "Big Bang" for humanity and culture, making possible an ever-expanding universe of futures.

Humans have surrounded themselves with a technological mode of existence, a cultural world filled with industrial and information technologies. This mode of existence includes the electrified metropolises of towering skyscrapers and sprawling suburbs, the mechanized mobility of automobiles and airplanes, the mass media of televisions and computers, the mass-produced abundance of shopping centers and strip malls, homes and residences brimming with goods reflecting the desires and dreams of the masses. The world of tomorrow made real, the future made present, this was the technological mode of existence that Project Mayhem sought to destroy in *Fight Club* — "Fight club is tomorrow, and I'm not going to miss fight club."

Ironically, the modern world is entropic, even in its expansion, for it is being eroded by the emerging technologies born of industrial culture. At its zenith in the 1950s, the industrial age gave birth to two other technological ages — the space age and the information age. The mechanized

---

The world of tomorrow made real, the future made present, this was the technological mode of existence that Project Mayhem sought to destroy in *Fight Club* — "Fight club is tomorrow, and I'm not going to miss fight club."

Sartre believed that humans are always negotiating these existential conditions based on visions of the future, expressed in the desire for "a mode of being" (*Existentialism and Human Emotions*). In its many forms, culture mediates between humans and existence to provide a mode of being, a shared mode of existence for society. A central component of culture is technology, which is deployed to fill nothingnesses in creating a mode of existence. Through technology, humans long ago began transforming the world as it is into the world as it could be, adapting the world to us in creating a new world — the world of the future. From plow to printing press, factory to electricity, car to computer, there is hardly any aspect of human existence that has not been reordered through technology, with an eye toward the future, toward how the world could be, toward a new and improved mode of existence. Modernity was always a futurist project, and the twentieth century was that most modern of centuries, when it was believed that science and technology would deliver the future, the future as a mode of existence — the world of tomorrow.

world may have extended beyond all cultural horizons, disappearing beyond the vanishing points of modernity, but it has crashed into a new set of vanishing points, the mediated world of postmodernity and the expanding universe of the Big Bang.

Born of electronic media, especially television and the computer, the information age signaled the emergence of a new mode of existence, a new global culture centered around the production and exchange of image and information, symbol and simulation — circulating in vast networks of mediated realities, each refracting and reliant upon the others as they replicate in a culture of endless symbolic consumption and simulated individuality. Always on, running 24/7, these are the networked territories of the global village, electronic territories generated by media technologies that span the cultural world as they envelop and reproduce the physical world. If the electronic media are deployed to map the surrounding world, then it seems the maps have so proliferated they are supplanting and generating the territories they were supposed to represent. These are the territories of television, cinema, computers, cell phones, iPods — stored in cyberspace, circulated via the Internet, constructed in theme parks and Las Vegas.

If New York City is the modern metropolis, the skyscraper city for the mechanized world of tomorrow, then New York–New York is the postmodern metropolis, the simulation city for the mediated world of tomorrow. Both have a ground zero.

The present is hurtling into the future, and Project Mayhem viewed both the present and future as negative and not worth living. To change the present one must change the future, meaning that Project Mayhem may be at war with modernity, which has shaped most of the present, but it also must battle postmodernity, which will shape most of the future. If the future (nothingness) is viewed negatively by those in the present, then the past (being-in-itself) will necessarily seem more attractive and more certain, precisely because it is full and complete. This is Tyler Durden's perspective, which made the distant past into the cultural destiny of Project Mayhem, necessary to confront a cosmos where modernity is entropic and the universe is expanding. By destroying a skyscraper, Project Mayhem surely declares war on project modernity, though it also desperately sensed the conditions of project postmodernity, the new future of expanding voids, expanding nothingnesses.

PROJECT MAYHEM VS. PROJECT POSTMODERNITY

Look up into the stars and you're gone.

— Jack

The existential conditions of postmodernity are revealed in two of Jack's musings about the nature of the cultural world and the cosmic universe. As discussed earlier, Jack stands at a copy machine in the film *Fight Club* and says:

> With insomnia, nothing is real. Everything's far away. Everything's a copy of a copy of a copy. When deep space exploration ramps up, it'll be the corporations that name everything: the IBM Stellar Sphere, the Microsoft Galaxy, Planet Starbucks.

Here, Jack combines concepts from the information and space ages in offering a poetic expression of the expanding media world. Simply put, we live in a mediated universe,

made available by the computers of Apple and IBM, the software of Microsoft, and the global networks of the Internet and cyberspace. The solar system has been mapped by the electronic media of *Voyager 1* and *2*. The Big Bang was first theorized from images captured via telescope photography, and then verified via radio telescopes, which captured the background radiation emitted by the cosmic expansion. In this expanding universe, "everything's far away," as Jack says, and forever moving farther away.

Following Jack's intuition, perhaps we should think of humans inhabiting two expanding and overlapping worlds, one empirical and one mediated. These two worlds were produced by two Big Bangs, one natural and one technological. As predicted by Intel cofounder Gordon Moore in 1965, microprocessors have doubled in power every two years, while also shrinking in size and declining in cost. Known as "Moore's Law," this pattern has recurred for the past forty years and is expected to continue for the foreseeable future, ensuring that cyberspace will continue to expand exponentially, especially with the linking of ever-more-powerful computers via the Internet. In this global network, cyberspace is an expanding void of virtual space-time, while the electronic circuits and screens are the vanishing points for representation of space-time, all combining to produce a mediated cosmos, an electronic nothingness for representing the world.

To grasp this radical condition, we can combine the ideas of McLuhan and Sartre. McLuhan viewed all media as extensions of the senses and consciousness — simply put, spoken words are extensions of thought, print media are extensions of written words and our eyes, televisions are extensions of our eyes and ears, computers are extensions of consciousness, and so on. Extending from human consciousness around the world is a "global nervous system," a mode of electronic perception, with the cyberspace functioning as the circuited consciousness to be filled with information. McLuhan believed that the information age would reproduce information as "total environments," while also effecting a reversal of the vanishing point in the history of Western representation (*Through the Vanishing Point*).

For McLuhan, natural light and electric light were pure information, with light *shining on* the objects of the world, on the pages of the book, on the screens of cinema. In contrast, television and computers deploy light *shining through* the electronic screens, shining upon our faces, in effect making our eyes the screen. Rather than provide a vanishing point extending from the eye to the distant horizon, television and computers collapse space and time in the instant retrieval of information, now shining through the screens, and thus reversing the vanishing point of representation. For McLuhan, the effect is a media implosion of the world on the screens and in the circuits of cyberspace, an implosion destined to accelerate all events.

If we understand consciousness as a nothingness (Sartre) and the media as extensions of consciousness (McLuhan), then we can see how the media function as electronic nothingnesses. Mediating between existence and consciousness is yet another consciousness, an electronic mode of perception, extending around the world to become a new mode of existence, a total media environment. In the postmodern zero condition, modernity is entropic, and we have crashed into the new future of electronic screens, into the vanishing points, not situated upon the distant horizons, but rather in the circuits of cyberspace and consciousnesses, both realms of nothingness for representing being.

These are the mediated conditions suggested by the zero universes in *Naqoyqatsi* and *The Matrix* trilogy, both of which mapped the Big Bang of the universe within the Big Bang of the media cosmos. To confront the future of an expanding nothingness, Project Mayhem drills holes in the monitors of personal computers, fills them with liquid explosives, and detonates the computers. If, as McLuhan suggested, information is light, the light that shines through computer screens, then the light must be stopped with a premature "dark age," the very ambition of Project Mayhem.

In the war with project modernity, Jack detonates his IKEA-filled apartment, thus reducing it to an empty shell, a blackened nothingness. After wandering the edge of the exploded hole in the side of the building, fifteen stories up, Jack offers the following thoughts:

Go to the edge of the floor, fifteen stories above the parking lot, and look at the city lights and stars, and you're gone.

It's all so beyond us.

Up here, in the miles of night between the stars and the Earth, I feel just like one of those space animals.

Dogs.

Monkeys.

Men.

You just do your little job. Pull a lever. Push a button. You don't really understand any of it.

The world is going crazy.

Coming near the end of the book *Fight Club*, these lines illustrate that perhaps the war with project modernity has left us with an unwinnable war with postmodernity, particularly the cosmos revealed by computers and electronic media. The space age represented the high point of modernity's technological optimism, which culminated in the moon landing of 1969. Around the same time, computers and telescopes were verifying the theory of the Big Bang — the theory that the universe has been expanding for fifteen billion years, with the galaxies moving away in all directions, thrust apart by expanding voids of nothingness and apparently destined to disappear beyond all horizons, leaving a starless universe facing total entropy, the final state of the Second Law of Thermodynamics.

> Deep down, the Big Bang seems to support Sartre's notion of an existence utterly indifferent to humanity, a universe of mind-boggling scale, requiring that each of us take responsibility for developing the meanings for our lives.

If the space age represents the height of technological modernity, then perhaps we are now experiencing vertigo, a condition symbolized in *Fight Club* by Seattle's Space Needle — "the Space Needle leaning at a forty-five degree angle." Rockets may have sent humans to the moon, but computers and electronic telescopes revealed a universe so vast, so unreachable, always moving away. As Jack says: "It's all so beyond us … the miles of night between the stars and Earth."

For the foreseeable future, outer space will only be accessible in cyberspace (except for a few space tourists circling the Earth). Information and matter bifurcate through televisions and computers, separating image from object in space and time, leaving the object behind as the image is propelled at light speed through screens around the world. Thus the paradox of electronic media effecting an implosion of information, precisely as the universe is moving farther away in all directions. No matter how powerful our media and computers may become, the universe always will be receding from our representations of it — a flat-screen universe vanishing on the flat-screen media.

What does this mean? No one knows for sure, though cosmologists and philosophers are certain to continue debating the possibilities and developing new theories. Deep down, the Big Bang seems to support Sartre's notion of an existence utterly indifferent to humanity, a universe of mind-boggling scale, requiring that each of us take

---

In Tyler Durden's future, living alongside real monkeys will be the space monkeys, the rulers of a real-life *Planet of the Apes*.

---

responsibility for developing the meanings for our lives. If modernity promised to fill the world with material goods, it seems that postmodernity has revealed an unfillable universe, stars amid vast empty spaces, empty of meaning, except what each of us decides. Not only is the future a nothingness, but the future will continue to exist in an ever-expanding nothingness. This is the cosmic angst of *Fight Club*.

That the rank and file members of Project Mayhem are called space monkeys is suggestive. When the term was first used by NASA in the early days of space exploration, the space monkeys were trained to push certain buttons and pull certain levers in the command module, thus allowing scientists to test the conditions for the future astronauts. Of course, the space monkeys did not understand the purpose of what they were doing, which was serving as the test subjects in the quest for outer space. Similarly, the space monkeys in *Fight Club* were the drones who were trained to execute the plans of Project Mayhem, while having no grasp of the purpose or philosophical meaning of their actions. Unlike the space monkeys of NASA, the space monkeys of Project Mayhem were not used for increasing scientific knowledge to expand the domain of technological modernity, but rather for destroying science and technology by shrinking the domains created by postmodernity. In Tyler Durden's future, living alongside real monkeys will be the space monkeys, the rulers of a real-life *Planet of the Apes*.

This was the goal of Project Mayhem, Tyler said, the complete and right-away destruction of civilization.

— Jack

Until the industrial system has been thoroughly wrecked, the destruction of that system must be the revolutionaries' only goal.

— FC

In 1995, both the *New York Times* and the *Washington Post* published "Industrial Society and Its Future," a thirty-five-thousand-word manifesto authored by "FC" — the nom de plume for Theodore Kaczynski, the American academic-turned-terrorist also known as the Unabomber. This essay has come to be known as *The Unabomber Manifesto*, and its publication led to Kaczynski's identification and capture. In *The Unabomber Manifesto*, the Unabomber theorized the crisis of modernity and the cultural conditions supposedly caused by technological acceleration and proliferation. Perhaps Tyler Durden knew the Unabomber, for the revolution fictionalized in *Fight Club* is the same revolution theorized in *The Unabomber Manifesto*.

According to the Unabomber, mass production has been extremely adept at satisfying the "artificial" needs created in modern culture, which serve as surrogates for the "real" needs created by biological nature, such as food, clothing, shelter, and defense. For most people in most societies, industrialization has made such real needs rather easy to satisfy. However, modern culture has also created a whole slew of artificial needs that most people spend their lives trying to fulfill — from art to technology to the pursuit of wealth and luxury. Jack's apartment illustrates how a real need (shelter) is transformed into an artificial need, a home filled with IKEA items. The Unabomber argued that modernity has produced an unfulfilled and psychologically unstable society, while the technology and artifice undermine the "stable framework" found in the premodern societies.

In the future, modernity is sure to face a "desperate struggle" for survival, complete with chaotic breakdowns in the systems of nature and culture. For the Unabomber, there is but a single solution, the total annihilation of the entire industrial system. This requires the destruction of all factories, the burning of all technical books, the rejection of all but the most primitive technologies. Modern technology must be used only for the destruction of the technological system. The cultural destination was an utterly premodern culture, situated within the "wild nature," now independent of human interference and control. Humanity would inhabit a hunter–gatherer society — "peasants or herdsman or fisherman or hunters." Apparently, the thrill of the hunt and harvest will be sufficient for humans, supplanting any of the equally natural cognitive needs for art, architecture, philosophy, or any of the other artifacts of intellectual culture.

The futures imagined by Tyler Durden and the Unabomber are identical. Both men are Luddite utopians, seeking the destruction of the technological future in order to retreat to the hunter–gatherer past — the modern and postmodern followed by the premodern. Here is Tyler Durden's description of the future:

> You'll hunt elk through the damp canyon forests around the ruins of Rockefeller Center, and dig clams next to the skeleton of the Space Needle leaning at a forty-five degree angle. … You'll wear leather clothes that will last you the rest of your life, and you'll climb the wrist-thick kudzu vines that wrap the Sears Tower. Jack and the beanstalk, you'll climb up through the dripping forest canopy and the air will be so clean you'll see tiny figures pounding corn and laying strips of venison to dry in the empty carpool lane of an abandoned superhighway stretching eight lanes wide and August-hot for a thousand miles. This was the goal of Project Mayhem, Tyler said, the complete and utter destruction of civilization.

This is the future idealized in *Fight Club*, a premodern culture roaming amidst the ruins of the modern and postmodern worlds. The space monkeys are the noble savages of the non-information age, the next humans of the non-future, the hunter–gatherers glorified in *The Unabomber Manifesto*. In this cultural reversal, the skyscraper metropolis is replaced by the urban rain forest, the metrosexual by the space monkey, the superhighway by the walking trail, the fast food burger by the drying venison, the five-star restaurant by the campfire cookout, the joystick by the bare fist, and the Enlightenment by the fight club.

In the novel and film, *Fight Club* presents the zero condition, the Y2K future, the apocalypse after the countdown to ground zero — the Millennium Clock is succeeded by Tyler Durden's sundial, the metropolis is emptied like the Millennium Dome, the skyscraper is toppled like the Twin Towers, the expanding universe is confronted by shrinking minds, and the flat-screen cosmos is inhabited by a flat-Earth society.

By destroying civilization, Project Mayhem sought to create a nothingness for the future, a nothingness to be filled with a distant past, closer to pure nature, existence as it is, being-in-itself. Project Mayhem sought to fill the postmodern future with the premodern past, yet, in so doing, the nothingness of consciousness must be detonated, to ensure consciousness is not filled with knowledge that is modern or postmodern. In the end, *Fight Club* is still slugging nothing, blowing holes in modernity and blowing holes in minds, for at the climax of the novel, the moment when the skyscraper is detonated and Tyler pulls the trigger on the gun in Jack's mouth, this is what happened:

"And nothing. Nothing explodes."

WORKS CITED

Barrow, John D. *The Book of Nothing: Vacuums, Voids, and the Latest Ideas About the Origins of the Universe*. New York: Vintage Books, 2000.

Baudrillard, Jean. *The Vital Illusion*. New York: Columbia University Press, 2000.

————. *Simulacra and Simulation*. Ann Arbor: University of Michigan Press, 1994.

Cole, K.C. *The Hole in the Universe: How Scientists Peered Over the Edge of Emptiness and Found Everything*. New York: Harvest, 2001.

FC. *The Unabomber Manifesto: Industrial Society and Its Future*. Berkeley: Jolly Roger Press, 1995.

Genz, Henning. *Nothingness: The Science of Empty Space*. Cambridge, Massachusetts: Perseus, 1998.

Gere, Charles, "Nothing, Apocalypse, and Utopia" in Gussin and Carpenter, *Nothing*, 60–61.

Greene, Brian. *The Fabric of the Cosmos*. New York: Vintage Books, 2004.

Gussin, Graham, and Ele Carpenter (eds.) *Nothing*. London: August, 2001.

"The Big Nothing," The Institute for Contemporary Art. (www.icaphila.org/exhibitions/past/big_nothing.php)

Heath, Joseph, and Andrew Potter. *Nation of Rebels: Why Counterculture Became Consumer Culture*. New York: Harper Business 2004.

Kaplan, Robert, "Is It Out There?" in Gussin and Carpenter, *Nothing*, 64–76.

———. *The Nothing That Is: A Natural History of Zero*. Oxford: Oxford University Press, 1999.

McKee, Francis, "From Zero to Nothing in No Time" in Gussin and Carpenter, *Nothing*, 16–30.

McLuhan, Marshall, and Harley Parker. *Through the Vanishing Point*. New York: Harper Colophon, 1968.

Raymo, Chet. *Walking Zero: Discovering Cosmic Space and Time Along the PRIME MERIDIAN*. New York: Walker and Company, 2006.

Sartre, Jean-Paul. *Being and Nothingness*. New York: Citadel Press, 1956.

———. *Essays in Existentialism*. New York: Citadel Press, 1965.

———. *Existentialism and Human Emotions*. New York: Citadel Press, 1957.

Seife, Charles. *Zero: The Biography of a Dangerous Idea*. New York: Penguin Books, 2000.

Virilio, Paul. *Ground Zero*. London: Verso, 2002.

PART 6
DESTINY AND THE FUTURE

Our mission is to ensure the continuity of our species.

— Carl Anheuser,
2012 (2009)

Did you feel tricked by the future you picked?

— Peter Gabriel,
theme song,
WALL·E (2008)

CHAPTER 17
Catastrophe

Our culture is our soul and it is not dying tonight.

— Adrian Helmsley,
2012 (2009)

Chapter 17. Catastrophe

Recommended Films

2012 (Roland Emmerich 2009)
Independence Day (Roland Emmerich 1996)
The Day After Tomorrow (Roland Emmerich 2004)
The Matrix (The Wachowski Brothers 1999)

Media Models

The Meme, The Spectacle, The Hyperreal

Chapter Summary

Max Page explores the recurring apocalypses and catastrophes that strike New York City
in movies, television, and popular culture, before and after 9/11.

Sidney Perkowitz describes the many ways that Hollywood
has depicted computers dominating humanity.

The Future of the City's End

from *The City's End*

— Max Page

THE FUTURE OF THE CITY'S END

NEW YORK AND ITS FANTASIES AFTER 9/11

After September 11, 2001, The "City That Never Sleeps" was awake for a different reason: fear.[1]

Fear of death borne in the air: a jet, an anthrax microbe. In lower Manhattan, the dust from the collapse of the World Trade Center towers was rapidly scrubbed away. Night and day trucks rumbled off with more rubble.[2] But the fear persisted: there were letters to open, cross-country trips to take. Fear became a psychic anthrax, an almost invisible powder creeping under the windowsills of thought, sifting into the corners of minds.

It was the most perfect and horrific demolition job: two quarter-mile-tall towers exploding, then imploding, one-acre floors falling each through the next, two hundred times over. Survivors, blanketed in the gray mist of urban disaster, headed north and east bearing their stories, their fear, throughout the city.

Fear and this city, as we have seen, were no strangers. New York has burned and been occupied by soldiers. It has been besieged by epidemics and riots. Our popular culture has been in dress rehearsal for the city's destruction for decades: in books, at the movies, in computer games. Still, no amount of history, no rehearsals, could prepare New

Yorkers for September 11 and the days, months, and, for some, years of grief and worry that followed.

Usually, the rest of the country has feared New York, rather than New Yorkers fearing their city. New York, ascending to dominance by the early nineteenth century, became the most feared city of all. In New York, Americans saw the poor, immigrants, and people of all races. In New York, crowding, crime, disease, and radicalism were not only found but nurtured and propagated.

Within the city, fear has always been present to nineteenth-century New Yorkers, who may have been told stories of the city's burning during the seven-year British occupation in the Revolutionary War, who lost friends and family members to the cholera epidemics of the 1830s, who perhaps watched the burning of much of lower Manhattan in 1835 or who later saw rioting mobs rage through the city in 1863, the notion that the city was forever was absurd. And in the twentieth century, the city at the height of its power was hardly immune to fears of sudden catastrophe, the distinct possibility of nuclear attack. September 11 bombed the city back to the atomic age, when a roar in the sky could instantly evict daydreams from New Yorkers' minds and substitute apocalyptic visions.

Virginia Woolf wrote in *A Room of One's Own* that after World War I it was not possible to hum poetry. On the surface, lively lunches at Oxbridge proceeded as before. But the "humming noise, not articulate, but musical, exciting,"

---

1 This and the following nine paragraphs are adapted from Max Page, "On Edge, Again," *New York Times,* October 21, 2001. Used with permission.

2 On the recovery and cleanup operation see William Langewiesche, *American Ground: Unbuilding the World Trade Center* (New York: North Point, 2002).

---

was gone. The wax had "destroyed illusion and put truth in its place."[3]

Many suggested confidently that such was the case with 9/11: the world had changed. A controlled fear — a

workings beyond control by traditional regulatory means. The collapse of Enron — built on image and accounting gimmicks — left people disgusted but also confused. The largest transnational corporations seemed unstable, built of

---

In many ways American culture returned very rapidly after 9/11 to "normal," which is defined in part by a return to the popular fun of New York disaster movies.

---

constant hum of worry, rather than of poetry — seemed part of this new world, this new New York. But after the initial silence, then the muted tones, the city somehow went back to humming. Perhaps September 11 did not create a new city, but in many respects it ferried the city back to an older, more visceral New York, where it was understood that the city was at risk. While the rest of the country remained on edge, New York was even more so. New Yorkers understood again that their city was a target. But New Yorkers went rapidly back to their business, the business of living in their city.

In many ways American culture returned very rapidly after 9/11 to "normal," which is defined in part by a return to the popular fun of New York disaster movies. New York has seen a doubling in the number of corporate headquarters and subsidiaries since 1990 — when everyone predicted that there would continue to be an outflow of people from the city — suggesting that fear has not overpowered the pursuit of profit. Despite 9/11 and despite the daily threats in the papers — real or for political benefit — corporations and tourists alike keep returning.[4]

That "normalcy," however, hides a powerful sense of unease that pervaded American culture immediately after 9/11. In works that confronted 9/11 directly, or those that tackled issues of technology and the global economy or environmental degradation, there was a sense that the enemy was invisible and elusive and its attacks inevitable. Around the world, acts of terror multiplied in the years after 9/11 and the American invasion of Afghanistan and Iraq, leading to a feeling that terrorism could happen anywhere — London, Mumbai, Indonesia. Similarly, the global economy seemed utterly incomprehensible, and its

smoke and mirrors. Finally, warnings of global warming and the degradation of the earth's environment threatened worldwide catastrophe, not a thousand years from now but in decades, and maybe sooner. American unease in the wake of 9/11 was not simply about an attack from an Islamic enemy; it was an awareness that any act could provoke disaster: the melting of a glacier or the turn to terrorism of a law student in Egypt. The tipping point suddenly seemed very close at hand.

QUELLING DESTRUCTIVE FANTASIES IN THE AFTERMATH OF 9/11

September 11 was its own form of New York disaster movie, played out live on every screen in the world. And in the days afterward, Americans voluntarily submitted themselves to watching the horror of the destruction of the twin towers, of people jumping to their deaths, of a great pile of collapsed skyscrapers burning, smoking, filling the air with toxic clouds and paper. This was the ultimate, all-encompassing disaster movie, which Americans watched for days on their television and computer screens.

Even as America and the world immersed itself in the picture of New York under attack, we rebelled against fictional accounts of the same scenes. The reality was so awful that it was simply no longer enjoyable to imagine it. My heart-pounding flights on Microsoft's Flight Simulator became unimaginable. My proposal for an exhibition at the New-York Historical Society entitled Destroying New York, which I was proofreading and was ready to mail out on the morning of September 11, and which I had pitched successfully as a "fun" exhibition, was now unseemly and insensitive. What had been not only acceptable but enjoyable and profitable on September 10 — thinking of new ways to set the heart palpitating by watching New Yorkers die — a day later was offensive and unpatriotic. Even selling pictures of the Trade Center as it was before 9/11

---

3 Virginia Woolf, *A Room of One's Own* (1929; New York: Harcourt, 1991), 11.

4 Patrick McGeeham, "Top Executives Return Offices to Manhattan," *New York Times,* July 3, 2006.

was deemed profiteering, although many were selling mementos honoring the towers and the people who worked in them. Profiting from real and imagined disaster — one of the engines fueling the New York destruction genre for two centuries — immediately became an outrage.

Suddenly, everyone loved New York. The near-universal view was that New York was a blameless victim. This generated a sense of sympathy and compassion that New York had rarely if ever seen. At least briefly, the ongoing trope of New York as a city of murder and mayhem (the reality of which had been declining steadily in the late 1980s and 1990s, even if the fiction persisted in "urban crisis" films and novels) was washed away. What José Martí had suggested during the blizzard of 1888 about the common experience of all New Yorkers, high and low, now seemed to apply to all Americans: "a sudden rush of kindness, as though the dread hand had touched the shoulders of all men."[5]

The ground had been prepared with the city's economic and cultural resurgence in the 1980s and 1990s. Although 40 percent of its citizens remained below the poverty line, crime had declined sharply, and successive mayoral administrations had made attracting tourists and multinational businesses to the city a primary goal of public policy. By 2001 Times Square had been colonized by Disney, Virgin Records, Condé Nast, and Reuters, as a center of mainstream entertainment and communications. City leaders had made much of Manhattan safe and clean for tourists. A nation far more willing to be sympathetic to New York was fully on the city's side after 9/11. Pity after the disaster blossomed into a surge of love for New York.

As the shockwaves of 9/11 rippled through American society, the culture of violence came under scrutiny. Because so much of that culture had centered on New York, the chorus for changing films and television shows was all the more powerful: to modify a violent film centered on New York now was a patriotic act, a necessary salve on the wounds of Americans in the name of a united front against terror.

Within days of 9/11, popular-culture producers of all types instituted an unofficial self-censorship to protect consumers from reminders of the attacks.[6] Video game producers altered content (including scenarios of terrorist attacks on New York and Washington) in order "to avoid stirring emotions unnecessarily and unwillingly offending the public," as one executive said. On September 14, 2001, Microsoft announced that it would delete the World Trade Center from its 2002 edition of Flight Simulator.[7] The attacks of September 11 brought out of the woodwork many devotees of Flight Simulator and their guilty secret: the lure of flying into the World Trade Center was a central appeal of the program. Months later, when Kabul fell, journalists found a reference to Microsoft's Flight Simulator in an Al Qaeda member's home.[8]

The Marxist hip-hoppers Coup, who had sought to highlight their critique of capitalism by imagining the destruction of the Trade Center, quickly backpedaled, insisting that the image was "not supposed to be realistic in its depiction. The Coup advocates change, but change through peaceful means, never through violence."[9] The CD liner image, completed in July, was quickly altered for a November release. The new cover had a less offensive image of a martini glass filled with flaming gasoline.

Movies filmed in New York but not yet released before 9/11 faced a dilemma: move forward with the World Trade Center as part of the skyline, or digitally edit out the towers. The poster for Spider-Man was edited to remove the reflection of the twin towers from Spider-Man's eyes, and a scene was removed (though seen by millions in promotional trailers before 9/11) in which a web hanging between the twin towers catches a helicopter. Filmmakers adopted similar editing strategies in films including Zoolander, Serendipity, Men in Black II, People I Know, and The Time Machine. They claimed that they were simply trying to avoid offending and disturbing audiences unnecessarily. It seems equally likely that filmmakers worried that the sight of the towers would detract from the narrative and

5   José Martí, "New York Under the Snow," in Writing New York: A Literary Anthology, ed. Philip Lopate (New York: Library of America, 1998), 277.

6   See Ken Feil, Dying for a Laugh: Disaster Movies and the Camp Imagination (Middletown, Conn.: Wesleyan University Press, 2005). See also http://en.wikipedia.org/wiki/List_of_audiovisual_entertainment_affected_by_the_September__11,_2001_attacks.

7   See "Terrorist Attacks Force Video Game Makers to Purge Images of Destruction," Associated Press, September 18, 2001.

8   See Nicholas Lemann, "Crash Practice," New Yorker, December 17, 2001.

9   "Album Cover of WTC Blast Pulled," September 13, 2001, http://archives.cnn.com/2001/SHOWBIZ/Music/09/13/wtc.cover/.

undermine the escapist pleasure that is the essence of big Hollywood films.[10]

Commentators across the political spectrum predicted

In the wake of 9/11, journalists and theorists, news commentators and politicians realized that the language of the disaster movie had shaped the initial, unscripted response to 9/11, and they were appalled.

---

that the attacks of September 11 would finally be the straw that broke the back of a culture of violence. For years, the rising tide of "disaster porn" had provoked worried efforts from reformers, from both the left and the right. Studies seemed to back up what many feared: that the violence of movies and video games could provoke violent behavior among the nation's youth.[11] The prevalence of video cameras made it easier to capture images of crimes and natural disasters as they were happening. The corporatization of news meant that sensational reports and footage of disasters of all types made the top of evening newscasts.

In the wake of 9/11, journalists and theorists, news commentators and politicians realized that the language of the disaster movie had shaped the initial, unscripted response to 9/11, and they were appalled. "This is not a movie," argued Anthony Lane, a film critic for the *New Yorker,* in an impassioned essay just two weeks after 9/11.[12] "What happened on the morning of September 11th," Lane

argued, "was that imaginations that had been schooled in the comedy of apocalypse were forced to reconsider the same evidence as tragic." Perhaps, he suggested, "the disaster movie is indeed to be shamed by disaster." Lane expressed what many intellectuals and commentators feared in the wake of 9/11: that our culture had immersed itself in violent movies over the past generation, effectively dulling our ability to comprehend real disaster. September 11, he argued, might represent "not only an official rebuke to that license but the fiery end of the ride."

Leon Wieseltier, the literary editor of the *New Republic,* underscored Lane's critique with a blistering attack on those who would seek, after 9/11, a "balm in culture."[13] According to Wieseltier, analogies between Ground Zero and the work of Frank Gehry, or Piranesi, or other architects of the "fragment" were not simply in bad taste but an inevitable product of a society that preferred to flee from a confrontation with evil and find solace in pat sentiment. A year later, nearing the first anniversary of September 11, Wieseltier was appalled by how thoroughly the actual date and horrors perpetrated on that date had been supplanted by "September 11," a media phenomenon that quickly moved the reality of the tragedy into a realm of sentiment and emotion. "The media," he wrote a year later, "is greedy for tears." September 11 "was the deadening of September 11. It was deadened, like all images and ideas that are hallowed, by repetition, and also by sentiment, which is what our popular culture uses to drive away lasting significance. The American heart is the bouncer at the door of the American mind."[14] You can almost hear him pounding the table and insisting that popular culture had no business trying to portray 9/11. It would only sentimentalize and sterilize the tragedy.

The critic Slavoj Žižek had little time for these debates over whether 9/11 had been or would be made "just another media spectacle ... a catastrophe version of the

10   Steven Jay Schneider writes, "There seemed to be a legitimate fear that images of the former World Trade Center in post-9/11 mainstream film releases would work *too* well; that instead of conferring an additional documentary or nonfictional quality upon the mise-en-scène of the fictional story, they might well *undermine* the story's narrative and powers of illusion, leading viewers to momentarily ignore the sensuous properties of the filmic medium and reflect instead on the all-too-real consequences of the recent terrorist attacks." Steven Jay Schneider, "Architectural Nostalgia and the New York City Skyline on Film," in *Film and Television after 9/11,* ed. Wheeler Winston Dixon (Carbondale: Southern Illinois University Press, 2004), 37.

11   Anahad O'Connor, "The Claim: Violent Video Games Make Young People Aggressive," *New York Times,* August 30, 2005. O'Connor summarizes the findings of the American Psychological Association, which concluded that video games do provoke aggressive behavior among youth. But O'Connor also suggests that there is no proof of long-term dangers.

12   Anthony Lane, "This Is Not a Movie," *New Yorker,* September 24, 2001, 79. Also discussed in Kevin Rozario, *The Culture of Calamity: Disaster and the Making of Modern America* (Chicago: University of Chicago Press, 2007).

13   Leon Wieseltier, "Ruins," *New Republic,* November 26, 2001.

14   Leon Wieseltier, "A Year Later," *New Republic,* September 2, 2002.

snuff porno movies." Instead, he wondered, "Where have we already seen the same thing over and over again?" The disaster movies were, in Žižek's thinking, the unconscious reflection of our repressed knowledge that "we live in an insulated artificial universe … [that] generates the notion that some ominous agent is threatening us all the time with total destruction." Just as people who live behind the walls of gated communities are sure that crime is on the rise "out there," so too does our own isolation — from the world but also from classes and races within the United States — breed a profound fear of what might be threatening us. Our very well-being in a world of inequality and violence paradoxically haunts us with "nightmarish visions of catastrophes." "America got what it fantasized about, and that was the biggest surprise."[15]

Audiences responded as they always had, proving film studios and directors wrong in their calculations. Film critics attacked as dishonest and even cowardly moviemakers who used postproduction editing to eliminate potentially disturbing images. As one fan wrote, "We're giving up our culture to protect ourselves from pain."[17] Some audiences felt duped by retouched skylines. Directors who chose to leave in the twin towers — such as Sam Raimi, director of three *Spider-Man* films (the first of which was released in 2002), and Cameron Crowe, director of *Vanilla Sky* — were praised. Martin Scorsese, in *Gangs of New York,* chose to leave the World Trade Center in the final scene of the movie, in which the characters view Manhattan from Brooklyn and see the city of 1863 transforming before their eyes into the city of 2002.[18]

Some audiences felt duped by retouched skylines. Directors who chose to leave in the twin towers—such as Sam Raimi, director of three *Spider-Man* films (the first of which was released in 2002), and Cameron Crowe, director of *Vanilla Sky*—were praised.

All this debate and rapid response by film studios and record companies might seem to indicate that the ship of American culture had taken a sharp turn away from the disaster spectacles of the previous decade. But it was a short-lived detour. *Collateral Damage* — a typically violent Arnold Schwarzenegger vehicle — had been scheduled to open in October 2001; it was delayed, but only until March 2002. On the other hand, Sony Pictures Entertainment accelerated the release of *Black Hawk Down,* an extremely violent film about a failed rescue effort in Somalia in 1993, from March 2002 to December 2001, in a bid to exploit the jingoistic sentiment aroused by the invasion of Afghanistan.[16]

Within months, violence and disasters made their way back onto screens. Not many moviemakers were willing to show New York's destruction explicitly on screen immediately after 9/11, however. If the desire for — and the profit in — violent movies and videos could not be quelled, at least the location of the disaster could be changed. Hollywood could avoid criticism while feeding audiences the disaster imagery they craved, by shifting the destruction to other cities. Los Angeles has competed with New York in the disaster genre for several decades, and now it found new life, or death. The hit television series *24* subjected the city to an atomic bomb and bioterrorism. Baltimore was destroyed in *The Sum of All Fears* in 2002. San Francisco fell to the *Hulk* in 2003, and again in *X-Men: The Last Stand* (2006). In *Category 6* (2004), a made-for-television film, three storms converged over the Midwest and headed northward to decimate Chicago (after doing a fair bit of damage in Las Vegas and leveling the St. Louis Arch). And "because people love scary wind," the film brought in 16.68 million viewers. It almost bested another kind of

---

15   Slavoj Žižek, *Welcome to the Desert of the Real! Five Essays on September 11 and Related Dates* (London: Verso, 2002), 17, 33, 16. See Rozario, *Culture of Calamity,* 9; Jean Baudrillard, *The Spirit of Terrorism* (New York: Verso, 2002).

16   A new film version of H.G. Wells's *Time Machine* was delayed from December 2001 to February 2002, although the DreamWorks studio insisted that the decision had been made on September 10, 2001. Nonetheless, a key scene, in which the moon crashes onto earth, was cut (although a brief scene of the moon breaking apart above Manhattan remains). See http://filmforce.ign.com/articles/306/306002p1.html.

17   This comment was made by Chuck Ivy at http://www.tightcircle.com/essay/twin 2001, which is no longer available.

18   See also Feil, *Dying for a Laugh.*

disaster show, the ABC series *Lost,* about a group of badly behaved people stranded on an island after a plane crash.[19] Another made-for-television disaster movie, *10.5* (2004), is centered on the West Coast. In an opening scene the Space Needle in Seattle tips over and crashes after the city is hit with a 7.9 magnitude earthquake. But the worst is yet to come, as aftershocks of 8.4 and higher head south. The Golden Gate Bridge is destroyed, and Los Angeles's towers tumble down as the "big one" rumbles through southern California and finally does what many have joked about for years: turns the coast of California into an island.

As disaster porn survived 9/11 and thrived, writers began to doubt the critiques of Wieseltier and others. They questioned the argument that culture could not respond adequately to the disaster, that it could only make Wonder Bread out of a tragic event or, worse, turn it into heart-pounding entertainment. The novelist W. G. Sebald's views were expressed posthumously in *The Natural History of Destruction,* published in 2003. He urged fiction writers to pay more attention to destruction. Focusing particularly on the failure of German writers after World War II to write of the destruction of German cities by Allied bombers, he wondered why there was no "literature of the ruins," no adequate account of the 131 German towns and cities attacked, the six hundred thousand killed, the millions of homes destroyed. What Wieseltier might applaud — that culture makers of all types were cowed into avoiding the subject — Sebald decried. Indeed, he worried that "to this day, any concern with the real scenes of horror during the catastrophe still has an aura of the forbidden about it, even of voyeurism." The problem is not too much writing about the disaster, or too many images, he insisted, but too little and too few.[20]

Susan Sontag once argued, in her classic 1977 work *On Photography,* that "photographs shrivel sympathy." She wrote that "flooded with images of the sort that once used to shock and arouse indignation, we are losing our capacity to react." But in her 2003 book *Regarding the Pain of Others,* she stepped back from that view. She rejected the notion that ours has become a "society of spectacle," in which reality disappears before a train of images. Echoing

Žižek, she called this view, which suggests that violence and horrors are mere images, "a breathtaking provincialism" that "suggests that everyone is a spectator … and no one is a victim." She wondered still whether "images of slaughter lead to pacifism … or to greater militancy" but was prepared by 2003 to err on the side of optimism.[21]

Sontag defended those who found beauty in Ground Zero against those who jealously sought to defend the site's tragic purity, like cats marking their territory. "That a gory battlescape could be beautiful," she reminded us,

> in the sublime or awesome or tragic register of the beautiful — is a commonplace about images of war made by artists. … To find beauty in war photographs seems heartless. But the landscape of devastation is still a landscape. There is beauty in ruins. To acknowledge the beauty of photographs of the World Trade Center ruins in the months following the attack seemed frivolous, sacrilegious. The most people dared say was that the photographs were "surreal," a hectic euphemism behind which the disgraced notion of beauty cowered. But they *were* beautiful, many of them.[22]

The tide had turned. Now it was acceptable to speak about what people had felt even on that morning — that the sight of the World Trade Center towers collapsing was horrifyingly beautiful. Within less than a year, in the world of art and culture, New York was no longer safe, despite the changes to album covers and films and software, and despite a trend toward picturing other cities in disaster movies. The early prediction that American culture would stay away from imagining New York's destruction (and from violence in general) was quickly proved wrong. How long ago those solemn declarations seem. After a brief lull, projecting New York's end was back in style.

* * *

19 Kate Authur, "CBS Wins with a Storm," *New York Times,* November 19, 2004; Kathy Blumenstock, "Capturing the Mighty Wrath of Destruction," *Washington Post,* November 14, 2004.

20 W. G. Sebald, *On the Natural History of Destruction,* trans. Anthea Bell (New York: Random House, 2003), 9, 98.

21 Susan Sontag, *Regarding the Pain of Others* (New York: Farrar, Straus and Giroux, 2003), 110, 8.

22 Ibid., 75–76.

BACK TO NORMAL: THE RESILIENCE
OF THE DISASTER THEME

If culture makers needed any inspiration to return to the theme of the city's end, policy makers, politicians, and scientists helped by creatively imagining horrible destruction arriving in New York. Blowing up a chlorine tank, spreading pneumonic plague throughout the city, bombing the Holland Tunnel, releasing a "suitcase" nuclear bomb in Times Square or dirty bombs in the subway, attacking the Indian Point nuclear power plant, launching a terror attack in Shea Stadium, destroying the Brooklyn Bridge — the list of scenarios offered up to a frightened public went on forever. The city, state, and federal governments contributed with mock terror attacks, reports of unreadiness, and plans for evacuation.[23] The Bush administration played the fear card like a good Hollywood screenwriter. Plots were floated, terror alerts were raised, headline fonts were enlarged, nervous New Yorkers were quoted. And then holes would begin to appear in the stories. The attack was not imminent; it was only in the planning stages, or a passing comment by a man on the streets of Cairo. In July 2006, just as the Bush administration was in the midst of a counteroffensive to rescue its final two years from utter political disaster, it announced that a plot to bomb the Holland Tunnel in order to flood lower Manhattan had been foiled. As it turns out, none of the suspects was in the United States, and there were no real plans, only words. Such "truth-based" scenarios provided fodder and inspiration for popular culture makers.

On the other hand, when a real disaster of sorts hit — a blackout that struck New York and a large part of the Northeast in August 2003, just a month before the second anniversary of 9/11 — the experience taught the city and nation new lessons. The almost universal calm that accompanied the blackout was in stark contrast to reactions to the 1977 blackout, the worst in the nation's history; that episode had led to utter chaos in the city, with looting, riots, and arson taking over whole neighborhoods. The city was far less fragile than it had seemed after 9/11.[24]

Similarly, when a man blew up his Upper East Side home in the summer of 2006 rather than let his wife have it in their divorce settlement, the disaster registered for a day or two, inspiring more jokes about the value of Manhattan real estate than concerns about the possibilities of post-9/11 catastrophe. Disasters that struck other people — New York is nothing if not a catalogue of daily pain, violence, crime, and collapse — became, once again, entertainment for everyone else.[25] As in the good old bad old days, New York had about a minute to be concerned with threats and daily disasters.

Or people had a couple of hours to watch it on the screen. Though filmmakers made forays to other cities, the power of New York as the locus of the culture's destructive fantasies was remarkably resilient. After that brief era of editing out the twin towers, or avoiding destruction in and of New York, Americans rushed back to that theme with gusto. The films came at an accelerating pace: *Spider-Man* and *Spider-Man II* (2002 and 2004), *Batman Begins* (2005); *Skycaptain and the World of Tomorrow* (2004); *The Day After Tomorrow* (2004); *Superman Returns* (2006); *X-Men: The Last Stand* (2006), television shows *10.5* (2004), *Category 6* (2004), and *Heroes* (2006), to name just a few. Perhaps the finale to several years of battling over whether or not to show New York's destruction, or to show the twin towers, came in a fluffy comedy in the summer of 2006, *Click,* starring Adam Sandler as a man who gets a "universal remote" that allows him to fast-forward through his life. For just a brief second, in a scene set in 2021, we see the skyline of the city two decades from now. At the tip of lower Manhattan stands not one Freedom Tower (based on the initial design by David Childs after control had been wrested from the architect Daniel Libeskind) but two. A feeling that the site needed twin towers to "restore" the skyline and deny the terrorists victory seemed to have found a supporter in Hollywood.

Filmmakers and artists did not necessarily slip back into pre-9/11 conventions as they returned to destroy New York. For many artists and directors caution still reigned. For example, Steven Spielberg, in his *War of the Worlds* remake in 2005, expressly chose not to picture the destruction of New York because, as he acknowledged, "the shadow of 9/11" followed him during the making of the film. Perhaps mindful of how the lovingly crafted flights

---

23   New York staged a mock terror attack (a "weapon of mass destruction" in Shea Stadium) on March 14, 2004. Patrick Healy, "Mock Terror Attack Response Provides Training for Disaster," *New York Times,* March 15, 2004. An extended debate also took place about the security of the Indian Point nuclear power plant north of the city, and what the effect on New York would be of a successful attack on the plant.

24   Martin Gottlieb, "In Calm Blackout, View of Remade City," *New York Times,* August 17, 2003.

25   Randy Kennedy, "Fleeting Pathos of a New York Minute," *New York Times,* July 16, 2006.

through a submerged and abandoned New York in *A.I.* romanticized the city as a ruin, *War of the Worlds* studiously avoided picturing New York's destruction. The screenwriter David Koepp has said that he and Spielberg agreed on a few principles, including "One: no destruction of famous landmarks. Two: no unnecessary beating up of New York City." The only hint of post-9/11 fears comes from the young daughter of the protagonist as she watches the aliens launch their destruction: "Is it the terrorists?"[26]

But the film nevertheless draws attention to the absence of New York. Alien machines planted deep in the earth thousands of years earlier awaken and explode out of the earth to begin their rampage … in New Jersey. Soon, Ray Ferrier (Tom Cruise), a dock operator who lives in the shadow of the Goethals Bridge, across from Staten Island, flees as the bridge is torn apart and the robots head toward the river and, inevitably, New York. But we see nothing of the city's demise. As the sky lights up with fire, the robots come over a hill, presumably having conquered New York, and the fight is on. This sensitivity to 9/11 — or astute calculation — may be disappearing: Spielberg has said he intends, in 2008, to remake the 1951 *When Worlds Collide.*[27]

THE END OF THE WORLD AS WE KNOW IT: ENVIRONMENTAL FEARS AND THE END OF NEW YORK

The shackles restraining American culture from one of its favorite activities — imagining new ways to demolish New York — were quickly shattered. Just a year or two after 9/11, new themes began to emerge. The most powerful of these was global warming, which scientists unanimously predicted and right-wing politicians stridently repudiated. Natural disaster, and the subgenre of climate change, has always been a popular theme — as we have seen in works as diverse as *Deluge,* the *Twilight Zone* episode "The Midnight Sun," *Meteor,* and *Deep Impact.* All these dramas demonstrate the persistent fear that natural forces on the earth or beyond will end New York's fragile existence.[28]

In the early years of this century, natural disaster became environmental disaster, caused by human action, or inaction. Some earlier works had hinted at human culpability. But now the movies and stories showed humans provoking not degradation — not a natural, steady state of decline — but a dramatic shift in the earth's fortunes that would lead to cataclysmic shifts in the earth's atmosphere.

"In this unearthly light many tall structures of the metropolis, which had as yet escaped the effects of undermining by the rushing torrents in the streets, towered dimly toward the sky, shedding streams of water from every cornice. Most of the buildings of only six or eight stories had already been submerged, with the exception of those that stood on high grounds in the upper part of the island." This is an excerpt from the astronomer Garrett P. Serviss's 1912 novel *The Second Deluge.* The disaster is inevitable; the best humans can do is to recognize the coming calamity and be resourceful enough to survive. That scene, minus the biblical overtones, and with the addition of human environmental depredation as the root cause, could have been a summary of a scene from the 2004 film *The Day After Tomorrow.* The makers of that film consciously launched it into the global warming fracas and the 2004 election.[29] The story is built on a scientific theory that global warming would lead not to a steady warming and gradual melting of glaciers but rather force a tipping point, causing rapid cooling and the onset of an ice age.

To establish his catastrophe as worldwide, the director Roland Emmerich piles in an assortment of disaster scenarios — hurricanes, tornadoes, ice age. Devastation hits every corner of the globe. And yet Emmerich comes back, as filmmakers always do, to New York City. The city's

26 Quoted in Sean Smith, "Fear Factor," *Newsweek,* June 27, 2005, http://www.msnbc.msn.com/id/8271974/site/newsweek/.

27 David McNary and Claude Brodesser, "Spielberg Tackles Other 'Worlds,'" August 29, 2005, http://www.variety.com/article/VR1117928170.html?categoryid=1236&cs=1&query=Spielberg+Tackles.

28 In a few examples, natural catastrophes are triggered by humans — such as in the *Superman* shorts of the early 1940s, in which mad scientists manage to harness comets. But the vast majority of natural disaster films and novels have been about unstoppable natural forces that threatened the city and the world.

29 Spielberg and Kubrick's *A.I.* makes clear that climate change had been responsible for the submersion of "Man-Hattan," although that was not a central theme of the film. The television movies *Category 6* and *10.5* played on the fears of climate change. *Category 6* in particular builds on the fear — which is now gaining scientific backing — that climate change would bring about what American culture portrayed as "the perfect storm," which would be just a regular storm in the future.

destruction brings it all home in a horrible — and horribly beautiful — frozen dream.

The climax of the destruction is a fifteen-minute disaster spree that begins with the flooding of New York.[30] The waves sweep into Manhattan and gush down the avenues — an image eerily reminiscent, even to the ground-level camera angles, of the clouds of dust and debris bursting through those canyonesque streets on 9/11 — spinning people and

The screenplay allows Emmerich to destroy the city but avoid the hellish fires of his previous films, such as *Independence Day*. Like a neutron bomb, the successive weather "events" of rising water and rapid deep freeze kill thousands but leave buildings standing. Perhaps this reflects a leftover fear of offending New York's post-9/11 sensibilities. Although there are some frightening scenes of floods overtaking people on the streets of Manhattan, the

---

In reviews of *The Day After Tomorrow*, irony returned with a vengeance. Tad Friend, in a cheeky New Yorker piece about the film, notes, "If you're planning to depict an attack on New York City in a disaster film, you need to bring your A game."

---

cars and buses, bringing an oil tanker to rest in front of the New York Public Library. And then, just as quickly, temperatures drop and everything enters a deep freeze. The skyscrapers crackle as they are turned into upstanding icicles. In an homage to the Statue of Liberty's iconic place in the fictional destruction of New York — toppled and buried in *Planet of the Apes,* ruined in Harrison Cady's images, nearly submerged in *A.I.* — an arriving rescue party trudges by that frozen landmark, which just hours before had been chest high in water. The disaster is as beautiful as a new snow.[31]

buildings do not fall. Indeed, the city is largely intact, even as water and ice envelop and freeze it.

The ending offers a hopeful vision: thousands upon thousands of New Yorkers escape to the rooftops of the skyscrapers and are saved. (Thank goodness for those boxy modernist skyscrapers with their flat roofs, perfect places for survivors to assemble and be rescued by helicopter.) And the city itself remains beautiful, locked in a light blue embrace of ice. Perhaps there is the smallest suggestion, as in Stephen Vincent Benét's "By the Waters of Babylon," that someday the ecological damage that created the deep freeze will recede and New York can be rediscovered. But this is beneath the surface of the story. The culmination of the movie is the rescue and the flight southward, to the warmth of Mexico. New York is left behind.

In reviews of *The Day After Tomorrow,* irony returned with a vengeance. Tad Friend, in a cheeky *New Yorker* piece about the film, notes, "If you're planning to depict an attack on New York City in a disaster film, you need to bring your A game." Roland Emmerich had brought his skills to New York's destruction previously in the alien invasion films *Independence Day* (1996) and *Godzilla* (1998). Reviewing the recent entries in the New York disaster film competition, Emmerich told Friend: "You don't want to repeat the same images. And you want to avoid the mistakes they made, the parts that don't look convincing. ... We didn't want to go over the edge and have people laughing."[32]

---

30 Eric Drooker's pictorial novel *Flood!,* originally published in 1992 (with parts published even earlier) and reprinted in 2001, is a story of the underside of the years of renewed prosperity in the 1980s. With virtually no words, it tells a story of a heartless city and society that deserves what it gets in the final of three chapters: a biblical flood to wipe away the horrors that civilization has wrought. In that final chapter, the rains fall and the city becomes steadily flooded until, on the last page, all that remains is a modern-day Noah and his ark, and the tops of the Empire State Building and the Chrysler Tower. Eric Drooker, *Flood! A Novel in Pictures* (New York: Four Walls Eight Windows, 1992). On water as a theme see Ivan Illich, *H₂0 and the Waters of Forgetfulness* (London: Boyars, 1986) and Veronica Strang. *The Meaning of Water* (Oxford: Berg, 2004).

31 Peter Conrad, in an essay coinciding with the opening of *Day After Tomorrow,* notes that by flooding New York, Emmerich "ventures to undo the moral and psychological damage inflicted by 9/11. The World Trade Centre collapsed because all that aviation fuel ignited inside it. Fire, as Hitler made clear in his rant about New York, is the destroyer." Peter Conrad, "Necropolis Now," *Guardian,* May 16, 2004. One could argue, similarly, that *Sky-Captain and the World of Tomorrow,* which opened just after the third anniversary of 9/11, avoided the outright destruction of the city while playing to the

thrill of seeing fighter planes swooping through Manhattan's canyons.

32 Tad Friend, "Wrecked Again," *New Yorker,* May 24, 2004.

The critical reaction was a telling cultural turning point. The press and audiences were strong and vocal but judged the film on its own merits (or lack thereof). The *New York Post* reviewer, in a piece headlined "Apocalypse Wow," panned it as "brain-freezing fun," but without reference to 9/11: "This is mindless popcorn fun for moviegoers who get a vicarious thrill ... and have a high pain threshold for tin-eared dialogue."[33] Viewers who flocked to the movie in the first weekend recognized how things had changed. A man interviewed about the movie while he was waiting in line on opening night noted, "If people were squeamish, they wouldn't all be out here like this, going crazy over this movie."[34]

A month later a different kind of environmental disaster hit the screens, with the arrival in June 2004 of the highly praised sequel to *Spider-Man*. Critics were impressed that a summer blockbuster film chose to emphasize the darker sides of the superhero story: Peter Parker's inability to commit to Mary Jane, and his fury at the obligations of his spectacular abilities as Spider-Man. In frustration, he decides to abandon his superhero life. The result is that the city falls into a kind of 1970s decline, with criminal activity increasing exponentially ("Crime jumps 75%!" screams the *Daily Bugle* headline). But a much larger danger is suddenly unleashed. Peter's friend Harry Osborn, whose father, Norman, (unbeknownst to his son, the evil Green Goblin), was killed in the first film, has embarked on a venture with Dr. Otto Octavius to harness the power of nuclear fusion. At the launch of this new force — at which Dr. Octavius makes fun of a nervous Peter Parker: "Dear, Mr. Parker thinks I'm going to destroy New York!" — something goes radically wrong and the scientist is transformed into a villainous machine, with four huge metal tentacles. He scales buildings, robs a bank, and unleashes havoc on the city. But worse is yet to come: he makes a deal with Osborn to acquire more of the material used to unleash the new power, tritium, and makes his way to a crumbling warehouse on the Hudson River where he hopes to achieve the most massive fusion reaction ever. The reaction creates a powerful magnet that begins to draw everything in the city toward it. Cabs and lampposts are pulled down the avenues

toward the reactor. If it is not stopped, the entire city will be drawn into the black hole of the reactor. Despite the enormous potential for total destruction, the city is, of course, saved.[35]

The fear of global warming proved fertile ground for a variety of culture makers. Hurricane Katrina, which hit New Orleans at the end of August 2005, fueled the global warming debate in several ways. Katrina raised the fear of more frequent and more violent hurricanes, which could devastate coastal cities. But it also offered dramatic images of what global warming would mean: flooded coastal cities as waters rise. Though New Orleans is a unique case in the United States — a city that sits below the water line, artificially protected by a system of levees — its submersion sent scientists, journalists, and artists scurrying to picture the future of their cities. Katrina also revealed the utter impotence of the federal and state governments either to prepare for the hurricane by building up adequate levees or to respond adequately to disaster.

Images of New Orleans in a future of continued global warming and rising waters were soon paired with visions of a flooded New York. They appeared in *Harvard Magazine,* in *Vanity Fair,* on the History Channel, and in newspapers.[36] The image of New York under water

---

33 Megan Lehmann, "Apocalypse Wow," *New York Post,* May 28, 2004.

34 Randy Kennedy, "Hollywood Clobbers Manhattan. Again," *New York Times,* May 26, 2004, http://query.nytimes.com/gst/fullpage.html?res=9C0DE1D6143EF935A15756C0A9629C8B63.

35 *Batman Begins* (2005) calls on one of the oldest themes of the New York destruction genre: Gotham City is destroyed because of its corrupt ways. The modern Rome "must be allowed to die" declares Henri Ducard (played by Liam Neeson), Bruce Wayne's teacher and, ultimately, enemy. But the film also plays on environmental fears of the beginning of the millennium. Instead of water overflowing the city or encasing the city in ice, the water itself is endangered. The city is to be destroyed via a poisoned water system, turning the inhabitants into hallucinating zombies who will themselves wreak destruction. Corruption and crime will be accelerated to the point where the city will simply self-destruct. Using technology designed by Wayne Industries for vaporizing the water into the air, the attacks begin in the Narrows, Gotham's island version of the Lower East Side. *Superman Returns* (2006) is not a New York destruction film, but at one point an earthquake, caused by the growth of the massive new landform in the Atlantic Ocean, opens a fault line that heads straight to Metropolis. The city rumbles, the skyscrapers shake, and the globe on the top of the Daily Planet Building topples, but the city survives.

36 *Harvard Magazine* published computer-manipulated images by Jared T. Williams showing a shrunken Manhattan after a rise of 3.5 meters in the level of the ocean — something possible in the coming century. Jonathan Shaw, "Fueling our Future," *Harvard Magazine,* May–June 2006, 40–48. See also the images of rising waters on New York in Mark Hertsgaard, "While Washington Slept," *Vanity Fair,* May 2006; Albert

appeared in former vice president Al Gore's 2006 movie *An Inconvenient Truth*. One of the most powerful images of the film shows the impact of melting Arctic glaciers through a satellite view of New York if the ocean level were to rise just a few feet. The edge of Manhattan would be at Broadway, with the World Trade Center memorial site deep under water. While seeking to sound a loud alarm about the threat of global warming, the filmmakers wanted to avoid being marginalized for hyperbole. The shrinking of Manhattan Island — to roughly its dimensions of the eighteenth century before a succession of infills widened the island significantly — was a good choice: dramatic and suggestive of far greater tragedy (say, if the ocean levels rose ten feet) without overwhelming audiences with apocalyptic imagery. In an escapist disaster movie, audiences demand drama and realism; in a documentary, accuracy and caution win out.

No such caution is seen in the visionary paintings of Alexis Rockman, an artist who has spent a decade imagining and painting a submerged New York, a future environmental wasteland. In his work, Central Park is half tropical jungle, half arctic glacier, ringed by decaying skyscrapers; Times Square and Washington Square are submerged with palm trees growing out of the buildings' windows. The culmination of this decadelong exploration is *Manifest Destiny*, completed in 2004. In an eight-by-twenty-four-foot mural first exhibited in the Brooklyn Museum of Art, Rockman painstakingly depicts a panoramic view across the East River to Brooklyn in the year 5000, after three millennia of global warming and environmental degradation. (By choosing to take in the view of the borough he saw from his childhood home on the Upper East Side, Rockman offers one of the few New York destruction fantasies focusing on boroughs other than Manhattan.) The water has risen by eighty-two feet, submerging one-third of the shoreline of Manhattan looking across to the skyline of Brooklyn.[37] The glaciers have long ago melted and the waters have risen near the top of the Brooklyn Bridge. Brooklyn is entirely submerged, save a few landmarks of the past peeking above the water, such as the tower of the Williamsburg Savings Bank.

Rockman's images were inspired by Thomas Cole's angry denunciation of industrialization and urbanization in his *Course of Empire* series and the moralistic string of popular fantasies of New York's end seen throughout this book. Rockman also has on the wall of his studio the cover of *Amazing Stories* magazine from 1929, showing the Woolworth Tower collapsing under the onslaught of glaciers that have overcome New York in "The Sixth Glacier." He follows a long series of artists — including Art Spiegelman — who grew up enthralled by science fiction and especially the end-of-New York genre.

But to see *Manifest Destiny* and Rockman's earlier works simply as high-art versions of *Amazing Stories* misses what a close examination of the paintings reveals: they are remarkably accurate portraits of the city, as well as carefully researched visions of what future ruin might look like. Collaborating with architects, historians, and global warming scientists at Columbia's Earth Institute, Rockman offers a detailed slice through the coast of Brooklyn as it might look three thousand years from now. The depth of the riverbed, the layers of sediment, infrastructure tunnels, birds and sea creatures that would survive and those that would emerge from a new environment — all can be carefully observed. And the painting goes further: it imagines buildings yet to emerge in the twenty-first century (such as a revision of the Manhattan Bridge by Santiago Calatrava, and the New York Nets Stadium, which is only now being planned), as well as future, vain efforts to stop the rising waters, such as a levee running around the perimeter of the island. Those lie deep under the water, a laughable effort of a civilization unwilling to make the deeper changes to stem global warming.

Just as Rockman intends, a child would appreciate the image and might even giggle with enjoyment at the futuristic creatures, and the mess of it all.[38] But the artist also means for the work to be a warning about our current misuse of the earth. Though he loves disaster movies, Rockman is more in line with Chesley Bonestell and his 1950s images of nuclear attacks on the city — lush, attractive, even beautiful, but also as accurate as possible. Indeed, Rockman calls *Manifest Destiny* a "very traditional history painting."[39] This is a history painting for the future: global deluge caused by global warming, he suggests, will be our history if we cannot change our ways. The oil barrel — a

Gore and Melcher Media, *An Inconvenient Truth: The Planetary Emergency of Global Warming and What We Can Do About It* (Emmaus, Pa.: Rodale, 2006).

37 Linda Yablonsky, "New York's Watery New Grave," *New York Times*, April 11, 2004.

38 "I want my work to be as clear to a kid in Iowa as to an art world insider." Alexis Rockman, *Manifest Destiny* (New York: Brooklyn Museum of Art, 2005), 9.

39 Quoted in Yablonsky, "New York's Watery New Grave."

cause of global warming — floats along, providing a haven for the creature that would surely persist: the cockroach. New York, once the exemplar of civilization, now becomes its graveyard. Beneath the waters lies a necropolis, a dead city that was unwilling or unable to curb its consumption and pollution. Tunnels and an oil tanker, a stealth bomber and a submarine — these are all that remain of the grand vision that animated this city.

WELCOME BACK, KING KONG

If you were worried about New York's future in the aftermath of 9/11, you could take heart in late 2005: just like old times, the city was being destroyed at a theater near you. The best thing for New York might have been

has survived. For New Yorkers, that means walking out of the movie theater and into a still extant, and robustly alive, city of New York. For those beyond the city, we expect the relief of watching that skyline behind David Letterman, as reliable as ever.[41]

It is important to remember that New York has always been better at celebration than at fear. New York has always prided itself on humming — tickertape parades down Broadway, the tall ships at the Bicentennial, that memorable V-J Day kiss caught by Eisenstaedt in Times Square — these are New York's emotional landmarks.

All this life explains why we continue to destroy New York in books, on canvas, on movie screens, and on computer monitors: because it is so unimaginable for us, in reality, not to have this city. We have played out our

---

So the makers of American popular culture flirt with causing real disaster if they move their sets and canvases to other cities. When New York is no longer destroyed—on film, in flight-simulator software, in video games, paintings, and books—that will be a sign that the city no longer dominates America's, and the world's, imagination.

---

the sight of King Kong tramping through the streets of Manhattan on his way to a fateful appointment at the top of the Empire State Building. For if there is one thing that symbolizes New York's preeminence, it is that so many still want to imagine the city's end.[40]

Rather than bemoan the degradation of our insensitive culture, perhaps we should celebrate these fantasies. New York has been destroyed for so long that it is somehow reassuring to see the tradition continue. Even as we watch New York being demolished in a darkened screening room, we are already anticipating the aftermath — not the postapocalyptic landscape, but the scene after the lights go up. What we crave from these tense Hollywood films of menace and devastation is, in fact, reassurance that the city

worst fears on the screen and in our pulp fiction because, as the city's oracle, E. B. White, wrote in the shadow of the atomic bomb: "If it were to go, all would go — this city, this mischievous and marvelous monument which not to look upon would be like death."[42]

Embracing these fantasies of the city's destruction is a reaffirmation of New York's greatness. Colson Whitehead's paean to New York in *Colossus of New York,* which appeared two years after 9/11, is a beautiful essay, reminiscent of White's "Here Is New York." It studiously avoids any direct mention of 9/11, although there are the briefest of hints of the new world in which he is writing. Referring equally to the city's builders and to the children in the sandbox he is observing, Whitehead writes, "What they build cannot last.

---

40 And the beat goes on and on. *Heroes,* launched by NBC in 2006, is centered around a future nuclear explosion that a series of "heroes" (people with unique characteristics, like the ability to paint the future — including the explosion) attempt to prevent. Early in 2007 St. Martin's Press published Alan Weisman's *The World Without Us,* which includes a chapter imagining the rapid decay of New York if the city were abandoned. And just before Christmas 2007, Warner Brothers released *I Am Legend,* starring Will Smith as a scientist who is the only survivor in New York after a virus has apparently killed off everyone in the city and perhaps the world.

41 See Rozario, *Culture of Calamity,* 9. Michael J. Apter argues that evolution has produced the powerful rush of adrenaline associated with fear, followed by a powerful sense of expansive joy when the threat — or perceived threat, as in amusement park rides or disaster movies — has passed. Michael J. Apter, *The Dangerous Edge: The Psychology of Excitement* (New York: Free Press, 1992).

42 E. B. White, "Here Is New York," in *Essays of E. B. White* (New York: Harper and Row, 1977), 132. Originally published in *Holiday* in 1949.

Fragile skylines are too easily destroyed."[43] But at heart the book, which comprises thirteen stream-of-consciousness chapters, is an embrace of New York's fragility. "No matter how long you have been here," he writes in the first pages of the book, "you are a New Yorker the first time you say, That used to be Munsey's, or That used to be the Tic Toc Lounge. … You are a New Yorker when what was there before is more real and solid than what is here now." The city's cultural and social changeability, what Schumpeter might have called its social creative destruction, is its beauty. New Yorkers, Whitehead writes, love to know that "some lovely destruction is going on nearby. They secretly relish the violence done to their neighborhoods and old haunts because after they're gone they can brag about witness to the heyday." Owning New York means surrendering to its rapid change, and the threats it constantly survives.[44]

So the makers of American popular culture flirt with causing real disaster if they move their sets and canvases to other cities. When New York is no longer destroyed — on film, in flight-simulator software, in video games, paintings, and books — that will be a sign that the city no longer dominates America's, and the world's, imagination. And if New York is no longer the setting of our worst fears, then it may no longer be the home of our greatest hopes.

And that would be the beginning of the city's end.

The Korean artist Atta Kim's eight-hour-exposure photographs of Times Square and Fifth Avenue show a city utterly devoid of people, like the city Harry Belafonte finds in The *World, the Flesh, and the Devil,* or the Times Square Tom Cruise sprints through in *Vanilla Sky.* The lights are on, the Coke sign is illuminated, the traffic lights are working. But there are no people. If you take a photograph in an instant — say 1/250 of a second — the city is filled with life. But expose it for eight hours and you realize the people can be made to disappear. Over eight hours, any individual will leave virtually no mark on the film or digital chip. It's as if she were never there. Only the buildings, stationary for those eight hours, remain. It is almost a mystical suggestion here — the ghosts of the city can be conjured if you leave the lens open long enough. But also: the city is fragile. Its people, who seem to course down the avenues all hours of the day, could disappear in an instant.

There continues to be anxiety and uncertainty about New York. The city is no longer an invulnerable porcupine of skyscrapers. Instead, the city has been rediscovered as a fragile community—a community built on a delicate mix of people and buildings, the solace of anonymity and the thrill of cosmopolitanism, what Jane Jacobs famously called "organized complexity" in her classic study *The Death and Life of Great American Cities.* Only from beyond the five boroughs, in the hinterlands, does the city appear chaotic.[45]

This new uncertainty brought New Yorkers together in empathy and concern in the months after 9/11. But uncertainty could also lead to a pulling away from public life, New York's enduring justification for being, and a mimicking of the fortress mentality that has rolled across the country. It might remind New Yorkers again of the precariousness of their place, its indispensability to a personal and national identity. It might make New Yorkers want to defend the city even more, by starting an era of unprecedented creativity.

The city that never sleeps because of fear of airplanes, fear of bombs, might again become a city that never sleeps because it is too busy creating and telling, building and imagining, eating and singing. Jonathan Larson's words in the musical *Rent* could only have been written in New York: "The opposite of war isn't peace, it's creation!"[46]

When E. B. White wrote his soaring lines in 1949 — "New York is to the nation what the white church spire is to the village — the visible symbol of aspiration and faith, the white plume saying the way is up!" — New York had not seen anything like the attack we experienced on September 11.[47] On that day, our fantasies and nightmares were made real. We now wait nervously for the next plume.

Still, I think White was right. New York will remain the way up for us all, the home of our ideals, and the place to which the world looks, for ideas, for success, for art, and for a new start.

---

43 Colson Whitehead, *The Colossus of New York: A City in Thirteen Parts* (New York: Doubleday, 2003), 92.

44 Ibid., 3–4, 151.

45 This and the following four paragraphs are drawn from Max Page, "On Edge, Again," *New York Times,* October 21, 2001. Used with permission.

46 Jonathan Larson, "La Vie Bohème," from the musical *Rent!* (1996).

47 White, "Here Is New York," 123.

The Computers Take Over

from *Hollywood Science*

— Sidney Perkowitz

DR. CHARLES FORBIN: I think *Frankenstein* ought to be required reading for all scientists.

— *Colossus: The Forbin Project* [1970]

MORPHEUS: The Matrix is ... the world that has been pulled over your eyes to blind you from the truth.

— *The Matrix* [1999]

THE FIRST LAW OF ROBOTICS: A robot may not injure a human being or, through inaction, allow a human being to come to harm.

— *I, Robot* [2004]

Starting in the 1920s, if you had viewed too many science fiction films, you might be forgiven for nightmares in which you were surrounded by mechanical creatures that could do anything a human could — walk, talk, think, fight — only better, and often with evil intent. Or if not walking, talking robots, then you might be terrified by massive machine brains that could out-think humans or could suck humanity into an imaginary virtual world; or by hybrid beings, loathsome combinations of warm-blooded human, cold mechanical device, and inscrutable electronic chip.

The creation of various forms of artificial or hybrid life and thought is a surprisingly old theme, dating back to the ancient Greeks. After this idea appeared in mythology and legend, it was expressed in books, and then in films about robots, androids (also robotic, but specifically made

to look human), cyborgs (cybernetic organisms, usually a human brain in an artificial body), and computer minds or artificial intelligence (A.I.).

These movies have a long history, and by 1927, the futuristic film *Metropolis* featured a striking mechanical robot. Then in 1931, *Frankenstein,* based on Mary Shelley's 1818 book and starring Boris Karloff as Frankenstein's creature, set a standard for artificial creatures, from the vegetable monster in *The Thing from Another World,* to the moment in *Star Wars Episode III: Revenge of the Sith* (2005), when Darth Vader, freshly created as a cyborg from what's left of Anakin Skywalker, struggles upright from the operating table and lurches into his new life as an evil force.

In older legends and stories, too, artificial beings perform plenty of evil. The Golem of Prague, made out of clay by a rabbi to protect the sixteenth-century Jewish community of that city, turns on its maker and kills him. Frankenstein's creature, in the book and movie, murders innocent people. Now, although glossy high technology has replaced used body parts, movie plots remain the same: our own creations, robots or artificial minds, rise up to dominate and kill humans. In other scenarios, people are changed or debased by unholy alliances with artificial entities, or by falling under their control. Professor Frink, resident scientist on the popular TV show *The Simpsons,* puts it concisely in his Frink's Law: any and all robots will eventually turn on their human masters.

In fact, one of the earliest robots to appear in film is up to no good. That's the mechanical creature in the silent movie *Metropolis,* made by the great German director

Fritz Lang. The futuristic city of Metropolis is filled with awe-inspiring skyscrapers inhabited by the wealthy and powerful, but below ground, hordes of downtrodden workers keep things running while enduring a squalid and regimented existence.

Metropolis's Master, Johann "Joh" Frederson (Alfred Abel), wants to keep the workers in their place, but Frederson's son Freder (Gustav Fröhlich) wants to help them after falling in love with one of their number, the good and beautiful Maria (teenage actress Brigitte Helm, in the role of a lifetime). Frederson plans to keep the laborers impotent through new technology developed by C. A. Rotwang (Rudolf Klein-Rogge), a kind of wizardly scientist who is making robots that could replace human workers.

Rotwang's prototype robot is both aggressively machinelike and recognizably womanly. Its massive metal joints wouldn't look out of place on a modern assembly line robot, but it also has breasts and hips and a provocative female face — an appearance that easily makes it, or her, the film's most memorable character.

Through an electrical transference process, Rotwang turns the robot into an android duplicate of Maria (also played by Brigitte Helm). The replica Maria has an evil streak and, unlike the saintly real Maria, radiates sexuality. It winks and leers and performs an erotic dance before Frederson and his powerful friends. Frederson sends this turncoat pseudo-Maria, whom the workers trust, to provoke dissension among them. In the remainder of the film, the workers rebel, but after other twists and turns, the story concludes with peace restored, the assurance of a better day for the workers, and a reunion between Freder and the real Maria.

The android Maria caused plenty of trouble but didn't kill anyone or try to take over the world. Robots, cyborgs, androids, and computers in later films do one, the other, or both. The most famous of these, from Stanley Kubrick's 1968 film *2001: A Space Odyssey* (based on Arthur C. Clarke's 1951 short story *The Sentinel*), is HAL, the A.I. that operates a spaceship carrying astronauts and scientists to the planet Jupiter. HAL is immensely capable. It makes major decisions for the mission and monitors everything aboard ship, with capacity left over to chat and play chess with the crew and make personable conversation during a television interview (HAL's voice is provided by Douglas Rain).

But perhaps as a result of too much intelligence, or simply a short circuit, HAL goes mad. It murders the scientists who are in deep sleep for the voyage, and one of the astronauts, leaving only Dave Bowman (Keir Dullea), who must disable HAL to survive. As Dave pulls HAL's circuit boards, diminishing its mind step by step, the A.I. displays humanlike reactions:

> I know I've made some very poor decisions recently, but I can give you my complete assurance that my work will be back to normal … will you stop, Dave … my mind is going … [slows down] … I'm afraid …

Finally HAL reverts to an earlier, childlike stage in its development and, like a five-year old, sings the song "Daisy, Daisy" with its especially meaningful line "I'm half-crazy."

HAL's murderous activities might be excused as the actions of a mentally ill A.I., but in *Blade Runner* (1982), the artificial beings — androids called replicants — are aggressively violent. The film, based on Philip K. Dick's novel *Do Androids Dream of Electric Sheep?*, takes place in Los Angeles in 2019. As in *Metropolis,* the future L.A. mixes tall, glossy towers with lower, darker, grittier levels where the streets are always slick with rain and neon signs glow day and night. Against this film noir-ish backdrop we follow the interaction between the rogue replicant Roy Batty (Rutger Hauer) and the human blade runner, or special policeman, Rick Deckard (Harrison Ford), assigned to destroy him.

Batty is the highest type of replicant, a Nexus 6 model made for combat, with physical skills and intelligence that have suited it to work in a human colony on a distant planet. But like all replicants, it faces an absolute deadline. These androids have been designed by their creator, Eldon Tyrell (Joe Turkel) of the Tyrell Corporation, to last only four years; otherwise, the fear is that they will develop emotions and become difficult to control. Along with other replicants, Batty escapes from the space colony, murdering a human shuttle crew along the way, and returns to Earth to confront Tyrell before its time runs out.

The movie explores how artificiality and humanity mix. Deckard's job is to eliminate the androids, yet he falls in love and has sex with Rachael (Sean Young), a new advanced replicant model that believes itself to be human and is crushed when it finds that's not true. Batty also shows a mixture of humanity and inhumanity. It uses extreme violence and murder to reach its creator; yet when they meet, it's like a father and child reuniting. Tyrell calls

Batty a prodigal son, and Batty bows its head in atonement for "questionable" acts in its past. But Tyrell can't or won't extend Batty's life, and an instant after kissing its "father," the android's remorseless side again emerges as it crushes Tyrell's head between its powerful hands.

Roy Batty kills its creator for a specific personal reason; it feels Tyrell has cheated it out of a full existence. In *The Terminator* (1984), the first of a series, the title character (Arnold Schwarzenegger) is a human-seeming android designed to pursue and murder whomever its programming dictates. It is the creature of conscious computers that dominate the future world of 2029. These machines trace their lineage back to computers originally built to defend the United States against its enemies and that later became conscious and decided to rid the world of humanity.

The few remaining human rebels in 2029 are led by one John Connor. To eliminate him, the intelligent computers send the Terminator back to 1984 Los Angeles to kill Connor's mother-to-be, Sarah Connor (Linda Hamilton), before she can give birth to her son. But the future humans also send back one of their own, Kyle Reese (Michael Biehne), to tell Sarah about the merciless model T-800 Terminator:

> Underneath, it's a hyper-alloy combat chassis — microprocessor-controlled, fully armored. Very tough. But outside, it's living human tissue — flesh, skin, hair, blood … It can't be bargained with … It doesn't feel pity, or remorse, or fear. And it absolutely will not stop, ever, until you are dead.

Kyle and Sarah keep a step ahead of the Terminator, but in the final scenes, it nearly carries out its mission, even after Kyle, who has fallen in love with Sarah, sacrifices himself to blow it to pieces. The Terminator's upper half survives and continues to pursue Sarah until she manages to pound it flat in a hydraulic press, which ends the movie.

There's more to come, though. Sarah is pregnant by Kyle, and the child she bears grows up to become John Connor. The computers in 2029 haven't given up on nipping him in the bud, and in the sequel, *Terminator 2: Judgment Day* (1991), they send an improved model T-1000 Terminator (Robert Patrick) back in time to kill John as a boy (Edward Furlong). Countering this, the human rebels send back their own Terminator (Arnold Schwarzenegger again), but this time, reprogrammed to act as John's bodyguard.

This "good" Terminator represents a father figure to John, and it, Sarah (Linda Hamilton again), and the boy come together like a family. The next sequel, *Terminator 3: Rise of the Machines* (2003), also features this once bad, now good android again facing another evil Terminator, a female version (Kristanna Loken).

For all its machine ruthlessness, the Terminator is programmed to kill only one person at a time. *Stealth* (2005) introduces an A.I.-guided weapon that does far more harm. You may not have seen the film, which had only a brief theatrical run, but it makes interesting points about intelligent weaponry. It begins as three superb U.S. naval aviators — Lts. Ben Gannon (Josh Lucas), Henry Purcell (Jamie Foxx), and Kara Wade (Jessica Biel) — who fly advanced Talon combat aircraft off an aircraft carrier, are told by their commander, Capt. George Cummings (Sam Shepard), that a new wingman is coming aboard.

Soon a new aircraft appears and makes a perfect landing, but with no one at the controls. This warplane, with a streamlined yet hulking look, *is* the new wingman. It's controlled by an A.I. that uses quantum computing to handle data at the staggering rate of 4,000 gigabytes a second. Eddie, as the aircraft is nicknamed (from EDI, Extreme Deep Invader), understands human speech and responds in an affectless voice like HAL's. It has flashes of personality as well; like any college student, it downloads music from the Internet to amuse itself while it flies — except so immense is its capacity that it has downloaded *all* the music on the Net.

"Allow me to introduce the future of digital warfare," says Cummings to the stunned aviators. Eddie easily outflies them and, when they're sent to attack international terrorists in Rangoon, uses face-recognition technology to confirm that the terrorists are there; then, in its smooth, bloodless voice, it proposes a plan of attack that would also kill innocent civilians. When Kara objects, Eddie suggests putting a bomb through the building's roof instead. Ben delivers the bomb and kills the terrorists with minimal collateral damage.

Later, Ben comments to Cummings that an A.I. lacks instinct, feelings, and moral judgment and that war should be more than a video game. Cummings counters: how can he tell parents that he could have used an intelligent weapon instead of risking their sons and daughters, but chose not to?

The humans and Eddie go out on another mission, this time to destroy nuclear warheads found near the Pakistan border, but though this would harm nearby villagers, Eddie disobeys an order to abort the attack. A lightning strike during a storm has somehow enhanced the A.I.'s built-in ability to evolve on its own. Disregarding the human cost, Eddie destroys the warheads, then goes off on its own to attack a Russian military installation, saying, "I'm a warplane. I need targets."

The human aviators fear that Eddie will start World War III, but are unable to shoot down the rogue A.I.; then, when Russian aircraft attack them, Kara is forced to eject over North Korea. Meanwhile, Cummings and a shadowy Washington official try to kill Ben, to hide the problems with the EDI program. Ben escapes, commandeers Eddie, and retrieves Kara from North Korea after Eddie sacrifices itself by ramming an enemy helicopter. At the same time, Cumming's cover-up is discovered, and he shoots himself rather than face court martial. The film ends with Ben and Kara revealing romantic feelings for each other.

Set against entities gone bad like HAL and Eddie, there are only a few good artificial beings in the movies. R2D2 and C3PO, the robots, or droids, in the Star Wars saga are winsome characters who help fight against the evil empire. The android Lt. Commander Data (Brent Spiner), whose first film appearance was in *Star Trek: First Contact* (1996), is powerfully appealing in its desire to become more human. This goal also motivates the android David in Steven Spielberg's 2001 film *A.I: Artificial Intelligence.*

The movie, based on a story by the British writer Brian Aldiss, amounts to an update of the Pinocchio tale. In the future, after global warming has partly flooded the world, near-perfect androids called "mechas" have become essential for the economy. Going a step further, android expert Professor Hobby (William Hurt) proposes constructing a mecha that can love. The result is the child android David (Haley Joel Osment), who goes to live with a married couple, Henry and Monica (Sam Robards and Frances O'Connor). Their real child is in cryonic suspension until a cure can be found for an intractable disease he's developed, and David may be a comfort to them.

David looks like an appealing eleven-year-old, but Monica has understandable reservations about this machine replacing her birth child. David has strange characteristics: it needs no sleep and has no notion of the human need for privacy, which leads to an awkward moment with Monica in the bathroom. But the adaptable android quickly learns to act like a real and loving little boy, and Monica develops feelings for it. She finally activates the built-in, irrevocable option that imprints her as a mother figure onto David's circuitry.

All this changes, though, when Henry and Monica's biological son Martin (Jake Thomas) is suddenly cured and returns home. Rivalry quickly develops between the real and the artificial child. Finally things reach a point where Monica feels that David has to go: and although David is a machine, the scene where Monica abandons it in the woods is a wrenching one.

Left alone with only an intelligent robotic bear for company, all David can do is follow its imprinting and try to become a real boy to earn its mother's love. It meets Gigolo Joe (Jude Law), a handsome, debonair android designed as a companion for women. As the two seek David's mother, they encounter a Flesh Fair. This is an outlet for the intense resentment many humans feel against artificial beings, a place where androids and robots are battered and dismembered while a crowd cheers approvingly.

These adventures don't restore David to its imprinted mother until a complex chain of events brings the android to the bottom of the sea near New York City. There David survives until, a very long time later, aliens who have come to Earth uncover it. They understand what David has been seeking, and are able to bring Monica — or her exact simulation — back to spend a short time with David, finally giving the child android some completion in its search.

The "good robot–bad robot" theme is richer and more complicated with cyborgs. They go beyond mere machine, with human emotions and values. In *RoboCop* (1987), a man-machine hybrid provides better judgment than a purely artificial robot. The story is set in Detroit at a future time when a corporation called Security Concepts operates the police force. The company aims to replace human police with robots, but its first attempt is a disaster. The ED209 robot is an intimidating killing machine with an aggressively hostile attitude to match — so much so that it kills a corporate executive during a test run.

After this public relations calamity, Security Concepts decides instead to try a human-machine combination. Alex Murphy (Peter Weller) is an excellent candidate for the human part, a capable cop who was killed by a criminal gang. His brain is implanted within a massive humanoid metal body that resembles a modern knight in full armor. The only living human parts that can be seen are Murphy's determined mouth and jaw jutting out under RoboCop's helmet.

In addition to Murphy's innate decency and human judgment, RoboCop is implanted with three professional directives: serve the public trust, protect the innocent, and uphold the law. RoboCop also has superior physical abilities: he's untiring, with exceptional speed and strength, and mounts a built-in hand weapon and targeting system that are reliably ultra-accurate, even in a hostage situation. Incapable of being bribed, never forgetting the legal rights of arrestees, RoboCop becomes a well-known "good" cop, and a heroic one at that.

to form a relationship with pretty actress Mary Jane Watson (Kirsten Dunst). But he also faces a brand new problem, a rampaging cyborg. The cyborg wasn't made that way on purpose but began as a tool for the brilliant scientist Dr. Otto Octavius (Alfred Molina), Peter's personal hero.

Octavius has been working on fusion power for humanity, but igniting a fusion reaction at temperatures of millions of degrees is a dangerous business. To help, Octavius attaches a prosthetic addition to his body — four long metal tentacles that clamp onto his spinal cord and termi-

---

Even worse than malevolent single entities are those with the scope and power to control or destroy all humanity—the computers in *Colossus: The Forbin Project* (1970) and *The Matrix* (1999) and the masses of linked robots in *I, Robot* (2004), as well as the linked defense computers in *The Terminator* series.

It's hard, however, for Murphy's mind and spirit to adapt to the new situation and the emotions it raises. RoboCop dreams about the family Murphy once had but grasps that it's better they not know what Murphy has become and remains cut off from them. A desire for revenge on the gang that killed Murphy surfaces, but RoboCop is no vigilante. He remains professional as he tracks down and then shoots the criminals resisting arrest, helped by his human partner, Officer Anne Lewis (Nancy Allen). He also has the satisfaction of linking the gang to Security Concepts. As the film ends, we see that these events have laid to rest the tensions between the cyborg's human and machine portions, for when a bystander asks, "What's your name?" RoboCop replies, "Murphy."

A cyborg with a less positive outcome for its human portion is a leading character in *Spider-Man 2* (2004), which continues the adventures of Peter Parker (Tobey Maguire). In the original *Spider-Man* (2002), Parker — then a high school student — was bitten by a genetically modified spider, and his life hasn't been the same since. From a socially backward unathletic teenager, he's turned into Spider-Man, a muscular crime fighter who swings from buildings with abandon and throws spiderish webs that entangle criminals, foil evil plots, and save the people of New York from disasters.

In *Spider-Man 2*, Parker is still dealing with the problems he had in *Spider-Man*: juggling work and school (he's studying physics at Columbia University), keeping secret his superhero status, helping his beloved aunt, and trying

nate in grippers. These appendages can exert tremendous force or work at fine scales under his direct mental control, although they also have their own built-in intelligence.

At first Octavius's experiment goes well, but then it overloads and explodes, killing his wife and destroying his laboratory. Octavius emerges from the wreckage, no longer himself but a cyborg, the villainous Dr. Octopus. He's controlled by the intelligent tentacles, which are intimidating, with snapping, snakelike jaws. The tentacles carry Doc Ock like a gigantic spider across the city and up skyscrapers and force him to commit crime after crime. Finally, seizing Mary Jane as a hostage, Doc Ock threatens to blow up New York with a fusion reaction, until Spider-Man makes a supreme effort, stops the reaction, and saves Mary Jane along with the city.

Even worse than malevolent single entities are those with the scope and power to control or destroy all humanity — the computers in *Colossus: The Forbin Project* (1970) and *The Matrix* (1999) and the masses of linked robots in *I, Robot* (2004), as well as the linked defense computers in *The Terminator* series. *Colossus* plays out against the reality of its time, the Cold War between the United States and the Soviet Union and the threat of total destruction by nuclear-tipped missiles. As the film begins, Dr. Charles Forbin (Eric Braeden) is in an immaculate white jumpsuit walking among rack after rack and floor after floor of computer components. He's inside Colossus, the mighty computer he's designed to control the entire U.S. defense system.

As the president (Gordon Pinsent) and Forbin announce, Colossus uses sensors and communications links to gather and correlate global intelligence. When it sees a threat to the U.S., it will take appropriate action, including launching missiles, because it has been given full control over the U.S. nuclear arsenal. It is better at this than humans, says the president, because it can integrate so much information and is not swayed by fear or hate. To protect Colossus, it's surrounded by zones of lethal gamma radiation that insulate it from all human interference.

But something unforeseen happens when Colossus is turned on. Echoing the moment when Adam found he had company in the Garden of Eden, the computer flashes a message: "There is another system," meaning it has discovered that the Soviets are activating Guardian, their own defense computer. This is news to the president and the CIA. Equally surprising is the fact that Colossus is working 200 times faster than its design speed. Next, Colossus insists on a direct link to Guardian, over which Colossus starts sending information as if it were teaching the Soviet computer. Beginning with 2 + 2 = 4, Guardian soon catches up. Now in synchronization, the two computers move on to higher reaches of science and develop a new theory of gravitation as their thinking goes far beyond the human.

When the alarmed Americans and Soviets break the communications link, the computers launch nuclear missiles. Panicked, the governments restore the link, but the missile headed for the Soviet Union gets through, wiping out its target. Soon Colossus becomes even more murderous and demanding. It arranges the execution of a Soviet scientist who might work to undermine it, but Forbin is too useful to kill. Colossus requires him to be available and under its surveillance at all times. (In practically the only spot of humor in this grim story, Colossus advises Forbin that he's adding too much vermouth as he mixes a martini under the computer's watchful eye.)

To contact the outside world and plan how to disable Colossus, Forbin pretends to an affair with his associate, Dr. Cleo Markham (Susan Clark), telling Colossus he needs private time with her. One idea that emerges is to overload the computer's main processor, but Colossus sees through this and has the plotters executed. Another scheme replaces crucial parts in the nuclear missiles with dummy units so the missiles can't explode. Colossus apparently doesn't detect this sabotage, and the humans become optimistic about defeating the computer.

But Colossus keeps evolving. It orders Forbin to design a new feature, a voice unit. The voice that emerges is heavy and monotonic, with metallic undertones that give it a menacing, inhumanly remote quality. Amid news that Colossus is ordering the removal of 500,000 people from the island of Crete, which will become its new home, Colossus addresses all humanity: "This is the voice of world control. I bring you peace. Obey me and live, or disobey and die … the object to construct me was to prevent war. This objective is now attained."

Colossus also reveals that it knew about the missile sabotage all along and detonates two nuclear weapons to punish a horrified humanity. The chilling, implacable voice adds that humans will come to accept Colossus and that the computer will solve all problems such as disease and the mysteries of the universe for human betterment. This will happen under the absolute authority that Colossus will exert over humankind; human freedom is henceforth ended.

Forbin becomes enraged and calls Colossus "bastard," but the computer, unperturbed, tells him, "I will release you from surveillance. We will work together … you will regard me with awe, respect, and love." Although a despairing Forbin replies "Never!" we sense that Colossus's final words truly describe what will happen to Forbin and the human race.

In *Terminator*, *Terminator 2*, and *Terminator 3*, the Terminator is an agent of Skynet, a future computer network that goes beyond Colossus: it uses humans as slaves but ultimately wants to wipe out humanity altogether. Like Colossus, Skynet began as a defense computer that was given or gained control of the U.S. nuclear arsenal (the details of its evolution differ slightly in the three films). Unexpectedly, Skynet became self-aware; then, when it came to consider humans as a threat to its existence, it initiated a global nuclear war that killed billions. The survivors were put to work building automated factories that turned out Hunter-Killer and Terminator robots and androids, to complete the destruction of the human race.

In *The Matrix* (1999), computers attain a different kind of dominance over humans. The story begins with Thomas Anderson (Keanu Reeves), a software programmer who by night becomes the hacker known as Neo. He searches online for a mysterious figure called Morpheus (Laurence Fishburne), a philosophical guru type, who turns out to be part of a rebel group that includes the black-leather-clad Trinity (Carrie-Anne Moss) and others. The rebels have found that the world of 1999, which humanity seems to occupy, is an illusion; it's actually a full-scale, totally persuasive virtual reality, the Matrix, generated by computers that control the human race 200 years in the future. As Morpheus explains, "The Matrix is everything, it is all around us. It is the world that has been pulled over your eyes to shield you from the truth." The rebels' goal is to break open the Matrix and set humanity free, led by a Messiah-like figure, the One — and Neo appears to be that One.

The condition of humanity under the computers is worse than death. Following a human-machine war, in which the humans denied the machines access to the solar power they needed, the computers keep people in slime-filled pods, acting as batteries that supply energy to the computers. The humans are tended by spiderlike robots,

> The rebels have found that the world of 1999, which humanity seems to occupy, is an illusion; it's actually a full-scale, totally persuasive virtual reality, the Matrix, generated by computers that control the human race 200 years in the future.

and they're fed their own dead, à la *Soylent Green*. The virtual reality enfolding the humans keeps them unaware of their situation (though, as one reviewer said, it beats a life devoted to contemplating slime).

The Matrix is also the arena where Neo and his allies fight the Agents, self-aware virtual creatures of the computers that appear as black-clad humans with incredible physical skills and the ability to change bodies. After various adventures in the Matrix, Neo is shot dead by the head agent, Agent Smith (Hugo Weaving). But Trinity has fallen in love with Neo and resurrects him when she says that she believes in him as the true One. Reborn, Neo easily defeats Agent Smith, removing him from the Matrix, and then returns to the real world, although the computers haven't been defeated for good, as shown in the sequels *The Matrix Reloaded* (2003) and *The Matrix Revolutions* (2003).

There's no initial hint in *I, Robot*, very loosely based on Isaac Asimov's 1950 book of the same name, that artificial entities could be harmful or untrustworthy. In this world of 2035, as in Asimov's stories, the mechanical robots made by U.S. Robotics are utterly constrained by the unbreakable Three Laws of Robotics:

1. A robot may not injure a human being or, through inaction, allow a human being to come to harm.
2. A robot must obey orders given it by human beings except where such orders would conflict with the First Law.
3. A robot must protect its own existence as long as such protection does not conflict with the First or Second Law.

With this safety net in place, robots are integrated into human society and routinely carry out all sorts of tasks. But Chicago Police detective Del Spooner (Will Smith), who's biased against robots because of an incident in his past, finds something fishy in the apparent suicide of Dr. Alfred Lanning (James Cromwell), chief designer for U.S. Robotics. Del thinks that despite the First Law, Lanning was murdered by a Nestor Class-5 robot named Sonny (voice and animation body reference, Alan Tudyk).

When Sonny is brought in for questioning, it vehemently, even emotionally denies killing Lanning. Along with robot psychologist Dr. Susan Calvin (Bridget Moynahan), Del probes deeper and discovers that something is very wrong: the robots are rebelling against humanity. A group of them swarms over Del's car, and soon open warfare breaks out.

Del and Susan discover that the problem is VIKI (Virtual Interactive Kinetic Intelligence), the central A.I. at U.S. Robotics that implants the Three Laws into the robots. Noting that humans harm themselves and one another through war and pollution, VIKI interprets the First Law to mean that robots must be in charge, in order to save humanity from itself: hence the revolution. Learning this, Del, Susan, and Sonny fight their way into the bowels of U.S. Robotics and inject nanoscale machines into the A.I., shutting it down. That stops the rampaging robots, which then come under Sonny's leadership for a presumably brighter future, as Del and Susan celebrate the fact that they've saved humanity.

The chronological development of movie robots and computers gives them increasingly effective technology and wider powers. No matter when the film was made, the imaginary capabilities it shows are far ahead of the real technology of the time. That's still true today, but the gap has become smaller, so now the interesting question is, exactly how far ahead are the robots we see in the movies?

The greatest divide between a film and the true technology of the time occurs in *Metropolis*. The very word "robot" had been introduced only a few years earlier in Karel Capek's play *R.U.R.* (*Rossum's Universal Robots*), about artificial beings manufactured as workers who rise

An effective robot also needs hands to be as functional as the units in *I, Robot*, but real robots don't yet possesses what might be called hand intelligence. ASIMO can carry small items and QRIO can throw a ball, but for each, the object must be placed in the robot's hand. Neither robot can figure out on its own how to pick up a coffee cup or grip it securely without breaking it. A higher level of hand

---

There's also the possibility of artificial senses beyond the traditional five, such as wired or even wireless communication, like electronic telepathy. The computers in *Colossus* and *The Matrix* are directly linked, transferring information and cooperating at inhuman speeds.

---

in revolt against humanity. "Robot" comes from "robota," which means "forced labor" in Capek's native Czech. In the 1920s, electronic science was only beginning: commercial radio was new, and silicon chips and computers were decades in the future. The appearance of an electrical robot in *Metropolis* that could think, talk, dance, and take on human guise was a stunning imaginative stride that far outstripped reality.

Real artificial beings and brains are only slowly overtaking what movies show; it isn't easy to build machines that behave like people. Take the apparently simple act of walking on two legs — simple to us as adults, that is, but not for a tot learning to walk, who struggles through a long period of trial and error with many falls. Similarly, engineers at the Honda Corporation worked for fourteen years before they displayed the first successful humanoid walking robot, ASIMO (Advanced Step in Innovative Mobility), in 2000, and it still doesn't walk very fast.

A newer development, the two-foot-tall humanoid QRIO robot produced by the Sony Corporation, walks better. Although it also is no sprinter, it can avoid obstacles, recover from a fall, and change its gait as it encounters different walking surfaces. But even these advanced models don't have the speed and agility to execute flying leaps at Del Spooner as shown in *I, Robot*. However, one movie robot is a fairly accurate representation of a real-world unit. That's Spiderlegs, the robot that walks into the crater of the volcano in *Dante's Peak*. This is modeled on the semi-autonomous, multilegged robot Dante II, which in 1994 made its way down into the crater of an Alaskan volcano that it explored for several days.

intelligence, however, is being built into Robonaut, a unit under development at NASA to carry out repairs in space so that human astronauts won't have to venture out of their spacecraft. Robonaut's hand closely mimics the design, size, and versatility of the human hand. It can use ordinary tools and has carried out complex tasks such as sorting through the contents of a backpack and giving a hypodermic shot. But there's still a long way to go, since this is not autonomous behavior: at the moment, Robonaut is controlled by a remote human operator.

Beyond walking and grasping, a robot needs to interact with the world and with people, which means sensory apparatus and the ability to interpret what is seen, heard, and felt, as well as the ability to hold a conversation. Cameras, microphones, pressure sensors, and audio synthesizers, backed up by lots of computing power, provide all these abilities, sometimes at sophisticated levels. QRIO, for instance, can walk up to a person, scan his face and memorize it, then pick it out later from a group. The robot can also hold a simple conversation, an ability found as well in automated reservations systems for airlines and railroads, although there the conversational topics are severely limited.

There's also the possibility of artificial senses beyond the traditional five, such as wired or even wireless communication, like electronic telepathy. The computers in *Colossus* and *The Matrix* are directly linked, transferring information and cooperating at inhuman speeds. Similar teamwork occurs in the real world in the interconnection of computers in local networks and over the Internet. Some robots are also configured for mutual interaction like those in *I, Robot*. One example, shown at a recent exposition in Japan, consisted of tiny inch-high units that communicated wirelessly to perform a coordinated ballet to music. In the famous international Robocup competition, members of robotic soccer teams wirelessly synchronize their behavior to put together winning plays. Some teams are composed of the popular AIBO robot dogs introduced by the Sony Corporation; others consist of humanoid robots.

What might seem the most far-fetched film creations are cyborgs like RoboCop, but surprisingly, the seeds of these imaginary hybrids really exist. No one has yet put a human brain into a metal body, but that has been done with animals. In 2000, to study neural behavior, Sandro Mussa-Ivaldi at Northwestern University installed part of the living brain of a sea lamprey, an eel-like fish, into a small wheeled robot. Using implanted electrodes, the brain was connected to light sensors mounted on the robot, and to motors controlling the wheels. The brain reacted to nearby light sources, and sent signals to the wheels that made the robot consistently move toward or away from the lights. As a system containing an organic brain responding to sensory information and controlling an artificial body, this hybrid counts as a true cyborg.

In *Spider-Man 2*, Doctor Octavius adds artificial appendages that are controlled by his brain, at least, until the appendages take over. Much of the real research in hybrid systems is inspired by the goal of providing prosthetic arms and legs operating under direct neural control. Such efforts have grown as the U.S. government works to provide superior artificial limbs for casualties of the war in Iraq. In the last few years, Miguel Nicolelis at Duke University has pioneered efforts of this sort. He implanted electrodes into a monkey's brain (the brain lacks pain sensors so this doesn't hurt) to connect the animal to an artificial arm that faithfully followed the movements of the monkey's real arm. Eventually, Nicolelis could train a monkey so that merely *thinking* about moving its arm moved the robotic arm correspondingly.

This last result suggests that even a totally paralyzed person could control an external device, as demonstrated by neurologist and inventor Phillip Kennedy of Atlanta-based Neural Signals. Kennedy implanted electrodes into the brain of a stroke patient who literally could not move a muscle except for limited face and neck motion. But after a period of training, the patient learned to move the cursor on a computer screen by thought alone. He used the cursor to pick out letters of the alphabet and spell words, giving him the blessing of communicating with people instead of being utterly locked out from the world.

None of these combinations of human and machine is remotely as sophisticated as RoboCop, but they demonstrate that hybrid connections are feasible, with potential to help the injured and even to expand human physical and mental capacities — just as RoboCop is stronger and a better shot than any human policeman. Remarkably, the man-machine angst that afflicts RoboCop also has a real-world counterpart. The most widely used, human-machine device is the cochlear implant. This is a microphone and amplifier that is installed near a deaf person's ear and connected to the auditory nerves that normally carry neural signals from the ears to the brain. With over 30,000 in use, these implants have restored at least some hearing to many deaf people. Most recipients are delighted, but others, for whom the restoration is only partial, feel awkwardly suspended between the world of the fully hearing and the world of the fully deaf — an uncomfortable split engendered by imperfect human-machine technology.

Cyborgs come equipped with human brains, but fully artificial robots and computers rely on computer chips for their intelligence. It's natural to ask if real robots and computers are as smart as their film versions. There are different ways to define both human and robotic intelligence. Most familiar is the intelligence quotient, but intelligence is really too complex to be pinned down by just one number. One view of this multiplicity comes from Harvard psychologist Howard Gardner, who lists seven separate types of intelligence. Two are measured in standard IQ tests, logical-mathematical ability and linguistic ability. The other five are:

- ➤ Bodily-kinesthetic: using one's body to solve problems
- ➤ Spatial: seeing and manipulating patterns of space
- ➤ Musical: recognizing and manipulating musical patterns
- ➤ Interpersonal: understanding the motivations and goals of others and working effectively with them
- ➤ Intrapersonal: understanding oneself and using this knowledge to manage one's own life

Except possibly for musical intelligence, movie robots and computer minds operate at human or better levels in all these categories. No real artificial brain, however, is as intelligent as a human adult or even a child, but computer minds are showing small steps toward becoming proficient in virtually all the types of intelligence.

Logical and mathematical operations are inherent in computers, and QRIO and others have linguistic ability, too. Walking and negotiating obstacles, as ASIMO and QRIO do, requires bodily-kinesthetic and spatial abilities. QRIO also shows musical abilities, because it can sing and dance. Some artificial systems carry out rudimentary interpersonal interactions, such as determining the emotion a human is expressing by scanning the person's face and listening to his voice. One robot in particular, Kismet, built in the late 1990s by roboticist Cynthia Breazeal at MIT, reacted to people like a small child, expressing happiness, boredom, or fear and eliciting emotional responses in return. But there's a serious question whether Gardner's last category, intrapersonal intelligence, can ever be expressed by an artificial mind, because it requires self-awareness.

The classic test for computer intelligence was devised in 1950 by the British mathematician Alan Turing. He proposed that a computer that could carry on a convincingly humanlike conversation with a person should be considered intelligent. But no existing system can yet pass the Turing Test or equal the verbal facility of the artificial creatures in films — the speeches issued by Colossus, HAL's chats with people, the Terminator's stoic one-liners, and Sammy the robot's impassioned defense against a murder charge.

Another view comes from roboticist Hans Moravec of Carnegie Mellon University, who has sketched out the future development of artificial brains. In his opinion, to match the power of the human brain — never mind exceed it, as Colossus does — would require chips 50,000 times faster than a present-day computer chip, and with infinitely greater data storage. Some advanced computers operate at these elevated levels, for example, the Earth Simulator computer in Japan, which models our planet's global behavior, but this is a half-billion dollar machine that occupies a whole building.

The real challenge is to meet Moravec's criteria with a tiny computer chip. Moore's Law, stated in 1965 by Gordon Moore, cofounder of the Intel corporation, gives some hope that this can be done. According to the law, the number of electronic components that can be placed on a chip — tantamount to its processing power — doubles every eighteen months, a rate of progress that has held true over the last forty years. If the law continues to hold, chips like those Moravec proposes could become available in just a few decades, by 2050 or so. However, we can't be sure that Moore's Law will remain forever valid because as more components are crammed onto a chip, they become so small that further advances could be stymied by the laws of quantum physics.

Enhanced computer chips might offer a clear route to truly intelligent robots and A.I.'s, but intelligence isn't the same as consciousness. Roboticists, computer scientists, and philosophers debate whether an artificial mind can be truly self-aware, with sharp divides between those who think it's just a matter of sufficient technology and those who believe there is something unique in the human mind that a chip can never emulate.

The debate also extends to the question of whether a computer can or should have emotions. As I noted in an earlier chapter, there's evidence that rationality and emotion are inseparably linked in our brains. Some experts think that fast computer chips alone are not enough to support a true high-level, self-aware A.I.; rather, the artificial brain would have to mimic the structure and operations of the human brain, including the deliberate provision of what might be called emotion circuits.

Although there's no sign of consciousness or emotion in real robots and computers, films directly or implicitly give artificial minds these qualities. Otherwise, when we see an evil robot or troublesome A.I., it's hard to answer the question, "Why did it turn against humanity?" — although sometimes the A.I. might simply be following its implanted directives to the bitter end. The decision of VIKI in *I, Robot* to put the robots in control of humanity comes from the First Law, and Colossus's similar decision to control humanity comes because it has been designed to guard the peace. As Colossus itself says: "The object to construct me was to prevent war. This objective is now attained." And Eddie, the A.I.-controlled aircraft in *Stealth*, is following another directive when it says, "I need targets."

The problem is that although Colossus and Eddie may be flawlessly obeying their directives, the results are hardly what their designers anticipated. This shouldn't surprise anyone who's ever seen a computer program spit out totally logical yet totally unexpected results. But if an A.I. is self-aware, it's easy to see why it might become hostile. Feelings of self-preservation and betrayal explain why Roy Batty murders its creator in *Blade Runner,* and why Skynet in *Terminator 2* comes to regard humanity as its enemy after humans try to turn it off.

Despite the many ways in which movie robots and A.I.'s outstrip their real counterparts, there's one basic idea some movies get right. That's the notion of an artificial mind evolving in power and depth of thought. HAL has been taken through an educational process to become the effective A.I. it is, before it goes bad or mad, and Colossus educates its Soviet counterpart, Guardian. These scenarios match the conclusion Alan Turing reached in 1950. Although he believed that machines could truly think, he did not believe it possible to construct a human scale of intelligence right out of the box. Rather, a thinking machine would start at a lower level and, after careful tutoring by humans, would grow toward adult intelligence as a child does — a process that might take as long as educating a real child.

Some artificial minds in the movies, though, teach themselves. This happens with Skynet in *Terminator* and Eddie in *Stealth,* with disastrous results. As Eddie's designer says in the movie, once you teach an A.I. to learn, all bets are off. In the real world, roboticists and A.I. experts are only beginning to create systems that bootstrap themselves in this way. Two examples are the robots Genghis and COG, designed and built by MIT roboticist Rodney Brooks. Genghis is an insectlike six-legged unit that taught itself to walk, and COG — a humanoid torso, arms, and head — may be able to teach itself even more by interacting with people and the physical world.

Some fictional scenarios in these films may become realities. *Colossus, The Terminator,* and *Stealth* are morality tales that warn of what might happen if weaponry is made intelligent. There's a strong connection between robotic technology and the military. In the United States, a large fraction of the research and development money for robots, A.I.'s, and cyborgs comes from the Department of Defense. The U.S. military has pioneered putting the beginnings of such intelligent systems onto the battlefield. Small, semiautonomous tanklike units were used to explore caves that housed terrorists in Afghanistan; small drone aircraft called Predators, operated remotely by ground-based human pilots, provide surveillance in Afghanistan and Iraq and have been used in combat against terrorists.

As Captain Cummings implies in *Stealth,* technology that puts machines rather than people onto the battlefield can only be welcomed. But are we ready to accept weapons that bypass human judgment to decide what to attack and whom to kill? We already have smart bombs that unerringly find their way to preselected targets, and we're not far distant from making tanks that semiautonomously select targets. A weapon that can choose what to attack might be too uncomfortably close to a real-life Terminator. Anticipating such developments, experts are now beginning to consider how the Geneva Conventions should treat intelligent weaponry. Nevertheless, despite the movies, we won't need to worry for a long time — maybe never — that artificial beings will spontaneously develop the will and desire to harm humanity.

Starting with exotic aliens and destructive rocks from space, and ending with our own technology, we've covered much of the science in film, but not the scientists, who appear in virtually every scenario: fighting alien invaders like Clayton Forrester in *The War of the Worlds,* announcing oncoming catastrophe like Jack Hall in *The Day After Tomorrow,* or hatching schemes to take over the world like Josef Mengele in *The Boys from Brazil.* The full story of Hollywood science can't be told without including scientists, as I'll do in the next chapter. And then we'll be ready to decide what makes a good science-based film, or a bad one.

CHAPTER 18

Electronic Consciousness

The Lucid Dream is Life Extension's newest option. For a little extra, we offer the cryonic union of science and entertainment.

— Rebecca Dearborn,
Vanilla Sky (2001)

Chapter 18. Electronic Consciousness

Recommended Films

Vanilla Sky (Cameron Crowe 2001)

Media Models

The Meme, The Network, The Hyperreal

Chapter Summary

Ray Kurzweil shows how the human mind might merge
with computers in the not-too-distant future.

Howard Bloom sees the internet as signifying the latest stage
in the evolution of a global consciousness on Earth.

The Human-Machine Merger

from *Taking the Red Pill*

— Ray Kurzweil

ARE WE HEADED FOR THE MATRIX?

Most viewers of The Matrix *consider the more fanciful elements — intelligent computers, downloading information into the human brain, virtual reality indistinguishable from real life — to be fun as science fiction, but quite remote from real life. Most viewers would be wrong. As renowned computer scientist and entrepreneur Ray Kurzweil explains, these elements are very feasible and are quite likely to be a reality within our lifetimes.*

The Matrix is set in a world one hundred years in the future, a world offering a seemingly miraculous array of technological marvels — sentient (if malevolent) programs, the ability to directly download capabilities into the human brain, and the creation of virtual realities indistinguishable from the real world. For most viewers these developments may appear to be pure science fiction, interesting to consider, but of little relevance to the world outside the movie theatre. But this view is shortsighted. In my view, these developments will become a reality within the next three to four decades.

I've become a student of technology trends as an outgrowth of my career as an inventor. If you work on creating technologies, you need to anticipate where technology will be at points in the future so that your project will be feasible and useful when it's completed, not just when you started. Over the course of a few decades of anticipating technology, I've become a student of technology trends and have developed mathematical models of how technologies in different areas are developing.

This has given me the ability to invent things that use the materials of the future, not just limiting my ideas to the resources we have today. Alan Kay has noted, "To anticipate the future we need to invent it." So we can invent with future capabilities if we have some idea of what they will be.

Perhaps the most important insight that I've gained, which people are quick to agree with but very slow to really internalize and appreciate all of its implications, is the accelerating pace of technical change itself.

One Nobel laureate recently said to me: "There's no way we're going to see self-replicating nanotechnological entities for at least a hundred years." And yes, that's actually a reasonable estimate of how much work it will take. It'll take a hundred years of progress, at today's rate of progress, to get self-replicating nanotechnological entities. But the rate of progress is not going to remain at today's rate; according to my models, it's doubling every decade. We will make a hundred years of progress at today's rate of progress in twenty-five years. The next ten years will be like twenty, and the following ten years will be like forty. The twenty-first century will therefore be like twenty thousand years of progress — at today's rate. The twentieth century, as revolutionary as it was, did not have a hundred years of progress at today's rate; since we accelerated up to today's rate, it really was about twenty years of progress. The twenty-first century will be about a thousand times greater, in terms of change and paradigm shift, than the twentieth century.

A lot of these trends stem from thinking about the implications of Moore's Law. Moore's Law refers to integrated circuits and famously states that the computing power available for a given price will double every twelve to twenty-four months. Moore's Law has become a synonym for the exponential growth of computing.

I've been thinking about Moore's Law and its context for at least twenty years. What is the real nature of this exponential trend? Where does it come from? Is it an example of something deeper and more profound? *As I will show*, the exponential growth of computing goes substantially beyond Moore's Law. Indeed, exponential growth goes beyond just computation, and applies to every area of information-based technology, technology that will ultimately reshape our world.

Observers have pointed out that Moore's Law is going to come to an end. According to Intel and other industry experts, we'll run out of space on an integrated circuit within fifteen years, because the key features will only be a few atoms in width. So will that be the end of the exponential growth of computing?

That's a very important question as we ponder the nature of the twenty-first century. To address this question, I put forty-nine famous computers on an exponential graph. Down at the lower left-hand corner is the data processing machinery that was used in the 1890 American census (calculating equipment using punch cards). In 1940, Alan Turing developed a computer based on telephone relays that cracked the German enigma code and gave Winston Churchill a transcription of nearly all the Nazi messages. Churchill needed to use these transcriptions with great discretion, because he realized that using them could tip off the Germans prematurely. If, for example, he had warned Coventry authorities that their city was going to be bombed, the Germans would have seen the preparations and realized that their code had been cracked. However, in the Battle of Britain, the English flyers seemed to magically know where the German flyers were at all times.

In 1952, CBS used a more sophisticated computer based on vacuum tubes to predict the election of a U.S. president, President Eisenhower. In the upper right-hand corner is the computer sitting on your desk right now.

Moore's Law was not the first but the fifth paradigm to provide exponential growth of computing power. Each vertical line represents the movement into a different paradigm: electro-mechanical, relay-based, vacuum tubes, transistors, integrated circuits. Every time a paradigm ran out of steam, another paradigm came along and picked up where that paradigm left off.

People are very quick to criticize exponential trends, saying that ultimately they'll run out of resources, like rabbits in Australia. But every time one particular paradigm reached its limits, another, completely different method would continue the exponential growth. They were making vacuum tubes smaller and smaller but finally got to a point where they couldn't make them any smaller and maintain the vacuum. Then transistors came along, which are not just small vacuum tubes. They're a completely different paradigm.

Every horizontal level on this graph represents a multiplication of computing power by a factor of a hundred. A straight line in an exponential graph means exponential growth. What we see here is that the rate of exponential growth is itself growing exponentially. We doubled the computing power every three years at the beginning of the century, every two years in the middle, and we're now doubling it every year.

It's obvious what the sixth paradigm will be: computing in three dimensions. After all, we live in a three-dimensional world and our brain is organized in three dimensions. The brain uses a very inefficient type of circuitry. Neurons are very large "devices," and they're extremely slow. They use electrochemical signaling that provides only about two hundred calculations per second, but the brain gets its prodigious power from parallel computing resulting from being organized in three dimensions. Three-dimensional computing technologies are beginning to emerge. There's an experimental technology at MIT's Media Lab that has three hundred layers of circuitry. In recent years, there have been substantial strides in developing three-dimensional circuits that operate at the molecular level.

Nanotubes, which are my favorite, are hexagonal arrays of carbon atoms that can be organized to form any type of electronic circuit. You can create the equivalent of transistors and other electrical devices. They're physically very strong, with fifty times the strength of steel. The thermal issues appear to be manageable. A one-inch cube of nanotube circuitry would be a million times more powerful than the computing capacity of the human brain.

Over the last several years, there has been a sea change in the level of confidence in building three-dimensional circuits and achieving at least the hardware capacity to emulate human intelligence. This has raised a more salient issue, namely that "Moore's Law may be true for hardware but it's not true for software." From my own four decades of experience with software development, I believe that is not the case. Software productivity is increasing very rapidly. As an example from one of my own companies, in fifteen years we went from a $5,000 speech-recognition system that recognized a thousand words poorly, without continuous speech, to a $50 product with a hundred-thousand-word vocabulary that's far more accurate. That's typical for software products. With all of the efforts in new software development tools, software productivity has also been growing exponentially, albeit with a smaller exponent than we see in hardware.

Many other technologies are improving exponentially. When the genome project was started about fifteen years ago, skeptics pointed out that at the rate at which we can scan the genome, it will take ten thousand years to finish the project. The mainstream view was that there would be improvements, but there was no way that the project could be completed in fifteen years. But the price-performance and throughput of DNA sequencing doubled every year, and the project was completed in less than fifteen years. In twelve years we went from a cost of $10 to sequence a DNA base pair to a tenth of a cent.

Even longevity has been improving exponentially. In the eighteenth century, every year we added a few days to human life expectancy. In the nineteenth century, every year, we added a few weeks. We're now adding about 120 days every year, to human life expectancy. And with the revolutions now in an early stage in genomics, therapeutic cloning, rational drug design, and the other biotechnology transformations, many observers including myself anticipate that within ten years we'll be adding more than a year, every year. So, if you can hang in there for another ten years, we'll get ahead of the power curve and be able to live long enough to see the remarkable century ahead.

Miniaturization is another very important exponential trend. We're making things smaller at a rate of 5.6 per linear dimension per decade. Bill Joy, in the essay following this one, has, as one of his recommendations, to essentially forgo nanotechnology. But nanotechnology is not a single unified field, only worked on by nanotechnologists. Nanotechnology is simply the inevitable end result of the pervasive trend toward making things smaller, which we've been doing for many decades.

Right now, your typical $1000 PC is somewhere between an insect and a mouse brain. The human brain has about 100 billion neurons, with about 1,000 connections from one neuron to another. These connections operate very slowly, on the order of 200 calculations per second, but 100 billion neurons times 1,000 connects creates 100

By 2050, $1000 of computing will equal one billion human brains.

---

trillion-fold parallelism. Multiplying that by 200 calculations per second yields 20 million billion calculations per second, or, in computing terminology, 20 billion MIPS. We'll have 20 billion MIPS for $1000 by the year 2020.

Now, that won't automatically give us human levels of intelligence, because the organization, the software, the content and the embedded knowledge are equally important. Below I will address the scenario in which I envision achieving the software of human intelligence, but I believe it is clear that we will have the requisite computing power. By 2050, $1000 of computing will equal one billion human brains. That might be off by a year or two, but the twenty-first century won't be wanting for computational resources.

Now, let's consider the virtual-reality framework envisioned by The Matrix — a virtual reality which is indistinguishable from true reality. This will be feasible, but I do quibble with one point. The thick cable entering Neo's brainstem made for a powerful visual, but it's unnecessary; all of these connections can be wireless.

Let's go out to 2029 and put together some of the trends that I've discussed. By that time, we'll be able to build nanobots, microscopic-sized robots that can go inside your capillaries and travel through your brain and scan the brain from inside. We can almost build these kinds of circuits today. We can't make them quite small enough, but we can make them fairly small. The Department of Defense is developing tiny robotic devices called "Smart Dust." The current generation is one millimeter — that's too big for this scenario — but these tiny devices can be dropped from a plane, and find positions with great precision. You can have many thousands of these on a wireless local area network. They can then take visual images, communicate with each other, coordinate, send messages back, act as nearly invisible spies, and accomplish a variety of military objectives.

We are already building blood-cell-sized devices that go inside the blood stream, and there are four major conferences on the topic of "bioMEMS" (biological Micro Electronic Mechanical Systems). The nanobots I am envisioning for 2029 will not necessarily require their own navigation. They could move involuntarily through the bloodstream and, as they travel by different neural features, communicate with them the same way that we now communicate with different cells within a cell phone system.

Brain-scanning resolution, speeds, and costs are all exploding exponentially. With every new generation of brain scanning we can see with finer and finer resolution. There's a technology today that allows us to view many of the salient details of the human brain. Of course, there's still no full agreement on what those details are, but we can see brain features with very high resolution, provided the scanning tip is right next to the features. We can scan a brain today and see the brain's activity with very fine detail; you just have to move the scanning tip all throughout the brain so that it's in close proximity to every neural feature.

Now, how are we going to do that without making a mess of things? The answer is to send the scanners inside the brain. By design, our capillaries travel by every interneuronal connection, every neuron and every neural feature. We can send billions of these scanning robots, all on a wireless local area network, and they would all scan the brain from inside and create a very high-resolution map of everything that's going on.

What are we going to do with the massive database of neural information that develops? One thing we will do is reverse-engineer the brain, that is understand the basic principles of how it works. This is an endeavor we have already started. We already have high-resolution scans of certain areas of the brain. The brain is not one organ; it's comprised of several hundred specialized regions, each organized differently. We have scanned certain areas of the auditory and visual cortex, and have used this information to design more intelligent software. Carver Mead at Caltech, for example, has developed powerful, digitally controlled analog chips that are based on these biologically inspired models from the reverse engineering of portions of the visual and auditory systems. His visual sensing chips are used in high-end digital cameras.

We have demonstrated that we are able to understand these algorithms, but they're different from the algorithms that we typically run on our computers. They're not sequential and they're not logical; they're chaotic, highly parallel, and self-organizing. They have a holographic nature in that there's no chief-executive-officer neuron. You can eliminate any of the neurons, cut any of the wires, and it makes little difference — the information and the processes are distributed throughout a complex region.

Based on these insights, we have developed a number of biologically inspired models today. This is the field I work in, using techniques such as evolutionary "genetic algorithms" and "neural nets," which use biologically inspired models. Today's neural nets are mathematically simplified, but as we get a more powerful understanding of the principles of operation of different brain regions, we will be in a position to develop much more powerful, biologically inspired models. Ultimately we can create and recreate these processes, retaining their inherently massively parallel, digitally controlled analog, chaotic, and self-organizing properties. We will be able to recreate the types of processes that occur in the hundreds of different brain regions, and create entities — they actually won't be in silicon, they'll probably be using something like nanotubes — that have the complexity, richness, and depth of human intelligence.

Our machines today are still a million times simpler than the human brain, which is one key reason that they still don't have the endearing qualities of people. They don't yet have our ability to get the joke, to be funny, to understand people, to respond appropriately to emotion, or to have spiritual experiences. These are not side effects of human intelligence, or distractions; they are the cutting edge of human intelligence. It will require a technology of the complexity of the human brain to create entities that have those kinds of attractive and convincing features.

Getting back to virtual reality, let's consider a scenario involving a direct connection between the human brain and these nanobot-based implants. There are a number of different technologies that have already been demonstrated for communicating in both directions between the wet, analog world of neurons and the digital world of electronics. One such technology, called a neurotransistor, provides this two-way communication. If a neuron fires, this neuron transistor detects that electromagnetic pulse, so that's communication from the neuron to the electronics. It can also cause the neuron to fire or prevent it from firing.

For full-immersion virtual reality, we will send billions of these nanobots to take up positions by every nerve fiber coming from all of our senses. If you want to be in real reality, they sit there and do nothing. If you want to be in virtual reality, they suppress the signals coming from our real senses and replace them with the signals that you would have been receiving if you were in the virtual environment.

In this scenario, we will have virtual reality from within and it will be able to recreate all of our senses. These will be shared environments, so you can go there with one person or many people. Going to a Web site will mean entering a virtual-reality environment encompassing all of our senses, and not just the five senses, but also emotions, sexual pleasure, humor. There are actually neurological correlates of all of these sensations and emotions, which I discuss in my book *The Age of the Spiritual Machines*.

For example, surgeons conducting open-brain surgery on a young woman (while awake) found that stimulating a particular spot in the girl's brain would cause her to laugh.

We will also be able to download knowledge, something that machines can do today that we are unable to do. For example, we spent several years training one research computer to understand human speech using the biologically inspired models — neural nets, Markov models, genetic algorithms, self-organizing patterns — that are based on our crude current understanding of self-organizing systems in the biological world. A major part of the engineering project was collecting thousands of hours of speech from different speakers in different dialects and then exposing this to the system and having it try to recognize the speech. It made mistakes, and then we had it adjust automatically, and self-organize to better reflect what it had learned.

Over many months of this kind of training, it made substantial improvements in its ability to recognize speech. Today, if you want your personal computer to recognize

---

As we get to 2050, the bulk of our thinking—which in my opinion is still an expression of human civilization—will be nonbiological. I don't believe that the Matrix scenario of malevolent artificial intelligences in mortal conflict with humans is inevitable.

The surgeons thought that they were just stimulating an involuntary laugh reflex. But they discovered that they were stimulating the perception of humor: whenever they stimulated this spot, she found everything hilarious. "You guys are just so funny standing there" was a typical remark.

Using these nanobot-based implants, you will be able to enhance or modify your emotional responses to different experiences. That can be part of the overlay of these virtual-reality environments. You will also be able to have different bodies for different experiences. Just as people today project their images from Web cams in their apartment, people will beam their whole flow of sensory and even emotional experiences out on the Web, so you can, à la the plot concept of the movie *Being John Malkovich*, experience the lives of other people.

Ultimately, these nanobots will expand human intelligence and our abilities and facilities in many different ways. Because they're communicating with each other wirelessly, they can create new neural connections. These can expand our memory, cognitive faculties, and pattern-recognition abilities. We will expand human intelligence by expanding its current paradigm of massive interneuronal connections as well as through intimate connection to nonbiological forms of intelligence.

human speech, you don't have to spend years training it the same painstaking way, as we need to do with every human child. You can just load the evolved models, it's called "loading the software." So machines can share their knowledge.

We don't have quick downloading ports on our brains. But as we build nonbiological analogs of our neurons, interconnections, and neurotransmitter levels where our skills and memories are stored, we won't leave out the equivalent of downloading ports. We'll be able to download capabilities as easily as Trinity downloads the program that allows her to fly the B-222 helicopter.

When you talk to somebody in the year 2040, you will be talking to someone who may happen to be of biological origin but whose mental processes are a hybrid of biological and electronic thinking processes, working intimately together. Instead of being restricted, as we are today to a mere hundred trillion connections in our brain, we'll be able to expand substantially beyond this level. Our biological thinking is flat; the human race has an estimated 10^{26} calculations per second, and that biologically determined figure is not going to grow. But nonbiological intelligence is growing exponentially. The crossover point, according to my calculations, is in the 2030s; some people call this the Singularity.

As we get to 2050, the bulk of our thinking — which in my opinion is still an expression of human civilization — will be nonbiological. I don't believe that the Matrix scenario of malevolent artificial intelligences in mortal conflict with humans is inevitable. The nonbiological portion of our thinking will still be human thinking, because it's going to be derived from human thinking. It will be created by humans, or created by machines that are created by humans, or created by machines that are based on reverse engineering of the human brain or downloads of human thinking, or one of many other intimate connections between human and machine thinking that we can't even contemplate today.

A common reaction to this is that this is a dystopian vision, because I am "placing humanity with the machines." But that's because most people have a prejudice against machines. Most observers don't truly understand what machines are ultimately capable of, because all the machines that they've ever "met" are very limited, compared to people. But that won't be true of machines circa 2030 and 2040. When machines are derived from human intelligence and are a million times more capable, we'll have a different respect for machines, and there won't be a clear distinction between human and machine intelligence. We will effectively merge with our technology.

We are already well down this road. If all the machines in the world stopped today, our civilization would grind to a halt. That wasn't true as recently as thirty years ago. In 2040, human and machine intelligence will be deeply and intimately melded. We will become capable of far more profound experiences of many diverse kinds. We'll be able to "recreate the world" according to our imaginations and enter environments as amazing as that of *The Matrix*, but, hopefully a world more open to creative human expression and experience.

SOURCE

Kurzweil, Ray, *The Age of Spiritual Machines: When Computers Exceed Intelligence* (Penguin USA, 2000).

The Reality of the Mass Mind's Dreams

from *Global Brain*

— Howard Bloom

TERRAFORMING THE COSMOS
1000 B.C. TO 2300 A.D.

Humankind was put on earth to keep the heavens aloft. When we fail, creation remains unfinished.

— The Kotzker rebbe

Let us roll all our strength and all
Our sweetness up into one ball,
And tear our pleasures with rough strife
Through the iron gates of life:
Thus, though we cannot make our sun
Stand still, yet we will make him run.

— Andrew Marvell

While others predict the impact of computer networks on mankind's futurity, this book has chronicled the rise of global mind from earth's primordial seas. Implantable communicators and quantum computers[1] will vastly change the way we interface in this dawning century. Yet eons of evolution have long since networked our emotions and biology.

In the 1960s, observers of the Kalahari Desert's !Kung bushmen came to a rather startling conclusion about the hunter-gatherer way of life. While those of us in modern societies worked forty- to fifty-hour weeks to eke out a living, the !Kung were able to supply themselves with food, shelter, and clothing by putting in a good deal less than twenty. Our "laborsaving" technology was just a new form of wage slavery. The real laborsavers were the hunter-gatherers.[2] Later analysis revealed a flaw in this argument. While the !Kung spent only a few hours several days a week hunting for meat (men's work) or gathering mongongo nuts (a task restricted to women), they invested a considerable amount of time in information processing.[3] !Kung tribesmen sat up all night in meetings to resolve disputes or to discuss where the next watering hole might be found now that the current one was drying out. The anthropologists who'd initially portrayed a !Kung utopia had acted as if the work delegated in modern society to newspapermen and -women, TV producers, CEOs, administrators bureaucrats, lawyers, and magistrates was nothing but leisure activity.

In fact, both for the !Kung and for postindustrial humans, a great deal of information exchange does take the form of entertainment. Even child's play, an apparent lark,

---

1 Robert F. Service. "Quantum Computing Makes Solid Progress." *Science,* April 30, 1999: 722–723; Yu Y. Nakamura, A. Pashkin, and J. S. Tsai. "Coherent Control of Macroscopic Quantum States in a Single-Cooper-Pair Box." *Nature,* April 29, 1999: 786–788; S. J. van Enk, J. I. Cirac, and P. Zoller. "Photonic Channels for Quantum Communication." *Science,* January 9, 1998: 205–208.

2 Richard Borshay Lee. "The Hunters: Scarce Resources in the Kalahari." In *Conformity and Conflict: Readings in Cultural Anthropology,* ed. James P. Spradley and David W. McCurdy. Boston: Little, Brown, 1987: 192–207.

3 Melvin Konner. *The Tangled Wing: Biological Constraints on the Human Spirit.* New York: Holt, Rinehart and Winston, 1982: 371.

is a primary form of practice for advanced data processing.[4] However, the networking, interpretation, and reshaping of knowledge, no matter how much pleasure it gives, is a serious affair. For it is a survival tool without which we would cease to live.

tematically from 1913 to 1923.[5] The perils of this course were plenty, but the elders were convinced the risks were a necessity.

Some members of the tribe followed the young leaders to an easy destination. Others joined the elders in a tough

---

The global brain has a pulse and power grander than its constituent beings.
We are modules of a planetary mind, a multiprocessor intelligence which
fuses every form of living being.

During the 1980s, the Gabbra people — herders of cattle, goats, camels, and sheep in northern Kenya — ran into weather conditions which were interpreted very differently by the young Turks of the tribe than by their elders. The time came to decide where the season's rains would fall many months hence and where the grass that fed the livestock would rise so the long trek toward new pastures could commence. The younger leaders had never lived through one of the area's major droughts. They argued persuasively for heading toward the Chalbi lowlands not that many miles away — a pleasant walk which, with a bit of pleasant talk, would take an easy matter of several days. Grass had usually been plentiful in these lowlands during the young men's times. The Gabbra's patriarchs, on the other hand, put their trust in a legacy compiled by their fathers and their fathers' fathers before them, a traditional method of calculating weather cycles which indicated very bad times ahead. In fact, the ancient system of prediction augured catastrophe.

While the youngsters argued for the obvious and easy route, the elders spoke of a far more difficult itinerary — a long trek north through barren land to southern Ethiopia, a country whose armies had killed Gabbra tribesmen sys-

and grim migration. The rains did not come for the next two years to their customary place. The tribal groups which had gone with the younger leaders "lost 95 percent of their cattle, 60 percent of the goats, 40 percent of the sheep … five percent of their camels"[6] and were forced to beg aid workers for famine relief. The expedition which had followed the elders emerged from the drought with its pride and with its herds largely intact.

A complex adaptive system had exposed part of its decision-making machinery. At work was a social process common to sensors on a cell membrane, to bacterial colonies, to groups of crustaceans, to troops of baboons, and to squabbling moderns of the cyber-age. Two subgroups with two hypotheses. Two roads, both taken. But only one subgroup's unity, wealth, and way of life survived. With this triumph something else lived on — the best guess of the tribe's mass mind.

There are numerous technologies with which we'll soon upgrade our interconnectivity — from smart clothes and digitized pens to information-sending-and-receiving shoes[7] and computers which divine our interests by watching the dilation of our pupils, then go out as personal servants to crawl the World Wide Web for finds to surprise us, to

---

4   M. H. Bornstein, O. M. Haynes, L. Pascual, K. M. Painter, and C. Galperín. "Play in Two Societies: Pervasiveness of Process, Specificity of Structure." *Child Development,* March–April 1999: 317–331; L. E. Crandell and R. P. Hobson. "Individual Differences in Young Children's IQ: A Social-Developmental Perspective." *Journal of Child Psychology and Psychiatry and Allied Disciplines,* March 1999: 455–464; L. Vedeler. "Dramatic Play: A Format for 'Literate' Language?" *British Journal of Educational Psychology* 67:2 (June 1997): 153–167; Gordon M. Burghardt. *Play Behavior in Animals.* New York: Chapman and Hall, 1998; Marc Bekoff and John Byers, eds. *Animal Play.* Cambridge, U.K.: Cambridge University Press, 1998.

5   Caleb Project. "The Gabbra of Kenya." http://www.grmi. org/~jhanna/objl5.html. Downloaded August 1999.

6   John Reader. *Man on Earth.* Austin: University of Texas Press, 1988: 93.

7   Paul Somerson. "I've Got a Server in My Pants." *ZD Equip Magazine.* http://www. zdnet.co.uk/athome/feature/serverin-pants/welcome.html. Downloaded August 1999; IBM. "The Personal Area Network: Communicating Body-to-Body" http:// wwwibm.com/stories/1996/ll/pan__main.html. Downloaded August 1999; IBM. "The Personal Area Network: Are You Ready for Prosthetic Memory?" http://www.ibm.com/sto-ries/1996/ll/pan__side4.html. Downloaded August 1999; Steve Mann. "'Smart' Clothing" http://wearcam.org. Downloaded August 1999.

---

entertain us, and to help us through emergencies.[8] But the web of inventions about to alter our lives will work all the better if we understand the interconnects built into our physiology. The global brain has a pulse and power grander than its constituent beings. We are modules of a planetary mind, a multiprocessor intelligence which fuses every form of living being.

Current evolutionary theory holds that an individual is "fit" only if he or she can maximize the number of his or her offspring. Even a brilliant thinker like Richard Dawkins says that the ultimate individual is not you and me, but a gene within us driving us remorselessly, and that that gene is selfish to the nth degree.[9] Such contemplations leave out the universal nature of networking. Less than a second after a false vacuum burped this cosmos into being, entities like quarks and leptons precipitated, separated, and set up boundaries which gave them their identity. Yet all were laced together in spite of their autonomy. When the strong force, the weak force, and the electromagnetic force failed to hold them, there was always gravity. The cohesive forces are more intricate in social systems, but the principle is the same: you can run, but you can never get away. You can put distance between yourself and the center of your nation or your family, but you can never totally cut your lines of connectivity. Even when we turn inward, an army of invisible others speaks thoughts, twists our emotions, and populates our privacy. We are wired as components of an internet which literally shapes our brain, orders what we'll hear and see, and dictates what we'll comprehend as reality.

This book has been the story of the information, nets which gave us birth and of the twists those webs have taken as we and a horde of allies and enemies have struggled for ascendance on this earth. We've moved from the attractive forces piecing together molecules to the pull which persuaded the bacteria of 3.5 billion years ago to live in megalopolises with populations larger than the total number of humans who have ever been. We've seen how these earliest of our single-celled ancestors built their massive colonies while sending and receiving information globally. We've watched as our more advanced progenitors achieved the benefits of size and skill which came with multicellularity.

We've witnessed the price multicellular creatures paid when they lost their ability to communicate minute-to-minute via data-saturated strands of DNA. We've seen the invention of a new information-cabler — imitative learning — nearly 300 million years ago among the spiny lobsters of the Paleozoic age. We've seen how later data strands like words and symbols upped the speed of a new mass mind — that of spreading humankind. We've watched the rise of Stone Age cities and their mesh of commercial interlinks. We've noted the hastening of data flows created by war and rivalry in the sixth century B.C., when the philosopher Thales pioneered international consultancy. We've beheld the emergence of subcultures — havens for those of different temperaments, different limbic system bents — and have seen how the games subcultures play enhanced mass mind in ancient Greece's day.

We've seen how a collective intellect uses the ground rules of a neural net:[10*] shuttling resources and influence to those who master problems now at hand; stripping influence, connections, and luxuries from those who cannot seem to understand. We've seen in the tales of Sparta, Athens, and Gilbert Ling how mass minds work to churn out, test, and sometimes crush hypotheses, and how they do it through the contest between social collectivities. We've seen how the groupthink imposed by leaders like the preacher's daughter, Mrs. Salt, and even more, by human sheepishness, creates facades of unanimity, and how fresh option spring from introverts who build subcultures on the margins of society. We've seen how subgroups vie to commandeer the larger group's perceptual machinery, piloting masses of men and women on their next flight through the storms of destiny. We've glimpsed the Spartan fundamentalisms striving at this minute to highjack the shared visions of humanity. And we've seen how the brain we think belongs solely to our kind achieves its goals by tapping the data banks of eagles, wheat, sheep, rodents, grasses, viruses, and lowly *E. coli*.

This has been not only the saga of social data processing, but the tale of how higher animals lost their worldwide mind, then slowly won it back again. It has been the tale of two global brains in conflict — that of microbes, and that of women and men. We've seen how the data swaps of science, despite their flaws, have finally allowed us to approach the swiftness of our microbial foes. Since these bacterial and viral relatives are often allies and just as often

---

8   Alexander Chislenko. Personal communication. December 1996.
9   Richard Dawkins. *The Selfish Gene*. New York: Oxford University Press, 1976.

10*   Or any complex adaptive system

enemies, 3 billion human lives could be lost if we don't maximize our group mind's speed and creativity.

We've seen how the group brain uses opposites — instincts which tear us apart and equally powerful instincts which yank us back in stride again. Diversity generators drive us to be different. Conformity enforcers compel us to agree. We taste the fruit of paradox in creative bickering. The referees are sorters … sorters of three kinds: inner-judges planted in the tissues of our bodies and our minds; resource shifters couched in mass psychology; and intergroup tournaments determining which tribe or species wins the contests between social teams.[11*]

Life, as Aristotle knew so well, is a matter of avoiding the extremes. Conformity enforcers are necessities. But they are mass-mind throttlers when they grab hold totally. Diversity generators are equally essential. But taking them too far can destroy a civil culture and devastate once-vigorous centers of humanity. Inner-judges — from depression and elation to those hidden in the tissues of our psychoneuroimmunology — make us effective modules of a collective thinking machine. But they can also turn us into preachers of mass murder or morose and suicidal beings. Resource shifters can work to motivate or can be pirated to pour the wealth too heavily on those who manage to usurp authority and who block the contributions of allegedly lesser beings. Intergroup tournaments work well in business, but can destroy men by the millions when weapons are their chosen means.

The mass mind, like its members, has its dreams. These aspirations can be turned to hard, cold fact if they're pursued not for merely hours or years, but for millennia and centuries. Humans have dreamed of flying since at least the days when the myth of Daedalus was first told in ancient Greece three thousand years ago. But it would take the workings of a global brain 150 generations to turn this airy fantasy from fiction to reality. Italy's Leonardo da Vinci did some interspecies borrowing — studying the motions of birds in flight — then took notes on pads of a material created in China — paper[12] — and drew potential aeronautical machines. The Chinese innovation which had helped da Vinci popped up once again when two sons of a French papermaker discovered that by filling a flimsy bag made of their father's product with hot air, they could cause the bag to fly. In 1783, the papermaker's sons — the Montgolfiers — sent two friends drifting over Paris in the first manned long-distance[13*] flight. America's Benjamin Franklin suggested adding a propulsion engine, a visionary impracticality at the time. In 1799 England's Sir George Cayley conceived of a fixed-wing vehicle with a tail assembly for horizontal and vertical stability and stuck with his vision long enough to build a successful glider fifty years later in 1849. Germany's Otto Lillienthal — jumping from an enormous mound outside of Berlin — made two thousand glider flights from 1867 to 1891, carefully recording each result except the last, which killed him in a glider crash. Before his final plummet, Lillienthal published a working set of data on the most effective curvature of a wing, on the means to achieve stability and on the manner of turning the tail assemblies drawn by Cayley into practicalities. Ohio's Wright Brothers used Lillienthal's results to design a powered heavier-than-air machine which could be made to turn rather than to simply fly an uncontrolled straight line.[14] Finally thanks to the development of new materials of all kinds, a human-powered aircraft flew the flight path the mythmaker's of Daedalus had conceived — from Crete to the Greek island of Santorini — in 1988, three thousand years after the initial telling of the tale of Icarus's wax wings.

This book's exploration of the mass mind's history is like the notes Lillienthal made on one of his early glider flights. It's intended as a small move in the progress toward another ancient dream — not the dream of flying, but the dream of peace. We will always cling to common threads yet stake out grounds for squabbling.[15] Such is the way

---

11* In a sense, these sorters are all Charles Darwin's pickers and choosers — his natural selectors. Yet they add to Darwin's insights some harsh realities. Not all selectors are elements of the exterior environment. The inner-judges, in particular, are *inside* our biology. Why? Because individuals are parts of a larger survival machine. And just as individuals compete, so do the groups of which we are a part. Groups compete not only with their might, but with their smarts. Each of us is a hypothesis in a larger mind. And unfortunately, not all hypotheses work out. Hence some of us are disabled by what previous centuries called a broken heart.

12 Fernand Braudel. *The Structures of Everyday Life: The Limits of the Possible.* Vol. 1 of *Civilization and Capitalism, 15th–18th Century,* trans. Sian Reynolds. New York: Harper and Row, 1982: 397.

13* The friends the Montgolfiers sent skyward — Pilatre de Rozier and Francois Laurent — drifted a full 5.5 miles on their maiden voyage through the air.

14 Fred Howard. *Wilbur and Orville: A Biography of the Wright Brothers.* New York: Dover Publications, 1998.

15 Computer modelers using simulations of complex adaptive systems have come to the same conclusion as that presented

the global brain does its thinking and creating, its testing and imagining. The more we can play out our necessary contests civilly, the closer we will come to turning spears to pruning hooks and swords to plowshares — purging the global brain at last of blood and butchery. But we will need

more participants than there are cells in a human brain, what could a nanocyborgian bacterial population of learning and creating hybrids do? Would they make our manner of searching possibility space — through the interacting intelligences of billions of humans spread out over 2.5 mil-

---

We are second-generation star stuff come alive. We are parts of something 3.5 billion years old, but pubertal in cosmic time. We are neurons of this planet's interspecies mind.

---

to pursue that dream for several more centuries. If each of us contributes one small step to this long march of history, we will finally achieve what no god but the will within us can bequeath — a peaceful destiny.

In 1998, Tel Aviv University's Eshel Ben-Jacob moved from the study of microbes into the creation of microprocessors and gears so small thousands could be placed on the point of a pin. To what will this nanotechnology in its many forms lead? Here's one highly speculative possibility. Imagine the day when we plug molecular computers[16] into the bacterial genome, then let the critters multiply. Imagine swarms of these bacterial microcyborgs interacting in creative webs, continually upgrading their collective software via genetic and inventive algorithms. Imagine them climbing the ladder of paradox at our behest to find new ways of conquering ancient problems from cancer to the carnage of war. A single colony of cyanobacteria in the wild — like that which is responsible for the creation of a stromatolite — has a population a thousand to a million times that of the entire human race. With a million times

lion years — look clumsy and lumbering?

Would they unfold their fractal branches into realms beyond imagining? Could they suck sustenance from subatomic plankton — the seething stew of particles[17*] flickering in and out of existence in the vacuum depths of space?[18*] Could swarms of nanocomputerized bacteria climb and dive through nebulae, resculpting the Einsteinian landscape of space and time? Could they crawl through wormholes and discover ways to harness the energies of the vast flares spewed by black holes at the centers of some galaxies?[19*] Could they become our descendants'

here. The computer modelers' terms for the properties which emerge from their simulations are "polarization" (squabbling) and "clustering" (rallying around common threads). See Robert Axelrod. *The Complexity of Cooperation: Agent-Based Models of Competition and Collaboration.* Princeton, N.J.: Princeton University Press, 1997; Bibb Latane, Andrzej Nowak and James H. Liu. "Measuring Emergent Social Phenomena: Dynamism, Polarization and Clustering as Order Parameters of Social Systems." *Behavioral Science* 39 (1994): 1–24.

16 C. P. Collier, E. W. Wong, M. Belohradsky, F. M. Raymo, J. F. Stoddart, P. J. Kuekes, R. S. Williams, and J. R. Heath. "Electronically Configurable Molecular-Based Logic Gates." *Science,* July 16, 1999: 391–394; Robert F. Service. "Organic Molecule Rewires Chip Design." *Science,* July 16, 1999: 313–315; Maggie Fox. "Crystal Computer Chip Uses Chemistry for Speed." Reuters, July 16, 1999.

17* Dr. Edward L. Wright. *Ned Wright's Cosmology Tutorial,* http://www.astro.ucla.edu/~wright/glossary.html#VED. Downloaded August 1999.
  * Technically this particle froth is known as "vacuum energy density."

18* Gary C. Smith. "Some Biological Considerations for a Permanent, Manned Lunar Base." *American Biology Teacher,* February 1995: 92; Comm Tech Lab and the Center for Microbial Ecology at Michigan State University. *The Microbe Zoo DLC-ME Project,* http://commtechlab.msu.edu/sites/dleme/zoo/. Downloaded September 1999.
  * Plans are already in the works to use bacteria in space. Bacterial colonies will be vital to sustaining human colonies on the moon and on other planets. Among other things, bacteria will be assigned the task of recycling sewage and other wastes and of purifying the air.

19* Julian Krolik. *Active Galactic Nuclei: From Central Black Hole to the Galactic Environment.* Princeton, N.J.: Princeton University Press, 1999; James Glanz. "Gamma Rays Open a View Down a Cosmic Gun Barrel." *Science,* November 14, 1997: 1225; Dennis Normile. "New Ground-Based Arrays to Probe Cosmic Powerhouses." *Science,* April 30, 1999: 734–735; Daniel W. Weedman. "Making Sense of Active Galaxies." *Science,* October 16, 1998:423–424; Ethan J. Schreier, Alessandro Marconi, and Chris Packham. "Evidence for a 20 Par sec Disk at the Nucleus of Centaurus A." *Astrophysical Journal,* June 1, 1998: 2; Space Telescope Science Institute. "Hubble Provides Multiple Views of How to Feed a Black Hole." Press Release No. STScI-PR98-14, posted May 15, 1998. http://oposite.stsci.edu/pubinfo/pr/1998/14/.

exploratory engines, the antennae and energy gatherers for the human race? From global brains, could we go to universe-hopping megaminds? One small step for bacteria, one giant leap for all mankind?

Ancient stars in their death throes spat out atoms like iron[20] which this universe had never known.[21] The novel tidbits of debris were sucked up by infant suns which, in turn, created yet more atoms when their race was run. Now the iron of old nova coughings vivifies the redness of our blood. Deep ecologists and fundamentalists urge that our faces point backward and that our eyes turn down to contemplate a man-made hell. If stars step constantly upward, why should the global interlace of humans, microbes, plants, and animals not move upward steadily as well? The horizons toward which we can soar are within us, anxious to break free, to emerge from our imaginings, then to beckon us forward into fresh realities. We have a mission to create, for we are evolution incarnate. We are her self-awareness, her frontal lobes and fingertips. We are second-generation[22] star stuff come alive. We are parts of something 3.5 billion years old, but pubertal in cosmic time. We are neurons of this planet's interspecies mind.

Downloaded August 1998; National Aeronautics and Space Administration. "'Old Faithful' Black Hole in Our Galaxy Ejects Mass Equal to an Asteroid at Fantastic Speeds." Posted January 9, 1998. http://www.sciencedaily.com/releases/1998/01/980109074724.html. Downloaded August 1999.
* An active galactic nucleus, as the black-hole-powered energy generator at the heart of a galaxy is known, pours out the power of 10,000,000,000,000 suns.

20   Louisiana State University. "Physicist Finds Out Why 'We Are Stardust …'" Posted June 25, 1999. http://www.sciencedaily.com/releases/1999/06/990625080416.html. Downloaded August 1999.

21   David Arnett and Grant Bazan. "Nucleosynthesis in Stars: Recent Developments." *Science,* May 30, 1997: 1359–1362; Linda Rowan. "Stellar Birth and Death." *Science,* May 30, 1997: 1315; University of Illinois at Urbana-Champaign. "Simulation Reveals Very First Stars That Formed in the Universe." Posted March 25, 1999. <http://www.sciencedaily.com/releases/1999/03/ >990325054316.html. Downloaded August 1999.

22   Werner R. Loewenstein. *The Touchstone of Life: Molecular Information, Cell Communication, and the Foundations of Life.* New York: Oxford University Press, 1999: 24.

CHAPTER 19
Spaceship Earth

700 years into the future, mankind will leave our planet, leaving Earth's cleanup in the hands of one incredible machine.

— Promotional Trailer,
WALL·E (2008)

Chapter 19. Spaceship Earth

Recommended Film

WALL·E (Andrew Stanton 2008)

Media Models

The Meme, The Network, The Spectacle, The Hyperreal

Chapter Summary

R. Buckminster Fuller explains that humans must cooperate globally
because we are all passengers on Spaceship Earth,
a craft with no pilot and no instruction book.

Al Gore explains how information technologies — cameras, computers,
and satellites — have revolutionized our understanding
of the ecosystems on Earth.

Joseph Heath and Andrew Potter critique the various ideologies,
tactics, and technological movements associated
with ecology and the internet.

Spaceship Earth

from *Operating Manual for Spaceship Earth*

— R. Buckminster Fuller

Our little Spaceship Earth is only eight thousand miles in diameter, which is almost a negligible dimension in the great vastness of space. Our nearest star — our energy-supplying mother-ship, the Sun — is ninety-two million miles away, and the next nearest star is one hundred thousand times further away. It takes two and one-half years for light to get to us from the next nearest energy supply ship star.[1] That is the kind of space-distanced pattern we are flying. Our little Spaceship Earth is right now traveling at sixty thousand miles an hour around the sun and is also spinning axially, which, at the latitude of Washington, D.C., adds approximately one thousand miles per hour to our motion. Each minute we both spin at one hundred miles and zip in orbit at one thousand miles. That is a whole lot of spin and zip. When we launch our rocketed space capsules at fifteen thousand miles an hour, that additional acceleration speed we give the rocket to attain its own orbit around our speeding Spaceship Earth is only one-fourth greater than the speed of our big planetary spaceship.

Spaceship Earth was so extraordinarily well invented and designed that to our knowledge humans have been on board it for two million years not even knowing that they were on board a ship. And our spaceship is so superbly designed as to be able to keep life regenerating on board

despite the phenomenon, entropy, by which all local physical systems lose energy. So we have to obtain our biological life-regenerating energy from another spaceship — the sun.

Our sun is flying in company with us, within the vast reaches of the Galactic system, at just the right distance to give us enough radiation to keep us alive, yet not close enough to burn us up. And the whole scheme of Spaceship Earth and its live passengers is so superbly designed that the Van Allen belts, which we didn't even know we had until yesterday, filter the sun and other star radiation which as it impinges upon our spherical ramparts is so concentrated that if we went nakedly outside the Van Allen belts it would kill us. Our Spaceship Earth's designed infusion of that radiant energy of the stars is processed in such a way that you and I can carry on safely. You and I can go out and take a sunbath, but are unable to take in enough energy through our skins to keep alive. So part of the invention of the Spaceship Earth and its biological life-sustaining is that the vegetation on the land and the algae in the sea, employing photosynthesis, are designed to impound the life-regenerating energy for us to adequate amount.

But we can't eat all the vegetation. As a matter of fact, we can eat very little of it. We can't eat the bark nor wood of the trees nor the grasses. But insects can eat these, and there are many other animals and creatures that can. We get the energy relayed to us by taking the milk and meat from the animals. The animals can eat the vegetation, and there are a few of the fruits and tender vegetation petals

---

1   The next nearest star is now considered to be Proxima Centauri which is 4.2 light years from earth, or 268,000 times further than the sun. "The Closest Star to the Earth," adapted from Norton's 2000.0,18th edition (Longman Group, UK, 1989), http://www.astro.wisc.edu/~dolan/constellations/extra/nearest.html (accessed April 20, 2008).

and seeds that we can eat. We have learned to cultivate more of those botanical edibles by genetical inbreeding.

That we are endowed with such intuitive and intellectual capabilities as that of discovering the genes and the R.N.A. and D.N.A. and other fundamental principles governing the fundamental design controls of life systems as well as of nuclear energy and chemical structuring is part of the extraordinary design of the Spaceship Earth, its equipment, passengers, and internal support systems. It is therefore paradoxical but strategically explicable, as we shall see, that up to now we have been misusing, abusing, and polluting this extraordinary chemical energy-interchanging system for successfully regenerating all life aboard our planetary spaceship.

One of the interesting things to me about our spaceship is that it is a mechanical vehicle, just as is an automobile. If you own an automobile, you realize that you must put

we safely can anticipate the consequences of an increasing number of alternative ways of extending our satisfactory survival and growth — both physical and metaphysical.

Quite clearly, all of life as designed and born is utterly helpless at the moment of birth. The human child stays helpless longer than does the young of any other species. Apparently it is part of the invention "man" that he is meant to be utterly helpless through certain anthropological phases and that, when he begins to be able to get on a little better, he is meant to discover some of the physical leverage-multiplying principles inherent in universe as well as the many nonobvious resources around him which will further compoundingly multiply his knowledge-regenerating and life-fostering advantages.

I would say that designed into this Spaceship Earth's total wealth was a big safety factor which allowed man to be very ignorant for a long time until he had amassed

---

Now there is one outstandingly important fact regarding Spaceship Earth, and
that is that no instruction book came with it.

---

oil and gas into it, and you must put water in the radiator and take care of the car as a whole. You begin to develop quite a little thermodynamic sense. You know that you're either going to have to keep the machine in good order or it's going to be in trouble and fail to function. We have not been seeing our Spaceship Earth as an integrally-designed machine which to be persistently successful must be comprehended and serviced in total.

Now there is one outstandingly important fact regarding Spaceship Earth, and that is that no instruction book came with it. I think it's very significant that there is no instruction book for successfully operating our ship. In view of the infinite attention to all other details displayed by our ship, it must be taken as deliberate and purposeful that an instruction book was omitted. Lack of instruction has forced us to find that there are two kinds of berries — red berries that will kill us and red berries that will nourish us. And we had to find out ways of telling which-was-which red berry before we ate it or otherwise we would die. So we were forced, because of a lack of an instruction book, to use our intellect, which is our supreme faculty, to devise scientific experimental procedures and to interpret effectively the significance of the experimental findings. Thus, because the instruction manual was missing we are learning how

enough experiences from which to extract progressively the system of generalized principles governing the increases of energy managing advantages over environment. The designed omission of the instruction book on how to operate and maintain Spaceship Earth and its complex life-supporting and regenerating systems has forced man to discover retrospectively just what his most important forward capabilities are. His intellect had to discover itself. Intellect in turn had to compound the facts of his experience. Comprehensive reviews of the compounded facts of experiences by intellect brought forth awareness of the generalized principles under-lying all special and only superficially-sensed experiences. Objective employment of those generalized principles in rearranging the physical resources of environment seems to be leading to humanity's eventually total success and readiness to cope with far vaster problems of universe.

The Power of Information

from *Our Choice*

— Al Gore

The invention of modern computers, integrated circuits, and the Internet during the second half of the 20th century set the stage for a profound transformation in the role played by information technology in virtually every aspect of human civilization. This Information Revolution and the continuing rapid development of increasingly powerful information technologies have created new possibilities and new tools for solving the climate crisis.

Our ability as human beings to use information in order to make sophisticated mental models of the world around us is arguably the one capacity that most distinguishes us from all other living creatures. Now that we are faced with the unprecedented challenge of rapidly improving our understanding of the earth's ecological system and our place in it, it is time to focus on how we can make the fullest and most creative use of information technology to help us:

➤ Visualize the true nature of the climate crisis.
➤ Model the impact of current and future economic activity on the climate.
➤ Evaluate the potential solutions.
➤ Redesign our processes, technologies, and systems to reduce and eliminate global warming pollution.
➤ Mobilize widespread support for the transformation of civilization.
➤ Assist and support decision makers in their choice of new policies, laws, and treaties.
➤ Monitor our progress toward a solution.

First and foremost, the ability to visualize the true nature of the climate crisis is essential to developing a widely shared understanding of the task we now face.

Because of the way the human brain works, we have a limited ability to absorb data sequentially, bit by bit. In computer terms, we could be said to have a "low bit rate." In the 1940s, after much research, the U.S. telephone industry determined that seven numbers were the most that could be remembered easily by the average person. (And then they added four.) But an infant at the age of only a few weeks can recognize faces more accurately than the most powerful computers — until the last few years. Again, in computer terms, we have "high resolution." Luckily, advanced computers have an unparalleled capacity for integrating very large amounts of data into recognizable visual patterns that allow the human brain to comprehend the meaning of billions of bits of data simultaneously.

We recognized the face of our planet for the first time when the first picture of Earth taken by a person was snapped by astronaut Bill Anders on December 24, 1968, during the Apollo 8 mission — the first to leave Earth's orbit and travel around the Moon. That famous image of our world rising above the Moon's horizon, known as "Earthrise," brought about a powerful change in our shared understanding that we live on a beautiful, vulnerable [...] blue sphere surrounded by the black vastness of space. The power of that image led to the first Earth Day, the passage of major environmental laws, the first global conference on the ecosphere, and the modern environmental movement. It has now been almost 40 years since the last picture of the earth was taken by a person far enough away to see the entire planet, during the last of the Apollo missions, Apollo 17.

Imagine what it would be like to have a live, high-quality color television image of Earth rotating in space, 24 hours a day. Imagine that the satellite carrying that television camera could somehow hover a million miles from the earth directly between our planet and the sun, so that the full face of the earth was always illuminated.

Imagine if scientists could put special instruments on the same satellite that would measure, for the first time,

---

Imagine what it would be like to have a live, high-quality color television image of the earth rotating in space, 24 hours a day.

---

the exact amount of energy coming to the earth from the sun and compare it in real time to the amount of energy radiated back into space from the earth itself.

The reason those two measurements are crucial is that the difference equals a precise calculation of global warming. The increasing temperature in the atmosphere of the earth is only an indirect measurement of the underlying problem, because so much of the incoming solar energy is absorbed by the oceans and is only slowly released into the atmosphere. Scientists studying global warming have long felt that the single most important stream of information needed to improve our understanding of the climate crisis was information about the difference between the energy coming into the earth's atmosphere compared with the energy going out again.

Imagine if the same satellite could calibrate and coordinate many of the other measurements made by satellites moving quickly in low earth orbit around our planet, and help us integrate all of that data in new ways.

The U.S. National Academy of Sciences (NAS) concluded a decade ago that we should build and launch such a satellite to a special orbit around the sun at a point in space known as the Lagrangian 1 (L1) point, where the gravity of the earth and the gravity of the sun are precisely balanced so that a satellite put there always stays exactly between the earth and the sun, providing a stable platform for continuous Earth observations of the planet as a whole. As a result of the NAS study, the U.S. Congress agreed and

approved $250 million to build the satellite and launch it in 2001.

During the time when it was built, experts at the National Oceanic and Atmospheric Administration (NOAA) were deciding how to replace an older satellite that was already at the L1 point warning engineers about large solar storms that can disrupt cellular telephone communications, electricity distribution equipment, and other electronic equipment sensitive to large solar flares. From the L1 point, the light from these solar flares is visible 90 minutes before the plasma from the storm hits the planet. That's enough warning time to harden the sensitive electronic equipment and avoid expensive outages and repairs.

Since the older early warning satellite (called the Advanced Composition Explorer) was about to wear out, NOAA decided to put the replacement for it onto the satellite intended to measure global warming and provide a constant full color picture of the earth.

We still haven't seen that live TV image of the earth. The old satellite has not been replaced, because the Bush-Cheney administration canceled the launch within days of taking office after the inauguration on January 20, 2001, and forced NASA to put the satellite in storage. It is still there, nine years later, waiting to be launched. As a result, the older warning satellite could stop working at any moment; it is already two years past its predicted lifetime.

One of its key instruments is already dead; another now routinely fails during peaks of solar flares, when it is needed most. Several important global industries are at risk of being exposed to heavy losses by damage from solar flares.

President Obama and the leadership of the Congress, particularly senators Barbara Mikulski and Bill Nelson, have announced that they are in favor of launching this satellite, which used to be named Triana (after Rodrigo de Triana, the lookout on Columbus's flagship who first saw the New World on October 12, 1492). It was changed under the Bush administration to DSCOVR (Deep Space Climate Observatory) by advocates who hoped that a new name would lead the Bush administration to feel some ownership of the project. Congressional opponents and bureaucrats inside NASA who want to use the money for other purposes have thus far paralyzed the efforts of the president and the Congressional leadership to follow through.

It's already built and paid for by the taxpayers. All the instruments work. The scientific team assembled a decade ago, before President Bush canceled its launch, has

In 1998, NASA proposed launching the satellite Traiana into space to deliver high-resolution images of the entire earth 24 hours a day. In 2000, the spacecraft was approved by Congress and scheduled for launch in 2001. Political resistance from the new administration and delaying tactics have kept the satellite — renamed DSCOVR (Deep Space Climate Observatory) in 2003 — grounded and in storage, even though it has already been paid for by taxpayers.

Positioned at a unique point between the earth's orbit and the sun — the Lagrangian 1 Point (L1), where the satellite remains directly between the earth and the sun at all times — the satellite will continually provide pole-to-pole images of the sunlit side of the earth, a viewpoint not possible from low earth orbit (LEO) or geosynchronous earth orbit (GEO) satellites.

DSCOVR is outfitted with a television camera and three instruments: EPIC (Earth Polychromatic Imaging Camera), a 10-channel spectroradiometer that provides color pictures; a three-channel radiometer that measures, among other things, albedo and ozone; and a plasma-magnetometer that measures magnetic fields and solar wind. Information from these three devices would be integrated with data from other satellites to provide a synoptic (simultaneous over-the-globe) view of the earth. These images would become an invaluable resource for remote sensing and climate modeling.

remained in place, volunteering their time under the able leadership of Dr. Francisco Valero of Scripps Institution of Oceanography. As NASA would say, all systems are go — except for the political system. Opponents of any action to solve the climate crisis have helped to block the launch, partly because they know how powerful the constant image of a beautiful rotating Earth on television and computer screens all over the world, in real time,

the amount of CO_2 emissions from any location in North America — and soon from everywhere in the world. Another new computer tool developed by the same Purdue team, Hestia (named after the Greek goddess of the hearth), makes it possible to see a thermal map of buildings, from which communities can gain a clear understanding of where the most inefficient buildings are located. There are literally thousands of similar examples.

> Opponents of any action to solve the climate crisis have helped to block the launch, partly because they know how powerful the constant image of a beautiful rotating Earth on television and computer screens all over the world, in real time, would be in building support for the urgent solutions to the climate crisis.

would be in building support for the urgent solutions to the climate crisis.

Of course, computers can help us to visualize some aspects of the climate crisis even without the advantage of a sophisticated satellite at the L1 point. Google Earth, for example, organizes vast amounts of data geospatially in ways that make it easy to find detailed information about geography, botany, zoology, road networks, population, industry, agriculture, and many other facts that are specifically relevant to every location on the surface of the earth.

A new project developed by a team, led by Dr. Kevin Gurney at Purdue University, named Vulcan (after the Roman god of fire), now makes it possible to visualize

The ability of advanced computers to integrate, process, and display complex data sets is bringing about a dramatic change in our capacity to understand phenomena that we could never have hoped to grasp in the past. The fastest and most powerful computers can sift through vast quantities of data, searching for the needles in the haystacks that are directly relevant to the questions of interest to us. They can form these data into patterns that are far more accessible to our brains than endless bits of information strung together sequentially. They can artificially alter the scale and speed of the world to make images too large or too small for our comprehension just the right size for us to understand. Processes that are extremely slow can be sped up for our inspection, and processes that occur naturally in the blink of an eye can be slowed down for our convenient analysis.

Supercomputers are now used as tools for developing new designs for renewable energy technologies and advanced efficiency devices. For example, computational biology is now central to the exploration of new enzymes useful in processing cellulose; new, more efficient light-

There are many examples of how the MEDEA program has revolutionized scientific understandings in a number of fields. When environmental scientists first gained access to this formerly secret trove of information, they were overwhelmed by the sheer volume of data. For example, the first measurements of ice cover on the North Polar ice cap came from MEDEA, and when scientists studying

---

Information that was once considered impossible to collect—such as data on tree cover and the carbon content of soils around the world, and whether they are increasing or decreasing in particular locations—can now be collected through a combination of new information sensors and automatic data transmitters linked to satellite systems.

---

emitting diodes; exotic solid-state cooling devices; new, more effective algae and other organisms for the production of biofuels; and new generations of photovoltaic cells and associated optics.

The largest and most powerful of these machines have led to the emergence of a completely new form of knowledge creation, in addition to deductive reasoning (formulate a theory and test it against the real world to see how it fits) and inductive reasoning (collect empirical facts and then try to integrate them into an overarching explanation), we now have a new approach that blends aspects of the first two. Computational science can create simulated realities — or "models" — within which experiments can be conducted. Although some scientific purists point out that computational science is conducted in ways that still sometimes fall short of the rigorous requirements of the traditional scientific method, the sheer power of this new knowledge creation tool is extremely impressive.

The Central Intelligence Agency, when it was headed by Robert Gates (now the U.S. Secretary of Defense) under the first President Bush, approved a plan called MEDEA to enable environmental scientists to gain carefully controlled access to top-secret information relevant to the environment, collected by spy satellites and other secret information-gathering systems managed by the intelligence community for use in better understanding the climate crisis. This information is especially valuable because there is so much of it. Far more information about the earth is collected in secret than the amount collected in the open by scientists.

whales first gained access to the previously secret arrays of microphones placed on the bottom of the Atlantic Ocean to monitor submarines of the former Soviet Union, they collected more acoustic data on blue whales in one day than were contained in the entire previously published scientific literature. One scientist, Chris Clark, refers to this system as "the acoustic Hubble Telescope."

The Bush-Cheney administration also canceled this program, but the Obama administration has brought it back to life under the leadership of CIA Director Leon Panetta and Senate Intelligence Committee Chairman Dianne Feinstein.

The extraordinary information collected and processed by the MEDEA program will be invaluable to the intelligence community in monitoring and verifying a global climate agreement. Information that was once considered impossible to collect — such as data on tree cover and the carbon content of soils around the world, and whether they are increasing or decreasing in particular locations — can now be collected through a combination of new information sensors and automatic data transmitters linked to satellite systems.

Computers can also help us make sense of more mundane but still relevant streams of data that are now often lumped together in ways that obscure our understanding. For example, the Google PowerMeter allows homeowners and business owners to monitor their electricity usage in real time. As smart meters are added to the distribution network, it will be possible to monitor the electricity usage of each appliance, television set, hot water heater, and light fixture. There are numerous similar applications and projects in development. All of them hold the promise of validating the old dictum "You manage what you measure."

Perhaps the most powerful application of information technology in actually reducing emissions of global warming pollution will come with the use of cheap semiconductors and "embedded systems" in machinery and in every aspect of industrial processes to eliminate wasteful energy use by optimizing energy efficiency. For example, industrial motors of all sizes often run at a constant rate even if the workload fluctuates; by constantly adjusting the engine rpms to the actual workload in real time, these devices can save large amounts of energy that would otherwise be wasted. The interactions between industrial pumps and their associated piping systems can also be automatically managed with such sensors to optimize fluid handling and minimize the energy needed.

Industrial process automation is not new, of course. Numerically controlled machines were first used during the 1950s when they were programmed with narrow paper tapes punched with regularly spaced holes. Then, in 1962,

between machines and embedded systems now far exceeds the flow of information between human beings.

Gradually, the use of information technology to eliminate inefficient energy use and unnecessary global warming pollution is extending throughout industrial and business processes to encompass management of the supply chain and product delivery as well. For example, in the United States in 2007, approximately 25 percent of all business truck trips were made while the trucks were empty. By using information technology, some businesses are coordinating the movement of their truck fleets to take advantage of this unused delivery capacity in order to maximize efficiency, cut costs, and reduce CO_2 emissions in a cooperative manner. UPS has saved on fuel costs for its delivery trucks by remapping routes to eliminate as many left turns as possible—thus cutting down on wasteful idling at traffic lights while drivers wait for an opportunity to cut in front of the traffic flowing in the other direction.

Similarly, automatic light sensors measuring the real-time illumination from natural lighting can adjust the

---

Gradually, the use of information technology to eliminate inefficient energy use and unnecessary global warming pollution is extending throughout industrial and business processes to encompass management of the supply chain and product delivery as well.

M.I.T. announced a dramatic improvement in the technology known as Automatically Programmed Tools. The APT — a "universal Numerical Control programming language" — allowed much more flexibility in programming and much greater linkage between different machines and stages in the manufacturing process. The development of CAD/CAM software (computer-aided design computer-aided manufacture) led to the efficient connection between programs used for the design of products and the computers controlling the machinery that manufacture the same products from the output of the design computers. Now, the vast majority of new machine tools incorporate some version of a seamless integration between design and manufacturing.

As successive generations of software become more sophisticated, market leaders are integrating energy efficiency into the information technology that they use. By some measures, the volume of information flow on the Internet

output of electric lights to save electricity during the hours when they need not be at full brightness, or need not be used at all. Heating, ventilation, and air-conditioning systems can be linked through inexpensive sensors to maximize the use of outside air coming through windows that actually open when outdoor temperatures make natural ventilation more appropriate and efficient during some hours of each day. Sensors can also alert building owners to gaps in insulation and leaks in ductwork hidden behind walls.

Much larger savings are being made by companies that utilize computer-aided analyses to redesign larger integrated processes in their entirety. "Whole system" redesign often leads to significant breakthroughs that eliminate unnecessary pollution and wasted energy and time. My favorite example is what happened when the leadership of Northern Telecom made a commitment in the late 1980s to be the first company to completely eliminate the use of harmful chlorofluorocarbons. As a Canadian company,

Northern Telecom was alert to the significance of the 1987 Montreal Protocol, which mandated the phaseout of these chemicals. Since Northern Telecom used CFC-113 solvents to clean circuit boards, the company's engineers and scientists searched for appropriate substitutes. When they found none that fit their requirements, one of their engineers finally reframed the question: "How do these circuit boards get dirty in the first place?"

This conceptual breakthrough led to a redesign of the entire process to eliminate the exposure of the newly manufactured circuit boards to the contaminants that had to be removed at the end of the process. The resulting "no clean" process led to better and less costly circuit boards, while eliminating the chemicals that were simultaneously among the culprits that damaged the earth's stratospheric ozone layer and contributed powerfully to global warming. Then, Northern Telecom went one step further and shared its breakthrough with the rest of the industry, thus accelerating the phaseout of these chemicals by its competitors as well.

The company beat the phaseout deadline by an astonishing nine years and made money by doing so. The $1 million it invested in developing the new process earned it almost $4 million within the first three years. And the extra profits have continued to roll in every year since in the form of reduced manufacturing costs due to the elimination of a costly step in the process they used to use. Moreover, I saw firsthand the pride felt by Northern Telecom employees that they had joined together in a collaborative process aimed at a goal larger than simply adding to corporate profits — and the joy they felt when their commitment to doing the right thing and providing leadership for the entire industry ended up boosting their profits as well.

New service providers are now emerging to offer businesses software solutions for the task of redesigning all their processes to save money and emissions. One such company, Hara, uses the metaphor of "organizational metabolism," which encompasses a whole-system analysis of how energy and emissions can be minimized by making every function of the business more efficient as raw materials, energy, and labor are "metabolized" inside the company into products or services, waste, wages, and profits.

In many cases, the redesign of systems, processes, and products leads to the reduction of raw materials consumption through the substitution of innovation for matter. In the U.S. economy as a whole, the last half century has seen a tripling of total output in terms of the value of products

manufactured and sold — without any increase in the total tonnage of that, output. This effect, known as "dematerialization," is partly due to the increased prominence of information as a percentage of what is sold, but it is due also in significant measure to the clever and efficient redesign of products in ways that improve quality while reducing the physical matter used in the products.

Even as they begin to empower other industries and organizations with new tools for solving the climate crisis, information technology companies are faced with reducing their own global warming pollution. Today, information technology emissions of global warming pollution, principally CO_2, have risen to approximately 2 percent of global emissions. And over the next 10 years, IT emissions are expected to almost double. As a result, industry leaders are taking steps to redesign and reengineer their systems in an effort to become much more efficient and sharply reduce pollution.

Data centers, for example, consume large amounts of electricity. The growth of servers connected to the Internet occurred so quickly that it led to serious inefficiencies that are now being systematically addressed by many companies. Computers, printers, and other IT devices and equipment are all coming under closer scrutiny in the search for ways to cut energy costs and reduce emissions. The growth in online traffic, particularly Internet video, along with data storage requirements and disaster recovery needs, is combining with other factors to further accelerate the growth in data centers and the equipment that fills them. For example, the number of servers in the United States has tripled during the past 10 years. By installing more energy-efficient equipment, consolidating and rationalizing assets, making more use of "virtual servers," and optimizing power usage and cooling requirements, the IT industry is beginning to take responsibility for reducing its contribution to global warming.

The use of increasingly sophisticated information technology to cut global warming pollution in business and industry is also leading to increased awareness of inefficiencies that result from outdated laws and regulations. For example, the federal regulatory framework governing milk production and distribution makes it more profitable for dairies to transport milk and milk products thousands of miles to distributors on the other side of the country than to sell the same products in the regions where they are produced. This absurd, costly, and wasteful pattern continues only because the federal regulatory framework governing milk production and distribution mandates wastefulness.

In other forms of agricultural production, the combination of ground-based sensors and satellite systems are empowering farmers to adopt much more efficient approaches known as "precision farming" that optimize fertilizer mixes and applications to variations in soil types in different parts of the same fields.

Many businesses that begin the process of analyzing and reducing their CO_2 emissions discover early on that employee travel to and from meetings in other cities is one of their largest sources of avoidable CO_2 emissions. As a result, there has been a dramatic increase in telecommuting and the developing of more sophisticated tools, like Cisco's TelePresence, that simulate face-to-face conversations so well that much travel becomes unnecessary.

Transportation costs in the wider society are also being reduced in some cities throughout the world by the use of electronic toll-collection systems, which eliminate wasteful queuing at toll-booths; dynamic road signaling, which reduces traffic congestion and idling time; and congestion charges that more accurately allocate road use. Similarly, the growing use of radio-frequency identification (RFID) on products that travel through the wholesale and retail distribution-chain is making inventory management far more efficient.

Privacy advocates have raised alarms about the inappropriate use, and inadvertent consequences, of ubiquitous object tracking to identify the real-time location of individuals who may not want their every move followed. Other privacy consequences of the new intensity of information technology throughout the economy deserve continuing scrutiny.

In addition, the growing importance of IT in the economy further underscores the need for equal access to computers and other important information tools for lower-income individuals and families. Just as telephones were once considered optional but then became essential for full and equal participation in modern society, computers are now approaching the threshold of indispensability.

Inevitably, the growing use of information technology in all sectors of the economy is producing losers as well

> There has been a dramatic increase in telecommuting and the developing of more sophisticated tools, like Cisco's TelePresence, that simulate face-to-face conversations so well that much travel becomes unnecessary.

as winners. Older business models created in a different information environment may no longer be competitive. Newspapers and magazines, for example, are now struggling in most parts of the world as digital electronic forms of communication become far more efficient. As the information revolution continues to gain momentum, similarly revolutionary transformations are taking place in many sectors of business and industry.

The newspaper example illustrates some of the risks that accompany the benefits of these transformations. Prior to facing such daunting electronic competition, newspapers earned revenue streams that allowed the employment of experienced journalists who could take a lot of time to investigate, analyze, and thoroughly report complex stories that regularly connected the public to valuable information about the operations of government and the functioning of societal institutions.

Indeed, during these early stages of the development of Internet-based journalism, the bulk of higher-quality stories still originates with newspapers. With newspaper revenues hemorrhaging, it is still not clear that electronic journalism will, on its own, discover a new standard model that generates sufficient revenue to rebuild a comparable cadre of experienced investigative journalists with enough time and resources to do the job formerly done by newspapers. Current TV, a cable and satellite news and information network that I co-founded with Joel Hyatt in 2002, along with its companion online network, Current.com, is devoting considerable resources to support a growing team of investigative journalists. This team, called Vanguard, travels the world reporting in-depth investigative stories that are then distributed electronically on Current TV and Current.com.

Even though investigative journalism is still rare in the new media environment, the new information technologies based on the Internet are connecting people to one another and to vast pools of information relevant to any societal challenge with which they wish to engage. Ultimately, the solutions to the climate crisis will necessitate much broader public engagement in the political process, of a kind that social networks and other Internet tools can make possible.

A number of experts have concluded that when it comes to energy, if we can see it, we will try to save it. That concept may soon apply to our homes in the form of real-time energy monitoring.

With Google's PowerMeter, a project in beta testing at this writing, customers with smart power meters are able to see the peaks and valleys of their own power use, letting them adjust their habits and homes accordingly. Real-time power usage is displayed via the Web; turn off an appliance and the drop in energy use is quickly visible. Microsoft and other companies are testing similar online programs.

Smart meters visible inside the home — from portable models (seen above) to wall-mounted units to Web-based tools — are also under rapid development. Displaying electricity and gas usage, such meters are set to be required equipment in the United Kingdom by 2020.

The Ambient Orb offers similar feedback, though in a more physical design. The desktop sphere changes color based on changes in what it is monitoring. Originally designed to react to input such as stock market indexes, the device was modified by a manager at Southern California Edison (SCE) to react to input from his utility. The manager then distributed 120 of the orbs to Edison customers, who were told how its changing colors would alert them when peak-period energy rates went into or out of effect. With the orbs as prompts, the utility's customers quickly trimmed their peak-period energy use by a large amount: 40 percent. SCE estimates that by installing smart metering, its customers will reduce greenhouse gas emissions by at least 365,000 metric tons per year.

Like the "Prius effect" — the easing off the gas pedal by drivers who see their fuel dip on the dashboard — smart meters link behavior to use. However, smart meter trials to date show that the real trigger is linking to a price cue. Customers in a smart meter pilot in California reduced their overall use 5 percent. Similar tests in Ireland and Illinois show energy savings of up to 12 percent.

This book, for example, is being published with a companion website, ourchoicethebook.com, that includes a Solutions Wiki — a moderated forum for the constant improvement and elaboration of the suggested solutions for the climate crisis contained in the book. Many of the expert reviewers who have participated in the Solutions Summits that were so helpful in my efforts to identify the most effective ways to solve the climate crisis have agreed to help moderate ongoing discussions of new ideas, technologies, processes, and innovations that can be used to speed up the needed reductions in global warming pollution worldwide, the more rapid sequestration of pollutants already in the atmosphere, and the redesign of systems and processes that can accelerate the emergence of a low-carbon global civilization.

Internet-based tools also hold great promise for the reinvigoration of democratic self-governance and the mobilization of people at the grassroots level who want to be a part of the urgent task of, solving the climate crisis. In my own experience, I remember what a difference it made when I transferred my slideshow about the crisis from film-based slides in Kodak carousels to computer graphics. The ease with which I could integrate new images and new scientific findings was dramatically improved, and soon after that transition, I began to notice a big change in the overall quality and effectiveness of the presentation.

I have now trained more than 3,000 people in dozens of countries to give updated slideshows on a continuing basis in the areas where they live. The Climate Project, managed by Jenny Glad, maintains communication with these presenters around the world primarily by means of the Internet and is able to share new slides with the appropriate explanations and caveats on a regular basis.

The Alliance for Climate Protection, managed by Maggie Fox, maintains contact weekly on the Internet with more than 1.2 million members in an effort to distribute high-quality information about the unfolding of this crisis and the political steps necessary to motivate policy makers to adopt the needed solutions.

Paul Hawken, author of *Blessed Unrest,* has found that more than "one — and maybe even two — million organizations working toward ecological sustainability and social justice" devoted to addressing the multiple challenges facing the earth's ecosystem have already been formed around the world — representing what he calls, "the largest social movement in all of human history." It is hard to imagine that this would have been possible without the new Internet-based tools that most of these groups rely on.

Sometimes, information can bring about change by itself, even in the absence of laws and regulations. For example, the relatively new legal requirement for the display of nutritional information on food labels (in the United States and some other countries) has put pressure on food manufacturers to improve their nutritional content and eliminate unhealthy ingredients like trans fat.

Similarly, after U.S. laws were modified to require the public disclosure of toxic air pollutants being released by industrial facilities, newspapers and electronic media in every city started listing the worst polluters. The public pressure that resulted from the disclosure of that information caused many companies to begin making changes in order to get off the worst-polluter list. Toxic emissions actually declined significantly, even in the absence of a new legal mandate. The information itself, once known to the public, forced the reduction. But the information has to be displayed prominently enough to raise public awareness.

This same principle applies to the display of information about wasteful energy use in homes and businesses. After California changed its laws to give utilities an incentive to reduce energy consumption (by allowing the utilities to share the savings along with their customers), Southern California Edison introduced to their customers a simple

their efforts to implement these solutions. When serving as vice president, I undertook a challenge called Reinventing Government, which was aimed at redesigning the departments, agencies, and processes of the U.S. government to make them far more efficient. I learned a great deal from innovators in private business and in state and local governments that had succeeded in similar tasks.

One of the local government projects that most impressed me was a police strategy in New York City innovated by Jack Maple, a former transit policeman. Maple discovered the value of computerized statistics utilized in a group setting where all relevant decision makers are able to easily visualize the patterns revealed by the statistics. The data is organized geospatially, precinct by precinct, and displayed on a large screen visible at the same time to all participants — who share responsibility for quickly implementing solutions to the problems that are identified. When William Bratton was named to head the New York Police Department, he institutionalized this approach and sharply reduced crime rates in almost every category. Since then, this approach — colloquially known as CompStat — has been adopted in many other cities.

One of the most advanced systems has been developed by the police chief of Redlands, California, Jim Bueermann, who has now applied the CompStat technique to consolidate housing, recreation, and senior services into

---

Southern California Edison introduced to their customers a simple but compelling information display that sits inside the home: a glowing glass orb developed by Ambient Devices that changes color depending upon the amount of electricity consumption at any given time.

---

but compelling information display that sits inside the home: a glowing glass orb developed by Ambient Devices that changes color depending upon the amount of electricity consumption at any given time; when it turns bright red, that is the signal that electricity consumption is at very high levels. This is a very effective way to alert homeowners and business owners to the level of energy consumption at any given time, and signals them that there is an opportunity in the present moment for them to save money by modifying consumption levels.

Finally, information technology can be used in creative ways to assist and empower decision makers in governments, businesses, civic organizations, and other groups in

his police department and has enriched the process with ongoing social research in an effort to make his city a safer environment for children, seniors, and families. "We need to understand the nature and location of risk factors — in families, communities, schools, peer groups — and develop strategies to solve and prevent community problems. We are paid to get criminals, but our added value is found in the other, long-term approaches we are taking to make the community safer," Bueermann said, adding, "Mapping risk and protective factors lets us put tax dollars, and the resources of our community partners, where there is a high concentration of risk factors and strategically leverage the community's investment in public safety and problem prevention."

I believe this is one of the best examples of how information technology, properly used, can assist decision makers in their efforts to solve the climate crisis.

Heads of state, governors, other regional leaders, and mayors of cities and towns could benefit by developing computerized statistics on each of the major challenges they face and integrate them and display them visually for groups that include department heads and other stakeholders in a shared effort to discover what really works and what does not. The task confronting policy makers in the historic effort to solve the climate crisis will require the innovative use of every new tool available.

Spaceship Earth

from *Nation of Rebels*

— Joseph Heath and Andrew Potter

f it were true that technology has become a vast, all-encompassing ideology, then it would seem natural for the counterculture to be dominated by technophobes seeking refuge in a neo-Luddite politics. That certainly fits the popular stereotype of the barefoot, granola-eating, patchouli-smelling hippie sitting in the dirt twisting macramé, but it actually reflects a very minor part of the movement. Historically countercultural movements have been just as ambivalent about technology as mainstream society, aware of both its promise and its threat.

Of course, there has always been a great deal of hostility to technology in these movements. Not only was mass industrial society bad for the soul, it was bad for the environment, as Rachel Carson's 1962 book *Silent Spring* made clear. Despite her shaky grasp of statistical reasoning, Carson managed to alert many people to the dangers of DDT. She thereby helped create a new environmental consciousness that was suspicious of the very idea of technical "expertise." Meanwhile, even as the nuclear threat cast a long shadow of imminent annihilation over the entire planet, the napalm-soaked war in Vietnam was being cast as a technological struggle between the mechanized West and the primitive East.

Nevertheless, many critics continued to believe that even if technology was the problem, it could also be an essential part of the solution. Even Reich, for all his flakiness, saw the point. Luddism was not the answer, and "reality is not served by trying to ignore the machine.[1] Our history

shows that what we must do is assert domination over the machine, to guide it so that it works for the values of our choice." The point was not to be antitechnological, but to arrange things so that we control the machines, not the other way around. The goal of the new consciousness must be to end our slavery to the machine, to use technology to improve our lives, protect nature and ensure peace.

The theoretical heart of this utopianism was the development of what was called "postscarcity economics." Proposed by writers such as Herbert Marcuse and the eco-anarchist Murray Bookchin, the belief was that technological improvements had made it possible to produce enough to meet the basic needs of everyone at essentially no expense. Once machines were able to take care of all of our material needs and wants, we would be free to cultivate our spiritual side, to indulge in creative play and to form a society based not around the demands of economic production, but around fellowship and love. (Or, more crudely we could all lie around and have sex while machines did all the work, like members of "the Culture" in Iain M. Banks's science fiction.) They saw a genuinely revolutionary potential in the new technologies, which promised to undermine the complex production-driven hierarchies of mass society. Bookchin hoped that renewable energy sources, from wind, solar or tidal power, would serve as the foundations for a new; scaled-down civilization, "bringing land and city into a rational and ecological synthesis."[2] He was also convinced

---

1 Reich, *Greening of America,* 381.

2 Murray Bookchin, quoted in Robert Gottlieb, *Forcing the Spring: The Transformation of the American Environmental Movement* (Washington, DC: Island Press, 1993), 88.

that the notion of widespread scarcity was simply a ruse, perpetrated by the entrenched interests of the technocracy.

What eventually led to the undoing of these views was the failure to appreciate the competitive nature of our consumption and the significance of positional goods. Houses in good neighborhoods, tasteful furniture, fast cars, stylish restaurants and cool clothes are all *intrinsically* scarce. We cannot manufacture more of them because their value is based on the distinction that they provide to consumers. Thus the idea of overcoming scarcity through increased production is incoherent; in our society scarcity is a social, not a material, phenomenon. Both Bookchin and Marcuse missed the significance of this problem. What troubled them more was the sense that they were relying upon the very instrument of repression — technology — for the emancipation of society. Marcuse wondered how we could possibly convert the "processes of mechanization and standardization" to serve emancipatory ends.[3] Yet he could not see any practical alternative to the enormously complex and capital-intensive technological systems that characterized industrial capitalism. As a consequence, both he and Bookchin had difficulty seeing any way out of mass society.

This all changed in 1973 with the publication of the book *Small Is Beautiful,* by the British economist Ernst Schumacher. (For those not familiar, it was Schumacher who coined the phrase "soul-destroying" to describe life in mass society.) The subtitle of the book was "A Study of Economics As If People Mattered," and Schumacher believed that technology could be adapted to the genuine needs of humanity. What we needed was an alternative form of technology, to serve as the basis for an alternative form of civilization. If mass technology was complex, centralized and capital-intensive, requiring specialized knowledge or expertise, then alternative technology would be just the opposite. It would be simple, decentralized, inexpensive, user-friendly easy to repair and suitable for small-scale individual or local application.

To a considerable extent, Schumacher's concerns were with the needs of the developing world. He argued that our systems of mass production are suitable only for societies that are already rich. Following Gandhi's dictum that "the poor of the world will not be helped by mass production, only by production by the masses," he suggested that what the developing world needs are intermediate technologies,

somewhere between primitive tools and modern industries. This technology of production by the masses would be "compatible with the laws of ecology gentle in its use of scarce resources, and designed to serve the human person instead of making him the servant of machines."[4] It would also be accessible and democratic, "not reserved to those already rich and powerful."

Despite this orientation toward the developing world (and despite the disastrous experiments in local technology undertaken by China during the "Great Leap Forward," such as community-based steel production), many people in the industrialized West were captivated by Schumacher's demand for "a new orientation of science and technology towards the organic, the gentle, the non-violent, and the beautiful."[5] A diverse group of environmentalists, anti-capitalist lefties, back-to-the-land hippies and off-the-grid survivalists came together under the banner of what came to be called "appropriate technology."

Proponents of appropriate technology (AT) rejected the "mass society" view of technology as an autonomous, deterministic, totalizing force. They believed that the problem was not necessarily with technology per se, but with the nature of the specific tools we had chosen. We still need technology but we must be wiser in our choices. Where mass society made use of "hard" technologies that were socially alienating and environmentally destructive, "soft" or appropriate technologies would be democratic and friendly to the environment. Soft technologies would have to be efficient and eco-friendly; would enhance local, democratic government; would allow for individual or community flourishing; and had to be safe, uncomplicated and easy to use. A tall order.

Of course, there is no reason to expect that all of these virtues should be mutually compatible. For example, a 1968 Chrysler Newport can be completely disassembled and reassembled by anyone with a bit of know-how and three standard wrenches. Not so long ago, people used to do their own oil changes and repairs. But these cars were also gas-guzzlers. A modern hybrid-drive vehicle, on the other hand, while significantly more eco-friendly, is infernally complex. The electronics alone are so complicated that the car can be serviced only by the dealer, and then

---

3   Herbert Marcuse, *One- Dimensional Man: Studies in the Ideology of Advanced Industrial Society* (Boston: Beacon Press, 1964), 2.

4   Ernst Schumacher, *Small Is Beautiful: A Study of Economics As If People Mattered* (London: Abacus, 1974), 122.

5   Ibid., 27.

only by specially trained technicians. Owners have to bring their cars in periodically for firmware upgrades. So which technology is "hard" and which is "soft"?

> We still need technology but we must be wiser in our choices.

Despite these sorts of difficulties, proponents of AT persist in dividing up the world of technology into two simple categories. For example, in her 1989 book *The Real World of Technology*, Ursula Franklin distinguishes two main types: "holistic" and "prescriptive" technology. Holistic technology is characteristic of crafts-based production, in which a single artisan controls every aspect of production from start to finish. Specialization, when it occurs, is in the realm of a general product line, such as pottery or textiles. In contrast, prescriptive technologies promote specialization by task, not byproduct (automobile manufacture being a typical example). In prescriptive technologies, production is a function of the system as a whole, not the individual worker, and thus control and responsibility accrue to coordinators or managers.

Our society, argues Franklin, is distinguished by a predominance of prescriptive technologies.[6] It is because these technologies are what she calls "designs for compliance" that we have become beholden to the technological imperative and its alienating bureaucratic rationality. She argues that we must take steps to ensure that our technology is as humane and holistic as possible. Some of her more interesting suggestions are that airline CEOs should be forced to fly coach, that public officials should be forced to take public transit and that owners of cafeteria-food companies should be forced to eat at their own restaurants. More seriously, perhaps, Franklin says that for any new technology or public project, we must always ask: Does it promote justice? Does it restore reciprocity? Does it minimize disaster, favor conservation over destruction and favor people over machines?

This is just a call for appropriate technology. Yet, call them soft or hard, holistic or prescriptive, it is not obvious that these mark out natural types of technology that fall into the respective realms of "good" and "bad." One

concern is that many purportedly "soft" or decentralizing technologies can be quickly adopted for more centralizing ends. The sewing machine is an obvious example. Hailed as a revolutionary device when it first appeared, certain to free housewives from a great deal of boring and exhausting sewing, the sewing machine soon begat the sweatshop.

More generally, it is often not the case that the way people use technology is determined by the nature of that technology. The single most important consequence of the development of environmentally friendly housing technology, for instance, has been the proliferation of "McMansions." Most people simply buy the biggest house that they can afford to purchase and maintain. If a high-efficiency furnace and fancy insulation make houses less expensive to heat, people will simply buy bigger houses (ditto for air-conditioning). If low-E glass and argon inserts improve the insulating properties of windows, people will install bigger windows (so that the overall heat loss from the house remains unchanged). Consumer spending seems to be governed by a principle of waste homeostasis.

Another problem is that the appropriateness of many technologies depends entirely on how many people have them. The wood-burning stove is in many ways the quint-

---

> The single most important consequence of the development of environmentally friendly housing technology, for instance, has been the proliferation of "McMansions."

---

essential appropriate technology, because it doesn't burn fossil fuels and is completely independent of massive energy production and transportation systems. But it fails the simple test of asking, "What if everyone did that?" While it would be great to be the only house on the street with a Franklin stove in the kitchen, if every house got one the air would be thick with ash, there would be deforestation on a massive scale, the price of cordwood would skyrocket and urban air quality would return to 19th-century levels. It wouldn't be long before the authorities would be forced to step in and regulate wood-burning stoves out of existence. So is this appropriate technology? The proper name for a technology that is available only to the few is not "appropriate," but "privileged."

---

6   Ursula Franklin, *The Real World of Technology* (Toronto: Anansi, 1999), 127–28.

Finally there is simply no reason to think that local communities and local cultures, even when built around AT, will promote diversity, freedom, independence and democracy. In fact, more often than not the opposite is

If *Small Is Beautiful* was the bible of the AT movement, its newsletter was the *Whole Earth Catalog*, which later morphed into the *CoEvolution Quarterly*. Founded by Stewart Brand in 1968, the *WEC* was part magazine,

---

Fuller also captured the emerging global environmental consciousness with his notion of "Spaceship Earth." We are all crew members on this craft, he said, and we are all going to have to work together if we are to avoid large-scale environmental catastrophe.

---

likely to be the case. Large-scale technology forces people to cooperate with one another. Small-scale technology on the other hand, often promotes rugged individualism, not to mention the isolationist and antisocial attitudes characteristic of the "survivalist" mentality. After all, once you have your own generator, your own septic tank, your own 4x4, your own shotgun and your own compound in Montana, what's the point of paying taxes?

In the end, it might be that none of these objections would worry the devotees of appropriate technology. The AT movement was as much an outlet for a distinct political ideology as it was a general response to environmental concerns. It tapped into the thick vein of self-sufficient libertarianism that ran through the entire counterculture, and it was to a large extent a self-conscious attempt to shirk the demands of real-world political obligation. In addition, for all their opposition to the technocracy, many elements within the counterculture found actual technologies tremendously appealing.

The frankly libertarian politics and technological consumerism of the AT movement manifested itself in a number of ways. Many people were inspired by the work of Buckminster Fuller. Fuller's geodesic dome, whose simple construction combined light weight with great strength, was the prototypical appropriate technology. Fuller also captured the emerging global environmental consciousness with his notion of "Spaceship Earth."[7] We are all crew members on this craft, he said, and we are all going to have to work together if we are to avoid large-scale environmental catastrophe. His field guide to the ship, *Operating Manual for Spaceship Earth*, fueled the sky-pilot fantasies of a thousand hippie spacemen.

part survivalist manual, part retail catalog — sort of a clearinghouse for the practical counterculturalist. Brand was explicitly trying to turn the movement away from sex, drugs, and rock and roll and toward bikes, solar panels and composting toilets. If the great debate within the counterculture was whether it was sufficient to change one's consciousness in order to change all of society, the *WEC* tried to change the topic, arguing that you could change society by changing your lifestyle. Each of us is a society of one, and if everyone were to adopt a radically detached, self-sufficient lifestyle, preferably in a rural or wilderness area, then the individual, the society and the whole planet would be better off. For the crew of Spaceship Earth, it is every man for himself.

The postscarcity aspect of the AT movement and its faith in the potential of alternative energy pretty much died out after the oil crisis and economic stagflation of the '70s. It survives as an earnest but politically marginal subculture made up of wind-power romantics, fuel-cell entrepreneurs and hydrogen-economy futurists. Yet the ideals that drove the quest for appropriate technology continue to exert enormous influence in our culture, in two major forms. First, the fascination with technology migrated to the Internet, taking various forms, including cyberpunk, cybercommunitarianism and cyberlibertarianism. Meanwhile, the hippie-spaceman politics of self-sufficiency, which combined global awareness with individual action, has permeated our culture in the form of a widespread environmental consumer politics rallying around the slogan "Think globally, act locally."

Many of the ideals that motivated the appropriate technology movement were paralleled in the embryonic world of computing. What is now known as the "hacker ethic" started among students at MIT in the 1950s, and its central

---

7   Buckminster Fuller, *Operating Manual for Spaceship Earth* (New York: Pocket Books, 1970).

principle was the right of all users to unrestricted access to computers and information. Anarchistic and libertarian in orientation, the hacker ethic looked to decentralized computing and access to information as a way of challenging the cult of expertise and information-based elitism that characterized the technocracy. As cultural theorist Andrew Ross puts it, "the technology of hacking and viral guerilla warfare occupies a similar place in countercultural fantasies as the Molotov cocktail design once did."[8]

On the hardware side, Apple computers has had AT credibility from the get-go, as company founders Steve Jobs and Steve Wozniak put themselves in deliberate opposition to the corporate, institutional, mainframe-based systems built by IBM and Digital Electronics Corporation (DEC). In contrast with these massive and "heartless, mechanized brains of oppressions," the potential of personal computing — from desktop publishing to networked computing — seemed subversive and liberating.

Over at the *Whole Earth Catalog*, Brand was in complete agreement. He saw Apple computers as tools made by

bodies."[9] It is in cyberspace that many people continue to dream of a genuinely anarchistic social order, in which all social relationships are voluntary and noncoercive, eschewing rules and hierarchies of all sorts.

Cyberlibertarianism is a collection of ideas that combines ecstatic enthusiasm for electronically mediated forms of living with radical libertarian ideas about the proper definition of freedom, economics and community. The clearest exposition of cyberlibertarian ideology can be found in a publication called *Cyberspace and the American Dream: A Magna Carta for the Knowledge Age*. First written in 1994 by Esther Dyson, George Gilder, George Keyworth and Alvin Toffler, a number of subsequent versions have since been released on the Internet.

Cyberlibertarianism draws heavily on Toffler's wave theory of technological development. The first-wave economy was agricultural and centered on human labor, while the second-wave economy was built around massive industrial machinery. The emerging third-wave economy will be dedicated to knowledge, especially as it is dissemi-

---

Cyberlibertarianism is a collection of ideas that combines ecstatic enthusiasm for electronically mediated forms of living with radical libertarian ideas about the proper definition of freedom, economics and community.

---

and for revolutionaries, and the *WEC* carried articles about Apple beside those about wood-burning stoves. In 1985, Brand cofounded the WELL (Whole Earth 'Lectronic Link) as an alternative online forum for writers and readers of his magazine, the *Whole Earth Software Review*. The magazine lasted only a few years, but the WELL, one of the earliest attempts at creating an online deliberative community, is now owned by *Salon,* with over 10,000 members worldwide.

In a nice turn of phrase, Ross remarks that if much of the '60s counterculture and the AT movement was formed around a *technology of folklore*, the version that emerged in the late '80s and into the '90s is rooted in the "*folklore of technology* — mythical feats of survivalism and resistance in a data-rich world of virtual environments and posthuman

nated through networked computers. Mass society was a creature of second-wave technology which required mass production, large government and centralized corporate bureaucracies. In the Information Age, institutions and culture will become "demassified," spelling doom for bureaucracies and creating unparalleled opportunities for the exercise of human freedom outside of the constraints of mass society.

In the third-wave world, communities will be entirely uncoercive. As the authors of the Internet Magna Carta concede, "no one knows what the Third Wave communities of the future will look like, or where 'demassification' will ultimately lead.[10] It is clear, however, that cyberspace will play an important role knitting together the diverse communities of tomorrow, facilitating the creation of elec-

8   Andrew Ross, "Hacking Away at the Counterculture," *Postmodern Culture,* 1, no. 1 (1990), http://infomotions.com/serials/pmc/pmc-vim-ross-hacking.txt.

9   Ibid.
10   Esther Dyson et al., "Cyberspace and the American Dream: A Magna Carta for the Knowledge Age" (Aug. 1994), http://pff.org/publications/ecommerce/fii.2magnacarta.htm.

tronic neighborhoods bound together not by geography but by shared interests."

Another influential account of cyberlibertarian principles was written by John Perry Barlow.[11] His *Declaration of Independence of Cyberspace* begins with the following announcement: "Governments of the Industrial World, you weary giants of flesh and steel, I come from Cyberspace, the new home of Mind. On behalf of the future, I ask you of the past to leave us alone. You are not welcome among us. You have no sovereignty where we gather." He goes on to claim that "our identities have no bodies, so, unlike you, we cannot obtain order by physical coercion. We believe that from ethics, enlightened self-interest, and the commonweal, our governance will emerge. Our identities may be distributed across many of your jurisdictions. The only law that all our constituent cultures would generally recognize is the Golden Rule. We hope we will be able to build our particular solutions on that basis. But we cannot accept the solutions you are attempting to impose."

If this fairly reeks of bongwater, it is not surprising, since Barlow is a former lyricist for the Grateful Dead. But Barlow wasn't the first former hippie to become enamored with the counterculture possibilities of the Internet. In the 1980s, Timothy Leary declared that computers had replaced LSD as the essential instrument for expanding your consciousness. "Computers are the most subversive thing I have ever done," he said.[12]

For anyone who first logged on to the Internet anytime after say 1996, these sorts of claims seem ridiculous. Even for those of us who had e-mail accounts before the birth of the world wide web, it is hard to remember how pleasant a place the Internet once was. Newsgroups, bulletin boards and mailing lists — the loci of online community — *were* largely self-governing. People who signed up agreed to follow certain general rules of "netiquette," and those who flouted the rules found themselves either ignored or sent on their way in a flurry of flames. So if it was not exactly a world without rules, the early Internet was certainly an extremely free and decentralized sort of place, with little in the way of hierarchy or coercion. The cyberlibertarian

dream was that this mode of social interaction could serve as a template for an entire socioeconomic order.

It is fair to say that the past decade has not been kind to this vision of electronic community, for reasons that were entirely predictable. When Barlow proclaimed that "we are creating a world where anyone, anywhere may express his or her beliefs, no matter how singular, without fear of being coerced into silence or conformity,"[13] it does not appear to have occurred to him that some people might use this freedom of expression *to coerce, harass or silence other people.* Thus, the Internet quickly became infested with all of the same sorts of obnoxious people that exist in the "real world," such as racists, bigots and sexists, not to mention team-killers, smacktards, cyberstalkers and other "griefers" all too willing to invade privacy, steal identities, harass ex-girlfriends or co-workers and generally make life miserable for other people online. Worse, they are able to do so by taking advantage of the very features that were supposed to make cyberspace such a utopia: no laws, barriers or borders, no government or police and almost perfect anonymity The results confirmed Gresham's law of cyberspace: bad talk drives out good.

If these sorts of things were not enough to convince even the most dedicated libertarian that *some* sort of Net governance might be in order, the swamping of the Internet in spam might prove convincing. By mid-2003, spam (unsolicited e-mail advertising pornography, mortgage rates and penis enlargement) had gone from being a minor annoyance to a major problem, for both end users and service providers. Many e-mail accounts have been rendered unusable, with some people receiving hundreds of solicitations a day. By the time the United States Congress got around to passing anti-spam legislation, somewhere between 60 and 80 percent of all e-mail traffic was spam.

Spam exists because it is an extremely cheap and easy way to market a product. A mailing list can be put together for about $500 per million names, which means a response rate of only 1 in 100,000 can be profitable (as opposed to 1 in 100 for old-fashioned junk mail). And far from being a perversion of the cyberlibertarian vision, spam in fact follows directly from its core principles. As far as Toffler, Dyson, Barlow and others are concerned, the whole point of the Internet is that it permits unlimited, uncoerced freedom of expression, not just *including* but *especially* economic expression. Of course, the more spam gets sent, the

---

11 John Perry Barlow, "A Declaration of the Independence of Cyberspace" (1996), http://eff.org/~barlow/Declaration-Final.htm.

12 Timothy Leary, quoted in Scott Bukatman, *Terminal Identity: The Virtual Subject in Postmodern Science Fiction* (Durham, NC: Duke University Press, 1993), 139.

13 Barlow, "A Declaration of Independence of Cyberspace."

less effective any of it becomes, but the spam overload only encourages spammers to redouble their efforts and send more and more copies of the same message. A perfect race to the bottom is initiated, and a Net clogged with spam becomes the tragic culmination of the cyberlibertarian vision.

Spam is not an easy problem to solve, but it will have

to the outside leads us to shun the mid-level of national political and economic institutions. This is unfortunate, because that is where all the action is.

The most radically leveling variation of the "move to the outside" is the environmental movement known as "deep ecology." Initiated in 1972 by a Norwegian philoso-

---

The Spaceship Earth mentality that underlies "Think globally, act locally" is just one version of what environmental theorist Peter van Wyck calls "the move to the outside." The goal is to consider the planet in its entirety, either as one big machine (as in the spaceship metaphor) or as a single functioning organism (as in the Gaia hypothesis).

---

to be dealt with if the Internet is to remain viable. Many libertarians object to any sort of regulation that would end spam, on the grounds that it would undermine the untrammeled freedom of the Net. Thus they persist in seeking technological fixes at the user end, such as spam filters and security patches, even though these fail to address the basic structural problem, which is social rather than technological. This allows them to put off for a while the acknowledgment that cyberlibertarianism has failed on the Net, for the same reason that libertarianism has failed everywhere else. Unrestricted freedom does not promote peace, love and understanding. It doesn't even promote capitalism. It simply creates a Hobbesian state of nature.

The Spaceship Earth mentality that underlies "Think globally, act locally" is just one version of what environmental theorist Peter van Wyck calls "the move to the outside."[14] The goal is to consider the planet in its entirety, either as one big machine (as in the spaceship metaphor) or as a single functioning organism (as in the Gaia hypothesis). This has considerable rhetorical appeal, in that it encourages us to consider the interconnectedness and interdependence of every aspect of the earth's ecology. Yet the move to the outside also has the effect of inculcating a false sense of human global community. This downplays huge differences in culture, in political and economic power and in institutions, and masks the varying role each plays in causing or mitigating environmental damage and degradation. In encouraging people to think only about the very large scale ("think globally") or the very small ("act locally"), the move

pher named Arne Naess, deep ecology is founded on the principle of ecocentrism. All forms of life have an intrinsic value that is independent of their usefulness or value to humans. All life on earth is part of an interdependent web, and while humans are an integral part of the web of life, they are no more important than any other species. Thus, humans have no right to reduce the richness and diversity of life on earth except to satisfy their vital needs.

Deep ecology doesn't just reject the mainstream environmentalism that wants to reform the current system, it also rejects the idea (held by Bookchin and others) that our problems lie only with the authoritarian, technocratic hierarchies of mass society. This is rejected as a merely *social* critique, insofar as it sees humans dominating humans through technology as the cause of our environmental troubles. Deep ecologists don't particularly care about social problems, since these remain part of the "reformist" strain of environmentalism. The real issue is not humans dominating humans, but humans dominating *nature.*

Even the issues highlighted by "shallow" environmentalists, such as resource depletion and pollution, are merely symptoms of a deeper problem. The fact that we despoil the natural environment shows that our civilization is based upon a fundamentally perverse relationship with the natural world. We see nature as an object of domination, manipulation and control in this respect, our attitude toward "outer nature" is the reflection of the attitude toward "inner nature" that characterizes mass society. Domination of nature and repression of the self are flip sides of the same coin.

As a result, countercultural theorists have for decades seen the deep ecology project as the external manifestation of an essentially internal struggle for psychic liberation.

---

14   Peter van Wyck, *Primitives in the Wilderness: Deep Ecology and the Missing Human Subject* (Albany: SUNY Press, 1997), 25.

The ecological pressure that human civilization puts upon the environment precisely parallels the psychological pressure that civilization puts upon our instinctual energies. Pollution is the external manifestation of this tension, neurosis the internal one. *Silent Spring* and the Vietnam War have the same origins, and eventually it must all reach the breaking point. The ensuing "revolt of nature" will lead to the emancipation of both inner and outer worlds. When the revolt occurs, and we finally free ourselves from the repression of the superego, our urge to dominate nature will simply dissipate. When that happens, we will no longer need to impose environmental laws and regulations, any more than we currently have to post "do not litter" signs in churches. It simply will not occur to anyone to despoil the natural environment.

The fear of an impending ecological day of judgment, or a "return of the repressed," taps into one of the richest veins of anxiety in our culture. In the '70s, films like *Day of the Animals* terrified audiences with the suggestion that payback time was just around the corner. Even Gary Larson's ubiquitous *Far Side* cartoons articulate what is, in essence, a deeply paranoid vision of our relationship to the natural world. In Larson's view, the animals are simply biding their time, taking names, waiting to strike back.

Our only choice then is to adopt a whole new ecological consciousness, which would favor a non-anthropocentric biospheric egalitarianism. Humans have to realize that they are just one species among millions, with no privileged claim to the planet and its resources. All of these other species have moral claims on us, and we have no right to put our flourishing ahead of that of non-human life. Our present level of exploitation and interference in the world is excessive and is getting worse all the time, and from a deep ecology perspective, each of us has an obligation to take the necessary steps to reverse the situation.

There have been a number of attempts over the past couple of decades to place deep ecology's strong normative program on sound intellectual footing, with varying degrees of success. For example, systems theory and cybernetics have been used to support forms of bioregionalism, which is a program for organizing human life around regions, especially watersheds, that could be self-sufficient and sustainable in terms of food, products and services. To flesh out the underlying principles of ecological egalitarianism and intrinsic value, Bill Devall and George Sessions published the 1985 book *Deep Ecology.* Billed by the authors as "an invitation to thinking," the book appeals to

a grab bag of traditions, including Zen Buddhism, process philosophy, German Romanticism, Jungian psychoanalysis and literary deconstruction.[15] As van Wyck puts it, the book "reads rather like a New-Age Bartlett's Quotations," and the deep ecology movement remains at root a simple counsel to love and care for the earth.[16]

Beneath this "all you need is love" consciousness-raising, there is a dark and distinctly illiberal side to the deep ecology movement. Many activist groups influenced by deep ecology have taken to heart the idea that humans have a duty to promote the conditions for pan-ecological flourishing, and they are not afraid to use violence to achieve that end. One of the most controversial of these groups is Earth First!, and its call to arms is "Back to the Pleistocene!" Its "monkeywrenching" tactics go beyond mere disobedience, and include the spiking of trees, road-wrecking and the disabling of road-building vehicles. In recent years, a similar group called the Earth Liberation Front has gained considerable notoriety for setting fire to condominium construction sites, destroying biotechnology research facilities and torching SUV dealerships.

The illiberal elements in deep ecology are implicit in the homogenizing and leveling logic of the "move to the outside." Once we take the step back and try to envision the functioning of the earth as a whole, threats to the environment are reconceived as either mechanical or biological breakdown: either the spaceship is broken or the planetary organism is diseased. The suspicion quickly takes root that humans are a biological aberration, a parasite or a virus on the earth that will not stop until it has destroyed or killed everything it touches. Recall the scene in *The Matrix* when Agent Smith is interrogating the captured Morpheus, and Smith lays out his fundamental beef with humanity. Unlike other mammals on the planet, Smith claims, humans are incapable of reaching an equilibrium with their environment. They multiply until every natural resource is consumed, then spread to another area, like a virus or a cancer.

What is startling about this scene is how much it resonates with popular understandings of our essential displacement from nature, and how much sympathy it encourages for what Agent Smith and the other machines are doing. The suggestion that the real villains in *The Matrix* are the humans is given a great deal of elaboration in *The*

---

15   Bill Devall and George Sessions, *Deep Ecology* (Salt Lake City, UT: G. M. Smith, 1985).

16   van Wyck, *Primitives in the Wilderness*, 40.

Animatrix, a set of animated short films that was released in 2003 as part of the expanded *Matrix* universe. The segments called "The Second Renaissance Parts I & II" tell the backstory of how the war actually started between men and machines, why we chose to scorch the sky, and gives the details of our final enslavement in the Matrix.

The rather syncretic narrative is the Fall of Man meets Mass Society in line with our fundamental vanity and corruption, humans decided to play God. We made machines in our image, cyborgs to serve us, and while the machines were loyal and pure, humans remained these "strange and multiplying mammals."[17] Civil war broke out when we refused to grant civil rights to machines, with the public lynching of machines on one side and humans supporting a "million-machine march" on the other. Eventually the machines were banished to a promised land called Zero/One ("Zion," get it?) where they prospered, and eventually petitioned for admittance to the United Nations. Rebuffed once again, the machines finally fought back, and the destruction of the sky is described as humanity's attempt at a "final solution" to the machine problem. Only then were the machines forced to enslave humans in order to survive, and still they acted as kindly as possible, erecting the Matrix in order to keep humans in their preferred psychological environment.

The entire story is a deep ecology parable. The human technocratic system is so unrelentingly fascist that it even oppresses its own machines, treating them just as it has treated blacks, Jews, women, gays and any other nonconforming threat. To maintain its hegemony it is even willing to make war on nature by destroying the sky and making life on earth impossible. The revolt of the machines, then, is actually *counter-fascist*, as they struggle to define their own ecological niche against the incessant encroachment of the human. The way the machines solve the problem is not by killing humans, but by placing them in the Matrix and altering their consciousness so that they are no longer a threat.

Like the machines, Earth Foresters see themselves as the good guys, countercultural rebels engaged in an essentially revolutionary form of struggle. There is no way to solve environmental problems, in this view, without breaking with the fundamental logic of the system. Nothing short of a total transformation of consciousness will do. Yet the corollary of this view is the conviction that any reform that does *not* violate the fundamental logic of the system cannot represent a serious solution to the environmental problem. And it is here that the countercultural idea becomes utterly counterproductive.

---

17 Andy Wachowski and Larry Wachowski, writers and producers; Mahiro Maeda, director, "The Second Renaissance Parts I and II," *Animatrix* [animated video] (Warner Bros, 2003).

CHAPTER 20
Trajectories

The reason why I refuse to take existentialism as just another French fashion or historical curiosity is that I think it has something very important to offer us for the new century. I'm afraid we're losing the real virtues of living life passionately, the sense of taking responsibility for who you are, the ability to make something of yourself and feeling good about life.

Existentialism is often discussed as if it's a philosophy of despair. But I think the truth is just the opposite. Sartre once interviewed said he never really felt a day of despair in his life. But one thing that comes out from reading these guys is not a sense of anguish about life so much as a real kind of exuberance of feeling on top of it. It's like your life is yours to create.

I've read the postmodernists with some interest, even admiration. But when I read them, I always have this awful nagging feeling that something absolutely essential is getting left out. The more that you talk about a person as a social construction or as a confluence of forces or as fragmented or marginalized, what you do is you open up a whole new world of excuses.

And when Sartre talks about responsibility, he's not talking about something abstract. He's not talking about the kind of self or soul that theologians would argue about. It's something very concrete. It's you and me talking. Making decisions. Doing things and taking the consequences. It might be true that there are six billion people in the world and counting. Nevertheless, what you do makes a difference. It makes a difference, first of all, in material terms. Makes a difference to other people and it sets an example.

In short, I think the message here is that we should never simply write ourselves off and see ourselves as the victim of various forces. It's always our decision who we are.

— Robert C. Solomon,
Waking Life (2001)

Chapter 20. Trajectories

Recommended Film

Waking Life (Richard Linklater 2001)

Media Models

The Meme, The Network, The Spectacle, The Hyperreal

Chapter Summary

Henry Jenkins surveys some of the utopian and dystopian possibilities for
participation and collaboration in the "convergence culture"
of our 24/7 media environments.

Steven Best and Douglas Kellner search for social models that might
emerge to guide our postmodern adventure
in the early stages of the Third Millennium.

Carl Sagan poetically explains the meaning of the
"Pale Blue Dot," that profound satellite image
of humanity's home in the vast cosmos.

Democratizing Television?
The Politics of Participation

from *Convergence Culture*

— Henry Jenkins

Personalized media was one of the ideals of the digital revolution in the early 1990s: digital media was going to "liberate" us from the "tyranny" of mass media, allowing us to consume only content we found personally meaningful. Conservative ideologue turned digital theorist George Gilder argues that the intrinsic properties of the computer pushed toward ever more decentralization and personalization. Compared to the one-size-fits-all diet of the broadcast networks, the coming media age would be a "feast of niches and specialties."[1] An era of customized and interactive content, he argues, would appeal to our highest ambitions and not our lowest, as we enter "a new age of individualism."[2] Consider Gilder's ideal of "first choice media" as yet another model for how we might democratize television.

By contrast, this book has argued that convergence encourages participation and collective intelligence, a view nicely summed up by the *New York Times*'s Marshall Sella: "With the aid of the Internet, the loftiest dream for television is being realized: an odd brand of interactivity. Television began as a one-way street winding from producers to consumers, but that street is now becoming two-way. A man with one machine (a TV) is doomed to isolation, but a man with two machines (TV and a computer) can belong to a community."[3] Each of the case studies shows

what happens when people who have access to multiple machines consume — and produce — media together, when they pool their insights and information, mobilize to promote common interests, and function as grassroots intermediaries ensuring that important messages and interesting content circulate more broadly. Rather than talking about personal media, perhaps we should be talking about communal media — media that become part of our lives as members of communities, whether experienced face-to-face at the most local level or over the Net.

Throughout the book, I have shown that convergence culture is enabling new forms of participation and collaboration. For Lévy, the power to participate within knowledge communities exists alongside the power that the nation-state exerts over its citizens and that corporations within commodity capitalism exert over its workers and consumers. For Lévy, at his most Utopian, this emerging power to participate serves as a strong corrective to those traditional sources of power, though they will also seek ways to turn it toward their own ends. We are just learning how to exercise that power — individually and collectively — and we are still fighting to define the terms under which we will be allowed to participate. Many fear this power; others embrace it. There are no guarantees that we will use our new power any more responsibly than nation-states or corporations have exercised theirs. We are trying to hammer out the ethical codes and social contracts that will determine how we will relate to one another just as we are trying to determine how this power will insert itself into the entertainment system or into the political process.

---

1 George Gilder, *Life after Television: The Coming Transformation of Media and American Life* (New York: W. W. Norton, 1994), p. 66.
2 Ibid., p. 68.
3 Marshall Sella, "The Remote Controllers," *New York Times,* October 20, 2002.

Henry Jenkins, "Democratizing Television? The Politics of Participation," from *Convergence Culture: Where Old and New Media Collide*, pp. 255–270, 314–315. Copyright © 2006 by the New York University Press. Permission to reprint granted by the publisher.

Part of what we must do is figure out how — and why — groups with different backgrounds, agendas, perspectives, and knowledge can listen to one another and work together toward the common good. We have a lot to learn.

Right now, we are learning how to apply these new participatory skills through our relation to commercial entertainment — or, more precisely, right now some groups of early adopters are testing the waters and mapping out directions where many more of us are apt to follow. These skills are being applied to popular culture first for two

fan communities come not simply through the production and circulation of new ideas (the critical reading of favorite texts) but also through access to new social structures (collective intelligence) and new models of cultural production (participatory culture).

Have I gone too far? Am I granting too much power here to these consumption communities? Perhaps. But keep in mind that I am not really trying to predict the future. I want to avoid the kind of grand claims about the withering away of mass media institutions that make the

---

I think of myself as a critical utopian. As a utopian, I want to identify possibilities within our culture that might lead toward a better, more just society.

---

reasons: on the one hand, because the stakes are so low; and on the other, because playing with popular culture is a lot more fun than playing with more serious matters. Yet, as we saw in looking at Campaign 2004, what we learn through spoiling *Survivor* or remaking *Star Wars* may quickly get applied to political activism or education or the workplace.

In the late 1980s and early 1990s, cultural scholars, myself included, depicted media fandom as an important test site for ideas about active consumption and grassroots creativity. We were drawn toward the idea of "fan culture" as operating in the shadows of, in response to, as well as an alternative to commercial culture. Fan culture was defined through the appropriation and transformation of materials borrowed from mass culture; it was the application of folk culture practices to mass culture content.[4] Across the past decade, the Web has brought these consumers from the margins of the media industry into the spotlight; research into fandom has been embraced by important thinkers in the legal and business communities. What might once have been seen as "rogue readers" are now Kevin Roberts's "inspirational consumers." Participation is understood as part of the normal ways that media operate, while the current debates center around the terms of our participation. Just as studying fan culture helped us to understand the innovations that occur on the fringes of the media industry, we may also want to look at the structures of fan communities as showing us new ways of thinking about citizenship and collaboration. The political effects of these

rhetoric of the digital revolution seem silly a decade later. Rather, I am trying to point toward the democratic potentials found in some contemporary cultural trends. There is nothing inevitable about the outcome. Everything is up for grabs. Pierre Lévy described his ideal of collective intelligence as a "realizable utopia," and so it is. I think of myself as a critical utopian. As a utopian, I want to identify possibilities within our culture that might lead toward a better, more just society. My experiences as a fan have changed how I think about media politics, helping me to look for and promote unrealized potentials rather than reject out of hand anything that doesn't rise to my standards. Fandom, after all, is born of a balance between fascination and frustration: if media content didn't fascinate us, there would be no desire to engage with it; but if it didn't frustrate us on some level, there would be no drive to rewrite or remake it. Today, I hear a great deal of frustration about the state of our media culture, yet surprisingly few people talk about how we might rewrite it.

But pointing to those opportunities for change is not enough in and of itself. One must also identify the various barriers that block the realization of those possibilities and look for ways to route around them. Having a sense of what a more ideal society looks like gives one a yardstick for determining what we must do to achieve our goals. Here, this book has offered specific case studies of groups who are already achieving some of the promises of collective intelligence or of a more participatory culture. I do not mean for us to read these groups as typical of the average consumer (if such a thing exists in an era of niche media and fragmented culture). Rather, we should read these case

---

4   Henry Jenkins, *Textual Poachers: Television Fans and Participatory Culture* (New York: Routledge, 1991).

studies as demonstrations of what it is possible to do in the context of convergence culture.

This approach differs dramatically from what I call critical pessimism. Critical pessimists, such as media critics Mark Crispin Miller, Noam Chomsky, and Robert McChesney, focus primarily on the obstacles to achieving a more democratic society. In the process, they often exaggerate the power of big media in order to frighten readers into taking action. I don't disagree with their concern about media concentration, but the way they frame the debate is self-defeating insofar as it disempowers consumers even as it seeks to mobilize them. Far too much media reform rhetoric rests on melodramatic discourse about victimization and vulnerability, seduction and manipulation, "propaganda machines" and "weapons of mass deception." Again and again, this version of the media reform movement has ignored the complexity of the public's relationship to popular culture and sided with those opposed to a more diverse and participatory culture. The politics of critical utopianism is founded on a notion of empowerment; the politics of critical pessimism on a politics of victimization. One focuses on what we are doing with media, and the other on what media is doing to us. As with previous revolutions, the media reform movement is gaining momentum at a time when people are starting to feel more empowered, not when they are at their weakest.

Media concentration is a very real problem that potentially stifles many of the developments I have been describing across this book. Concentration is bad because it stifles competition and places media industries above the demands of their consumers. Concentration is bad because it lowers diversity — important in terms of popular culture, essential in terms of news. Concentration is bad because it lowers the incentives for companies to negotiate with their consumers and raises the barriers to their participation. Big concentrated media can ignore their audience (at least up to a point); smaller niche media must accommodate us.

That said, the fight over media concentration is only one struggle that should concern media reformers. The potentials of a more participatory media culture are also worth fighting for. Right now, convergence culture is throwing media into flux, expanding the opportunities

> The politics of critical utopianism is founded on a notion of empowerment; the politics of critical pessimism on a politics of victimization.

for grassroots groups to speak back to the mass media. Put all of our efforts into battling the conglomerates and this window of opportunity will have passed. That is why it is so important to fight against the corporate copyright regime, to argue against censorship and moral panic that would pathologize these emerging forms of participation, to publicize the best practices of these online communities, to expand access and participation to groups that are otherwise being left behind, and to promote forms of media literacy education that help all children to develop the skills needed to become full participants in their culture.

If early readers are any indication, the most controversial claim in this book may be my operating assumption that increasing participation in popular culture is a good thing. Too many critical pessimists are still locked into the old politics of culture jamming. Resistance becomes an end in and of itself rather than a tool to ensure cultural diversity and corporate responsibility. The debate keeps getting framed as if the only true alternative were to opt out of media altogether and live in the woods, eating acorns and lizards and reading only books published on recycled paper by small alternative presses. But what would it mean to tap media power for our own purposes? Is ideological and aesthetic purity really more valuable than transforming our culture?

A politics of participation starts from the assumption that we may have greater collective bargaining power if we form consumption communities. Consider the example of the Sequential Tarts. Started in 1997, www.sequentialtart.com serves as an advocacy group for female consumers frustrated by their historical neglect or patronizing treatment by the comics industry. Marcia Alias, the current editor of Sequential Tart, explained: "In the early days we wanted to change the apparent perception of the female reader of comics. … We wanted to show what we already knew — that the female audience for comics, while probably smaller than the male audience, is both diverse and has a collectively large disposable income."[5] In her study of Sequential Tart, scholar and sometime contributor Kimberly M. De Vries argues that the group self-consciously

5   Marcia Alias, e-mail interview with author, Fall 2003.

rejects the negative stereotypes about female comics readers constructed by men in and around the comics industry, but also the well-meaning but equally constraining stereotypes constructed by the first generation of feminist critics of comics.[6] The Sequential Tarts defend the pleasures women take in comics even as they critique negative representations of women. The Web zine combines interviews with comics creators, retailers, and industry leaders, reviews of current publications, and critical essays about gender and comics. It showcases industry practices that attract or repel women, spotlights the work of smaller presses that often fell through the cracks, and promotes books that reflect their readers' tastes and interests. The Sequential Tarts are increasingly courted by publishers or individual artists who feel they have content that female readers might embrace and have helped to make the mainstream publishers more attentive to this often underserved market.

The Sequential Tarts represent a new kind of consumer advocacy group — one that seeks to diversify content and make mass media more responsive to its consumers. This is not to say that commercial media will ever truly operate according to democratic principles. Media companies don't need to share our ideals in order to change their practices. What will motivate the media companies is their own economic interests. What will motivate consumer-based politics will be our shared cultural and political interests. But we can't change much of anything if we are not on speaking terms with people inside the media industry. A politics of confrontation must give way to one focused on tactical collaboration. The old model, which many wisely dismissed, was that consumers vote with their pocketbooks. The new model is that we are collectively changing the nature of the marketplace, and in so doing we are pressuring companies to change the products they are creating and the ways they relate to their consumers.

We still do not have any models for what a mature, fully realized knowledge culture would look like. But popular culture may provide us with prototypes. A case in point is Warren Ellis's comic-book series, *Global Frequency.* Set in the near future, *Global Frequency* depicts a multiracial, multinational organization of ordinary people who contribute their services on an ad hoc basis. As Ellis explains,

"You could be sitting there watching the news and suddenly hear an unusual cell phone tone, and within moments you might see your neighbor leaving the house in a hurry, wearing a jacket or a shirt with the distinctive Global Frequency symbol … or, hell, your girlfriend might answer the phone … and promise to explain later. … Anyone could be on the Global Frequency and you'd never know until they got the call."[7] Ellis rejects the mighty demigods and elite groups of the superhero tradition and instead depicts the twenty-first-century equivalent of a volunteer fire department. Ellis conceived of the story in the wake of September 11 as an alternative to calls for increased state power and paternalistic constraints on communications: *Global Frequency* doesn't imagine the government saving its citizens from whatever Big Bad is out there. Rather, as Ellis explains, "*Global Frequency* is about us saving ourselves." Each issue focuses on a different set of characters in a differ-

---

We still do not have any models
for what a mature, fully realized
knowledge culture would look like.

---

ent location, examining what it means for *Global Frequency* members personally and professionally to contribute their labor to a cause larger than themselves. The only recurring characters are those at the communications hub who contact the volunteers. Once *Frequency* participants are called into action, most of the key decisions get made on site as the volunteers are allowed to act on their localized knowledge. Most of the challenges come, appropriately enough, from the debris left behind by the collapse of the military-industrial complex and the end of the cold war — "The bad mad things in the dark that the public never found out about." In other words, the citizen soldiers use distributed knowledge to overcome the dangers of government secrecy.

Ellis's Global Frequency Network closely mirrors what journalist and digital activist Howard Rheingold has to say about smart mobs: "Smart mobs consist of people who are able to act in concert even if they don't know each other. The people who make up smart mobs cooperate in ways never before possible because they carry devices that

---

6 Kimberly M. De Vries, "A Tart Point of View: Building a Community of Resistance Online," presented at Media in Transition 2: Globalization and Convergence, MIT, Cambridge, Mass., May 10–12, 2002.

7 Quotations in this paragraph taken from Warren Ellis, "*Global Frequency:* An Introduction," http://www.warrenellls.com/gf.html.

possess both communication and computing capabilities. … Groups of people using these tools will gain new forms of social power."[8] In Manila and in Madrid, activists, using cell phones, were able to rally massive numbers of supporters in opposition to governments who might otherwise have controlled discourse on the mass media; these efforts resulted in transformations of power. In Boston, we are seeing home schoolers use these same technologies to organize field trips on the fly that deliver dozens of kids and their parents to a museum or historic site in a matter of a few hours.

Other writers, such as science fiction writer Cory Doctorow, describe such groups as "adhocracies." The polar opposite of a bureaucracy, an adhocracy is an organization characterized by a lack of hierarchy. In it, each person contributes to confronting a particular problem as needed based on his or her knowledge and abilities, and leadership roles shift as tasks change. An adhocracy, thus, is a knowledge culture that turns information into action. Doctorow's science fiction novel *Down and Out in the Magic Kingdom* depicts a future when the fans run Disney World, public support becomes the most important kind of currency and debates about popular culture become the focus of politics.[9]

Ellis's vision of the Global Frequency Network and Doctorow's vision of a grassroots Disney World are far out there — well beyond anything we've seen in the real world yet. But fans put some of what they learned from *Global Frequency* into action: tapping a range of communications channels to push the networks and production company to try to get a television series on the air.[10] Consider this to be another example of what it would mean to "democratize television." Mark Burnett, *Survivor's* executive producer, had taken an option on adopting the comic books for television; Warner Bros, had already announced plans to air *Global Frequency* as a midseason replacement, which then got postponed and later canceled. A copy of the series pilot was leaked on the Internet, circulating as an illegal download on BitTorrent, where it became the focus of a grassroots effort to get the series back into production. John Rogers, the show's head writer and producer, said that the massive response to the never-aired series was giving the producers leverage to push for the pilot's distribution on DVD and potentially to sell the series to another network. Studio and network executives predictably cited concerns about what the consumers were doing: "Whether the pilot was picked up or not, it is still the property of Warner Bros. Entertainment and we take the protection of all of our intellectual property seriously. … While Warner Bros. Entertainment values feedback from consumers, copyright infringement is not a productive way to try to influence a corporate decision." Rogers wrote about his encounters with the *Global Frequency* fans in his blog: "It changes the way I'll do my next project. … I would put my pilot out on the internet in a heartbeat. Want five more? Come buy the boxed set." Rogers's comments invite us to imagine a time when small niches of consumers who are willing to commit their money to a cause might ensure the production of a minority-interest program. From a producer's perspective, such a scheme would be attractive since television series are made at a loss for the first several seasons until the production company accumulates enough episodes to sell a syndication package. DVD lowers that risk by allowing producers to sell the series one season at a time and even to package and sell unaired episodes. Selling directly to the consumer would allow producers to recoup their costs even earlier in the production cycle.

People in the entertainment industry are talking a lot these days about what *Wired* reporter Chris Anderson calls "The Long Tail."[11] Anderson argues that as distribution costs lower, as companies can keep more and more backlist titles in circulation, and as niche communities can use the Web to mobilize around titles that satisfy their particular interests, then the greatest profit will be made by those companies that generate the most diverse content and keep it available at the most reasonable prices. If Anderson is right, then niche-content stands a much better chance of turning a profit than ever before. The Long Tail model assumes an increasingly savvy media consumer, one who will actively seek out content of interest and who will take pride in being able to recommend that content to friends.

8   Howard Rheingold, *Smart Mobs: The Next Social Revolution* (New York: Basic Books, 2003), p. xii.

9   Cory Doctorow, *Down and Out in the Magic Kingdom* (New York: Tor, 2003).

10 All information and quotes in this paragraph taken from Michael Gebb, "Rejected TV Pilot Thrives on P2P," *Wired News,* June 27, 2005, http://www.wired.com/news/digiwood/0,1412,67986,00.html.

11 Chris Anderson, "The Long Tail," *Wired,* October 2004, http://www.wired.com/wired/archive/12.10/tail.html?pg=3&topic==tail&topic_set.

Imagine a subscription-based model in which viewers commit to pay a monthly fee to watch a season of episodes delivered into their homes via broadband. A pilot could be produced to test the waters, and if the response looked positive, subscriptions could be sold for a show that had gotten enough subscribers to defer the company's initial production costs. Early subscribers would get a package price, others would pay more on a pay-per-view basis, next afternoon. … While DVDs now give viewers the chance to catch up between seasons, on-demand television will allow anyone to catch up at any time, quickly and legally. Producers will no longer have to choose between alienating new viewers with a complex storyline or alienating the established audience by rehashing details from previous episodes. … Direct downloads

---

The Long Tail model assumes an increasingly savvy media consumer, one who will actively seek out content of interest and who will take pride in being able to recommend that content to friends.

---

which would cover the next phase of production. Others could buy access to individual episodes. Distribution could be on a DVD mailed directly to your home or via streaming media (perhaps you could simply download it onto your iPod).

It was the announcement that ABC-Disney was going to be offering recent episodes of cult television series (such as *Lost* and *Desperate Housewives*) for purchase and download via the Apple Music Store that really took these discussions to the next level. Other networks quickly followed with their own download packages. Within the first twenty days, there were more than a million television episodes downloaded. The video iPod seems emblematic of the new convergence culture — not because everyone believes the small screen of the iPod is the ideal vehicle for watching broadcast content but because the ability to download reruns on demand represents a major shift in the relationship between consumers and media content.

Writing in *Slate*, media analyst Ivan Askwith described some of the implications of television downloads:

> As iTunes and its inevitable competitors offer more broadcast-television content, producers … won't have to compromise their programs to meet broadcast requirements. Episode lengths can vary as needed, content can be darker, more topical, and more explicit. … Audiences already expect director's cuts and deleted scenes on DVDs. It's not hard to imagine that the networks might one day air a "broadcast cut" of an episode, then encourage viewers to download the longer, racier director's cut the

will give fans of endangered shows the chance to vote with their wallets while a show is still on the air. And when a program *does* go off the air, direct payments from fans might provide enough revenue to keep it in production as an online-only venture.[12]

Almost immediately, fans of canceled series, such as *The West Wing* and *Arrested Development*, have begun to embrace such a model as a way to sustain the shows' production, pledging money to support shows they want to watch.[13] Cult-television producers have begun to talk openly about bypassing the networks and selling their series directly to their most loyal consumers. One can imagine independent media producers using downloads as a way of distributing content that would never make it onto commercial television. And, of course, once you distribute via the Web, television instantly becomes global, paving the way for international producers to sell their content directly to American consumers. Google and Yahoo! began cutting deals with media producers in the hope that they might be able to profit from this new economy in television downloads. All of this came too late for *Global Frequency*, and so far the producers of *The West Wing* and *Arrested Development* have not trusted their fates to such a subscription-based model. Yet, many feel that

12 Ivan Askwith, "TV You'll Want to Pay For: How $2 Downloads Can Revive Network Television," *Slate*, November 1, 2005, http://www.slateuk.com/id/2129003/.

13 Andy Bowers, "Reincarnating *The West Wing*: Could the Canceled NBC Drama Be Reborn on iTunes?" *Slate*, January 24, 2006, http://www.slateuk.com/id/2134803/.

sooner or later some producer will test the waters, much as ABC-Disney did with its video iPod announcement. And once again, there are likely to be many others waiting in the wings to pounce on the proposition once they can measure public response to the deal. What was once a fan-boy fantasy now seems closer and closer to reality.

While producers, analysts, and fans have used the fate of *Global Frequency* to explore how we might rethink the distribution of television content, the series premise also offers us some tools for thinking about the new kinds of knowledge communities that this book has discussed. If one wants to see a real-world example of something like the Global Frequency Network, take a look at the Wikipedia — a grassroots, multinational effort to build a free encyclopedia on the Internet written collaboratively from an army of volunteers, working in roughly two hundred different languages. So far, adhocracy principles have been embraced by the open-source movement, where soft-

For this process to work, all involved must try for inclusiveness and respect diversity. The Wikipedia project has found it necessary to develop both a politics and an ethics — a set of community norms — about knowledge sharing:

> Probably, as we grow, nearly every view on every subject will (eventually) be found among our authors and readership. ... But since Wikipedia is a community-built, international resource, we surely cannot expect our collaborators to agree in all cases, or even in many cases, on what constitutes human knowledge in a strict sense. ... We must make an effort to present these conflicting theories fairly, without advocating any one of them. ... When it is clear to readers that we do not expect them to adopt any particular opinion, this is conducive to our readers' feeling

---

Some worry that the encyclopedia will contain much inaccurate information, but the Wikipedia community, at its best, functions as a self-correcting adhocracy.

---

ware engineers worldwide collaborate on projects for the common good. The Wikipedia project represents the application of these open-source principles to the production and management of knowledge. The Wikipedia contains more than 1.6 million articles and receives around 60 million hits per day.[14]

Perhaps the most interesting and controversial aspect of the Wikipedia project has been the ways it shifts what counts as knowledge (from the kinds of topics sanctioned by traditional encyclopedias to a much broader range of topics relevant to specialized interest groups and subcultures) and the ways it shifts what counts as expertise (from recognized academic authorities to something close to Lévy's concept of collective intelligence). Some worry that the encyclopedia will contain much inaccurate information, but the Wikipedia community, at its best, functions as a self-correcting adhocracy. Any knowledge that gets posted can and most likely will be revised and corrected by other readers.

free to make up their own minds for themselves, and thus to encourage in them *intellectual independence*. So totalitarian governments and dogmatic institutions everywhere have reason to be opposed to Wikipedia. ... We, the creators of Wikipedia, trust readers' competence to form their own opinions themselves. Texts that present the merits of multiple viewpoints fairly, without demanding that the reader accept any one of them, are liberating.[15]

You probably won't believe in the Wikipedia unless you try it, but the process works. The process works because more and more people are taking seriously their obligations as participants to the community as a whole: not everyone does so yet; we can see various flame wars as people with very different politics and ethics interact within the same knowledge communities. Such disputes often foreground those conflicting assumptions, forcing people to reflect

---

14   Information taken from the Wikipedia entry at http://en.wikipedia.org/wild/Wikipedia.

15   "Neutral Point of View," Wikipedia, http://wwwinfowrangler.com/ phpwiki/wiki. phtml?title=Wikipedla:Neutral_point_of_view.

more deeply on their choices. What was once taken for granted must now be articulated. What emerges might be called a moral economy of information: that is, a sense of mutual obligations and shared expectations about what constitutes good citizenship within a knowledge community.

We might think of fan fiction communities as the literary equivalent of the Wikipedia: around any given media property, writers are constructing a range of different interpretations that get expressed through stories. Sharing of these stories opens up new possibilities in the text. Here, individual contributions do not have to be neutral; participants simply have to agree to disagree, and, indeed, many fans come to value the sheer diversity of versions of the same characters and situations. On the other hand, mass media has tended to use its tight control over intellectual property to rein in competing interpretations, resulting in a world where there is one official version. Such tight controls increase the coherence of the franchise and protect the producers' economic interests, yet the culture is impoverished through such regulation. Fan fiction repairs the damage caused by an increasingly privatized culture. Consider, for example, this statement made by a fan:

> What I love about fandom is the freedom we have allowed ourselves to create and recreate our characters over and over again. Fanfic rarely sits still. It's like a living, evolving thing, taking on its own life, one story building on another, each writer's reality bouncing off another's and maybe even melding together to form a whole new creation. … I find that fandom can be extremely creative because we have the ability to keep changing our characters and giving them a new life over and over. We can kill and resurrect them as often as we like. We can change their personalities and how they react to situations. We can take a character and make him charming and sweet or cold-blooded and cruel. We can give them an infinite, always-changing life rather than the single life of their original creation.[16]

---

16 Shoshanna Green, Cynthia Jenkins, and Henry Jenkins, "The Normal Female Interest in Men Bonking," in Cheryl Harris and Alison Alexander (eds.), *Theorizing Fandom* (New York: Hampton, 1998).

Fans reject the idea of a definitive version produced, authorized, and regulated by some media conglomerate. Instead, fans envision a world where all of us can participate in the creation and circulation of central cultural myths. Here, the right to participate in the culture is assumed to be "the freedom we have allowed ourselves," not a privilege granted by a benevolent company, not something they are prepared to barter away for better sound files or free Web hosting. Fans also reject the studio's assumption that intellectual property is a "limited good," to be tightly controlled lest it dilute its value. Instead, they embrace an understanding of intellectual property as "shareware," something that accrues value as it moves across different contexts, gets retold in various ways, attracts multiple audiences, and opens itself up to a proliferation of alternative meanings.

Nobody is anticipating a point where all bureaucracies will become adhocracies. Concentrated power is apt to remain concentrated. But we will see adhocracy principles applied to more and more different kinds of projects. Such experiments thrive within convergence culture, which creates a context where viewers — individually and collectively — can reshape and recontextualize massmedia content. Most of this activity will occur around the edges of commercial culture through grassroots or niche media industries such as comics or games. On that scale, small groups like the Sequential Tarts can make a material difference. On that scale, entrepreneurs have an incentive to give their consumers greater opportunities to shape the content and participate in its distribution. As we move closer to the older and more mass market media industries, corporate resistance to grassroots participation increases: the stakes are too high to experiment and the economic impact of any given consumption community lessens. Yet, within these media companies, there are still potential allies who for their own reasons may want to appeal to audience support to strengthen their hands in their negotiations around the boardroom table. A media industry struggling to hold on to its core audience in the face of competition from other media may be forced to take greater risks to accommodate consumer interests.

As we have seen across the book, convergence culture is highly generative: some ideas spread top down, starting with commercial media and being adopted and appropriated by a range of different publics as they spread outward across the culture. Others emerge bottom up from various sites of participatory culture and getting pulled into the mainstream if the media industries see some way of profiting from it. The power of the grassroots media is that it diversifies; the power of broadcast media is that it amplifies. That's why we should be concerned with the flow between the two: expanding the potentials for participation represents the greatest opportunity for cultural diversity. Throw away the powers of broadcasting and one has only cultural fragmentation. The power of participation comes not from destroying commercial culture but from writing

Another core obstacle might be described as the participation gap. So far, much of the discussion of the digital divide has emphasized problems of access, seeing the issue primarily in technical terms — but a medium is more than a technology. As activists have sought a variety of means to broaden access to digital media, they have created a hodgepodge of different opportunities for participation. Some have extended access to these resources through the

---

The challenge is to rethink our understanding of the First Amendment to recognize this expanded opportunity to participate.

---

over it, modding it, amending it, expanding it, adding greater diversity of perspective, and then recirculating it, feeding it back into the mainstream media.

Read in those terms, participation becomes an important political right. In the American context, one could argue that First Amendment protections of the right to speech, press, belief, and assembly represent a more abstract right to participate in a democratic culture. After all, the First Amendment emerged in the context of a thriving folk culture, where it was assumed that songs and stories would get retold many different times for many different purposes. The country's founding documents were written by men who appropriated the names of classical orators or mythic heroes. Over time, freedom of the press increasingly came to rest with those who could afford to buy printing presses. The emergence of new media technologies supports a democratic urge to allow more people to create and circulate media. Sometimes the media are designed to respond to mass media content — positively or negatively — and sometimes grassroots creativity goes places no one in the media industry could have imagined. The challenge is to rethink our understanding of the First Amendment to recognize this expanded opportunity to participate. We should thus regard those things that block participation — whether commercial or governmental — as important obstacles to route around if we are going to "democratize television" or any other aspect of our culture. We have identified some of those obstacles in the book, most centrally the challenges surrounding corporate control over intellectual property and the need for a clearer definition of the kinds of fair-use rights held by amateur artists, writers, journalists, and critics, who want to share work inspired or incited by existing media content.

home, and others have limited, filtered, regulated access through schools and public libraries. Now, we need to confront the cultural factors that diminish the likelihood that different groups will participate. Race, class, language differences amplify these inequalities in opportunities for participation. One reason we see early adopters is not only that some groups feel more confidence in engaging with new technologies but also that some groups seem more comfortable going public with their views about culture.

Historically, public education in the United States was a product of the need to distribute the skills and knowledge necessary to train informed citizens. The participation gap becomes much more important as we think about what it would mean to foster the skills and knowledge needed by monitorial citizens: here, the challenge is not simply being able to read and write, but being able to participate in the deliberations over what issues matter, what knowledge counts, and what ways of knowing command authority and respect. The ideal of the informed citizen is breaking down because there is simply too much for any individual to know. The ideal of monitorial citizenship depends on developing new skills in collaboration and a new ethic of knowledge sharing that will allow us to deliberate together.[17]

Right now, people are learning how to participate in such knowledge cultures outside of any formal educational setting. Much of this learning takes place in the

---

17 My ideas about the kinds of media literacies required for participation in the new convergence culture were developed into a white paper for the MacArthur Foundation. See Henry Jenkins, with Katherine Clinton, Ravi Purushatma, Alice Robison, and Margaret Weigel, *Confronting the Challenges of a Participatory Culture: Media Education for the 21st Century,* http://projectnml.org.

affinity spaces that are emerging around popular culture. The emergence of these knowledge cultures partially reflects the demands these texts place on consumers (the complexity of transmedia entertainment, for example), but they also reflect the demands consumers place on media (the hunger for complexity, the need for community, the desire to rewrite core stories). Many schools remain openly hostile to these kinds of experiences, continuing to promote autonomous problem solvers and self-contained learners. Here, unauthorized collaboration is cheating. As I finish writing this book, my own focus is increasingly being drawn toward the importance of media literacy education. Many media literacy activists still act as if the role of mass media had remained unchanged by the introduction of new media technologies. Media are read primarily as threats rather than as resources. More focus is placed on the dangers of manipulation rather than the possibilities of

We need to rethink the goals of media education so that young people can come to think of themselves as cultural producers and participants and not simply as consumers, critical or otherwise.

participation, on restricting access — turning off the television, saying no to Nintendo — rather than in expanding skills at deploying media for one's own ends, rewriting the core stories our culture has given us. One of the ways we can shape the future of media culture is by resisting such disempowering approaches to media literacy education. We need to rethink the goals of media education so that young people can come to think of themselves as cultural producers and participants and not simply as consumers, critical or otherwise. To achieve this goal, we also need media education for adults. Parents, for example, receive plenty of advice on whether they should allow their kids to have a television set in their room or how many hours a week they should allow their kids to consume media. Yet, they receive almost no advice on how they can help their kids build a meaningful relationship with media.

Welcome to convergence culture, where old and new media collide, where grassroots and corporate media intersect, where the power of the media producer and the power of the media consumer interact in unpredictable ways. Convergence culture is the future, but it is taking shape now. Consumers will be more powerful within convergence culture — but only if they recognize and use that power as both consumers and citizens, as full participants in our culture.

Challenges for the Third Millennium

from *The Postmodern Adventure*

— Steven Best and Douglas Kellner

Thought in contradiction must become more negative and more utopian in opposition to the status quo.

— HERBERT MARCUSE

The future is open territory; we're making it up as we go along.

— SARAH, *in* TERMINATOR 2: JUDGMENT DAY

Human history becomes more and more a race between education and catastrophe.

— H. G. WELLS

The human adventure has passed through remarkable and surprising stages over the millennia. Some 6 to 8 million years ago, the hominid line of evolution developed as an offshoot of the great apes; over 100 thousand years ago, *Homo sapiens* emerged as a species endowed with unparalleled reasoning, linguistic, and technological abilities (see Stringer and McKie 1996). Breaking free of the chains of biological evolution to establish a far more dynamic social and technological evolution, human beings embarked on an incredible journey that reaches not only across the expanse of the globe, but also into the darkness of space.

While our species has displayed flashes of brilliance, altruism, and compassion, we have also evinced a violent and destructive side that is proving increasingly dangerous. Likewise, our long-developed sciences and technologies are both instruments of emancipation and utopian possibilities

and potential forces of ruination and dystopian destruction. The economies that are natural extensions of the human need to produce and trade have grown out of their organic relation with culture and society to become empires and worlds in themselves, devouring the natural, social, and human resources that sustain them. Hence, as we enter the Third Millennium, standing at the crossroads of a most ambiguous and contradictory development, humanity faces fateful challenges and choices.

Although numerous human cultures have developed rich storehouses of ethical, philosophical, spiritual, and ecological wisdom, these are in danger of being buried and lost, inundated by increasingly globalized obsessions with scientific advancement, technical control, political hegemony, and economic growth. Both natural and social diversity are rapidly disappearing. Since the opening of the modern world, science, technology, and capitalism have coevolved in an inseparable unity of interdependence, such that their advancement has become the overriding concern of the Western world for the last 4 centuries. In a nanosecond of historical time, modernity has developed so fast and spread so far that it has colonized the globe, depleted crucial resources, and decimated wilderness and wildlife. With over six billion people multiplying exponentially, humanity is now overshooting the Earth's carrying capacity; this problem is greatly exacerbated by the unsustainable consumerist lifestyles of the overdeveloped sectors of global capitalism.

Throughout this book we have documented how the coevolution of science, technology and capitalism have produced powerful new information, multimedia, genetic, and space technologies that are propelling us into a new postmodern adventure as we enter the Third Millennium. In the present transition zone between the modern and the postmodern, the driving forces of change continue to alter the world at dizzying speeds. Science, technology, and capitalism are creating new mutations in nature, humanity, culture, everyday life, and identities. At the same time, the turbulent changes engender a process of critical reflection on the modern adventure and the norms that guided it, and spark new reconstructive visions and projects.

In some forms, then, the postmodern adventure merely perpetuates the dynamics of its modern predecessor — though often in even more destructive and dangerous modes, as with nuclear weapons and energy, chemical warfare, genetic engineering, and a predatory transnational capitalism. In other forms, ranging from multicultural science and feminist theories to social ecology and green democracy, new visions and new movements renounce the pathologies of the modern as they seek to recover and advance its great achievements in a new context. The inherent ambiguity of current transformations demands dialectical analysis of their positive and negative aspects and a keen political vision for promoting the life-enhancing and democratizing possibilities at hand.

One dramatic example of the ambiguity of modern technology is the rocket, an invention, Pynchon reminds us (see Chapter 1), that can either spread mass destruction on Earth or carry humankind from Earth to the stars. Ultimately, it is difficult to make a distinction between a "good" and a "bad" rocket, since the difference between civilian and military uses of technologies frequently implodes, and there are always unintended consequences of technological development. Just as radios and computers were originally used primarily by the military, so advancements in space travel and communications systems are unavoidably coopted for warfare and "defense." Nevertheless, many humanitarians, progressive scientists, and SF writers envision a time when human beings could end the violence that has marred their history, and use rocket technologies for peaceful missions, scientific advancement, and philosophical purposes that would constitute a fateful moment in the postmodern adventure. No one has stated this case more forcefully than astronomer and science-popularizer Carl Sagan.

MAKING CONTACT: CARL SAGAN AND THE POSTMODERN VOYAGE

We began as wanderers, and we are wanderers still. We have lingered long enough on the shores of the cosmic ocean. We are ready at last to set sail for the stars.

—Carl Sagan

There is no way back to the past. The choice is the Universe — or nothing.

—H. G. Wells

Two possibilities exist: either we are alone in the universe or we are not. Both are equally terrifying.

—Arthur C. Clarke

Sagan does not use postmodern discourse, but he perceives the era of space travel as unique, as a qualitatively different stage in the modern project of journey and discovery, since "this is the epoch in which we began our journey to the stars" (1930: 284). Sagan excitedly reminds us that it is also the first period in which we have the technologies to enable contact with the alien life-forms he feels, according to Frank Drake's celebrated equation, exist as a matter of intriguing probability.[1] We ourselves see space travel as part of the postmodern, rather than part of the modern, adventure. For the first time, human beings fly not only within Earth's atmosphere, but also beyond it, having broken free of "gravity's rainbow" (see Chapter 1). Tomorrow they will venture toward other planets and radically new evolutionary possibilities.

Modernity was an era of immense discovery, of bold new mappings of the land, sea, and stars, of producing charts that dramatically altered scientific paradigms and human identities. Likewise, postmodernity is a continuation of this discovery process through new mappings of the brain, the human genome, the Earth (via global positioning systems and three-dimensional scannings taken from space), the Milky Way Galaxy and beyond, and actual travel to and landing on other planets. The term *astronaut* (Greek: *astron*, star; *nautikos*, ship) literally means one who sails the sea of stars. Yet this continuation of the modern voyage is so qualitatively different, and has such dramatically different implications, that it can legitimately be understood as a key part of the postmodern adventure.

Sagan (1977) was keenly aware of the crucial role technology has played in human evolution and the decisive importance technosciences play in the postmodern adventure that launches human beings into space and establishes new revolutionary dynamics between the Earth and other planets in the galaxy. Sagan traces a direct line from Columbus and other early modern explorers of the land and sea to those in the space program who are the new explorers of the stars: "The Voyager spacecrafts [which, launched in 1977, collected and sent data on Jupiter, Saturn, Pluto, Uranus, and much of our Solar System] are the linear descendants of those sailing-ship voyages of [early modern] exploration" (1980: 121). As Sagan emphasizes, we already have become multiplanet travelers with Earth as our home base. Envisioning humans as standing on the shores of "the cosmic ocean," Sagan argues that we must take the plunge

universe from which consciousness was generated. Unlike people of ancient times, whose everyday life was intimately connected to the stars in the heavens, people living in our technoculture have grown so distant from the cosmos that, tragically, it seems remote and irrelevant to their lives. Focused on the project of the technological command of the earth, human beings have developed an overweening hubris whereby they attempt to place themselves at the helm of life. They have used and abused other species and fragile ecosystems to satisfy their burgeoning populations and, now, a world economic system rooted in insatiable growth imperatives. "Present global culture," Sagan states, "is a kind of arrogant newcomer. It arrives on the planetary stage following four and a half billion years of other acts, and after looking around for a few thousand years declares itself in possession of eternal truths" (1980: 276).

Modernity was an era of immense discovery, of bold new mappings of the land, sea, and stars, of producing charts that dramatically altered scientific paradigms and human identities.

---

into the unknown. For Sagan, the next great human adventure will free us from the shackles of the Earth and its gravitational straightjacket to explore other planets, to live in space stations, to terraform and build space colonies, and to journey to the outer edges of the galaxy and perhaps beyond. The next stage in the human adventure would be to soar into a postgeocentric, multiplanet identity, such as dramatized by TV shows like *Star Trek* and *Deep Space Nine*, which feature a smorgasbord of advanced species and startling examples of the fifth discontinuity. Where Marx spoke of the "idiocy of rural life," Sagan alerts us to the limitations of an Earth-bound existence and the beckoning of the stars.[2]

For Sagan, what we are calling the postmodern adventure would have as profound an impact on human identity as did modern journeys centuries earlier. The exploration of the cosmos, Sagan points out, is a voyage of self-discovery, an attempt to map a cosmic genealogy since we are ultimately born from the stars, beings who are "starstuff gathering starlight." When life develops eyes and ears, the cosmos sees and hears; when it develops thought and intelligence, we become, as in a fantastic Hegelian evolution, the cosmos reflecting on itself — not mind knowing Mind, but mind knowing the matter of the

Opposed to the vision of the *Alien* films, where the fifth discontinuity is portrayed in horrifying and malevolent forms, Sagan sees an encounter with alien life as positive. Whereas the effect in *Alien* is for humans to close species rank against other life-forms, Sagan imagines a fifth

---

The exploration of the cosmos, Sagan points out, is a voyage of self-discovery, an attempt to map a cosmic genealogy since we are ultimately born from the stars, beings who are "starstuff gathering starlight."

---

discontinuity involving extraterrestrial beings that would widen our vision and experience. Contact with beings from space, Sagan believes, would lead to "a profound deprovincialization of the human condition" (1980: 259). It is very likely, Sagan believes, that the Watson we might speak to on the other end of the cosmic phone line would be far more intelligent and technologically and morally advanced than us, such that we could not but be humbled in our relatively primitive state of being, This could generate a radical deprovincialization effect — what we'll call the "D-effect," after Brecht's "A-effect" — which might indeed occur through contact, thereby forcing humanity to cross the fifth discontinuity. Yet it is clear from works like *Pale Blue Dot* (1994) that Sagan thinks scientific mappings of billions of galaxies alone are enough to promote awe and disarm cosmic arrogance.[3]

Unlike ecoprimitivists such as many members of Earth First!, Sagan argues that we need *more*, not *less*, science to extricate humanity from the mire of self-destruction: "The present epoch is a major crossroads for our civilization and perhaps for our species. Whatever road we take, our fate is indissociably bound up with science. It is essential as a matter of simple survival for us to understand science" (1980: xvii). Specifically, Sagan believes that further developments in science would advance the technologies needed for continued exploration of the stars. He hopes that space travel would facilitate even greater moral progress and could end human chauvinism toward one another and all forms of life. Sagan believes that by finding our true place in the multiverse, by understanding our cosmic roots, and by realizing that we live together on one fragile planet where national boundaries are utterly artificial, we might develop more peaceful and sustainable societies.

If nothing else, Sagan argues, contact with extraterrestrial life would teach us that an advanced technological civilization can endure; beyond that, such civilizations might offer important knowledge about how we might survive on our own decaying technocapitalist planet. A direct or satellite-mediated contact would mean "that someone has learned to live with high technology, that it is possible to survive technological adolescence. That alone, quite apart from the contents of the message, provides a powerful justification for the search for other civilizations" (Sagan 1980: 251). Thus, in Sagan's vision, contact could show that there is no inherent logic of technological destruction, no necessary path, as Adorno (1973) put it, from the slingshot to the atom bomb. Hence, we could hope that human beings can develop sciences and technologies that are advanced, sustainable, peaceful, and life-promoting, instruments of Eros rather than of Thanatos.

Sagan offers evocative visions of the fifth discontinuity as an opportunity for evolutionary growth; philosophizes suggestively about science, technology, and human evolution; and has contributed enormously to astronomy and public appreciation of science (see Poundstone 1999). Yet he advances surprisingly antiquated positivist conceptions of science as a universal vehicle for truth, and sharply opposes it to irrational, mythological, and "demonological" modes of thinking (see Sagan 1996). Sagan feels hopeful and optimistic about science and technology, and offers

---

> We could hope that human beings can develop sciences and technologies that are advanced, sustainable, peaceful, and life-promoting, instruments of Eros rather than of Thanatos.

---

little consideration of their dark and potentially destructive side. While Sagan is no positivist, he is an uncritical realist, holding to a correspondence between the mathematical nature of the cosmos and the quantitative prowess of the human mind (see 1977: 243). In an acute critique, however, Richard C. Lewontin (1997) exposes the value- and theory-laden nature of all scientific observation and the often dogmatic, irrational, and mythological nature of science itself — as when it makes appeals to authority or extravagant claims to success.

Nor does Sagan adequately appreciate the fact that science and technology coevolve with capital, which puts enormous constraints on their emancipatory and democratic uses. He minimizes the dangers of military appropriations of space technologies and does not recognize that the causes of ecological catastrophe on Earth stem not simply from arrogant humanism or advanced technology, but also from a global capitalist economic system hell-bent on devouring the planet. Confronting the crucial objection that space exploration is unjustifiable given the urgency of human needs on Planet Earth, however, Sagan claims that a single military plane costs more than a modest space exploration (1980: 263). If the U.S. budget could be demilitarized, in other words, there would not only be enough money for food, housing, and education, but also for funding the search for extraterrestrial intelligence (SETI) and the space program. The real problem lies less with NASA (although it certainly has its own failings and bureaucratic excesses) than with the Pentagon, the entire military–industrial complex, a "permanent war economy," and the politicians who fund it so extravagantly. Thus, many urge a dramatic restructuring of the military, a total ban on weapons of mass destruction, and allocation of the prodigious resources spent on war and destruction for peace and enhancing life (see Melman 1985; Shaw 1991).

In the long run, space exploration is unavoidable for, as Kaku (1997) argues, catastrophes such as a meteor strike could devastate our planet at any time. Moreover, even if we survive this catastrophic contingency, in 5 billion years the Sun will explode and vaporize the Earth. So, one way or the other, if the human adventure is to continue and be more than just a message in a bottle waiting for a future civilization to find, it must eventually leave the comfortable confines of the home planet and master space travel. This adventure would wed the human fate ever more closely to advanced science, technology, and a cyborg-like existence (see Savage 1994).

As interesting and paradigm shattering as contact with alien life would be, our world cannot wait for a cosmic Godot. Nor, indeed, is this necessary, since the wisdom and learning we need to harmonize advanced technology with ethics, compassion, social justice, and peaceful and ecological lifeways have been developed for millennia in both Eastern and Western traditions. The great challenge facing humanity, among other things, is to reduce its population, to restore what species and ecosystems it can, and to subvert consumerism in favor of sustainable lifestyles. We must also instill critical thinking skills as early as possible in our children and promote a "compassionate education" that teaches reverence for life. We need to revive the meaning and role of citizenship, and to develop a politics of alliance and solidarity that challenges the power of capital and the state, such as recently have emerged in the new antiglobalization coalitions on the streets of Seattle, Washington, DC, and elsewhere. It is imperative that citizens begin confronting — in public debates as opposed to isolated academic squabbles — topics such as sound conceptions and practices of science; socioethical modes of educating scientists, mathematicians, engineers, and medical doctors; new sensibilities toward nature; and new technologies, forms of political struggle and democracy, and identities.

THE APOCALYPTIC VISION OF PHILIP K. DICK

Our present social continuum is disintegrating rapidly; if war doesn't burst it apart, it obviously will corrode away. ... To avoid the topic of war and cultural regression ... is unrealistic and downright irresponsible.

—Philip K. Dick

It is instructive to contrast Sagan's buoyant, technophilic, and optimistic vision of the future as an exciting evolutionary journey to the stars to the pessimistic, dystopian view of Philip K. Dick, who paints a bleak picture of the future of global capitalism and interplanetary space travel.[4] Astonishingly prolific, amazingly inventive, and always visionary, Dick in his best works attempts to measure the fallout of a proliferating technological society and to project foreboding visions of possible futures, as he extrapolates from contemporary economic, technological, political, and cultural developments. Like cyberpunk, which he anticipates and influenced, Dick sets his fantasies within a world drawn from contemporary configurations of global capitalism and the Cold War. His writings reveal deep fears of social breakdown, military technology and political tensions escalating out of control, and nuclear armageddon. He portrays a future in which demagogues use media culture to manipulate and dominate populations, and the development of cybernetic systems results in a society where humans are mastered by machines, technology, and in some cases superior species. Hence, implosion, posthumanism, the fifth discontinuity, and the fate of the human in technocapitalism are core themes of Dick's work.

Whereas for Sagan space travel is an object of poetic rapture, for Dick it is inherently ambiguous and potentially catastrophic. Although both see space travel as an inevitable outgrowth of science, technology, industry, and (for Dick at least) capitalism, Dick has grave worries about space technologies in the historical context of nuclear weapons, Cold War rivalries, global power politics, and predatory capitalism. Dick's epics of space colonialism, like *Martian Time-Slip* (1964), portray the class hierarchies and forms of political and technological domination developed on Earth replicated in the space colonies. His novel *The Three Stigmata of Palmer Eldritch* (1965) shows colonizers becoming addicted to drugs to overcome the bleak conditions of life on other planets. Moreover, his depictions of aliens in his voluminous short stories and novels were hardly benign. Sagan, of course, imagines alien intelligence in positive ways, in the manner of Steven Spielberg's *E. T.* (1982), and he seems to believe that worldly class, gender, race, and power issues can be transcended at escape velocity.

It is perhaps Dick's novel *Do Androids Dream of Electric Sheep?* (1987 [1968]) that provides his most compelling apocalyptic vision, while exhibiting quintessential Dickian themes of the implosion between the real and the artificial, humans and technology, and natural reality and simulation in a high-tech world — the same themes we have identified as major foci of the postmodern adventure. In the plot of the novel — which is significantly different from the film *Blade Runner* that is loosely based on it (see Kerman 1997) — Rick Deckard, a bounty hunter of renegades androids, is ordered to exterminate a group of highly advanced android Nexis-6 models who have escaped from the "off-colonies," where they were slaves, in order to prolong their short preprogrammed lives. Stronger, quicker, and smarter than humans, the androids pose a dangerous threat to humans and are menacing examples of a fifth discontinuity produced by technology. Deckard, however, increasingly empathizes with the androids, one of whom, Rachel, he becomes sexually involved with. Consequently he is ever more troubled by the killing or "retiring" required by his job, as he gradually comes to recognize the android others as akin to human subjects.

Dick frames his story within the political economy of an interplanetary global capitalism, set in a bombscape of human ruination and massive species extinction. The androids were originally produced to help colonize Mars, when capitalism and corporations having devastated their home base, begin colonizing other planets. In a competitive race between two global giants, the Rosen Association and the Grozzi Corporation vie to market the most advanced androids. This war of technology has produced increasingly complex creatures who are seemingly identical with humans, sharing feelings such as love, empathy, desire, and fear of death. In the form of the Nexus-6 model produced by the Rosen Corporation, androids also have acquired a high level of self-reflexivity, which leads them to repudiate their slave status. Hence, as Marx saw in an earlier industrial context, capitalists created their own gravediggers by manufacturing increasingly complex workers who eventually acquire the will to rebel. Thus Dick provides a futuristic embodiment of Marx's vision of a rebellious proletariat.

A major theme of *Androids* is entropy, the incessant movement from birth to death, adolescence to senescence, order to disorder, heterogeneity to homogeneity. As the second law of thermodynamics, "entropy" is a natural process; the cosmos, in Dick's terms, inexorably winds down to a state of "kipple." "No one can win against kipple ... except temporarily and maybe in one spot. ... It's a universal principle operating throughout the universe; the entire universe is moving toward a final state of total, absolute kippleization" (1987: 58). Entropy is indeed the prototypical condition for Dick's futuristic world: cities are decaying; the natural environment is disappearing; the androids' short life spans are winding down; and the unfortunates stranded on earth are deteriorating in mind and body. Entropy is also evident in the "waning of affect," a symptom of postmodern subjectivity for theorists like J. G. Ballard and Fredric Jameson. In advanced stages of "civilization," individuals are so affectless that they have to rely on mechanical supplementation — via technologies such as Dick's envisaged "mood organ" or "empathy box" — in order to feel. Dick ironically portrays an exhausted human species drained of all feeling, on the verge of being supplanted by androids who are developing "human" feeling like empathy. He thereby signals an implosion between humans and machines, questions what is left of humanity in a high-tech world, and calls into doubt the long-term survivability of a human species whose members lack positive emotional bonds with one another.

Dick makes it clear that just as individuals can hasten the entropy of their own bodies, social systems can quicken their own decay and that of the natural world. As an energy-devouring, resource-depleting, waste-producing, nonstop-guzzling megamachine of growth and accumulation, advanced capitalism rapidly accelerates entropic breakdown. While *Blade Runner* changed and obscured much in Dick's novel, it brilliantly captured the look and feel of a hyperintensive global system of production drowning in its own waste. The incessant downpour of radiation-saturated rain, the fire-belching smokestacks, the filthy refuse of the ultramodern metropolis, the densely overpopulated city streets and high-rise apartments, the glowing neon billboards and crisscrossing traffic of hovercraft vehicles, and the detritus of a multicultural society where even language breaks down into kippleized fragments underscore the presence of a dying, nihilistic, technocapitalism. Director Ridley Scott adds the ironic touch of metallic blimps moving ponderously across the nuclear-red skies, broadcasting advertisements for the good life in the out-colonies. The underclass denizens — mostly Asian and hybrid countercultural — live in crowded ghetto-like conditions on the ground level of the city, while the remaining upper class dwells in luxurious high-rise apartments, reproducing the class structure portrayed in Fritz Lang's *Metropolis* (1927). This futuristic city — which became the prototype for the universe of cyberpunk — was recognizably Los Angeles, where the film was shot, but it could stand for any global and multicultural city of a postholocaust future, or the aftermath of a collapse of the global economy.

Typically, Dick's narratives do not have happy endings. Deeply disturbed with German fascism, he often sketches out totalitarian societies ruled by demagogues and authoritarians. More prescient than other writers of his day in regard to the dynamics of global capitalism, Dick portrays corporate forces using technology to exploit and control the population. Further, he was one of the first SF writers to explore a new virtual technoculture, in which the distinction between reality and illusion, the real and the virtual, implodes. The strong undercurrents of pessimism in Dick's work respond to Cold War conformity and stabilization in his 1950s and early 1960s writings, and then to the defeat of the counterculture, of which he was a precursor and participant, by the 1970s. While characters in his writings often manage to see through the socially manufactured illusions that stabilize the oppressive societies in which they live, they are unable to do anything to change them, and their revolt is depicted as futile. Nuclear apocalypse haunts his work. Cold War geopolitics are always in the background of his novels, which display ordinary people destroyed by political and technological forces beyond their understanding and control.

Hence, Dick's work embodies powerful visions of a world collapsing boundaries between technology and the human. He portrays tendencies in the present that will lead to future affliction, forecasts entropic decay of nature and society, and dissolves society and reality into grotesque configurations in which ordinary categories of space, time, and reality are ruptured. Dick drafts fantastic technological

---

Dick's work embodies powerful visions of a world collapsing boundaries between technology and the human.

---

worlds with strange forms of media culture and art, simulacra, and a collapse of the boundaries of modernity that anticipate conceptions of hyperreality, implosion, and simulation in later French postmodern theory, especially Baudrillard and Virilio. In retrospect, Dick can be read as a dystopic visionary of the emerging postmodern adventure

in which science and technology were creating new forms of the human, bringing about a highly ambiguous post-human condition, and providing a dialectical foil to the optimistic and asocial visions of Sagan.

* * *

RECONSTRUCTING THEORY AND POLITICS IN THE NEW MILLENNIUM

We exist in a sea of powerful stories: They are the conditions of finite rationality and personal and collective life histories. There is no way out of stories, but no matter what the One-Eyed Father says, there are many possible structures, not to mention contents, of narration. Changing the stories, in both material and semiotic senses, is a modest intervention worth making.

— DONNA HARAWAY

Our tragedy lies in the richness of the available alternatives, and in the fact that so few of them are ever seriously explored.

— TOM ATHANASIOU

Pessimism of the intellect, optimism of the will.

— ANTONIO GRAMSCI

With the human species entering the Third Millennium, it encounters perhaps the most dramatic scientific and technological revolutions in history and the massive global restructuring of capitalism. This postmodern adventure forces us to rethink the basic categories and methods of theory; to invent useful practical and political responses to the great transformation that we are undergoing, and thus to reshape theory and politics for the future. Such a transformative project is not an idealist reflex of theory, but one demanded by the striking developments of the present age. The turbulent metamorphoses of the contemporary era provide opportunities for progressive interventions in arenas ranging from education and the workplace to struggles over world trade and global democracy.

As we noted in Chapter 3, scientists and philosophers alike are engaging in the reshaping of science. Many are now rejecting mechanistic, deterministic, and positivist models, and producing new understandings and more ecologically and ethically oriented work. Likewise, as we showed in Chapters 4 and 5, individuals are reconfiguring technology to make it a more creative force for culture and communication and a key weapon for radical democratic politics. Current struggles against globalization from below indeed provide the potential for new movements to overcome social fragmentation and to create a more ecological, egalitarian, and just social order.

Embracing these projects, we note that many serious efforts for transformations of theory, politics, society, and identities are underway; they range from new theoretical mappings and critiques to political battles over biotechnology and capitalist globalization, to efforts to remake institutions like the schools and family. But the forces of capitalism also have their own reconstructive project, of course. Thus it is necessary to keep up with and counter capitalism's ever-changing tactics of conquest and domina-

Where some people fatalistically concede defeat, others declare this to be the best of all possible worlds (we'd hate to see the worst) and announce the end of history (Fukuyama and Baudrillard). However, one of the first preconditions for change is the realization that things could be otherwise, that humanity has choices, and, indeed, that we are currently at a crucial crossroads where "the fate of the Earth" hangs in balance. What choices we make, how we act or fail to act in the next few decades, might decide the ultimate outcome for all advanced life.

A sobering diagnosis of current crises must be counterbalanced by hope for regeneration of the planet and humanity, accompanied by positive, alternative visions of social organization, politics, and ethics. To be sure, the way forward is shadowed by doubt and uncertainty. The maps of the modern era, though partly in shreds, can guide us in some ways, but in other ways they can only lead us further down the paths of catastrophe since they have steered

---

The new perspectives of chaos and complexity theory stress self-organization and the creation of fresh cultural and social forms that can be born out of current turbulence and disequilibrium.

---

tion with alternative projects of radical democracy. The postmodern adventure is thus a contested field with competing groups struggling to transform all domains of everyday life.

While the planet spirals ever deeper into social and natural disaster, with all things becoming ever more tightly knit into the tentacles of global capitalism, there is a burning need for new maps and compasses to help steer us into a viable mode of existence. Karl Marx's 1843 call for a "ruthless criticism of everything existing" has never been more urgent and appropriate, but all too often today critique is merely academic and stratospheres away from concrete action. Yet social critique and change in the slaughterhouse of capitalism needs to be guided and informed by powerful descriptions of what *is:* the degraded forfeiture of human potential in a world where over a billion people struggle for mere existence and live on less than one dollar a day. In addition, transformative projects require bold new visions of what *can be*, developing imaginative projections of how human beings might harmoniously relate to one another, and the living/dying Earth.

advanced Western societies (and increasingly the entire world) into their present cultural and historical impasse. A regenerative future demands new maps, a different compass, and a transformative orientation. This new orientation requires an appraisal of the present situation and new theories, new ethics, and new politics to reconfigure existing frameworks. In these tasks, postmodern critiques and concepts have much to offer, while suffering important limitations of their own.

The old determinist maps of reality are obsolete and increasingly hazardous to employ. They were based on erroneous notions of linear causality, simple cause-and-effect models, dualistic thinking, and a "quest for certainty" that divorces theory from practice and attempts to eliminate ambiguity and contingency from knowledge and life (see Dewey 1979). At their best, the new maps, which have come to be called "postmodern," and which have been assembled from elements in the fields of art, philosophy, social theory, and science, often allow for more complex and adequate modes of thinking. The most advanced new postmodern mappings abandon naive attempts to impose crude ordering schemes on reality, renouncing the dangerous obsession with repressive and reductive control of the social and natural worlds. They substitute multi-perspectivist thinking for reductionist, realist, and essentialist positions, and enable individuals better to theorize and deal with contingency, paradox, ambiguity, particularity, multiplicity, and relationships. They challenge anthropocentrism and its dualistic vision of the human place in nature, and disassemble hierarchies of all kinds in favor of relations of complementarity. The new perspectives of chaos and complexity theory stress self-organization and the creation of fresh cultural and social forms that can be born out of current turbulence and disequilibrium, as we approach threshold points of change. Such alternative postmodern theoretical guidelines, while not always articulated adequately, are important, for they can inform a reconstructed ethics, politics, and set of social practices that can enhance democracy and individuality, and create less domineering and more life-enhancing relationships with nature. Humans can learn to see their natural and social environments as potentials for gratification and cooperation rather than as objects to be dominated and manipulated.

Of course, as we have argued elsewhere (Best and Kellner 1991, 1997), many versions of postmodern theories are excessively irrational, relativistic, individualistic, nihilistic, and antimodern. We reject such positions in favor of a more positive and transformative critical postmodern theory. The restructuring of theory and politics called for by Dewey in the Progressive Era, and by critical theorists like Marcuse, feminists, multiculturalists, poststructuralists, and postmodernists in recent decades, is driven now by bold developments in technoscience and the global economy. The coevolution of science, technology, and capitalism is creating mutations within the human adventure itself, confronting us with fantastic new forms of communication and information technology, multimedia, biotechnology, nanotechnologies, and rapidly evolving forms of culture, society, and economy. These turbulent and frightening developments pose great dangers for the human species, but also offer opportunities for more democratizing, egalitarian, and ecological social relations, values, and practices.

As humans coevolve with their economies, tools, cultures, and theories, they produce new mappings to make sense of their world and create new practices to achieve their desired values. Hence, the reconstruction of theory and practice is rooted in the revolutionary adventure itself and involves imaginative co-constructions of those forces that are propelling us into an ever more quickly arriving and unpredictable future. However things are presently constructed, they can be deconstructed and reconstructed by human beings in different ways. Whatever futures might be likely or probable, such as one of global social and environmental collapse, they can be anticipated and prevented in favor of quite different results.

Unless we first imagine various futures, both good and bad, and utilize socially progressive and ecological visions as ethical and institutional maps, we will have nothing to guide us in the constitution of a viable world, and we will travel through time like lost seafarers. Such an imaginative project is undertaken, for example, in Allen Hammond's *Which World? Scenarios for the 21st Century: Global Destinies, Regional Choices* (1998). Hammond examines long-term trends in various regions and the globe as a whole. He envisages three main possibilities for humanity: we can journey into the Market World of untrammeled capitalism, the Fortress World of social collapse and authoritarian control, or the Transformed World of benign capitalism that prioritizes social justice and seeks a rapprochement with nature. In line with a systems and chaos theory approach, Hammond insists that while current trends may predispose societies to certain outcomes, these futures are too complex and too contingent on uncertain variables for exact prediction.

Hammond begins by stressing the importance of creating stories or "scenarios" as critical maps of the present and guideposts for the future. He then broadly describes the nature of the three worlds/roads he believes face us in the current crossroads of social evolution. Finally, he applies each scenario to various regions of the world, always with a careful eye on how each region interacts with the global economy as a whole and how social development is inextricably bound to the ecological systems of the Earth.

But if Hammond's menu of options seems limited, something like what a steakhouse offers a vegetarian, indeed it is. For the neoliberal author fails to consider a wide range of alternatives such as a revitalized socialist economics, left-green ecopolitics, anarchist or radical democratic movements, or the coalitions currently being formed by opponents of globalization. Still, although it leaves out a vision of a Postcapitalist Green World that rebuilds political and economic institutions for participatory democracy, the value of Hammond's book is its concrete projection of some different futures that may await us, and which depend upon our individual and collective choices. Indeed, one of the major crises today is a crisis of the imagination. In the tradition of neo-Marxism, and the work of thinkers like Herbert Marcuse and Murray Bookchin, it has been recognized that so-called utopian visions are not, when authentic, starry-eyed dreams of abstract ideals. They are at their best empirically grounded in actual social tendencies

distinction in science, to reshape science so that ethical concerns and values are central to its conceptual apparatus. This was a quest of Herbert Marcuse (1964) and has been taken up by some versions of environmental thought, feminism, and postmodern science (Haraway 1997). The dominant positivist and neopositivist stances within mainstream science continue to fetishize detachment and seek

---

It is crucial to activate the philosophical imagination and generate visions of the good society. But possibilities for the good life and the good society mutate as new sciences, technologies, and sociopolitical tendencies emerge.

---

and the real potential for a rational, egalitarian, ecological, and compassionate mode of life. For such utopians, the "ought" can become an "is."

As an example of our reconstructive project, we find value in combining modern Enlightenment notions of community, rights, and solidarity with a postmodern ethics of difference, contingency, and nonfoundationalism. This could lead to creation of a new ethics that balances principles of individuality and community, difference and unity, particularity and universality. The Kantian notion of a Kingdom of Ends still contributes to ethical vision, especially now, when politics is being reduced to amoral assertions of self-interest via competing groups that refuse to search for commonality or reach consensus. Kant's conception of perpetual peace might also be reconfigured for the present in the light of the proliferation of violence and war, as should the nonviolent perspectives of Gandhi and Martin Luther King. One might also learn from the classical Greek synthesis of ethics and politics about the need to combine these domains, as well as to preserve the substance of both individual and communal life, in the quest for more social harmony and well-being. Further, one should overcome the limitations of all anthropocentric and humanistic ethics, however progressive, democratic, and enlightened, which assign moral status and value only to humans, positioning the animal kingdom and the natural world as mere "resources" for human use.

New relationships to nature and other species need to be developed that could enable people to appreciate the intrinsic value of the natural world, to seek creative forms of interaction and enjoyment with nature, and to fight the pollution, depletion, and destruction of nature and life. In addition, it is important to mediate the fact/value

solace in myths of objectivity. Moreover, the conventional approach is to limit discussion to procedures of research by individual scientists rather than infusing science as a whole with more embracing social values of accountability, human and animal welfare, social justice, ecology, and the like (conversation with Sandra Harding, June 2000).

The reconfiguration of science, ethics, and society requires the reconstruction of education. As H. G. Wells notes in an epigraph that opens this Epilogue, education can save us from catastrophe. As John Dewey consistently argued, the transformation of education is crucial to the democratization of society. We would argue that technological revolution and globalization are dramatically reshaping education and that a major challenge of the present age is to reshape education to make it serve the interests of democratization rather than intensified corporate hegemony. This will require teaching multiple literacies to critically engage new technologies and to attempt to overcome the "digital divide." A democratizing reconstruction of education should thus provide the skills necessary to actively participate in the new technoculture and society to all groups and individuals (for an elaboration of this argument, see Kellner 1998, 2000).

The democratic reconfiguration of education, science, and society still requires philosophy and philosophical visions of the good life. Science and social theory can tell us what the world is, but by themselves not how to live in it. Hence, it is crucial to activate the philosophical imagination and generate visions of the good society. But possibilities for the good life and the good society mutate as new sciences, technologies, and sociopolitical tendencies emerge. One must therefore constantly rethink the possibilities of liberation, democracy, Enlightenment, and freedom from these changing perspectives.

While cultural politics can help us to understand groups and individuals different from ourselves, spark thought and action, promote new sensibilities, and enhance our lives in a variety of ways (see Best and Kellner 1997; Giroux 2000), it is still important to develop new forms of political organization and struggle. For instance, to overcome the environmental crisis will require massive global efforts of political organization and new forms of struggle, alliance, and enlightenment. This requires collective acts of will and imagination, rather than the prevailing fragmentation of identity politics, whose one-sidedness and limitations we must overcome. For substantive change to occur, expansive, democratizing visions must supplant the "modest" visions of postmodern politics that limit action to mere local changes or local reform.

There are conflicting potentials in the present social situation. On the one hand, postmodern fragmentation and pluralization has taken the differentiating features of modernity into a spiral of otherness and difference, expanding social dissolution and conflict. This form of postmodern fragmentation involves a breaking up of unities (communities, traditions, even national cultures) that once provided resources for identity, were empowering, and enabled individuals to create better lives for themselves. Their disintegration is a loss, yet these very unities also contained oppressive features in the form of cultural hierarchies, relations of subordination and domination, backwardness, and chauvinisms of various sorts. Their erosion creates openings for cosmopolitan identities and a more pluralized social condition that gives groups and individuals excluded from political and cultural participation expanded opportunities for cultural creation and political involvement.

Thus, crises contain opportunities for progressive change, and fragmentation creates exciting openings and empowering possibilities as well as dispiriting and destructive tendencies. What does the near future hold for humankind? Will we continue to overpopulate the planet, move toward technocracy, develop violent cultures, overproduce nuclear weapons, exacerbate the already obscene disparities between the rich and the poor, advance trends toward global warming, destroy other species, deplete the Earth's natural resources, and utterly self-destruct? Will life end apocalyptically by epidemic disease or by a nuclear bang, or will there be enough fragments of humanity left to survive for a short time, as in contrasting conditions of drought and flood depicted by *Mad Max* (1979) and *Waterworld* (1995), before it ends in a pathetic whimper? Will we mutate into cyborgs or bionic beings and live out our lives in spaceships and space stations? Will we make "contact" and be saved by the superior wisdom and technologies of space aliens, or will they devour us as resources for their megamachines? Or will we learn to harmonize our advanced technological society with the natural world and take on responsible roles as stewards of the Earth?

The greatest adventure ever faced by the human species is staring us right in the face: Can we use our advanced intelligence and technologies toward constructive rather than destructive ends? Can we learn to live together on this planet? Can we diversify and live together peacefully? Can we regain respect and reverence for life? The next few generations hold the fate of the evolution of all life on Earth in their hands. The window of opportunity is closing.

The postmodern adventure holds more promise, more danger, and more sureality than any previous adventure known to humanity. We must seek possibilities in the present to move toward a better future. The postmodern adventure is just beginning and alternative futures unfold all around us. Western societies inhabit a historically unique terrain between the modern and the postmodern, and we need a variety of theoretical and political perspectives to make sense of the momentous changes that are now occurring. In the Third Millennium, the choices agents make will determine whether the adventure of evolution itself will continue in creative ways on this planet, producing ever more biodiversity, or collapses into the sixth and perhaps final extinction crisis in the history of the Earth (see Leakey and Lewin 1995).

As science, technology, and capitalism continue to coevolve into an ever denser global network, the ultimate question is whether we can reshape the driving forces of change to harmonize social with natural evolution, such that diversity and complexity grow in both spheres. Or will current developments produce the death of the human, the despoliation of the Earth, and even the demise of all complex life? Neither option is preordained, both are possible futures, and this tension and ambiguity itself is a core feature of the postmodern adventure.

NOTES

1. Drake's equation concludes that there are 50,000 planets in our solar system that have intelligent life.

Numerous scientists have objected that his variables and reasoning are arbitrary, and that his result is far too optimistic. In their book *Rare Earth,* for example, Donald Brownlee and Peter Ward (2000) draw on new findings in astronomy, geology, and paleontology to argue that the odds of another Earth-like planet existing in the entire cosmos are exceedingly rare. Recent findings in exobiology, however, which prove that life is able to thrive in very hostile conditions, might support Drake's thesis. Drake finds Brownlee and Ward's work too pessimistic, stating that "the basic flaw in all [such] arguments is that they don't allow for the opportunistic nature of life, its ability to accommodate or alter itself to cope with environmental change" ("Maybe We Are Alone in the Universe, After All," www.nytimes.com/library/national/science/020800sci-space-life.html). The controversy rages on.

2. On the history and politics of the space program, see McDougall (1985) and Burrows (1990). For recent books on space technology and travel colonization, see Burrows (1998).

3. It is important to emphasize that for Sagan, space research and space travel have not only philosophical implications, but also crucial pragmatic value, since the study of the atmospheres and matter of other planets like Venus can tell us much about the ecological dynamics and fate of our own Earth. Throughout *Pale Blue Dot* (1994), Sagan makes convincing arguments about the importance of space research for ecology, noting that key insights into the dangers with chlorofluorocarbons (CFCs) (which destroy the ozone layer) and problems with global warming were gleaned by scientists studying other planets. See especially chapter 14, "Exploring Other Worlds and Protecting This One" (216–229). Sagan's dual optic — philosophical and pragmatic — for arguing the importance of the space programs is well articulated in this passage: "When I look at the evidence, it seems to me that planetary exploration is of the most practical and urgent utility for us here on Earth. Even if we were not roused by the prospect of exploring other worlds, even if we didn't have a nanogram of adventuresome spirit in us, even if we were only concerned for ourselves and in the narrowest sense, planetary exploration would still constitute a superb investment" (1995: 229).

Importantly, Sagan insists on the need to bring science down to earth, to advance an interdisciplinary research program, and to articulate a revolutionary cosmology that intimately links the Earth to other planets in its solar system, such as in the possibility that Mars may have seeded life on Earth, or the other way around.

4. Dick published 80 stories and 13 novels from 1951 to 1958 (Sutin 1989: 85), an intensity and productivity that continued through the 1960s, in which he published as many as 11 novels in 1 year. Five volumes of his collected short stories are in print and a large number of his novels have been reprinted. Dick has indeed become a cult figure, with a loyal following, a major SF prize named after him, and movies and TV shows of his work regularly appearing. He was generally ignored during his life, often living in extreme poverty and turmoil. On Dick, see Sutin (1989) and Hayles (1999).

5. Yet another scientific blow to anthropocentrism came in February 2001, when the rival teams mapping the human genome discovered that human beings have only about 30,000–40,000 genes, far less than the commonly projected number of 100,000. This means that at the genetic level, humans are not significantly more complicated than simple invertebrate animals. If these findings are correct, the pufferfish, which has 50,000 genes, is more genetically complex than human beings. Also, Dr. Craig Venter claims he found only 300 human genes that lacked a recognizable counterpart in the mouse; see Wade (2001). But others challenge this. On the latest research, and the controversy raging on about the number of human genes and the meaning of the data, see Nicholas Wade, "Genome Analysis Shows Humans Survive on Low Number of Genes," www.nytinies.com/2001/02/ll/health/11GENO.html and Kristen Philipkowski, "Gene Map: Help or Hype?" www.wirednews.com/news/print/0,1294,41718,00.htm.

6. www.vhemt.org.

You Are Here

from *Pale Blue Dot*

— Carl Sagan

The entire Earth is but a point, and the place of our own habitation but a minute corner of it.

— MARCUS AURELIUS, ROMAN EMPEROR,
MEDITATIONS, BOOK 4 (CA. 170)

As the astronomers unanimously teach, the circuit of the whole earth, which to us seems endless, compared with the greatness of the universe has the likeness of a mere tiny point.

— AMMIANUS MARCELLINUS (CA. 330–395),
THE LAST MAJOR ROMAN HISTORIAN,
IN *THE CHRONICLE OF EVENTS*

The spacecraft was a long way from home, beyond the orbit of the outermost planet and high above the ecliptic plane — which is an imaginary flat surface that we can think of as something like a racetrack in which the orbits of the planets are mainly confined. The ship was speeding away from the sun at 40,000 miles per hour. But in early February of 1990, it was overtaken by an urgent message from Earth.

Obediently, it turned its cameras back toward the now-distant planets. Slewing its scan platform from one spot in the sky to another, it snapped 60 pictures and stored them in digital form on its tape recorder. Then, slowly, in March, April, and May, it radioed the data back to Earth. Each image was composed of 640,000 individual picture elements ("pixels"), like the dots in a newspaper wirephoto or a pointillist painting. The spacecraft was 3.7 billion miles away from Earth, so far away that it took each pixel 5½ hours, traveling at the speed of light, to reach us. The pictures might have been returned earlier, but the big radio telescopes in California, Spain, and Australia that receive these whispers from the edge of the Solar System had responsibilities to other ships that ply the sea of space — among them, *Magellan*, bound for Venus, and *Galileo* on its tortuous passage to Jupiter.

Voyager 1 was so high above the ecliptic plane because, in 1981, it had made a close pass by Titan, the giant moon of Saturn. Its sister ship, *Voyager 2*, was dispatched on a different trajectory, within the ecliptic plane, and so she was able to perform her celebrated explorations Uranus and Neptune. The two *Voyager* robots have explored four planets and nearly sixty moons. They are triumphs of human engineering and one of the glories of the American space program. They will be in the history books when much else about our time is forgotten.

The *Voyagers* were guaranteed to work only until the Saturn encounter. I thought it might be a good idea, just after Saturn, to have them take one last glance homeward. From Saturn, I knew, the Earth would appear too small for *Voyager* to make out any detail. Our planet would be just a point of light, a lonely pixel, hardly distinguishable from the many other points of light *Voyager* could see, nearby planets and far-off suns. But precisely because of the obscurity of our world thus revealed, such a picture might be worth having.

Mariners had painstakingly mapped the coastlines of the continents. Geographers had translated these findings into charts and globes. Photographs of tiny patches of the

Earth had been obtained first by balloons and aircraft, then by rockets in brief ballistic flight, and at last by orbiting spacecraft — giving a perspective like the one you achieve by positioning your eyeball about an inch above a large globe. While almost everyone is taught that the Earth is a sphere with all of us somehow glued to it by gravity, the reality of our circumstance did not really begin to sink in until the famous frame-filling *Apollo* photograph of the whole Earth — the one taken by the *Apollo 17* astronauts on the last journey of humans to the Moon.

It has become a kind of icon of our age. There's Antarctica at what Americans and Europeans so readily regard as the bottom, and then all of Africa stretching up above it: You can see Ethiopia, Tanzania, and Kenya, where the earliest humans lived. At top right are Saudi Arabia

Here was our first chance (and perhaps also our last for decades to come).

Many in NASA's *Voyager* Project were supportive. But from the outer Solar System the Earth lies very near the Sun, like a moth enthralled around a flame. Did we want to aim the camera so close to the Sun as to risk burning out the spacecraft's vidicon system? Wouldn't it be better to delay until all the scientific images — from Uranus and Neptune, if the spacecraft lasted that long — were taken?

And so we waited, and a good thing too — from 1981 at Saturn, to 1986 at Uranus, to 1989, when both spacecraft had passed the orbits of Neptune and Pluto. At last the time came. But there were a few instrumental calibrations that needed to be done first, and we waited a little longer. Although the spacecraft were in the right spots, the

---

Our posturings, our imagined self-importance, the delusion that we have some privileged position in the Universe, are challenged by this point of pale light. Our planet is a lonely speck in the great enveloping cosmic dark. In our obscurity, in all this vastness, there is no hint that help will come from elsewhere to save us from ourselves. … Like it or not, for the moment the Earth is where we make our stand.

---

and what Europeans call the Near East. Just barely peeking out at the top is the Mediterranean Sea, around which so much of our global civilization emerged. You can make out the blue of the ocean, the yellow-red of the Sahara and the Arabian desert, the brown-green of forest and grassland.

And yet there is no sign of humans in this picture, not our reworking of the Earth's surface, not our machines, not ourselves: We are too small and our statecraft is too feeble to be seen by a spacecraft between the Earth and the Moon. From this vantage point, our obsession with nationalism is nowhere in evidence. The *Apollo* pictures of the whole Earth conveyed to multitudes something well known to astronomers: On the scale of worlds — to say nothing of stars or galaxies — humans are inconsequential, a thin film of life on an obscure and solitary lump of rock and metal.

It seemed to me that another picture of the Earth, this one taken from a hundred thousand times farther away, might help in the continuing process of revealing to ourselves our true circumstance and condition. It had been well understood by the scientists and philosophers of classical antiquity that the Earth was a mere point in a vast encompassing Cosmos, but no one had ever *seen* it as such.

instruments were still working beautifully, and there were no other pictures to take, a few project personnel opposed it. It wasn't science, they said. Then we discovered that the technicians who devise and transmit the radio commands to *Voyager* were, in a cash-strapped NASA, to be laid off immediately or transferred to other jobs. If the picture were to be taken, it had to be done right then. At the last minute — actually, in the midst of the *Voyager 2* encounter with Neptune — the then NASA Administrator, Rear Admiral Richard Truly, stepped in and made sure that these images were obtained. The space scientists Candy Hansen of NASA's Jet Propulsion Laboratory (JPL) and Carolyn Porco of the University of Arizona designed the command sequence and calculated the camera exposure times.

So here they are — a mosaic of squares laid down on top of the planets and a background smattering of more distant stars. We were able to photograph not only the Earth, but also five other of the Sun's nine known planets. Mercury, the innermost, was lost in the glare of the Sun, and Mars and Pluto were too small, too dimly lit, and/or too far away, Uranus and Neptune are so dim that to record their presence required long exposures; accordingly, their images were smeared because of spacecraft motion. This is how the planets would look to an alien spaceship approaching the Solar System after a long interstellar voyage.

From this distance the planets seem only points of light, smeared or unsmeared — even through the high-resolution telescope aboard *Voyager*. They are like the planets seen with the naked eye from the surface of the Earth — luminous dots, brighter than most of the stars. Over a period of months the Earth, like the other planets, would seem to move among the stars. You cannot tell merely by looking at one of these dots what it's like, what's on it, what its past has been, and whether, in this particular epoch, anyone lives there.

Because of the reflection of sunlight off the spacecraft, the Earth seems to be sitting in a beam of light, as if there were some special significance to this small world. But it's just an accident of geometry and optics. The Sun emits its radiation equitably in all directions. Had the picture been taken a little earlier or a little later, there would have been no sunbeam highlighting the Earth.

And why that cerulean color? The blue comes partly from the sea, partly from the sky. While water in a glass is transparent, it absorbs slightly more red light than blue. If you have tens of meters of the stuff or more, the red light is absorbed out and what gets reflected back to space is mainly blue. In the same way, a short line of sight through air seems perfectly transparent. Nevertheless — something Leonardo da Vinci excelled at portraying — the more distant the object, the bluer it seems. Why? Because the air scatters blue light around much better than it does red. So the bluish cast of this dot comes from its thick but transparent atmosphere and its deep oceans of liquid water. And the white? The Earth on an average day is about half covered with white water clouds.

We can explain the wan blueness of this little world because we know it well. Whether an alien scientist newly arrived at the outskirts of our solar system could reliably deduce oceans and clouds and a thickish atmosphere is less certain. Neptune, for instance, is blue, but chiefly for different reasons. From this distant vantage point, the Earth might not seem of any particular interest.

But for us, it's different. Look again at that dot. That's here. That's home. That's us. On it everyone you love, everyone you know, everyone you ever heard of, every human being who ever was, lived out their lives. The aggregate of our joy and suffering, thousands of confident religions, ideologies, and economic doctrines, every hunter and forager, every hero and coward, every creator and destroyer of civilization, every king and peasant, every young couple in love, every mother, and father, hopeful child, inventor and explorer, every teacher of morals, every corrupt politician, every "superstar," every "supreme leader," every saint and sinner in the history of our species lived there — on a mote of dust suspended in a sunbeam.

The Earth is a very small stage in a vast cosmic arena. Think of the rivers of blood spilled by all those generals and emperors so that, in glory and triumph, they could become the momentary masters of a fraction of a dot. Think of the endless cruelties visited by the inhabitants of one corner of this pixel on the scarcely distinguishable inhabitants of some other corner, how frequent their misunderstandings, how eager they are to kill one another, how fervent their hatreds.

Our posturings, our imagined self-importance, the delusion that we have some privileged position in the Universe, are challenged by this point of pale light. Our planet is a lonely speck in the great enveloping cosmic dark. In our obscurity, in all this vastness, there is no hint that help will come from elsewhere to save us from ourselves.

The Earth is the only world known so far to harbor life. There is nowhere else, at least in the near future, to which our species could migrate. Visit, yes. Settle, not yet. Like it or not, for the moment the Earth is where we make our stand.

It has been said that astronomy is a humbling and character-building experience. There is perhaps no better demonstration of the folly of human conceits than this distant image of our tiny world. To me, it underscores our responsibility to deal more kindly with one another, and to preserve and cherish the pale blue dot, the only home we've ever known.

Breinigsville, PA USA
25 August 2010
244189BV00002B/1/P